Cognition and Second Language Instruction

THE CAMBRIDGE APPLIED LINGUISTICS SERIES

Series editors: Michael H. Long and Jack C. Richards

This series presents the findings of recent work in applied linguistics which are of direct relevance to language teaching and learning and of particular interest to applied linguists, researchers, language teachers, and teacher trainers:

Cognition and Second Language Instruction

EDITED BY

Peter Robinson
Aoyama Gakuin University

CAMBRIDGE
UNIVERSITY PRESS

PUBLISHED BY THE PRESS SYNDICATE OF THE UNIVERSITY OF CAMBRIDGE
The Pitt Building, Trumpington Street, Cambridge, United Kingdom

CAMBRIDGE UNIVERSITY PRESS
The Edinburgh Building, Cambridge CB2 2RU, UK
40 West 20th Street, New York, NY 10011–4211, USA
10 Stamford Road, Oakleigh, VIC 3166, Australia
Ruiz de Alarcón 13, 28014 Madrid, Spain
Dock House, The Waterfront, Cape Town 8001, South Africa

http://www.cambridge.org

First published 2001
Second printing 2003

Printed in the United Kingdom at the University Press, Cambridge

Typeface Sabon (*The Enschedé Font Foundry*) 10.5/12 pt.   *System* LaTeX 2_ε [TB]

A catalogue record for this book is available from the British Library.

ISBN 0 521 80288 1 hardback
ISBN 0 521 00386 5 paperback

Contents

Series editors' preface

Second language acquisition is first and foremost a mental process – one that occurs in a behavioural and social context, to be sure, but fundamentally a matter of acquiring a new knowledge system. Cognition and cognitive factors, therefore, are central to any account of how and why SLA works, or so often fails, and equally central to the theory and practice of second language instruction, given that it is the SLA process that instruction is designed to facilitate.

Section 1 of Professor Peter Robinson's new book, *Cognition and Second Language Instruction*, offers the reader six detailed surveys of what is thought to be known about some of the cognitive resources, processes and constraints SLA researchers consider most crucial, including attention, memory, automatization, processing, and learnability. Six chapters in Section 2 describe current work in several areas where the models and empirical findings are being drawn upon (and new knowledge often simultaneously created) in the design, delivery and evaluation of second language instruction: task design, task classification and sequencing, the provision of focus on form, intentional and incidental vocabulary learning, syllabus and materials design, individual differences, and protocol analysis. Given the undeniable importance of cognitive factors, the authors in this section explore how best to adapt instruction to putative universals and empirically attested variability in learning processes.

A leading authority on SLA and language teaching, Professor Robinson has assembled an impressive line-up of recognized experts on the issues covered. While differing in theoretical allegiances, they share a respect for the importance of theory, accountability to empirical findings, and rational argument. These are qualities sought in all volumes in the *Cambridge Applied Linguistics Series*. *Cognition and Second Language Instruction* is a very welcome addition to the series, and should prove invaluable to SLA researchers, language teachers, and all those involved in the practice of language teaching.

Michael H. Long
Jack C. Richards

Preface

What are the cognitive correlates and components of learning, and to what extent are these affected by instructional manipulations, and different learning conditions? Answers to these questions concerning the influence of cognitive learner variables on second language acquisition (SLA), and on the development of effective second language (SL) instruction, are a subject of major interest to both SLA researchers and those involved in SL pedagogy alike. Cognitive theory has influenced SLA theory and SL pedagogy in the past, for example through the work of such researchers as Carroll (1962, 1990), on the measures of cognitive ability predicting aptitude for language learning; Lado (1965) and Stevick (1976), on the role of memory in language learning; McLaughlin (1965, 1987), on information processing approaches to SLA theory; O'Malley and Chamot (1990), on learning strategies; and Krashen (1982), on the role of consciousness during instructed and naturalistic SLA.

More recently, both theoretical research into SLA and SL pedagogy have shown renewed interest in the role of cognitive variables. Articles on attention, memory, and automaticity, as well as on connectionism, learnability and language processing have increasingly appeared in the major SLA journals in the field, reflecting in part the rapid pace of development of the relatively new fields of cognitive science and cognitive psychology, and research findings arising within them. Such articles include those referred to throughout many of the papers in this collection by Schmidt (1990) and Tomlin and Villa (1994) on the role of attention and awareness during SLA; N. Ellis (1996a), and Robinson (1995b) on the role of memory processes; N. Ellis and Schmidt (1997) and Gasser (1990) on connectionist approaches to modeling SLA; DeKeyser (1997) on the development of automaticity and control of language use as a result of extended practice, and Gregg (1993) on linguistic theory, learnability and SLA theory development. Concurrently with this reawakening of theoretical interest in cognitive issues a number of SLA researchers have been developing techniques for laboratory research into SLA, and the effect of L2 instruction, which attempt to operationalize and control one or more of these variables and study their effects on learning under different conditions of exposure. These experimental studies began to appear regularly in the major journals throughout the 1990s. For example, two special issues of Studies in Second Language Acquisition, Volume 15 no. 2 (1993) and Volume 19 no. 2 (1997), have been dedicated to the issues of cognitive influences on instructed SLA, and laboratory studies of SLA respectively. Books drawing on cognitive theory, some with a pedagogic orientation, have also appeared recently, including for example the edited collections by N. Ellis (1994d), Schmidt (1995b) and Healy and Bourne (1998), and also full length books by de Graaff (1997b), Johnson (1996), Robinson (1996b), Skehan (1998a) and VanPatten (1996).

There is thus likely to be considerable interest in a collection which contains chapters summarizing the latest theoretical thinking about cognitive variables, and chapters relating these issues to SL instruction and research. This collection is in two sections. Section 1 (Theoretical Issues) deals with central cognitive resources and processes. This section includes (in this order) chapters by Schmidt on attention; Nick Ellis on memory; MacWhinney on connectionist models of representation and learning; Harrington on sentence processing; DeKeyser on automaticity and automatization; and Gregg on learnability and SLA theory. This section therefore moves from a focus on key cognitive resources drawn on in SLA, attention and memory, to broader issues of their implication in second language processing and learning. Section 2 (Cognition and Instruction) draws on the concepts and constructs introduced in Section 1 and attempts to relate them to issues in instructed SLA. This section includes chapters on the design of pedagogic tasks (Skehan & Foster); the cognitive processes triggered by focus on form (Doughty); the intentional and incidental learning of vocabulary (Hulstijn); cognitive complexity, task sequencing and syllabus design (Robinson); aptitude, individual differences and program design (Sawyer and Ranta); and the insights provided by protocol analysis into the cognitive processes underlying second language skill acquisition (Jourdenais). As with the first section this section also moves from a relatively narrow focus, i.e., on issues of L2 task design and methodology, to broader pedagogic issues such as syllabus and program design and skill learning.

The ordering of the sections and papers in this book therefore reflects the belief that many aspects of decision making during second language instruction should be motivated by theories of, and research into, the cognitive processes instructional treatments attempt to manipulate. The book as a whole, as well as the contributions of individual authors, is an attempt to demonstrate how this important connection can be made.

SECTION I

THEORETICAL ISSUES

1 Attention

Richard Schmidt

Introduction

The essential claim of this chapter is that the concept of attention is necessary in order to understand virtually every aspect of second language acquisition (SLA), including the development of interlanguages (ILs) over time, variation within IL at particular points in time, the development of L2 fluency, the role of individual differences such as motivation, aptitude and learning strategies in L2 learning, and the ways in which interaction, negotiation for meaning, and all forms of instruction contribute to language learning.

The theoretical issues dealt with in this chapter are organized around the basic assumptions, definitions, and metaphors concerning attention in psychology and include the idea of attention as a limited capacity, the notion of selective attention, and the role of attention in action control, access to awareness, and learning. It turns out that, like most psychological concepts initially based on common experience, attention is not a unitary phenomenon, but refers to a variety of mechanisms. These include alertness, orientation, preconscious registration (detection without awareness), selection (detection with awareness within selective attention), facilitation, and inhibition. This does not diminish the centrality of attention, in its several manifestations, for learning. Although recent evidence, discussed towards the end of this chapter, indicates the possibility of some unattended learning, this appears limited in scope and relevance for SLA. There is no doubt that attended learning is far superior, and for all practical purposes, attention is necessary for all aspects of L2 learning.

A secondary goal of this chapter is to provide some of the details of the role of attention as that fits within a broader cognitive approach to understanding SLA, one that relies on the mental processes of language learners as the basic explanation of learning. I am particularly concerned with those mental processes that are conscious, under the working hypothesis that SLA is largely driven by what learners pay

3

attention to and notice in target language input and what they understand the significance of noticed input to be. This stands in opposition to what Jerome Bruner (1992) has called the 'magical realist' view, that unconscious processes do everything.[1]

A full understanding of the ways in which awareness may shape SLA is beyond the scope of this chapter. Specifically, the issue of explicit and implicit learning and related questions concerning the role of explicit and implicit knowledge in SLA are not discussed here at any length. Both implicit and explicit learning surely exist, and they probably interact. Implicit learning (learning without awareness) is shown by numerous demonstrations that the result of allocating attention to input results in more learning than can be reported verbally by learners. Knowledge of the grammar of one's L1 is an obvious case. Native speakers of French 'know' the rules for using the subjunctive, even if they know none of them explicitly. In experimental studies, it has also been shown that people can learn to control complex systems without recourse to an explicit mental model of how the system works (Berry, 1994). Various theories have been proposed to account for this common phenomenon. In SLA, those most discussed at the present time are the Universal Grammar (UG) account, which argues for unconscious deductive reasoning from innate principles (Gregg, this volume), and the connectionist account, in which automatic, implicit learning results from the strengthening and inhibition of connections in an associative network – a simple, 'dumb' process that leads to a complex and intelligent result (Elman, Bates, Johnson, Karmiloff-Smith, Parisi, & Plunkett, 1996; MacWhinney, this volume). On both accounts, the learning is unconscious.

Explicit learning (learning with awareness) is also common. Probably most readers have learned a language recently enough to remember some of the experience or have learned some other cognitively demanding skill and can verify that learners commonly form (conscious) hypotheses about the target of their learning and modify those hypotheses as they encounter more information. What these two kinds

---

[1] This chapter is a revised version of presentations at PacSLRF (Aoyama Gakuin University, Tokyo, March, 1998) and SLRF '97 (Michigan State University, East Lansing, October, 1997), under the titles 'The centrality of attention in SLA' and 'There is no learning without attention', respectively. The SLRF presentation was part of a point-counterpoint plenary with Jacquelyn Schachter of the University of Oregon, who presented the view that multiple types of evidence for unconscious learning of various kinds converge on the notion that unconscious adult learning can and does take place in some, though presumably not all, areas of language. My own view is that conscious and unconscious processes probably interact in all domains of language, but that there is little evidence for learning without attention (one reading of 'unconscious') in any of them.

of learning, implicit and explicit, have to do with each other continues to be a topic of great debate within SLA and elsewhere. In SLA the question has frequently been posed in terms of whether or not 'learned' knowledge can become 'acquired' or whether the learner's conscious hypotheses can become internalized (Krashen, 1982; R. Ellis, 1993). Another, possibly more productive, way to pose the question is in terms of learning processes (rather than types of knowledge), to ask whether bottom–up, data driven processing, and top–down, conceptually driven processing guided by goals and expectations (including beliefs and expectations concerning the target language grammar), interact; to which the answer is probably yes, they do (Carr & Curran, 1994; N. Ellis, 1994a, 1996a, 1996b, this volume; Robinson, 1995b).

Since the concerns dealt with in this chapter concern the role of attention in SLA, it might be desirable to simply exclude all issues of awareness (Anderson, 1995). Unfortunately, it is probably impossible to separate attention and awareness completely, because of the common assumption that attention and awareness are two sides of the same coin (Carr & Curran, 1994; James, 1890; Posner, 1994), the emphasis in psychology on attention as the mechanism that controls access to awareness (discussed later in this chapter), and the reliance, in many experimental studies, on verbal reports as a method of assessing the allocation of attention. The solution adopted to this problem in this chapter is to limit the discussion of attention and its subjective correlate of 'noticing' to awareness at a very low level of abstraction. 'Noticing' is therefore used here in a restricted sense, as a technical term equivalent to 'apperception' (Gass, 1988), to Tomlin and Villa's (1994) 'detection within selective attention', and to Robinson's (1995b) 'detection plus rehearsal in short term memory.' My intention is to separate 'noticing' from 'metalinguistic awareness' as clearly as possible, by assuming that the objects of attention and noticing are elements of the surface structure of utterances in the input – instances of language, rather than any abstract rules or principles of which such instances may be exemplars. Although statements about learners 'noticing [i.e., becoming aware of] the structural regularities of a language' are perfectly fine in ordinary language, these imply comparisons across instances and metalinguistic reflection (thinking about what has been attended and noticed, forming hypotheses, and so forth), much more than is implied by the restricted sense of noticing used here.[2]

---

[2] As Truscott (1998) has pointed out, for some in SLA, rules are considered to be the targets of noticing (R. Ellis, 1993; Fotos, 1994).

Attention in current accounts of SLA

Even a cursory review of the SLA literature indicates that the construct of attention appears necessary for understanding nearly every aspect of second and foreign language learning.

Understanding development

Some accounts of L2 development emphasize the importance of attention much more than others. If one is concerned only with linguistic competence and subscribes to a strong innateness position, that development is the mere triggering of innate knowledge (which is not only unconscious but inaccessible in principle to consciousness), then the role of input is minimized and the role of attention to input even more so. Perhaps the only role for attention is that, presumably, at least the crucial evidence that triggers changes in the unconscious system must be attended (Schmidt, 1990). Connectionist models of learning, which are based on the processing of input and do not distinguish between competence and performance, also have little to say about attention, since input and output units are usually simply assumed to be attended. (Most connectionist accounts are silent on this issue; for one that is explicit, see Cohen, Dunbar, & McClelland, 1990).

The role of attention is emphasized most in cognitive accounts of L2 development, especially those that are strongly psycholinguistic in approach (Bialystok, 1994; Carr & Curran, 1994; N. Ellis, 1994b, 1994c, 1996a; R. Ellis, 1997; Gass, 1988, 1997; Hatch, 1983a; Pienemann, 1989; Pienemann & Johnston, 1987; Robinson, 1995b; Skehan, 1998a; Swain, 1993, 1995; VanPatten, 1990, 1994, 1996; Wolfe-Quintero, 1992), within which attention to input is seen as essential for storage and a necessary precursor to hypothesis formation and testing. Common to these approaches is the idea that L2 learners process target language input in ways that are determined by general cognitive factors including perceptual salience, frequency, the continuity of elements, and other factors that determine whether or not attention is drawn to them (Slobin, 1973, 1985; Towell & Hawkins, 1994). It has also been pointed out that attention is what allows speakers to become aware of a mismatch or gap between what they can produce and what they need to produce, as well as between what they produce and what proficient target language speakers produce (R. Ellis, 1994a; Gass, 1988, 1997; Schmidt & Frota, 1986; Swain, 1993, 1995, 1998).

Most discussions concerning the role of attention in L2 development focus exclusively on morphology and syntax, although a few have dealt with lexical learning (N. Ellis, 1994b) and pragmatic development (Bialystok, 1993; Schmidt, 1993b). Peters (1998) proposes that in every domain of language learning (phonology, grammar, semantics, pragmatics, vocabulary, discourse structuring), learners must attend to and notice any source of variation that matters, whatever makes a difference in meaning. For example, in syntax, one may say in English both 'I turned the covers down' and 'I turned down the covers', but there is no difference in meaning that depends on the position of the direct object. Native speakers do not attend to this difference, and non-native speakers do not have to attend to it either, at least for comprehension. However, if an utterance contains a pronoun, there is a difference: 'I turned it down' is possible, but 'I turned down it' is possible only in the sense of 'I turned down the road', while 'I turned the road down' makes sense only with the semantic reading of a road being offered but rejected as a gift. In this case, Peters argues that learners do have to notice the difference in ordering and be aware that it matters as they map forms with their appropriate meanings. Moreover, since beginning learners are cognitively overloaded, they cannot pay attention to all meaningful differences at once. If they have not learned what is simple, they cannot learn what is complex, but as simpler processing routines are over-learned, they have more capacity to attend to details, eventually being able to attend to whatever native speakers pay attention to. In the multidimensional model of Pienemann and Johnston (1987), developmental features and natural orders are related to the learner's gradually expanding processing space and the freeing of attentional capacity. For example, the crucial point for accurate production of third person singular – s is that the learner must have enough processing space available to generate a third person marker and keep it active in working memory until the appropriate moment arrives for attaching it to a verb.

VanPatten (1994) has argued that attention is both necessary and sufficient for learning L2 structure:

Bob Smith is a learner of Spanish, a language that actively distinguishes between subjunctive and indicative mood...He begins to notice subjunctive forms in others' speech. He attends to it. Soon, he begins to use it in his own speech, perhaps in reduced contexts, but none the less he is beginning to use it. If you ask him for a rule, he might make one up. But in actuality, he doesn't have a rule. All he knows is that he has begun to attend to the subjunctive and the context in which it occurs and it has somehow begun to enter his linguistic system...Bob did not need to come up with a conscious rule; he only needed to pay attention. (p. 34)

Others who emphasize the importance of attention do not claim that attention is necessary for all learning. Carr and Curran (1994) claim that focused attention is required for some types of structural learning, but restrict this to cases where complicated or ambiguous structures are the object of learning. Gass (1997) argues against the principle that all L2 learning requires attention (attributing some learning to UG), but cautions that her arguments are not intended to weaken the claim that attention is important, merely to show that attention and awareness are not the only factors (p. 16).

Understanding variation

Mellow (1996) has argued that, when non-automatized knowledge is target-like but automatized knowledge is not, tasks for which attentional resources are abundant will result in more accurate language use than tasks for which attentional resources are limited. For example, redundant grammatical elements that have not been automatized are likely to be omitted in tasks that make high demands on attention such as comprehension tasks, but will be supplied more consistently in tasks such as writing, which does not make as high demands on attention. Variability can also be induced by task constraints and instructions. Hulstijn and Hulstijn (1984) showed that performance on two Dutch word-order rules in a story retelling task improved when the subjects' focus of attention was experimentally manipulated towards grammatical correctness. From a different perspective, Tarone (1996) has argued that language learners should not be viewed solely as decontextualized information processors, emphasizing that social context (including interactional pressures) is what causes a speaker to pay more or less attention to one or another linguistic form. However, the information-processing account and the social variationist account agree that variations in attention underlie variations in use.

Understanding fluency

Attention is a key concept in accounts of the development of L2 fluency that are related to the psychological concept of automaticity (DeKeyser, this volume; Schmidt, 1992). Models that contrast controlled with automatic processing posit a transition from an early stage in which attention is necessary and a later stage (after practice) in which attentional resources are no longer needed and can be devoted to higher level goals (McLaughlin, Rossman & McLeod, 1983; Shiffrin & Schneider, 1977). According to Logan's instance theory (1988; Logan, Taylor, & Etherton, 1996), a competitor to the standard information processing view, the transition to fluency is not the result of developing automatic routines that do not require attention, but rather the replacement of slower algorithmic or rule-based procedures by faster memory-based processing. However, this theory is also based on crucial assumptions about attention: encoding into memory is an obligatory consequence of attention (representations in memory are not complete and accurate snapshots, but only encode what subjects pay attention to), and retrieval is an obligatory consequence of attention at the time of retrieval. Similarly, chunking theories of fluency assume a role for attention; chunking is a mechanism that applies automatically, but only to attended input (N. Ellis, 1996a, this volume; Servan-Schreiber & Anderson, 1990). Other models of fluency emphasize executive control and skilled selective attention. Bialystok has argued that the basis of fluency is the ability to focus attention on relevant parts of a problem to arrive at a solution, an ability that develops as the result of age, experience, practice, and bilingualism (Bialystok, 1994a; Bialystok & Mitterer, 1987).

Understanding individual differences

Attention is a useful construct for understanding individual differences in SLA. As Tremblay and Gardner (1995) have pointed out with respect to motivation, a statement that some aspect of motivation leads to higher proficiency or better performance does not answer the question of why such a relationship exists. Models of motivation and learning can be improved by the identification of mediators that explain why one variable has an effect on another. In a revised version of Gardner's well-known socio-educational model, Tremblay and Gardner propose that three 'motivational behaviors' – effort, persistence, and attention – mediate between distant factors, including language attitudes and motivation, and achievement. Tremblay and Gardner found support for a LISREL structural equation model linking these variables in a study of achievement in French courses. In addition, three studies to date (MacIntyre & Noels, 1996; Oxford & Nyikos, 1989; Schmidt, Jacques, Kassabgy, & Boraie, 1997) have found strong links between motivation and learning strategies, particularly cognitive and metacognitive strategies. These strategies are either strategies for focusing attention on some aspect of the target language or for sustaining attention while doing something else in addition – inferencing, looking for patterns, monitoring (paying attention to one's output and to the process of learning itself), and other types of active conscious processing (O'Malley, Chamot, & Walker, 1987; Oxford, 1990).

At least one aptitude factor, short term or working memory capacity (Baddeley, 1986; Cowan, 1996; N. Ellis, 1996a, this volume; Harrington & Sawyer, 1992), is closely related to attention. Robinson (1995b) has suggested that my concept of 'noticing' can be redefined as detection plus rehearsal in short-term memory. Baddeley, Papagno, and Vallar (1988) have reported that such rehearsal is necessary for learning unfamiliar verbal material, although not necessary for forming associations between meaningful items that are already known. In the model of Baddeley (1986), there are three components of working memory: a 'central executive', explicitly related to attention and responsible for controlling the flow of information into working memory; a 'visuospatial sketchpad', a passive storage buffer for visual and spatial information; and an 'articulatory loop,' storing rich, detailed, and temporarily held information about the surface properties of language and allowing the relatively effortless recycling of the items currently in memory (Cowan, 1996). Another model relating attention to aptitude is that of Skehan (1998a), who suggests that the ability to notice what is in input is one of three factors in foreign language aptitude (see Sawyer & Ranta, this volume). The others are language analytic ability and the ability to retrieve chunks from memory to support fluent speech production.

Understanding the role of instruction

Sharwood Smith (1995) points out that input salience can be internally derived (when input becomes noticeable to the learner because of internal cognitive changes and processes) or externally derived (when input becomes more noticeable because the manner of exposure is changed). One major role of explicit instruction is that, by changing expectations, it helps focus attention on forms and meanings in the input, a prerequisite for subsequent processing (de Graaff, 1997; N. Ellis, 1993; R. Ellis, 1994a; Hulstijn & de Graaff, 1994b; Long, 1988; Schmidt, 1990; Schmidt & Frota, 1986; Sharwood Smith, 1993, 1994; Terrell, 1991; Tomlin & Villa, 1994; VanPatten, 1994). It can be argued that task requirements, task instructions, and input enhancement techniques affect what is attended to and noticed in on-line processing, thereby causing their effects (Doughty, 1991, this volume; Doughty & Williams, 1998a; Skehan, 1996, 1998a).

Similar characteristics of informal instruction, ranging from immersion contexts to natural interaction with native speakers of a language, have also been widely commented upon (Pica, 1994, 1997). Long

(1983, 1992, 1996) has argued that interactional modifications such as clarification requests and recasts are more consistently present than are input modifications (e.g., linguistic simplification) in interaction between native and non-native speakers and that the nature of interactional modifications as attention-focusing devices is what makes them likely to be helpful for acquisition. Gass and Varonis (1994) have proposed that interaction serves to focus learners' attention on form in instances where there is perceived difficulty in communicating, 'raising to awareness that area of a learner's grammar that deviates (either productively or receptively) from native speaker usage.' Swain (1985, 1993; Swain & Lapkin, 1995) has proposed that one reason learners in immersion contexts exhibit weaknesses in grammatical accuracy even after receiving years of comprehensible input is that they are not called upon to produce much, arguing that 'producing the target language may be the trigger that forces the learner to pay attention to the means of expression needed in order to successfully convey his or her own intent' (1985: 249).

If all these accounts are correct, attention is a crucial concept for SLA. The allocation of attention is the pivotal point at which learner-internal factors (including aptitude, motivation, current L2 knowledge, and processing ability) and learner-external factors (including the complexity and distributional characteristics of input, discoursal and interactional context, instructional treatment, and task characteristics) come together. What then happens within attentional space largely determines the course of language development, including the growth of knowledge (the establishment of new representations), fluency (access to that knowledge), and variation.

However, it could be argued that attention in these accounts is merely a *deus ex machina* that does not actually explain anything. At the least, one must wonder whether a unitary concept of attention based on ordinary experience or folk psychology can be the explanation of so many varied phenomena. To gain a better understanding of what attention is and how it works, it is necessary to turn to psychology, where attention has been a major focus of theory and empirical research for over a century, and to examine some of the assumptions, definitions, metaphors, theoretical disputes, and empirical findings from that field.

Attention in psychology: basic assumptions

In psychology, the basic assumptions concerning attention have been that it is limited, that it is selective, that it is partially subject to voluntary control, that attention controls access to consciousness, and that attention is essential for action control and for learning. All of these basic points were raised early on. The classic work on attention is that of William James (1890), who noted that 'Everyone knows what attention is. It is the taking possession by the mind, in clear and vivid form, of one out of what seem several simultaneously possible objects or trains of thought. Focalization, concentration of consciousness, are of its essence. It implies withdrawal from some things in order to deal more effectively with others' (p. 403). The nature and mechanisms of attention turned out not to be so self-evident, however, and the topic continues to be discussed within an enormous literature, most of which is experimentally based.

Attention is limited

The classic view in psychology is that limited capacity is the primary characteristic of attention (Broadbent, 1958; Kahneman, 1973), and this view has been taken on by many in SLA (McLaughlin et al., 1983; VanPatten, 1994). Within this general view, some have stressed that there are two general human information processing systems. Such accounts contrast effortful, attention-demanding ('controlled') processes with capacity-free ('automatic') processes (Shiffrin & Schneider, 1977). Another variant of the basic notion of capacity limitations in attention is that of Wickens (1984, 1989), who proposed multiple, specific resource pools for processing stages, brain hemispheres, and modalities (visual, auditory, vocal, manual). This model accounts for the fact that attention-demanding activities can be carried out at the same time more easily if they call upon different modalities than if they draw upon the same modality. In other words, there is some flexibility to capacity limitations, though each resource pool is assumed to have limited capacity.

Since the 1960s, when computers with limited memory systems began to come into widespread use, the primary metaphor for the limited capacity notion of attention has been memory (CPU). Another influential variant of the limited capacity metaphor for attention was influenced by psychoanalysis; Kihlstrom (1984) proposed that 'effort' (analogous to Freud's libido) was the limited resource.

Attention is selective

In the classical account of attention, the common view is that a second characteristic of attention, that it is selective, is a corollary of limited capacity. Because there is a limited supply of attention and because any activity that draws upon it will interfere with other activities requiring it, attention must be strategically allocated. The basic metaphor here is economic (Shaw & Shaw, 1978). When resources are limited, a cost-benefit analysis determines the focus of attention. VanPatten has drawn upon this metaphor in SLA, arguing that what is important in most SLA contexts is the meaning of messages. Limited attentional resources are directed first at those elements that carry message meaning, primarily lexicon, and only later, when the cost comes down, towards communicatively redundant formal features of language (VanPatten, 1990, 1994, 1996; Lee, Cadierno, Glass, & VanPatten, 1997).

In the selective attention literature, the most enduring controversy has been whether selection happens early or late in processing. One influential early view held that attending to one message eliminated perception of another (Broadbent, 1958). The metaphor here is that of a filter, gate, or bottle-neck. Later findings showing that individuals process highly meaningful words outside an attended channel (for example, in dichotic listening studies, in which different messages are played to the two ears) led some researchers to make the strong assumption that all information in the input stream is perceptually processed and that selection happens late (Deutsch & Deutsch, 1963).

Whether or not early selection occurs is still controversial (LaBerge, 1995), but more recent work in psychology has moved away from this issue and from the notion of selection as a corollary of limited capacity, identifying selection itself as the basic function of attention and emphasizing that selection may have other functions in addition to the allocation of scarce resources. Treisman (1992) argues that visual attention serves to integrate the features that belong to the same visual object, that is, to coalesce the properties of an object into a coherent perceptual representation (see also Shapiro, Arnell, and Raymond, 1997). Within the language acquisition field, Bialystok (1994a) has also emphasized the importance of selection ('control' in her framework) rather than limited capacity as the primary characteristic of attention.

Attention is subject to voluntary control

LaBerge (1995) emphasizes the importance of preparatory attention, which includes such things as being ready to step on the gas when a traffic light turns green or waiting to applaud at the exact moment the last sound of a musical performance ends. The benefits of preparatory attention include accuracy in perceptual judgment and categorization, as well as accuracy and speed in performing actions. Preparatory attention has not been discussed directly within SLA, but is relevant to studies of planning, comparing the complexity, accuracy, and fluency of learner language under conditions in which learners do or do not have time to plan before performing (Crookes, 1989; R. Ellis, 1987; Ortega, 1999; Skehan & Foster, this volume). More generally, with or without time to plan, we have some freedom to pay attention to one stimulus (or some feature of a complex stimulus) over another. A great deal of language teaching practice is founded on the premise that learners can attend to different aspects of the target language and that one of the important functions of teaching is to help focus learners' attention. Hulstijn and Hulstijn (1984) have suggested that certain tasks can be repeated, with the teacher telling learners each time to pay attention to different features, such as grammar, pronunciation, rate of speech, completeness of information, and so on.

The idea that we can control the focus of attention is an ancient one, often equated with the soul or will. In the 19th century, Wundt and James were the most prominent proponents of this view of attention (Neumann, 1996), while recognizing as well that there is also a passive, involuntary form of attention. For example, one attends to a loud noise, whether one wants to or not. In the well-known Stroop effect, the printed name of a colour word like 'red' or 'green' tends to interfere with the ability to name the colour ink in which the word is printed, e.g., 'brown', when the word 'red' is printed in brown ink (Dalrymple-Alford & Budayr, 1966). Involuntary attention is data driven, elicited bottom–up. Voluntary attention is top–down in the sense that attention is directed to outside events by inner intentions.

Attention controls access to consciousness

To quote William James again, 'My experience is what I agree to attend to' (1890: 403). The idea that one of the roles of attention is to control access to consciousness is an old one (Baars, 1988: 301–324; Shapiro et al., 1997). Ever since Aristotle described the phenomenon of selective attention, consciousness (awareness) has been identified with the phenomena of selective access. Neumann (1996) provides an excellent historical account of these views. Descartes assumed that selectivity occurred at a specific place, the pineal gland, between the mechanical brain processes shared with all animals and higher mental processes that are unique to humans. Neumann points out that the idea that attention and awareness are essentially two sides of the same coin also played a prominent role in most nineteenth century theorizing in psychology. For Wundt, the focus of consciousness was determined by the direction of attention, what he called apperception.[3] Theodore Ziehen argued against Wundt's concept of apperception, but also identified attention with access to awareness. In Ziehen's model, attentional selection was based on competition. Sensations and latent (non-conscious) ideas compete for access to consciousness (a very contemporary view). Only the most strongly activated ideas and their associated sensations actually enter consciousness; those that do not remain unconscious and have no effect at all. A modern version of these ideas is that of Marcel (1983), who identifies focal attention as the mechanism that establishes the boundary between an early processing stage that produces nonconscious representations of all stimuli and a higher state of phenomenal experience which consists of the imposition of a particular interpretation. Neisser's (1967) model of attention was similar, in the sense that he viewed the essential function of focal attention as a constructive, synthetic activity that makes stimuli available for further analysis. Baars (1988, 1996) also views attention as the mechanism responsible for access to awareness, distinguishing between autonomous, specialized processors that operate out of awareness and consciousness as a global workspace that broadcasts currently active information to any processor that can make use of it.

In reviewing two independent research traditions used in psychology to investigate attention, one rooted in filter theory and largely investigated through dichotic listening studies, the other based on paradigms from visual information processing, Neumann (1990, 1996) identified the following assumptions in common:

- Selection is the mechanism that moves information from one stage of processing to a subsequent stage.
- The locus of selection is situated between the unlimited-capacity and the limited-capacity portions of the information processing system.
- Selected stimuli are represented in conscious awareness, and unselected stimuli are not so represented.

The predominant metaphor of this view of selection as access to consciousness is that of the spotlight or zoom lens (Baars, 1996; Eriksen & St. James, 1986; Posner & Peterson, 1990). Various SLA theorists have also stressed the role of attention as the process that brings things into awareness. Bialystok has proposed a model of the development

---

[3] Gass (1988, 1997) refers to apperception as the first stage of L2 input processing, defining it as 'to perceive in terms of past perceptions' (1988: 200) and relating it to selective attention. Her use of 'apperception' is equivalent to my use of 'noticing' in this chapter.

of L2 proficiency built around two cognitive processing components, called analysis and control. Analysis is the process by which internal, formal representations are constructed. Relatively unanalyzed representations (e.g. formulaic chunks useful for conversational purposes) gradually evolve into more analyzed representations which are required to support higher literacy skills. Control refers to access to these representations, the basis of fluency. For Bialystok (1994a), awareness (consciousness) is the result of an interaction between analysis and control; the process of focusing attention onto internal representations 'gives rise to the subjective feeling of awareness that has been called consciousness' (p. 165).

Attention is essential for the control of action

The essential contrast here is between novice behaviour, for which controlled processing is required, and expert behaviour, which can be carried out automatically (without attention) except at critical decision points (Reason, 1984). Schneider and Detweiler (1988) have proposed a model in which automatization is viewed as a gradual, continuous transition through five identifiable phases: fully controlled processing, context-maintained controlled comparison, goal-state-maintained controlled comparison, controlled assist of automatic processing, and fully automatic processing.

Attention is essential for learning

The orthodox position in psychology is that there is little if any learning without attention (Baars, 1988, 1996; Carlson & Dulany, 1985; Fisk & Schneider, 1984; Kihlstrom, 1984; Logan, 1988; Nissen & Bullemer, 1987; Posner, 1992; Shiffrin & Schneider, 1977; Velmans, 1991). This claim is often related to models of memory. It is argued that unattended stimuli persist in immediate short-term memory for only a few seconds at best, and attention is the necessary and sufficient condition for long-term memory storage to occur. In SLA as well, the claim has been made frequently that attention is necessary for input to become available for further mental processing (Carr & Curran, 1994; Gass, 1988; van Lier, 1991, 1994; VanPatten, 1994; Schmidt, 1995).

Attentional mechanisms

Metaphors for attention (attention as an economic resource, pipeline, gate, computer, spotlight, or executive) are useful and often drive research programs, but recent approaches to the study of attention have attempted to move beyond such metaphors to identify mechanisms that may be more explanatory. In a widely read article in SLA, Tomlin and Villa (1994) have drawn upon the work of Posner (1994; Posner & Peterson, 1990) to identify three mechanisms or subsystems of attention (each with identifiable neurological correlates): alertness, orientation, and detection.

Alertness vs orientation

In Posner's account of attention, orienting refers to committing attentional resources to sensory stimuli. In earlier accounts (Pavlov, 1927), orienting was traditionally studied as a reflexive response (e.g. attending involuntarily to a loud noise), and Posner comments that the orienting system responds to involuntarily processed stimuli during early visual processing, but for Posner the essential characteristic of orienting is the alignment process itself (attributed to the posterior cortex), not whether such alignment is voluntary or involuntary. Orientation can therefore be modulated by a second attentional subsystem, the alertness or executive attentional system (in the mid-frontal lobe), which maintains a state of vigilance to increase the rate at which high priority information is detected. Attending, in the sense of orienting, 'is therefore jointly determined by environmental events and current goals and concerns' (Posner, 1994: 620).

Tomlin and Villa argue that both orientation and alertness are important in SLA. Alertness is related to motivation, interest in the L2, and classroom readiness to learn. Orientation is related to such instructional techniques as input-flooding and VanPatten's notion of attention to form: 'that is, the learner may bias attentional resources to linguistic form, increasing the likelihood of detecting formal distinctions but perhaps at the cost of failing to detect other components of input utterances' (Tomlin & Villa, 1994: 199). The notion of focus on form as presented by Doughty (this volume) also relates more directly to orientation than to either alertness or detection.

Detection: non-conscious registration vs conscious perception

For Tomlin and Villa, both orientation and alertness enhance the likelihood of detection, but it is detection itself, the cognitive registration of stimuli (mapped to an anterior attention network that includes the anterior cingulate gyrus and nearby motor areas), that is the necessary and sufficient condition for further processing and learning. Tomlin and Villa stress that, in their view, detection is not equivalent to awareness. It is therefore necessary to distinguish between detection without awareness (for which 'registration' seems a non-controversial choice of labels) and detection within focal attention accompanied by awareness (conscious perception or noticing).

Making this distinction, unfortunately, immediately raises some thorny methodological issues:

- How can we know whether some stimulus (or a feature of it) has been attended?
- How can we know whether some stimulus (or a feature of it) has been noticed?
- How can we know whether some stimulus (or a feature of it) has been registered, even if not attended or noticed?

Evidence that some part of target language input has or has not been attended and noticed is sometimes available from learner productions (in either naturalistic or classroom settings), as in the following exchange, reported by VanPatten (1990):

Interviewer: Cómo están ellos? (How are they?)
Subject: Son contento. (They are happy.)
Interviewer: Y ellos, cómo están? (And them, how are they?)
Subject: Son contento también. (They are happy too.)

VanPatten argues that the learner in the above example was so intent on meaning that features in the input that were not crucial to meaning (verb choice between *ser* and *estar*) were neither attended to nor noticed. It is impossible to tell whether verbs in the input might have been unconsciously detected (i.e., detected without awareness).

Learner reports, for example in diary studies, provide another source of information about what learners pay attention to and notice. Schmidt and Frota (1986) reported the results of a diary study in which there were so many instances of L2 use matching the learner's reports of what had been noticed when interacting with native speakers that the study was taken to support the hypothesis that there is no language learning without attention and noticing. On the other hand, Warden, Lapkin, Swain, and Hart (1995) found no particular relationship between the quantity and quality of linguistic observations recorded by high school students of French in their journals during a summer exchange program and their progress as reflected in test scores. This might be because some learners found their language observations more worthy of report than did others, but as Tomlin and Villa point out, the essential weakness of diary studies is that their temporal granularity is too coarse: 'Diary studies encompass spans of time as large as several weeks, but the cognitive processing of L2 input takes place in relatively brief spans of time, seconds or even parts of seconds' (1994: 185). Once again, such studies cannot shed any light on what might have been detected without being noticed, since making diary entries requires not only noticing but reflexive self-awareness (awareness that one has noticed).

Leow (1997) has used data from think-aloud protocols produced by learners of Spanish while completing a problem-solving task (an L2 crossword puzzle) to gather finer-grained data and to distinguish between two levels of awareness, illustrated below by two responses to the same item (the stem changing verb *mintieron*): simple noticing (registration with awareness, indicated by a report or repetition) and noticing with metalinguistic awareness:

Simple noticing:

'...the opposite of no, so it is supposed to be sí, so 11 across is gonna be *mintieron* (fills in *mintieron*)'

Noticing with metalinguistic awareness:

'...now let's see where is number 17 down? oh *se durmieron, con* a with a *u...repetir, ellos repitieron?* I think it has a stem change, 25 down *ir*, yes!...four down would be *tu*, so *durmi ó* (writes in *durmi ó*) done cool, I like this. Number 5 *ellos* of *pedir*, that asked, *pidieron* and it's good ... nine is gonna be *sí* again *mintieron* and obviously I spelled number 11 wrong so I can fix that (changes *mentieron* to *mintieron*)'

This technique appears to have been successful in distinguishing between two levels of awareness (those who showed higher levels of awareness learned more than those whose protocols showed that they merely attended and noticed), but once again it is difficult to see how such techniques could show that subjects did not attend or notice something, since verbal reports (even when concurrent) cannot be assumed to include everything that is noticed (see Jourdenais, this volume, for further discussion).

Jourdenais, Ota, Stauffer, Boyson, and Doughty (1995) have also used think-aloud protocols to see whether learners in a focus-on-form instructional treatment (target items were textually enhanced) would notice and learn more than subjects in a comparison group. Enhancement participants did notice more target forms and did produce more target features in production, but the methodology cannot identify all examples of target features that were noticed, or any that were not noticed but non-consciously registered. In computer-assisted learning contexts, instructional treatments can be designed to focus learners' attention on crucial aspects of input, and the success of such efforts can be assessed not only through learners' reports of what they notice (Chapelle, 1998) but also with programs that track the interface between user and program, for example by recording mouse clicks and eye movements (Crosby, 1998). However, while such records can provide additional information about orientation, detection still remains invisible.

Nevertheless, it is possible to operationalize the distinction between non-conscious registration and conscious noticing within focal attention in some experimental settings. Merikle and Cheesman (1987) have introduced a distinction between the objective and subjective thresholds of perception. The clearest evidence that something has exceeded the subjective threshold and been consciously perceived or noticed is a concurrent verbal report, since nothing can be verbally reported other than the current contents of awareness. After the fact recall is also good evidence that something was noticed, but only if prior knowledge and guessing can be controlled. For example, if beginning students of Spanish are presented with a series of Spanish utterances containing unfamiliar verb forms, are forced to recall (immediately afterwards) the forms that occurred in each utterance, and can do so, that is good evidence that they did notice them. However, many have argued that it is unreasonable to assume that failure to provide a verbal report (whether concurrent or retroactive) signals the absence of noticing. Learners of Spanish may well notice the forms that are presented, fleetingly, without processing them sufficiently to be able to retrieve them from memory. Failure to achieve above-chance performance in a forced-choice recognition test is a much better indication that the subjective threshold of perception has not been exceeded and noticing did not take place. If subjects, such as these students of Spanish, cannot identify (with better than chance accuracy) which forms occurred in input when forced to choose between alternatives, that would be much stronger evidence for the absence of noticing than their inability to produce them. If it could then be shown, using more indirect measures that tap the objective threshold of perception, that these subjects did, nevertheless, register those forms, then we would have a strong case for pre-attentive, unconscious detection.

One widely accepted indirect measure of registration is priming, the facilitation of responses to a stimulus by the prior presentation of the same or a related stimulus. Marcel (1983) showed that subliminally presented words that subjects could not consciously see could prime semantic associates. Eich (1984) reported dichotic listening experiments in which pairs of words were both presented to the unattended ear, one of which was ambiguous (e.g., 'fair' or 'fare') while the other biased its less common interpretation (e.g., 'taxi'). Recognition of both members of the pair was poor (indicating that the subjective threshold of perception was not exceeded), but in a spelling test subjects were biased in the direction of the disambiguated meaning (indicating that the objective threshold of perception had been reached). However, these studies used well-known native language words and are not inconsistent with the claim that novel material (such as foreign language input) cannot be unconsciously registered (MacKay, 1990). Before turning to some recent evidence that unfamiliar information might also be processed without exceeding the subjective threshold of perception, it is necessary to discuss two additional mechanisms of attention.

Facilitation vs inhibition

The theories discussed so far have assumed that attention directly facilitates or enhances processing (LaBerge, 1995). Automatic processing is assumed up to some level. Attention then enables selected information to receive further processing (Neill, Valdes, & Terry, 1995), and ignored stimuli are not processed further (Van der Heijden, 1981). However, there is an alternative. The mechanism of attention might inhibit the processing of irrelevant information, so that processing of relevant information simply proceeds without interference.

The inhibition construct played an important role in early psychological theories (Harnishfeger, 1995). Luria (1961), for example, demonstrated a developmental sequence of action control via verbal regulation. Very young children are not able to guide their own behaviour by inhibiting irrelevant behaviour either through external or internal speech. Later, toddlers become capable of using external verbal commands to direct their behaviour, yet they continue to be unable to regulate their behaviour with their own verbal instructions (internal or aloud). However, until recently most psychological models paid little attention to inhibition. Inhibition was ignored by behaviourists and not seen as particularly useful in information processing models of cognition (Harnishfeger, 1995).

Selective attention probably cannot be exclusively an inhibition mechanism, because outside of laboratory experiments there are just too many things that would have to be inhibited. However, resistance to interference from potentially attention-capturing processes is clearly important in understanding many real life phenomena, such as school children who cannot keep their attention on class, adults with obsessive-compulsive disorder (who cannot inhibit the intrusion of unwelcome thoughts), and older adults with Alzheimer's disease (Kane, Hasher, Stolzfus, Zacks, & Connelly, 1994). Considerable evidence has accumulated in support of the suppression position in general (Tipper, 1985; Tipper & Baylis, 1987; Tipper & Cranston, 1985), and research on inhibitory processes is probably the most active and theoretically interesting work within attention theory at the present time. The reasons for this probably include the growing preference among cognitive psychologists for the brain metaphor rather than the computer metaphor, the impact of studies relating the frontal cortex to resistance and interference, and connectionist models in which simple processing units send both excitatory and inhibitory signals to each other (Bjorklund & Harnishfeger, 1995; Dempster, 1995; Posner, 1994).

Evidence for facilitation and inhibition effects comes from positive and negative priming, respectively (Neill et al., 1995). Suppose that a subject must attend and respond to one source of information, while ignoring another, and must later unexpectedly respond to the previously ignored information or to entirely new information. According to facilitation theories, the effects of the ignored information dissipate over time, but if those effects have not yet dissipated completely, then processing of the previously ignored information should show an advantage over completely new information (positive priming). However, if the processing of ignored information is inhibited when processing attended information, subsequent processing of the ignored information must overcome that inhibition. Inhibited information should be more difficult to process than new information (negative priming).

Negative priming has been demonstrated in a great variety of selective-attention tasks. For example, research on lexical ambiguity has focused heavily on the question of whether sentence context is able to constrain processing only to the meaning that is appropriate in the context, or whether multiple meanings become activated in all contexts. Data supporting the latter view (temporary non-conscious activation of multiple meanings) are frequently cited as evidence for the modularity of lexical processing. However, Simpson and Kang (1994) and Yee (1991) report recent studies that are concerned with the fate of meanings *after* the processing of an ambiguous word has run its course, reporting several studies showing that one meaning of an ambiguous word is suppressed following the selection of the other for a response.

Can there be learning without attention?

It is necessary to deconstruct this question somewhat in order to find the essential issues, since different variants of the question may well have different answers. For example, Gass (1997) has countered the claim that 'attention to input is a necessary condition for any learning at all' (Schmidt, 1993b: 35) with the observation that some learning does not even depend on input. Gass cites studies showing that ESL learners who are instructed on one type of relative clause perform well not only on that type but also on other types of relative clauses that are higher up in the universal relative clause accessibility hierarchy (Gass, 1982; Eckman, Bell & Nelson, 1988). Gass points out that input on those structures was not available to the learners in the study, and asks, 'If no input existed, how could attention to input be a necessary condition for all aspects of learning?' (p. 16).

Gass is certainly correct in pointing out that not all aspects of second learning depend on input. Leaving aside the issue of whether innate universals guide SLA and, if so, how, the L1 is a source in addition to target language input that can assist learners and that clearly influences IL development (Zobl & Liceras, 1994). It is equally clear that successful L2 learning goes beyond what is present in input. However, it seems to me that this argument misses the main point of the argument concerning attention, which is not 'Can there be learning that is not based on input?', but rather 'Can there be learning based on unattended input as well as attended input?'

Even restricting the question to whether or not it is necessary to attend to input in order for it to become intake, further clarification of the question is necessary. For example, one might paraphrase the question as 'Is it necessary to pay attention, deliberately, to some aspect of L2 input in order to learn it?', with a focus on intentionality, alertness, and voluntary orienting to specific stimuli. Because we know that attention can be involuntarily attracted to stimuli, it cannot be claimed that learners must intentionally focus their attention on each particular aspect of L2 input in order to learn it. Even if it is true that in order to learn anything one must attend to it, that does not entail that it is necessary to have either the intention to attend or the intention to learn. On the other hand, we know that preparatory attention and voluntary orienting vastly improve encoding (LaBerge, 1995; Cowan, 1995) and since many features of L2 input are likely to be infrequent, non-salient, and communicatively redundant, intentionally focused attention may be a practical (though not theoretical) necessity for successful language learning. Language learners who take a totally passive approach to learning, waiting patiently and depending on involuntary attentional processes to trigger automatic noticing, are likely to be slow and unsuccessful learners. As Hulstijn (this volume) points out, most vocabulary is learned from context, but relying on reading and listening alone for vocabulary learning is very inefficient. We also know that learners are not free to allocate their attention wherever they wish. VanPatten (1990) has carried out experiments showing that learners have great difficulty in attending to both form and content simultaneously, although they need to do both in order to map form and meaning (see Doughty, this volume, for a detailed discussion of this issue).

Another way to paraphrase the question is to ask whether all aspects of L2 input must be attended in order to learn them, or whether some kind of global attention to input is sufficient (Truscott, 1998). For example, is it sufficient for attention to be focused on meaning, with message form picked up without any attention to it (Paradis, 1994), or is Gass (1997) correct in arguing that apperceived input that is processed only semantically (for example, with the help of non-linguistic cues, isolated lexical items, and contextual expectations) and receives no syntactic processing will not lead to development of syntax? It has been suggested that aspects of language may differ in their attentional requirements; perhaps learning lexicon and morphology require attention and awareness in ways that learning syntax does not (VanPatten, 1994; Schwartz, 1993). Based on a review of vocabulary learning studies by amnesics, Ellis (1994b) concludes that attention (but not awareness) is necessary and sufficient for learning the perceptual aspects of novel word forms, while learning word meanings requires both attention and explicit awareness.

The psychological literature provides much less help in resolving this question than some others concerning attention, because relatively few studies have assessed the effects of focusing attention on different features of stimulus sets (as opposed to dividing or sharing attention between two sources of stimuli). The few studies that address this issue suggest that stimulus attributes are filtered by attention and only those that are relevant to the experimental task and receive attention are represented in stored instances (Logan et al., 1996). There are sufficient grounds to motivate an attentionally determined encoding specificity hypothesis for SLA, but insufficient to settle the issue, which clearly requires research within SLA itself, focused on different domains of language.

The question of whether global attention to L2 input might be sufficient is also reflected in the sentiment expressed by many SLA researchers that many features of language could not possibly be attended to, because they are too subtle and abstract (Sharwood Smith, Internet posting to PSYCHEB@listserve.uh.edu, 11/3/97). If these features of language are taken to be those that modern linguistic theory makes explicit – such as abstract principles of government, constraints on movement, and the like – this must surely be true, since many of these are unrecognizable in any conscious way simply by attending to input. On the other hand, assuming that abstract grammars of the type described by linguists are what L2 learners acquire (itself not an uncontroversial assumption), it may well be necessary for learners to attend to the evidence for these principles, including the presence of morphological material, the order of elements, and the ways in which specific utterances map onto meanings. That is, the issue may be resolved in terms of the distinction made at the beginning of this chapter between attention to the surface structure of utterances as distinct from an understanding of abstract rules or principles.

Another way to resolve this issue is suggested by Sharwood Smith's (1994b) distinction between competence, held to be elusive, intuitive, and essentially subconscious, and the on-line production and reception processes of actual language performance. Sharwood Smith gives as an example the position of a verb in a sentence. As far as competence is concerned, there is no rule as such for positioning a verb. Its position falls out from some general principles of UG which prevent it from going anywhere but its one position. However, language processing takes place in real time, so a verb (whose position in the structure of a sentence may not be governed by a rule) must be positioned appropriately (by a rule or routine) in real time utterances generated by a language processor. In order to establish such routines, attention must be allocated to the order of elements (sequences) in both input-processing and in production.

Probably the most interesting variant of the question of whether attention is necessary for learning in all cases concerns detection in Tomlin and Villa's sense and the distinction that can be made between non-conscious registration and conscious perception, 'noticing', or – in Tomlin and Villa's terms – 'detection within selective attention'. Tomlin and Villa's claim that detection is necessary for learning but that detection need not result in awareness is somewhat anticlimactic, since it is self-evidently true that some aspect of language that is not registered in any sense will not lead to learning. The most interesting question, and the hardest to answer conclusively, is whether selection accompanied by awareness is necessary, or whether pre-consciously detected information is sufficient for learning.

There is evidence for the cognitive registration of stimuli without focal attention or awareness, both from subliminal perception studies and from studies using measures of implicit memory to establish the registration of unattended information (Schmidt, 1990, 1993a, 1994a, 1994b, 1995). These studies clearly show cognitive activation (for about a tenth of a second) of previously well-learned information present in long-term memory. However, the vast majority of these studies do not show learning of anything new. On the basis of this distinction, I have proposed a strong version of the 'noticing hypothesis,' a claim that while there is subliminal perception, there is no subliminal learning.

Several types of studies have the potential to falsify this claim, but each entails methodological difficulties. The most straight-forward would be to demonstrate the existence of subliminal learning directly, either by showing positive priming of unattended and unnoticed novel stimuli or by showing learning in dual task studies in which central processing capacity is exhausted by a primary task. Unfortunately, in positive priming studies one can never really be sure that subjects did not allocate any attention or have at least fleeting awareness of what they could not later report (DeSchepper & Treisman, 1996; Merikle & Daneman, 1998). Similarly, in dual task experiments one cannot be sure that *no* attention is devoted to the secondary task, and in experiments using this paradigm, selective attention procedures vary considerably in the extent to which they permit subjects to divide attention between two information sources rather than focusing exclusively on one (Greenwald, 1992).

Schachter, Rounds, Wright, and Smith (1996) have reported learning of complex WH-questions by ESL learners in a non-attentional condition, based on a paradigm used by Curran and Keele (1993) in psychology, although 'non-attentional' is a very misleading label when applied to these experiments. Subjects in this condition were required to read the target structure sentences out loud while performing online a substitution of an earlier seen word for its synonym in the target sentence. Since reading aloud requires attention to the sequence of words and since Schachter et al. define the learning task as one of serial learning, it is very difficult to accept the claim that this was truly a nonattentional condition. If not (and both Schachter et al. and Curran and Keele comment that their use of 'nonattentional' does not mean that no attention at all is devoted towards the secondary task) then the results are consistent with the idea that performance under conditions of divided attention results in some learning (though less than in single task learning), as long as the competing task does not completely deplete attentional resources. The general point is that both positive priming and dual task learning are likely to be contaminated by conscious processes (Loftus & Klinger, 1992).

As a way out of this bind, Jacoby, Lindsay, and Toth (1992) have argued that the way to demonstrate true non-attentional learning is to use the logic of opposition, to arrange experiments in which unconscious processes oppose the aims of conscious processes. DeSchepper and Treisman (1996) have recently used this logic to produce what may be the most solid demonstration to date of unattended learning, using an experimental paradigm devised by Rock and Gutman (1981). Rock and Gutman presented two overlapped nonsense shapes and asked subjects to attend to one of them (e.g., the green one, not the red one) and rate it for aesthetic quality. After a series of trials, they gave participants a surprise recognition test, found that recognition was at chance, and concluded that attention is needed to form new representations of shape. DeSchepper and Treisman's innovation was to add an implicit memory measure (response time) to the paradigm and to restructure the experimental procedure based on an inhibition mechanism model of attention. After a series of trials in which subjects attended to green shapes (ignoring red ones) and matched them to other shapes, target and distracter were reversed, i.e., a shape that previously appeared in red (distracter) now appeared in green (target). DeSchepper and Treisman report that previously ignored shapes were subsequently responded to more slowly than control shapes (never before exposed). This can only be accounted for by assuming that representations of these unattended novel shapes were formed in memory.

One could perhaps argue that the 'unattended' shapes in experiments like these are in fact attended and briefly noticed before being suppressed, that inhibition is by definition an attentional mechanism, or that learning in this case is an example of unconscious detection (without alertness, orienting, or awareness), which is itself a form of attention. However, it would be unwise to make such arguments, for this would raise the very serious question of whether the hypothesis that attention is necessary for all learning could ever be falsified, even in principle. It seems wise to conclude, therefore, that there can be representation and storage in memory of unattended novel stimuli, something frequently claimed but not convincingly demonstrated in the past.

The DeSchepper and Treisman experiment counts even more heavily against the strong form of the noticing hypothesis, that there is no learning whatsoever from input that is not noticed, because stimuli that were shown in a previous experiment (Rock & Gutman, 1981) not to have exceeded the subjective threshold of perception were shown in this experiment to have exceeded the objective threshold and to have led to learning. This is an important study, therefore, although there are some limitations to these findings that make it questionable how relevant such learning could be for SLA. The effect has been found so far only with visual perception and only when ignored stimuli compete directly and strongly for attention, which is probably not generally the case with L2 input. There was no build up of memory strength with multiple presentations in the distracter role, making it unlikely that preconsciously established traces gradually build in strength until they are finally noticed. Not all subjects showed negative priming, suggesting strategy differences, but for those subjects who did demonstrate negative priming, a single act of attention was sufficient to change from inhibition to facilitation, which is necessary if knowledge is to be available for use. This study did not assess subject awareness, but other priming studies have, and the general finding is that unaware subjects show negative priming of ignored stimuli, while aware subjects show facilitation (Driver & Baylis, 1993; Hasher, Stolzfus, Zacks, & Rympa, 1991; Neill & Valdes, 1992). Similar effects have been found in other studies contrasting conscious and unconscious perception (Merikle & Daneman, 1998). Unconsciously perceived stimuli can influence affective reactions; when the same stimuli are consciously perceived, these reactions are neutralized. Unconsciously perceived stimuli lead to automatic reactions; consciously perceived stimuli allow subjects to modify their reactions.

However interesting the finding of storage of non-consciously stored novel information is theoretically, it appears to be of little potential benefit for language learning. Kellogg and Dare (1989), who argue that both attended and unattended encoding are possible, emphasize that this 'does not imply that unattended encoding has any practical value ... [since] the degree of elaboration resulting from unattended encoding appears to be too limited to have any substantive influence on human cognition or behaviour' (p. 412). In fact, if we are less able to access previously ignored information than completely new information, we might have an explanation, not for development in language learning, but for non-learning through habituation of the self-instruction to ignore something.

Conclusions

Like most psychological constructs based initially on common experience, attention does not refer to a single mechanism but to a variety of mechanisms or subsystems, including alertness, orientation, detection within selective attention, facilitation, and inhibition.[4] What these have in common (and do not share with the mechanisms of unattended, preconscious processing) is the function of controlling information processing and behavior when existing skills and routines are inadequate (Neumann, 1996). Learning in the sense of establishing new or modified knowledge, memory, skills, and routines is therefore largely, and perhaps exclusively, a side effect of attended processing.

The question of whether *all* learning from input requires attention to that input remains problematic, and conceptual issues and methodological problems have combined to make a definitive answer illusive, even after a century of psychological experimentation. If the issue is seen as one of intention or the voluntary orientation of attention onto stimuli, the answer seems to be that intention is not a general requirement. However, because goals and motivation are such important determinants of the focus on attention (Baars, 1988), paying deliberate attention to less salient or redundant aspects of L2 input may be a practical necessity. Since task demands are an equally important determinant of attentional focus, instructional practices that focus learners' attention on things that they are less likely to attend to or notice on their own also have a solid justification.

There may be some cases where intentionally focused attention is a requirement. One type of case is when the target language requires that sources of information be attended that are not attended in the L1. An example from phonology would be lexical tone in Vietnamese, which not only requires that six new categories of phonological representation be established, but also requires that learners attend to an aspect of speech that non-tonal languages do not make use of. The other type of case arises when information that is automatically processed in the L1 (without reaching awareness) must be suppressed or treated differently in the L2. Flege (1991) and Valdman (1976) have argued that the learning task is harder in the long run for sounds that are similar in the L1 and L2 than for those that are different. Adult L2 learners are eventually more successful in producing new than similar sounds because they are able to establish phonetic categories for new phones, whereas similar sounds are perceived as equivalent to L1 sounds and

---

[4] This is probably not an exhaustive list. Posner, Walker, Freidrich and Rafal (1987) have suggested that the orientation subsystem itself has three mechanisms: disengaging from one stimulus, shifting to a new one, and re-engaging with the new stimulus. Tom Scovel (personal communication) has alerted me to a study by Casey, Gordon, Mannheim and Rumsey (1993) that accounts for the attentional strengths and weaknesses of autistic savants in terms of these mechanisms. Autistics do not have a problem noticing new stimuli but do have deficient orienting abilities, specifically in disengaging, which gives them their savant ability to perform elaborate calculations.

therefore escape further attention. It is difficult both to detect and to produce the subphonemic details of L2 categories because automatic processing is fast and difficult to modify. To do so requires the inhibition of well established routines so that new ones can be established. The examples given here have been from phonology, but there are parallel cases in all domains of language where it is necessary to attend to new kinds of information or to suppress the automatic processing of other information, both of which require selective attention or control (Bialystok, 1994a).

The important issue of whether there can be any learning (as opposed to activation of known information) on the basis of unattended, subliminal processing remains recalcitrant. Some recent evidence that appears to falsify the claim that attention is necessary for any learning whatsoever has been presented in this chapter. However, many psychologists have expressed the opinion that this dispute will never be settled conclusively, because zero-point questions are not answerable (Baars, 1988; Merikle & Daneman, 1998). Baars argues that the important question is not whether there can be any learning without attention and conscious involvement (unanswerable) but rather whether more attention results in more learning. There does not appear to be any evidence at all against the weaker (but much more easily falsifiable) claim that people learn about the things they attend to and do not learn much about the things they do not attend to (Logan et al., 1996).

If the focus of inquiry is on what specifically in L2 input must be attended, there is a conflict between the encoding specificity hypothesis and the global attention hypothesis. The former claims that only those stimulus attributes that are attended in processing are encoded (Logan et al., 1996). The latter derives from the belief that some aspects of L2 input are so subtle and abstract that they cannot possibly be attended to. The solution proposed in this chapter is that attention must be directed to whatever evidence is relevant for a particular learning domain, i.e. that attention must be specifically focused and not just global. Nothing is free. In order to acquire phonology, one must attend to the sounds of target language input, especially those that are contrastive in the target language, and if one's goal is to sound like a native speaker, one must attend to sub-phonemic details as well. In order to acquire vocabulary one must attend to both word form (pronunciation, spelling) and to whatever clues are available in input that can lead to identification of meaning. In order to acquire pragmatics, one must attend to both the linguistic form of utterances and the relevant social and contextual features with which they are associated. In order to acquire morphology (both derivational and inflectional), one must attend to both the forms of morphemes and their meanings, and in order to acquire syntax one must attend to the order of words and the meanings they are associated with (Schmidt, 1990, 1993b, 1995).

What is noticed or apperceived is not the raw data of the input (the phonetic stream of speech) to which attention is directed, but input as interpreted by existing schemata (Gass, 1988; N. Ellis, this volume). Learners do not notice such aspects of the phonetic stream as voice onset time or vowel frequencies directly, but perceive these phonetic features only as filtered by an existing phonological system (L1-based in the earliest stages, modified as learning progresses) which is itself implicit. The fact that such features are subliminally detected (without orientation or awareness) is important, but so is the principle that non-conscious registration applies to well learned rather than new information. Syntactic categories may also be non-consciously activated once they are well established. MacKay (1990) has reported that highly familiar meanings and syntactic categories of words (in the L1) receive unconscious processing (as shown by priming of semantic and syntactic associates) without entering awareness; however, comprehending what is new requires conscious processing.

While what learners notice (in the restricted sense in which I have been using this term) is not the raw data of input, it is still relatively concrete, i.e., utterances (and parts of utterances) that may be exemplars of higher level categories and principles of the linguistic system, but not the principles or the system itself. Noticing is therefore the first step in language building, not the end of the process. In syntax, Bley-Vroman (1997) has argued that in SLA (unlike L1 acquisition), learners do not reset parameters based on abstract features but accumulate constructions or patterns, and noticing is the interface between the input and the developing set of such constructions. For example, although inversion and the positioning of adverbs in German are seen in the UG perspective to be linked, different learners may notice different things in the input: one learner may notice that adverbs can occur pre-sententially but not notice that there is inversion in such cases, while a different learner may notice the inversion along with the preposed adverbial. However, this use of noticing already goes somewhat beyond the restricted sense in which I have been using the term here, because the only obligatory consequence of attention to input is that learners become aware of sounds, words (recognizable sequences of sounds associated with meanings) and sequences of words. These words are examples of lexical categories such as noun, adverb, and so on, but the input does not come labelled that way. Going beyond purely formulaic use so that one is able to use such constructions productively requires that utterances be syntactically analyzed or parsed (Gass, 1988; Gregg, and Harrington, this volume) and that the learner eventually comes to 'know' (implicitly) that individual words are exemplars of lexical categories. The way in which learners acquire knowledge of lexical categories, constructions, and rules is a central issue in SLA, but it is being viewed here as a question related to the contrast between implicit and explicit learning, rather than to the contrast between attended vs unattended input.[5]

---

[5] There are at least five ways in which lexical categories and constructions could be established in a second language. They may be innate or transferred from the L1 (not learned from L2 input in either case). Alternatively, they may be learned from input based on an implicit, associative, inductive learning mechanism (N. Ellis, this volume). Or they may be learned explicitly, either through instruction or through active, conscious hypothesis testing. Bley-Vroman (1997) proposes that only the L1 and categories 'evidently present' in the input can be the source of such construction. What is evidently present or obvious from input clearly needs to be independently defined. For derivational and inflectional morphology, Bybee (1985) has argued that morphemes whose meanings are centrally related to the meanings of the stems to which they are attached are more obvious and will be acquired earlier than morphemes whose meanings are only peripherally related to that of the stem. For verbs – which deal mainly with events (actions, processes, and states) – the most important semantic distinctions are (in order): aspect, tense, mood, number, and person, and they are predicted to be acquired in that order. Cognitive linguistics constitutes a more general attempt to relate linguistic and cognitive categories and discuss the relationships of these to attention (see N. Ellis, this volume, for discussion).

2 Memory for language

Nick C. Ellis

Working memory

Consider the flow of your conscious experience. At any point in time you may choose to focus your attention on (i) the speech of your conversation-partner, (ii) a section of conversation which you've recreated in your mind's speech from information previously stored in long-term memory (LTM), (iii) a part of the visual scene before your eyes, (iv) a part of a visual scene which you have recreated in your mind's eye from information previously stored in LTM. Of course, you have potential access to a wider range of percepts and memories than these (Baddeley, 1997; Baddeley & Hitch, 1974; Gathercole & Baddeley, 1993).

Baddeley and Hitch (1974) identified three components of working memory (WM):

1. The *central executive*, or *supervisory attentional system (SAS)*, regulates information flow within WM, allocates attention to particular input modalities or LTM systems, activates or inhibits whole sequences of activities guided by schemata or scripts, and resolves potential conflicts between ongoing schema-controlled activities. The processing resources used by the central executive are limited in capacity, and the efficiency with which the central executive can fulfil a role depends upon the other demands that are simultaneously placed upon it. We have limited attentional resources (see Schmidt, and Skehan & Foster, this volume). The central executive is supplemented by two slave systems, each specialised for the short term memory (STM) and manipulation of material within a particular domain: the *phonological loop* holds verbally coded information; the *visuo-spatial sketchpad* deals with visual and spatial material.
2. The phonological loop itself comprises two components: a *phonological store* which represents material in a phonological

code and which decays over time, and a process of *articulatory rehearsal* where inner speech can be used to refresh the decaying representations in the phonological store in order to maintain memory items. If you imagine someone telling you a new phone number they wish you to ring for them: as you hear the information, it is first registered in the phonological store whence it will rapidly decay; to combat this your natural inclination may be to repeat the string to yourself in order to maintain it while dialling; once you stop this rehearsal and start talking on the phone, it is likely that the number will rapidly decay from your memory.

3. The visuo-spatial sketchpad is involved in generating images, temporarily maintaining them, and manipulating information with visual or spatial dimensions. If you try to describe the route from your kitchen to your car, you will place heavy demands on this system – accessing mental maps, perhaps rotating perspective, zooming in on particular areas, and orienting through this mental space.

These slave systems are of limited capacity. Articulatory rehearsal is a serial process and can only say one thing at a time – try saying the phone number and 'the, the, the . . .' simultaneously. Decay from the phonological store in conjunction with a serial refresh process results in the capacity of the phonological loop for novel verbal material being approximately the amount of this material which can be articulated in about two seconds. The visuo-spatial sketchpad can only focus on one image at a time – you may well have found that you closed your eyes in the previous route-description exercise so that there was less competition from concurrent visual perception.

Perception, as input to WM, is automatically filtered and patterned by our existing LTM schema. Consider three examples: (1) As children learn about analogue clocks they closely attend to the features and relative positions of hands and numerals; when experienced adults consult their watch they are aware of *the time*, and have no immediate access to such lower-level perceptual information (Morton, 1967). (2) You do not consciously see the letter features on this page (unless you choose to) as you read this paragraph – you do not see the ascenders, the dots of the i's or the crosses of the t's, you don't even see the letters, you see the words, or groups of words (more likely still, you may not even be aware of the words, instead being conscious of their meaning). It was far from so as you learnt to read. (3) When looking up a new phone-number, if it contains 'chunks', you cannot fail to perceive them. Thus your STM for a patterned phone number

(0800–123999) is much better than that for a more random sequence (4957–632512) even though both strings contain the same number of digits. Therefore, our model of WM must acknowledge the intimate connections and mutual influences of long-term phonological memory and the phonological loop, and of long-term visual memory and the visuo-spatial sketchpad. These interactions underpin the development of automaticity and fluency (see DeKeyser, this volume). Thousands of experiments have investigated the properties of these components of WM (Baddeley, 1986) and the theory is considerably more than as it is described here. Readers should note that in the present character-isation of WM, in emphasising the filtering of input to WM through LTM, I lean more towards interactive views where STM reflects the ac-tivated and attended subsets of LTM (Cowan, 1995), as does Doughty (this volume) than would be the natural inclination of Alan Baddeley and his associates. Also there are alternative models of memory which differ in focus, emphasis or content (for review see Baddeley, 1997; Schacter, 1991). But most of them, like the WM model, acknowledge different modalities of storage, separations between activated short-term and consolidated long term representations, and the role of atten-tional processes in learning and recollection. Thus the WM model will do as a modal view, and the simple summary architecture described in Figure 1 serves as a foundation for describing the role of memory in language acquisition.

The essence of the Working Memory Model is that we have special-ist systems for perceiving and representing, both temporarily and in the long term, visual and auditory information,[1] along with a limited resource attentional system. Given the rich sophistication of language and its linguistic descriptions, this may seem a rather banal starting point for a description of the memory systems that underpin language acquisition. But it will do. It has to do. Because that's just about all there is.

Constructivist approaches to language acquisition

Constructivist views of language acquisition hold that it is primarily these systems that the child uses in bootstrapping their way into lan-guage. None the less, simple learning mechanisms operating in these systems as they are exposed to language data as part of a rich human

---

[1] The working memory model concentrates on the major perceptual modalities of vision and audition. But it acknowledges that the SAS also has access to other slave systems such as those for representing motor schema, kinaesthetics, tactile information, emotion, etc. As we will discuss in the forthcoming section concerning Cognitive Linguistics, these other modalities also have influence on language.

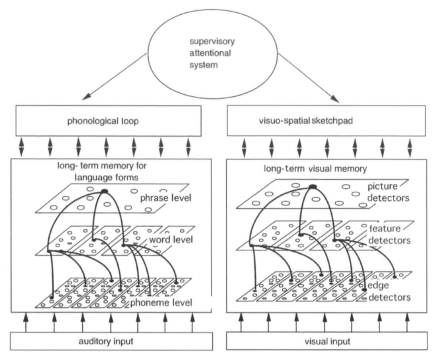

Figure 1. The model of working memory for language acquisition

environment by an organism eager to exploit the functionality of language is enough to drive the slow acquisition of complex language representations. Constructivists deny any innate linguistic universals.[2]

Fluent language users have had tens of thousands of hours on task. They have processed many millions of utterances involving tens of thousands of types presented as innumerable tokens. The evidence of language has ground on their perceptuo-motor and cognitive apparatus to result in complex competencies which can be described by formal theories of linguistics such as UG. It is more than a 'simplifying assumption' that language learning 'can be conceptualised as an instantaneous process' (Chomsky, 1976, pp. 14–15). It is an error which compounds into the fallacy of predeterminism. Language is *learned*. Various theories of language acquisition, including connectionist approaches (Levy, Bairaktaris, Bullinaria &

---

[2] Note that this claim concerns innate *linguistic* universals. It is a specific denial of representational innatism whilst acknowledging the influence of our particular endowment of perceptual transducers, inherited general neuronal architectural constraints, chronotopic constraints, computational capacity constraints and very general attentional biases (Elman et al., 1996; O'Grady, 1997).

Cairns, 1995; MacWhinney, this volume; McClelland, Rumelhart & Hinton, 1986), functional linguistics (Bates & MacWhinney, 1981; MacWhinney & Bates, 1989; see also Harrington and MacWhinney, this volume), emergentist approaches (Elman, Bates, Johnson, Karmiloff-Smith, Parisi, & Plunkett, 1996), and cognitive linguistics (Lakoff, 1987; Langacker, 1987), believe that as the study of language turns to consider ontogenetic acquisition processes, it favours a conclusion whereby the complexity of the final result stems from simple learning processes applied, over extended periods of practice in the learner's lifespan, to the rich and complex problem space of language evidence.

Apparent complexity may come more from the problem than from the system which learns to solve it. Simon (1969) illustrated this by describing the path of an ant making its homeward journey on a pebbled beach. The path seems complicated. The ant probes, doubles back, circumnavigates and zigzags. But these actions are not deep and mysterious manifestations of intellectual power. Closer scrutiny reveals that the control decisions are both simple and few in number. An environment-driven problem solver often produces behaviour that is complex only because a complex environment drives it. Language learners have to solve the problem of language. Thus in this case, like that of Simon's ant, it is all too easy to overestimate the degree of control, sophistication and innate neurological predisposition required in its solution.

The complexity is in the language, not the learning process: 'Many universal or at least high-probability outcomes are so inevitable given a certain "problem-space" that extensive genetic underwriting is unnecessary ... Just as the conceptual components of language may derive from cognitive *content*, so might the computational facts about language stem from nonlinguistic *processing*, that is, from the multitude of competing and converging constraints imposed by perception, production, and memory for linear forms in real time.' (Bates, 1984: 188–190).

Constructivists are unhappy with nativist explanations simply because they may not be necessary – why posit predeterminism, like magic, when simpler explanations might suffice (Sampson, 1980; Tomasello, 1995)? They are additionally unhappy because the innateness hypothesis has no process explanation; our current theories of brain function, process and development do not readily allow for the inheritance of structures which might serve as principles or parameters of UG (Elman et al., 1996; Quartz & Sejnowski, 1997; cf. Gregg, this volume). Without such a process explanation, innatist theories are left with a 'and here a miracle occurs' step in their argumentation.

Incompleteness of explanation is not a fatal flaw – Mendel was correct long before Crick and Watson provided a process explanation – but we do expect the gaps to be filled eventually, and current neuroscience makes implausible any assumptions about inherited parameter 'switches'. Finally, they are unhappy with arguments about learnability and the poverty of the stimulus. If the definition of language is revised to include statements of likelihood, Gold's (1967) [see editor's footnote] theorem cannot be proven, and the consequential limits to positive evidence-only learning are not established (Ellison, 1997; Quartz & Sejnowski, 1997).

Thus the constructivist view is that language learning results from general processes of human inductive reasoning being applied to the specific problem of language. There is no language acquisition device specifiable in terms of linguistic universals, principles and parameters, or language-specific learning mechanisms. Rather, language is cut of the same cloth as other cognitive *processes*, but it is special in terms of its cognitive *content*. Learners' language comes not directly from their genes, but rather from the structure of adult language, from the structure of their cognitive and social cognitive skills, and from the constraints on communication inherent in expressing non-linear cognition into the *linear* channel provided by the human vocal-auditory apparatus (Bates, Thal, & Marchman, 1991). Language is like the majority of complex systems that exist in nature and which empirically exhibit hierarchical structure (Simon, 1962). And like these other systems, its complexity emerges from simple developmental processes being exposed to a massive and complex environment. We are enlightened when we substitute a process description for a state description, when we describe development rather than the final state, when we focus on the language acquisition process (LAP) rather than language acquisition device (LAD).

Chunking as the LAP

The term *chunking* was coined by George Miller in his classical review of STM (Miller, 1956). It is the development of permanent sets of associative connections in long-term storage and is the process that underlies the attainment of automaticity and fluency in language. Newell (1990) argues that it is the overarching principle of human

Editor's footnote: Gold's theorem is a Mathematical Model of first language learnability describing the difficulties of inducing any target language from a 'hypothesis space', which is gradually narrowed on the basis of input to the learner, both in the form of 'text presentation' (positive evidence) and 'informant presentation' (negative evidence) (see Pinker, 1995: 147, and Saxton, 1997: 141, for discussion).

cognition: 'A chunk is a unit of memory organisation, formed by bringing together a set of already formed chunks in memory and welding them together into a larger unit. Chunking implies the ability to build up such structures recursively, thus leading to a hierarchical organisation of memory. Chunking appears to be a ubiquitous feature of human memory. Conceivably, it could form the basis for an equally ubiquitous law of practice.' (Newell, 1990: 7). *The power law of practice* describes the rate of acquisition of most skills (see DeKeyser, this volume): for example, Anderson (1982) showed that this function applies to cigar rolling, syllogistic reasoning, book writing, industrial production, reading inverted text, and lexical decision. The critical feature in this relationship is not just that performance, typically time, improves with practice, but that the relationship involves the power law in which the amount of improvement decreases as a function of increasing practice or frequency. For the case of language acquisition, Kirsner (1994) has shown that lexical recognition processes (both for speech perception and reading) and lexical production processes (articulation and writing) are governed by the relationship $T = PN^{-\alpha}$ where T is some measure of latency of response and N the number of trials of practice. Newell (1990; Newell & Rosenbloom, 1981) formally demonstrated that the following three assumptions of chunking as a learning mechanism could lead to the power law of practice. (1) People chunk at a constant rate: every time they get more experience, they build additional chunks. (2) Performance on the task is faster the more chunks that have been built that are relevant to the task. (3) The structure of the environment implies that higher-level chunks recur more rarely. Chunks describe environmental situations. The higher the chunk in the hierarchy, the more subpatterns it has; and the more subpatterns, the less chance there is of it being true of the current situation. For example, if one chunk is the trigram 'the' and another the bigram 'ir' then one will see each of these situations more frequently than the higher level chunk 'their'. These three assumptions interact as follows: the constant chunking rate and the assumption about speedup with chunking yields exponential learning. But as higher level chunks build up, they become less and less useful, because the situations in which they would help do not recur. Thus the learning slows down, being drawn out from an exponential towards a power law.

Although many lexical phenomena, because they involve relatively idiosyncratic memories, follow simply the power law of practice, other aspects of language acquisition, particularly those involving systemic generalisations, may seem at first sight to violate it. Thus there are classic exceptions like U-shaped learning curves and apparent backslidings in the acquisition of inflectional morphology and syntax more generally. Connectionist accounts of these phenomena hold that they result from the interactions in learning of many individual exemplars in a system, along with their components. The learning of each component follows a power law of practice, but systemic regularities may follow different non-linear growth curves which arise from interactions (both competitive and facilitatory) between the multiple components in the system and the combinations of their form-function mappings (Elman et al., 1996, Chapter 4). Thus, for example, a learner might learn *went* as the past tense of *go* initially as a lexical item. Its acquisition follows the power law. As time progresses more and more 'regular' past tense mappings are learned and the collaboration of these exemplars of form-past tense mapping pull the learner back to the *go-ed* form. There is not scope here to do more than introduce this matter – a more complete explanation for the particular case of regular and irregular morphosyntax can be found in Ellis and Schmidt (1998: 330–333) and we will return to the general issues in subsequent sections of this chapter which concern cognitive linguistics and the connectionist modelling.

So chunking, the bringing together a set of already formed chunks in memory and welding them together into a larger unit, is a basic associative learning process which can occur in all representational systems. Its operation in both phonological and visual LTM systems is acknowledged in Figure 1 by the arcs which gather recurring patterns of several units at a lower level together into one unit at the next-higher plane. The next section fills in some details of chunking in phonological memory as a key aspect of language acquisition.

Chunking in phonological memory

Language is sequential. Speech is a sequence of sounds. Writing is a sequence of symbols. Learning to understand a language involves parsing the speech stream into chunks which reliably mark meaning. The naturalistic learner doesn't care about linguists' analyses of language. They don't care about theories of grammar or whether words or morphemes are the atomic units of language. From a functional perspective, the role of language is to communicate meanings, and the learner wants to acquire the label-meaning relations.

This task is made more tractable by the patterns of language. Learners' attention to the evidence to which they are exposed soon demonstrates that there are recurring chunks of language. There are limited sets of sounds and of written alphabet. These units occur in more or less predictable sequences (to use written examples, in English 'e' follows 'th' more often than 'x' does, 'the' is a common sequence, 'the [space]' is frequent, 'dog' follows 'the [space]' more often than it does 'book', 'How do you do?' occurs quite often, etc.). A key task for the learner is to discover these patterns within the sequence of language. At some level of analysis, the patterns refer to meaning. It doesn't happen at the lower levels: 't' doesn't mean anything, nor does 'th', but 'the' does, and 'the dog' does better, and 'How do you do?' does very well, thank you. In these cases the learner's goal is satisfied, and the fact that this chunk activates some meaning representations makes this sequence itself more salient in the input stream.

The learner is searching for sequential patterns with reliable reference, and throughout this process, they are acquiring knowledge of the sequential aspects of language. From this perspective, language acquisition is essentially a sequence learning problem: the acquisition of word form, collocations, and grammatical class information all result from predominantly unconscious (or implicit) processes of analysis of sequence information (see forthcoming section on 'Sequences in learner talk'). Phonology, lexis, and syntax develop hierarchically by repeated cycles of differentiation and integration of chunks of sequences. With the benefit of hindsight, it comes as no surprise that language is acquired in this way. The formation of chunks, as stable intermediate structures, is the mechanism underlying the evolution and organisation of many complex hierarchical systems in biology, society, and physics (Dawkins, 1976; Simon, 1962).

Chunking and lexical acquisition

Learning lexical structure involves identifying the categorical units of speech perception, their particular sequences in particular words, and their general sequential probabilities in the language. Melton (1963) demonstrated for digit sequences like phone numbers that the more they are repeated in the phonological STM, the greater the LTM for these items, and in turn, the easier they are to repeat as sequences in STM. The same process of chunking allows us to bootstrap our way into lexis (Ellis, 1996a). Repetition of sequences in the phonological loop allows their consolidation in phonological LTM. Perception of frequent sequences, and the more frequent subsequences within them, allows their chunking in phonological LTM. The same cognitive system which does the LTM for phonological sequences does the perception of phonological sequences. Thus the tuning of phonological LTM to regular sequences allows more ready perception of input which contains regular sequences. Regular sequences are thus perceived as chunks and, as a result, individuals' phonological STM for regular sequences is greater than for irregular ones.

Experience of our environment leads to modification of our schemata, our schemata direct our exploration of the environment, our exploration samples the available information in the environment, and thus the cycle continues. The same systems which perceive language represent language. Thus the 'cycle of perception' (Neisser, 1976) is also the 'cycle of learning'; bottom–up and top–down processes are in constant interaction.

These processes result in sequences of language which are *potential* labels, but what about reference? In addition to implicit learning within input modalities, attentional focus in WM can result in the formation of cross-modal associations. The most basic principle of association is the Law of Contiguity: 'Objects once experienced together tend to become associated in the imagination, so that when any one of them is thought of, the others are likely to be thought of also, in the same order of sequence or coexistence as before.' (James, 1890: 561). Nodes which are simultaneously or contiguously attended in WM tend to become associated in the long term. The implicit pattern-detection processes that occur *within* these modalities of representation entail that any such *cross-modal* associations typically occur between the highest chunked level of activated node. Thus, to extend Morton's (1967) example, the adult looking at their watch when post falls through their letter-box each morning learns an association that *mail-time* is 08.30, not one between envelopes and the big hand of their watch.

Similar processes occur within the language system. Consider for illustration two learners of differing levels of proficiency hearing the complaint 'I have a headache' while they observe salient visual input (Figure 2). The more proficient leaner, who knows the words *hEd* and *eik*, attends to the sequence of these *two* chunks along with the visual pattern. The less proficient learner, who has neither heard such words nor syllables before, has to attend to a much longer sequence of chunks: // h // E // d // ei // k //, and there is concomitantly greater chance of errors in sequencing (for example, Crystal (1987) describes a child who pronounced *blanket* as [bwati], [bati], [baki], and [batit] within a few hours of each other). Three occurrences for the more proficient learner might well result in three pairings of the image with // hEd // eik // and a concomitantly strengthened association between the visual and phonological representations. For the less proficient learner there might be much less commonality in the language sequences between trials, with // h // E // d // ei // k // on one trial, but // h // ei // k // on another and // E // d // h // ei // k // on a third (Treiman & Danis, 1988). No strong cross-modal association between the attended unit in the visual module and a common representation in the language module

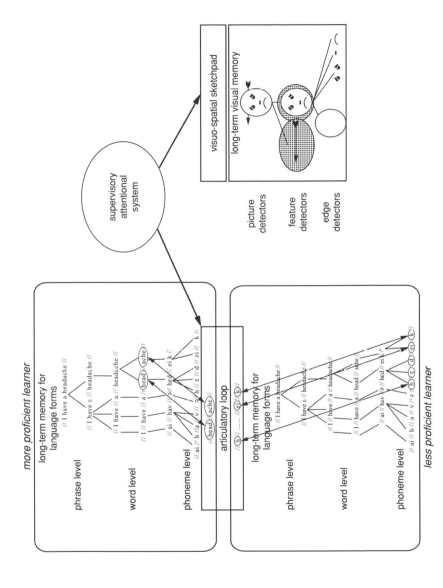

Figure 2. Cross-modal associations for less and more proficient learners bearing the term 'headache' for the first time while viewing its referent

43

can result. The more the units of language come as packaged wholes, the greater the possibility of attentional focus and resultant association.

The more any novel word, be it L1 or L2, is repeated in phonological WM, the more its regularities and chunks are abstracted, and the more accurately and readily these can be called to WM, either for accurate pronunciation as articulatory output or as labels for association with other representations. It is from these potential associations with other representations that interesting properties of language occur. Links with conceptual representations underlie reference and grounded semantics. Links with frequent local collocations underlie syntax and idiomatic meaning. Links with local and more distant lexical neighbours underlie lexical semantics. Links between L2 and simultaneously active L1 representations underlie translation and language transfer effects. These simple associations amass over the learner's language-input history into a web of multimodal connections which represent the complexities of language.

Chunking and idiom acquisition

The cycle of learning that underpins vocabulary acquisition operates at all levels of language. Language reception and production are mediated by learner's representations of chunks of language: 'Suppose that, instead of shaping discourse according to rules, one really pulls old language from memory (particularly old language, with all its words in and everything), and then reshapes it to the current context: "context shaping", as Bateson puts it, "is just another term for grammar"' (Becker, 1983: 218).

As we analyse language performance, so the underlying chunks become readily apparent. Sinclair (1991), as a result of his experience directing the Cobuild project, the largest lexicographic analysis of the English language to date, proposed *the principle of idiom* – 'a language user has available to him or her a large number of semi-preconstructed phrases that constitute single choices, even though they might appear to be analysable into segments. To some extent this may reflect the recurrence of similar situations in human affairs; it may illustrate a natural tendency to economy of effort; or it may be motivated in part by the exigencies of real-time conversation. However it arises, it has been relegated to an inferior position in most current linguistics, because it does not fit the open-choice model' (Sinclair, 1991: 110). Rather than it being a rather minor feature, compared with grammar, Sinclair suggests that for normal texts, the first mode of analysis to be applied is the idiom principle, since most of text is interpretable by this principle. Comparisons of written and spoken corpora demonstrate that collocations are even more frequent in spoken language (Butler, 1995). Collocations and stock phrases are viewed with just the same importance in SLA and FL research where they are known as holophrases (Corder, 1973), prefabricated routines and patterns (Hakuta, 1974), formulaic speech (Wong-Fillmore, 1976), memorised sentences and lexicalized stems (Pawley & Syder, 1983), lexical phrases (Nattinger & DeCarrico, 1992), or formulas (R. Ellis, 1994a).

Pawley and Syder (1983) give good reason to believe that much of language is in fact closed-class. They provide two sources of evidence: native-like selection and native-like fluency. Native speakers do *not* exercise the creative potential of syntactic rules of a generative grammar (Chomsky, 1965) to anything like their full extent. Indeed if they did, they would not be accepted as exhibiting native-like control of the language. While such expressions as (a) 'I wish to be wedded to you', (b) 'Your marrying me is desired by me', and (c) 'My becoming your spouse is what I want', demonstrate impeccable grammatical skill, they are unidiomatic, odd, foreignisms when compared with the more ordinary and familiar (d) 'I want to marry you'. Thus native-like selection is not a matter of syntactic rule alone. Speaking natively is speaking idiomatically, using frequent and familiar collocations, and learners thus have to acquire these familiar word sequences. That native speakers have done so is demonstrated not only by the frequency of these collocations in the language, but also by the fact that conversational speech is broken into fluent units of complete grammatical clauses of four to ten words, uttered at or faster than normal rates of articulation. A high proportion of these clauses, particularly of the longer ones, are entirely familiar memorized clauses and clause sequences which are the normal building-blocks of fluent spoken discourse (and at the same time provide models for the creation of (partly) new sequences which are memorable and in their turn enter the stock of familiar usages – for example 'I'm sorry to keep you waiting', 'Mr. Brown is so sorry to have kept you waiting', etc. can allow the creation of a lexicalised sentence stem 'NP be-*tense* sorry to keep-*tense* you waiting'). 'In the store of familiar collocations there are expressions for a wide range of familiar concepts and speech acts, and the speaker is able to retrieve these as wholes or as automatic chains from the LTM; by doing this he minimises the amount of clause-internal encoding work to be done and frees himself to attend to other tasks in talk-exchange, including the planning of larger units of discourse' (Pawley & Syder, 1983: 192).

Learners don't care about the units of language as long as they map onto accessible meanings (Peters, 1983) and language learning involves learning sequences of words (frequent collocations, phrases, and idioms) as much as it does sequences within words. For present purposes, such collocations can simply be viewed as big words – the role of WM in learning such structures is the same as for words. It is a somewhat more difficult task to the degree that these utterances are longer than words and so involve more phonological units to be sequenced. It is a somewhat less difficult task to the degree that the component parts cluster into larger chunks of frequently-encountered (at least for learners with more language experience) sequences comprising morphemes, words, or shorter collocations themselves (e.g., 'I've a _'). Despite these qualifications the principle remains the same – just as repetition aids the consolidation of vocabulary, so it does the long-term acquisition of phrases (Ellis & Sinclair, 1996).[3]

Chunking and creativity

There are two major aspects of language creativity. One is the ability to express ideas in a novel grammatical surface form (grammatical creativity). The other is the ability to express novel ideas (conceptual/semantic creativity). In both cases, the creative act involves the original and interesting combination of two or more pre-existing ideas or representations. It is the combination of pre-existing chunks. For interesting creative behaviour to occur, there must be a substantial

---

[3] A natural question might then be, 'Why then, in L1 and L2 acquisition, doesn't frequency in the input correlate in every case with acquisition orders for, say, morphemes?' The initial response to this is that frequency may not be the only explanation, but it takes us a large part of the way. Larsen-Freeman (1976) was the first to propose that the common acquisition order of English morphemes to which ESL learners, despite their different ages and language backgrounds, adhere is a function of the frequency of occurrence of these morphemes in adult native-speaker speech. But we must then qualify this answer as follows: for morpheme acquisition orders we are talking about the acquisition of regularities in *systems of form-function mapping* and thus there is something that overrides the mere effect of frequency of exposure to a particular form, and that is the effects of frequency of 'friends' (those exemplars which conspire in this form-function mapping) and 'enemies' (those which use different mappings). It is the summing of these competitions which result in the cue reliabilities, consistencies and validities which underpin relative learnabilities. Ellis and Schmidt (1998) and DeKeyser (1997) show that the power law applies to the acquisition of morphosyntax and that it is this acquisition function which underlies interactions of regularity and frequency in this domain. As described by MacWhinney, this volume, the Competition Model sees all of language acquisition as the process of acquiring from language input the particular cues which relate phonological forms and conceptual meanings or communicative intentions, and the determination of the frequencies, reliabilities and validities of these cues. This information then serves as the knowledge base for sentence production and comprehension in lexicalist constraint-satisfaction theories which hold that sentence processing is the simultaneous satisfaction of the multiple probabilistic constraints afforded by the cues present in each particular sentence (MacDonald, Pearlmutter & Seidenberg, 1994; MacWhinney & Bates, 1989).

knowledge base so that there is something to and from which transfer of information can occur. Thus a high level of prior knowledge acquisition is necessary. Quantifying this is difficult, but the 10-year rule has been suggested as an estimate of time-on-task needed for expertise, with, for example, 50,000 'kitchen facts' needed for an expert cook, and 50,000 board positions for a grand master at chess (Norman, 1980; Simon, 1980). There is some exploitable mileage in the observations (a) that the ball-park estimate of the size of vocabulary of an average college student is also around 50,000 words, and (b) that vocabulary development is a strong predictor of subsequent achievements in morphology and syntax (Marchman & Bates, 1994).

Memory chunks (schema, scripts, frames, stereotypes, etc.) lie at the core of creativity in all domains of cognition.[4] In drafting this chapter I am building structures from my pre-existing knowledge: sometimes they are low level clichés ('at the core of' in the previous sentence); sometimes they are high-level chunks (the earlier large quotation from Sinclair); sometimes they are surface form representations; sometimes they are conceptual ones (whole theories, like that of Neisser). Sometimes, 'thinks', like things, just click into place. Like pieces of a jigsaw, they have their own structure. My representations of my science, like those of my language, have evolved hierarchically by repeated cycles of differentiation and integration – identifying the smaller chunks and building up the larger ones. My available representations are tuned by the content and frequency of my lifespan intake. The intelligibility of this account for you, the reader, is determined by your system of constructs, which reflects your experience. The present account will thus sound more foreign to some linguist readers than to some psychologists. The point about the idiom principle is that maximally rapid intelligibility is afforded by the use of frequent, pre-existing chunks in the parole.

---

[4] Besides schema, scripts, frames and stereotypes, there is one other general class of abstractions from input data, namely syntax. Does syntax also lie at the core of linguistic creativity? Well, it depends on what is meant by 'syntax'. The more syntax is conceived as systems of form-function mapping, as in systemic functional or lexical functional grammars, the more I would agree that syntax contributes, along with any of the other types of abstraction that are relevant to the communicative task in hand. But the more a conception of syntax isolates abstractions which relate signifiers, but divorces them from the signifieds, from semantics, the functions of language, and the other social, biological, experiential and cognitive aspects of the humankind who invented and used language ever since, the less I believe that such syntactic descriptions have any causal creative role (Ellis, 1998). Even so, there would still be some influence. Because humans, in their everyday making sense of the world, also abstract patterns which relate lexical forms. And thus, as shown by Epstein (1967), 'A vapy koobs desaked the citar molently um glox nerfs' is more readily read and remembered than 'koobs vapy the desaked um glox citar nerfs a molently'!

Individual differences in phonological STM predict language aptitude

One advantage of this account is that individual differences in phonological STM ability explain individual differences in language learning aptitude. Individuals differ in their ability to repeat phonological sequences (this is known as phonological STM span). In part this can result from constitutional factors – some individuals are born with better phonological abilities than others. Language impaired and dyslexic individuals have poorer phonological STM spans (Ellis, 1990, 1996a; Ellis & Large, 1987; Gathercole & Baddeley, 1993). Other reasons for having a poor phonological STM span for a particular type of material are due to the learner not having any prior experience of the content of the to-be-recalled material, and thus having no LTM representations which aid the chunking of the incoming material. Examples of these interactions in the domain of language include the effects of: long-term lexical knowledge on STM for words (Brown & Hulme, 1992), long-term phonological knowledge on STM for non- and foreign-language words (Ellis & Beaton, 1993b; Gathercole & Baddeley, 1993; Treiman & Danis, 1988;), long-term grammatical knowledge on STM for phrases (Epstein, 1967), and long-term semantic knowledge on STM for word strings (Cook, 1979). This is also the reason why elicited imitation tests serve so well as measures of second-language competence (Bley-Vroman & Chaudron, 1994; Lado, 1965).

This ability to repeat verbal sequences (for example, new phone numbers or non-words like 'sloppendash') immediately after hearing them, is a good predictor of a learner's facility to acquire vocabulary and syntax in first, second, and foreign language learning. Ellis (1996a) reviews a wide range of evidence for this: (i) phonological STM span predicts vocabulary acquisition in L1 and L2, (ii) interfering with phonological STM by means of articulatory suppression disrupts vocabulary learning, (iii) repetition and productive rehearsal of novel words promotes their long term consolidation and retention, (iv) phonological STM predicts syntax acquisition in L1 and L2, (v) phonological rehearsal of L2 utterances results in superior performance in receptive skills in terms of learning to comprehend and translate L2 words and phrases, explicit metalinguistic knowledge of the detailed content of grammatical regularities, acquisition of the L2 forms of words and phrases, accuracy in L2 pronunciation, and grammatical fluency and accuracy (Ellis & Sinclair, 1996). Thus phonological sensitivity, chunking and segmentation are key components of language learning aptitude (see Sawyer & Ranta, this volume).

Let us consider L2 vocabulary learning as a detailed example. The novice L2 learner comes to the task with a capacity for repeating native words. The degree to which the relevant skills and knowledge are transferable to immediate L2 word repetition depends on the degree to which the phonotactic patterns in the L2 approximate to those of the native language (Ellis & Beaton, 1993b). Thus long-term knowledge affects phonological STM. The reverse is also true: repetition of L2 forms promotes long-term retention (Ellis & Beaton, 1993a; Ellis & Sinclair, 1996). As learners practise hearing and producing L2 words, so they automatically and implicitly acquire knowledge of the statistical frequencies and sequential probabilities of the phonotactics of the L2. In turn, as they begin to abstract knowledge of L2 regularities, they become more proficient at short-term repetition of novel L2 words. And so L2 vocabulary learning lifts itself up by its bootstraps. Although learners need not be aware of the *processes* of such pattern extraction, they will later be aware of the *product* of these processes since on the next time they experience that pattern it is the patterned chunk that they will be aware of, not the individual components.

Working out how words work (i): distributional analysis of memorized collocations to derive word-class information and morphology

But of course, language learners do not simply recombine surface elements of previous input in their novel productions. There is creativity in the transition to L1 competence and in L2 interlanguage which demonstrates the abstraction of systematicity from prior input, a systematicity which is certainly rule-like if not rule-governed. The following examples from my son Gabe's productions are utterances which he has certainly never heard before: 'Give it to he' (2 years, 6 months), 'That's good of I' (2:11), 'We're coming soonly', 'Rain is falling straightly', 'I like you because you don't shout at me oftenly' (3:0–3:2), 'Dad had a lot of them, but I had a lotter' (3:3). Such errors are not limited to learners – even Gabe's dad has been prone to overcorrect to produce such cringe-worthy utterances as 'Thank you kindlily'. Learners abstract structural regularities from previously experienced utterances which share structural and functional similarity (see section 'Sequences in learner talk').

As we analyse word sequence chunks, so we discover that they have characteristic structural types. Linguists call these regularities grammar. And if we take a bottom–up approach, and simply describe the distributional properties of words and morphemes in chunks, so we discover that something very close to traditional grammatical word-class and inflectional morphological information emerges. I will describe four demonstrations for illustration: (1) Kiss (1973) which was the first analysis of this type. (2) Elman (1990) which used a neurologically plausible connectionist model to analyze the sequential dependencies in miniature language systems. This work is important because it demonstrates how one single process of sequential acquisition can give rise to useful representations at all levels from phonetics, through phonotactics and lexis, and up to syntax. (3) The Cobuild Project (Sinclair, 1991), a corpus linguistic analysis of English-as-it-is-used to determine the collocational streams that are frequent in the input data. (4) Recent connectionist work concerning acquisition of regular and irregular morphology.

Kiss

Kiss (1973) provided the first computational model of the acquisition of grammatical word class from accumulating evidence of word distributions. An associative learning program was exposed to an input corpus of 15,000 words gathered from tape recordings of seven Scottish middle class mothers talking to their children who were between one and three years of age. The program read the corpus and established associative links between the words and their contexts (here defined as their *immediate successor*). Thus, for example, the program counted that *the* was followed by *house* 4.1% of the time, by *horse* 3.4%, by *same* 1%, by *put* never, etc., that *a* was connected to *horse* 4.2%, to *house* 2.9%, to *put* never, etc. Next a classification learning program analyzed this information to produce connections between word representations which had strengths determined by the degree of similarity between the words in terms of the degree to which they tended to occur together after a common predecessor (i.e., the degree of similarity based on their 'left-contexts'). This information formed a level of representation which was a network of word similarities. Finally the classification program analyzed this similarity information to produce a third network which clustered them into groups of similar words. The clusters that arose were as follows: (*hen sheep pig farmer cow house horse*) (*can are do think see*) (*little big nice*) (*this he that it*) (*a the*) (*you I*). It seemed that these processes discovered word classes which were nounlike, verblike, adjectivelike, articlelike, pronounlike, etc. Thus the third level of representation, which arises from simple analysis of word distributional properties, can be said to be that of word class. Kiss argues that in this way language learners can boot-strap their way into discovering word classes. More recent, and much larger, demonstrations show that such bootstrapping results from a variety of analysis methods including statistical, recurrent neural net-work, or self-organizing map models (Charniak, 1993; Elman, 1990; Finch & Chater, 1994; Sampson, 1987).

Elman

Elman (1990) used a simple recurrent network to investigate the tem-poral properties of sequential inputs of language. In simple recurrent networks, the input to the network is the current letter in a language stream, and the output represents the network's best guess as to the next letter. The difference between the predicted state and the correct subsequent state (the target output) is used by the learning algorithm to adjust the weights in the network at every time step. In this way the network improves its accuracy with experience. A context layer is a special subset of inputs that receive no external input but which feed the result of the previous processing back into the internal representa-tions. Thus at time 2 the hidden layer processes both the input of time 2 and, from the context layer, the results of processing at time 1. And so on, recursively. It is by this means that simple recurrent networks capture the sequential nature of temporal inputs. Note that such net-works are not given any explicit information about the structure of language.

Elman's network had 5 input units (binary coding one letter at a time – thus *m* was represented as 01101, *a* as 00001, *e* as 00101, etc.), 20 hidden units, 5 output units (again coding individual letters), and 20 context units. It was fed one letter (or phoneme) at a time and had to predict the next letter in the sequence (akin to asking you to predict the next letter at the following example choice points marked!: Once upo!n a! time). It was trained on 200 sentences of varying length from 4 to 9 words. There was no word or sentence boundary information; thus part of the stream was:

Manyyearsagoaboyandgirllivedbytheseatheyplayedhappily . . .

The error patterns for a network trained on this task illustrate that the network abstracted a lot of information about the structure of English. If the error is high, it means that the network had trouble predicting this letter. Error tends to be high at the beginning of a word and decrease until the word boundary is reached. Thus the model is learning the word units of the language (compare these abilities in eight-month-old infants – Saffran, Aslin & Newport, 1996). Before it is exposed to the first letter in the word, the network is unsure what is to follow. But the identity of the first two phonemes is usually sufficient to enable the network to predict with a high degree of confidence subsequent phonemes in the word. The time course of this process is as predicted by cohort models of word recognition (Marslen-Wilson, 1993). Once the input string reaches the end of the word, the network cannot be sure which word is to follow, so the error increases – hence the saw-tooth shape of the error function. But some word sequence information is evidently extracted too. For example, the segmentation error '*aboy*' which the network made is simply a function of the distributional characteristics of these words in the language sample – *boy* often followed *a*, just like the phonemes within a word occurred together. Such word sequence information is important in the extraction of syntactic information. It is also implicated in the acquisition of formulaic phrases (once upon a time, etc.), and in the segmentation errors of language learners – *a nelephant for an elephant, ife* for *knife, dult* for *adult*, etc. There are both overshooting errors (*aboy* at 13th position) and undershooting errors (*the* rather than *they* at 39th position). The model also showed implicit categorization of units. Although at first the network's predictions were random, with time the network learned to predict, not necessarily the actual next phoneme, but the correct category of phoneme, whether it was a vowel or consonant, etc. (see also Elman & Zipser, 1988, on this with networks trained on a large corpus of unsegmented continuous raw speech without labels). Thus the network moves from processing mere surface regularities to representing something more abstract, but without this being built in as a pre-specified phonemic or other linguistic constraint.

Elman (1990) also trained a larger network of similar architecture (31 input nodes, 31 output nodes, hidden and context vectors 150 units each) with sequences of words following a simple grammar. A 27534 word sequence formed the training set and the network had to learn to predict the next word in the sequence. At the end of training, Elman cluster analyzed the representations that the model had formed across its hidden unit activations for each word+context vector. It is clear that the network discovered several major categories of words: large categories of verbs and nouns, smaller categories of inanimate or animate nouns, smaller still categories of human and non human animals, etc. (for example, 'dragon' occurs as a pattern in activation space which is in the region corresponding to the category animals, and also in the larger region shared by animates, and finally in the area reserved for nouns). These categories emerge from the language input without any semantics or real world grounding. The category structure is hierarchical, soft, and implicit.

The same network architecture which discovered sublexical regularities of language discovers important grammatical and semantic information from the same processes of sequential analysis. The network moves from processing mere surface regularities to representing more abstract aspects such as word class, but without this being built in as a pre-specified syntactic or other linguistic constraint. Relatively general architectural constraints give rise to language-specific representational constraints as a *product* of processing the input strings. These linguistically relevant representations are an *emergent* property of the network's functioning.

The Cobuild project

The Cobuild project represents the largest descriptive enterprise of the English language as it is used. Over 250 million words of representative English have been analyzed for the sequential patterns that are present. The three key conclusions of this research are (i) that it is impossible to describe syntax and lexis independently, (ii) that syntax and semantics are inextricable, and (iii) that language is best described as being collocational streams where patterns flow into each other (often going over the clause boundary). 'Through the reliability and objectivity of the computer evidence, verbs can be divided according to the pattern, and pattern can be seen to correlate with meaning – that is to say, verbs with similar patterns have similar meanings... We can now see that this relation between meaning and pattern is inevitable – that meaning and usage have a profound and systematic effect on one another.' (Sinclair, foreword to Cobuild Grammar Patterns: Verbs, 1991: iv). Thus the Collins Cobuild (1996) analysis of English verbs shows that there are perhaps 100 major patterns of English verbs (of the type, for example, V *by* amount: the verb is followed by a prepositional phrase which consists of the preposition *by* and a noun group indicating an amount as in 'Their incomes have dropped by 30 per cent', 'The Reds were leading by two runs', etc.). Verbs with the same Comp (Complementizer) pattern share meanings (the above-illustrated pattern is used by three meaning groups: (i) the 'increase' and 'decrease' group (inc. 'climb', 'decline', 'decrease', 'depreciate', etc.), (ii) the 'win' and 'lose' group (inc. 'lead', 'lose', and 'win'), (iii) the 'overrun' group (inc. 'overrun', 'overspend'). Any Comp pattern is describable *only* in terms of its lexis.

Perhaps surprisingly, Chomsky's recent accounts of syntax in the Minimalist Program for Linguistic Theory (MPLT) (Chomsky, 1995) shares this emphasis on lexis and sequence analysis. Chomsky (1989, emphasis added) stated: 'There is only one human language apart from the lexicon, and *language acquisition is in essence a matter of determining lexical idiosyncrasies*'. Within the MPLT, '*differences between languages are attributed to differences between the features of lexical items in the languages* and specifically between the features of lexical items belonging to the functional categories AGR and Tense... Vs and Ns are taken from the lexicon fully inflected with inflectional affixes... specific bundles of these features of the category AGR and T are lexical items and *differences between the sets of bundles available in the lexicon account for cross-linguistic syntactic differences between languages*.' (Marantz, 1995: 366).

Over the last twenty years theories of grammar have increasingly put more syntax into the lexicon, and correspondingly less into rules. The corpus linguistic approach and the MPLT alike both represent a natural culmination of this trend where lexis is at the very centre of syntax. In both accounts, syntax acquisition reduces to vocabulary acquisition – the analysis of the sequence in which words work in chunks.

Inflectional morphology

As described at the beginning of this section, distributional analysis generates words, fuzzy word-class clusters with prototypical structure (like 'nounlike' rather than 'noun'), and letter sequences which are fairly reliable morphological markers (like -*s*, -*ing*, -*ed*, etc. in English). If particular combinations of these are reliably associated with particular temporal perspectives (for tense and aspect) or number of referents (for noun plural marking) for example, then we have the information necessary for the beginnings of a system which can generate inflectional morphology. But how could an associative system ever generalise to allow it to mark tense, aspect, case, etc. for words it has never previously experienced in a marked form? How could an associative system abstract regularities in order to operate grammatically with novel words? Can human morphological abilities be understood in terms of associative processes, or is it necessary to postulate rule-based symbol processing systems underlying these grammatical skills? This question has generated considerable debate in the literature over the past decade, much of it focusing on the behaviour of 'regular' and 'irregular' inflectional morphology. There are broadly two contrasting accounts. Dual-processing models (for example

Marcus, Brinkmann, Clahsen, Wiese & Pinker, 1995; Pinker & Prince, 1988; Prasada, Pinker & Snyder, 1990) take the differences in behaviour of regular and irregular inflections to represent the separate underlying processes by which they are produced: regular inflections are produced by rules (for example, for the past tense 'add -*ed* to a Verb'), while irregular inflections are listed in memory. Associative accounts, whether connectionist (e.g., MacWhinney & Leinbach, 1991; Plunkett & Marchman, 1993; Rumelhart & McClelland, 1986) or schema-network (Bybee, 1995) models, assume that both regular and irregular inflections arise from the same mechanism, a single distributed associative network, with the differences in behaviour being due to statistical distributional factors.

There have been a number of compelling PDP models of the acquisition of morphology. The pioneers were Rumelhart and McClelland (1986) who showed that a simple learning model reproduced, to a remarkable degree, the characteristics of young children learning the morphology of the past tense in English: the model generated the so-called U-shaped learning curve for irregular forms; it exhibited a tendency to overgeneralize, and, in the model as in children, different past-tense forms for the same word could co-exist at the same time. Yet there was no 'rule' – 'it is possible to imagine that the system simply stores a set of rote-associations between base and past-tense forms with novel responses generated by "on-line" generalisations from the stored exemplars.' (Rumelhart & McClelland, 1986: 267). This original past-tense model was very influential. It laid the foundations for the connectionist approach to language research; it generated a large number of criticisms (Lachter & Bever, 1988; Pinker & Prince, 1988), some of which are undeniably valid; and, in turn, it thus spawned a number of revised and improved PDP models of different aspects of the acquisition of the English past tense. The successes of these recent models in capturing the regularities that are present in associating phonological form of lemma with phonological form of inflected form (Daugherty & Seidenberg, 1994; MacWhinney & Leinbach, 1991; Marchman, 1993; Plunkett & Marchman, 1991), and between referents (+past tense or +plural) and associated inflected perfect or plural forms (Cottrell & Plunkett, 1994, Ellis & Schmidt, 1997); in closely simulating the error patterns, profiles of acquisition, differential difficulties, false-friends effects, reaction times, and interactions of regularity and frequency that are found in human learners (both L1 and L2); as well as in acquiring a default case allowing generalisation on 'wug' tests, all strongly support the notion that acquisition of morphology is also a result of simple associative learning principles operating in a massively distributed system abstracting the regularities of association using optimal inference. That morphology can be described as being rule-like behaviour does not imply that morphology is rule-governed (Ellis, 1996b; Harris, 1987).

Much of the information that's needed for syntax falls quite naturally out of simple sequence analysis.

Working out how words work (ii): distributional analysis of word co-occurrences to derive lexical semantic information

Recent work by Landauer and Dumais (1997) demonstrates that a large part of semantics can also come from sequence analysis. Although much of semantics comes from the grounding of lexical meaning in conceptual/imagery-perceptual representations, there is clearly another source of lexical meaning, particularly important for more abstract words, which arises from a word's associations with the other words with which it tends to co-occur. This is the aspect of meaning which drives the collocational analysis of meaning (see earlier section concerning 'the Cobuild project') stemming from Firth's (1957; Bazell, Catford, Halliday, & Robins, 1966) dictum: 'You shall know a word by the company it keeps.' The lexical context which surrounds a lexeme is crucial to the determination of its meaning and its grammatical role. The telling evidence that this is a potent source of lexis is the fact that people who read more know more vocabulary (Anderson, Wilson, & Fielding, 1988). This relationship between print exposure and vocabulary appears to be causal in that it holds even when intelligence and even reading comprehension ability – an excellent measure of general verbal ability – is controlled (Stanovich & Cunningham, 1992).

Landauer and Dumais (1997) present a theory and mechanism of acquired similarity and knowledge representation called Latent Semantic Analysis (LSA) which simulates both L1 and L2 acquisition of vocabulary from text. By inducing global knowledge indirectly from local co-occurrence data in a large body of representative text, LSA acquired knowledge about the full vocabulary of English at a comparable rate to school children. Yet LSA has no prior linguistic or perceptual similarity knowledge, and is based solely on a general mathematical learning method that achieves induction by extracting about 300 dimensions to represent words-as-letter-strings in the context of other words-as-letter-strings. Conceptually, LSA can be viewed as a large symmetrical three-layered connectionist network linking every word type encountered in layer 1, through several hundred hidden units in layer 2, to a layer 3 which comprises nodes for every text window context ever encountered. After the model had been trained by exposing it to text samples from over 30 thousand articles from Groliers Academic American Encyclopaedia, it was tested with 80 items from the synonym portion of the Test of English as a Foreign Language (TOEFL). Applicants to US colleges from non-English speaking countries who took tests containing these items averaged 64.5% correct on this test. LSA got 64.4% correct.

LSA closely mimics the behaviour of a group of moderately proficient English readers with respect to judgements of meaning similarity. Yet it acquired this competence without any other information than simple exposure to words (as sequences of letters) and other such words as tend to co-occur as their neighbours. Interestingly, the input to LSA was, as Landauer and Dumais put it, 'a simple bag of words'; all information from word-order was ignored, and there was therefore no explicit use of grammar or syntax. All it had was the frequency profile of co-occurring words in 30,000 text samples comprising roughly 150 words each. It appears that word co-occurrence data in sequence is important for the derivation of syntactic information (see previous section), but that simple word co-occurrence statistics, ignoring order, is at least sufficient for the derivation of lexical semantics. It remains to be seen if the performance of LSA given ordered information is superior to that given unordered input.

The performance of LSA will be surprising to many readers. The model could not see or hear, and thus could make no use of phonology, morphology, or real-world perceptual knowledge. It was provided with no prior linguistic or grammatical knowledge. But from a large corpus of simple lexical-string co-occurrence data it acquired latent semantic information to allow it to perform at levels expected of a good ESL learner.

In this account, lexical semantic acquisition reduces to the analysis of word co-occurrences, i.e. the words that tend to chunk together (ignoring order).

Collocations, slot-and-frame patterns, and sequences in learner talk

We have seen that as powerful computers are used for distributional analysis of large language corpora, so they demonstrate the underlying chunks of language and the ways in which lexical items, with their particular valences and subcategorization requirements, operate in these patterns. Is there parallel evidence that *learners* acquire collocations on their path to fluency, and that their analyses of these chunks gives them the information about lexical idiosyncrasies that allows later more open-class productions?

Collocations and patterns in L1 acquisition

Tomasello (1992) begins his book, *First Verbs: A Case Study of Early Grammatical Development*, with the following observation from Wittgenstein: 'Language games are the forms of language with which a child begins to make use of words... When we look at the simple forms of language the mental mist which seems to enshroud our ordinary use of language disappears. We see activities, reactions, which are clear-cut and transparent. On the other hand we recognize in these simple processes forms of language not separated by a break from our more complicated ones. We see that we can build up the more complicated forms from the primitive ones by gradually adding new forms.' (Wittgenstein, The Blue Book).

Tomasello (1992) kept a detailed diary of his daughter Travis' language between 1 and 2 years old. On the basis of a fine-grained analysis of this corpus he proposed the Verb Island hypothesis: young children's early verbs and relational terms are individual islands of organization in an otherwise unorganized grammatical system. In the early stages the child learns about arguments and syntactic marking on a verb-by-verb basis, and ordering patterns and morphological markers learned for one verb do not immediately generalize to other verbs. The reason for this is that nascent language learners do not have any adultlike syntactic categories or rules, nor do they have any kind of word class of verb that would support generalizations across verbs. Particular summary observations supporting this claim were as follows:

'There is individuality and contextedness everywhere, signs of broad-based rules nowhere. T did bring order and systematicity to her language during her 2nd year of life, but it was a gradual, constructive process. It did not resemble in any way the instantaneous and irrevocable setting of parameters...

T's earliest three-or-more-word sentences (18–21 months) were almost all structured by verbs. The vast majority of these involved straight-forward coordinations of already produced word combinations (93%), preserving in almost all cases the established ordering patterns of the constituents (99%).

T began marking the syntagmatic relations in these three-or-more-word sentences through the use of contrastive word order and prepositions. She did this, however, on a verb-by-verb basis. By far the best predictor of the arguments and argument markings that T used with a particular verb at a particular time was previous usage of that verb, not same time usage of other verbs' (Tomasello, 1992: 264–266).

Tomasello concludes:

'It is not until the child has produced or comprehended a number of sentences with a particular verb that she can construct a syntagmatic category of 'cutter', for example. Not until she has done this with a number of verbs can she construct the more general syntagmatic category of agent or actor. Not until the child has constructed a number of sentences in which various words serve as various types of arguments for various predicates can she construct word classes such as noun or verb. Not until the child has constructed sentences with these more general categories can certain types of complex sentences be produced' (Ibid.: 273–274).

Other analyses of child language corpora point to similar conclusions. For example, Lieven, Pine and Dresner Barnes (1992) show formulae to be both frequent (children's first 100 words typically contain about 20 formulae) and productive (in providing templates which, following analysis, are converted into lexically based patterns). Pine and Lieven (1997) and Lieven, Pine and Baldwin (1997) show that a lexically based positional analysis can account for the structure of a considerable proportion of children's early multiword corpora. The corpus-analyses of Pine and Lieven (1997) suggests that the development of, for example, an adult-like determiner category may be a gradual process involving the progressive broadening of the range of lexically-specific frames in which different determiners appear. These data are all broadly consistent with constructivist models of children's early grammar development.

Collocations and patterns in SLA

No observation is entirely theory-free. Yet we are fortunate to have some descriptions of stages of L2 proficiency which were drawn up in as atheoretical way as possible by the American Council on the Teaching of Foreign Languages (ACTFL) (Higgs, 1984). The ACTFL (1986) *Oral Proficiency Guidelines* include the following descriptions of novice and intermediate levels which emphasise the contributions of patterns and formulae to the development of later creativity:

Novice Low: Oral production consists of isolated words and perhaps a few high-frequency phrases . . .
Novice Mid: Oral production continues to consist of isolated words and learned phrases within very predictable areas of need, although quantity is increased. Vocabulary is sufficient only for handling simple, elementary needs and expressing basic courtesies. Utterances rarely consist of more than two or three words and show frequent long pauses and repetition of interlocutor's words.

Novice High: Able to satisfy partially the requirements of basic communicative exchanges by relying heavily on learned utterances but occasionally expanding these through simple recombinations of their elements. Can ask questions or make statements involving learned material . . . Speech continues to consist of learned utterances rather than of personalized, situationally adapted ones . . . Pronunciation may still be strongly influenced by first language.

Intermediate: Characterized by an ability to create with the language by combining and recombining learned elements, though primarily in a reactive mode; initiate, minimally sustain, and close in a simple way basic communicative tasks; and ask and answer questions.

Intermediate-Mid: Able to handle successfully a variety of uncomplicated, basic communicative tasks and social situations. Can talk simply about self and family members. Can ask and answer questions and participate in simple conversations on topics beyond the most immediate needs; e.g., personal history and leisure-time activities. *Utterance length increases slightly, but speech may continue to be characterized by frequent long pauses, since the smooth incorporation of even basic conversational strategies is often hindered as the speaker struggles to create appropriate language forms. Pronunciation may continue to be strongly influenced by first language* and fluency may still be strained.' (ACTFL, 1986, emphases added).

Thus the ACTFL repeatedly stresses the constructive potential of collocations and chunks of language which are slowly analysed on a word-by-word basis to allow the determination of L2 grammatical word class and grammatical dependencies. This is impressive because the ACTFL guidelines were simply trying to *describe* SLA as objectively as possible; there was no initial theoretical focus on formulae, yet none the less the role of formulae became readily apparent in the acquisition process. Wong-Fillmore (1976) presented the first extensive longitudinal study which focused on formulaic language in L2 acquisition. Her subject, Nora, acquired and overused a few formulaic expressions of a new structural type during one period, and then amassed a variety of similar forms during the next: previously unanalysed chunks became the foundations for creative construction. These observations closely parallel those of Lieven et al. (1997) for L1 acquisition. But Nora was just one child, and there is clearly need for larger sampled, detailed collection and analysis of SLA corpora, although there is some recent progress: Myles, Mitchell and Hooper (1999) studied the first two years of development of interrogatives in anglophone French L2 beginners and tracked the breakdown of interrogative chunks, the creative construction of interrogatives, and the ways in which formulae fed the constructive process (see also Myles, Hooper & Mitchell (1998) for the constructions that stem from three other formulae during this period). Other useful reviews of formulae in SLA include Hakuta (1974), Nattinger and DeCarrico (1992), Towell and Hawkins (1994), Weinert (1995), and Wray (1992).

Working out how words work (iii): cognitive linguistics and grounded lexical meaning

Much of traditional linguistics views language as a closed modular system where syntax can be described as a body of logical rules for generating the sentences of a language that are grammatically correct. This enterprise had largely studied syntax in isolation from semantics, the functions of language, or the other social, biological, experiential, or cognitive aspects of the humankind who invented and used language ever since. But the meaning of the words of a given language, and how they can be used in combination, depends on the perception and categorization of the real world around us. Since we constantly observe and play an active role in this world, we know a great deal about the entities of which it consists, and this experience and familiarity is reflected in the nature of language. Language reflects our *experience* and our *embodiment*. The different degrees of *salience* or *prominence* of elements involved in situations which we wish to describe affect the selection of subject, object, adverbials, and other clause arrangement. Figure/ground segregation, which originated from Gestalt psychological analyses of visual perception, and *perspective taking*, again very much in the domains of vision and attention, are mirrored in language and have systematic relations with syntactic structure. We have expectations of the world which are represented as complex packets of related information (schemata, scripts, or *frames* for, for example, how the parts of a chair inter-relate, a trip to the dentist, buying and selling, indeed, everything we know – Schank, 1982). What we express reflects which parts of an event attract our *attention*. Depending on how we direct our attention, we can select and highlight different aspects of the frame, thus arriving at different linguistic expressions.

All of these concerns – the experiential grounding of language, our embodiment which represents the world in a very particular way, the relations between our perceptual and imagery representations and the language which we use to describe them, our perspective and attentional focus – lie at the heart of an alternative view of language: cognitive linguistics (Fillmore, 1977; Lakoff,

1987; Lakoff & Johnson, 1980; Langacker, 1987, 1991; Talmy, 1988):

In cognitive linguistics the use of syntactic structures is largely seen as a reflection of how a situation is conceptualised by the speaker, and this conceptualisation is governed by the attention principle. Salient participants, especially agents, are rendered as subjects and less salient participants as objects; verbs are selected which are compatible with the choice of subject and object, and evoke the perspective on the situation that is intended; locative, temporal and many other types of relations are highlighted, or 'windowed for attention' by expressing them explicitly as adverbials. Although languages may supply different linguistic strategies for the realisation of the attention principle, the underlying cognitive structures and principles are probably universal (Ungerer & Schmid, 1996: 280).

It seems possible that much of our knowledge of language structure emerges from the analysis of chunks of language form. The research described in earlier sections demonstrates how orthographic and phonological regularities, lexical and morphological form, collocations, word class, and even aspects of lexical semantics might so arise. However, other aspects of language, like the grounding of lexical semantics and the communicative use of syntactic structures, derive from the frequency and regularity of cross-modal associations between chunks of phonological surface form and, particularly visuospatial, imagery representations. But these visual representations are not fixed and static; rather they are explored, manipulated, cropped and zoomed, and run in time like movies under attentional and scripted control (Kosslyn, 1983; Talmy, 1996a). Cognitive linguistics reminds us that the prominence of particular aspects of the scene and the perspective of the internal observer (i.e. the attentional focus of the speaker and the intended attentional focus of the listener) are key elements in determining regularities of association between elements of visuo-spatial experience and elements of phonological form. We cannot understand language acquisition by understanding phonological memory alone. All of the systems of WM, the slave systems and the SAS, are involved in collating the regularities of cross-modal associations underpinning language use. Cognitive linguistics aims to understand how the regularities of syntax emerge from the cross-modal evidence that is collated during the learner's lifetime of using and comprehending language. The difficulties of this enterprise are obvious. Acknowledging the importance of embodiment, perspective, and attention entails that to understand the emergence of language we must also understand the workings of attention, vision, and other representational systems (Talmy, 1997). And then we must understand the regularities of the mappings of these systems onto particular languages. And the mappings in question are piecemeal; it's the content of the mappings that is important, not simply the modalities concerned. Which is why cognitive linguistics focuses on one particular construction and representational aspect at a time, for example motion event frames (Langacker, 1991; Talmy, 1996b), spatial language (Bowerman, 1996; Regier, 1996), verb aspect (Narayanan, 1997), or inflectional morphology.

Attention and language learning: implicit and explicit learning, memory and instruction

One area of WM which, because of its centrality in language learning and language use, deserves much more consideration than it has been given here, is the role of attention in language learning. Since our fluent language use is unencumbered by metalinguistic descriptions of sufficient complexity to allow its generation, so much of the representation and processing that generates language must be unconscious. But what is the role of attention and consciousness in language learning? This complex and long-standing question cannot be dealt with adequately here, but it is nevertheless important to highlight some relations between this chapter's emphasis on memory and theories of attention in language learning and processing.

Attention, as the SAS, is the most central element of the Working Memory Model, yet it is the least-well understood. One must look elsewhere to the research on consciousness and attention (Ellis, 1994a, and chapters in this volume by Doughty, Hulstijn, Robinson, and Schmidt) for more detailed specification of its role in language learning.

Language understanding and language production utilise the many millions of associations that the learner has acquired in their history of language use. Thus language is learned in the course of using language, and the best predictor of language facility will simply be time-on-task. Research on implicit learning and implicit memory suggests that at least some of the relevant associations can be acquired from the input without the learner being consciously aware of the contingency, although the relevant aspects of the input must be attended for processing (see Ellis, 1994b; Hsaio & Reber, 1998; Schmidt, this volume). In acquiring associations, some parts of the input environment can be made more salient, and learners are more likely to learn about the part of the environment which they selectively attend. Thus there are ways of speeding learners' L1 or L2 acquisition from a given amount of language exposure, to increase the quality of the learning (see Ellis & Laporte, 1997, for review). These ways, which include grammatical consciousness raising or input processing, as well as corrective feedback and recasts, promote the acquisition of sophisticated grammatical proficiency. There is some benefit in a focus on form in L2 instruction (see Doughty & Williams, 1998b; R. Ellis, 1994a; Long, 1988, 1991; Terrell, 1991, for reviews of instructional programs which incorporate these ideas).

Communicative approaches give input, time-on-task, and opportunity for relating form and function. Of course, all of this is necessary for developing the associations necessary for language learning. Naturalistic environments provide motivation and plenty of opportunity for output practice as well. These are situations which guarantee sufficient quantity of language. But without any focus on form, formal accuracy is an unlikely result. Focus on forms alone can teach some declarative rules of grammar, but at its worst can be accompanied by too little time on the task of language use itself (see Skehan & Foster, Doughty, and Robinson, this volume). At its worst it is insufficient to support language development. But focus on form instruction, which is rich in communicative opportunities and which also makes salient the associations between structures (which the learner is already at a stage to be able to represent) and functions, can facilitate language acquisition. Instruction must build on the levels of representation which the learner has already acquired. Just as there is the issue of Learnability in L1, so there is that of Teachability in L2 – any empirical findings about natural (in terms of epistemics, not biology – see Ellis, 1996a, b) developmental sequences should be respected in the design of instructional materials (Pienemann, 1985), and attempts to teach structures or strategies which build on still-to-be acquired representations are likely to fail.

Conclusions and overview: the different connections and the need for connectionist simulations

The proper study of language acquisition is to chart the course by which perceptual, motoric, and cognitive functions induce structure, from undifferentiated novice performance to that remarkably differentiated nativelike competence. The history of linguistic science demonstrates language to be an extremely complicated set of evidence. To remind us of the enormity of the representational database, consider just the four lines of nursery-book language shown in Figure 3. Processing this simple 18 word sentence taps into a rich abundance of

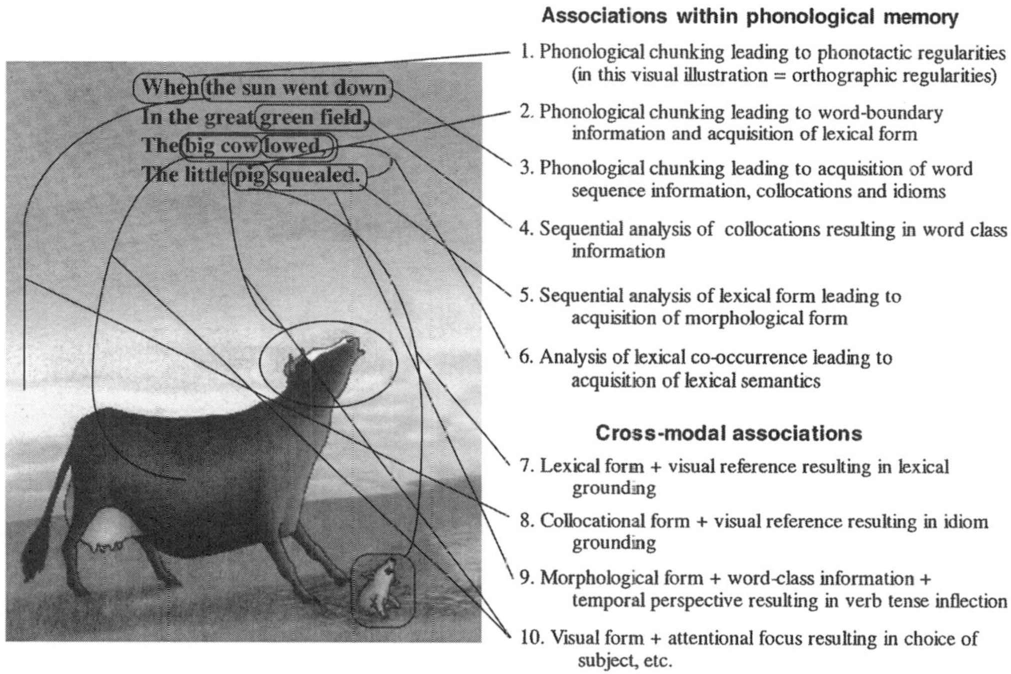

Associations within phonological memory

1. Phonological chunking leading to phonotactic regularities (in this visual illustration = orthographic regularities)

2. Phonological chunking leading to word-boundary information and acquisition of lexical form

3. Phonological chunking leading to acquisition of word sequence information, collocations and idioms

4. Sequential analysis of collocations resulting in word class information

5. Sequential analysis of lexical form leading to acquisition of morphological form

6. Analysis of lexical co-occurrence leading to acquisition of lexical semantics

Cross-modal associations

7. Lexical form + visual reference resulting in lexical grounding

8. Collocational form + visual reference resulting in idiom grounding

9. Morphological form + word-class information + temporal perspective resulting in verb tense inflection

10. Visual form + attentional focus resulting in choice of subject, etc.

When the sun went down
In the great green field
The big cow lowed
The little pig squealed.

Figure 3. An overview of the range of language-relevant associations. (Original picture taken from Big Red Barn (p. 21) by Margaret Wise Brown (pictures by Felicia Bond), HarperFestival, A Division of Harper Collins Publishers. Text copyright 1956, 1989 by Robert Brown Rauch. Illustrations copyright 1989 by Felicia Bond.)

associations, some associative chunks in phonological memory, some cross-modal associations. The types of association are also illustrated in Figure 3. Since the 'cycle of perception' is also the 'cycle of learning', the processing of the sentence itself also results in some language acquisition; associations which are used in the processing of this sentence are forged or strengthened in LTM, making them more accessible in the future (short term implicit memory or priming effects (Ellis, 1994b) and long term life-span practice effects (Kirsner, 1994). If we just consider the orthographic chunks that are potentially activated from this 72 character sequence, there are 71 bigrams to be processed, each much more likely than chance although individually varying in their likelihood; 70 trigrams; 18 lexemes, which are common but varying in their individual likelihood of occurrence; three common verb inflections; 17 biword sequences, and collocations ranging in size from *the sun*, through *when the sun went down*, up to, for me, *the father who has read these words so many nights before*, the whole sentence, etc. If we then consider the various ways in which these varying sizes of chunk map onto phonology, syntax and semantics it is clear that there is a combinatorial explosion of associations potentially activated in processing this simple sentence. Although there are not many modalities of representation involved here, the many representations within each modality, richly interconnected by associations of varying weight, affords a massively complex database.

This type of analysis will surely leave many linguists aghast, observing that there are just too many associations, that anything is possible from such complexity, and that it is yet more psycholinguistic research lacking any but the most naive linguistic content (see Gregg, this volume). This would be fair comment indeed. None the less, the research outlined here, along with four decades or so of psycholinguistics, demonstrates that language learners do indeed possess this richness of association. The computational work outlined in this chapter also shows that analysis of these associations results in generalization and emergent linguistically relevant representations. Thus it seems worthwhile investigating how connectionist or constraint probability models might allow single interpretations to result from the competition between all of these available cues, in the same way that somehow, as we read the nursery text in Figure 3, we settle on-line on one interpretation.

We need to understand the active competition between the cues available in input and their representational associations. And we need dynamic models of the acquisition of these representations and the emergence of structure. Connectionism provides a set of computational tools for exploring the conditions under which such emergent properties arise. Advantages of connectionism include: neural inspiration; distributed representation and control; data-driven processing with prototypical representations emerging rather than being innately pre-specified in nativist accounts; graceful degradation; emphasis on acquisition rather than static description; slow, incremental, non-linear, content- and structure-sensitive learning; blurring of the representation/learning distinction; graded, distributed and non-static representations; generalization and transfer as natural products of learning; and, since the models must actually run, less scope for hand-waving. We have already discussed the millions of potential connections that map between orthographic structure and phonological structure. When connectionist models of reading acquisition learn these mappings, so highly plausible models of reading acquisition arise (Seidenberg & McClelland, 1989). We have described the associations between stem form and past tense form involved in inflectional morphology. When connectionist models learn these mappings, so close simulations of acquisition and performance result. The problem with modelling the totality of language knowledge is that we need to understand, thus to be able to model, representation in other modalities as well – the visual, motor and other systems which underpin conceptual knowledge. This is very hard, although some useful progress is being made: see, e.g., Regier (1996) on spatial language; Narayanan (1997) on how the semantics of verbal aspect are grounded in sensori-motor primitives abstracted from processes that recur in sensori-motor control (such as goal, periodicity, iteration, final state, duration, force, and effort); more general work on embodied language development by the L_0 project (Bailey, Feldman, Narayanan & Lakoff, 1997; Feldman, Lakoff, Bailey, Narayanan, Regier & Stolcke, 1996); and MacWhinney's competition model (this volume).

Gregg (this volume) is correct in reminding us of the essential need for linguistic analysis, and the UG framework has provided the most complete description of language competence to date. But, like Studdert-Kennedy (1991), I believe that UG is neither a prescription nor a program for development, but rather it is a partial and *a posteriori* description of the phenotypic product of the developmental system. In this view, UG is a consequence, not a condition of development. The types of association described in this chapter are pretty much all we have as far as language representation is concerned. But out of these associations comes systematicity. There is a more relevant Universal which concerns process and learning rather than content: it is to be found in efforts to rationalize intelligence in terms of models of optimal (Bayesian) inference in the presence of uncertainty. My money's on connectionism to help us solve the riddle, more complex even than that of Samson (*Judges, 14*), of how, out of the strings, came forth syntax.

3 The competition model: the input, the context, and the brain

Brian MacWhinney

Introduction

Language learning is a three-way interaction between the input, the learner, and the interactional context (Bloom, 1974). This three-way interaction provides a general framework for understanding first and second language acquisition (SLA), in both naturalistic and formal contexts. In order to elaborate this general framework, we need to model its three components:

1. The input. We need to know how the linguistic input can be structured to maximize effective learning. What aspects of the phonology, syntax, semantics, and morphology of the input does the learner use to 'crack the code' of the new language?
2. The learner. We need to understand exactly how the cognitive abilities of the learner shape the process and outcome of L2 instruction.
3. The context. Traditionally, the classroom environment maintains a rather uniform structure in which interaction is controlled by the instructor. How does this framework affect learning and how can it be varied to improve the learning process?

This paper will examine these three components within the framework of the Competition Model (MacWhinney, 1987; MacWhinney & Bates, 1989). To quantify the role of the input in L2 learning, the model relies on the concepts of cue reliability and availability. To characterize the cognitive abilities of the learner, the model relies on findings from cognitive neuroscience. To understand the role of the context, the model elaborates the concepts of environmental and social support. The Competition Model views both L1 and L2 learning as constructive, data-driven processes that rely not on universals of linguistic structure, but on universals of cognitive structure. It attributes development to learning and transfer, rather than to the principles and parameters of Universal Grammar (Chomsky, 1965).

The input

The Competition Model is designed to quantify the ways in which distributional properties of the input control language learning and language processing. The basic claim of the model in regard to input is that language comprehension is based on the detection of a series of cues and the reliability and availability of these determines the strength of cues in comprehension. The model contrasts sharply with generative grammar in this regard. Generative grammar views language through the lens of abstract trees in a universal deep structure. The Competition Model recognizes the importance of surface phrase structure, but relates all sentence processing to cue detection and interpretation. Those cues that are highest in reliability and availability are the ones that most strongly control comprehension and which are acquired first during language learning.

In order to elaborate this simple relation between cues and comprehension, we need to specify how languages distribute cues across sentences. To do this, the Competition Model has turned to crosslinguistic studies of sentence processing. In particular, the forms or cues that we have studied empirically include nominal case-marking, word order patterns, stress patterns, noun-verb agreement markers, clitic pronouns, and verb voice markings. We have studied the use of these cues in Arabic (Taman, 1993), Bulgarian (Andonova, 1998), Chinese (Bates, Chen, Tzeng, Li & Opie, 1991; Liu, Bates & Li, 1992), Dutch (Kilborn & Ito, 1989; McDonald, 1986, 1987a, 1987b), English (Bates, McNew, MacWhinney, Devescovi & Smith, 1982; MacWhinney & Bates, 1978; MacWhinney, Bates & Kliegl, 1984), French (Kail, 1989), Hebrew (Sokolov, 1988), Hindi (Vaid & Pandit, 1991), Hungarian (MacWhinney & Pléh, 1988, 1997), Italian (Bates et al., 1982), Japanese (Kilborn & Ito, 1989; Sasaki, 1994, 1997), Russian (Kempe & MacWhinney, 1998), Spanish (Kail, 1989), Turkish (MacWhinney & Leinbach, 1991), and Warlpiri (Bavin & Shopen, 1989).

Much of the cross-linguistic work conducted in the Competition Model framework has focused on the use of cues to agent identification. To illustrate the ways in which surface cues mark grammatical functions, let us focus on the case of agent identification in simple sentences with two nouns and a verb, such as 'The boy is annoying the parrots'. Figure 1 presents a simple connectionist model for the cues to agent identification in English. This network takes as input various combinations of these seven cues:

1. **pre:** preverbal positioning (placing 'the boy' before 'is annoying' in 'the boy is annoying the parrots');

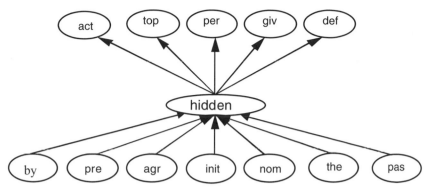

Figure 1. A network for relating subject-marking forms to subject functions in English

2. **agr:** verb agreement morphology (marking 'is' to agree in number with 'the boy', rather than 'the parrots');
3. **init:** sentence initial positioning (placing 'the boy' at the beginning of the sentence);
4. **nom:** nominative case-marking for pronouns ('I' vs 'me' as a marker of the subject in English);
5. **the:** use of the article 'the';
6. **by:** the attachment of the preposition 'by' to mark the agent in a passive;
7. **pas:** the presence of passive morphology in the verb.

For example, if the input sentence is 'the boy is annoying the parrots', then the input nodes activated are 'pre', 'agr', 'init', and 'the'. The node for 'nom' is not activated because 'boy' is a noun and there is no case-marking for nouns in English. The nodes for the 'by' and 'pas' cues are not activated, because the sentence is not passive. In a connectionist neural network, activation of the input units is passed on to the hidden units and, from there, to the output units at the top of the figure.

The network produces as output a series of functional interpretations, including actor (act), topicality (top), perspective (per), givenness (giv), and definiteness (def). In our cross linguistic experiments, we are usually most interested in finding out which of two or three nouns in a sentence ends up being selected as the actor. This means that the activations of the output nodes at the top of Figure 1 also feed into additional nodes that arbitrate between a series of word competitors. In the sentence 'the boy is annoying the parrots', the 'act' output unit is turned on more strongly for the noun 'boy' than for the noun 'parrots'. As a result, 'the boy' wins the competition for assignment to the role of actor. It is this competition that gives the Competition Model its name.

Variations in the pattern activated across the input units will lead to variations in the output. For example, if the input were 'He was chased by the dog', the 'pre', 'agr', 'init', and 'nom' units would be activated for 'he'. However, the units for 'by', 'agr', 'the', and 'pas' would be activated for 'the dog'. A young child might have trouble understanding the passive. However, by the age of four or five, the child has learned that, when the 'by' and 'pas' units are turned on, they must dominate the other units and select 'the dog' as the agent in the output.

During sentence production, the connections in Figure 1 operate in the opposite direction. Unlike the Garrett-Levelt model (Levelt, 1989; and see Doughty, this volume), the Competition Model assumes that lexical items are activated before full syntactic frames are composed. This means that, when production begins, we may have a couple of nominals available, such as 'the boy' and 'the parrots'. We know that 'the boy' is the actor and the topic. Our goal is to figure out which forms to activate in order to express this fact. Because the functions of 'actor' and 'topic' are not dissociated in this case, we will want to treat 'the boy' as a subject by assigning it to the preverbal position and making the verb agree with it. Thus, 'the boy' wins out in the competition for preverbal positioning and the nominal 'the parrots' wins in the competition for postverbal positioning.

Figure 1 includes an additional layer of connections called 'hidden units'. Connectionist models use these additional units to facilitate the learning of nonlinear associations between inputs (functions) and outputs (forms). Non-linearities arise when cue A has one effect in the presence of cue B, but an exactly opposite effect in the presence of cue C. A good example of such non-linear associations occurs in the choice of the passive voice in English. In the active voice, the actor wins the competition for preverbal position. However, in the passive voice, it loses out to the object and is forced to take a backseat in the 'by-clause'. This 'flip-flop' between two competing interpretations of the same surface cue of preverbal positioning is mediated by the presence or absence of the additional cue of passive morphology on the verb. If the verb has the passive morphology, the normal interpretation is reversed. This relation between the cues involved is a good example of a non-linear association.

The architecture of connectionist systems of the type diagrammed in Figure 1 provides us with several ways of thinking about the interplay between cooperation and competition. In natural dialogue,

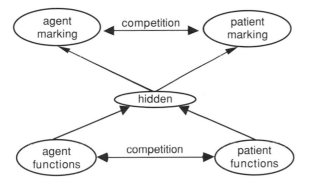

Figure 2. A network illustrating the competition between case roles in English

communicative functions tend to co-occur in a state of **peaceful coexistence**. For example, it is often the case that the topic of a sentence is also agential, given, definite, and perspectival. Together, these five functions form a cluster of co-occuring, mutually compatible relations that activate a set of parallel linguistic devices such as preverbal positioning and unmarked stress. These correlations between functions are reflections of real correlations in the world. Because the functions we choose to talk about are highly correlated in real life, the forms we use to talk about these functions also become highly correlated. This makes it so that no single form expresses any single function and the relation between forms and functions is both fluid and complex. There are also important correlations on the level of forms. For example, words that take the article 'the' are also capable of taking the plural suffix, and so on (Maratsos & Chalkley, 1980). The cooperation that exists in coalitions is balanced by the **competition** that exists between major form alternatives. For example, only one noun phrase in a sentence can be the agent and only one can be the patient. This means that there is a direct competition between agent marking and patient marking, as schematized in Figure 2. Competitions of this type exist on all levels of language processing. Words compete for lexical activation, phrases compete for syntactic ordering position, and sounds compete for insertion into syllabic slots. In comprehension, alternative sound forms compete for lexical activation, and alternative interpretations compete for phrase and case role assignments.

All of this cooperation and competition works against a background of probabilistic activations that leads to a system rich in **category leakage**. Leakage arises when a form that is normally associated with a certain function starts to be viewed occasionally as expressing some related, but different function. The root cause of category leakage is the fact that, even before the leakage becomes obvious, there is often no single function that is uniquely associated with a given form. Instead, several allied functions may coexist peacefully, because they coexist peacefully in the world around us. For example, it is typically the case that a 'causor' is also an 'initiator', and the functions of 'causor' and 'initiator' tend to coexist peacefully. Over time, the functional weight of a given marking can change so that what was originally a secondary function starts to emerge as the primary function. MacWhinney (1987) examines cases of reinterpretation of this type in the historical development of case-marking in Hungarian.

The basic empirical claim of the Competition Model is that the learning of the system of form-function mappings we have discussed is driven by **cue reliability**. Reliability is the conditional probability that an interpretation X should be selected given the presence of a cue Y, i.e. $p(X|Y)$. If this probability is high, then Y is a reliable cue to X. The most straightforward prediction from this initial analysis is that forms with a high conditional probability should be acquired early and should be the strongest determinants of processing in adults. A more complete treatment of the general topic of cue validity distinguishes four cue distribution dimensions. We are particularly interested in the ways in which these four dimensions end up contributing to cue strength as measured in our psycholinguistic experiments.

1. **Task frequency.** The most basic determinant of cue strength is the raw frequency of the basic task. Some tasks are incredibly frequent. For example, the task of locating an object in space is something that we routinely do as frequently as once each second. Other tasks may be quite rare. For example, we are seldom called upon to determine the rotational momentum of planetary bodies. Linguistic tasks are often of intermediate frequency. The task of determining the agent of the verb occurs with virtually every transitive verb. The task of determining anaphoric reference occurs every time a pronoun is encountered. Because most basic linguistic tasks are well above threshold frequency, the dimension of task frequency is seldom an important determinant of relative cue strength. However, in the case of a second language that was used extremely infrequently, task frequency could become a factor determining a general slow-down in acquisition.
2. **Availability.** Within a given task, cues will vary in their relative availability. We can call the relative availability of a cue for a given task its 'simple availability'. Usually, however, we are interested not just in knowing whether a cue is present, but also

whether or not it has any contrastive effect. This is called 'contrast availability'. For example, the cue of subject-verb agreement in English is present in nearly every English clause. However, in many sentences, the verb agrees with two or more candidate subjects. In a sentence like 'The cat chases the dog', the fact that the verb is marked for a singular subject tells us nothing about the status of the subject, since both nouns are singular. In this example, the agreement cue is available, but not contrastively. However, in a sentence like 'the cat chases the dogs', only the first noun agrees with the verb and the agreement cue is both available and contrastive. This example shows that an available cue is only useful if it is also contrastive.

3. **Simple reliability.** The most important and most basic cue validity dimension is the dimension of reliability. A cue is reliable if it leads to the right functional choice whenever it is present.

4. **Conflict reliability.** In addition to simple reliability, cues can be characterized in terms of their conflict reliability *vis à vis* some other particular cue.

Most Competition Model experiments use a simple, basic, sentence interpretation procedure. Subjects are given a sentence with two nouns and a verb and are asked to say who was the actor. In a few studies, the task involves direct-object identification (Sokolov, 1988), relative clause processing (MacWhinney & Pléh, 1988), or pronominal assignment (MacDonald & MacWhinney, 1990), but most often the task is agent identification. Sometimes the sentences are well-formed grammatical sentences like 'the cat is chasing the duck'. Sometimes they involve competitions between cues, as in the ungrammatical sentence '*the duck the cat is chasing'. Depending on the language involved, the cues varied in these studies include word order, subject-verb agreement, object-verb agreement, case-marking, prepositional case marking, stress, topicalization, animacy, omission, and pronominalization. These cues are varied in a standard orthogonalized ANOVA design with three or four sentences per cell to increase statistical reliability. The basic question being asked is always the same: What is the relative order of cue strength in the given language and how do these cue strengths interact?

These studies have yielded a remarkably consistent body of results. The most important finding is that the order of cue strength found in our experiments with adults always corresponds with the order of cue reliability yielded by text counts in the language. In different languages, we find different cue dominance patterns. In English, the dominant cue for subject identification is preverbal positioning.

For example, the English sentence 'the eraser hits the cat' is interpreted as having 'the eraser' as the agent. However, a parallel sentence in Italian or Spanish, would have 'the cat' as the agent. In Spanish, the prepositional object marker 'a' is a clear cue to the object and the subject is the noun that is not the object. An example of this is the sentence 'El toro mató al torero' (The bull killed to-the bullfighter). No such prepositional cues exists in English. In German, case marking on the definite article is a powerful cue to the subject. In a sentence such as 'Der Lehrer liebt die Witwe' (The teacher loves the widow), the presence of the nominative masculine article 'der' is a sure cue to identification of the subject. In Hungarian, the subject is the noun not marked by any suffix or postposition. In Russian, the subject often has a case suffix. In Arabic, the subject is identified as the noun that agrees with the verb in number and gender and this cue is stronger than the case-marking cue. In French, Spanish, and Italian, when an object pronoun is present, it can help identify the noun that is not the subject.

Figures 3 and 4 illustrate the types of empirical data collected in these studies. In Figure 3, we see a comparison of English, German, and Italian in terms of the strength of use of the preverbal positioning word order cue in adults. In these graphs, percentage choice of the first noun as actor is graphed on the y-axis with sentence types varied on the x-axis. It is clear that only English makes strong use of the word order cue. When the sentence has NVN order, English speakers interpret it overwhelmingly as SVO, despite the possible presence of agreement or animacy cues pointing in other directions. When the order is NNV, listeners interpret it as OSV, relying on the fact that the noun before the verb is the actor. When the order is VNN, they interpret it as VOS, relying on the fact that the noun after the verb is the object. Germans and Italians make no strong use of any of these cues. In Figure 4, on the other hand, we see that Italians rely intensely on the agreement cue whenever it is present, despite possible contradictory signals from word order or animacy. It is cue usage patterns of this type that indicate the unique 'footprint' of each of the languages we have studied.

The Competition Model provides a minimalist, empiricist prediction for the ways in which cues are acquired during L1 acquisition. The prediction is that the first cue learned by the child should be the most reliable cue in the language and the order of acquisition of cues across the span of development should be determined by relative cue reliability. In general this prediction has held up. Figure 5 presents developmental data from three languages. In this graph, we see that word order is the predominant cue for children learning English and case-marking is the predominant cue for children learning Hungarian.

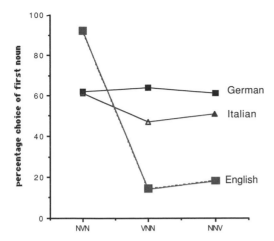

Figure 3. Language by word order interaction for English, German, and Italian
(Bates et al., 1982)

However, we encountered a major violation of the predictions of the Competition Model for Italian children. If the children were to behave in accord with the cue reliability patterns found in text counts for adult Italian and the cue strengths evidenced by adult Italians, they would make far more use of agreement and far less use of word order. We

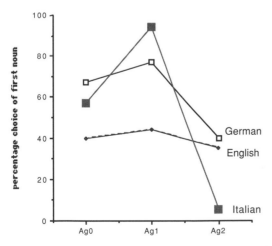

Figure 4. Language by agreement interaction for English, German, and Italian
(MacWhinney et al.,1984)

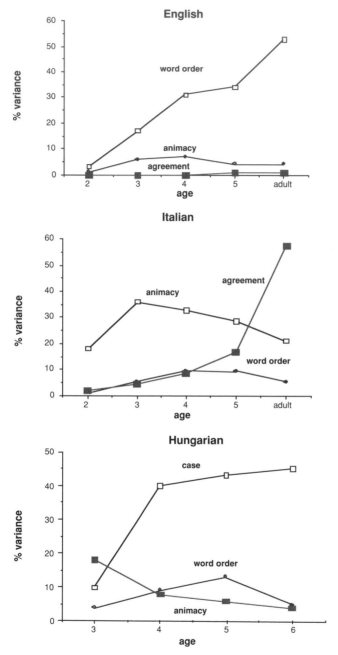

Figure 5. Changes in cue strength through development in English, Italian, and Hungarian (The y-axis in each panel is percentage variance accounted for in the ANOVA)

have interpreted this failed prediction as evidence for additional **cue cost** factors that make it difficult for Italian children to pick up and use the agreement cue. These cue cost factors will be discussed in the section that deals with the characteristics of the learner.

In addition to these basic findings regarding primary cue use, we have also found strong support for those aspects of the model that emphasize the ways in which cues interact through strength summation. Traditionally, interactive cue summation has been viewed as evidence for information integration (Anderson, 1982; Massaro, 1987; Oden & Massaro, 1978). In fact, the Competition Model uses the same maximum likelihood mathematical modeling tools found in information integration theory (McDonald & MacWhinney, 1989). What this means is that when there is a sentence in which the cues for subject disagree, choice is inconsistent. For example, people might disagree about the identity of the actor in an ungrammatical sentence like 'are pushing the erasers the cat.' In this sentence, the choice of 'the erasers' is favoured by the agreement cue, but the choice of 'the cat' is favoured by the animacy cue and the fact that 'the erasers' is in object position. In this particular sentence, the crucial preverbal positioning cue is missing, so only weak cues are determining performance. If we look at a sentence like 'The cats are pushing the erasers' we have no cue competition at all, since agreement, word order, and animacy are now all favouring 'the cats'. In general, by looking in detail at cells in which cues either compete or cooperate, we have found uniform support for the predictions of the Competition Model.

The learner

Students of SLA have long recognized the importance of the learner. SLA models have often incorporated ideas from cognitive psychology regarding individual differences in attention, automaticity (DeKeyser, Schmidt, this volume), phonological rehearsal (Service & Craik, 1993: Hulstijn, this volume), short term memory (Harrington, 1992a; McLaughlin, 1982), long term memory, auditory acuity, motivational levels, and learning styles (O'Malley & Chamot, 1990; Sawyer & Ranta, this volume). This 'skills' approach to language learning has led to solid advances in our understanding of the L2 process. However, it has not yet been tightly linked to information from the rapidly expanding field of cognitive neuroscience (Gazzaniga, 1997). In this section, I will suggest some ways in which facts about the human brain can help us build fuller models of SLA.

The human brain is basically a huge collection of neurons. These neurons are connected through axons. When a neuron fires, it passes activation or inhibition along these axons and across synapses to all the other neurons with which it is connected. This passing of information occurs in an all-or-none fashion. There is no method for passing symbols down axons and across synapses. Brain waves cannot be used to transmit abstract objects such as phrase structures. Rather, it appears that the brain relies on a type of computation that emphasizes patterns of connectivity and activation. Models based on this type of computation are called 'connectionist' models (Fausett, 1994), and they can be developed to offer computationally explicit accounts of L2 learning. A fundamental feature of these models is that they view mental processing in terms of interaction and connection, rather than strict modularity and separation. Although connectionist models often postulate some types of modules, they tend to view these modules as emergent and permeable (MacWhinney, 1998), rather than innate and encapsulated (Fodor, 1983).

Transfer

The interconnected nature of the brain has a crucial consequence for SLA theory. It means that the brain is structured in a way that promotes the transfer of information between emergent modules. Having acquired a first language during childhood, the learner comes to the task of learning the L2 with a well-organized neurolinguistic system. Initially, the learning of the L2 is highly parasitic on the structures of the L1 in both lexicon (Kroll & Sholl, 1992) and phonology (Flege & Davidian, 1984; Hancin-Bhatt, 1994). When the learner first acquires a new L2 form, such as 'silla' in Spanish, this form is treated as simply another way of saying 'chair'. This means that initially the L2 system has no separate conceptual structure and that its formal structure relies on the structure of L1. The learner's goal is to build up L2 representations as a separate system. This is done by increasing the direct linkage between the new L2 forms and conceptual representations.

Given the fact that connectionism predicts such massive transfer for L1 knowledge to L2, we might ask why we do not see more error in L2 learning. There are several reasons for this.

1. A great deal of transfer occurs smoothly and directly without producing error. Consider a word like 'chair' in English. When the native English speaker begins to learn Spanish, it is easy to use the concept underlying 'chair' to serve as the meaning for the new word 'silla' in Spanish. The closer the conceptual, material, and linguistic worlds of the two languages, the more successful this sort of positive transfer will be. Transfer only works smoothly

when there is close conceptual match. For example, Ijaz (1986) has shown how difficult transfer can be for Korean learners of English in semantic domains involving transfer verbs, such as 'take' or 'put'. Similarly, if the source language has a two-colour system, as in Dani, acquisition of an eight-colour system, as in Hungarian, will be difficult. These effects underscore the extent to which L2 lexical items are parasitic on L1 forms.

2. Some types of transfer are quickly corrected. For example, when a learner tries to form a cognate in Spanish for the English noun 'soap' the result is 'sopa' which means 'soup'. Similarly, an attempt to transfer the English form 'restrictions' to Spanish will run into problems, since the required target is 'limitaciones', not 'restriciones'. Once an error like this is made, it will be quickly detected. Moreover, the learner will become increasingly sensitive to possible errors in cognate transfer.

3. Error is minimized when two words in L1 map onto a single word in L2. For example, it is easy for an L1 Spanish speaker to map the meanings underlying 'saber' and 'conocer' onto the L2 English form 'know.' Dropping the distinction between these forms requires little in the way of cognitive reorganization. It is difficult for the L1 English speaker to acquire this new distinction when learning Spanish. In order to correctly control this distinction, the learner must restructure the concept underlying 'know' into two new, related structures. In the area of lexical learning, it is these cases that should cause the greatest transfer-produced errors.

By building direct links between sound and meaning in L2, and by restructuring underlying concepts, the learner is able to increase the automaticity of lexical access in L2. This automaticity constitutes a 'fire wall' against ongoing interference effects from L1 to L2. Consider the case of the English word 'table' and the Spanish word 'mesa'. The construction of this fire wall in an adult learning Spanish as a second language requires the formation of links between the new Spanish word and other related Spanish words. At the same time, the concept underlying 'mesa' will become linked to phrases and meanings that are more closely associated with the Spanish-speaking world than the English-speaking world. The more these two synonymous nouns can be linked into separate worlds and to other words in the same language, the stronger will be the fire wall that can prevent interference. This type of separation must be achieved not only on the lexical level, but also on the phonological, syntactic, and semantic levels. In effect, this work undoes the early parasitic association of concepts that the beginning L2 learner used to bootstrap the first phases of learning. The end result of this process is the tightening of within-language links in contrast to between-language links. In this way, a certain limited form of emergent linguistic modularity is achieved. However, the establishment of a non-parasitic L2 lexicon does not produce full insulation between languages, even in the most advanced bilinguals (Grainger & Dijkstra, 1992). The interactive nature of language processing continues to promote transfer and interference, even when the lexicons and grammars of both languages are fully established.

For those bilinguals and multilinguals who acquire their languages simultaneously during childhood, separate lexicons and grammars are constructed directly and there is no need to go through a process of undoing the initial connections formed through transfer (de Houwer, 1995; Grosjean, 1982). However, even in simultaneous bilinguals, some transfer and interference is predicted, due to the interactive nature of cognitive processing.

In phonology, the transfer of L1 articulatory patterns to L2 produces a foreign accent. In effect, the learner treats new words in L2 as if they were composed of strings of L1 articulatory units. This method of learning leads to short term gains at the expense of long term difficulties in correcting erroneous phonological transfer. However, even the most difficult cases of this negative transfer can be corrected through training and rehearsal (Flege, Takagi & Mann, 1995).

Transfer also affects the acquisition of grammar. If we think in terms of the Competition Model account of subject-marking devices presented earlier, we would say that the initial setting of weights in the parasitic L2 network is based on the weights in L1. However, learning of L2 involves more than simple weight-tuning. In some cases, the L2 requires the learner to seek out entirely new conceptual or discourse distinctions that were ignored in the first language, but which are now obligatory grammatical contrasts in the new language. A prime example of this type of restructuring might be the foreigner's attempts to pick up the category structure underlying the two major verbal conjugations of Hungarian. Every time a speaker of Hungarian uses a verb, he or she must decide whether it should be conjugated as transitive or intransitive. Making this choice is not a simple matter. The intransitive conjugation is used not only when the verb is intransitive, but also when the direct object is modified by an indefinite article or by no article at all. It is also used when it is in the first or second person, when the head of the relative clause is the object within the relative clause, when the direct object is quantified by words like 'each', 'no', and so on. For example, the 'intransitive' conjugation is used when a Hungarian says 'John runs', 'John eats an apple', 'John eats your apple', and 'John eats no apple'. On the other hand, the transitive conjugation is used when the object is definite, when it is modified by a third person possessive suffix, when it is possessed by a third person nominal phrase, and so on. Thus, the 'transitive' or 'definite' conjugation is used when the Hungarian wants to say 'John eats the apple' or 'John eats Bill's apple', whereas the intransitive is used to say 'John eats an apple'. There are some 13 conditions which, taken together, control the choice between the transitive and intransitive conjugations (MacWhinney & Pléh, 1997). There is no single principle that can be used to group these 13 conditions. Instead, transitivity, definiteness, and referential disambiguation all figure in as factors in making this choice. This way of grouping together aspects of transitivity, definiteness, and possession is extremely foreign to most non-Hungarians. Not surprisingly, L2 learners of Hungarian have a terrible time marking this distinction; errors in choice of the conjugation of the verb are the surest syntactic cue that the learner is not a native Hungarian.

In order to acquire this new category, the L2 learner begins by attempting to transfer from L1. To some degree this can work. The learner attempts to identify the intransitive with the English intransitive. However, the fact that many sentences with objects also take the intransitive if the objects are somehow 'indefinite' tends to block the simple application of this conceptual structure. In the end, the learner must be resigned to picking up the pieces of this new category one by one and restructuring them together into a working system. Here is an area where attempts at formal linguistic analysis on the learner's part only make matters worse. If the learner had proceeded like a Hungarian child (MacWhinney, 1974), he or she would have learned the conjugations by generalizing from a rich database of collocations and phrases. The adult needs to amplify this case-based approach to learning with a way of focusing on contrastive structures in which cues are competing. For the adult, such focusing on particularly difficult parts of a grammatical system will increase the efficiency of acquisition.

In many cases, the transfer of syntactic patterns from L1 to L2 is structurally correct, but pragmatically inaccurate. For example, Trévise (1986) observes that French speakers make excessive use of topicalization structures in English in the form of structures corresponding to left-dislocations, right-dislocations, and 'c'est... que' in French. Although these structures are all permissible in English, the actual conditions on their usage are far more restrictive than in French. Similarly, Seliger (1989) notes that Hebrew learners of English tend to systematically underuse the passive. He attributes this underusage to the relatively tighter, genre-dependent conditions on the use of the passive in Hebrew. In general, it is clear that simple transfer of an L1 structure to L2 is not sufficient to guarantee correct usage, since both under-utilization and over-utilization can occur until the full conditions governing the use of a construction in L2 are learned.

Our first investigations of L2 processing effects (Bates & MacWhinney, 1981) examined the comprehension of English sentences by a few of our academic colleagues. One subject was a native speaker of German who had lived in the United States for thirty years, was married to an American, and had published several important textbooks in experimental psychology written in English. Remarkably, we found that this subject processed simple English sentences using the cue strength hierarchy of German. This is to say, that he used agreement and animacy cues whenever possible, largely ignoring word order when it competed with agreement and animacy. This first evidence for the preservation of a syntactic 'accent' in comprehension has now been supported in over a dozen studies across a wide variety of L2 learning situations (Bates & MacWhinney, 1981; de Bot & van Montfort, 1988; Gass, 1987; Harrington, 1987; Kilborn, 1989; Kilborn & Ito, 1989; Liu et al., 1992; MacWhinney, Leinbach, Taraban & McDonald, 1989; McDonald, 1987a, 1987b; McDonald & Heilenman, 1991; McDonald & MacWhinney, 1989).

These Competition Model studies have used the sentence interpretation technique discussed earlier to estimate the strength of cues in L2 learners. Because the experimental design places cues into competition, we can use mathematical techniques to estimate the strength of each cue in terms of its ability to determine the shape of our experimental data. We find uniformly that the learning of sentence processing cues in a second language is a gradual process. The process begins with L2 cue weight settings that are close to those for L1. Over time, these settings change in the direction of the native speakers' settings for L2. The pattern of results found in this research is perhaps most clearly represented by data from McDonald's studies of English–Dutch and Dutch–English L2 learning (McDonald, 1987b). Figure 6 shows the decline in the strength of the use of word order by English learners of Dutch over increased levels of competence. In this graph the monolingual cue usage pattern for English is given in the first column and the monolingual Dutch pattern is given on the right. Between these two patterns, we see a declining use of word order and an increasing use of case inflection across three increasing levels of learning Dutch. In Figure 7, we see exactly the opposite pattern for Dutch learners of English. These results and others like them constitute strong support for the application of the Competition Model to L2 learning.

Figure 1 depicted a set of connections between forms and functions for the processing of cues to sentence interpretation. It is possible to

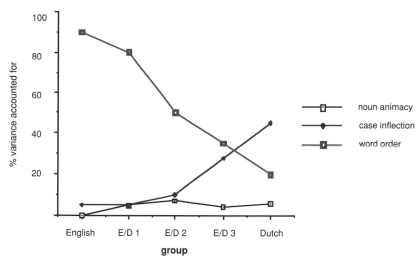

Figure 6. Changes in cue strength as English speakers learn Dutch (McDonald, 1987b)

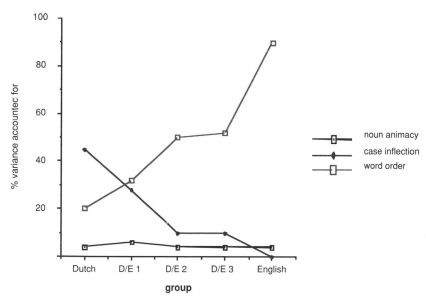

Figure 7. Changes in cue strength as Dutch speakers learn English (McDonald, 1987b)

convert this intuitive analysis of the subject-marking system into an actual running network model. Janice Johnson and I have done this by giving the various surface cues specified in Figure 1 as input to a 'recurrent' network of the type developed by Elman (1990) (described in detail by Ellis, this volume). This network is able to simulate the learning of Dutch and English. The model takes as input a corpus of over 1,000 sentences in each language. This corpus contains grammatical sentences from a wide variety of sentence types, including relative clauses, simple transitives, imperatives, subordinates, pronominalizations, and grammatical word order variations. After training in either language as L1, the model is given ungrammatical Competition Model sentences as test materials. At this point, we find exactly the types of cue interpretation patterns we saw in graphs like Figures 3 and 4. In order to model L2 learning, we then continue with a period of training with sentences from both languages and we then see exactly the pattern of cue development reported in Figures 6 and 7 by McDonald (1987b).

Neuronal commitment

Facts about brain development lead to a second major consequence for SLA theory. As development progresses from childhood through adolescence, the various areas of the brain lose their plasticity and their capacity for radically new forms of learning (Booth, MacWhinney, Feldman, Thulborn, Sacco and Voyvodic, 1999). When children are young, they can easily recover from the loss of large areas of cerebral cortex. However, similar losses in adulthood can lead to aphasia. This declining plasticity of the brain is at the root of the difficulties that older adults have in acquiring full competence in L2. This slow decline in flexibility is often discussed in terms of the theory of critical periods (Lenneberg, 1967). The idea that adults cannot learn second languages is easily over-stated. None the less, it is important to recognize that the plasticity of the brain places important limits on what the adult has to do to achieve successful L2 acquisition. Johnson and Newport (1989, 1991), and DeKeyser (this volume) have emphasized the extent to which adult learners may fail to achieve successful control over the L2. For these learners, continued exposure to English does not appear to lead to continued learning. In practice, the language attainment of these learners becomes fossilized or frozen at a fairly low level.

These findings can be understood in terms of the theory of neuronal commitment. We know that, even during infancy, areas involved in auditory processing and motor control are under intense pressure toward neural 'commitment' (Werker, Gilbert, Humphrey & Tees,

1981). Once a local neural area has been committed, it then begins to accept input data which lead toward a fine-tuning of the activation weights governing processing. If a second language is then to be imposed upon this pre-existing neural structure, it would directly interfere with the established set of weights. In fact, the parasitic nature of second language learning blocks any such 'catastrophic' interference of L2 onto L1. However, a full control over L2 requires the learner to reduce this parasitism and to automatize L2 processes apart from L1 processes.

Automaticity

Like other cognitive accounts, the Competition Model recognizes the importance of basic principles of learning such as the power law, and the fact that the best predictor of level of learning is time on task. These principles underscore the fact that learning a second language involves developing an automatic level of access to words and syntactic patterns that can guarantee fluency and accuracy (see Skehan & Foster, this volume). There are several Competition Model demonstrations of this fact. Kilborn (1989) has shown that even fully competent bilinguals tend to process sentences in their L2 more slowly than monolinguals. However, when monolinguals are asked to listen to sentences under conditions of white noise, their reaction times are identical to those of bilinguals not subjected to noise. Similarly Blackwell and Bates (1995) and Miyake, Carpenter, and Just (1994) have shown that, when subjected to conditions of noise, normals process sentences much like aphasics not subjected to noise. Parallel results for the effects of noise on simultaneous interpretation have been reported by Gerver (1974) and Seleskovitch (1976).

The Competition Model provides an account of sentence processing difficulty that stems directly from the notion of competition. Consider a German sentence that begins with an initial noun that is ambiguously marked for case, such as 'Die Mutter küsst der Vater' (The father kissed the mother). Because a noun like 'die Mutter' could be in either the nominative or accusative case, the listener does not know initially whether to establish the perspective as agent or patient. Because there is a strong tendency for initial nouns to be agents in German, this reading is favoured. However, a cautious listener will continue to maintain the alternative assignment in memory until the clause is complete. There are many examples of competing interpretations of this type. The parsing model promoted by Frazier and colleagues (Frazier, 1987; Frazier & Rayner, 1990) treats ambiguity resolution in terms of garden-pathing, rather than competition (as described by Harrington, this volume). However, other researchers (e.g., Altmann & Steedman,

1988; Juliano & Tanenhaus, 1994; Taraban & McClelland, 1988) have found that linguistic processing is best viewed in terms of an ongoing competition between alternatives.

Functional circuits

In order to solve the problems caused by commitment and parasitism, the adult L2 learner must rely on another dimension of neuronal processing. This is the use of the functional neural circuits that support rehearsal, monitoring, imagery, and reinforcement. These circuits allow the adult learner to maintain focused contact with crucial pieces of the input that can be used to correct problems with negative transfer and to reduce the parasitism of L2 on L1. By listening to high-quality input, working on meaningful relations in dialogues, and shadowing native speaker productions, the learner is able to make repeated use of the phonological loop and mental imagery. We know that neural networks can be effectively trained through repeated presentation of stimuli. This suggests that repeated use of these functional circuits should help recruit the residual neuronal resources that are still available to adult learners.

The prototypical case of a functional neural circuit is the phonological or rehearsal loop (Gathercole & Baddeley, 1993; Geschwind, 1970). This loop involves an activation of auditory cortex in the temporal lobe, processing of this input through parietal and temporal cortex, activation of the corresponding articulatory form of the word in motor cortex or premotor cortex, and storage of this material in dorsolateral prefrontal cortex (Cohen et al., 1997). We can think of individual differences in working memory (WM) as variations in the extent to which people make use of this particular circuit. King and Just (1991) present evidence that individual differences in WM are correlated with sentence processing in Competition Model type sentences, as well as variations in relative clause structure (MacWhinney & Pléh, 1988, and see Ellis, and Sawyer & Ranta, this volume).

Researchers in neuropsychology have only just now begun to explore the ways in which positive effect can help support mental processing in the phonological loop or in similar processing loops. When we consider the long hours that a teenage boy will spend absorbed in video games, we begin to think about the ways in which this activity may release rewarding substances such as dopamine in the brain. The release of these chemicals provides further support for the activity.

There is evidence that people find language use itself reinforcing. Many of us love to talk, even when there is nothing important to talk about. Language use is reinforcing, physically, socially, and cognitively. Bedtime monologues, word games, songs, and poems provide further evidence for the reinforcing nature of language. How this reinforcement actually works in terms of structures like the amygdala and the basal ganglia is something we are only now beginning to understand. To the degree that adult L2 learners can use reinforcing loops to participate in this self-rewarding use of language, they may succeed in overcoming declining neuronal plasticity and the parasitism of L2 on L1. Whether classroom use of language serves to promote these reinforcing loops is a matter that needs to be studied more closely.

Perspective-taking

A final aspect of neural processing that we need to consider is the way in which language imposes demands on memory during sentence interpretation. For language learners, these demands will interact with other aspects of their cognitive system, including WM, vocabulary size, and automaticity. Our raw memory for strings of nonsense words is not more than about four. However, when words come in meaningful groups, we can remember dozens of words, even when the message is unfamiliar. The most likely candidate for this additional storage is some form of conceptual representation (Lombardi & Potter, 1992). This process begins with the identification of a starting point (MacWhinney, 1987) or perspective from which the entire clause can be interpreted. In English, this is usually the subject. As new elements come in, they are linked up to this starting point. For example, if the initial phrase of the utterance is 'the black dog', then the noun 'dog' is taken as the perspective and the adjective 'black' is linked to 'dog' through the relationship of modification. The formation of the link between 'black' and 'dog' involves more that the simple positional relation of two words. Instead the adjective is applied to the noun on the conceptual level and an image of a black dog is activated. As long as verbal material can successfully access an integrated conceptual representation, it exacts no additional storage cost. However, sometimes verbal elements will 'stack up' in a way that exceeds a learner's capacity. Even a single centre-embedding like 'the dog that the flea bit chased the cat' involves more storage and restructuring than a subject relative like 'the dog that bit the flea chased the cat'. Studies of Hungarian (MacWhinney & Pléh, 1988) and Japanese (Hakuta, 1982) show that the stacking up of unlinked noun phrases can be even worse in SOV languages. L2 learners who have problems coping with such conceptually opaque structures may well have problems with these particular languages (MacWhinney, 1995).

The context

The third component of the language learning system is the interactional context. To some degree, this context is given by the facts of social life. If a young child is reared in isolation, language acquisition will be difficult (Curtiss, 1977). If the child is given strong scaffolding and support, acquisition will be facilitated (Snow, 1995). For the L2 learner, the situation is very different. In the classroom, a learner has little control over the interactional context. In this framework, successful learning strategies amount to little more than paying attention to the teacher, taking good notes, and keeping up with assignments. The goal in all of this is to maximize input and to occasionally get a chance to produce utterances. If there is a language learning laboratory, the student can use videotapes, audiotapes, and computerized lessons as further sources of input.

Even in more naturalistic contexts, the adult often does not have access to the rich system of social support that provides high quality language input to the child (Locke, 1995; Snow, 1995). In some situations, the learner is overtly excluded from close personal interactions. In such cases, it becomes difficult to engage in the type of rich ongoing use of language that can maximally support learning. To compensate for this, the learner can develop a system of 'autosupport' that uses functional neural circuits and carefully recruited social contexts as ways of maximizing the outcome of language learning. Concrete strategies include listening to television, radio, and movies, rehearsing taped dialogues, practising new lexical items, and direct study of grammatical theory. These activities allow the adult learner to remain in contact with the input in ways that promote the functioning of neuronal loops for rehearsal, memory, and learning.

In summary, the Competition Model framework we have examined provides several tools for understanding L2 learning. First, the underlying functionalist model of language processing makes direct predictions about impact of the input on the course of acquisition of specific structures in comprehension and production. Second, the neuronal model of learner emphasizes the roles of transfer, automatization, and parasitism in learning of the L2. Third, findings regarding plasticity and commitment can help us understand why adults have difficulties blocking transfer and parasitism in certain cases. At the same time, learning practices can provide forms of auto-support that compensate for the adult learner's loss of neuronal plasticity and full social support.

4 *Sentence processing*

Michael Harrington

Introduction

Sentence processing research seeks to understand the processes responsible for the comprehension and production of sentences in real time. Second language (L2) processing research complements that devoted to understanding language *structure*, in which the focus is on describing the phonological, lexical, and syntactic knowledge in the L2. It also complements investigations of language *function*, in which the interest is in how language is used in communicative contexts. Processing research differs from research on language structure and function in that it is primarily concerned with understanding the mental processes responsible for language as a dynamic, real-time entity. All three components are essential elements in a complete theory of second language acquisition (SLA).

Research on sentence level processing is a central focus in psycholinguistics, computational linguistics and artificial intelligence (Clifton, Frazier, & Rayner, 1994). Of central concern is how the different sources of linguistic and extralinguistic knowledge interact in real time to yield meaning. Like all cognition, the processes involved in sentence comprehension are only indirectly available to examination, and unfold on a millisecond timescale. This presents a great challenge to researchers in the field, as both theoretical and technical issues must be adequately addressed if progress is to be made. The insights derived from this research afford an important window both into the workings of the human speech processing mechanism and into the organization of the mind and behaviour (Carpenter, Miyake, & Just, 1995).

Although a major enterprise in psycholinguistics, sentence processing issues have received only limited attention in the SLA literature. This is due, in part, to the fact that mainstream sentence processing research has been mainly concerned with the development of normative models of the human speech processing system, that is, with how mature speakers use the language. As a result, correspondingly less attention has been given to developmental aspects, or to individual differences in processing (MacDonald, 1997). The lack of interest in learning and individual variation has meant that the issues occupying mainstream sentence processing research have been seen as peripheral to the central concerns of SLA. In addition, interest in processing issues among SLA researchers has been limited by the lack of technical resources and methodological expertise required to carry out the research. However, this has started to change. Research on L2 sentence processing has started to appear, and the studies to date have served to establish the relevance of sentence processing research for SLA theory (Harley, Howard, & Hart, 1995; Juffs, 1998; Juffs & Harrington, 1995, 1996; Myles, 1995; Sasaki, 1991, 1994; Ying, 1996).

The aim of this chapter is to describe the goals, methodology, and current theoretical approaches in sentence processing research, and to consider implications this field has for our understanding of SLA. The chapter will deal only with sentence comprehension processes, and will not consider recent work on L1 or L2 sentence production (for discussion of this see especially Doughty, this volume). The first section introduces the basic research paradigm and the experimental logic used in sentence comprehension research. In keeping with traditional practice, sentence comprehension is characterized here as a process of structure building. The sentence processor (or 'parser') builds a syntactic interpretation that leads to an interpretation of the sentence. Fundamental insights into how this structure building comes about has been obtained by examining the processing of ambiguous language structures (e.g., *'visiting relatives'*), where structural alternatives are thrown into sharp relief. Ambiguity resolution has been a key testing ground for competing processing accounts, as it provides a window on processes that are difficult to observe in normal comprehension processes. The central place of sentence processing research in cognitive science is also established by introducing key issues of cognitive organization and representation that are critical to understanding sentence processing in particular, and cognition in general.

In the second section, three approaches to sentence processing are described and models representative of each are examined. The respective approaches can be distinguished by assumptions they make concerning the role of syntax, its interaction with other sources of knowledge in real-time interpretation, and the manner in which processing is carried out. *Principle-based* models of sentence comprehension accord syntax a privileged role in representation and interpretation, with the parser and the grammar assumed to be closely linked (Frazier, 1987). Syntactic knowledge is assumed to be autonomous, that is, represented independently of other sources of knowledge (e.g, syntax, semantics, prior discourse context, frequency). Syntactic principles are applied prior to other sources of knowledge, which only become available later in the course of interpretation. *Constraint-based* models characterize sentence comprehension as a process of constraint satisfaction, in which the various knowledge sources serve as constraints on how a sentence is interpreted (Trueswell & Tanenhaus, 1994). All constraints are assumed to interact simultaneously in the course of processing, with prior frequency of exposure and context important factors in processing outcomes. Alternative structural possibilities are developed in parallel, with the most likely interpretation finally winning out on the basis of the support received from the various kinds of information. *Referential* models combine elements of the first two approaches. They assume that syntactic knowledge is modular, but emphasize the importance of discourse information in selecting among competing syntactic interpretations (Crain & Steedman, 1985).

Following the survey of the three approaches, the final section will conclude with a discussion about the contribution that sentence processing research can make to SLA theory and pedagogy. Future research in this area will provide a more grounded, mechanism-explicit account of *processing*, a term which is used in the current SLA literature with varying degrees of rigour (Juffs, 1998; Sharwood Smith, 1993). Sentence processing research also embraces as a central issue the relationship between processing and learning mechanisms, with the implications this will have for a transition account of L2 development (Gregg, 1996, this volume). Finally, greater insight into on-line processing by L2 learners will inform individual differences models of L2 development (Sawyer & Ranta, this volume), and provide a window on transfer in interlanguage (IL) development.

Sentence processing research

Research on sentence comprehension investigates how a listener converts an incoming string of sound (or orthographic) cues into a meaningful interpretation. This operation encompasses a complex series of steps that begins with the segmentation of incoming speech and ends with the recovery of the speaker's intentions. In Figure 1 this process is broken down into the major steps involved. The figure is adapted from Caron (1992: 38). The picture of sentence interpretation presented here is highly schematic, but it does serve to fix the place of sentence processing models in the more global process of language understanding. Note that the scheme does not necessarily represent the order in which the actual processing takes place.

1. Segment sound stream into string of linguistic units
2. Access individual lexical items in segmented string
3. Assign a syntactic structure to the word string
4. Derive a meaning for the words and syntactic structure as a unit
5. Establish the real-life referent of the string
6. Recover the speaker's intention.

Figure 1. The sentence comprehension process

Sentence processing research focuses on the interpretation of sentence level meaning (Steps 3 and 4). Processing involves a range of surface lexical and syntactic information, including the grammatical function of the individual words, morphological affixes, word order information, etc., as well as contextual and pragmatic information. How this information is integrated, and at what point the various information types become available in the course of processing, are questions the respective approaches address and resolve in different ways. Of particular importance is the role syntax is assumed to play in the process (Frazier, 1987).

The other steps in the process have been accorded less attention in the psycholinguistic literature. Word recognition and lexical access processes (Steps 1 and 2) are assumed as inputs to the sentence interpretation process, with little concern as to how they develop or their internal structure (Caron, 1992). The separation of levels should not be overstated, though, as the line between lexical and syntactic processes is quite tenuous in the constraint-based approach examined below (MacDonald, Pearlmutter, & Seidenburg, 1994). Higher order interpretative processes (Steps 5 and 6) have also been ignored generally by the mainstream sentence processing research, as pragmatics has traditionally been considered of little relevance to processing issues (Clark, 1992).

Sentence comprehension as structure-building

Sentence comprehension has traditionally been characterized as a structure building activity, in which the listener or reader builds a structure from incoming information (Mitchell, 1994). The incoming speech stream consists of a set of successively accumulating cues that the individual, under the pressures of real-time performance, incorporates into a developing meaning representation. For explanatory purposes, the structure-building operation can be divided into an assembly phase and an evaluation phase (Trueswell & Tanenhaus, 1994). In the assembly phase the processor can either build a single, structural representation in a serial manner (Frazier, 1987), or create a number of alternative candidates in parallel (Taraban & McClelland, 1990). In the evaluation phase the structure or structures are then evaluated in terms of semantic and discourse appropriacy. Principle-based models (Frazier & Fodor, 1978) assume that the assembly and evaluation stages are highly discrete, while in constraint-based models (MacDonald, 1993), they are interactive.

The structure building process begins by analyzing the input string into constituent structures. The listener starts with a provisional and partial analysis of the acoustic signal, and internally produces a string of phonemes which are interpreted as words. These lexical units are then integrated into a partial structure which is constantly being compared with the incoming information. A range of cues are used to identify and assign words to parts of speech, define the constituent boundaries, and then to integrate the constituents into the developing structure (see MacWhinney, this volume). These cues include lexical category information (e.g., whether a word is a noun, verb or adjective); thematic role information (e.g., the role a word plays in an event, as agent, source, goal, etc.); information concerning phrase structure (noun phrase (NP), verb phrase (VP), prepositional phrase (PP), as well as lexico-semantic information concerning who can normally do what to whom (e.g., trees don't sing)); and frequency information concerning how likely a particular form yields a specific interpretation. All these elements contribute to the ultimate interpretation of the sentence, but the various models differ greatly as to when and how this information is used.

The integration of successive elements into a structural representation requires the identification of which adjacent constituents combine with one another, the order in which they combine, and the phrasal category to which the combination belongs. Central to this process is the grammar of the language, as it specifies what are permissible constituents and relationships in the language. Grammatical representations can be portrayed as a tree diagram (also called a *phrase marker*) that captures the important structural relationships among the elements in the sentence. Figure 2 presents a tree diagram for an analysis of the string *The spy saw the cop with the binoculars*. The nodes represent the hierarchical relationships between the constituents in the sentence, and serve to indicate where processing decisions must be made in the course of structure building. These decision points are thus of primary interest to researchers seeking to model the sentence comprehension process.

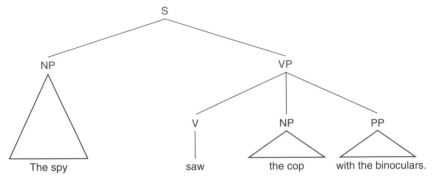

Figure 2. A phrase marker interpretation for The spy saw the cop with the binoculars

Ambiguity resolution in sentence processing research

The creation of a structure like that in Figure 2 from the incoming speech stream involves a complex set of processes and knowledge representations that interact rapidly in real time. Given the serial nature of the input string, and the millisecond timescale in which the processes unfold, and – in oral language – the evanescent nature of the speech signal, investigating how this operation works presents a great challenge. It has proved extremely difficult to directly tap into the basic structure-building operations which underlie the normal comprehension process. Attempts to infer underlying processing operations by 'working backwards' from the relative difficulty of processing specific structures (e.g., comparing global reading times on active versus passive structures) have provided little insight into the processes involved in comprehension (Mitchell, 1994: 376).

One way in which researchers have surmounted this problem is to study how individuals interpret structures that represent syntactic and semantic ambiguities. Figure 2 presents an interpretation of the sentence in which the spy uses the binoculars to see the cop, that is, the prepositional phrase (PP) *with the binoculars* is attached to the verb phrase (VP). However, this is not the only interpretation of the sentence possible. Consider an alternative phrase marker interpretation for the *The spy saw* ... in Figure 3.

In this instance the binoculars are no longer an instrument used by the spy to see the cop, but are interpreted as belonging to the cop. Note that the second reading becomes more likely if *the binoculars* is replaced with *a gun*, as in *The spy saw the cop with a gun*. Here *the gun* NP makes only one of the interpretations possible, as it cannot be an instrument of *saw*. The type of ambiguity evident in Figure 2

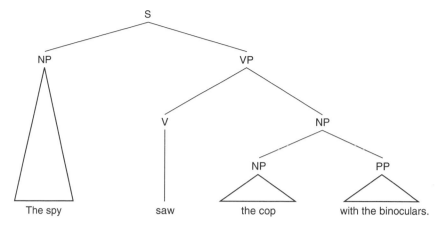

Figure 3. An alternative phrase marker interpretation for The spy saw the cop with the binoculars

is referred to as an *attachment ambiguity*, as it involves parsing decisions concerning where the word or phrase will be attached to the developing structure.

Another commonly studied attachment ambiguity involves 'garden path' effects that are evident in structures like (1), first discussed in Bever (1970).

(1) The waiter served the calzone complained.

When first encountered in the left-to-right pass through the string, *served* is usually interpreted as the main verb of a simple transitive sentence, in which the waiter is the Agent. However, this interpretation must be reconsidered when *complained* is finally encountered. At this point the listener/reader senses that she has been 'led down the garden path', and that the verb must be re-interpreted as part of a reduced relative clause, as in (2).

(2) The waiter who was served the calzone complained.

In addition to attachment ambiguities, there are two other areas of ambiguity resolution that have received extensive attention in the sentence processing literature. *Syntactic category* ambiguity occurs when a word is temporarily ambiguous among two or more syntactic categories, as in the phrases *visiting relatives* and *landing planes* (Farrar & Kawamoto, 1993; Tyler & Marslen-Wilson, 1977). Such ambiguities arise because multiple syntactic categories are initially accessed automatically, or 'primed' (Seidenberg, Tanenhaus, Leiman, & Bienkowski, 1982). The ambiguities are resolved rapidly on the basis of syntactic and semantic context, and are often the basis of the relative frequency of one alternative in a particular context (MacDonald, 1993).

The other type of ambiguity resolution that has been studied extensively is the processing of *empty categories*, an area of particular interest to linguists (Fodor, 1989). In this instance the ambiguity is of a temporary structural nature, and arises from the absence of an expected element, as in the long distance dependency constructions in (3a) and (3b) (Tanenhaus & Trueswell, 1995, p. 243). An empty category is assumed to be posited for structures where there appears to be a missing syntactic argument in the surface form of the sentence, as in:

> (3) a. I wonder which book$_i$ Tom read___$_i$ to us?
> b. I wonder which book$_i$ Tom read about___$_i$?

The missing element is termed the *gap*, and the phrase that serves as the argument of the gap in the interpretation is the *filler*, the two elements co-indexed by *i*. In (3), the interpretation of the filler *which book* depends on identifying the nature of the gap. In (3a) *which book* serves as the object of the verb *read*, which is used in a transitive sense, that is, it specifies what Tom is reading. In (3b) *read* is used intransitively, and *which book* is the object of the preposition *about*, that is, indicating what is being read about. Empty categories play an important role in Government & Binding theory (Chomsky, 1981), and much research has been devoted to establishing their psychological reality in sentence processing (Bever, 1988; Gibson, Hickok, & Schütze, 1994; Nicol & Swinney, 1989). The effects of empty categories on L2 processing is the focus of the Juffs and Harrington (1995) study discussed below.

Mechanisms of sentence comprehension

The goal of sentence processing research is to understand how sentences are comprehended and produced in real time. Central to achieving this goal is the identification of the cognitive mechanisms that are responsible for processing. Processing mechanisms consist of three elements: algorithms, heuristics, and knowledge representations.

Algorithms are formal information processes that operate on knowledge representations. Algorithms have been described as a 'recipe' for achieving specific processing outcomes. They are exemplified in IF–THEN production rules, in which a given computation or step is carried out when a condition is fulfilled, 'IF the bottom of Stack A is reached, THEN go to the top of Stack B' (Harel, 1992). Algorithms are responsible for transforming linguistic input into meaning, although the manner in which they carry this out is still largely unknown. There is, however, increasing refinement in our understanding of the manner in which these algorithms work, including whether they are carried out in a top–down or bottom–up manner; whether specific processes like the generation of syntactic structures are carried out in a parallel or a serial manner; or whether interpretations are immediate or delayed (Carpenter et al., 1995).

Heuristics are *apriori* principles that limit, or constrain, how the algorithms operate, usually serving to bias the processor in some way (Caron, 1992). Heuristics can be expressed in terms of principles specifying how sentence structure is developed, as in the *minimal attachment* and *late closure* heuristics used in Frazier's garden path model (Frazier, 1987). These heuristics bias the processor towards constructing the simplest syntactic structure that is consistent with the input. Heuristics can also reflect more general limitations that general cognitive capacities place on sentence processing, as in the perceptual 'operating strategies' that guide the individual's attention to specific parts of the input, as in, 'pay attention to the ends of word strings', (Bever, 1970; Slobin, 1985; and Doughty, this volume). The explication and testing of various heuristic proposals has been a central activity in sentence processing research.

Representations are the linguistic and extralinguistic knowledge structures in the mind of the learner. They are the 'stuff' on which the algorithms and heuristics operate. Representations include rules governing morphosyntax and phrase structure, as well as lexical, semantic and real-world knowledge (Caron, 1992). Syntactic and lexical representations have received most of the attention in sentence processing research, but the contribution of other types of knowledge (e.g., pragmatics) to sentence interpretation is attracting increasing interest (MacDonald, 1997).

The goal of sentence processing research is to understand the mechanisms and representations responsible for comprehending sentences in real time. The research thus has direct implications for linguistic and psychological models of language knowledge and use, as well as for how that knowledge is developed. In addition, sentence processing research also has profound implications for our understanding of cognitive organization and representation, and thus has an important place in the cognitive sciences.

Sentence processing research as a cognitive science

Processing models embody fundamental assumptions about cognitive organization and representation, or what is referred to as the *cognitive architecture*. The cognitive architecture defines the information processing capacities and mechanisms that are assumed to be built in to the mind/brain (Stillings, Weisler, Chase, Feinstein, Garfield, & Rissland, 1995). A number of different cognitive architectures have been proposed, and each makes basic assumptions about the nature of the subsystems involved in cognition. These subsystems include the peripheral sensory registers, the central systems of memory and attention, and the motor control systems, as well as the way in which information is represented and processed. Four aspects of the cognitive architecture are particularly important for sentence processing models, as they help define the way in which the proposed processing mechanisms are structured internally, and the way these elements are organized in a larger system. The four aspects can be characterized in terms of oppositions that capture how knowledge is represented (*symbolic* versus *distributed*), the nature of knowledge representation (*discrete* versus *graded*), the degree of interaction among processing components (*modular* versus *interactive*), and the manner in which processing proceeds (*serial* versus *parallel*). The models examined below can be distinguished by the specific assumptions made concerning these four aspects (Clifton et al., 1994). Each will be briefly considered in turn.

Symbolic versus distributed knowledge   The traditional view of cognition characterizes the mind as a general purpose computational system that is best understood as a symbol manipulation process (Newell, Rosenbloom, & Laird, 1989). A *symbolic* architecture assumes that knowledge is represented directly in symbols, and that computations are carried out on these representations. In natural language computation these symbols include phonemes, morphemes, grammar rules, etc., and the processor works directly on these elements to yield an interpretation. The comprehension process can be described as something akin to a predicate logic in which rules are applied to a string of input representations to yield an output. Thus the string *the man runs quickly* is understood as (is *transformed* into) the structured symbolic proposition RUNS(MAN, QUICKLY). The assumption is that there are processes that reliably generate these arguments and predicates at a level of syntactic representation that is independent of the semantics of the specific items involved (Stillings et al., 1995). Many – although not all – cognitive scientists view the rule-governed processing of structured symbolic representations as indispensable to carrying out higher order cognitive processes by humans, most notably for the processing of syntax or the use of number systems (Fodor & Pylyshyn, 1988).

A challenge to the classical symbolic view has appeared in the form of *connectionist* models of cognition. In this approach language is represented and computed via a network of linked nodes (Rumelhart,

1989). Language knowledge is not represented as symbols as such, but rather as patterns of neural activations that emulate symbolic knowledge (e.g., words, grammar rules) and rule-governed behavior. Connectionist models are thus sometimes referred to as 'subsymbolic', and computation is characterized as a process of transforming activations on a set of input unit weights into a set of output units (Clark, 1989). For example the phonological input string [kʰiːp] represents a specific pattern of units at varying strengths that serves as input to the system. For English speakers this phonological input is mapped onto the meaning representation of 'keep', which is the output. It is important to note that what is represented in the mind is not phonemes or words, but patterns of activation that link input and output mappings. Connectionist models have been particularly successful at capturing processes at the word and intraword level, as, for example, in resolving ambiguities in lexical access (Kawamoto, 1993), but less successful at capturing higher-order syntactic processes (Plunkett, 1998). The respective strengths of symbolic and connectionist approaches has led to interest in *hybrid* models that seek to incorporate the complementary strengths of the two approaches (Bever, 1992; Dijkstra & di Smedt, 1996).

Discrete versus graded knowledge representation   Closely related to the form of the cognitive architecture is the nature of knowledge representations. Symbolic approaches have traditionally assumed that the knowledge of words, rules, etc., is *discrete*, that is, one either knows the word or one doesn't. In contrast, connectionist approaches assume that knowledge of words or rules is represented in a pattern of activation strengths in a network. These activation levels increase and decrease over time as a function of exposure and experience. The notion of graded representations is particularly useful for explaining instances of processing ambiguity resulting from failure to identify clear boundaries among knowledge representations, as in the case of lexical ambiguity (Rumelhart, 1989). Although graded representations are characteristic of connectionist models, recent symbolic accounts have also incorporated the notion of gradedness within a symbolic representation framework (MacDonald, 1997).

Interaction among levels   Comprehension is a multi-level phenomenon that involves perceptual, lexical, syntactic, and discourse knowledge. The multi-level nature of processing means that a satisfactory processing account must specify how the different levels interact in real time comprehension. Approaches to sentence processing vary in the degree to which the levels are formally differentiated. *Modular* architectures assume that the different levels, notably syntax, are independent and interact in a highly constrained manner. Extreme modular versions (e.g., Frazier, 1987) assume that syntactic processing is encapsulated from other non-syntactic sources of knowledge. A syntactic interpretation alone is computed on the first pass through the sentence, with sentence semantics or discourse information taken into account only when evaluating the output of the initial parse. In contrast, *interactive* models of processing assume that multiple sources of information interact, more or less immediately, in the on-line interpretation of sentence meaning (Marslen-Wilson & Tyler, 1987). Syntax is viewed as just another source of information, along with semantic, pragmatic and discourse factors, that the processor uses to yield an interpretation. Although all these sources of information ultimately contribute to sentence comprehension, a key issue in the interactivity/modularity debate is the time-course of processing, that is ascertaining when the various kinds of information become available (Mitchell, 1994).

Serial versus parallel processing   Sentence processing approaches differ in their explanations of how the structure-building process takes place. *Serial* models immediately build one structure at the expense of alternative interpretations. The output is then submitted to a checker that evaluates the output for appropriacy in the given discourse or processing context (Frazier, 1987; Frazier & Fodor, 1978). *Parallel* models, in contrast, assume that the processor immediately constructs and stores all possible alternative interpretations in parallel, and then waits for disambiguating information to yield the appropriate outcome (Crain & Steedman, 1985; Marslen-Wilson & Tyler, 1987). Modular approaches can be either serial (Frazier, 1987; Frazier & Fodor, 1978) or parallel (Altmann & Steedman, 1988; Crain, Ni & Conway, 1994), while interactive approaches, particularly connectionist models, assume parallel processing.

The models examined in the next section make specific commitments on all four aspects of cognitive architecture. These commitments serve to frame the respective approaches to sentence processing, and have important implications for the processing problems addressed and the scope of explanation offered.[1] As will become evident the

---

[1] Although the dimensions have been presented here as dichotomies, the attempt to support or refute one position versus the other is not considered a useful research strategy (Carpenter et al., 1995). Setting up competing positions as, for example, modular versus interactive processing, can lead to an oversimplification of the issues in question and often sterile arguments. It is often the case that empirical evidence presented in support of a specific model cannot be directly compared with findings used to support the 'opposing' position. Rather, a more productive tack has been to investigate the nature of these processes in specific domains, as in assessing the degree of interaction between lexical knowledge and syntactic processing (Mitchell, Corley, & Garnham, 1992).

sentence processing research program represented in three approaches provides insight not only into the human speech processing capability, but also into the organization of the mind.

Three approaches to sentence processing

Three approaches to sentence comprehension are presented in this section, with the main focus on the problem of ambiguity resolution. Representative models of each approach are described, and studies are discussed that applied these models to domains of L2 sentence processing. As there is a vast and growing literature on sentence processing, the survey does not attempt to be exhaustive. The three approaches surveyed here: the *principle-based* approach; the *constraint-based* (or *interactive*) approach; and the *referential* (or *discourse-based*) approach, represent the principal currents in sentence processing research (Boland, 1997; Mitchell, 1994; Tanenhaus & Trueswell, 1995), and the issues raised in the course of examining the various models represent key concerns in the current sentence processing literature – concerns that also have direct implications as well for SLA theory development.

Principle-based approach

The principle-based approach accords a central role to syntactic structure in accounting for the resolution of ambiguity (Berwick, Abney, & Tenny, 1991). The language processor is assumed to be modular, which means that syntactic knowledge is applied prior to, and independently of, other types of linguistic and real world knowledge in the course of on-line interpretation. One of the most influential principle-based models is Frazier and Fodor's two-stage model of comprehension (Frazier & Fodor, 1978). Dubbed the 'sausage' model, the first stage consists of a syntactic parse of the incoming word string based only on information about major syntactic categories (e.g., determiner, noun, verb). The output of the syntactic parse is then fed to a thematic processor, where lexical, semantic, and discourse information is brought to bear on the interpretation of the sentence (Frazier, 1987; Frazier & Fodor, 1978). The initial commitment to a particular structural interpretation can result in the listener or reader being 'led up the garden path' when the selected alternative turns out to be incompatible with the ultimate interpretation of the structure, as in *The waiter served the calzone complained.*

The two-stage model makes a basic representational distinction between lexical entries and syntactic rules. Lexical entries are assumed to be stored and accessed as discrete entities, while syntactic structure is computed in real time. Other lexical information, such as how an item subcategorizes, and how frequently it occurs in the given structures only available at a later stage. Such a 'lexically blind' arrangement, it is argued, allows sentence comprehension to be carried out rapidly and efficiently – two features of modular systems (Fodor, 1983; Frazier, 1989).[2] The model did much to set the agenda for two decades of sentence processing research. Among other things, it defined as a central research issue the time course in which the different sources of knowledge becomes available, particularly in the initial parsing decisions (MacDonald, 1997).

Empirical support for the garden path model has come from studies that examined the processing of ambiguous sentences like *The waiter served...* and *The spy saw the cop with the binoculars*. For the latter type of ambiguity, the model predicts a bias toward the instrumental reading of the sentence (i.e., in which the spy uses the binoculars to see the cop) on the basis of the minimal attachment heuristic. Refer to Figures 2 and 3 above. Minimal attachment stipulates that the processor constructs the simplest structure that is consistent with the incoming information, and the model assumes that structural complexity predicts processing demands (Frazier, 1987). The non-instrumental reading of the sentence (in which the binoculars are an attribute of the cop) is assumed to require the creation of a more complex structure with six terminal nodes ((NP(VP(V)(NP(NP, PP))), in contrast to the five nodes needed to represent the preferred instrumental reading ((NP)(VP(V, NP, PP))). The need to posit an additional node is assumed to make a greater demand on processing capacity, and hence is avoided by the processor (Crocker, 1994).

A number of experimental studies have supported the main predictions of the garden path model (Clifton, Speer & Abney, 1991; Frazier, 1989; Frazier & Rayner, 1987; Mitchell et al., 1992; Rayner, Carlson, & Frazier, 1983). However, the model has also been challenged. Other principle-based models have appeared that differ from the garden path model in a number of aspects, notably the increased role that lexical information is assumed to play in syntactic processing (Abney, 1989; Pritchett, 1992), and the number of syntactic interpretations output by the syntactic processor (Gibson et al., 1994; Crocker, 1994). There is also a growing body of literature that suggests a much greater interaction among the various knowledge sources (lexical, semantic, contextual, etc.) than the garden path model allows (Boland, Tanenhaus & Garnsey, 1990; Juliano & Tanenhaus, 1993; Marslen-Wilson & Tyler, 1987). This literature will be examined more closely in the discussion of the constraint-based approach below.

[2] See Pinker (1991) for an analogous processing account for irregular and regular verbs in English.

The garden path model has been modified considerably since it was first introduced, but remains the strongest version of principle-based parsing, given the highly restrictive role it ascribes to lexical information in sentence interpretation (Frazier & Clifton, 1996). Although other principle-based models have appeared, all such models are unified in the assumption that the parser directly utilizes grammatical rules in the course of real time interpretation. Also referred to as the *strong competence hypothesis* (Bresnan, 1978), the posited direct relationship between the grammar and the parser is highly compatible with formal theories of autonomous syntax (Chomsky, 1995), and principle-based models have been particularly attractive to researchers working in this framework.

Juffs and Harrington (1995, 1996) applied a principle-based processing model to examine L2 on-line reading processes. The *Generalized Theta Attachment* (GTA) model (Pritchett, 1992) was used to assess the relative contribution of processing difficulty and (UG-based) grammatical knowledge to learner performance in on-line reading and grammaticality judgement tasks.[3] The GTA characterizes the structure-building process in terms of the assignment of thematic roles to elements in the input string (Pritchett, 1992). The thematic role of a phrase is the general semantic role that the phrase (called an *argument*) plays in relation to its predicate, with the various thematic roles possible for the phrase described by the argument structure of the predicate. Thematic roles (also called theta roles) include such entities as *Theme* (or Patient), which signals the entity undergoing the effect of some action, as *Tom* does in *Tom fell over*; Agent (or Causer), in which *Tom* is the instigator of an action, as in *Tom killed Bob*; and Goal, which is the entity toward which something moves, as in *home* in *Tom went home* (Radford, 1997). Lexical items can appear in more than one argument structure, and it is the possibility of multiple argument structure interpretations that leads to the ambiguity encountered.

The NP in the string *The waiter served...* can either be an agent (an interpretation consistent with either a transitive or intransitive argument structure for *served*), or a theme (consistent only with a transitive reading of the verb). The parser seeks to build as complete a structure as possible by assigning all thematic roles as soon as possible. As each word comes through the parser, syntactic principles (e.g., Theta Attachment, Case, Binding) are assigned so as to realize the most complete structure possible for the local string (see Juffs & Harrington, 1995, for details). It is assumed that every NP must eventually be associated with a specific thematic role, and that the parser

---

[3] Generalized Theta Attachment (GTA): Every principle of the Syntax attempts to be maximally satisfied at every point during processing (Pritchett, 1992: 138).

selects the reading that imposes the lowest cost on the system. Processing difficulties thus arise as the result of unfulfilled thematic role assignments. The thematic assignment model differs from the garden path model in the central role that subcategorization information plays in parsing, particularly the thematic information that is allocated by the verb (see also Abney, 1989; and for non-GB motivated approaches that emphasize the lexical nature of parsing, Ford, Bresnan & Kaplan, 1982; Tanenhaus, Carslon & Trueswell, 1989).

Juffs and Harrington (1995) investigated the asymmetry evident in L2 learner performance on grammatical judgements for *wh*-structures exemplified in (4) and (5).

(4) *Who did Ann believe__likes her friend?* (Subject extraction from finite clause)

(5) *Who did Ann believe her friend likes__?* (Object extraction from finite clause)

The sentences differ in that (4) is assumed to require the extraction of the pronoun *who* from the subject site (indicated by the gap), while (5) involves extraction from the object site. Earlier research showed that ESL learners experience more difficulty judging the acceptability of subject extraction sentences like (4) than their object extraction counterparts in (5) (Schachter & Yip, 1990; White & Juffs, 1997). Structures involving constraints on *wh*-movement are interesting because they provide a testing ground for the availability of UG-based constraints in adult L2 processing, given that these constraints are not assumed to operate in all languages (Epstein, Flynn, & Martohardjono, 1996). Poor performance on the subject extraction sentences by adult L2 learners from languages in which *wh*-movement constraints are not assumed to operate (e.g., Chinese) have thus been used as evidence for lack of access to these principles by L2 learners (Schachter & Yip, 1990). Juffs and Harrington questioned whether the difficulties encountered by learners on these particular structures might be due to processing deficits rather than knowledge deficits, given that the learners demonstrated sensitivity to *wh*-constraints in judgements on other types of *wh*-structures, including the object extraction types in (5).

Juffs and Harrington (1995) examined the ability of Chinese advanced ESL learners to read and judge the grammaticality of sentences like (4) and (5) in an on-line reading task. The key comparison in the study was between processing times for the region immediately following the verb 'believe' in both sentence types. Reading times were sharply higher in the post-gap region for the subject extraction from finite clauses (4); the slowdown in processing mirroring the observed decline in accuracy for these forms. Given that the Chinese learners in the study showed sensitivity to *wh*-movement constraints in general, the relative difficulty encountered on the subject extraction sentences was attributed to greater processing demands that resulted from the re-analysis involved in the correct assignment of thematic roles in these structures.[4] In Sentence (4), GTA predicts that the parser will initially interpret the main verb *believe* as an NP complement, and will posit a complete grammatical sentence with an object gap as in *Who does Ann believe___?* The appearance of the finite verb *like* then forces the object gap to be reanalyzed as an embedded subject trace, *Who does Ann believe___likes?* The authors thus concluded that it was the demands of the on-line re-analysis, and not the availability of the *wh*-movement constraints, that may be responsible for the observed differences in performance on the respective structures evident in the research reported to date.

The use of a competency-based grammar (the strong competence assumption) in the Juffs and Harrington study allows the interface of syntactic knowledge representations and processing mechanisms to be systematically examined. The grammar provides a formal, testable set of predictions that permits the researcher to isolate and identify the relative contribution of the grammar and the processor to real time language comprehension. In adult L2 comprehension, the understanding of this interaction is made more complex by the wide range of individual differences in knowledge and processing across learners, and the potential effect of the first language on both these dimensions (Juffs, 1998).

Principle-based models provide important insights into the working of the human speech processing mechanism. However, many researchers find the assumptions made by these models, particularly the garden path model, to be overly restrictive or even misplaced. The prediction that contextual and semantic effects are confined to the latter stages of processing, that is when the thematic processor evaluates the initial syntactic interpretation, has been challenged by research demonstrating contextual effects much earlier in comprehension process (Tanenhaus & Trueswell, 1995). Manipulation of prior discourse context has been shown to bias responses to garden path sentences like

---

[4] The Chinese ESL participants in the study performed at levels comparable to native speaker controls on grammatical extractions of objects from finite clauses as in (5), but were less accurate than the native speakers on grammatical extractions of subjects in finite clauses (4), and grammatical extractions of objects and subjects in finitival clauses, as in *Who does Tom expect to fire___?* and *Who does Tom expect___to fire the manager?*, respectively. Note, however, that learner performance was well above chance for all these structures (Juffs & Harrington, 1995: 501).

The waiter served... both toward and away from the predicted main verb-minimal attachment reading. For example, the reduced relative clause reading can be elicited by prefacing the test sentence with *Two waiters were served different types of Italian food. The waiter served calzone...* (Altmann & Steedman, 1988; Trueswell & Tanenhaus, 1994). Semantic effects on initial parsing have also been found. The fact that *waiter* in *The waiter served...* is animate makes an ambiguous reading more likely than the presence of an inanimate noun would, compare *The spaghetti served...* (Ferreira & Clifton, 1986; Trueswell et al., 1994). Frequency effects have also been shown to bias sentence interpretations. For example, the frequency with which a verb occurs in a given argument structure can bias interpretation toward one of the alternatives made available by the subcategorization information. The main verb interpretation of *served* in the example sentence is possible with both a transitive and intransitive argument structure, while the reduced relative clause reading requires a transitive argument structure. Verbs that appear more frequently in transitive argument structures are less likely to be given an intransitive reduced relative interpretation, despite the fact that both structural interpretations are available (MacDonald et al., 1994). These issues are examined in more detail in the next section.

Finally, there is also a methodological limitation to the principle-based approach that arises from its dependence on an explicit theory of linguistic structure. Syntactic theory is a complex, constantly changing entity, and the attempt to apply the theory to processing issues means the researcher runs the risk of solving yesterday's problem, as the theory evolves and changes (White, 1996).

Constraint-based approach

Principle-based models emphasize the role of syntactic representations in the structure building process, whether as the basis for the complexity-based parsing decisions in the garden path model (Frazier, 1989), or as the well-formedness conditions driving thematic role assignment (Pritchett, 1992). The constraint-based approach, in contrast, describes ambiguity resolution as an interactive process, in which syntactic, lexical, and semantic-conceptual information interacts to constrain on-line comprehension (Tanenhaus & Trueswell, 1995). Several of these sources of information have already been introduced. Lexical constraints include both major syntactic category and argument structure information, that is, *The waiter...* is an NP that can be associated with an agent role, appearing in either a transitive or intransitive argument, or as a theme in a transitive structure alone (Boland,

Tanenhaus, Garnsey, & Carlson, 1995; MacDonald et al., 1994). Semantic-conceptual constraints include information in the preceding discourse that can serve to bias interpretations (Altmann & Steedman, 1988; Spivey-Knowlton & Tanenhaus, 1994; Trueswell & Tanenhaus, 1994), the frequency with which an item appears, both alone and in particular structures (MacDonald et al., 1994; Mitchell, 1994), as well as real world knowledge and beliefs. For example, given the expectation that animate things typically do the acting, while inanimate things are acted upon, it is more likely that *The waiter serves the pizza* than it is that *The pizza serves the waiter*.

Sentence interpretation in the constraint-based approach is described as an interactive process of *constraint-satisfaction* (McClelland, Rumelhart & Hinton, 1986).[5] Constraint-satisfaction models are most readily associated with connectionist perspectives on cognition, and current constraint-based models draw heavily on connectionist architecture and processing principles.[6] A prime example is the 'lexicalist' constraint-based model developed by MacDonald and her co-workers (MacDonald, 1997; MacDonald et al., 1994). In a connectionist implementation of the lexicalist model the various types of knowledge are represented in a graded, distributed network of units or sets of units (Rumelhart, 1989). Units corresponding to the various information types are activated in parallel, with the strength of activation of a particular unit or set of units reflecting the type, number, and strength of the links it shares with other units in the system. Alternative structures are activated to differing degrees, and the interpretation depends on which alternative the system ultimately settles on (Rumelhart, 1989).

A distinguishing feature of the lexicalist constraint-based model is the assumption that the principles governing syntactic ambiguity resolution (and processing) are identical to those governing lexical ambiguity resolution (Kawamoto, 1993; MacDonald et al., 1994). Both processes are assumed to be the outcome of an interactive, constraint-satisfaction process in which multiple, interdependent sources of probabilistic information serve to interact to facilitate certain outcomes and inhibit others.[7] The ambiguity encountered in structures like

---

[5] See Rumelhart and McClelland, 1986, for a description of constraint satisfaction models of language and cognition. See also the chapters by Ellis and MacWhinney in this volume.

[6] There are constraint-satisfaction models in non-connectionist architectures as well (Mackworth , 1977).

[7] The terminology can be confusing. Pritchett's 1992 model has also been called a constraint-satisfaction model, although the constraints that are satisfied are strictly defined in terms of grammatical principles (Crocker, 1994: 249). This, however, is an exception, as constraint-satisfaction models are usually associated with the interactive approach discussed here.

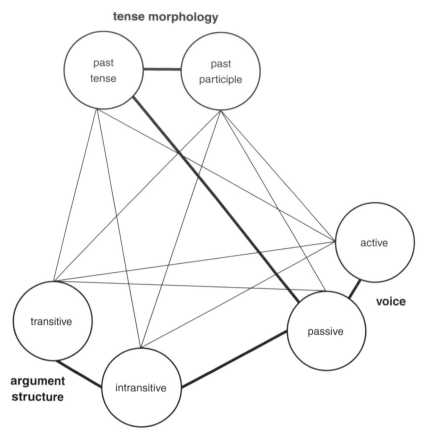

Figure 4. Three levels of lexical ambiguity for the verb served

The waiter served the calzone complained are recast as a problem of lexical ambiguity (at three levels) rather than a structural parsing or thematic role assignment problem. Figure 4 presents a hypothesized representation of the three levels of lexical ambiguity that must be resolved in order to interpret *served* in *The waiter served...* The figure is adapted from MacDonald et al. (1994: 135), and is based on a connectionist interactive-activation model of processing (Elman & McClelland, 1984; Kawamoto, 1993).

Three levels of representation are shown in Figure 4. The circles (nodes) represent the feature units and the lines representing the links between the units. The thick lines represent inhibitory connections, in which activation of one unit will inhibit activation of the other unit(s) with which it shares links. The thin lines represent excitatory connections between units that serve to raise activation levels or linked units.

Both types of connections are defined by the grammar of the language, which specifies which combination of units is possible. Each pair of circles represent the alternatives that are available for the verb *served* in the structure *The waiter served* . . . The argument-structure level alternates between transitive (in which both an agent and a thematic role can be assigned), and intransitive (in which only an agent role is possible); the tense morphology level between the past tense and past participle; and the voice level between active and passive (MacDonald, 1994).

The interdependencies between these levels is schematically represented in the pattern of connections. For example, the reduced relative clause reading (*The waiter who was served* . . .) requires that the *waiter* is in the passive voice. This places a constraint on the other two levels, as only one possible alternative exists at each of the other two levels, namely the past-participle tense morphology and the transitive argument structure. The conjunction of the passive voice and the simple past tense is not allowed (*The waiter was flew by the pilot*), nor is the passive possible with intransitive argument structure (*The waiter was slept*).

Ambiguity resolution is the result of spreading activation between units in the system (a process initiated by phonological and orthographic inputs not shown in the figure). The favoured interpretation is the one receiving the highest level of activation and represents the cumulative effects of all units on all the other units. It is assumed that all sources of information are taken into account during processing, and that all levels of ambiguity must be resolved before the interpretation is complete (McDonald et al., 1994b).[8]

Frequency and context effects also act on this lexical information to bias interpretation. As noted, the reduced relative clause reading requires a transitive reading. Studies manipulating the frequency of verb and structure concurrence in test sentences indicate that frequency has a reliable effect on interpretations (MacDonald, 1994). Verbs that occur in transitive argument structures much less frequently than in intransitive structures overall are less likely to be given a reduced relative interpretation (MacDonald et al., 1994; Trueswell et al., 1994).

The constraint-based approach thus contrasts sharply with principle-based accounts. In the garden path model an initial commitment is made to a particular syntactic representation, and thematic and

---

[8] The authors acknowledge that the assumption that all information must be processed, that is that processing is *analytically exhaustive*, is probably too strong, given that the goals of the reader or listener may be satisfied at times with only a partial analysis (MacDonald et al., 1994b: 137).

semantic information used only to guide the re-analysis. The lexicalist model, in contrast, assumes an immediate contribution from lexical, thematic, and semantic information in a process in which sentence interpretation emerges from the simultaneous interaction of interpretations at a number of levels (MacWhinney, 1998). In fact, *structure-building* itself may not be the appropriate metaphor for capturing the highly interactive nature of the constraint satisfaction process that drives comprehension in the constraint-based approach (Tanenhaus & Trueswell, 1995).

A constraint-based model that has received considerable attention in the SLA literature is the Competition Model (CM) (see MacWhinney, this volume). The CM characterizes sentence interpretation as a cue-based process in which linguistic knowledge is represented as a complex set of links between available surface cues (form) and the meaning in a particular context (function). Surface linguistic forms, like word order and case markings, serve as cues that the speaker maps onto underlying language functions. For example, the position of the noun before the verb in a canonical subject-verb-object (SVO) English sentence is a strong cue that the noun is the subject/actor of the sentence, as in *Bill read a book*. Positional cues are particularly important in English, where word order plays a central role in conveying structural information (e.g., thematic roles), but are less important in languages where this information is signalled by other means, like case marking. The strength (or *weight*) of a given cue is the result of its frequency in the language and the manner in which it interacts with other cues.

The CM has been used to model thematic role assignment, specifically the interpretation of the sentential agent. The main experimental methodology used in CM research is a sentence interpretation task that requires an individual to identify the agent in simple two-argument sentences in which cues are systematically varied (e.g., word order cue contrasts include SVO/*Betty kissed Jack*, SOV/*Betty Jack kissed*, and VSO/*Kissed Betty Jack*). This task allows the effect of specific cues and cue combinations on agent assignment to be systematically compared and contrasted across learners and groups.

The CM has generated a sizeable body of cross-linguistic research that has produced a cross-linguistic typology of language-specific cue strengths, and has established the universality of the model. The CM has been applied with success to L2 processing as a model of IL development and L1 transfer (e.g., Harrington, 1987; Kilborn, 1989; MacWhinney, 1987; Rounds & Kanagy, 1998; Sasaki, 1991, 1994). The characterization of language knowledge as cue strengths allows IL development to be described in quantitative terms, that is, as the development of the requisite cue strengths in the target L2 (MacWhinney, 1992). The individual learner develops the cue strengths for expressing a particular linguistic function (e.g., assigning agenthood) through experience with the language, and is either facilitated or inhibited in this process by the strength of the cue in her L1. For most linguistic domains and functions, IL development can thus be described as the position of the individual learner or group of learners somewhere along a cue-strength continuum bounded by the cue strengths in the L1 and those in L2 (Harrington, 1987, forthcoming). At the same time, the model provides the means to quantify the role of the L1 on L2 development.

Harrington (1987), for example, examined sentential agent interpretations by groups of native English, native Japanese, and native Japanese ESL learners (the IL group), for evidence of L1-influenced processing strategies in L2 performance. Accuracy and reaction time results on sentences in which word order, animacy, and contrastive stress cues were varied suggested that the IL subjects did transfer L1 processing preferences in the interpretation of the L2 English sentences. The result for word order effects is plotted in Figure 5. It is evident that in the canonical NVN (= SVO) order, the IL responses on the English sentences (68% of the first nouns were selected as Agent) were midway between the two L1 response means (81% for the L1 English, and 59% for the L1 Japanese). This suggests that the IL participants were moving from the L1 to the L2 cue strengths in this domain. However, for the non-standard word orders (NNV and VNN), the word order cues were not as strong, since the IL responses remained closer to the L1 Japanese – a finding attributed to the interaction of animacy cues with these two types of word order (Harrington, 1987: 368–9).

The complex interaction of cues in the CM means that the patterns of convergence and competition among the various cues in yielding particular interpretations can be difficult to interpret. However, a number of CM-based L2 studies have established the usefulness of the model in understanding L1 transfer effects (Harrington, forthcoming; Kilborn, 1989; Sasaki, 1994; Rounds & Kanagy, 1998). Although the CM shares fundamental assumptions about the cognitive architecture underlying sentence comprehension with other constraint-based models (see Mitchell, 1994 or MacDonald, 1997), it has received limited attention in the sentence processing literature. This is due, in part, to the fact that the CM has not directly addressed ambiguity resolution and on-line time course issues involved in interpretation, issues that have driven the mainstream research agenda. Also, empirical support for the model is almost exclusively drawn from a single linguistic

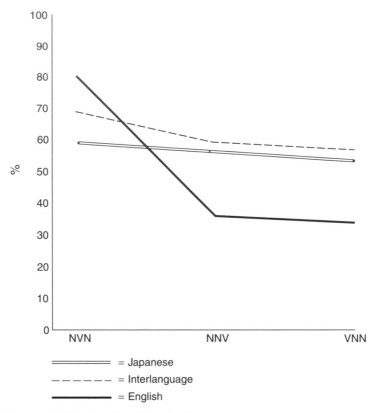

*Figure 5. Word order effects by learner groups
(Harrington, 1987)*

domain (the assignment of the sentential agent), which makes it difficult to assess the generalizability of the major theoretical claims. This
particularly is problematic as an account of the development of complex syntactic relationships that are not directly marked in the surface
form (Harrington, 1992b).[9]

---

[9] This is an issue for bottom–up models of processing in general. For example, consider the
following four sentences that express pronominal agreement (taken from White, 1989).
Note that *Mary* and *she* refer to the same person in all the sentences.

(a) *Mary* watched television before *she* had her dinner.
(b) Before *Mary* had her dinner *she* watched television.
(c) Before *she* had her dinner *Mary* watched television.
(d) *She* watched television before *Mary* had her dinner.

It is difficult to see, on the basis of surface cue distribution alone, how the learner could
know that (d) is not allowed. In (a), (b), and (c), *Mary* and *she* appear to be interchangeable,

Constraint-based models provide a parsimonious account of sentence comprehension that is particularly attractive to researchers working in a connectionist framework (MacDonald, 1997). Lexical and syntactic processing are assumed to be guided by a single constraint satisfaction mechanism that works on multiple sources of information. The increased role that lexical information plays in constraint-based sentence interpretation is also compatible with the ongoing trend in both sentence processing research and linguistic theory in general to locate more of the representational and processing burden at the lexical level (Chomsky, 1995; Juffs, 1996; MacDonald et al., 1994; Pritchett, 1992).

The limitations of constraint-based models have also been noted (Frazier, 1995). Specific models have demonstrated that frequency and context effects influence sentence interpretation (e.g., Trueswell et al., 1994), yet they have failed to make explicit predictions as to how these elements affect the course of on-line processing. This is due, in part, because the models have lacked sophisticated accounts of grammatical representation, which is needed to delimit which constraints are important in sentence processing outcomes (Tanenhaus & Trueswell, 1995: 233). Finally, claims made concerning the data-driven nature of sentence processing have proved difficult to test in the absence of large scale corpora on which to establish the frequency counts used to make the processing predictions; and even if the effect of frequency in processing is demonstrated, the differences in frequency themselves need to be explained in a principled way if the account is to have the desired explanatory adequacy (Frazier, 1995).

Referential approaches

Principle-based and constraint-based approaches to ambiguity resolution diverge sharply on key issues of representation and processing. A third approach, the referential (or *discourse-based*), shares features with both approaches. Referential models focus on the role that prior context plays in on-line processing outcomes, particularly in the resolution of the types of ambiguity discussed in this chapter (Altmann & Steedman, 1988; Crain & Steedman, 1985; Steedman & Altmann, 1989). A key element in interpreting *The waiter served calzone complained* is the identification of the referent for the definite noun phrase

that is, they map onto the same underlying functions within the clauses, and there appears to be no restriction on the order in which the clause containing *Mary* and one containing *she* can appear, as in (a) and (c) However, sentence (d) is not permitted, indicating that a more abstract level of syntactic representation is also needed that is not directly recoverable from surface features of the input.

The waiter. Crain and Steedman (1985) note that the referent can either be located in prior discourse, as is normally the case in everyday discourse contexts, or is created by the listener mentally in the absence of context, as is common in experimental treatments of these structures (e.g., Frazier & Rayner, 1987; Juffs & Harrington, 1995). The interpretation of *The waiter* as a reduced relative clause, as required by the final verb *complained*, presupposes a set of possible discourse referents from which the modifying relative clause then identifies a unique referent, that is, *The waiter that was served calzone* as opposed to *The waiter that was served pizza*. The bias away from the reduced relative clause reading in 'null' context settings reflects not the need to minimize structural complexity but the lesser degree of *presuppositional complexity* involved in positing a single discourse referent, which is all that is needed for the main clause interpretation (Crain & Steedman, 1985).

Like principle-based accounts, referential models assume that syntactic processing is autonomous. But unlike the garden path model, it is assumed that the syntactic processor builds all possible structural interpretations in parallel, on a word-by-word basis. When it encounters an ambiguous word like *served* in the *The waiter served . . .* it automatically generates the alternatives, which are then fed to a semantic/discourse processor that evaluates and selects among the alternative analyses on the basis of how well they fit the immediate discourse context. Immediate discourse information has precedence in guiding the interpretation, but if that is not available real world knowledge can also play a role (Ni, Crain & Shankweiler, 1996). Crain and Steedman describe this as a *weak interaction* approach, in which referential information is used to select between alternatives generated by the parser, but that this information is not available to guide the parser at the initial stages (Crain & Steedman, 1985). This approach is in contrast to the *strong interaction* view embodied in constraint-based models, where various sources of information are available to guide the interpretation from the outset (Spivey-Knowlton & Sedivy, 1994). Both the weak and strong interaction versions contrast with the garden path model by sharing the assumption that contextual information plays a more immediate role in sentence interpretation.

Support for the model has come from studies demonstrating that varying prior context can systematically bias sentence interpretation (Steedman & Altmann, 1989; Taraban & McClelland, 1990). Referential context can overcome the structural biases predicted in principle-driven approaches (e.g., minimal attachment, Frazier, 1987), and override general knowledge or frequency effects in some contexts (Altmann, Garnham, & Dennis, 1994; Marslen-Wilson & Tyler, 1987;

Mitchell, 1994). However, there are studies where context-based predictions are not borne out (Ferreira & Clifton, 1986; Mitchell, Corley & Garnham, 1992), and an ongoing debate concerning when the influence of context comes to bear on parsing decisions (see Ni et al., 1996; Spivey-Knowlton & Tanenhaus, 1994).

Ying (1996) compared predictions made by referential and garden path models in the interpretations by ESL learners on PP attachment ambiguities (structures like *The spy saw the cop with the binoculars*, see Figures 2 and 3 above). The ambiguity arises in the attachment alternatives possible for the PP *with the binoculars*: attachment to the VP results in the instrumental reading (the spy using the binoculars to see the cop), while attachment to the NP results in the attributive interpretation (the binoculars belong to the cop). Frazier's minimal attachment principle predicts that the VP reading will be preferred on the grounds of structural simplicity, regardless of context (Frazier, 1995). Ying compared ESL learner interpretations across three conditions: a null context condition in which no preceding context was provided; a context condition in which a biasing context was given; and a prosodic condition in which prosody cues were used to bias the interpretation. In the null context condition the participants simply listened to test sentences, and indicated whether the PP modified the VP or the NP. An example of a test sentence used in the null-context condition follows (all examples taken from Ying, 1996: 690):

> The girl [$_{VP}$ saw [$_{NP}$ the man[$_{PP}$ with a special pair of glasses]]].

In the context condition, a discourse context was presented that biased the responses toward the NP reading. This was done by introducing a set of discourse referents prior to the experimental sentence:

> There were two girls. One of them had a sense of humor, and the other did not. The man [$_{VP}$ talked to [$_{NP}$ the girl [$_{PP}$ with a sense of humor]]].

The prosodic condition involved presenting a prosodic break immediately after the verb, and a single unbroken intonation contour over the remaining constituents. The prosodic break was intended to signal the closing off of the current constituents and, along with the single intonation contour over the remainder of the utterance, biased the listener toward attaching the PP to the adjoining NP. An example sentence in the prosodic condition follows ('. .' denotes prosodic break):

> The man talked . . to the girl with a sense of humor.

Ying's results replicated earlier findings (Ying, 1996: 697). Principle-based parsing predictions were supported in the null context condition, where a bias toward the VP interpretation was evident in learner responses (Frazier, 1987). However, learner responses were strongly biased toward the NP interpretation when a biasing context was provided (Altmann & Steedman, 1988; Trueswell & Tanenhaus, 1994), and to a lesser extent when prosodic information was included (Harley et al., 1995; Marslen-Wilson, Tyler, Warren, Grenier, & Lee, 1994). The results again underscore the importance of accounting for multiple sources of information in models of sentence interpretation.

Summary of the three approaches to sentence processing

Three approaches to sentence comprehension, specifically to understanding the resolution of on-line ambiguity, have been examined in this section. Defining characteristics of the respective approaches were described and models representing each approach were discussed. The models examined make varying assumptions about cognitive architecture and the processing mechanisms responsible for on-line interpretation. Principle-based and referential models assume a modular architecture, in which syntactic interpretations are generated autonomously. In the garden path model this process is carried out in a serial manner (Frazier, 1989), while in the thematic role assignment model (Pritchett, 1992), and in the referential model (Altmann & Steedman, 1988), alternative analyses are generated in parallel. In all three models the ultimate interpretation is either confirmed (in the case of the serial models), or selected (in parallel approaches) by a distinct, second stage parser. In the principle-based model it is a thematic processor that selects for suitability (Crocker, 1994; Ferreira & Clifton, 1986), and in referential models the preferred structural alternative is selected on the basis of the relative fit to the prior discourse context, if available (Steedman & Altmann, 1989). Both principle-based and referential models make a principled distinction between the mechanisms responsible for lexical processing (e.g., word recognition and lexical access) and syntactic processing.

Constraint-based models, in contrast, are highly interactive and do not assume autonomous syntactic representations. Multiple sources of knowledge (syntactic, lexical, referential, frequency-based) interact from the first stages of processing in a massively parallel manner. Comprehension is the result of a continuous process of constraint satisfaction based on correlated information from the various knowledge sources, and both lexical and syntactic processing are assumed to be guided by a single constraint satisfaction mechanism (MacDonald et al., 1994).

The various approaches can differ greatly as to how they account for processing outcomes, but one finding that emerges from all the surveys is that lexical information appears to play an increasingly important role in accounts of ambiguity resolution, although the different approaches characterize the role of lexical information in different ways.

Sentence processing research and SLA theory

The sentence processing research surveyed in this chapter seeks to understand how mature speakers (native L1 adult or advanced L2) comprehend language in real time. The underlying aim of the enterprise is to develop a normative model of language comprehension, both for its own intrinsic value and for the insights it will provide for theories of mind. As a result, there has been correspondingly less interest in how the capacity develops, or in understanding the variation apparent in language learning and use.

SLA theory, in contrast, is primarily occupied with explaining how individuals acquire proficiency in an L2, a domain characterized by a great range of individual outcomes, both quantitatively and qualitatively. A complete theory of SLA will provide both a property theory describing what the L2 learner must learn, and a transition theory explaining how the learner acquires that knowledge (Gregg, 1996). An integral part of that transition theory will be an account of the cognitive mechanisms responsible for language learning and use. The sentence processing research program examined here has produced an increasingly sophisticated understanding of real-time comprehension processes, and it seems reasonable to assume that the conceptual and methodological tools developed as part of that endeavour will also help us understand the development of L2 proficiency.

Contributions that sentence processing research can make to a cognitive theory of SLA theory are sketched out in this section. The point of departure for the discussion is the assumption that models of L2 sentence processing will be of increasing importance to the development of a SLA transition theory. However, while the processing research is likely to provide insight into L2 development, there is nothing in terms of logic or empirical evidence that require learning and processing be governed by the same mechanisms (see, e.g., Crain, Ni, & Conway, 1994). The relevance of the sentence processing research to a transition theory of SLA is an empirical question, and one that is only beginning to be addressed in SLA research.

Three ways will be briefly considered in which this influence might manifest itself. First, L2 sentence processing research can provide an explicit account of the mechanisms responsible for language process-ing; elements that are largely absent from current theoretical and peda-gogical treatments of processing in SLA. Second, and the central issue here, L2 sentence processing research provides the methodological framework for addressing the relationship between processing and learning. Although early sentence processing models largely ignored developmental issues, there is a growing recognition that the under-standing of processing and learning is closely intertwined, if not, as in the case of constraint-based models, identical. Thirdly, sentence processing is also an important dimension of IL variation, both in its sensitivity to individual differences in the ability to learn and use language, and as a source of L1 influence on L2 development. All three areas are important for the development of a cognitive theory of SLA.

An explicit account of processing

Studies addressing L2 sentence processing are a recent – and still limited – addition to the SLA research literature. However, processing-based accounts, particularly those from the information-processing perspective, have been an integral part of SLA theory (Bialystok, 1990; Hulstijn, 1990; McLaughlin, 1987; McLaughlin & Heredia, 1996; McLaughlin, Rossman, & McLeod, 1983). Information-processing models describe learning and processing in terms of a system that is decomposable into a set of simpler subsystems and processes (Palmer & Kimchi, 1986). The emphasis in these models has been on describing cognitive states and the transformation of information (e.g., from controlled to automatic processing, from state A to state B via restructuring), with very little attempt to account for the mechanisms responsible for the real-time transformation processes. A better un-derstanding of real-time comprehension and production mechanisms would complement these global models.

Processing-based L2 pedagogical theory also draws on processing constraints as a motivation and a rationale. Instructional process-ing accounts include consciousness-raising (Rutherford & Sharwood Smith, 1985), comprehensible input (Krashen, 1982), input-processing (VanPatten, 1996), and output-processing (Swain & Lapkin, 1995). These accounts make minimal assumptions about the underlying mechanisms responsible for the proposed learning pro-cesses, and a more complete account of the actual on-line processes will provide a principled basis for evaluating the tenability and scope of these proposals (Juffs, 1998; Sharwood Smith, 1993).

The relationship between processing and learning mechanisms

The core of an SLA transition theory is an account of the on-line mechanisms responsible for learning. At issue here is the relationship between synchronic processing mechanisms and diachronic learning mechanisms, and what research on one might tell us about the other. Principle-based and referential models make a sharp distinction between the two mechanism types. Sentence comprehension processes are driven by grammatical knowledge, which takes the form of discrete, rule-based representations that develop independently and are then used by the parser (Frazier & De Villiers, 1990). The rich syntactic representations that are central to the account allow these models to make and test explicit predictions about the structural aspects of comprehension, but have little to say about development. In addition, the research findings are based on performance by mature speakers, whether they are psychology undergraduates or fluent L2 speakers (Juffs & Harrington, 1995; Myles, 1995; Ying, 1996). Note that this is also typical of most constraint-based research to date, with the CM being a notable exception (MacWhinney & Bates, 1989). The nature of the model and the subject pool used raises the issue of whether processing effects obtained in these instances also generalize to learners at differing stages of proficiency. To date this issue has not been addressed in the principle-based literature, but evidence from other perspectives, particularly CM research, suggests that there may be significant developmental differences at the processing level (MacWhinney & Bates, 1989; also Harley et al., 1995).

Learning mechanisms for the principle-based and referential approaches must thus come from other sources. For researchers working in the generative framework, the learning mechanisms are structurally defined, and include parameter-(re)setting (Hyams, 1987), triggering (Lightfoot, 1989), or the Subset Principle (Wexler & Manzini, 1987). How these mechanisms actually work in real-time processing remains largely a matter of conjecture (Gregg, 1996, this volume; White, 1996).

The relationship between processing and learning mechanisms is more direct in the constraint-based approach, where they represent two sides of the same representational coin. The knowledge that subserves sentence processing is stored in a distributed network of activations that are graded, thus varying in strength as a function of the individual's experience. Processing outcomes are the result of the interaction of multiple sources of information (lexical, syntactic, frequency, context) that are a direct reflection of the individual's knowledge at that point. That knowledge, expressed in levels of activation, changes in principle every time the processing mechanism is engaged. In this view processing is learning. The learning/processing mechanism responsible for the development of this knowledge is the accretion of patterns of activation through associative learning (Elman, 1990; MacDonald, 1997).

Associative learning plays an important role in the development of L2 proficiency, but the extent of that role is a matter of debate (for one side of the debate, see Ellis or MacWhinney this volume; for the other side, see Gregg, 1996, this volume). Associative learning is directly implicated in the strengthening of existing knowledge representations, most readily evident in the 'practice effects' that result from the improvement in performance due to exposure or practice (Kirsner, Lalor, & Hird, 1993; Schmidt, 1992; and DeKeyser, this volume). More controversial is the role of associative learning in the development of new knowledge, particularly syntactic knowledge. Connectionist models of syntactic development have emerged that have successfully demonstrated the capacity to learn a specific class of syntactic structures (MacWhinney, 1998, this volume), but the adequacy of these input-driven associative models as a general learning account for syntax remains very much an open question (Fodor & Plyshyn, 1989; Sharkey, 1996).

Parsimony favors the constraint-based approach, as it provides a unified account of learning and processing. The importance of associative-based processes in SLA indicates that constraint-based models will be a necessary part of a complete SLA transition theory. Whether it can be shown to be a sufficient account – particularly for the development of complex syntax – is not clear. The fact that principle-based models are well-suited for understanding just those aspects of processing which cause problems for constraint-based models suggests that a hybrid approach, in which elements of both approaches are combined, may be a productive research strategy. At the very least we need to see more L2 research with both models in order to understand the limits of the respective approaches as accounts of processing and learning.

Processing and interlanguage variation

Sentence processing is also directly implicated in IL variation. The effect of capacity differences on quantitative and qualitative aspects of sentence processing have been documented. Marcel Just and co-workers, for example, have shown that the likelihood of being 'garden-pathed' on structures like *The waiter served...*, is systematically related to the individual's working memory capacity, that is, individuals with a larger working memory capacity can consider more structural alternatives (Just & Carpenter, 1992; MacDonald, Just, & Carpenter, 1992). We would expect the same relation between individual capacity and processing outcomes to hold for L2 learners, and it may turn out that capacity-based processing differences may be more important in understanding L2 individual differences than it is for the L1. Research addressing this question is clearly needed. Both principle-based and constraint-based approaches to L2 processing also need to incorporate capacity constraints.

The final area to consider is the effect of L1 sentence processing strategies on L2 processing. CM research has demonstrated the systematic effect of L1-based strategies on L2 processing performance, and the substantial role that processing strategy transfer plays in accounting for IL variation in the model (Kilborn, 1989). Likewise, Juffs (1998) has also found evidence for L1 based processing influences on L2 sentence interpretation processes in the principle-based processing framework. This indicates that processing will play a role in SLA transfer accounts, though more research is certainly needed.

Conclusion

The aim of this chapter has been to provide a survey of the sentence processing literature, and to consider the implications this research might have for our understanding of SLA. Representative models from three approaches to sentence processing were discussed. The strengths and limitations of respective approaches were described, and initial attempts to apply them to domains of L2 processing were examined.

In keeping with the common practice in the literature, sentence comprehension has been described in this chapter as a structure-building task. This metaphor may have outlived its usefulness for describing comprehension from the constraint-based perspective, given the highly interactive nature of sentence comprehension. It may be time to move away from the conception of sentence comprehension as a product, that is, as a structure-building exercise, to a more dynamic, process-oriented view that emphasizes the central goal of the process, namely, comprehension (Clark, 1992).

Research on ambiguity resolution has generated a large body of empirical findings and has been a primary source of evidence for current models of sentence comprehension. It has been a key testing ground for competing processing accounts, providing a window on processes that are difficult to observe in normal comprehension processes. However, with more interest directly on learning processes, the focus is starting to shift to modelling acquisition processes (e.g., Ellis & Schmidt, 1997), in which the focus is on modelling normal learning processes.

Sentence processing research in SLA is still in its infancy. Findings from the limited number of L2 studies to date, along with the vast psycholinguistic literature, indicate that a better understanding of on-line L2 processes will become increasingly important as researchers take more seriously the need to develop a transition theory of SLA.

5 Automaticity and automatization

Robert M. DeKeyser

Introduction: concepts and issues

In a very general sense, everybody knows what automaticity means. Some doors slide open automatically, some cars shift gears automatically, some VCRs rewind automatically; in other words these objects perform their functions without requiring any physical or mental effort on our part (the meaning of the Greek adjective *automatos* is self-acting). In the psychological sense, every layman has had experience with automaticity too. When typing, driving a stick-shift car or using a word-processor to edit a text, we perform a complex series of tasks very quickly and efficiently, without having to think about the various components and subcomponents of action involved; sometimes we are even unable to think of them explicitly, and therefore we may have trouble visualizing the keyboard or explaining to somebody else how to use a piece of software, even though – or rather just because – we use the keyboard or the software with great ease. Initially, though, we may have found typing, driving a stick-shift car or using a spreadsheet to be slow, tricky, and tiring. The automaticity, that is the speed and ease with which we ultimately carry out these tasks, is the result of a slow process that we call automatization. Once this process has run its course, the chain of actions involved in the automatized tasks can even become hard to suppress, as we experience when forced to shift from a querty to an azerty keyboard, from a stick-shift to an automatic car, or from one kind of accounting software to another.

The ultimate example of automaticity is probably our ability to use language. Through a complex chain of mental operations, carried out in a fraction of a second, we can convert complex thoughts and feelings into soundwaves; and our interlocutor can convert them back into thoughts and feelings with the same amazing speed. Given the complexity of this skill and the speed with which it is used, it is not surprising that it takes years to acquire, and that learning a new language in adulthood is a slow and frustrating process.

125

The aim of this chapter is to investigate in some depth how psychologists conceptualize the layman's experiences with automaticity and automatization, to assess how automatization operates in second language (L2) learning, and to draw at least tentative conclusions about what classroom activities and what curricular sequences are conducive to the automatization of second/foreign language skills. A better comprehension of these issues is essential for the language teaching enterprise, because without automatization no amount of knowledge will ever translate into the levels of skill required for real life use, and because '[t]heories which relate [interlanguage] variation to cognitive processes capable of manipulation or change are of particular importance, since they may be directly applicable to the teaching/learning situation' (Crookes, 1989: 367).

However important automatization may be for the acquisition of all complex skills, including L2 skills, it has not been the object of much empirical research in the field of applied linguistics. To some extent this is due to developments within the field (lack of appropriate methodology before 1980, lack of theoretical interest between 1980 and 1990; see DeKeyser, 1997), but probably also to the complexity of the concepts of automaticity and automatization themselves. It is difficult to find a definition of the terms that cognitive psychologists can agree on; in fact, at first sight several conceptualizations seem outright contradictory. Some researchers use the term automatization for a process of gradual quantitative change (speed-up) in the execution of the same task components, while others see automatization as a qualitative change (restructuring, i.e., selection and configuration of task components). However, Cheng (1985), for instance, argued that certain phenomena that appear to be automatization are not because restructuring of the task is going on. Schneider and Shiffrin (1985) appeared to agree with that distinction when they replied to Cheng that the phenomena they had documented in their landmark (1977) study *were* instances of automatization because what appears to be evidence against speed-up of simple components in fact reflects a complex mixture of components, only some of which have been automatized. Carlson, Sullivan and Schneider (1989) provide further evidence for a process that has constant structure, but whose components become faster. Logan (1988, 1992) also clearly sees automatization as a gradual improvement of the same process (retrieval from memory in this case). On the other hand, Segalowitz and Segalowitz (1993) state that automatization implies a change of task components, not just a speed-up, citing high correlations between means and standard deviations sampled at different stages of the learning curve (such as the ones documented by Logan and used as a crucial element in his theory of automatization; see below under 'Item-based approach') as evidence that what is going on is *not* automatization.

Another source of initial confusion is the concept of skill acquisition as taking place in a discrete number of stages. While Schneider and Shiffrin (1977; cf. also Shiffrin & Schneider, 1977, 1984; Schneider, Dumais & Shiffrin, 1984) present a dichotomy of controlled versus automatic processes, most researchers now see skills on a continuum between controlled and automatized (see esp. Cohen, Dunbar, & McClelland, 1990; Cohen, Servan-Schreiber, & McClelland, 1992; Logan & Etherton, 1994; Strayer & Kramer, 1990); and while researchers such as Fitts and Posner (1967) or Anderson (1982, 1983, 1987, 1993) see skill acquisition as a three-stage process, Anderson, Fincham and Douglass (1997) as well as Schneider (1985) describe four stages, and Schneider and Detweiler (1988) five.

Some of these apparent contradictions are merely terminological in nature or follow from a focus on substages of the skill acquisition process, as will become clearer in the second and third sections. One distinction is rather fundamental, however, and currently is the focus of much debate: that between automatization as the ever more efficient use of rules (cf. esp. Anderson, 1993) and automatization as the ever faster retrieval of instances from memory (cf. esp. Logan 1988, 1992). Even though these two views have converged to some extent recently (Anderson, et al., 1997; Palmeri 1997; see below under 'A modicum of convergence'), they do remain fundamentally different, and are beginning to be reflected in the second language acquisition (SLA) literature (e.g., DeKeyser, 1997; Robinson, 1997b), as illustrated below under 'Empirical research on automatization in SLA'.

Given the terminological confusion and conceptual complexities that prevail in the literature on automaticity and automatization, we will begin the next section with an overview of what different authors have considered to be criteria of automaticity, and then we will define automatization 'in terms of manifest properties' (Logan & Klapp, 1991: 179) rather than positing one underlying defining mechanism from the outset.

Criteria and characteristics

Criteria for automaticity

What are the characteristics of performance that lead to the conclusion that it is automatic? Table 1 presents an overview of what different researchers have mentioned explicitly as criteria of automaticity.

Table 1. *Criteria for automaticity*

	fast	parallel	effortless	capacity-free	unintentional (hard to control/alter, suppress)	result of consistent practice	little interference from/with	"unconscious" (no attention, no monitoring)	always memory retrieval	OTHER (see below)
LaBerge & Samuels, 1974	x					x		x		
Posner & Snyder, 1975								x		
Hasher & Zacks, 1979			x	x	x		x	x		no benefit from further practice
Schneider & Shiffrin, 1977	x		x	x	x	x		x		
Shiffrin & Schneider, 1984		x	x	x	x	x				
Schneider et al., 1984				x				x		
MacKay, 1982	x		x				x	x		error-free and flexible
Kahneman & Treisman, 1984	x			x	x	x		x		
Levelt, 1989	x	x		x	x					
Schneider & Detweiler, 1988							x			
Treisman et al., 1992						x				
Bargh, 1992								x		
Cohen et al., 1992	x					x	x	x		
Anderson, 1992	x			x	x	x	x	x		strong production rule
Logan, 1988									x	
Strayer & Kramer, 1990			x						x	no WM interference
Palmeri, 1997			x						x	
Segalowitz & Segalowitz, 1993	x									no correlation between mean and stand. dev.

Individual researchers are represented by one publication only, unless a substantial shift occurred in their thinking. The table shows clearly that a wide variety of criteria have been used. To some extent this may simply be due to the fact that sometimes authors do not mention all criteria explicitly, even when they would not disagree with them, but in large part the table does reflect the inability of the field to agree on a definition applicable to all tasks. Bargh (1992), Klapp, Boches, Trabert and Logan (1991), Newell (1990), Phillips and Hughes (1988), and Strayer and Kramer (1990), in particular, argue that many of the criteria used in the earlier research (largely before 1985) do not apply across all studies or tasks.

Up to Shiffrin and Schneider (1984) the predominant view was that automatic processes were characterized by their high speed, their very low error rate, the lack of effort required, the absence of general capacity use (as reflected, for instance, in the absence of an effect of memory set size[1] in a visual detection task, and other forms of load independence), and the difficulty of controlling the process, that is, the difficulty of suppressing the process once started, of altering it in the future or of ignoring stimuli relevant to it. These characteristics were the result of large amounts of consistent practice, as illustrated in great detail in Schneider and Shiffrin (1977; for good summaries of that study see Barsalou, 1992; Newell, 1990; Shiffrin & Schneider, 1984).

A shift in thinking then occurred which is made particularly obvious from a comparison of Shiffrin and Schneider's (1984) criteria for automaticity with those listed in Schneider et al. (1984). The latter explicitly rejected many of the previously suggested criteria as neither necessary nor sufficient to distinguish controlled from automatic processing, and reduced the list to two. Kahneman and Treisman (1984) mark a further step away from the controlled/automatic dichotomy by stating that the 'criteria probably co-vary in most situations but may be separable' (p. 42), and by distinguishing three levels of automaticity (at least in perception): strongly, partially, and occasionally automatic, depending on how much attention is required.

Most authors since then have listed far fewer criteria. Schneider and Detweiler (1988), Treisman, Vieira, and Hayes (1992), and Bargh (1992) each list only one explicitly; and proponents of memory-based theories, such as Logan (1988), Strayer and Kramer (1990), and

---

[1] Memory set size refers to the number of elements to be kept in WM at the same time. If the number of elements has no influence on task performance, this is evidence that the elements are not processed individually (serially), and thus that their processing has been automatized.

Palmeri (1997) only agree on one criterion: performance of a task has become automatic when it is always accomplished through single-step memory retrieval. This criterion is one that follows from the theory rather than a directly observable criterion, of course, as is the case with Anderson's main criterion of a strong production rule (see the next section for full discussion of these mechanisms).

Perhaps the most important change reflected in Table 1 is that from theories which present automaticity as an issue of how much *attention* is given to a task to theories that present it as an issue of how *memory* is used. While all of the pre-1990 publications list either unintentional or unconscious as an important criterion, only three of the post-1990 publications do, and only one presents it as central.

Segalowitz and Segalowitz (1993; see also Segalowitz, Segalowitz & Wood, 1998) are a special case by insisting that automaticity is characterized not by a quantitative change in existing task components, but by a qualitative shift in components[2] (operationalized as a low correlation between means and standard deviations for reaction time, and a high correlation between means and co-efficients of variation). This criterion is unique in the literature; it is, however, one of several examples of how researchers have started to think of automaticity as the end result of a process of automatization (which has well-known characteristics) rather than of automatization as the process leading up to automaticity (which has proven hard to define). The next sub-section, therefore, will present a set of phenomena that characterize the automatization process.

Characteristics of automatization

The most ubiquitous finding about the acquisition of cognitive skills, recognized by proponents of any kind of theory of automatization, is the *power law of practice*. Newell and Rosenbloom (1981; cf. Newell, 1990; Rosenbloom & Newell, 1987) documented in great detail how many fine-grained longitudinal studies had established how the

---

[2] The qualitative shift in components (as opposed to a mere quantitative change in the same components) is operationalized by Segalowitz and Segalowitz (1993: 374) as a relatively low correlation between the means and the standard deviations for reaction time and a high correlation between the means and co-efficients of variation. The latter is the standard deviation for reaction time divided by the mean for reaction time, and indicates variability for a given level of response latency. As the least efficient processes tend to have the highest variability, qualitative improvement tends to reduce the variability (as measured by the co-efficient of variation). Therefore, as the mean reaction time declines, the co-efficient of variation declines too, and the two are correlated more than reaction time and standard deviation.

acquisition of a cognitive skill is reflected in not just any kind of gradual learning curve, but in a curve defined by a power function. Power functions come in a variety of shapes, but the most general and most intuitive formulation for our purposes is given by the equation $RT = a + bN^{-c}$, where RT = reaction time, N reflects the amount of practice the subject has had, *a* represents the asymptote (the RT the subjects would reach after an infinite or at least very large amount of practice, a level determined by the physical limits of human biology and tools used in carrying out a task), *b* is the difference between initial and asymptotic performance level, and *c* is the rate of learning. Most studies have documented how RT follows a power function; some show the same power function learning curve for error rate (e.g., Anderson, 1995, Chapter 6; DeKeyser, 1997). Furthermore, while most studies use means for reaction time and error rate in fitting power functions to learning curves, standard deviations appear to follow the same power function as means, a point which is of great importance for Logan's (1988, 1990, 1992) theory of automaticity (see the next section). Several studies have reported that the initial section of the learning curve deviates from the power function, a fact which has led to a number of different interpretations, several of which are of great theoretical interest themselves.

Another important fact that has been documented repeatedly is that the automatized behavior that results from consistent practice is highly specific. This means, for example, that practice in writing computer programs has only limited impact on the skill to read them and vice-versa (Anderson, 1993; cf. Carlson, 1997: 61; Singley & Anderson, 1989), that understanding sentences in a language quickly does not mean that one can produce them fast and vice-versa (DeKeyser, 1997), and that rules for relating one kind of information to another may only work well in the practised direction (Anderson et al., 1997).

Finally, the load independence (elimination of the memory set size effect), which was mentioned as a criterion of automaticity in early studies such as Schneider and Shiffrin (1977) and MacKay (1982), has more recently been shown to develop equally gradually as the decline in reaction time or error rate (Anderson, 1992, 1993; Strayer & Kramer, 1990).

Clearly, the observable characteristics of automatization described above have proven easier for psychologists to agree on than the criteria for the automaticity/control distinction. Theories differ widely, however, in the mechanisms they invoke to explain the agreed-on phenomena. The next section first presents the most important contemporary theories of automatization, and then discusses in detail how they explain the characteristics just described.

Theories of automatization

Anderson's ACT-R theory and the rule-based approach

For some 25 years, John Anderson and his associates have been working on a model of human cognition called ACT (Adaptive Control of Thought). From ACTE in Anderson (1976) and ACT* in Anderson (1983) to ACT-R in Anderson (1993) and Anderson and Lebiere (1998), the basic idea has remained the same: a production system[3] coupled with a three-stage theory of skill acquisition. Knowledge usually[4] starts out in declarative form, goes through a stage of compilation/proceduralization, and then finally through a long stage of fine-tuning of procedural knowledge before performance reaches the asymptote of the learning curve. The theory posits two separate long-term memories: declarative and procedural. Declarative knowledge is knowledge THAT, e.g., Washington DC is the capital of the US; procedural knowledge is knowledge HOW to do something, e.g., shifting gears in a car or using the right form of a verb. Procedural knowledge takes the form of production rules: condition-action pairs of the form if x is the case, then do y.

Any kind of behavior can be performed in principle by using general-purpose production rules to retrieve relevant chunks of knowledge from declarative memory and assembling them in working memory (WM) – which is just another name for currently available declarative knowledge in this theory (Anderson, 1993: 20). As a result of practice, however, chunks of declarative knowledge that are often called by a production rule can become incorporated into it; the rule can then operate faster and with less risk of error, bypassing retrieval of information from long-term declarative memory. See Anderson et al. (1997) for a particularly clear example.

This qualitative change in knowledge, called proceduralization or production compilation, can only take place in one way, according to the 1993 ACT-R model,[5] viz. by compiling the process of analogy to

---

[3] Production systems are computer programs that make use of IF ... THEN statements to model cognitive phenomena computationally. See, e.g., Anderson (1983); Keane (1990).

[4] Anderson and Fincham (1994) state: 'It is too strong to argue that procedural knowledge can never be acquired without a declarative representation or that the declarative representation always has to be in the form of an example that is used in an analogy process. None the less, the research does indicate that this is a major avenue for the acquisition of procedural knowledge' (p. 1323). See also Anderson and Lebiere (1998: 21).

[5] In ACT*, compilation consisted of two parts: composition and proceduralization. In ACT-R, however, complex production rules are compiled by analogy to complex examples rather than through composition of simpler production rules (see Anderson, 1993, section 4.4). Anderson and Lebiere (1998) no longer use the term 'proceduralization', but use 'production compilation' instead (1998, esp. p. 106 ff.).

an example. In the process of going through all the steps involved in carrying out a task (while keeping the example in mind to guide the process), a separate routine is built which incorporates all the minute elements necessary to carry out the task without referring to knowledge outside of this routine anymore.[6] It is not possible for the system to follow instructions without examples. These examples do not need to be committed to long-term memory; all that is needed is that the declarative representation be active in WM during the analogy process (cf. Anderson & Fincham, 1994: 1323). Anderson et al. (1997) present evidence for a less radical point of view, where a declarative rule forms a transition stage between analogy to examples and the procedural rule. Anderson and Lebiere (1998, see esp. Ch. 10) claim that the process of analogical reasoning consists of many 'atomic components' that can be modeled equally well by a system of fine-grained production rules as by a system of retrieval of analogical mappings as declarative chunks.

Once knowledge has been compiled/proceduralized, the skill acquisition process becomes a matter of slow and quantitative rather than fast and qualitative change. The production rules go through a fine-tuning process: four changing parameters determine the likelihood that a production rule will be instantiated: cost of executing the production, probability that the production will achieve its intended effect, estimated further cost of other productions that have to apply before the goal is achieved, and the probability that the goals will be achieved if the production has its intended effect (Anderson, 1993, section 4.5; Anderson & Lebiere, 1998, Ch. 4).

During this stage, the learner can also develop the strategy of retrieving frequently encountered examples directly from declarative memory; this process is even more direct and faster than production rule use (Anderson et al., 1997). This last element brings Anderson's theory somewhat closer to the item-based theories to be discussed in the next section.

Logan's instance theory and the item-based approach

A radical alternative to rule-based theories is found in item-based theories of automatization. The best-known formulation of the item learning approach is Logan's (1988) instance theory of automaticity. The

---

6 The concept of compilation is a metaphor from computer science. A compiler is a special type of computer program that 'translates' programs written by humans in more convenient, more abstract computer languages into elementary machine language suitable for a particular computer.

central ideas of this theory are that 'Automaticity is memory retrieval: performance is automatic when it is based on single-step direct-access retrieval of past solutions from memory' and that 'automatization reflects a transition from algorithm-based performance to memory-based performance' (Logan, 1988: 493). In other words, early performance or decision-making is carried out on the basis of an algorithm or rule. Later, automatized performance is based not on the rule but on retrieval of previously encountered instances. The theory makes three assumptions: 1. Encoding into memory is an obligatory, unavoidable consequence of attention; 2. Retrieval from memory is also an obligatory, unavoidable consequence of attention; 3. Each encounter with a stimulus is encoded, stored, and retrieved separately.

The third point is what makes the theory an instance theory as opposed to other item-based theories (e.g., Schneider, 1985; Schneider & Detweiler, 1988), where consistent practice serves to increase the likelihood of retrieving an item by strengthening its representation. In an instance theory, consistent practice increases the probability of (fast) retrieval by increasing the number of representations (instances encoded). During initial stages of skill acquisition, the number of instances represented in memory is very small. Initially, retrieval time for instances is slow, and decisions and actions are performed on the basis of a rule processing algorithm. However, once a large number of instances have been stored it becomes likely that at least one instance will be retrieved in a time that is shorter than what is required by the algorithm.[7] Memory retrieval, from then on, almost always wins the race against algorithm application.

Logan (1988) argues that the power law of learning observed so often in reaction times (see the above section on 'Characteristics of automatization') is the result of two counteracting factors. On the one hand, as more and more instances are stored in memory, the likelihood of observing an extremely low retrieval time keeps increasing, so the mean reaction time goes down gradually. On the other hand, the lower the reaction time, the lower the likelihood of sampling a still lower retrieval time, so the decreasing process slows down. The two combined yield the power law.[8]

---

[7] As the time needed for any retrieval of *any* instance is variable, following a probability distribution, the likelihood is very small that the time needed for retrieving any instance will be very short. As more and more instances accumulate, however, the chance that at least one of them is retrieved at a speed far below the average of the distribution becomes bigger and bigger.

[8] Moreover, Logan (1988) argues, the same factor that limits the reduction in the mean limits the reduction in the range that can be expected for the minimum, so the standard deviation should follow the same power law as the mean. Lexical decision as well as

Given that in Logan's theory all learning is encoding and storing of instances and performance is retrieval of instances, it is important to determine what constitutes an instance. Essentially, an instance is a representation of co-occurring events; which co-occurrences are remembered is determined by what the learner pays attention to. Logan and Etherton (1994) tested this prediction of the theory with two-word display experiments, for example, experiments with word pairs such as *Canada* and *steel*, in which words were presented together on a screen. As the theory predicts, co-occurrences were not learned in focused-attention conditions in which subjects only attended to one word, but they were learned in divided-attention and dual-task conditions in which subjects attended to both words. Logan, Taylor, and Etherton (1996) extended the attention hypothesis beyond encoding to retrieval: subjects show transfer of what they learned if they attended to the same things in the same way at encoding and retrieval time. The next section will describe some recent developments that constitute an extension of Logan's work in the direction of theories that posit that something more abstract than an instance is learned, as well as research in the rule paradigm that acknowledges the importance of instance retrieval.

A modicum of convergence

The applicability of Logan's theory is limited by the fact that it is a pure instance model; only stimuli identical to the ones in memory can be categorized by the retrieval process. Clearly, in daily life, and in language comprehension in particular, we constantly have to deal with stimuli that are somehow similar but certainly not identical to instances we have encountered before. Palmeri (1997; cf. also Nosofsky & Palmeri, 1997) developed a model to account for the observed effect of item similarity on the development of automaticity. By combining elements of the instance theory of automatization with a generalized context model of categorization (Nosofsky, 1986),

---

alphabet-arithmetic experiments (i.e., experiments where subjects perform simple arithmetic with letters that stand for a number corresponding to their position in the alphabet) confirmed these predictions. Logan (1992) goes a step further by arguing that reaction time minima follow a Weibull distribution (an exponential distribution in which the independent variable is raised to some power; see Logan (1992: 885)), and that the entire distribution of reaction times, not just means and standard deviations, decreases as a power function of practice. The shape of the power function is determined by the same parameter that determines the shape of the reaction-time distribution: the exponents of the Weibull distributions are the reciprocals of the exponents of the power functions. These theoretical predictions were borne out by extensive analyses of data from an alphabet-arithmetic and a dot-counting task.

Palmeri (1997) developed what he calls the exemplar-based random walk model. In this model, automatization is still an issue of item retrieval, but this retrieval is similarity-based: responses are determined by the relative similarity of a stimulus to members of different categories. Furthermore, in this model responses are not determined by the first instance to be retrieved. Instead, the effect of various instances retrieved (of potentially several categories) is additive: a response is not made till the number of similar instances retrieved from one category sufficiently outweighs the number of similar instances retrieved from other categories to warrant a classification decision. This means that the theory incorporates an element of response competition, where Logan's model is based on a strict first-instance race process.

Palmeri's exemplar-based random walk model predicts that: 1. RTs get faster with practice; 2. similarity of an item to other exemplars of the same category decreases RT; 3. similarity of an item to exemplars of other categories increases RT. All three predictions were borne out in Palmeri (1997), both through computer simulations and experiments with human subjects. The exemplar-based random walk model clearly is more powerful than the pure instance model because it can account for the development of automaticity in the categorization of non-identical instances. The experiments reported in Palmeri (1997) are still limited in several ways, however: for instance, within-category and between-category similarity were never manipulated at the same time, and all exemplars within a category were equally similar to each other. It would be interesting to see how within-category and between-category similarity would interact in the automatization process, how differing item similarity within a category would affect retrieval of individual items, and how well the model would predict the phenomena observed under much more realistic conditions.

While Palmeri (1997) marks a departure from the most radical form of item-based theories, Anderson et al. (1997) mark a departure from the most radical form of rule-based theories. Not only do they stress the importance of analogy to examples in the first (declarative) stage of skill acquisition, as Anderson (1993) and Anderson and Fincham (1994) already did, but they also acknowledge the possibility of item retrieval after the relevant procedural rule has been compiled. Their evidence from experiments where subjects learned a number of simple correspondence patterns showed both directional asymmetry (see above under 'Characteristics of automatization'), even with new examples, and a speed advantage for repeated examples. The former supports the hypothesis that production rules were being used, and the latter suggests that some of the examples were handled by simple retrieval from memory. Furthermore, Anderson et al. (1997)

document how the directional asymmetry developed over time, thereby providing strong evidence for the interpretation of automatization as increasingly efficient use of production rules.[9]

Even though Palmeri (1997) is less radical than Logan, by allowing for the existence of item retrieval that is not pure instance retrieval, and even though Anderson et al. (1997) are less radical than Anderson (1993) by allowing for a mixture of production rule use and item retrieval instead of production rule use only, the two approaches remain far apart, as one still sees the use of rules as primary, and the other excludes it from the concept of automatization. The degree of convergence remains limited.

Rickard (1997), however, marks a further rapprochement between the two by showing that the learning curves he found for some pseudo-arithmetic tasks can be analyzed as a relatively long period of speed-up of an algorithm, followed by a period of increasingly fast item retrieval. This approach gives more importance to algorithms than Logan's or Palmeri's, and more importance to instance retrieval in later stages than Anderson's, and thus implies a certain convergence of the two models. At the same time, however, it marks a radical departure from both models because of its claim that a given power law applies to improvement in algorithm use or item retrieval, but not both, and that many learning curves should really be analyzed as two separate power functions, the first half for algorithm use, and the second half for item retrieval. Similar conclusions were independently reached by Delaney, Reder, Staszewski, and Ritter (1998).

The explanatory potential of the different theories

How well do the various theories of automatization account for the phenomena described above, i.e. the power law for reaction time and error rate, the initial deviation from the power function learning curve, the increasing directional asymmetry of skill, and the decreasing effect of memory set size? Many researchers have attempted to provide an explanation for the ubiquitous power law, especially Logan (1988, 1992) and Newell (1990; cf. also Newell & Rosenbloom, 1981; Rosenbloom & Newell, 1987). As was pointed out above, Logan explains the power law by referring to the distribution of minimal reaction times for retrieval of instances: as more and more instances accumulate, reaction times decrease, but this decrease is slowed down

---

[9] Incidentally, by listing abstractions (declarative rules) as a transitional stage between analogy and production rules, Anderson et al. (1997) appear to take a step back compared to Anderson (1993), where declarative rules are not mentioned and production rules are always compiled by analogy to an example. See also Footnote 4.

because the likelihood of an even shorter RT becomes smaller and smaller as RTs decrease (Logan, 1988)[10]. Cohen et al. (1990) explain the power function by two factors: learning is error-driven (therefore, as the appropriate set of strengths develops, and the error gets smaller, so will the changes made to the connections in each training trial), and activation functions are non-linear (i.e., as connections get stronger, subsequent increases in strength have less of an influence on activation). Anderson (1992) argues that the power function reflects the gradual build-up of strength of both chunks of declarative knowledge and production rules. By treating strength as a rate parameter for an exponential distribution of reaction times, Anderson can explain changes in means, standard deviations and entire distributions of reaction times. Logan (1992), however, argues that Cohen et al. only obtain power-function learning by arbitrarily setting some connection weights, and that Anderson's exponential distribution leads to predictions that are not borne out by the facts. At any rate, Logan appears to be right when he states that in his theory, the power law follows directly from the core concepts of the theory, while Cohen et al. (1990) or Anderson (1992) can only obtain these results by making specific implementation decisions that do not follow directly from the theory.

Newell, on the other hand, does present an alternative account of the power law that is central to his theory of skill acquisition. Newell and Rosenbloom (1981: 42) argued that the most likely interpretation of the power law was in terms of the following three assumptions: 1. The performance program of the system is coded in terms of high-level chunks, with the time to process a chunk being less than the time to process its constituent chunks; 2. The probability of recurrence of an environmental pattern decreases as the pattern size increases; 3. Chunks are learned at a constant time rate on average from the relevant patterns of stimuli and responses that occur in the specific environments experienced.

As the smaller, lower-level chunks occur by far the most frequently, they are the first to be learned. By the same token, as these newly formed time-saving devices are used very frequently, they lead to a dramatic improvement in reaction time at the beginning. Subsequently, however, even though chunks are learned at a constant rate according to the third assumption, the ones learned later and later are used less and less frequently and therefore lead to an ever smaller reduction in reaction time. Rosenbloom and Newell (1987) showed that a

---

[10] The precise shape of the specific learning curve within the family of power functions is determined by the precise shape of the distribution of minimal reaction times, which is a Weibull distribution whose exponent equals the reciprocal of the exponent of the power function (Logan, 1992). See Footnote 8.

fully specified form of the chunking theory could form the basis for a production-system learning mechanism whose simulations of skill acquisition produced power-law practice curves (see Ellis, this volume). For overviews of other attempts to explain the power law, see Anderson (1982), MacKay (1982), and Newell and Rosenbloom (1981).

The initial deviation from the power-law practice curve has also been subject to various interpretations. For Logan (1988: 496), the initial deviation reflects the fact that at the beginning few instances have been stored in memory, and therefore usually the algorithm wins over instance retrieval (see above). As this algorithm application is a qualitatively different process from instance retrieval, it does not follow the same learning curve. For Anderson, the large improvement from the first to the second data point 'would reflect the compilation of the production rule, and the remaining power-law learning would reflect the accumulation of producing strength' (Anderson & Fincham, 1994: 1324). For Newell, the deviation is simply due to the fact that one never obtains pure base-line pre-practice performance on the first trial, because there is always transfer of training from everyday experience (Rosenbloom & Newell, 1987: 223). For MacKay (1982: 493), mental practice produces a fast initial rate of improvement because there are many unpractised, and therefore quickly improving, 'nodes' in the task component hierarchy. What stands out in many empirical studies, however, is not so much the fast initial learning, but the slowness of the very initial task performance; it seems that neither MacKay's nor Newell's explanation would account for that. Logan's explanation seems to account for the data better, but of course applies only to skills that can be explained entirely as instance learning. Rickard's (1997) model is really just an extension of Logan's in the sense that according to him there is often more than an initial deviation at play (the learning curve consists of two separate power functions, one for algorithm use, and one for item retrieval); both models explain the fact that there is not one perfect power function by positing a transition from rules to items. Thus, Anderson's concept of initial use of declarative knowledge before production rules have been formed seems to be the only descriptively adequate and theoretically interesting explanation of the initial deviation that applies to situations where more than instance learning must be taking place in later stages of skill development.

The increasing directional asymmetry of skill is a point that only Anderson (1993; Anderson & Fincham, 1994; Anderson et al., 1997; Anderson & Lebiere, 1998; Singley & Anderson, 1989) tries to account for. Asymmetry of skill is predicted by his theory as a consequence of the building of very specific production rules; as pointed out earlier, Anderson et al. (1997) demonstrated that this asymmetry develops gradually in parallel with other aspects of the automatization process. Some researchers claim to have counter-evidence on this point (Klapp et al., 1991; Logan & Klapp, 1991; Palmeri, 1997), but they used very specific kinds of tasks (alphabet arithmetic and judging the numerosity of dot patterns) that may reflect pure memorization of facts rather than skill acquisition. Still others, such as MacKay (1982) or Newell (1990), do not address the point at all, although a more recent elaboration of Newell's SOAR model (NL-SOAR, designed to handle natural language), also builds separate productions for comprehension and generation, in different contexts, with potential asymmetries as a result, in spite of the many interactions between comprehension and generation skills (Lehman, personal communication, September 29, 1997; for broader information on NL-SOAR see Lehman, Laird & Rosenbloom, 1998). Finally, the gradual reduction of the set size effect has been addressed specifically only in the item-based approach. Strayer and Kramer (1990), especially, argue that the reduction of the set size effect is the result of decreased reliance on WM (which is required for algorithm application but not for direct retrieval of items from long-term memory). (See also Schneider & Shiffrin, 1977.)

An overall evaluation of how well the various theories account for the range of empirical phenomena is a complex matter. Compared to Newell's explanation of the power law, Logan's theory is more explicit on the exponents in the power functions (he shows how they follow from his theory), but Newell's view is embedded in a more comprehensive model of skill acquisition. Anderson's account appears to strike a balance between the two: it is embedded in a broad model of skill acquisition and it explains the power law in detail, even though Anderson's account of the exponents follows less directly from his model than is the case for Logan's theory (cf. Anderson, 1992; Logan, 1992).

More importantly, however, it can be argued that the different theories apply to different learning situations. While Anderson's theory aims to provide a complete model of cognitive skill acquisition (see esp. Anderson & Lebiere, 1998, Ch. 12), Logan (e.g., 1988: 518; Logan & Klapp, 1991: 194) has repeatedly made clear that he does not claim to account for all kinds of task performance (cf. also Cohen et al., 1992: 263; Rabinowitz & Goldberg, 1995: 230–231).

While item retrieval appears to be an important part of skilled performance even in contexts where algorithms are applicable (e.g. Anderson et al., 1997), transfer to new items clearly shows a directionality effect that can only be explained by rules (Anderson, et al., 1997; DeKeyser, 1997 [see below]). Ultimately, the relative frequency and efficiency of reliance on rule application versus item retrieval depends on the number of instances of a given item encountered in proportion to the number of instances of rule application, and on the similarity of task context in the training and transfer situations (Rabinowitz & Goldberg, 1995).

Finally, neither the rule-based account nor the item-based account easily accommodates data such as those of Haider and Frensch (1996), who showed that practice led subjects to ignore irrelevant aspects of the stimuli. As this ignoring transferred to new instances, it cannot be accounted for by Logan's view; on the other hand, as it developed slowly over time, it also does not seem to fit with a short-term qualitative change such as production compilation in Anderson's view.

Empirical research on automatization in SLA

The empirical research on automatization of L2 skills is very limited at this point. A few studies have dealt with grammar skills, and a few with word recognition and reading. Some studies have adopted a more global perspective and documented the development of fluency, interpreting certain phenomena as automatization of grammar and vocabulary. No studies exist on the automatization of pronunciation.

DeKeyser (1997) documented how the development of L2 grammar skills shows the same characteristics as the development of automatization in other domains: power-law learning, initial deviation from the power function, and directional asymmetry of skill after automatization. Participants in that study were taught the grammar rules of a miniature linguistic system, as well as the vocabulary, and tested thoroughly on their knowledge of what they were taught. Then they started a series of 15 sessions spread over eight weeks, in which they practised some rules in a comprehension exercise format and others in a production format. For both comprehension and production, the learning curves for reaction time and error rate followed a power function. An initial deviation from the power curve was found, which was interpreted as a stage of proceduralization of the explicitly taught rules. Moreover, at the end of the study, a large difference was found in both reaction time and error rate between items that required participants to use rules in the skill in which they had practised them (either comprehension or production) and items that required them to use the rules in the opposite skill.

Not only does this latter finding corroborate in the L2 domain the directional asymmetry that studies such as Anderson et al. (1997; cf. also

Anderson, 1993; Carlson, 1997: 61; Singley & Anderson, 1989) found in the development of other skills, but it also provides evidence against an instance retrieval interpretation of automatization in this kind of learning task. The directional asymmetry can only be explained by the concept of a directional production rule (cf. esp. Anderson, 1993), and not by retrieval of instances, because such retrieval is a declarative memory process (cf. Klapp et al., 1991: 208), and therefore symmetrical (Rabinowitz & Goldberg, 1995; cf. also Anderson et al., 1997). Klapp et al. (1991) show that, in their alphabet-arithmetic experiments, training need not be on the verification task itself to produce automaticity effects at testing; it is only necessary that the true statements be memorized. Klapp et al. interpret this as evidence that automatization is memorization. In the light of the data from Anderson et al. (1997) and DeKeyser (1997), however, one can come to a different conclusion: automatization of rules is a directional phenomenon, and the fact that Klapp et al. (1991) did not find a task-specific effect shows that the alphabet-arithmetic task is of a special kind that can be performed exclusively by memory storage and retrieval. The same reasoning can be made for the overlearning (improvement of performance due to continued practice after automatization was achieved) documented in Klapp et al. (1991). DeKeyser (1997) shows that subjects with twice the amount of practice (in terms of number of items practiced) for one of the two skills did not do any better than the other subjects, showing again that overlearning does not occur when automatization takes the form of production rule learning; the overlearning documented in Klapp et al. and labeled as a typical memory phenomenon, therefore, must be limited to the narrow set of tasks where item memorization is all that is required for successful performance of the target task.

Peter Robinson (1997b; Robinson & Ha, 1993) has tested Logan's instance theory explicitly with data from L2 grammar learning tasks. Robinson and Ha (1993) presented ESL learners with an explicit explanation of the morphological criteria for dative alternation in English, and then trained them on a number of sentences with nonsense verbs illustrating the morphological criteria. The results of the study were mixed: while it provided evidence for a speed-up for old as opposed to new instances, which is compatible with Logan's theory, it also failed to show any effect on reaction time for number of presentations of the old items, which is not predicted by Logan's theory. This fact, along with the observation that familiarity with the sentence frame in which the verb occurred was a better determinant of response time than familiarity with the verb itself, suggests that neither rule application nor instance retrieval were at work, but a similarity-based item retrieval process like the one proposed by Palmeri (1997). Furthermore, as Robinson and Ha (1993) indicate, the fact that no accuracy differences obtained between old and new instances indicates that the learners used the algorithm successfully for the new instances; this is only evidence for rule use, however, and not for rule automatization.

Robinson (1997b) went a step further in assessing the interaction between the speed-up effect as a result of practice and the effect of different learning conditions (instructed, enhanced, incidental and implicit). The results for speed-up as a function of practice were the same as in Robinson and Ha (1993): old instances are judged significantly faster, but number of previous presentations has virtually no effect. No difference in reaction time to old items was found between the instructional conditions. For new items, however, the instructed group was significantly faster, probably because they had a clear rule they could use as opposed to the other groups. Therefore, this speed difference does not necessarily reflect an automatization effect.

The fact that no gradual improvement as a function of number of previous presentations of an item was found in either Robinson (1997b) or Robinson and Ha (1993) could possibly be explained by Rickard's (1997) and Delaney et al.'s (1998) finding that the power law only applies to pure item retrieval or to gradual shifts in strategies, and not to situations where a discrete shift from algorithm to item retrieval takes places (Robinson, personal communication, February 18, 1998).

In conclusion, the existing research on automatization of L2 grammar rules has shown that they can be automatized according to the same power law as other cognitive skills, that the learning curve shows the same initial deviation, which can be interpreted as a production compilation stage, and that they show the same directional asymmetry, which is most easily interpreted as the result of specific production rules (see DeKeyser, 1997). While evidence was also found for memory effects, these memory effects were not sensitive to the number of previous exposures, and therefore do not support Logan's instance theory of automaticity. Thus, the existing L2 experiments not only draw on the cognitive literature, but also contribute to it by providing evidence for the limited applicability of Logan's instance theory (see Robinson, 1997b; Robinson & Ha, 1993). Palmeri's theory of similarity-based item retrieval may explain some of the findings better, but it is doubtful that it could ever account for a substantial percentage of L2 learning, given that so often superficially (lexically) similar sentences call for the application of different rules, while superficially different sentences call for the application of the same rule.

Ultimately, an integration of the rule account and the similarity-based item-retrieval account will probably be necessary. As Robinson and Ha (1993) suggest, both structural complexity and stage of learning may determine whether the learner relies on item retrieval or rule application. A major structural factor is probably the degree to which a rule reflects more abstract characteristics of distant elements or more concrete characteristics of contiguous elements in the sentence (DeKeyser, 1998; cf. also DeKeyser, 1995; Hulstijn & de Graaff, 1994).

Studies of automaticity and automatization in L2 reading are somewhat less scarce than in the domain of grammar. In particular, several studies have investigated word recognition in L2 reading. Favreau and Segalowitz (1983) showed how differences in L2 reading speed among highly fluent French-English bilinguals were due to differential automaticity of word recognition. Segalowitz and Segalowitz (1993) reflect the aforementioned shift in focus from the controlled/automatic dichotomy to documentation of the automatization process. They interpret a change in task components (inferred from the lack of correlation between reaction time means and standard deviations) as evidence of automatization. It is doubtful whether gradual change over time can be inferred from the between-subjects analyses in this study, but Segalowitz et al. (1998) also provide longitudinal evidence for a gradual change in task components. The interpretation of the correlations between reaction times and standard deviations should still be treated with caution, however: as stated above (see under 'Characteristics of automaticity'), these two studies are unique in their conceptualization of automatization as change of task components.

McLeod and McLaughlin (1986) showed how advanced ESL learners, who were about halfway in-between beginners and native speakers in terms of errors in a read-aloud task and a cloze test, made virtually the same proportion of meaningful as opposed to non-meaningful errors. They inferred from this that no restructuring of task components had taken place. Their findings do not necessarily contradict those of Segalowitz and Segalowitz (1993) and Segalowitz et al. (1998), however, because the latter investigated the possibility of fine-grained restructuring of components within word recognition, while McLeod and McLaughlin looked at more holistic tasks, where change or lack of change of various components of reading, at the level of word recognition, is at issue. The highly complex, hierarchical, parallel, and interactive nature of task components in reading makes research on automatization of L2 reading a highly complex task itself. (For more information about the development of L2 reading, and automatization in particular, see Segalowitz, Poulsen & Komoda (1991); for information regarding the automatization of orthographic knowledge, see Koda (1994); for more information on restructuring and its implications for SLA, see McLaughlin & Heredia (1996) and Schmidt (1992); for more information about restructuring in general, see Carlson (1997).)

While these studies provide a fair amount of information on the automaticity of L2 lexical access in comprehension, and reading in particular, studies on the equivalent in listening or in production are not available (see Ellis, and Hulstijn, this volume).

Finally, a number of studies have provided global and longitudinal documentation of the development of fluency in foreign language learners, particularly after an extended stay abroad (e.g., Möhle, 1984; Raupach, 1987; Towell, Hawkins, & Bazergui, 1996). These studies show marked improvements in oral fluency after substantial real life practice (see discussions in DeKeyser, 1997; Griffiths, 1991a; Schmidt, 1992; Towell & Hawkins, 1994, Ch. 12). However, the inevitable lack of precision in documenting the amount, nature and spread of practice in such longitudinal and essentially naturalistic studies makes it difficult to interpret the findings within the framework of any given theory of automatization. Therefore, a great need exists for research that could combine to some extent the experimental control, methodological refinement, and relatively large number of subjects of laboratory research with the longitudinal and ecologically valid character of the 'semester abroad' studies.

Fostering automatization through the second language curriculum

Given the scarcity of research into the automatization of L2 skills, recommendations to practitioners about classroom activities to foster automatization have to rely on extrapolation from research in cognitive psychology, the laboratory-type SLA research mentioned in the previous section, and the applied linguistics literature on syllabus and curriculum design. Moreover, the experimental literature discussed in the previous sections mainly focuses on characteristics of automatization, and the question of conditions for promoting automatization has received far less attention. There seems to be agreement among cognitive psychologists, however, that besides amount of consistent practice, two other factors play a major role: spread of practice and feedback (e.g., LaBerge & Samuels, 1974; Anderson, 1992). It is the task of applied linguists, then, to determine how consistent practice, distributed practice, and quality feedback can be incorporated into the curriculum and reconciled with other desiderata for classroom activities, such as communicativeness and variety, not to mention how activities designed to automatize grammar can be integrated with the automatization of vocabulary.

In recent years applied linguistics has seen a tendency to shift away from a linguistic syllabus (whether structural or functional-notional) to a curriculum built around the sequencing of real life tasks (Long & Crookes, 1992; Prabhu, 1987; Robinson, this volume; Skehan, 1996, 1998a). However, there is still a widely perceived need for some kind of systematicity in the curriculum beyond that provided by the non-linguistic content, especially for an analytical component to foster the development of accuracy in production (see, e.g., Ellis' (1997) arguments in favour of a structural syllabus). The idea of a task-based syllabus is not, however, incompatible with the idea of psycholinguistic systematicity. One fundamental principle of task-based language teaching, at least in Long's interpretation of the term (Long, 1985; Long & Crookes, 1992; Long & Robinson, 1998), is that instead of teaching *formS* in a sequence determined by a syllabus of structures, one teaches *form* as it becomes relevant /useful /necessary to do so because of the linguistic demands of the learning activities determined by a syllabus of tasks. Once tasks have led learners to notice certain elements of form and once the learners attempt to use them, explicit intervention is often required, depending on the nature of the structure, the relationship with L1, and the learner's ability. Furthermore, once an aspect of form has been taught, in order for that treatment to be successful, it has to be sustained throughout the curriculum by means of continued attention to form, including feedback (Doughty, this volume; Doughty & Williams, 1998b). This is where it becomes important to look toward the literature on skill acquisition in general and automatization in particular, in order to ensure that tasks are chosen and sequenced not only because of their non-linguistic content and their interactional demands, but also as a function of their potential for systematic, yet truly meaningful and context-embedded practice of forms that have previously been in focus. Such an integration of the task-based syllabus with attention to systematic skill development will ensure both a natural progression of real life communication tasks with the range of forms they imply, and an equally natural progression of skillful use of these forms with the range of interactional uses that implies.

What are the implications of skill theory, then, for long-term sequencing in the sense of curriculum development? If authentic practice leading to production compilation and further automatization requires that students engage in activities that make them communicate certain meanings while the necessary forms are easily available, first in declarative, and later in partially automatized procedural form, then we have to make sure that we provide many activities of this kind throughout the curriculum. This goes against an idea that some applied linguists (e.g., Harmer, 1983: 46) have advocated, viz. that there should be very different emphases on meaning vs. form at different stages in the curriculum. Rather, both should be in focus throughout; the main change over time then consists of increasing requirements on the complexity of form that go hand in hand with increasing requirements of meaning (see Robinson's proposal, this volume, that increasing the cognitive demands of tasks may lead to such change). The learning curves reported in DeKeyser (1997) certainly show how the development of fluency and accuracy (reduction of both reaction time and error rate) occur hand in hand, rather than being incompatible. For a given individual at a given point in time, fluency and accuracy may be hard to reconcile, but that does not imply that these two components of skill are each other's enemies in the process of skill development over time (see Skehan & Foster, this volume, for further discussion).

A two-dimensional model of the curriculum may then look somewhat like the front part of Figure 1: we have requirements on meaning on the X-axis and requirements on form on the Y-axis. In the lower left-hand corner we have communicative drills to practise the basic

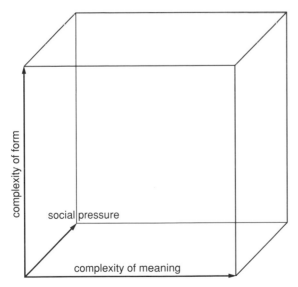

Figure 1. The three dimensions of curricular sequencing

structures of the language. As the students are a bit more advanced, we can make increased use of role plays, scenarios and information gap activities, which require more complex forms to express more complex meanings, and for the really advanced students we can begin to think of tasks that are truly challenging on both dimensions, such as formal presentations with serious scientific or cultural content. Still beyond that – and here we are going beyond what is done in the classroom, and getting into the sort of L2 use that only some learners will eventually engage in – we have tasks such as giving a job talk in a foreign language, or having a quick-paced decision-making conversation with multiple native speakers in a business meeting. The last two tasks are very demanding both from the point of view of meaning and form, because the speaker does not want to run the risk of his/her message being misunderstood, nor does he/she want to give a bad impression by using clumsy or error-ridden language. This last point suggests that there is a third dimension along which the student moves through the curriculum, viz. that of requirements on social functioning, from the simple dialogues in communicative drills to the highly decontextualized formal job talk, which makes audience awareness very challenging, and the fast-paced multiple-speaker conversation, which requires very fast and explicit hook-ups with the interlocutor's discourse and the individual's view behind it. In other words, the curriculum can be represented as a cube, the three sides of which represent requirements on form, requirements on meaning, and social pressure. Efficient skill development, then, can be represented as travelling from the bottom left front corner of the cube, through the centre, to the upper right back corner, rather than traveling along the ribs of the cube.

Skehan (1998a; Skehan & Foster, this volume) comes to a similar conclusion after reviewing the literature on the choice and sequencing of pedagogical tasks for L2 learning. He emphasizes that the three goals of fluency, accuracy and complexity are in a state of mutual tension, that balanced development should be a priority, and that this can be achieved in part by recycling certain tasks and by explicit monitoring of certain forms by both teacher and student. His three dimensions of fluency, accuracy, and complexity correspond respectively to our dimensions of social pressure, requirements on form, and requirements on meaning. Interestingly, Skehan's view on curricular sequencing, derived largely from the applied linguistics literature on tasks, and the one presented here, derived largely from the cognitive psychology literature on skill automatization, are very similar. This shows once more that the two perspectives are not incompatible, and that the two bodies of literature complement each other nicely.

Where specific instructional units rather than long-term sequences are at issue, several authors have proposed activities conducive to automatization. Gatbonton and Segalowitz (1988) advocated communicative activities that make (groups of) learners use the same expressions and formulas repeatedly; this approach fits in with item-based theories of automaticity. Arevart and Nation (1991), on the other hand, found positive effects in the sense of increased speed and reduced number of hesitations for learners who had told a story several times, under increasingly strict time limitations (4, then 3, then 2 minutes; a technique first proposed by Maurice (1983), quoted in Arevart & Nation (1991)). While such a technique undoubtedly has the effect of having learners use the same vocabulary items and formulas many times in a row, as do the activities proposed by Gatbonton and Segalowitz, it also makes learners draw on some grammar rules repeatedly, without having the disadvantage of disconnecting form and meaning, an often-cited disadvantage of other kinds of repetitive practice of forms, especially mechanical drills (cf. DeKeyser, 1998). It seems likely that such repeated use of rules in a context where the link between form and meaning is guaranteed would transfer to new contexts, but as Arevart and Nation themselves point out, further research is needed to test this hypothesis. Skehan (1996: 44) takes a somewhat intermediate point of view, acknowledging the importance of the proceduralization of rules, but leaning towards the item-based view of skill acquisition. Skehan (1998a) stresses that rule automatization and item automatization necessarily have to alternate in the long process of L2 development:

Learners need to be led to engage in cycles of analysis and synthesis. In other words, if meaning primacy and communicational pressure make for exemplar-based learning, it is important that there should be continual pressure on learners to analyze the linguistic units they are using, so that they can access this same material as a rule-based system. Equally, it is important that when material does become available as such a system, learners should engage in the complementary process of synthesizing such language so that it will then become available in exemplar, memory-based form as well (p. 91).

This point of view is strongly reminiscent of the research reported in Anderson et al. (1997).

On this point, then, the applied linguistics literature reflects the above-described dichotomy in the psychological literature between rule-based and item-based approaches. To the extent that quick access to formulas is important at various stages of language acquisition, an instance-based model can inspire classroom activities. As few people would claim that (second) languages can be learned through formulas alone, however, activities that follow from a rule-based model are certainly desirable. More applied research along the lines of Arevart and Nation (1991) is needed to assess the success of various concrete activities in this respect. Meanwhile, among commonly used classroom techniques, communicative drills (e.g., Paulston & Bruder, 1976) stand out as an activity that is likely to lead to production compilation, because of the repeated execution of the target routine while the relevant declarative knowledge is highly active (cf. Anderson, 1993; DeKeyser, 1998). A variety of techniques, such as role play, or the 4/3/2 story-telling task described in Arevart and Nation (1991), may then lead to gradual automatization by making the learner go through the same production routines under conditions of increased time pressure and increased integration with other cognitive demands. Johnson (1996), in particular, emphasizes the importance of modulating speed as a technique for 'form defocus', which he sees as a more viable alternative to the 'meaning focus' that has characterized so much communicative methodology. Computer-assisted instruction holds special promise on this point, because it is relatively easy 'to control/vary amounts of time available for particular tasks' (1996: 176).

Conclusions and perspectives for further research

Research in cognitive psychology has shown that tasks can be carried out with various degrees of automaticity. It appears that both rule automatization and increased speed of instance retrieval are responsible for the improvement in performance that results from large amounts of consistent practice. The scant amount of (laboratory) research on automatization reported so far in the SLA literature indicates that grammar rules can be automatized through the same mechanisms that are at work in other cognitive domains. Virtually no empirical research exists, however, on the learning conditions that are conducive to automatization.

Fine-grained longitudinal classroom research on variables such as quantity, consistency, and distribution of practice, as well as error feedback, is needed to establish the conditions that foster automatization in contexts that are representative of real life language teaching and learning. Special attention should be given in such research to the relative efficiency of rule automatization versus increasingly efficient item retrieval. The relative efficiency of these two processes will probably depend on the psycholinguistic nature of the elements of language to be learned as well as on the conditions under which the language is learned in the classroom and used outside of the classroom, but the attainment of high levels of skill probably requires the interaction of both kinds of automatization.

Research on L2 speech production has been primarily descriptive in nature (Crookes, 1991). Classroom research on automatization of L2 rules provides an opportunity for focused hypothesis-testing, in an area that is of interest not only to theory-building in cognitive psychology and SLA research, but also of great practical importance for language teachers and learners.

Acknowledgements

This chapter was written while the author was in residence at the National Foreign Language Center in Washington, DC, as a Mellon Fellow under the Institute for Advanced Studies program. The financial support of the Mellon Foundation and the cheerful assistance of the NFLC staff is gratefully acknowledged. Thanks are also due to Peter Robinson and Joyce Tang Boyland for their comments on a previous version. A shorter version was presented at the Pacific Second Language Forum in Tokyo on 28 March, 1998.

6   Learnability and second language acquisition theory

Kevin R. Gregg

Introduction: SLA theory

The fundamental goal of a theory of second language acquisition (SLA) is to explain the acquisition of competence in a second language. This may seem a straightforward enough formulation, but it includes some not-so-innocent presuppositions that should be made explicit. Especially we need to be careful with the terms 'explain', 'acquisition', and 'competence'.

I am assuming that a theory, any theory, has as its aim the *explanation* of some phenomena within its domain; not mere description, and not just prediction (Gregg, 1993). Of course, a sufficiently precise description of the phenomena is a requisite for a satisfying explanation, and successful predictions are useful evidence that the explanation is in fact correct. But the goal is explanation. I belabour this point because in fact it is anything but easy to agree on whether an explanation has been offered, let alone a successful one. I return to this question in the next section.

In our case the phenomenon in question is linguistic *competence* – that is to say, knowledge of a language. This means that our domain is centrally and inevitably mental; while we are necessarily interested in the behaviour of L2 learners on the one hand, and in the characteristics of individual languages on the other, what the SLA theorist in fact wants to explain is not why L2 learners say such-and-such, or why certain languages have such-and-such a construction, but rather why learners have the knowledge they do have of an L2, and of course how they come to have it.

An SLA theory is by definition a theory of *acquisition*, or learning. If this seems too obvious to need stating, I can only point to the numerous papers in the SLA literature that seem to overlook this obvious point; indeed, there is a whole school of writers who object to certain SLA research precisely for its 'cognitive bias'. (For some egregious examples, see Block, 1996; Firth & Wagner, 1997.)

Thus an SLA theorist attempts to explain certain cognitive states and changes in those states. It should be clear that this will not be an easy task; so difficult is it, indeed, that I would argue that an even minimally satisfying SLA theory simply does not exist. The difficulty is compounded by the variation in L2 competence one finds across learners, and by what would appear to be the general failure of any learner to achieve native-like competence. The SLA theorist thus has to explain both success and failure.

It should also be clear from the above that the goal of an SLA theorist is a good deal different from the goal of an L2 learner or an L2 instructor; this book ostensibly being about, *inter alia*, L2 instruction, it's just as well to call attention to the difference in goals. Most of us who are interested in SLA theory have had occasion to hear, or even be the target of, complaints about the irrelevance of SLA theory to the classroom. And on the other hand some theorists have perhaps been overly concerned to show, or at least allege, a direct theory-practice connection. In fact the connections between SLA theory and L2 instruction are indirect, complex, and tenuous at best, when they are not non-existent, and we may as well face that fact. In what follows I will try to indicate what I see as possible connections, but I caution readers not to get their hopes up about 'implications for classroom practice'. And to those who may be prone to whine about absence of relevance, all I can say is, if you can't stand the theorizing, get the hell out of the armchair.

Now, here's my plan: I propose to lay before you the main problems of SLA theory construction within a so-called learnability framework, and to illustrate the main proposals that have been offered for solving these problems. Section 2 outlines the learnability model as proposed for first-language acquisition, and extends and emends it to deal with SLA. I then offer a couple of basic criteria for assessing SLA theories within this framework. Section 3 examines the question of the learner's initial and final cognitive states with respect to knowledge of an L2; specifically, we will look at the question of modularity in characterizing the initial state of linguistic competence, and we will look at the question of 'access to Universal Grammar'. In Section 4 we take up the question of input; specifically we will examine the question of so-called negative input (correction, explanation) and the question of modified input; the question in each case being whether such input plays a significant role in L2 acquisition. Section 5 discusses the problem of learning mechanisms and learning principles that might act on the input to produce new knowledge.

Learnability

Elements of a learnability model

Formal learnability theory is a complex mathematical enterprise, but the idea behind it is simple enough: all normal humans learn their native language, and hence a successful acquisition theory must be able to explain this fact. This is known as the Learnability Condition (Pinker, 1979) on (L1) acquisition theories. A learnability model (see e.g., Atkinson, 1992) deals with this condition by positing a small set of parameters or components that must be taken into consideration when constructing a theory of acquisition:

Elements of a learnability model for L1 acquisition

The initial state of the learner   This is the learner's (language-related) cognitive state prior to receiving any linguistic input. In L1 acquisition this is in effect the cognitive equipment the infant brings with it into the world. One proposal, of course, is that an innate Universal Grammar (UG) constitutes the initial state.

The final state of the learner   This will be the adult's native language (NL) grammar. This 'final' state is actually reached, to a first approximation, by puberty; such changes as occur later – new vocabulary, the learning of minor, literary constructions, etc. – can safely be ignored for our purposes.

Input   In L1 acquisition input consists essentially – perhaps exclusively – of utterances in context addressed to the learner, especially by caregivers and siblings.

Learning mechanisms   Some sort of mechanism, e.g., a sentence parser, is needed to analyze input and convert it into permanently recorded information about the target grammar.

An evaluation metric   The learning mechanism must know when to stop learning; once it has established a grammar, it must be able to reject input that violates that grammar, rather than continually adjusting to such input.

Even with such a bare-boned outline as this, it can be seen that there is ample room for a theorist to tinker, and for different theorists to disagree. For instance, as we will see, there is major disagreement over whether the child's initial state includes any specifically linguistic knowledge, over whether the learning mechanism is a 'dedicated' one, dealing only with linguistic information, and over the role of input.

In any case, this model can also be applied to SLA, but a number of interesting problems immediately arise:

Elements of a learnability model for adult SLA

The adult L2 learner's initial state vis-a-vis the L2   The adult now has a complete L1 grammar; does he have anything else? For instance, does he still have UG as such, in addition to a UG-governed L1 grammar? Conversely, has the adult learner lost anything that existed in the child's initial state? The adult has also gained a vast amount of other knowledge; could that acquired knowledge be of use, or be a hindrance, in acquiring an L2?

The L2 learner's final state   Not only do L2 learners start in a different cognitive state than the infant's, they also notoriously end up in different final states. This fact burdens the SLA theorist with an additional explanatory task.

L2 input   L1 acquisition proceeds to a successful conclusion in the virtually total absence of negative evidence such as correction or explanation. This difference in terminal states raises the possibility that negative evidence might be of use in SLA; perhaps it's only the learner who has received sufficient negative input that succeeds in L2 acquisition. Or conversely, the fact that L1 acquisition succeeds without negative evidence may simply underscore the impossibility of successful L2 acquisition even with it. Again, it has been proposed (and denied) that mothers address their young children in a characteristic way (so-called 'motherese'), and that this special input serves an important function in L1 acquisition (see, for example, papers in Heath, 1983; Snow & Ferguson, 1977). Similarly, it has been proposed that various kinds of simplification or other modification of input to L2 learners are of use in SLA.

L2 learning mechanisms   Just as we can ask if UG survives puberty, we can ask whether the learning mechanisms employed by children in L1 acquisition are the same as those employed by adults. And just as it is possible that UG atrophies in the adult, it might be that the learning mechanisms cease to function or weaken in their function.

Evaluation metric   Although there is plenty of talk in the L2 literature about 'fossilization', I know of no proposals that would show how a non-fossilized learning mechanism could be prevented from abandoning the 'correct' decision for some aspect of L2 grammar once it had learned it. Thus I will simply say nothing more about this element of a learnability model.

Assessing SLA theories from a learnability perspective

It will be noticed that the above parameters of a learnability model apply either to the process of acquisition (the interaction of learning mechanisms with linguistic input) or to the object of that process (the cognitive system before and after the acquisition process has produced its effects). This distinction, between cognitive system and cognitive process, corresponds nicely to a distinction, made by Cummins (1983), in theory types: *property theories* and *transition theories*.

A **property theory** deals with the instantiation within a given system of various properties of that system; it is intended to answer questions of the form, 'In virtue of what does system S have property P?' (Cummins, 1983 p.15). To use an example of Cummins's, the kinetic theory of gases is a property theory with which we can explain why a gas has a temperature, or in virtue of what property a gas has a temperature. A genetic theory would explain how heritable traits are instantiated in an organism; a sociological theory would explain how, say, authority is instantiated in a society. The domain of interest here being L2 competence, an SLA theory would include, as one component, a property theory explaining how L2 knowledge is instantiated in the mind of a learner.

A **transition theory**, on the other hand, is intended to explain changes of state in a system; rather, say, than explaining why a gas has a temperature, it would explain why the gas expanded when heated. Similarly, we would need transition theories to explain how traits are inherited, or how authority is acquired or transferred. Given a specific cognitive state – for instance, the state of knowledge obtaining in a learner who has yet to receive any information about the L2 to be acquired – we need a transition theory to explain the transition from this state to a state where the learner has L2 knowledge. The varying states themselves will be accounted for in a property theory, but it is the transition theory that will provide the mechanism for moving from state to state.

Looking at our outline of a learnability model, it is easy to see that insofar as we are dealing with initial and final states of the learner, we require a property theory of those states; whereas in dealing with input and the learning mechanism that operates on that input to produce linguistic competence, we require a transition theory. We can in fact specify these requirements in the form of criteria to be met by any theory offering itself as an SLA theory, and we can assess such a candidate theory according to the success with which it meets these criteria. Atkinson (1982) offers a number of such criteria for asssessing L1 acquisition theories (and, incidentally, finds all such theories wanting), but I will limit myself to those two which correspond neatly to Cummins's property/transition distinction; I will call them the Theoretical Framework Condition and the Mechanism Condition:

Two criteria for assessing SLA theories

Theoretical Framework Condition An SLA theory is explanatory only if it can account for each state of a learner's competence within the framework of a satisfactory property theory of linguistic competence, as defined by that theory.

Mechanism Condition An SLA theory is explanatory only if it includes a transition theory that has a mechanism or mechanisms to effect changes of state in L2 competence.

Note that I say 'only if' and not 'if and only if'; these conditions are necessary, but not sufficient, conditions on a successful SLA theory. (Atkinson, for instance, further requires that an explanatory acquisition theory explain acquisition sequences.) Note further that these are criteria for determining whether a theory is explanatory, not whether it is correct; it will be difficult enough to create a theory that provides even an inadequate and incorrect explanation of SLA. And indeed, there are, to my knowledge, no criteria for the correctness of a theory, such that a theory meeting them must be adjudged to be correct, although there are, of course, standards against which to compare competing theories (see Long, 1993, for a detailed proposal for SLA). Thus all I am saying in laying down these two criteria – and it hardly seems unreasonable, after all, to lay them down – is that an SLA theory must meet both of these criteria in order to be accepted as explanatory. And, since SLA theories are intended to be explanatory – a non-explanatory SLA theory is a contradiction in terms – it follows as the night does the day that no SLA theory that fails to meet these criteria can qualify as an SLA theory. In the following sections we will look at the elements of our learnability model in the light of these two criteria; but to let the cat out of the bag, I think we will find that, as of this writing, no theory of SLA exists.

Initial state and final state in SLA

Modularity and the homunculus problem

The initial and final cognitive states of the L2 learner (as well, of course, as the various intermediate states) are to be accounted for by some sort of property theory. Since the cognitive states are knowledge states, and since the domain of the knowledge is language, it might seem reasonable enough to assume that the property theory needed here is a linguistic theory. That seems reasonable to me, certainly, and even correct; but it is not necessarily the case. If we require that the property theory needed for an SLA theory be a linguistic theory, we are assuming 1) that a linguistic theory is a theory of linguistic knowledge; 2) that linguistic knowledge is categorically different from other kinds of knowledge; and 3) that the linguistic theory in fact *explains* the knowledge. All three assumptions are controversial.

The idea that a linguistic theory is a theory of knowledge is, of course, Chomsky's idea of competence; and, like most of Chomsky's ideas, it is not unanimously accepted. One can view language as a form of behaviour, for instance, in which case the idea of knowledge can be treated as irrelevant. Or one can view linguistic theory as an explanation of individual languages or the set of such languages, however defined, abstracted away from speakers of the language, and indeed irrespective of whether or not the language has speakers. That is, one can study what Chomsky (e.g., 1986) calls 'E-language', where the 'E' indicates 'external' to human minds. Typological theories of language, for instance, and in fact most descriptive linguistics to this day, take this approach. There is nothing wrong with these approaches, which indeed have produced a great deal of useful knowledge, but it is very hard to see how one can use them if one wishes to explain language acquisition, which inescapably involves individual minds. So I'm going to proceed on the assumption that our property theory must of necessity be a theory of knowledge, not of behaviour, not of skill, and not of disembodied languages.

But that does not mean that the knowledge involved is of a different type than knowledge of, say, arithmetic or ballroom dancing or bridge. Most psychologists, for instance, would deny that language has some privileged, distinct position among the objects of human learning. Not simply the behaviourists, but also more mainstream psychologists, such as most researchers who talk of 'learning theory', assume that the object of the learning is pretty much irrelevant. And of course connectionism is a prime example of a theory of knowledge and knowledge acquisition that denies any special status to knowledge of language (see Ellis, and MacWhinney, this volume). Thus if we are to claim that our property theory is a theory specifically of linguistic knowledge and no other, we need to show some reason for making language a special case. It's not that hard to do.

Theoretically, one can try to show that the theoretical concepts necessary for a successful description of language phenomena are simply not reducible to, or useable in, other knowledge domains. This certainly seems to be the case with such concepts as 'sentential subject', or 'c-command', for instance. Empirically, one can try to show cases where learning in the domain of language is grossly different in an individual from learning in other domains. Again, this seems to be the case with certain pathologies, e.g., Williams Syndrome or Downs Syndrome, where grammatical competence exists in the absence of all but minimal learning in other areas (Bellugi et al., 1991; Smith & Tsimpli, 1995); or conversely in cases like that of Genie (a normal child, deprived of language exposure by being locked in solitary confinement between the ages of 20 months and $13\frac{1}{2}$ years), whose syntactic knowledge is minimal but who made a good deal of progress in other areas, including personal interaction (Curtiss, 1977). I have no time to offer a detailed defence of the **modular** view of language, and indeed for the purposes of this chapter it isn't necessary to defend it. It is enough to show how the view might be defended, and what's at stake in the dispute. For detailed discussion of the question of modularity, see e.g., Fodor, 1983; Newmeyer, 1983; Pinker, 1994.[1]

So, let's assume that our SLA theory requires a property theory of linguistic competence specifically. Will that theory *explain* the knowledge? Indeed, what does it mean to say that a property theory explains a phenomenon? Consider the ancient joke about the man who had the ability to tell you at a glance the exact number of cows standing in a field; when asked how he could do it, he replied that it was simple: you just count the teats and divide by 4. What makes this an unsatisfying explanation, of course (and what makes it a joke), is that the

---

[1] It is, of course, a separate question whether the mind starts off modular or becomes modular. And it is yet a further question whether the putative development of modularity is internally (maturationally) or externally driven. See e.g., Karmiloff-Smith (1992) for a proposal for – in effect – *learned* modularity. With regard to the language faculty in particular, O'Grady (1987, 1996, 1997) makes a useful distinction between 'special nativism' (*à la* Chomsky) and 'general nativism', which he favours. O'Grady's proposals deserve a far more thorough discussion than this skimpy footnote; for one thing, O'Grady is one of the few anti-modularists in language acquisition who is fully cognizant of the explanatory challenges facing a non-modular account of language acquisition, and who faces them directly. As yet, however, there has been virtually no SLA research conducted within an O'Gradyan framework (but see Wolfe-Quintero, 1992); and this must be my – insufficient – excuse for giving general nativism short shrift here.

knowledge underlying his talent is more complicated than the talent itself. This is sometimes called the homunculus problem: explaining complex knowledge by appealing to equally complex knowledge is like appealing to the existence of a homunculus inside one's head. The problem is that one then must explain the knowledge inside the homunculus's head, and so on. This problem can be circumvented only if the homunculus is dumber than we are.

A satisfying property theory, in other words, is a theory that explains a complex system by breaking it down into less complex parts. By describing the various converging conveyor belts in an automobile factory, for instance, and the step-by-step attachment of part to part by robots that do nothing but, for example, bolt a frammis to a whizbang, one can explain the composition of the automobile. The car itself is a complex system, but it can be analyzed as a product of a fairly small set of very simple, indeed mindless, operations.

In the same way, linguistic theory is a way of reducing linguistic knowledge, which is horribly complex, down to the product of the interaction of a set of very simple operations. Consider, for instance, passivization in English as described in an early transformational grammar: converting a sentence from active to passive involved applying a set of highly specific rules. But to say that knowledge of English passive meant knowledge of these rules would be like the man counting the cows: we've gained nothing in the way of an analysis of our knowledge. On the other hand, current generative theory would posit the existence of a few very general, mindless principles whose interaction can lead to the production of a passive sentence from an active or vice versa: a principle which simply says that a constituent can move, a principle that sticks the agreement marker in a specific location in the sentence structure, another principle that chooses markers from a tiny list according to what is in the subject position, etc.

The *mindlessness* of the principles is essential: we must be able to reduce the complex knowledge we have to simple primitive components. This is because our knowledge is not God-given; it is either learned or innate, and in either case, irreducibly complex knowledge is an embarrassment to a theory. If our knowledge, say, of the old-fashioned 'passive transformation' were not analyzable into a set of independently existing simple operations, it could hardly be innate: after all, the 'passive rule' is a rule of English, not of human language. And how could it have evolved? But how could it have been learned, either?

It's also worth noting that this search for mindless rules, and as few of them as possible, is a characteristic of generative linguistic theories and of connectionist theories alike. It's worth noting this, because connectionists and generative linguists tend to disagree sharply on most other issues.

'Access to UG'

Tentatively, then, we can posit that the initial state of the infant *vis-à-vis* its L1-to-be is to be characterized by a theory of UG. What is the initial state of the adult *vis-à-vis* the to-be-acquired L2? In the SLA literature, the debate has tended to be framed within the question of whether UG 'operates' in SLA, or whether UG is 'available' to the L2 learner, or whether the learner has 'access' to UG. These formulations tend to obscure more than they illuminate: How does UG 'operate'? In what sense is UG available or unavailable? In what would 'access' to UG consist? Indeed, what is UG that one can have, or lose, access to it?

In practice, research on this subject has ignored such questions and left the question of 'access' in its metaphorical state, while looking at L2 learners and trying to determine 1) whether their L2 grammars obey, or violate, principles of UG, and 2) whether L2 learners are able to 'reset' parameters of UG – parameters being principles that can be instantiated in two (perhaps more) ways. Thus, for instance, one can look at learners of an L2 which instantiates a given principle of UG that is not instantiated in the learners' L1. (A language 'instantiates' a principle just in case there are phenomena in that language which are in some way constrained by the principle.) Or one can compare two languages that exemplify different values of a given parameter: Language X may permit null subjects, for instance, while Language Y forbids them; or X may restrict anaphoric reference to subjects while Y has no such restriction. One can then test whether or not native speakers of X learning Y, or vice versa, learn the restriction, or learn not to impose it.

Research here has been extensive, and generally inconclusive.[2] On the one hand, there is no good evidence that L2 grammars are 'rogue grammars' (Finer, 1991); there is no good evidence, in other words, that the L2 competence of adult learners violates principles of UG. On the other hand, though, it is hard to find compelling evidence of truly

---

[2] UG-oriented SLA research has proliferated over the last several years, to the degree that there is no longer any point in citing individual items. For a magisterial survey of early research (as well as a lucid exposition of the research program), see White, 1989; for a more recent review, see White, 1996. Major collections of generative SLA research include Eubank, 1991 and Flynn, Martohardjono and O'Neil, 1998. The journal *Second Language Research* has become the gathering place for UG/SLA researchers; virtually every issue has relevant material.

native-like success in the acquisition of an L2, such that one could say with confidence that the learner has a grammar essentially identical to that of a native speaker of the L2. What typically occurs in this kind of research is that the subjects score significantly better than chance, indicating that they have learned something, while scoring significantly worse than native-speaker controls, indicating that if they've learned something they haven't learned it very well. In a way, such results are the worst of all possible worlds, in that UG is not supposed to be a question of degree; languages do not sort of obey a principle, or tend to obey it, and native competence is supposed to be not statistical but categorical.[3]

In any case, the empirical results themselves are not at issue here; what is at issue is whether or not SLA theories whose property theory component is a theory of UG can supply us with an explanatory account of the initial state and/or of the final state of L2 acquisition. It would seem that they can, although once again I stress that the criterion here is explanitoriness, not correctness. Insofar as we need a theory of linguistic competence to explain the L2 competence of a learner – even of a rather unsuccessful learner – then an SLA theory that claims that the learner's L2 knowledge is represented by the same kinds of representations as his L1 knowledge will have met the Theoretical Framework Condition. And this is true regardless of what more specific claims are made about the initial state.

The 'access' debate, for instance, has generally boiled down to a debate between a small number of positions, with variations that we will have to gloss over:[4]

Full access   UG as such is fully accessible to the adult learner. The L2 learner should, *ceteris paribus*, acquire an L2 grammar comparable to that of a native speaker of the L2. Principles not relevant to the L1 but functioning in the L2 will be obeyed; parameters that differ from L1 to L2 will be 'reset'. Note that this position distinguishes between UG itself and a grammar produced in accordance with UG, and assumes that the two coexist in a learner's mind/brain.

No access   UG itself is no longer available, but the L1 grammar, which developed in the individual under UG constraints, is. This is sometimes known as the Fundamental Difference Hypothesis (FDH; Bley-Vroman, 1990). The term is misleading, though, in that, as far

---

[3] Cf. Crain & Thornton, 1998, who stress the point with respect to L1 acquisition; they refuse in principle to accept any but the narrowest range of variation in results.

[4] See e.g., White, 1996. Epstein, Flynn and Martohardjono, 1996 contains a defence of 'full access', along with a large number of criticisms of their position.

as the property theory goes, the difference is not fundamental. Here too a distinction is being made between UG and a given grammar; but where the 'total access' position sees the two as coexisting, the FDH claims that UG as such no longer exists, and that its functions are exercised – imperfectly – by the L1 grammar.

Limited access   UG as a whole is not available, but certain elements of it are. Specifically, the claim here is that parameters cannot be 'reset', although the L2 grammar will conform to other principles of UG (Eubank & Gregg, 1999; Schachter, 1990, 1996).

What must be stressed here is that all three positions, insofar as they accept the idea of UG as the property theory for L1 acquisition, are claiming that the L2 grammar too is describable, and indeed explainable, by UG. In this sense they all meet the Theoretical Framework Condition.

Not only do these UG-related SLA theories meet this condition, **no other SLA theories do.** This is the ugly little secret of SLA studies: as far as property theories of linguistic competence go, UG is the only game in town, and yet most SLA theoreticians simply decline to play the game. For a field that likes to use the term 'applied linguistics', it is truly astounding to see the degree to which linguistic analysis of any sort is shunned in the non-UG literature. If we are to take the Theoretical Framework Condition seriously – and I see every reason to do so – then advocates of non-UG SLA theories must either show how their theories can interact with UG, or else must propose a property theory of something like the scope, detail, and internal consistency of UG. Failing that, there is little reason to take them seriously as contenders.

Rejecting UG

It is, of course, possible for a theoretician to deny the need for UG in the first place; we will still need a property theory, of course, but not a modular one. Just about the only serious, non-modular challenge to UG-type theories of competence – aside from 'general nativism' (see footnote 1) – comes from connectionism, which denies the existence (the non-epiphenomenal existence, at least) of a language module, or rules, or principles, and for which the mind is essentially uniform and learning is essentially associative. Attempts to apply connectionist principles to SLA are still few (see e.g., Ellis & Schmidt, 1998; Gasser, 1990; Schmidt, 1988; Shirai, 1992; Sokolik, 1990; Sokolik & Smith, 1992; for critical comment, see e.g., Carroll, 1995; Carroll & Meisel, 1990; Fantuzzi, 1993), but this could easily change. Perhaps the fundamental problem with connectionism from a learnability perspective is its apparent inability to explain how we know that such-and-such a linguistic form, say, is *impossible*. Rule-like knowledge in a highly structured mind – as posited, e.g., by UG-based SLA theory – supports counterfactuals: thus *if* X were a noun in English, its plural form would be Y. A connectionist mind lacks rules, and can only produce Y as a statistically very highly probable form associated with X. Gasser (1990) is to my knowledge the only SLA connectionist even to have addressed this question, and all he says is that it is an 'empirical question'. Which it is, of course; but one to which we already seem to have an answer. Until connectionists can give an account of how L2 learners acquire knowledge of what is not possible in the L2, or can give us reason to believe that in fact L2 learners lack such knowledge, connectionist SLA theory is not going to get off the ground, as it will lack an explanatory property theory.

There is one other way for an SLA theory to bypass UG: finesse it altogether by appealing to underlying neural systems (cf. e.g., Jacobs, 1988; Jacobs & Schumann, 1992; Pulvermuller & Schumann, 1994; for critical comment see Eubank & Gregg, 1995). After all, it is agreed that knowledge, including L2 knowledge, is instantiated in the brain; why not eliminate the UG middleman and get to the heart of the matter? Why not, in other words, reduce SLA theory to a more basic level, the neurological level? The problem is that in fact no one has the slightest hint of an idea how to go about such a reduction.

In order to successfully reduce a theory – in this case a theory of linguistic competence – one must show that the terms of the theory to be reduced are translatable into terms of the reducing theory (Fodor, 1981; Hempel, 1966). Needless to say, no one has found a way to replace, for example, such terms as 'empty category', 'clause', 'subject', etc. with terms from neurobiology. But since a theory that uses such terms is currently able to explain a good deal about linguistic knowledge – although it can't tell us anything about how that knowledge is instantiated in the brain – it would be the height of folly to discard that theory because it's not 'basic' enough.

And it's not simply that neuroscience hasn't advanced sufficiently, hence that we have to make do for the time being with a linguistics that is disconnected to the neurons. If the day ever comes when we can locate the Empty Category Principle in some nook or cranny of Broca's area (and there are good reasons for pessimism), we will still not likely be in a position to discard the more abstract UG theory. This is because that more abstract level will almost certainly continue to be the best level for making certain kinds of explanatory generalizations.

To take an example adapted from Fodor (1981), any economic theory will have to account, *inter alia*, for such phenomena as debt and payment. Would it make sense to reduce economics to physics? Every act of payment is of course a physical act and hence conforms to the laws of physics. But payment can be instantiated in any of many grossly different physical actions: handing metal objects to another person, making marks on a piece of paper and putting the envelope containing the paper into a metal box, punching computer keys, etc. This variety precludes us from making any useful statement about payment as such, at the physical level; which is to say that if there are laws of economics, we will not be able to phrase them in the language of physics, even if we wanted to (cf. Pylyshyn, 1984). And *mutatis mutandis* for SLA theory.

So the bottom line appears to be that as things stand today, it would seem that an explanatory SLA theory will need to have as its property theory a UG type of theory of linguistic competence. Thus the learner's initial state, final state, and all the intervening states should be explicable within such a theory. This leaves open the question of what the initial and final states are at a more detailed level of analysis. In particular, we need to confront the evident *variation* in the cognitive states of adult learners, both initial and final.

Variation in initial and final states

In first language acquisition (and disregarding pathology), the initial state is the same across individuals regardless of L1 to be learned. And, within a given speech community, the final state is also essentially the same across individuals. (The kind of individual variation one of course sees – vocabulary size, rhetorical skill, that sort of thing – is taken to be theoretically irrelevant to UG.) But in SLA, the situation is much less clearcut. Given that a learner has an L1 grammar, and given that L1 grammars vary, it would seem to follow that initial states vary also. And of course the variation in final states is notorious. In the face of this kind of variation, it would appear difficult to apply the Learnability Condition to SLA theories; which would mean that we have lost an important constraint on theory-construction. In any case let us look at how the three positions on 'access to UG' might deal with variation in initial and final states.

In one sense, of course, none of the positions is embarrassed by variation, provided that the various cognitive states or grammars can all be accounted for by a theory based on UG; provided, that is, that there are no 'rogue' grammars. An IL grammar that violated UG would be a major problem for a theory that claims 'full access', but an IL grammar which conforms to UG while not matching the target language grammar in all respects need not be. One would have to explain these mismatches, of course, but in principle one could explain them without impugning UG. One could save the property theory, for instance, by appealing to problems in the domain of the transition theory, as we will see below when we look at learning mechanisms. Still, there is a limit to how much we can explain away in this manner; after all, the more UG-related mismatches there are between the TL grammar and the IL grammar, the harder it becomes to talk about 'access' to UG.

The 'no access' position naturally welcomes mismatches between TLG and ILG, at least as long as those mismatches reflect the L1 grammar. The problems arise here when the learner succeeds in acquiring knowledge (acquiring principles, resetting parameters) not available in the L1 grammar. But here, too, it may be possible to shift the blame to elsewhere in the theory: an adult might have access to learning mechanisms, say, that a child acquiring an L1 lacks, and that could compensate in some cases for the absence of UG.

But in either case – 'full access' or 'no access' – there is a conceptual problem, it would appear, insofar as UG is being conceived of as something in the mind that produces grammars, and either continues to exist independently of the grammar(s) it produces or else disappears and is replaced by the L1 grammar. Certainly current generative linguistic theory does not countenance this sort of picture: it is generally, although not unanimously, held that what we have been calling L1 grammars are essentially epiphenomena, useful for descriptive purposes but having no psychological reality (Chomsky, 1995). What we call a speaker's L1 grammar simply *is* UG, as modified by interaction with input. From this point of view the idea of UG and a grammar existing independently is incorrect; the idea of UG being replaced by a grammar is at least misleading; and the idea of UG making a grammar, or of an L1 grammar making an L2 grammar, is incoherent.

After all, the claim is that UG is a part of the mind/brain; as part of the mind, it must be represented in the brain. And the brain, especially the cortex, undergoes profound changes over the course of maturation. It would be odd indeed to find UG unchanged from birth to adolescence; and in fact it has been proposed in the L1 acquisition literature (e.g., Borer & Wexler, 1987; Radford, 1990) that UG matures, so that the competence of the young child is not fully constrained by UG. By the same token, it has often been claimed, both from within and from outside the UG perspective, that there is a critical period for language acquisition; which is to say that the brain, after a period of development, loses the plasticity necessary for learning, at least in the domain of language. We cannot go into the debate here (for recent discussion see the papers in Birdsong, 1999 and the references therein), but it should be stressed that much of the debate has been vitiated by a failure to specify just what areas of language are claimed to be affected by a critical period (but see Long, 1990). Eubank and Gregg (1999) offer a version of the limited access position that limits lack of 'access' to a failure to reset parameters, and point to some suggestive evidence in favour of this position.

Claiming (or denying) that the L2 learner has 'access to UG' is at best a shorthand way of claiming (or denying) that the L2 learner's L2 competence is constrained by UG, hence describable by the same property theory used in an L1 acquisition theory. At worst, the 'access' metaphor can muddy the waters by begging the question of what UG actually does. In other words, the 'access' issue cannot be settled, or even framed with sufficient clarity, until we look at the transition theory component of an SLA theory. To that component we now turn.

Input

It is uncontroversial that a learner needs input in order to acquire a language; you learn Swahili not by reading about it, or by staring at a colour chart, or by sitting in a comfy chair listening to Vivaldi, but by actually hearing it or reading it. Unfortunately, the consensus stops about there. How much input is necessary? What kind of input? Under what conditions need it be provided? For that matter, what is input?

To start with that last question, input is information that is fed into an input-output device; the output is a grammar. (The device itself is whatever the language learning mechanism turns out to be.) The input information is conveyed by – but not identical with – oral or written utterances in the TL (Carroll, 2000). Since the input-output device is a cognitive mechanism inside the learner's head, the input too is some sort of mental representation. Thus strictly speaking it makes little sense to talk of 'comprehensible input', 'modified input', etc.; what is actually intended, usually, is 'comprehensible utterances', 'modified utterances', etc. An ideally detailed transition theory for SLA would need to show how utterances are transduced into grammatical information for the input-output device; but I'm going to be much less demanding here, and deal with 'input' in the more common SLA sense of interlocutor utterances, with the tacit understanding that these utterances are but the first step in a series of transformations that lead to mental representations of linguistic knowledge. In the SLA literature, 'input' has been the object of a number of controversies, of which I will discuss two: the question of modified input, and the question of negative input.

Modified input

There is an enormous literature on modified input and its putative role in acquisition (see e.g., Day, 1986; Gass & Madden, 1985; Long, 1983a), whether on 'foreigner-talk' (Ferguson, 1975) or other forms of simplification, or on the role of discourse and 'negotiation of meaning' in SLA (e.g., Hatch, 1978, 1983a; Larsen-Freeman, 1980). The idea behind much of this research and discussion is that modification is necessary or useful in order to provide 'comprehensible input' to the learner. But – since no one has proposed that SLA can take place in the absence of comprehensible input – comprehensible input in SLA theory is like edible input in a theory of digestion; a given. And the claim that input must be made comprehensible is roughly comparable to B. Kliban's eminently sound, but probably unnecessary, advice: never eat anything bigger than your head. The problem is to get beyond platitudes to see how comprehensible input actually works.

From a practical point of view, of course, it's extremely important to learn how to make input more comprehensible, as when preparing pedagogical materials. But practical considerations are not theoretical considerations; and the theoretical question is not why learners learn more when exposed to utterances they understand than when exposed to gobbledygook, but why (and when) exposure to understood utterances leads to gains in competence. And nothing in the modified-input literature tells us much about that. Indeed, much of the input-modification literature seems not to be interested in acquisition at all: there is a largeish body of putative L2 acquisition research, for instance, that seems to be more discourse analysis or perhaps sociolinguistics than acquisition research.

The more theoretically (at least, acquisition-theoretically) relevant modified-input SLA research (see e.g., Long, 1991, 1996) tends to assume the following logic: comprehensible input is a necessary condition on acquisition; input can vary in comprehensibility; hence determining the factors that make input more or less comprehensible should tell us something about how input is used for acquisition. Such research has suggested that, in Long's terms (Long, 1991), 'focus on form' – drawing the learner's attention in some non-explicit way to a given form or structure, e.g., by repeating it, placing it in perceptually more salient positions within an utterance, etc. – is superior, in terms of increasing the comprehensibility of input containing those forms focussed on, both to 'focus on forms' and to simple conveying of comprehensible input without any focus on elements of the input. The logic underlying the research is compelling as far as it goes, and the results, if valid, certainly have implications for language pedagogy. Is there theoretical import as well?

Probably there is, although it is likely to be limited. Insofar as 'focus on form' seems to work better than unfocussed presentation of comprehensible input, this would seem to be evidential support for claims such as Schmidt's (1994b, 1995, this volume) about the role of attention and consciousness in SLA, and hence to be a contribution to a transition theory of SLA. Insofar as 'focus on form' seems to work better than 'focus on forms' – the latter being a kind of negative evidence (see below) – this could be evidential support for a modular view of language acquisition, in that 'focus on form' need not implicate the participation of higher-level 'central' processes, whereas 'focus on forms' certainly would.

Still, what has yet to be done in SLA research is to show any interesting – that is, theoretically relevant – relation between some specific type of input modification on the one hand, and some specific bit of acquisition on the other. It's one thing, after all, to show that the learner comprehends what you say better when the two of you are in the same room, or when you take the chewing gum out of your mouth, or when you say everything twice; and it's one thing – pretty much the same thing, in fact – to show that the learner's proficiency increases when comprehensibility increases. But it's quite another thing to show, say, that learners acquire free relatives in English more quickly or more securely when they are presented with input containing free relatives made salient than when they are not. And it is yet another thing again to show that presenting the learner with comprehensible input where, say, expletives are 'focussed on' will lead to the re-setting of the learner's IL parameter value for the Null Subject Parameter. That in itself, of course, wouldn't meet the Mechanism Condition, but it would at least provide an explanandum for a theoretical learning mechanism to explain. And indeed here we have the weakness of the modified-input research (that is, of the modified-input research that is even relevant to an SLA theory): the research is conducted in essential isolation from a grammatical theory. Which is to say that this kind of research tends to ignore the Theoretical Framework Condition.

Negative input

Given a system (that is, a learner) at stage i (e.g., thinking that whales are fish, or thinking that the past tense of *teach is teached*), and the same system at stage $i + 1$ (thinking that whales are mammals, thinking that the past tense form is *taught*), one obvious way to explain the change of state is to hypothesize that someone told the learner about whales, or about *taught*. This is negative evidence, and it seems reasonable enough to imagine that it plays some sort of role in at least some aspects of SLA.

There are various ways to characterize negative evidence in language acquisition (see Birdsong, 1989, for a thoroughgoing discussion). Most commonly, negative evidence is defined as evidence that some form or structure is ungrammatical, while positive evidence is evidence that some form or structure is grammatical. In first language acquisition, positive evidence is generally equated with so-called primary linguistic data (PLD); that is, the utterances addressed to the child. Since parents and caregivers normally don't address metalinguistic explanation and correction to their child, this positive-negative distinction works fairly well.[5] But adult learners often do receive such explanation, and it has seemed to some researchers to be inappropriate to include explanation or correction as positive evidence.

Thus it might be more fruitful to divide the two along the traditional use vs. mention axis: Positive evidence is language used; that is, utterances in context. Negative evidence is language mentioned. From this categorization it follows that negative evidence includes not just correction of learner errors, but also instruction and metalinguistic explanation; what Schwartz and Gubala-Ryzak (1992) refer to as explicit positive evidence. Thus, just as one can think whales are fish and be disabused, one can also not know a thing about whales and be enlightened. And one can either think that *jejune* means puerile and be told that it means sterile, or one can have not a clue as to what *jejune* means and look it up. In either case *jejune* is no more being used than whales are.

Why should this distinction, however drawn, matter? Well, in first language acquisition we know that negative evidence is unnecessary; it's not provided, and yet all children successfully acquire their first language. But of course not all adults acquire a second language successfully; this fact may at least open up the possibility that negative evidence is of use, or even necessary, for successful SLA.

We must distinguish here, as always, between theoretically relevant and theoretically irrelevant negative evidence. It may well be that one can learn that *gokiburi* means 'cockroach' by being told explicitly, just as effectively as by hearing the word used in an appropriate context;

---

[5] Of course, positive evidence for X can, in at least some circumstances, be information that Y is ungrammatical. Parameter setting presumably works this way; e.g., positive evidence that the head of a noun phrase comes at the beginning of the phrase is also presumably ('negative') evidence that heads do not come at the ends of their phrases.

just as effectively, and far less traumatically. It may even be the case that certain larger aspects of language, say honorifics, will *need* to be explicitly taught, at least to some extent, at least in an SLA context. And in any case, of course, explicit instruction and correction in such areas may well be useful even if not necessary, in terms of efficient use of learning time, for instance.

But the theoretically interesting question is whether or not negative evidence is necessary in SLA in those domains defined as central by our property theory; in other words, does negative evidence have a role to play in the construction of a UG-based IL grammar? For instance, is negative evidence either necessary or effective in getting the learner to reset parameters? Of course, no one thinks that one should explicitly give instruction in UG theory itself, e.g., pointing out to francophone learners of English that the difference in the value of AGR[6] is what's responsible for their saying things like, 'John drinks often coffee'. The question rather is, if you tell a learner that 'John drinks often coffee' is ill-formed, or that English adverbs cannot be inserted between verb and direct object, will that negative evidence suffice to reset the relevant parameter (see White, 1991)?

That, at least, is the theoretical question. A more practical question, of course, is, would this kind of explanation or correction lead to the learner's ceasing to produce utterances of the form, 'John drinks often coffee', IL grammar be damned? If the answer to this question is yes, learners and their teachers may perhaps be forgiven if they pass over the theoretical question. But then it's not at all clear whether or when the answer to the practical question is yes. If, or insofar as, the answer is no, then learners and their teachers as well as SLA theoreticians have a stake in answering the theoretical question.

In any case, the question of the effectiveness or otherwise of negative evidence is theoretically fraught. Scholars like Schwartz, for instance (e.g., 1986), following Fodor's concept of a mental module, stress the *cognitive impenetrability* of linguistic competence.[7] However much we know that the moon doesn't actually grow bigger as it sets, our knowledge has no effect on our (modular) visual system, which persists in seeing the moon as bigger. The visual module, in other words, is unaffected by input from 'above', from the higher-level intellectual

---

[6] AGR is agreement between two words regarding a grammatical feature, such as, in English, a noun and a verb and the feature third person-s.

[7] The notion of cognitive (im)penetrability is Pylyshyn's (e.g., 1984): Perception, for instance, is cognitively impenetrable in the sense that 'the output of the perceptual systems is largely insensitive to what the perceiver presumes or desires' (Fodor, 1983 p. 68). Schwartz's claim (e.g., 1986), following Fodor, 1983, is that the language module is cognitively impenetrable in a similar way.

functions of the central processor. By the same token, claims Schwartz, higher-level information *about* linguistic input should be as useless as higher-level information about the moon. Hence negative evidence should be ineffective by definition, if linguistic competence constitutes a module.

Ironically enough, it would seem that a connectionist would also be unwilling to attribute much efficacy, if any, to negative evidence. In connectionist theory, after all, learning is associative; it is the strengthening of connections between associated nodes. And this strenghtening occurs with repeated input of the relevant stimulus. Thus, for example, a connectionist might want to claim that a learner learns not to drop subjects from English sentences by exposure to a sufficiently large number of sentences with overt subjects (sufficiently large, and sufficiently larger than any input of subjectless sentences). But being told explicitly that English sentences must have subjects would merely amount to one single input of a sentence with a subject; hardly enough to affect the learner's grammar.

In any case, we have accepted – tentatively and *faute de mieux* – a UG-type of grammar as the basis of our property theory, and UG theories are definitely modular. Does this force us to deny, on pain of inconsistency, any role to negative evidence in the transition theory?

Not necessarily. For one thing, there is modularity and there is modularity; there is, for instance, Chomsky's concept of language as modular, and there is Fodor's, and they are not necessarily the same concept. For instance, as Chomsky (1986) has pointed out, Fodor's modules are 'input systems', but language includes more than input processing. Especially, language output – saying something, in other words – tends to originate in some sort of *intention* to express some sort of *thought*, and intention and thought are non-modular on Fodor's own view. So when Chomsky talks about language as modular, he means something like that language is a distinct mental faculty from others, with its own rules and procedures; but he also means that it interacts with other mental faculties. It does not follow, however, that a Chomsky-modular language faculty is Fodor-modularly deaf to higher-level, e.g., metalinguistic, input. It could be, of course, but it need not be. The question, in other words, is an empirical one, not a metatheoretical one. And, like all the other empirical problems we've come across here, it's an open one.

The learning mechanism

As a property theory, UG can only establish constraints on development. The explananda of a UG theory include such phenomena as the grammaticality, ungrammaticality, ambiguity, possible and impossible interpretations, scope, etc., of sentences, or (which is the same thing) the native speaker's knowledge of the grammaticality, ungrammaticality, etc. They do not include the acquisition of this linguistic knowledge; this is the domain of an acquisition theory in the wider sense, that is, the property theory plus the transition theory. The Mechanism Condition requires that we have a transition theory that includes some sort of learning mechanism or mechanisms to interact with UG on the one hand, and with input on the other.

Non-linguistic mechanisms

Ironically enough, the SLA literature is chock full of causal theories; in fact most of what passes for SLA theorizing is causal in intent. The problem, as we have seen, is that these theories fail to meet the Theoretical Framework Condition: they don't interface in any useful way with what I have claimed is the unique property theory in our domain, UG. The plausibility of such theoretical explanations as have so far been offered depends largely on taking a sufficiently broad and superficial view of either the initial or final state or both. It *may*, for instance, be possible to appeal to acculturation as a cause of SLA, *if* we define L2 competence in the broadest, vaguest terms like 'proficiency'. So we can say, for example, that overall proficiency is a function of acculturation to the culture of the speakers of the target language. And this may even be true, for all I know. True or not, it is not satisfactory. We certainly cannot appeal to acculturation to explain e.g., parameter-resetting; we couldn't make such an appeal even if there were a perfect correlation between degree of acculturation and success in resetting parameters.

And note that even to the extent that such non-UG causal theories can be seen as explanatory, they provide at best contrastive explanations, not causal ones. It might be plausible to assume that, *ceteris paribus*, the more highly motivated a Korean learner of English is, the greater his chance of acquiring Subjacency, thus explaining why Kim but not Paik can handle Subjacency in English. But this is a far cry from saying that the motivation was the cause of the acquisition. Indeed, to say that Kim acquired Subjacency because he was motivated is not even the beginning of an explanation.

In other words, if we are to postulate language acquisition mechanisms, they are going to have to be more specifically linguistic mechanisms, or at least mechanisms that can act on linguistic input to create a grammar. Thus not only are motivation, acculturation and such non-starters as candidate mechanisms, so are most of the more general mechanisms that have been proposed that apply equipotentially to linguistic and non-linguistic learning situations.

For example, McLaughlin (1987, 1990) talks of 'restructuring', where information acquired piecemeal is later reorganized and integrated into a system. Restructuring is intended as a general process in that it can apply in any cognitive domain; just as the English past tense marker is first learned verb by verb and then later converted to a past-marking rule, so, for example, is mathematical knowledge restructured when a child goes from adding 7 ten times to multiplying 7 × 10 (McLaughlin, 1987). Again, there is a burgeoning literature on so-called 'learning strategies'; e.g., O'Malley and Chamot (1990: 46) offer inferencing ('using information in text to guess meanings of new linguistic items'), rehearsal ('repeating the names of items . . . to be remembered'), deducing ('applying rules to the understanding of language'), and imagery ('using visual images . . . to understand and remember new verbal information').

This is rather a mixed bag, but one thing is fairly clear already: whether or not such 'strategies' operate in SLA, and for all I know all of them do, they either will not satisfy the Mechanism Condition or else they will not satisfy the Theoretical Framework Condition. Restructuring or automatization, for instance, are not mechanisms, they are processes; to say that -*ed* is restructured as a rule is a statement that the past tense rule is acquired, not an explanation of how. On the other hand, while inferencing, deducing, and so on can indeed be seen as mechanisms, no one has shown how these mechanisms operate on input that can be characterized within the property theory (UG theory).

Learning principles

More relevant to the Mechanism Condition, perhaps, are the various learning principles that have been proposed, both in the UG-related acquisition literature and in the non-modular literature. Probably the best-known proposal is Slobin's Operating Principles (OPs) (e.g., Slobin, 1973, 1985; cf. Andersen, 1989 for related work in SLA, and Doughty, this volume, for discussion). OPs are in effect instructions to the learner as to how to perceive, store, or organize input, as well as how to produce speech. Slobin has proposed a couple of dozen principles, such as the following:

Pay attention to stressed syllables in extracted speech units.
Keep track of the frequency of occurrence of every unit and pattern
   that you store.

Store together ordered sequences of word classes and functor classes
that co-occur in the expression of a particular proposition type,
along with a designation of the proposition type.
Keep the order of morphemes in a word constant across the various
environments in which that word can occur. (from Slobin, 1985:
1251–54)

There are several problems with Slobin's proposal, aside from whether
or not the OPs are accurate descriptions of what learners in fact do.
For one thing, the OPs are awfully numerous, and there seems to be
no principled limit to the number; this makes for an inelegant and
implausible learning mechanism. Worse, the OPs do not seem to form
a natural class, which reinforces the sense that the OPs are *ad hoc*
descriptions of various language-related phenomena. Keeping track
of frequency and paying attention to stressed syllables, for instance,
seem like two very different mental operations. The adhocness becomes more apparent when one notes that, for instance, there are
three separate OPs calling for attention to be paid to the first syllable, the last syllable, and any stressed syllables in a speech unit. This
means there are two OPs for paying attention to the first syllable of
'blackboard', say; while on the other hand all three OPs join to focus
attention on the entire word 'banana' (but on only 3 of the 4 syllables
of 'banana boat').

It's not that the OPs don't exist, although they may not (Pinker
claims that OPs 'are almost certainly not implemented in the child's
mind' [1989a p.458]); learners no doubt do pay attention to stressed
syllables, store frequently heard forms in memory, keep track of frequency of input forms, etc. It is rather that they don't go very far in
showing how the input leads to the formation of a grammar, let alone
a grammar describable in UG terms.

Other learning principles that have been offered include the Subset
Principle (SP) and the Uniqueness Principle (UP). The Subset Principle
(Berwick, 1985) essentially is a principle of conservatism in grammar
construction: 'the learner should hypothesize languages in such a way
that positive evidence can refute an incorrect guess' (p. 37). In other
words, given two possible grammars – G_1 and G_2 – where G_1 allows
only a subset of the sentences allowed by G_2 (the Subset Condition), the
Subset Principle tells the learner to choose G_1. In the absence of such
a principle, there is the danger that an over-general grammar would
be chosen, which could then be corrected only by negative evidence.

In SLA, White (1989) has argued that the Subset Principle is no
longer operative; and indeed, she has used this claim as a principled
way to get UG off the hook in explaining failure to achieve nativelike

L2 competence: UG itself is still implicated in SLA, as evidenced e.g., by the conformity to UG of IL grammars; but unlike L1 acquisition, the constraint on learning imposed by the SP is gone, allowing for overgeneral IL grammars. This is an attractive proposal, but of course it depends on the existence of a Subset Principle in the first place, and that is not a given. Fodor and Crain, for instance, insist that the SP is 'a guiding principle for linguists to follow in devising theories. It is not, presumably, a principle that a learner can abide by in constructing his grammar...' (1987: 54).

White (1989) herself points out some of the difficulties. One problem is the scope of the SP. It has usually been seen as applying to parameter-settings, but of course there are other, non-parametric, phenomena where the Subset Condition seems to obtain. For instance, the English conditional works both for 'If I go to Chicago, I'll meet Mary' and 'If I go to Chicago, I'll go by plane', whereas the Japanese conditional (or one of them, the *-eba* form) disallows the second. Does the SP apply in this case? There is a problem whether the answer is yes or no. If no, and the SP is applicable only in parameter-setting cases, then we have a possibly large body of phenomena where the Subset Condition seems to apply but where we have no explanation for failure to overgeneralize (of course, if L2 learners consistently do overgeneralize, there's no problem for the theory).

If the answer is yes, and our acquisition theory uses the SP to explain successful acquisition of conditionals as well as of parametric values, we have the daunting problem of explaining how a learner could possess such a principle (hence Fodor & Crain's demur): as White (1989) points out, either the SP is in some way innately specified to start off with the more conservative of two possible choices, or else the learner has the capacity to judge (unconsciously, of course) which choice would be more conservative. The former *might* be plausible for a strictly limited set of parameters, but totally out of the question for the whole array of possible subset phenomena (and, as White points out, if all the conservative parameter settings were 'wired in', as it were, then there would in fact be no SP). But the latter, too, seems highly unlikely at best: How *could* a learner implement a general learning principle, Be conservative?

All this would seem to lead to the conclusion that the Subset Principle, if it exists, can't do the job that has been attributed to it. The subset *problem* is a real one, definitely; and indeed one of the differences between L1 acquisition and SLA is precisely that adults frequently fail to solve the problem. But it is one thing to say that adults cannot overcome the subset problem, and a very different thing to say that adults do not have the Subset Principle, especially if no one else has it either.

The Uniqueness Principle has been proposed in various forms, both within a generative-linguistic framework and as a more general principle of language and language acquisition. Clark's Principle of Contrast, for instance, simply states that 'Every two forms contrast in meaning' (Clark, 1987: 2). Pinker (1984: 113) suggests that when a (child) learner 'is faced with a set of alternative structures fulfilling the same function, only one of the structures is correct unless there is direct evidence that more than one is necessary.' In SLA, Andersen has proposed his One to One Principle: 'An interlanguage system should be constructed in such a way that an intended underlying meaning is expressed with one clear invariant surface form (or construction)' (Andersen, 1984: 79).

However phrased, the Uniqueness Principle (UP) is intended as a means for the learner to eliminate incorrect forms from his developing grammar. Hearing 'ate', for example, in a context where he has been using 'eated', the learner will discard 'eated' in favour of 'ate', on the principle that they can't both be right (combined, as Pinker points out, with the further principle that in a conflict between learner form and input-form, input-form wins). Conversely, hearing both, e.g., 'will' and 'be-going-to' in what seem like identical contexts, the learner can use the same UP to infer that there must be some distinction between the two forms. If Clark and others are correct in thinking that languages have virtually no true synonyms, the learner will normally be correct in making such an inference; and in the few cases of true synonymy (*anyone/anybody, almost/nearly*), the learner will presumably give up eventually and accept both forms as true synonyms.

As with the Subset Principle, the UP seems like a useful tool for a learner to have, but there are problems. One problem, as with the SP, is the scope of the UP. While the UP seems plausible enough when applied to lexical items or inflectional morphology, it seems hard to apply to syntax. It would be hard, to start with, to determine what the same 'function' would be for two syntactic structures, if we use Pinker's definition, or what the 'meaning' of a syntactic structure is, if we use Clark's or Andersen's. And indeed it appears that those three scholars at least are restricting the UP to lexis and morphology (but see Trahey & White, 1993).

A more serious problem, and again one faced by SP proposals, is the problem of how the UP is supposed to work. How can we guarantee that the learner, rather than purging a self-generated form in the presence of a competitor in the input (*eated – ->ate*), will not look for a dimension on which to distinguish the two? For instance, a learner whose L1 has more than one morphological past tense – say a preterite and an imperfect – could theoretically assign *ate* to one and *eated* to the other. After all, even though *eated* hasn't appeared in the input, there's still very powerful evidence in the input for its existence, in the thousands of tokens of regular past-tense verbs.

Putting aside the question of how it works, we may ask *if* it works in SLA (see Rutherford, 1989 for detailed discussion). There are next to no empirical data (but see Trahey & White, 1993), but there are some anecdotal data from Bley-Vroman (1986) that are not encouraging. And I can add my own experience of learning Japanese, more or less naturalistically, where I seem to have both honored and ignored the UP: I have persisted for several years, for instance, in looking for a principled meaning difference between *kamosirenai* and *kamowakaranai* ('perhaps'), where evidently it's only a dialectal difference, and I did the same thing with *kuu* and *taberu* ('eat'), although I got the distinction wrong at first. But on the other hand, especially as a beginner, I ignored gross differences in pairs of forms, such as *tokorode/tokoroga* ('by the way'/'however') and *sikasi/sikamo* ('however'/'moreover'), again for years. Based on this admittedly meager evidence, it would seem that the UP, if it exists, ceases to operate, or at least ceases to operate effectively, in SLA.

Learning principles vs. learning mechanisms

Of course one thing we have been glossing over in discussing learning principles is the fact that whether they exist or not, and whether, if they exist, they operate with the same or less efficiency in SLA as in L1 acquisition, learning principles are not learning mechanisms. At best they are constraints on the operation of the mechanism(s), guiding attention mechanisms, for instance, to certain parts of the input, forcing memory to record two forms separately in long-term storage, and so on. They therefore cannot play a central role in a transition theory of SLA.

It might be objected here that we do have mechanisms already, mechanisms that I've even touched on from time to time, such as attention, memory, inferencing, generalization, and so on. Indeed, just such an objection is likely to be made by anyone outside UG theory, for instance most psychologists. And of course we do have such mechanisms, and they are essential components of any explanation we may wish to offer of SLA. The problem is that while essential, they are not sufficient. The reason lies in the property theory of linguistic competence, in effect the theory of UG.

UG theory is motivated by the fact that L1 linguistic competence is both incredibly complex and incredibly speedily acquired. This fact leads to the positing of innate principles that constrain the forms of sentences and that explain their (un)grammaticality, ambiguity, etc. Further, these principles are framed in terms that are for the most part restricted to the domain of language – terms like subject, c-command, binding, etc. Now, if we are going to accept this kind of theory as the property theory for SLA – and at the moment, for better or worse, there are no other candidates – and if we want to content ourselves with general learning-theoretical mechanisms like attention and memory, we are going to have to show how they can interact with input to produce L2 knowledge, i.e., a grammar.

Clearly, L2 learning involves storing new information in long-term memory, for instance. But since a learner can't simply memorize all sentences, there needs to be a way to extract grammatical information from those sentences in such a way as to produce new grammatical information. Again, learning requires attention to input; but one cannot pay attention to rules or principles, since these are not perceptible. Thus in order to specify the role of attention in an acquisition theory – in order, that is, to go beyond the truistic point that one can't learn from input without attention to that input – we have to show how the relevant information conveyed by the input attended to can be converted into part of competence. What we need, in effect, is some sort of transducer that can take sound or visual signals and convert them into information consistent with a grammatical theory.

What we need, in short, is a **parser**, a device that subjects incoming input to grammatical analysis within the constraints of a grammar; and, where the grammar is still inchoate, revises that grammar upon dealing with unparseable input (see e.g., White, 1987). At the same time, we need a theory of **triggers**; that is, a theory of precisely what kinds of unparseable input should trigger a revision of the learner's grammar (for L1 acquisition, see e.g., Fodor, 1998; Gibson & Wexler, 1994). To take a simple example, a learner whose IL English grammar lacks a passive could, on encountering a sentence like 'The soup was made by Max', use that input to trigger the inclusion of a passive 'rule' (assuming of course sufficient attention to the little grammatical morphemes and such, etc.). A more difficult example is anaphora: what sort of input would be necessary or sufficient for a learner of English (either native child or, say, adult Japanese, whose language differs from English in this respect) to learn that in a sentence like 'John thinks Max will introduce himself to Greta' *himself* cannot refer to John? Acquiring this kind of information definitely involves attention, memory, inferencing – noticing 'was … by …', remembering that passive agents are marked by *by*, inferring that since soup can't make a person it must be Max who made the soup, etc. – but it needs more than that. Our theory must be able to say what sort of input should lead to restructuring the grammar, and to be able to say that requires having some sort of theory of parsing and triggers.

The problem is that SLA theory doesn't have anything like such a theory. Indeed, the SLA literature is almost devoid of discussion of parsing and its relation to grammar-formation (but see Bley-Vroman, 1991; Juffs & Harrington, 1995, 1996; Harrington, this volume; and Zobl, 1988). Virtually the only research program in SLA where there is evident awareness of the problem is, unsurprisingly, UG/SLA theory; but these researchers have tended to concentrate on the 'access' problem, while bypassing or glossing over the trigger problem. Finer (1991), for instance, in an interesting and important study, says that 'the *realization* that the [Proper Antecedent Parameter] takes on the marked value in the target language would entail the further *recognition* that failure to shift away from the marked position... on the [Governing Category Parameter] could eventuate a violation of [binding theory]' (p.367; emphasis added). 'Realization' and 'recognition', of course, are metaphors here, since Finer is certainly not claiming that learners are or could be aware of the relevant facts. But that means that a homunculus has intruded into the discussion; and we expressly wanted to exorcise homunculi from our theory. This can be done only when we have a transition theory that can translate the realizing and recognizing into mindless, but successful, cognitive activities.

SECTION II

COGNITION AND INSTRUCTION

7 Cognition and tasks

Peter Skehan and Pauline Foster[1]

Introduction

Unlike any other skill that you could care to mention (algebra, tennis, driving, playing the bagpipes), language can work well despite poor execution. Its meaning is recoverable even when its form is incorrect. 'Me Tarzan, you Jane', or 'ET phone home' are not grammatical, nor particularly subtle, but they get the job done. This useful characteristic of language means that learners can decode and encode the semantic contents of a message without attending to all of its syntactic packaging. Anderson and Lynch (1988), for example, show how contextual and discourse knowledge-sources enable comprehension to proceed for native and non-native speakers without exhaustive bottom-up analysis of a message. Schematic knowledge enables the redundancy in language to be exploited for meaning-extraction. Productively, it is clear that second language (L2) users draw upon a range of communication strategies (Bygate, 1988; Faerch & Kasper, 1983; Kasper & Kellerman, 1997) enabling them to communicate meanings despite limited resources. Individual case studies, e.g., of Wes (Schmidt, 1983) and Schmidt (Schmidt & Frota, 1986), as well as larger scale research such as that evaluating immersion education in Canada (Harley, Allen, Cummins & Swain, 1990; Swain & Lapkin, 1982) also indicates how the need to engage in output does not automatically lead to acquisitional progress. In evolutionary terms, it is entirely plausible that the language system should be robust in this way – requiring crystalline precision in all communication could well have been decidedly dangerous for our ancestors' health and survival. Unsurprisingly therefore, a strategy of prioritising the meaning of the message over its form is not uncommon among language users.

---

[1] The authors would like to thank Peter Robinson for comments on an earlier version of this chapter.

Some linguists (e.g., Givon, 1985) would say that this prioritisation is pre-eminently natural and can explain the ease and speed with which humans create pidgin languages. Others (e.g., Corder, 1973; Selinker, 1972; Schumann, 1978) would say it helps to explain why the learning of second or foreign languages almost invariably falls short of complete success. What these different accounts are predicated upon is the existence of a critical period for language learning. First languages are acquired incidentally despite a lack of focus on form by the child. L2 learners no longer seem to have this capacity for incidental learning (Newport, 1990) such that an automatic, 'by-product' development of syntax no longer seems available. From a communicational perspective, older learners can exploit their superior cognitive resources, their awareness of how messages can achieve communication without syntax. From a developmental perspective, problems are posed, since something interventionist has to be done to compensate for this lack of automatic engagement.

In any case, taking these different views into account, the claim we are led to is that native-like morphosyntactic competence is an expensive optional extra. The redundancy of much syntax in successful second or foreign language communication serves to underline warnings about a task-based approach to language instruction (Harley & Swain, 1984; Skehan, 1992). Unless it is appropriately handled, a task-based approach can over-emphasise the importance of just 'getting the job done' at the expense of the central purpose of pedagogy: improving target language ability. As a consequence, it is more likely to have the effect of encouraging comfortable fossilisation than that of promoting interlanguage (IL) development.

Injecting a concern for language form without compromising the communicative nature of the task has been the focus of a great deal of interest over recent years. This has concerned itself almost entirely with the matter of getting the right task design. A number of suggestions have been produced. Fotos and Ellis (1991) make grammatical structures the subject of the task itself, with the intention that the learners will be attending to particular forms at the same time as engaging in meaningful communication. A different tack is taken by Loschky and Bley-Vroman (1993) and Samuda, Gass and Rounds (1996) who say it is possible to design communicative tasks in such a way that the use of certain grammatical structures is unavoidable. Loschky and Bley-Vroman (1993) discuss three types of relationship between specific language forms and task design. *Naturalness* applies if a particular structure can be used in a task in an unforced manner, but where the structure is not particularly required, or probabilistically more likely.

Helpfulness describes the situation where a structure is probabilistically more likely but nevertheless quite possible to circumvent. Finally, *necessity* applies to a task where a particular structure has to be used unavoidably. Clearly, Loschky and Bley-Vroman (1993) and Samuda et al. (1996) are optimistic that this third, most stringent condition can be met, and as a result, a marriage of form and function are arranged so that naturalness of communication is not compromised while planned and systematic instruction can take place. For example, speculating on the identity of the owner of a jacket by considering the contents of its pockets will lead inevitably to the use of modal auxiliaries. Teachers are thus able to maximise the chances that a particular structure (selected by them) will be used in a meaningful situation, and that the learners will thereby be drawn into paying attention to its form.

Willis (1996) rejects such a 'structure trapping' approach as impractical, noting how very adept learners are at avoiding the chosen structure a teacher or task designer has built the task around.[2] She proposes instead an extended task sequence in which the design characteristics of the task are of less significance than its implementation. This involves several stages of task planning, execution, and reflection and, uniquely, a comparison with native speaker norms. The role of the teacher is not to push learners towards using particular structures but to help them notice what language is required to do a particular task, and then provide help with this where necessary. The stages of planning, reflection and native speaker comparison keep up a focus on form thereby combating any tendency on the part of the learner just 'to get the job done'.

There are similarities here with an approach advocated by Swain (1998). She argues that tasks should get students to produce language and then allow them to reflect upon its structure. Tasks of this type would include reconstructing a passage from a few prompts; a cloze test on verb tenses; or preparing a short oral presentation. Each of these activities   involves the learners collaborating on a

---

[2] It should be noted that the different positions on the feasibility of structure-trapping are essentially evidence-free. Loschky and Bley-Vroman (1993) and Samuda et al. (1996) assert the feasibility of this approach without advancing strong evidence that (a) structures are trapped in any systematic way, or (b) the approach to design can be generalised, through creative task design, to a wide range of structures. Willis (1996) draws on informal investigations of task trialling prior to the publication of the Cobuild course (Willis & Willis, 1988) which show how 'plausible' tasks that targeted particular structures were indeed subverted by speakers who completed the task very well but with structures other than those intended.

piece of writing, and discussing together what is most appropriate and correct. The important feature of the design is that learners are enabled to focus on the forms in their own output through writing them down collaboratively, and thus are helped to notice gaps in their knowledge.

A rather different approach, and perhaps the most currently influential, is to see a task not as the vehicle for drawing attention to particular language forms, nor as an opportunity for extended target language consciousness-raising, but as a powerful catalyst for IL development (Long, 1989; Pica, 1994; Varonis & Gass, 1985). Engaging in a task with one or more partners will typically lead learners into episodes of communication breakdown in which either they do not properly understand what is being said, or they themselves are not properly understood by the others. At such moments, negotiation of meaning devices such as clarification requests, confirmation checks, and the like are seen as triggering vital 'comprehensible input' (Krashen, 1982) for learners at precisely the point where they may have realised that there is a gap in their knowledge of the target language. In such a negotiation of meaning approach, there is no attempt to 'seed' such tasks with particular structures deemed ripe for attention. Indeed, the teacher has no part at all in determining where a learner's attention should be directed; this depends entirely on where communication breakdowns occur during the task. It is therefore considered important to design tasks which increase the chances that meanings will have to be negotiated among the task participants, producing plenty of comprehensible input.

According to various researchers (see Long, 1989; Pica, Kanagy & Falodun, 1993 for a review), task types vary in the incidence of negotiation of meaning that they provoke. Pica et al. categorise tasks in terms of *interactional activity* and *communication goal*. Regarding the former, they argue that there is more negotiation of meaning with tasks where each interactant holds different and necessary information for task completion and where this information is required. Where there is some degree of optionality in information supply, negotiation of meaning is reduced. Regarding communication goal, negotiation of meaning is promoted where interactants have shared convergent goals, rather than divergent goals. Similarly, where one acceptable outcome is possible, rather than more than one, greater negotiation of meaning is predicted (Pica et al., 1993, p. 15). Positive tasks advocated by Pica et al. are jigsaw and information gap tasks (which promote interaction and the achievement of convergent goals) compared to (say) an opinion-exchange task, which does not require interaction, and, moreover, allows divergent goals.

Negotiation of meaning has come to be highly valued as a peculiarly effective way of providing targeted comprehensible input, and a lot of energy has gone into designing tasks that will promote it (Duff, 1986; Long, 1989; Pica et al., 1993). There are problems, however, with this line of thought. First is the lack of empirical studies that show a causal link between negotiated interaction and IL development (although see Mackey, 1999). Negotiation studies have appeared for the last fifteen years or so, but they are still preoccupied with a descriptive level of research which seeks to identify when negotiation is more likely to occur. There has been ample time during this period to demonstrate some sort of empirical link between negotiation and acquisition. This has not been done. Second is the point (made at the beginning of this section) that communication is effective even when morphosyntax is far from perfect because many grammatical inflections are redundant and context can often substitute for syntax. It is unlikely that missing or mistaken morphemes that should be marking plurals or verb tenses are going to cause serious communication problems and become the focus of negotiations of meaning. It should be noted that this is not an argument based on limited attentional capacities where form becomes out of reach because attention is absorbed by meaning. It is simply that form is not sufficiently motivated since the redundancy of language, not to mention conversational principles such as brevity (Grice, 1975), leads to whatever use of form is necessary to get the job done, without automatic need to be correct, complete, or complex.

Finally, there is the undeniable dislike people feel for owning up to not understanding something which another person has expected to be understood, and the undeniable irritation people feel when constantly asked to repeat or explain something. Aston (1986) has pointed out that a task which has been designed to maximise such episodes is likely to result in annoyance and demotivation all round. If Aston's criticisms are right (and it is striking that negotiation of meaning researchers have not responded to this criticism with any empirical work which counters it[3]), it is not surprising that a classroom study into the negotiation of meaning (Foster, 1998) showed very little of it going on, even during tasks which required information to be transferred. Although a few subjects sought clarification or confirmation of problem utterances, most played a very insignificant negotiating role, suggesting that gaining comprehensible input through checking and

---

[3] Editor's footnote: See Robinson (2001), and the summary in Robinson, this volume, where it was shown that complex interactive tasks which resulted in significantly greater numbers of confirmation checks than simpler tasks, were rated by learners as equivalent in level of interest, and motivation to complete them was also rated equivalently.

clarifying is not a popular strategy even in situations designed to promote it.[4] Significantly, the study also showed (in common with Pica et al., 1993) that where the negotiation of meaning does occur it is more likely to result in lexical rather than morphosyntactic adjustments, i.e. the theoretically most valuable type of negotiated comprehensible input is the least common. This may be because it is a gap in lexis, not in syntax, that is perceived to be the most common cause of a communication breakdown.

Most recently, researchers in the negotiation of meaning literature have turned their attention to the functioning of recasts (Long & Robinson, 1998), i.e. the provision of implicit negative evidence as the teacher (usually) preserves the meaning a learner intended, but provides a correct version of an ill-formed utterance. Doughty and Varela (1998) report encouraging results for this sort of feedback as learners incorporate the feedback they are given into reformulated utterances. Lyster and Ranta (1997), in contrast, report little incorporation of this sort. We have to wait for further research to see if the recast based interpretation of feedback (a) can lead to effective incorporation when provided in certain ways, (b) will generalise in its effects beyond teacher-cued situations, and (c) influences acquisition (see Doughty's discussion of this issue, this volume).

Performance demands of tasks

In none of the approaches above has the cognitive difficulty of the task been considered a particularly significant characteristic of its design. From an information processing perspective, however, it is a very important feature. Issues of cognitive difficulty have important implications for our understanding of how attention is deployed during task completion. There are competing accounts of how this is done. Robinson (this volume), for example, proposes a multiple-resources view of attention where performance is partly a consequence of task complexity demands, i.e. the task demands push learners to certain sorts of performances. In support of his claims for the effects of tasks on production he cites Givon (1985, 1989), for example, who proposes that structural complexity and functional complexity are associated with one another. In this view complex tasks would promote

---

[4] This raises the additional point that group-based comparisons may attain statistical significance. However, the significance may be achieved by a small number of individuals exerting considerable influence on the results which are obtained. To put this another way, the typicality of the effects reported in negotiation of meaning studies may not be very great. Most learners, if we extrapolate from Foster's (1998) results, may be unscathed by the experimental conditions that have been manipulated.

greater accuracy *and* greater complexity while simple tasks would lead to lower complexity and accuracy.

A contrasting viewpoint (Skehan, 1992, 1998a) is that humans have limited information processing capacity and must therefore prioritise where they allocate their attention. If a task demands a lot of attention to its content (because it is complex or puzzling, or someone else possesses information you don't have), there will be less attention available to be devoted to its language. This is not much of a problem for native speakers, whose knowledge of their language forms is proceduralised (Anderson, 1983) and can be executed automatically without requiring much, if anything, in the way of attentional resources. It can, however, be a considerable problem for language learners. Their knowledge of many target language forms is likely to be more or less declarative, and executed through controlled processing that takes up attentional resources. A study by VanPatten (1990) has demonstrated that learners cannot pay attention to language forms without a loss of attention to language content, and that when allowed to allocate attention freely, they will prioritise concern for content over concern for form. In this view, tasks which are cognitively demanding in their content are likely to draw attentional resources away from language forms, encouraging learners to avoid more attention-demanding structures in favour of simpler language for which they have already developed automatic processing (the 'safety first approach'). Conversely, very cognitively demanding content might result in learners paying insufficient attention to language forms which still require controlled processing and which are therefore likely to be poorly done (the 'accuracy last' approach). These two contrasting views of attentional use, and of the consequences for different features of performance, will be explored empirically below. For now it is worth pointing out that the two accounts might function differently for native and non-native speakers. In the former case, with fewer attentional demands because underlying language abilities are greater, complexity and precision may be associated. This may not be the case for the non-native speaker, since the language resources available are so different. Hence it is an open question as to whether functional and structural complexity and accuracy go together when *learners* are concerned.

We can look at essentially the same tension through the perspective of performance itself. Approaches to communicative language teaching have tacitly assumed that there is a tension between accuracy and fluency (Brumfit, 1984). But there has been little theorising about the different *dimensions* of performance, still less any systematic empirical investigation. In this section of the chapter, exactly such an analysis will be developed, considering first a more theoretical basis for the

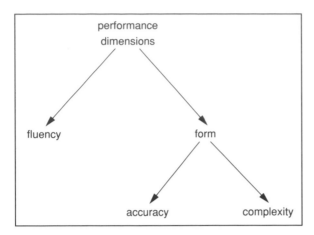

Figure 1. Theorising dimensions of performance

nature of communicative performance, and second, empirical work based on codings of actual L2 use in a task-based context. This analysis then underpins the more detailed discussion of task characteristics and of task implementation conditions in later sections.

Skehan (1992, 1998a) proposes a three-way distinction between complexity, accuracy, and fluency. The initial distinction here is between a focus on form and a focus on meaning/fluency (reflecting VanPatten's (1990) proposal that these enter into significant competition with one another). This is shown in Figure 1. This distinction captures the tension between, on the one hand, getting a task done, represented by the fluency/meaning emphasis, and on the other, using the task for language focus and development. A commitment of attention to simply transacting a task would lead to a concern to use whatever comprehension and communicative strategies are effective, and enable the pressures of real-time communication to be met. A commitment of attention to form requires more complex analysis, since it permits both a concern for complexity, on the one hand, and accuracy on the other. Complexity concerns the learner's willingness to use more challenging and difficult language. This may be because the language concerned is at the upper limit of his or her IL system, and so reflects hypothesis testing with recently acquired structures. It may also mean that a wider repertoire of structures is drawn on, even though many of these structures, while not completely controlled, may not be at the cutting edge of development. It may be that learners vary in how willing they are to take risks and explore new alternatives – some learners may be consistently more likely to experiment and engage in linguistic hypothesis testing. If this were the case, a willingness to use more complex language could be seen as an individual difference variable, related perhaps to the analysis oriented learners described by Wesche (1981) and Skehan (1986a).

Most importantly, complexity is seen to operate in tandem with the attendant language learning process of restructuring. It is assumed that when learners are in the process of realising that their IL systems are limited and require modification, they are more likely not simply to use more complex language, but also to attempt to pressure their own language systems. In other words, greater complexity is taken to be a surrogate of a willingness to experiment, and to try to extend or make more elaborate the underlying IL system. In contrast, a focus on accuracy is seen to reflect a greater degree of conservatism, as the learner tries to achieve greater control over more stable IL elements. In this case, the emphasis is not on hypothesis testing so much as avoiding areas where error may occur, and using an IL repertoire to achieve communication while avoiding more extending (even though possibly more appropriate) aspects of IL. Again, individual differences (IDs) may play a part, with some learners more concerned to avoid error, leading them to avoid risks and pressure, and to rely instead on a narrower but more familiar linguistic repertoire (see Sawyer & Ranta, this volume).

Analyses such as these, although theoretically motivated, are somewhat speculative. Nevertheless, they have the virtue of being susceptible to empirical investigation. In particular, it is possible to examine L2 learner performance on tasks to explore what sort of relationships emerge between the different areas. To that end, the data that is the basis for a series of studies at Thames Valley (reported separately in Foster & Skehan, 1996; Skehan & Foster, 1997; Skehan, Foster, & Mehnert, 1997) have been pooled and subjected to a large scale analysis of the relationship between dimensions of performance. Each of the studies included measures of fluency (indexed as pauses), accuracy (measured as the proportion of error free clauses), and complexity (essentially a measure of subordination, using the c-unit as the basic unit of performance, where a c-unit is an utterance consisting of either an independent simple clause, or sub-clausal unit, together with any subordinate clause(s) associated with either).[5]

[5] The research programme explored the use of a number of different operationalizations in each of these areas. Exploring the measurement choices available suggests that general measures were more sensitive to experimental manipulations than specific measures, e.g., accuracy of a specific language subsystem such as articles, or complexity assessed through theoretically motivated developmental scales. Further, pausing seemed the most direct measure of fluency since it emerged consistently as central in factor analyses of a range of fluency measures, including repetition, false starts, reformulations, etc. Complexity was assessed through subordination because, in pilot work, the measure correlated with, but was more robust than, measures of range of structure use. For further details, see Foster and Skehan (1996) and Foster, Tonkyn and Wigglesworth (1997).

In all these studies data was collected from task-based performance. The studies all used three tasks: a personal information exchange task, a narrative, and a decision-making task. The exponents of these three task types varied from study to study. The two personal tasks used were (a) instructing someone on how to go back to one's house to turn off an oven which had been left on, and (b) comparing what is found to be surprising, pleasantly and unpleasantly, about life in Britain. The two narrative tasks were (a) to tell a story from a given set of pictures, where the picture set had common characters but no obvious storyline (this had to be invented from imagination), and (b) to tell a story from a cartoon picture strip, where the story told in the picture series conveyed, wryly, the frailties of human nature. The decision making tasks were (a) to agree on judicial sentences for the perpetrators of a series of crimes, where the crimes were described in such a way as to hint at extenuating circumstances, and (b) to agree on the advice that should be given by an Agony Aunt to the authors of several letters that had been sent to her.

To address the issue of how performance dimensions inter-relate the pooled data from Foster and Skehan (1996a) and Skehan and Foster (1997) was subjected to a factor analysis. The results of this analysis are presented in Table 1. The table demonstrates that a three factor solution is appropriate for this data. Factor One loads positively (and highly) on the three measures of fluency, with noteworthy negative loadings on one accuracy and one complexity measure. Factor Two has high loadings on two of the complexity measures, while Factor Three is defined principally by the two high positive accuracy loadings, and one moderate and negative loading on a complexity measure. Interestingly, there is no suggestion of a task interpretation with, for example, the three measures on the Decision-making task loading together. Nor was there evidence of a proficiency effect, with high loadings on just one factor reflecting pervasive characteristic levels of performance derived from consistent performance across tasks and across measures. Factor analyses were also carried out on subsets of the grand dataset. For example, the tasks completed under planned conditions were analysed separately, as were the tasks completed under unplanned conditions. Virtually identical solutions were arrived at, suggesting that the structure concerned is fairly stable.

Results such as these could have a major impact in the development of a theory of performance. But more immediately, the implications of these results for task-based instruction and research are considerable. The results do not sit well with the multiple resource pools view of attention (Wickens, 1989) since there is little evidence that accuracy and complexity load on the same factor. Where there is such a joint

Table 1. *Factor analysis of pooled data from Foster and Skehan (1996, 1999a) and Skehan and Foster (1997)*

	Factor One	Factor Two	Factor Three
Narrative: Fluency	.73	.38	.19
Personal: Fluency	.88	.08	.15
Decision-making: Fluency	.71	.49	.09
Narrative: Accuracy	.18	.18	.83
Personal: Accuracy	.52	.06	.08
Decision-making: Accuracy	.24	.02	.72
Narrative: Complexity	.50	.16	.53
Personal: Complexity	.03	.88	.12
Decision-making: Complexity	.26	.81	.08

loading (in Factor Three) the complexity loading is negative, while the accuracy loadings are positive, suggesting that higher accuracy is associated with lower complexity.[6] In contrast, the results do suggest that the limited attentional capacity model outlined earlier has reality within the contexts of task performance. It is clear that performance is not defined simply by overall proficiency, with more able learners simply performing at higher levels across the board. Rather, prioritisation or predisposition (or both) seem to orient performance towards one (or two) of the three areas theorised to be important, with the result that the other(s) suffers. If we relate this to the acquisitional dynamic outlined earlier, it would appear that performance on a particular task can, at most, help *some* of the areas of language development, not all – for example, in one context complexity might be promoted, but this may well have damaging effects upon accuracy.

If we assume that the goal in language instruction is improvement in all the three areas (with perhaps the dynamic of restructuring-led change producing greater complexity, followed by greater control and accuracy, with fluency and lexicalised communication achieved last), then it is clear that the individual task has to be located, in a principled way, in longer-term instructional sequences which seek to promote balanced development, such that improvements in one area will be consolidated by improvements in others. To put this another way, it is important in designing instruction sequences (a) to monitor profiles of

---

[6] Clearly we can offer no direct interpretation of the multiple resource pools theory here since there is no systematic comparison of accuracy-complexity relationships with easier and more difficult tasks. However, the independence of the two areas (shown in Factor Two) or their opposition to one another (in Factor Three) is hardly consistent with such a view of attentional use.

performance, and (b) to be able, following the results of such monitoring, to adjust instruction to foster balance in IL and performance. To achieve this, knowledge of task factors which promote development in the different areas is essential, as is knowledge of how different conditions of task implementation similarly have selective effects. The next section reviews research relevant to these issues.

Task characteristics and task difficulty

It was argued above that being able to assess a task's difficulty is crucial to understanding how it might be performed. Knowing what demands the task will make opens up the possibility of using task design to manipulate the learner's attention between form and meaning in ways that may help IL development. In this section we will explore how tasks can best be categorised to reflect their cognitive load, and then how these categories might be used in planning a task-based approach to language instruction. Let it be said at once that assessing a task's difficulty is far from straightforward. For one thing it is not merely a matter of how difficult its content might be. This in itself is inevitably somewhat subjective: every teacher has had the uncomfortable experience of setting an 'easy' task only to find half the class utterly baffled by its content, and the even more uncomfortable experience of being unable to figure out how to do an intermediate level textbook task (say, some form of jigsaw reasoning), which the task designers have presumably regarded as unproblematic. Of course, it is often possible to say with some degree of certainty how a task's contents may be more or less cognitively taxing: talking about how many people there are in your family could be confidently described as less taxing for most learners than discussing euthanasia, and speculating on what is happening in some bizarre photograph is probably a lot more taxing for most learners than describing a story told explicitly in a cartoon strip.

But aside from this rather obvious assessment of a task's difficulty, depending as it does on a learner's general intelligence, breadth of imagination and personal experience, there are other less obvious dimensions to tasks that need to be taken into account. Skehan (1996), building on previous categorizations by Nunan (1989) and Candlin (1987) proposes an analysis of task complexity in three principal areas: language, cognition and performance conditions.

1. *Code complexity*
   linguistic complexity and variety
   vocabulary load and variety

2. *Cognitive complexity*
   cognitive familiarity
       familiarity of topic
       familiarity of discourse genre
       familiarity of task
   cognitive processing
       information organization
       amount of 'computation'
       clarity of information given
       sufficiency of information given
3. *Communicative stress*
   time pressure
   scale
       number of participants
       length of texts used
   modality
   stakes
   opportunity for control

The first area, language, is concerned with the linguistic demands of the task. Tasks which require more advanced structures, or which require the use of wider repertoires of structures, or greater densities of advanced structures, such as complex tenses or subordination or embeddings, are likely to be more complex. The same goes for judgements of task difficulty based on lexical level or repertoire or density.

The second area, cognition, is concerned with the cognitive complexity of the task's content and how this has to be manipulated. For example, the on-line processing demands of solving a riddle or a jigsaw *whodunnit* are likely to consume considerable attention while the task is being done, whereas the processing demands of recounting a simple story are likely to be far less. Another consideration is how far the task material is inherently structured. An account of a journey, with a clear beginning, middle and end, could be seen as easier to process than an account of a complex situation in which several narrative strands have to be cross-referenced. Also important is the degree to which the task participants already possess the knowledge that will be needed to transact the task, or the extent to which they must absorb and use entirely new information. For example, does the task require the participants to talk about themselves and their own lives, or does it require them to express views on imaginary people and situations which they have only just been presented with. In this regard, the task type is important also: have the participants ever done a similar task before (or even the same task before) so that they are already aware of what is expected of them and don't need to waste attentional resources on figuring this out? Finally, have all the participants been given all the information they require, or are crucial parts of it missing or hidden?

The third area, performance conditions, is concerned with a task's communicative stress and includes three potential sources of stress that could affect performance. There could be pressure on getting a task finished within an allotted time, especially if that allotted time is very short; the task could include listening, reading, writing or speaking, or any combination of the four, thus demanding real-time or slow-time processing, or both; the task may include several participants, all of whom have to be kept involved because they have information the others lack; the task may be viewed as a lighthearted affair at the end of an exhausting class, or as a pre-exam classroom activity in which target language accuracy is very important; the task may or may not allow the participants any scope to control or change its implementation.

From an information processing point of view it is possible that all of these factors, embracing as they do task code, content and conditions, have some bearing on how a learner's attention during a task is likely to be shared out and how performance is likely to be affected. What is needed then is empirical research that will explore factors such as these and determine what effect, if any, they actually have. Numerous lines of inquiry into task types have been going on for some years and their findings will be discussed below. But before turning to these research studies it is as well to acknowledge a very important question: *What do you measure to find out if task A was more difficult to do than task B?*

Of course, there is no simple answer to this, nor could there be. Language is not like reciting multiplication tables with easily identifiable right and wrong answers, nor (to use a better analogy perhaps) is it like reciting tongue twisters where difficulty could be measured simply by assessing speed and accuracy of articulation. Task difficulty has to do with the amount of attention the task demands from the participants. Difficult tasks require more attention than easy tasks. We know that content is prioritised over form (VanPatten, 1990), so difficult content is likely to absorb lots of attentional capacity and only what is left over can be devoted to language form. Researchers trying to measure task difficulty have tended to reason that inadequate attention to form will be manifested in a greater degree of dysfluent, or inaccurate (Skehan, 1998a), or uncomplex language during task performance. We argue this results from the strategies language learners adopt when unable to give proper attention to form:

- *slow down*
- *forget accuracy*
- *be simple*

While one can imagine that a task of awesome code and cognitive difficulty undertaken in extreme communicative stress might lead to the poor learner adopting all three strategies at once in order to get the task done, it is unlikely that this would be necessary for most tasks. It is then a question of which strategy is chosen by the learner to compensate for insufficient attentional resources. Mehnert's (1998) research, for example, shows that giving different lengths of pre-task planning time facilitates different patterns of performance, consistent with a prioritization sequence of first accuracy, then fluency, and finally complexity. But this is an area where there are far more questions than answers, reflecting how important it will be to conduct relevant research in the future. For example: are individual learners predisposed to an accuracy orientation, or a complexity orientation, or fluency orientation that causes them to allocate resources to one performance dimension at the expense of the other two? Or is it possible that task design itself could be responsible for a general shift to more accurate, or more complex, or more fluent language? Is it the case, for example, that tasks with 'difficult' content (e.g., a discussion of a particularly hot and controversial issue) will prompt learners into trying to express themselves through complex language forms because it makes them realise that simple language will not do the job?

Nevertheless, it is possible to discern some consistent patterns in the research findings that have been reported so far. A number of researchers (Brown, Anderson, Shillcock & Yule, 1984; Foster & Skehan, 1996) report that tasks based on concrete and immediate information are easier (i.e., result in more fluent and accurate language) than tasks which are based on abstract and remote information. Bygate (1996) showed that familiarity with a task's contents has an effect upon learners' syntax and lexis. Repeating a cartoon narrative after a three-week gap resulted in the subjects producing more complex and precise language than they had used to tell the story the first time around. Skehan and Foster (1997) also researched storytelling tasks and report that a narrative containing a well structured and obvious storyline resulted in significantly more fluent language (measured by false starts, repetitions and reformulations) than a narrative with a less structured storyline. Other research has looked at the way different task goals can affect the language produced to transact them. Brown (1991) concludes that tasks requiring learners to *interpret* information lead to greater complexity in language and a willingness to hypothesize. Similarly, Skehan and Foster (1997) report that a decision-making task involving tricky dilemmas of one sort or another are likely to lead to more complex (i.e. more subordinated) language than a problem-solving task where the available solutions are straightforward and more circumscribed. Robinson, Ting and Urwin (1995) conclude that a task set in the 'here and now' imposes a lighter cognitive load than one set in the 'there and then' as it produced significantly more fluent but less accurate language.

Taken together, these studies and others like them suggest that the performance of L2 learners in terms of their fluency, accuracy and complexity is sensitive to the cognitive demands of tasks, and that therefore the cognitive dimension of task design is a very important consideration. From the complex pattern of the evidence it is clear, however, that an assessment of the cognitive demands of particular tasks is not a matter of a simple taxonomy.

Three major issues need to be resolved if progress is to be made in this area. First, conceptual and empirical research is needed to better distinguish between the effects of IDs on task performance and the effects of tasks themselves. Given that performance priorities are unavoidable, different learners may characteristically commit attention, when limited, to one of the three areas covered here, e.g., the conversational risk-taker. Conversely, the task itself may lead to selective attentional commitments, e.g., structured tasks and greater fluency. It is difficult to know at present how to distinguish between these different sources of influence without additional experimental study, e.g., assessing whether dependable processing-based IDs exist. Performance dimensions in themselves are unrevealing.

Second, if one is to use measures of fluency, accuracy, and complexity, it is important to know how to inter-relate them if one is to establish overall task difficulty. The data reported in Figure 1 brings out clearly that performance is multidimensional. Proficiency is not reflected in across-the-board levels of performance. A choice needs to be made, therefore, between establishing one measure as pre-eminent (although it would not be clear which particular measure should be elevated in importance in this way, or why), or to derive some weighted composite index based on fluency, accuracy, and complexity. Progress is necessary in one of these two routes if one is not to regard task difficulty as simply an artifact of the measurement choices made.

Third, we need greater understanding of how task effects are altered by the conditions under which the tasks are done. The research reported in the next section shows that the cognitive load imposed by a task can be manipulated by the way the task is carried out. In other words, task qualities in themselves do not have automatic influences on performance, since such performance is mediated by what happens before and after the task itself. This interaction between the task and task conditions is not unpredictable, but it cannot be taken for granted either. It is to a consideration of task condition effects that we turn next.

The implementation of tasks: the roles of pre- and post-task activities

This section will review work that has been done in the area of pre-task planning and, to a lesser extent, post-task activities.

Planning

In principle, a wide range of pre-task activities are possible, including:

Teaching

- actual presentation of linguistic material, in an expository way, and then demonstration of the utility of this language for the task to come

Implicit learning activities

- inductive learning activities, with, e.g. particular forms highlighted
- concordance-based problems, where learners search for regularity in the material presented

Parallel or modelled or pre-tasks

- simplified versions of the task to come
- exposure to others, e.g. native speakers, carrying out the task which learners will do

Consciousness-raising activities

- giving learners problems to solve through concordance work, e.g. the difference between 'for' and 'since' with present perfect expressions

• mobilization of schematic knowledge, through, for example, the use of splash diagrams to organize ideas on a particular topic

As it happens, though, it is pre-task planning which has received the most extensive research activity. In this respect, two early studies have proved both seminal and illuminatively contrasting. Ellis (1987) used three related narrative tasks: (1) a written story related to a set of pictures, (2) an oral story told from the same set of pictures, and (3) an oral story told from a new set of pictures. Ellis hypothesized that the three tasks engaged progressively less planned discourse. Focussing on the specific measure of past tense morphology, he reported an accuracy effect for the regular form of the simple past – accuracy decreased as one went from the first to the third task. Crookes (1989) defined planning as giving subjects ten minutes' planning time prior to completing two information-gap tasks. Compared to a control group, the subjects who had planning time produced a performance which was more complex and more fluent, but not significantly more accurate.

Subsequent to these two publications, many other studies of planning have been published. Foster and Skehan (1996), using three tasks – a personal information exchange, a narrative, and an interactive decision-making task – reported significant effects for planning on complexity and fluency for all tasks, as did Crookes, but also for accuracy with two of the tasks, the personal and the decision making. In addition they report that the use of what is termed a 'detailed' planning condition led to the greatest level of complexity, whereas the greatest effect on accuracy was reported for the undetailed (standard) ten minute planning. Skehan and Foster (1997) confirmed these effects, as regards the contrast between control groups and undetailed planning, but in a new study with different subjects. In a subsequent study, they have shown that teacher-led planning is also effective, although in this later study, a distinction between language and content-oriented planning did not yield any significant differences (Foster & Skehan, 1999a).

Wigglesworth (1997), exploring planning effects on language *test* performance, has shown that we must also consider the importance of interactions between planning and other variables. She used FACETS (Linacre, 1992) to establish task difficulty on the basis of performance ratings by expert judges. Then she divided her sample into high and low proficiency groups. She reports that there was a greater planning effect on complexity measures with high proficiency students doing the most difficult task. A similar pattern is reported for accuracy where this concerns an aggregated morphology measure. However, when accuracy was assessed in terms of target-like use of the article system, it is the low proficiency students who show the greatest effect. The (not unreasonable) implication is that planning influences can be subtle as well as show more global effects. Probing these more complex interactions will be a challenge for planning research in the future. Mehnert (1998), questioning the 'standard' use of ten minutes' planning time, explored the effects of varying the amount of time available for planning, using, besides a control group, one, five, and ten minute planning conditions. She showed that an effect for accuracy was evident with as little as one minute planning, while an effect for complexity only emerged with the ten minute planning condition. Fluency was greater with increasing time available for planning, although the amount of gain in fluency decreased as the amount of planning time decreased. Ting (1996) investigated the effects of planning on spoken and written description tasks. The planned oral descriptions were longer than the unplanned, but, in the main, no more accurate. No significant effects were found for the written tasks. Finally, Ortega (1999), using narrative tasks, reported significant differences for complexity and fluency, and one of two accuracy measures.

Both methodological and substantive issues emerge readily from this literature. Methodologically, a first issue is that some investigators define planning as time provided pre-task (e.g., Crookes, 1989; Foster & Skehan, 1996), whereas others provide activities which engage learners in pre-task processing (Ellis, 1987). A second issue is that some researchers use generalized measures of actual task performance (e.g., Foster & Skehan, 1996), whereas others prefer specific indices (e.g., Crookes, 1989; Ortega, 1999). Finally, in terms of the findings themselves, there is considerable agreement that complexity and fluency are enhanced by pre-task planning. Virtually every study has delivered similar results for these aspects of performance. Effects for accuracy seem more fragile, however. Some studies (Foster & Skehan, 1996; Mehnert, 1998; Wigglesworth, 1997) demonstrate effects here, while others (Crookes, 1989; Ortega, 1999) do not. It is one of the most interesting challenges facing this research tradition to explore how an accuracy effect can be more reliably obtained, and what variables may influence it.

What this burgeoning literature does suggest, though, is the need for a clearer conceptualization of the nature of planning and how it might impact upon performance. The discussion that follows is somewhat speculative, but this may be a stage which is unavoidable if we are to better understand how exactly planning operates. Three aspects of planning can be distinguished:

- rehearsal
- activation/foregrounding
- task interpretation

Clearly, the activities which occur during the planning period and the mental processes they engage are crucial. First of all, we may consider the importance of rehearsal activities, in which the planning time is used to bring into working memory (WM) elements of long term memory which are perceived to be relevant to the task at hand (Anderson, 1995). Such elements may then be rehearsed, possibly in the articulatory loop (Gathercole & Baddeley, 1993; Ellis, this volume), so that they can be accessed virtually instantly during task performance. If this were the case, IDs in speed and capacity of phonological WM might come into play as some learners are able to do this more effectively than others (Robinson, personal communication). In any case, this rehearsal may well involve both language and content elements, although from the range of research evidence, one would expect that the material is more likely to be language oriented, and indeed, if rehearsal is effective, one would expect accuracy to be mostly strongly affected.

But it is also possible that planning time will be used not so much to assemble ready-made linguistic elements as to activate and foreground relevant material which may then be more accessible, even though it is not being rehearsed in WM. Anderson (1995), for example, discusses the way that WM may be conceptualized as holding in a greater state of readiness activated records from long term memory. In this respect, planning may not impact upon specific language, so much as make available a wider repertoire which may be drawn on during a task. In this case, one would expect the effects of planning to impact upon complexity rather than accuracy (cf. the more robust findings in this area).

Finally, it is possible that planning time may enable learners to engage with the content of the task, with the interpretation of what it entails (Coughlan & Duff, 1994), and with the schematic knowledge which is relevant for its effective completion. This may lead to the transformation of material and ideas in preparation for the task which is to be completed. This is unlikely to have a strong effect upon accuracy, but it is likely to influence other aspects of performance in two ways. First, the organisational changes that are achieved may drive the learner to using more complex language to reflect the different ideas that are involved, as well as their more complex internal organization. Second, it is possible that if preparation of the ideas and schematic knowledge underlying the way a task is done is effective, it may lead to a greater amount of attention being available during task completion. The result may be that other areas, such as fluency and accuracy, may benefit in indirect fashion.

Looking at task-planning in this way complexifies the nature of actual task performance. Wendel (1997) and Ortega (1999) argue for the relevance of a distinction between strategic and on-line planning. The former occurs in the pre-task planning phase, and reflects the processes such as rehearsal and engagement of strategic competence. The latter occurs during the task itself, and is concerned with whatever (snatched) planning opportunities are available while the real-time demands of the task are being met. Ortega (1999) draws on this distinction to argue that strategic planning is unlikely to have any appreciable effect upon accuracy during task performance.

The strategic vs. on-line planning distinction is a useful one, but it does little more than distinguish between the pre- and during-task phases on the basis that they occur at different times. The analysis from the earlier paragraphs shows that understanding planning is more complex than such a distinction implies. In particular, learners who set priorities between different aspects of task performance may use activity at the strategic planning level to prepare the ground for the greater accuracy that they wish to achieve while the task itself is running. For example, Robinson (personal communication) points out that learners may use planning time to help them avoid structures they are not comfortable with 'and', as a result, achieve higher levels of accuracy. This is an extension of a point made by Schachter (1974) that error analysis is a difficult undertaking precisely because learners avoid structures on which they may make errors. Planning may enable them to do this more efficiently! Rehearsal activities may similarly make greater accuracy more likely. The same would follow from learners who plan the *content* of a task effectively since the attention that is liberated by such careful planning may be directed to enabling greater accuracy, perhaps through engagement of on-line planning.

What this discussion implies above all is that our understanding of planning is now much greater than it was some ten years ago. The cost of this progress however is a much greater complexity in the set of influences which we now recognise as important. Unfortunately, we cannot always predict exactly how these influences will impact upon performance. One consequence of this may be that we will need to revise the research methodologies that are used in planning studies. Up to now, the research effort has been towards establishing functional relationships between planning conditions, task types, and different aspects of performance. Ortega (1999) calls for a much greater use of introspective techniques to establish what processes are implicated during the planning periods. Given the analysis of planning in this section, the time for this now seems right, given (a) that we have a range of functional relationships to draw upon, and (b) the wider range of processes that are hypothesized will enable introspection-based studies to be carried out which can be more targeted in the areas where introspections are solicited (see Jourdenais, this volume). If this is done, we are likely to gain a much deeper understanding of the cognitive operations which have an impact upon task performance and – the ultimate goal – the nature of the IL change which takes place.

Post-task effects

Even though the greatest research effort in the task literature has been towards the investigation of planning, there have also been studies that focus on post-task effects. Skehan and Foster (1997) and Skehan, (1998a) have proposed that foreknowledge of a post-task, if sufficiently salient in the learner's mind, may influence the allocation of attention while a task is being done. In particular, it is proposed that if the post-task emphasizes a focus on form, either through the 'threat' of subsequent public re-performance of a task, or through an awareness that there will be some later analysis of the task performance, then the meaningful communication during the task will prioritize accuracy to a greater extent than would otherwise be the case.

Skehan and Foster (1997) explored the effects of a post-task operationalization in the form of the threat of a subsequent public performance on three tasks, a personal information exchange task, a narrative, and a decision-making task. They showed that, as predicted, the post-task condition did not influence complexity or fluency. It did, however, selectively increase accuracy, but although means for all tasks were in the predicted direction, the only significant result was obtained for the decision-making task. In a subsequent study (Foster & Skehan, 1999b) narrative and decision-making tasks were investigated through a different post-task operationalization, a requirement that subjects transcribe one minute of their own recorded performance. Once again, it was the decision-making task which generated a significant result in favour of accuracy. In addition, it was found that the post-task condition led to a greater degree of reformulation on the part of the subjects, although there was no particular tendency for this reformulation to be associated exclusively with corrections from inaccurate to accurate. Skehan and Foster speculate that interactive tasks are particularly supportive of such an accuracy effect, although at this stage it is difficult to tell whether this is because of the communicative precision such tasks require, the discourse scaffolding that they provide, or simply the greater planning time that is available while the task is developing.

These post-task studies are consistent with the attention-based interpretation of performance argued in this chapter and the attention-driven view of learning argued elsewhere in this book (see the chapter by Schmidt). They show that learners make choices when they are transacting tasks, and that these choices are not neutral as regards instructional goals. It would seem that, although some planning studies do suggest accuracy effects, the more robust effect in this area is in terms of complexity and fluency. Contrastingly, with post-task conditions, the more consistent effects seems to be towards accuracy.

Conclusion

The central claim of this chapter is simply that attentional limitations for the L2 learner and user are such that different areas of performance compete for one another for the resources that are available. An analysis of performance has been proposed in which a basic tension between meaning and form is complexified by a further tension within form between conservatism and risk-taking, with the former manifested in a greater attention to accuracy, and the latter in a prioritization of complexity, and the use of more demanding (and extending) language. Viewed in this light, the central challenge in task-based approaches to instruction is to learn how to enable or predispose the learner to direct adequate attention to form, and how this directed attention can lead to higher levels of accuracy *and/or* the use of more cutting-edge language. The discussion of task characteristics and of task conditions explored how this might be achieved, as well as surveyed the growing body of empirical research which is becoming available to illuminate the nature of L2 development and provide principles which may guide pedagogic decision making. Particular stress was laid on the role of pre-task planning, since this is an area that has attracted a considerable quantity of research.

Several problems remain in our attempt to understand cognitive functioning when tasks are used in language teaching. There is certainly considerable scope to research the selective effects of different task characteristics on the nature of performance. There is also the challenging question of how one may conceptualize task difficulty when performance itself is multi-dimensional, with learners prioritising one area at the expense of others.

8 Cognitive underpinnings of focus on form

Catherine Doughty[1]

Introduction

The purpose of this chapter is to examine focus on form in cognitive processing terms by postulating plausible, psychologically real, cognitive correlates for a range of L2 learning processes that have become prevalent in the instructed second language acquisition (SLA) literature. Progress in adult SLA is thought often to depend crucially upon cognitive processes such as paying attention to features of target input, noticing interlocutor reactions to interlanguage (IL) output, and making insightful comparisons involving differences between input and output utterance details. To be effective, these cognitive comparisons must be carried out under certain conditions of processing meaning, forms, and function, i.e., conditions which promote *processing for language learning*. Whereas pedagogically oriented discussions of issues – such as noticing the gap and L2 processing – abound, psycholinguistically motivated rationales for pedagogical recommendations are still rare.

Focus on form is proposed as an instructional expedient for addressing pervasive, systematic, remediable or persistent L2 learning problems (Long, 1991); for instance, pervasiveness and systematicity as evidenced in emerged L2 developmental errors, persistence as evidenced in the less-than-targetlike production of advanced immersion learners (Doughty & Williams, 1998b; Long, 1991; Long & Robinson, 1998), and remediability in the sense of not fundamentally determined by immutable acquisition processes (Long, 1991; Pienemann, 1989). Such pedagogical intervention is claimed to be more effective and efficient than would be leaving learners to their own devices to solve these L2 problems (Doughty & Williams, 1998b). In general, these

[1] This chapter is an expanded version of a plenary address delivered at the 18th annual Second Language Research Forum, October, 1998, University of Hawaii at Manoa. I thank Jessica Williams, Michael Long, Kees de Bot, Peter Robinson, and an anonymous reviewer for insightful comments on earlier drafts.

focus-on-form (FonF) recommendations make pedagogical sense and are consistent overall with findings of SLA research. However, I believe that particular focus-on-form constructs, as expressed in pedagogical terms, are in need of greater scrutiny in cognitive processing terms in order to ascertain the validity of the intuitive recommendations and to inform more specific decisions, such as determining when best to 'intrude' into the ordinary language processing by the L2 learner.

The organization of the chapter is as follows. First, four definitions of focus on form are examined with a view to identifying the likely-to-be integral cognitive constructs, for instance, cognitive *micro-processes*, such as working memory (WM) and noticing; cognitive *macroprocesses*, such as input processing, output production; and cognitive *resources* such as the long-term memory (LTM) mental representation of the learner's developing IL knowledge. Next, a consideration of two schematic models (Figures 1 and 2) – one of memory and one of speech processing – is undertaken to facilitate discussion of determining the optimal points of intervention for focus on form.

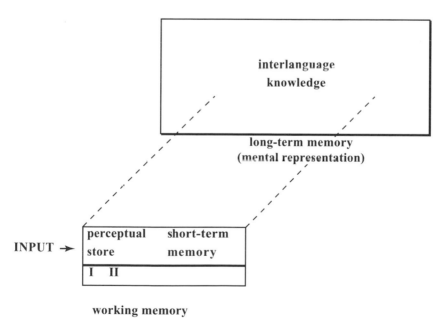

Figure 1. Memory in language processing (adapted from Cowan, 1995)

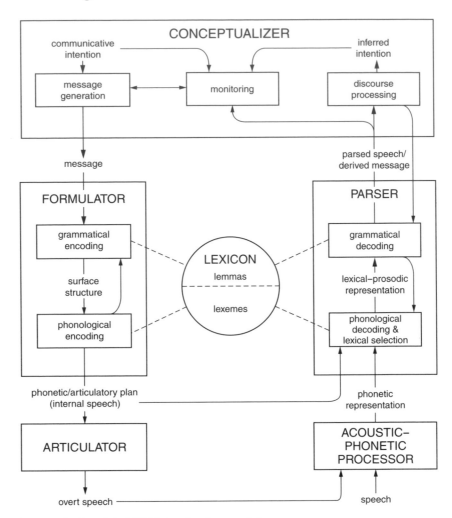

Figure 2. Levelt's (1993) Production model

Throughout the examination of definitions and the two models, the cognitive correlates of focus on form are identified[2] and then cumulatively represented in Figure 3. (Readers may find it useful to examine Figure 3 at this point and to refer back and forth from Figures 1 and 2 as terminology is introduced). The discussion then turns briefly to a set of specific pedagogical recommendations before finally taking up, in cognitive terms, three fundamental issues concerning the feasibility

---

[2] In the following discussion, terminology referring to cognitive correlates appear in bold-face. These terms are then represented together with the pedagogical constructs in Figure 3. Terminology referring to pedadogical constructs is underlined.

focus on form concepts	cognitive correlates
1. micro-processes	
focus	selective attention, expectation, orientation
focus on form (by learner)	simultaneous processing of forms, meaning, and use in working memory
focus on forms	explicit learning (often metalinguistic in practice)
noticing the gap	detection, cognitive comparison
focus on form, pedagogical intervention (by teacher or another learner)	cognitive 'intrusion', directing or attracting attention
2. macro-processes	
focus on meaning	implicit (experiential) learning
processing for language learning (Intake)	segmentation, acoustic, lexico-semantic, syntactic encoding; abstraction; monitoring; planning; rehearsal; memory search
language use	speech processing, i.e., production, comprehension
language learning (Interlanguage development)	internalization of input, analysis, mapping among forms, meaning, and use restructuring
3. resources	
interlanguage knowledge	mental representation in long-term memory
world knowledge	discourse and encyclopedic knowledge

Figure 3. The cognitive correlates of focus on form

and timing of recommended FonF interventions: (1) *The noticing issue*: Do learners have the cognitive resources to notice the gap between their IL utterances and the TL utterances around them?; (2) *The interruption issue*: Is a pedagogical intervention that does not interrupt the learner's own processing for language learning even possible?; (3) *The timing issue*: If so, then precisely 'when', in cognitive terms, should the pedagogical intervention occur?

Pedagogical definitions of focus on form

Of the four definitions of focus on form cited below, the first is the original theoretical construct, and the second is an operational definition derived from that construct:

- (1) '... focus on form ... overtly draws students' **attention** to linguistic elements as they arise incidentally in lessons whose overriding focus is on meaning or communication' (Long, 1991, pp. 45–46)
- (2) 'focus on form involves ... an occasional shift in **attention** to linguistic code features – by the teacher and/or one or more students – triggered by perceived problems with **comprehension** or **production**' (Long & Robinson, 1998, p. 23).

From both the theoretical and the operational definitions, it is clear that the key cognitive construct in focus on form is **focus,** or more specifically, **selective attention** (for further discussion, see Long & Robinson, 1998). In the second pedagogical definition, Long & Robinson (1998) suggest that any shift of attention from meaning processing to forms processing should be a brief response to problems in on-line communication. Similarly, Lightbown (1998) and Doughty and Williams (1998b) recommend further that the pedagogical intervention should not interrupt language use, or, stated in cognitive terms, that the teaching intervention should not interfere with the larger macroprocessing involved in speech **comprehension** or **production**.

The third and fourth definitions cited below have recently been proposed in order to clarify the crucial difference between the more cognitively integrated microprocess, <u>focus on form</u>, in comparison both with the more circumscribed microprocess known as <u>focus on forms</u>, involving **explicit learning** (often, in practice, time-consuming metalinguistic learning), and the more global macroprocess, <u>focus on meaning</u>, involving **experiential learning**. (See also Long, 1998.) The term 'form-focused instruction' (see definition 3), ever problematic in the literature, encompasses *both* focus on forms and focus on form (Doughty & Williams, 1998b). As shown in definition 4, however, whereas focus on form entails focus on forms, the reverse cannot be true.

- (3) *form-focused instruction* is 'any pedagogical effort which is used to draw the learners' **attention** to language form either implicitly or explicitly. This can include the direct teaching of language (e.g., through grammatical rules) and/or reactions to learners' errors (e.g., corrective feedback) ... The essential difference [between form-focused instruction and *focus on form*] ... is that Long's definition of focus on form is restricted to meaning-based pedagogical events in which **attention** is drawn to language as a perceived need arises rather than in predetermined ways' (Spada, 1997, p. 73).

- (4) 'focus on formS and focus on form are *not* polar opposites in the way that "form" and "meaning" have often been considered to be. Rather, a focus on form *entails* a focus on formal elements of language, whereas focus on formS is *limited* to such a focus, and focus on meaning *excludes* it. Most important, it should be kept in mind that the fundamental assumption of focus-on-form instruction is that meaning and use must already be evident to the learner at the time that **attention** is drawn to the linguistic apparatus needed to get the meaning across' (Doughty & Williams, 1998a, p. 4).

Taken together, these four definitional proposals point to the importance of what happens uniquely in **working memory** during <u>focus on form</u>. In other words, the factor that consistently distinguishes focus on form from the other pedagogical approaches is the requirement that focus on form involves learners' briefly and perhaps simultaneously attending to form, meaning, and use during one cognitive event. This kind of joint processing is claimed to facilitate the cognitive **mapping** among forms, meaning and use that is fundamental to language learning. It is the overall purpose of this chapter to try to examine the nature of joint processing in WM and to specify the kinds of pedagogical interventions that potentially can facilitate it.

Cognitive correlates of the components of focus on form

Memory and speech processing

It goes almost without saying that, to be comprehended, produced and/or acquired, language must be cognitively processed. However, the details of this are little understood and enormously complex, involving automatic, invariant processes as well as processes that are attuned to the conditions (both cognitive and social) under which the language input is being processed. Focus on form procedures potentially *can* influence any of these processes, but probably *will* do so only if the intervention conforms sufficiently with the nature of the language **encoding** underway (where encoding refers to the transformation of linguistic information at one stage of processing for use in the next) and *will* do so only if the intervention manages not to disrupt or halt the fundamental and ongoing cognitive macroprocessing that comprises comprehension and production. For example, when the learner is encoding a message for production, if the teacher were to interrupt the learner's utterance with a correction, the utterance encoding would likely break down completely at that point of intervention. On the other hand, if the teacher were to provide an unobtrusive backchannel, any new linguistic information could potentially be integrated to the speech plan in progress. In other words, although it may be intuitive to assume that overt and explicit guidance is the most efficient aid to L2 processing, focus on form starts from the assumption that pedagogical interventions that are overly intrusive actually hinder language learning.

To understand these issues further, it will be useful to examine two essential cognitive constructs – **memory** and **speech processing** – although an exhaustive consideration of these is well beyond the scope of this chapter. Nevertheless, some explication of the constructs as represented in the two models shown in Figures 1 and 2, taken in conjunction, is needed to enable the identification of potentially optimal intervention points for focus on form during particular cognitive processes or events. In different ways, both of these models depict the manner in which language input is **encoded** when going either from thought to speech, as in **production**, or from speech to understanding, as in **comprehension**. Together, the models schematize the cognitive resources that are utilized along the way. Figure 1 emphasizes the contribution of memory to language processing, and Figure 2 provides considerable detail regarding the nature of the language encoding that is carried out at each stage of processing.

As can be seen in Figure 1, **working memory** consists of a perceptual store for initial and rather automatic acoustic processing. Once the input is encoded acoustically, it then passes to the short-term memory (STM) store for further encoding. Rather than being in linear alignment as in earlier models of memory and processing (e.g., Baddeley, 1986; Broadbent, 1984), the current psycholinguistic conceptualization of WM is one of a presently activated segment of LTM (Cowan, 1988, 1993, 1995). In this conceptualization, the contribution to **processing for language learning** of already stored knowledge can be accounted for, since new information encoding processes have continual access to (activated) **IL mental representations** from LTM.

Figure 2, which is Levelt's well-known and generally accepted speech processing model (Levelt, 1989, 1993), shows (a) on the right-hand side, moving upwards, that language can be decoded for **comprehension** (for instance, during listening and reading); and/or (b) on the left-hand side, moving downwards, encoded for **production** (for instance, during speaking and writing). Applying and modifying the two models to handle the case of **processing for language learning**, first on the incoming, **comprehension** basis, it can be seen that language input is encoded roughly in the following ways (and see the right side of Figure 2, working up from the bottom):

- 1. Input moves from the environment into the perceptual store of **working memory** (see Figure 1) via acoustic phonetic **encoding**.
- 2. Acoustically processed input moves into the short-term store of WM (see Figure 2) via a little understood process of **analysis**. The input in the short-term store is available for use by **comprehension** and/or **learning** processes.
- 3. During **comprehension**, input is parsed via phonological, lexical selection, and grammatical decoding (where decoding refers essentially to encoding on an incoming basis). During **interlanguage development, internalization** of new input and **mapping** processes are continually underway. In Levelt's terms, new lemmas[3] are being constructed in the IL lexicon.
- 4. Parsed speech is understood via processes that utilize **discourse knowledge and encyclopedic knowledge** as resources, and speech plan **monitoring** to check for success of processing at earlier stages.
- 5. During IL development, offline **restructuring** of the **mental representation** of IL knowledge is continually underway. New forms-meaning-function mappings are made, and existing ones are fine-tuned in accordance with the linguistic evidence in the input. As for **processing for language learning**, on a moment-to-moment basis, **cognitive comparisons** of input, internal representations, and output can be made. Sometimes these comparisons can result in new insights.

On the outgoing, **production** basis, speech is processed roughly in the following ways (see the left side of Figure 2, moving from the top down, this time):

The conceptual content of a speech act is planned. Concepts (ideas) are then moved to the utterance formulator via message generation involving encoding into propositions.

Propositional messages are moved to the articulator via formulation, which involves grammatical and then phonological encoding, resulting in an internal, partially encoded speech plan.

Internally formulated utterances are moved to the environment (i.e., 'produced') via phonetic encoding and articulatory processes.

Simultaneously, the internal speech plans are returned to the conceptualizer for monitoring of the degree of success of the conceptualization, formulation and articulation of the message intent, in light of the relevant discourse and encyclopedic knowledge of the speaker.

---

[3] Lemmas are similar to subcategorization frames for constituents in generative grammars and to lexical entries in lexical-functional grammars.

In **processing for language learning**, a special kind of monitoring
involving **cognitive comparisons** of the intention, the input, and
the output is sometimes engaged in. Such comparisons are made
in the STM store.

It is important to note that, while the models of memory and speech
processing have been represented separately, any and all of these
cognitive micro- and macroprocess and resources are or can be simultaneously in operation during speech processing. Crucially, the
extent to which they interact becomes an important issue to consider
in planning any pedagogical intervention.

Processing for language learning

The processes and memory resources that are involved in processing language for comprehension, for production, and for learning are
grouped together in Figure 3 in columns opposite their L2 pedagogical counterparts. Some of these cognitive processes are the continual,
more or less automatic macroprocesses of IL development, such as
internalization of input, mapping, analysis, and **restructuring**. Others are shorter-term, sometimes momentary, cognitive microprocesses,
such as **selective attention, cognitive comparison**, and focus on form.
The key question for FonF pedagogical intervention is whether the
latter can have any significant positive effect on the former.

Macroprocessing and focus on form

Taking the case of cognitive macroprocessing first, it is generally agreed
that the default mode for L2 learners is processing for meaning. Insofar as the meaning is clear to the learner, and the language forms
that encode the meaning have already been acquired, then, typically,
it is hypothesized, no other processing mode is necessary[4] (VanPatten,
1989, 1990). When the language being processed is beyond the
learner's L2 ability, then processing for language learning is possible. Processing for language learning has been discussed in a number
of, by now, familiar ways in the SLA literature. Three well-known
examples are found in discussions of the notions of intake for acquisition (Corder, 1967; Gass & Selinker, 1994), processing instruction
(VanPatten, 1996), and $i + 1$ input comprehension (Krashen, 1982).

In cognitive processing models of SLA, intake is defined as that
portion of the available input that is selectively attended to and extracted from the stream of speech for further processing (Corder, 1967;
Leow, 1993, Sharwood Smith, 1985; VanPatten, 1996). Specifically,

---

[4] An exception to this would be metalinguistic processing of already acquired L2
knowledge.

this extraction requires the segmentation and selection from the stream of speech of those 'bits' of language that are morpho-phonologically and/or semantically salient. Among other cognitive operating principles (OPs) proposed for L1 acquisition, Slobin (1985) defines an extraction operating principle called OP (Attention) Sounds: Store any perceptually salient stretches of speech. To accomplish this, learners extract chunks that are larger than words at first, but eventually component words and morphemes also become perceptually salient. At the word level, morphemes located in word-final position are perceptually most salient to learners, followed by stressed morphemes, and finally, preposed morphemes. Hardest to perceive and, therefore, not likely readily to become intake are bound, contracted, unstressed, asyllabic, and allophonic morphemes (Slobin, 1985). An example of semantic transparency during IL development may be found in Zobl's (1982) discussion of the acquisition of English articles by an L1 Chinese speaker (Huang, 1971), a case of zero contrast, i.e., in which the L1 does not have a structure analogous to the target. The L1 Chinese speaker is forced by the zero contrast to employ a basic developmental form. The data reveal that the learner sometimes selects a deictic form to be used in the context of the definite article (for example, *I want this bike*), but never uses the targetlike article. Zobl (1982: 178) argues that

[t]he use of deictic forms as an initial approximation to the definite article represents an extension of the developmental continuum.... One can say that zero contrast obliges the Chinese child to begin the continuum with a more basic developmental structure. This means that the semantic motivation on the form is more transparent. While both deictic forms and the definite article contain the feature *definite* (Lyons, 1975), the deictic forms retain more transparently the pointing function to an entity in a reference situation.[5]

Gass and Selinker (1994) describe the intake component of language learning as a process of assimilating linguistic material, 'It is that component where psycholinguistic processing takes place. That is, where information is matched up against prior knowledge and where, in general, processing takes place against the backdrop of the existing internalized grammatical rules' (p. 303). Through repeated instances of segmentation or grammaticization on the basis of perceptual salience or semantic transparency, together with other cognitive principles of storage, mapping and analysis, learners gradually internalize the target structure of the input into the developing language system (see Slobin, 1985 for details).

---

[5] Zobl (citing Lyons, 1969: 279) also goes on to note that English, French and Spanish articles have evolved historically from demonstrative pronouns.

input   ⇒   intake   ⇒   developing system   ⇒   output

⇑

processing mechanisms

processing instruction

Figure 4. Processing instruction
(adapted from VanPatten, 1996)

Assuming such a chunking-and-segmentation cognitive processing theory for SLA, VanPatten and colleagues have developed a model of processing instruction which includes a pedagogical intervention designed to influence L2 learners' processing of input such that it more readily and efficiently becomes intake. In particular, processing instruction aims to make salient to L2 learners those aspects of the input which, as noted above, are hardest or least natural to pay attention to. Figure 4 shows the processing instruction model.

The most well known among the studies in this series attempt to modify L1 English learners' tendency to segment L2 Spanish speech input according to rigid English SVO word order rather than according to the actual features of the Spanish input (see VanPatten, 1996). Sometimes this processing strategy is adequate because Spanish word order can match English word order. At other times, however, since Spanish word order is quite flexible, and subjects can be omitted by virtue of its rich morphology, the strategy forms a processing barrier insofar as it results in apperceiving the wrong meaning. For example, L1 English learners of L2 Spanish tend to process the first noun or pronoun encountered in the input as the subject of the utterance. As can be seen in the examples below, the morphological cues to meaning differences (e.g., pronoun case, presence or absence of prepositions, and verb number marking) are not perceptually salient in Spanish.

A. *Te busca el señor.*   vs.   B. *Tu buscas al señor.*
   OBJ V SUBJ   SUBJ V OBJ
   2nd-sing 3rd-sing 3rd-sing 2nd-sing 2nd-sing 3rd-sing
   Pronoun V Det+N   Pronoun V Prep+Det+N
   'The man is looking for   'You are looking for the
   you.'   man.'

A. *Le llama el señor.*   vs.   B. *El llama al señor.*
   OBJ V SUBJ   SUBJ V OBJ
   3rd-sing 3rd-sing 3rd-sing 3rd-sing 2nd-sing 3rd-sing
   Pronoun V Det+N   Pronoun V Prep+Det+N
   'The   man   is   calling   'He is calling the man.'
   him/her.'

By informing them of the flexibility of Spanish word order and of their own natural tendency to process language according to their L1's rigid word order, processing instruction makes these differences explicit to L2 learners and then provides numerous opportunities for structured input processing practice during which, typically, sentences containing morphological clues such as those in examples A and B must be matched to pictures according to the known reality of the situation. Despite some methodological difficulties in individual studies (DeKeyser & Sokalski, 1996), overall the research to date indicates that processing instruction facilitates IL change in the direction of the TL, as measured by both comprehension and production measures.

Perhaps the best known of the initial processing-for-language-learning proposals is Krashen's $i + 1$ hypothesis, one among five hypotheses comprising his Monitor Theory of SLA (Krashen, 1982). According to this hypothesis, SLA occurs if and only if an L2 learner needs to process input that is currently beyond his or her current level of processing ability and, somehow extralinguistically, this slightly-too-difficult input becomes comprehensible. Although intuitively appealing and consistent with the intake and processing instruction constructs just discussed, the $i + 1$ hypothesis has been judged to be unfalsifiable given that there are no specific proposals for the mental representation of i (the current interlanguage processing level) nor for determining $i + 1$ (the next level up in terms of processing difficulty) (Gregg, 1984). Furthermore, no cognitive mechanisms for the conversion of comprehended $i + 1$ input into IL mental representation are proposed. And finally, the overemphasis on meaningful and extralinguistic contexts overstates the value of simplified input in solving the problem of the acquisition of formal features of language (White, 1987).

Inherent in all three of the above notions of processing for language learning is an assumption that the learner is somehow utilizing the input such that the input details which are processible become integrated into the IL system. To make progress in our understanding of SLA, however, any cognitive theory of such processes is in need of far greater specification. For instance, whereas intake processes are dependent upon the quality of the input *vis à vis* the learner's IL ability, other integrative cognitive macroprocesses – such as analysis with its component subprocess, mapping, as well as restructuring (see 2 in Figure 3) – are thought to be automatic in the sense that they are continually in operation regardless of the fluctuations of the quality of the input in the linguistic environment.

Little is known about these invisible, mysterious cognitive macroprocesses. None the less, there are a number of important theoretical proposals concerning the nature of analysis, mapping, and restructuring. According to Bialystok (1994b, p. 561):

Analysis is the process by which linguistic and conceptual representations become more explicit, more structured, and more accessible to inspection. Analysis proceeds on implicit unstructured representations and converts them to an increasingly explicit form. This process uncovers the basic categories of knowledge and is similar to what Bowerman (1987) calls 'off-line' change. It is the means by which cognitive processes are responsible for altering mental concepts of grammar in the absence of any ongoing input or correction.

Mapping is a key component of analysis. For L1 learning, Slobin has hypothesized that children engage in mapping basic cognitive notions onto a fixed set of phonological forms which they extract from the input. For instance, children consistently interpret the highlights of scenes around them as prototypically involving agents, actions, objects, patients, figures, ground, etc. Three examples of this are (a) the manipulative activity scene (Agent/Object), (b) the object transfer scene (Figure/Ground), and (c) the object placement scene (Figure/ Ground) (Slobin, 1985). In the prototypical manipulative activity scene through which the child acquires the grammatical notions of transitivity and causality, both the Agent (usually the child using his own hands) and the Object (the physical object manipulated by the child) as well as the relationship between them (transitivity) are cognitively salient. The two object-salient scenes (b & c) involve Figure and Ground and enable the child to acquire semantic notions like location, path, and direction. The basic figure-ground scene has been described as follows:

'The Figure is a MOVING or conceptually MOVEABLE object whose site, path, or orientation is conceived as a variable, the particular value of which is the salient issue. . . . The Ground is a reference object (itself having a stationary setting within a reference frame) with respect to which the Figure's site, path, or orientation receives characterization'.

(Talmy, 1983, cited in Slobin, 1985, p. 1178)

Slobin assumes that the scene information that is stored during input processing has to be stored in a way that permits mapping of extracted phonological forms and salient scene highlights. What ensures the mapping of forms to meaning and grammatical functions is the support of the physical context, as can be seen in the following examples:

(1) That's good. Give the   (Agent/Object; transitivity)
    ball to Mommy.
(2) Look, the ball is rolling   (Object placement; location)
    away!
(3) Look, the ball is rolling   (Object transfer; location)
    to Mommy!

Lending support to the proposal that context is essential to mapping, a study comparing the processing of event representations during interaction in familiar vs. unfamiliar events demonstrated via lexical and grammatical measures that language acquisition is facilitated only by familiar events (Farrar, Friend & Forbes, 1993). Similarly, Barton and Tomasello (1991) have shown that actions that are jointly attended to by mother and child, as measured by eye gaze, influence the order of acquisition of the verb types involved. Although Slobin's proposals for mapping- and storage-related cognitive OPs are complex (and not without their critics; see Bowerman, 1987; Gregg, this volume), several are shown in Figure 5 to illustrate the (as yet theoretical) mapping construct. Whether these particular formulations of the mapping macroprocess can be considered valid need not concern us excessively here.

Underlying this account of mapping is an assumption that language learners are predisposed to systematization. This systematization involves an expectation for meaning and function and that these should be mapped in some organized fashion onto forms. This view is generally held by cognitive SLA researchers, with the caveat, of course, that adults are not developing the bulk of the cognitive notions contemporaneously with forms-function-meaning mapping, as are children.

Perhaps the most cogent discussion of OPs for SLA is found in Andersen's (1989) cognitive-interactionist theory of SLA, in which he discusses the processes of mapping (as one of the composite of processes involved in 'nativization') and restructuring (which he calls 'denativization') in an attempt to explain variation in SLA. Andersen divides a set of 12 cognitive OPs for SLA into two groups. The first group of four principles are termed 'Basic psycholinguistic processes of perception and storage', such as the following: OP1. Attention (sounds): store any perceptually salient stretches of speech (Slobin 1985: 1165); OP2. Attention (stress): pay attention to stressed syllables in extracted speech units. Store such syllables separately and also in relation to the units with which they occur (Slobin 1985: 1166).

OP(MAPPING): CONTENT WORDS AND ROUTINES

Look for prototypical activities and interactions (predisposition). Assume that all words are content words, holophrases, or interactional routines. Continually try to assign new strings to content words.

OP(MAPPING): DICTIONARY

Store the meaning in conjunction with some representation of the context in which the item was encountered.

OP(MAPPING): FUNCTIONS

Map the leftover bit to an accessible grammaticizable notion that is related to the nearest referential words.

OP(MAPPING): EXTENSION

When you figure something out, try to map it to all members of that word class.

OP(MAPPING): AFFIX-CHECKING

Do not add an affix to a word that already appears to have one.

OP(MAPPING): UNIFUNCTIONALITY

If you discover that a form expresses two closely related but distinguishable notions, use available means in your language to mark the two notions distinctly.

OP(MAPPING): ANALYTIC FORM

If you discover that a complex notion can be expressed by a single, unitary form (synthetic) or by a combination of several separate forms (Analysis), prefer the analytic form.

OP(MAPPING): VARIABLE WORD ORDER

If you find more than one word order for a clause type, attempt to find a distinct function for each order.

Figure 5. Cognitive mapping principles (based on Slobin, 1985, appendix)

The second group of eight 'Additional principles' have the first set as prerequisites, and include the following: OP5. The one-to-one principle: an IL system should be constructed in such a way that an intended underlying meaning is expressed with one clear invariant surface form (or construction). (Andersen, 1984: 79); OP6. The multi-functionality principle: (a) Where there is clear evidence in the input that more than one form marks the meaning conveyed by only one form in the IL, try to discover the distribution and additional meaning (if any) of the new form. (b) Where there is evidence in the input that an IL form conveys only one of the meanings that the same form has in the input, try to discover the additional meanings of the form in the input (see Andersen, 1989, pp. 50–56).

Andersen's approach was to adopt those of Slobin's OPs that clearly provided insight into problems of SLA and then to postulate additional principles based on his own analysis of L2 data.[6] The case for the explanatory value of these twelve principles is made through examination of the well-documented developmental sequence for L2 negation, in which learners progress from sentence-external negation, through pre-verbal negation, finally arriving at the targetlike, analyzed system for negation of main and auxiliary verbs (Cazden, Cancino, Rosansky & Schumann, 1975). Andersen demonstrates clearly how the details of the sequence can be explained on the basis of cognitive processing and mapping.

In their discussion of the complexity of mapping that is inherent in focus on form, Doughty and Williams recognize that the term 'meaning', which is often equated only with its lexical component, in fact, subsumes lexical, semantic and pragmatic. To be more precise, Doughty and Williams note that focus on form includes forms, meaning and function (or use), and, following Larsen-Freeman (1995), they illustrate the mapping involved in acquiring the form, meaning and function of the passive (see Figure 6), noting in particular that both meaning and function mapping elements are often overlooked in instruction: Doughty and Williams suggest that the degree of effectiveness (especially over the long term) of focus on form, as measured by successful mapping leading to analysis, ultimately depends on the level of integration of the learner's attention to all three aspects of form, meaning, and function in the target language (TL), although this dependence may be mediated in some ways by individual differences (see Sawyer & Ranta, this volume).

Whereas the mapping component of analysis is continual and cumulative, the cognitive macroprocess of restructuring is a more abrupt change through which some aspect of IL knowledge suddenly becomes more efficient in mental representation. An example of the process of restructuring is the skill-building model embodied in ACT theory which makes explicit the difference between declarative rules and procedural or production rules (Anderson, Fincham & Douglass, 1997; DeKeyser, this volume). In this work, subjects are given examples of

---

[6] Andersen explicitly rejects the criticisms leveled by a number of researchers against Slobin's operating principles as being a case of throwing the baby out with the bath water:

'My position on this criticism is that rather than rejecting the OPs (with nothing comparable to replace them), we should work with them as they are and improve on them with further research. More important, however, it is quite possible – I would say probable – that the difficulties faced in testing some of the operating principles such as the interrelatedness of certain of the principles with each other are the result of the complexity of language and human cognition, not necessarily a weakness in the operating principles themselves or of the theoretical framework' (1989, p. 61).

Examples

A. The bill was paid by the company.

B. The wallet was stolen.

C. The data were collected and analyzed.

D. Spare toilet paper is stored here.

E. A mistake was made.

Forms

[NP-theme] [Aux + Past Participle of Transitive Verb ([by + NP-Agent])

Meaning

The events (the action expressed in the verb); the entities (the lexical meaning of nouns); and the semantic relations (Agent; Theme)

Function

Use when: theme is the topic (A, B); agent is unknown (D), agent is unimportant (C); want to conceal the agent (E).

Figure 6. Forms-meaning-function mapping for English
(Doughty & Williams, 1998b: 244–245)

regular relationships and then are asked to solve problems involving this relationship. Each time a problem occurs, a subject has an opportunity to codify abstractly the relationship in the form of an initial declarative encoding. An example (based on Anderson et al., 1997: 933) of such a declarative encoding would be: *Skydiving was practised on Saturday at 5 p.m. and Monday at 4 p.m.*: Declarative Rule – 'The second day is 2 days later and 1 hour earlier than the first.' After about fifty such examples, reaction times (RTs) in problem solving show a directional asymmetry, which Anderson et al. interpret as evidence of proceduralization (or what Anderson, 1982 called compilation), a process that results in a more efficient production rule: – IF the question is about skydiving, and the second day is D2 and the second hour is H2, and D1 is two days before D2, and H1 is one hour after H2, THEN the first day is D1 and the first hour is H1.

Inspired by Anderson's ACT theory of learning, DeKeyser (1997) designed a computer-mediated investigation of the learning of an artificial language, Autopractan (developed to instantiate testable language rules), in which it was demonstrated that 'learning of L2 grammar rules can proceed in very much the same way that learning in other cognitive domains from geometry to computer programming, has been shown to take place.' The evidence for this is found in examining the learning curves (as measured by RTs at each experimental session) of subjects who participated in 15 sessions of instruction on four grammar rules and 32 vocabulary items. Results showed a dramatic decrease in RTs between sessions 1 and 2, followed by a continuing, very gradual reduction in RT. DeKeyser argues that this reflects, in the first instance, qualitative restructuring, in which declarative knowledge becomes procedural knowledge, and then, in the second instance, gradual automatization of the now restructured, procedural knowledge as a consequence of repeated practice. The latter change is a quantitative one within the same knowledge components.

Another example of what is meant by the mysterious process of restructuring can be found by taking up, once again, Zobl's (1982) discussion of the effects of zero contrast on language transfer. To this, we can add the concept of congruence between the L1 and L2 and inspect the stages of the development of L2 English definite articles:

1. All learners go through a stage of absence of articles. For example, both L1 Chinese (− articles) and L1 Spanish (+ articles) learners omit articles in early IL.
2. When the L1 matches the L2 (congruence), the category of article emerges quickly, but the competence is usually variable. When the L1 does not match the L2 (zero contrast), there will be a delay in the emergence of the category (and sometimes there is emergence of a more basic form, as discussed earlier in the case of Chinese L1 learners of English L2 who sometimes use a deictic in the definite article context). Once emerged, competence is also variable for the zero contrast learners.
3. After the category has emerged, if there is congruence, it is not unusual for a delay in restructuring to occur at this point, where restructuring refers to the sorting out of the variable competence in the category to match the details of L2 rather than the hypothesis of the L1. For example, Spanish L1 learners of English L2 quickly overgeneralize the definite article to all prenominal contexts, even to the non-targetlike abstract and generic contexts: this seems to delay restructuring. No such restructuring delay is experienced by learners whose L1 does not match the L2. Once they have noticed the category, albeit late, they may be in a better position to notice the distributional details and, hence, restructure and move to targetlike use faster than learners with L1–L2 congruence.

4. After restructuring, competence is less variable and more targetlike (though not necessarily to the same degree) for both congruent and zero contrast learners (in other words, L1 Chinese learners still omit articles to a greater extent than do L1 Spanish learners).

Although interesting, further discussion of the 'off-line' changes that occur in mental representation – for present purposes, in IL development – is beyond the scope of this chapter, particularly given the still more or less theoretical status of this aspect of cognitive development (but see Karmiloff-Smith, 1992, for detailed proposals). For present purposes, it should be sufficient to note that mapping and restructuring appear to be both continually in operation and not subject to conscious reflection, although once the insight has occurred, the knowledge itself may become increasingly available for metalinguistic comment (Bialystok, 1994b). Both of these observations, however tentative, may need to be taken account of in pedagogical considerations.

Microprocessing and focus on form

Still other processes, such as **selective attention** and **cognitive comparison** occur on a moment-to-moment basis, are dependent upon current processing conditions, and may be more accessible to conscious awareness, though obtaining reports thereof is notoriously difficult (see Jourdenais, 1998; this volume). Whereas the cognitive macroprocesses discussed in the previous section are normally automatic and inaccessible, moment-to-moment microprocessing may be open to immediate influence – for instance by a pedagogical intervention such as focus on form – and this may, in turn, ultimately influence the macroprocessing. What needs to be determined is whether or not this influence facilitates L2 learning. For example, focus on form (in this case, but not necessarily, a pedagogical intervention by the L2 teacher), appears in the box at the center of Figure 3 with the cognitive correlate of 'cognitive intrusion' (Harley, 1984). This term emphasizes that directing or attracting learner attention to formal features of language is potentially an intrusion on ordinary cognitive processing, which may or may not be advantageous, depending upon degree of intrusiveness or congruence with the processing underway (Doughty & Williams, 1998b). We will return to this issue later in a discussion of how to determine optimal language processing intervention points.

    As noted briefly earlier, from the four definitions of focus on form that were examined at the outset of this chapter, it is evident that the cognitive microprocess, **selective attention**, is the key cognitive correlate in learner focus on form. A clear understanding of attention and its relationship to language encoding is fundamental to any discussion of the cognitive underpinnings of focus on form. The centrality of attention is also claimed by some for all aspects of SLA. Schmidt, for example, holds the strongest version of the claim that attention is central. Schmidt's Noticing Hypothesis states essentially that 'learners need to pay attention to (and notice) details and differences in order to learn' (Schmidt, this volume). For some fifteen years now, this crucial process of noticing details and differences has been referred to as *noticing the gap* (Schmidt & Frota, 1986; Swain, 1995), and by this is meant that learners must notice the difference between what they themselves can or have said (or even what they know they cannot say) and what it is that more competent speakers of the TL say instead to convey the same intention under the same social conditions.

For it to be cognitively possible for learners to notice gaps, they must have sufficient and coordinated working and long-term memory resources to enable the **cognitive comparison**. On the one hand, their own IL utterance or, on the other, a propositional message that perhaps could not be formulated into a speech plan for an utterance due to insufficient IL knowledge, each must be compared with the relevant data available from the contingent utterances of their more competent interlocutors. In other words, in the case of a non-targetlike but propositionally complete utterance, the learner would have to compare TL and IL differences (i.e., noticing mismatches), and in the case of an incomplete utterance, the learner would have to notice the additional linguistic material in the TL utterance (missing from the IL resources) which might have been relevant to the speech plan (i.e., noticing holes). The ability to make such a comparison suggests (a) that there is some continual relationship or connection between STM and LTM as shown in Figure 1, and (b) that WM, where the actual comparison is made, can hold more than the notorious seven bits of information (Miller, 1956).

In fact, as noted in the discussion of Figure 2, recent studies of memory (Cowan, 1992, 1993) suggest that WM is far more complex and integrated than held by earlier conceptualizations (Broadbent, 1984). Whereas earlier views depicted STM as 'either (1) the set of representations from long-term memory currently in a state of heightened activation or (2) the focus of attention or the content of awareness,' a more coherent view, according to Cowan, would be to say that WM involves both currently activated portions of LTM and attentional focus, arranged in a hierarchical fashion, with the focus of attention being a subset of the activated portion of long-term memory (Cowan,

1993: 162). In sum, Cowan (1988) suggests that *working memory is the sum of all activated information.*

Another definition of WM that Cowan offers is 'the temporary state of memory representation that would allow these representations to have a priming effect on subsequent stimuli' (Cowan, 1988, p. 165). Numerous psycholinguistic experiments demonstrating priming effects are evidence of the relationship between LTM and its activation in the short-term store. For example, in lexical priming studies, the mean time to recognize two items that have appeared in an experiment is positively related to how many times either of the pair has earlier appeared in another. These studies show that, at the very least, previously attended items stay active in STM in some capacity for a while after they leave awareness. A stronger claim made by Cowan on the basis of the lexical priming studies is that recently attended items may even be reactivatable from LTM. For present purposes, this kind of heightened activation of previously attended input items suggests an important cognitive resource for focus on form and task sequencing. If learners have just been attending to input that has already been identified as relevant to their language learning needs, the L2 teacher may take advantage of the fact that these items may be especially amenable to pedagogical intervention in this heightened state of activation, particularly if the learner microprocessing involved is cognitive comparison.

Another important and potentially relevant psycholinguistic finding concerning the nature of WM is that the length of retention of encoded input in both the perceptual store and the STM store may be longer than originally thought. Whereas it had previously been held that a subject can recall – i.e., hold in STM – about as many items of a particular type as can be pronounced in two seconds (known as the speech rate effect; see Baddeley et al., 1975), more recent studies have shown that subjects can retain material in memory for up to 20 seconds in each phase (see Figure 2, phases I and II) by utilizing cognitive processes of rehearsal and rapid searching through activated LTM resources (Cowan, 1993). Evidence for the latter is found in studies showing that the length of memory span and speech rate effect are greatly influenced if the items used in the experiment are already known words.

Taken together, findings such as these are suggestive of the length of duration of what Doughty and Williams (1998b) have called the cognitive window for provision of focus on form. This may be as long as 40 seconds, if the learner is able to rehearse material in the perceptual store and if already-stored IL knowledge is engaged. Furthermore, this brief review of studies has shown that the earlier conceptualization of STM involved an unfortunate separation between mechanisms of storage and mechanisms of processing. Theoretically, as Cowan (1992) claims, 'short-term memory serves as the interface between everything we know and everything we perceive or do.' Making connections between the known and the unknown eventually leads to knowledge restructuring. Consequently, the aim of focus on form should be facilitating the making of such connections, taking advantage of the potential of heightened activation and the more enduring cognitive window for intervention.

Determining optimal language processing intervention points

The pedagogical recommendations

Ideally, focus on form should come at cognitively opportune times, i.e., when the intervention can somehow be seamless with processing for language learning, rather than at overtly intrusive moments. This notion has been expressed in general ways in pedagogical discussions of focus on form (Long & Robinson, 1998: 21–26). Drawing upon this work, Doughty (1997) cites three criteria which must be met if a pedagogical intervention is to be considered unobtrusive: (a) the primary focus is on meaning; (b) the FonF targets arise incidentally[7]; and (c) learner attention is drawn to forms briefly (and perhaps overtly). An overarching pedagogical recommendation in all the above proposals is that focus on form should be carried out in response to learners' needs. There are two possible conceptualizations of responding to learner needs: curricular learner needs assessment (for instance to facilitate the identification of target tasks in task-based language teaching – see Long, 1998) and/or a contemporaneous, classroom discourse-based or other diagnostic analysis of L2 learning problems. The latter learner-needs-as-a-starting-point recommendation is meant to contrast with more formal and/or synthetic approaches to language teaching that are based upon notions of linguistic complexity (Long, 1991, 1998). Instead, learners' needs are defined globally in terms of long-term developmental needs, often referred to as the 'learner's internal syllabus' (Corder, 1967; Lightbown, 1992b, 1998) and/or in terms of short-term task-related or communicative needs (Long, 1998). The overall

---

[7] Although the requirement is that the target of focus on form must arise incidentally during the task, it is conceivable that the target be identified in advance through an analysis of learning problems. None the less, the teacher should wait until the problem actually does occur during the course of a communicative task (which may have been designed to increase the chances for use of a particular form).

recommendation stresses the futility of attempting a pedagogical intervention for which the learner is not ready or for which the learner has no purpose. Beyond this, however, it remains for cognitive SLA theory and research to determine the cognitively optimal intervention points for focus on form.

Assuming the efficiency of addressing developmental and communicatively relevant L2 learners' needs, cognitively opportune moments can be identified somewhat more precisely by examining four somewhat more specific focus-on-form proposals (Long & Robinson, 1998, pp. 22–25): (1) Focus on form 'draws learners' attention to mismatches between input and output.'; (2) Focus on form should take place at 'a crucial site for language development,' for example during 'interaction between learners and more proficient speakers or certain types of texts.'; (3) Focus on form should use 'pedagogical devices' that are appropriate for learners; (4) Focus on form must be 'timed appropriately.' With the exception of much useful consideration of the role of attention in focus on form (Schmidt, 1992, this volume; Tomlin & Villa, 1994), the remaining pedagogical recommendations have not been elaborated sufficiently in cognitive SLA terms. Accordingly, the following section examines focus on form during processing for language learning in considerably more detail.

Cognitive processing concerns

Taken together, the FonF pedagogical recommendations seem to raise at least the following three cognitive processing concerns: (1) *The noticing issue:* Do learners have the cognitive resources to notice the gap?; (2) *The interruption issue:* Is a pedagogical intervention that does not interrupt the learner's own processing for language learning even possible? If so, how can this be accomplished?; (3) *The timing issue:* If so, then precisely 'when', in cognitive terms, should the pedagogical intervention occur? The discussion will now turn to a psycholinguistic research-based consideration of each of these issues, using the cognitive correlates to focus on form proposed in Figure 3 as the point of departure.

The noticing issue

Do learners have the cognitive resources to notice the gap? To address the noticing issue, it is necessary to draw upon the cognitive constructs of attention, selective attention (noticing), STM, cognitive comparison and mapping. Focus on form pedagogy recommends drawing learners' attention to gaps. From the learner's perspective, this implies that

IL–TL mismatches or IL holes are noticeable (Swain, 1995; Schmidt, 1990, 1992, this volume; Schmidt & Frota, 1986), which implies, in turn, that the learner can hold a representation of the output utterance (learner's own or interlocutor's), as well as keep the relevant input utterance in memory. This begs the question of whether learners simultaneously (or at least within a specified cognitive window) can pay attention to input and output during speech processing. Based on current conceptualization of L2 learner STM capacity, there are at least three possibilities for how this kind of cognitive comparison could work: (1) Representations of the input and output utterances are held in STM and compared there; (2) Only a deeper (semantic) representation of the already-processed utterance is held in LTM, but it leaves useable traces in the STM against which new utterances may be compared; and (3) The memory of the utterance passes to the LTM but readily can be reactivated if there is any suspicion by the language processor that there is a mismatch between stored knowledge and incoming linguistic evidence.

All three of these proposals involve the language processor according special status to speech input that has recently occurred in the discourse. Therefore, evidence for a cognitive preference for re-utilizing recent speech would provide a strong underpinning for focus on form pedagogy aimed at helping learners notice the gap. Such evidence is found in three different kinds of research: conversational analysis of adult–adult and child–adult discourse, examination of naturally occurring speech errors, and controlled psycholinguistic experimentation.

Conversational evidence for the preference for recent speech At the discourse level, a detailed formal conversational analysis by Schenkein (1980, p. 46) has led to the claim that 'the systematic use of resources from prior talk in current talk apparently organizes the conversation'. Schenkein terms these *repeating resources* and documents through analyses of ten different kinds of conversation that topical, inflectional, structural and thematic resources that occur in the prior turn are used to organize ensuing conversation. The most fascinating examples of these are to be found in a taped conversation between two bank robbers:

A band of thieves had burrowed through the basements of a handbag shop and fast food outlet into the vault of a Lloyds Bank [to get at private safe deposit boxes] . . . A ham radio operator was dialing through his megacycles just before retiring on Saturday night when he happened to hear a suspicious remark about 'sitting on 300 grand'. He had intercepted a walkie-talkie communiqué between a man already in the bank vault and another man acting as a lookout on a nearby rooftop. (Schenkein, 1980, p. 21)

According to Schenkein's analysis, many of the repeating resources carry a theme over from one turn to the next, using the same discourse speech act (i.e., a complaint followed by a complaint). This occurs either within the same speaker's clause, across turns, or even minutes later. Furthermore, many of the repeats 'conduct inflectional and structural features down through the interaction', such that the previous turn provides an automatic format for the following turns, as can be seen in this example, where each interlocutor is complaining about his respective 'working conditions' (A is drilling into safe deposit boxes and B is the roof-top lookout) (from Schenkein 1980, p. 27):

A. Cor, the noise downstairs, you've got to hear and witness it to realise how bad it is.
B. You have got to experience exactly the same position as me, mate, to understand how I feel.

Here, the speech act that is reiterated is the complaint, and the sentence format (i.e., roughly the underlined part in the examples) that is carried forward is something like: You've got to do X terrible thing to understand how Y my situation is. In terms of noticing, it seems possible that interlocutors notice, retain, and utilize speech plan formats from the prior discourse, rather than expend the cognitive resources needed to encode a new plan.

Evidence from child-directed discourse   Further evidence for preference for utilizing earlier topics and language in conversation is found in studies of child-directed discourse, this time with the advantage of being consistent with a language development model, whereas the previous prior-utterance preference data have come from the speech of already competent speakers. A central issue in L1 developmental research is whether children can make use of negative evidence (defined as information indicating what is not possible in the adult language) provided to them during interaction. To determine this, it must be ascertained whether negative evidence is provided at all and, if it is, whether it is supplied in a reliable fashion, whether children notice this consistent evidence, and whether child language development is affected in any way by provision and noticing of negative evidence. These questions, well known in current controversy concerning the role of negative evidence in language learning, are presented in Figure 7, together with relevant empirical evidence (adapted from Doughty, 1994).

This cumulative evidence points to a conclusion that parents differentially fine-tune their feedback to the accuracy of child utterances,

Do parents provide negative evidence?

Adults are more likely to:

> • recast or request clarification of children's ill-formed utterances than of the well-formed ones (Demetras, Post & Snow, 1986).
>
> • recast ill-formed utterances with one error than those with many (Bohannon & Stanowitz, 1988).
>
> • provide "specific contrastive evidence" by giving exemplars (in their recasts) of the correct syntactic form or pronunciation immediately after the child error has been uttered (Bohannon & Stanowitz, 1988).
>
> • repeat well- rather than ill-formed utterances (Demetras et al., 1986).

Do children differentiate feedback types (i.e., notice negative evidence)?

Children show their sensitivity to parental feedback by being more likely to:

> • repeat recasts than to repeat adult repetitions (Bohannon & Stanowitz, 1988; Farrar, 1992).
>
> • imitate the grammatical morphemes contained in corrective recasts than to imitate the identical information contained in other discourse categories (all constituting positive evidence) (Farrar, 1992).

Does negative evidence contribute to child language acquisition?

Parental discourse types provide reliable information to the child insofar as:

> • 90% of adult exact repetitions follow well formed utterances (Demetras et al., 1986).
>
> • 100% of corrective recasts (those that supply contrastive evidence) follow illformed child utterances (note that this is by definition).

Effects on language acquisition:

> • children whose parents repeat after them more often learn faster (Nelson, Denninger, Bonvillian, Kaplan & Baker, 1984)
>
> • parental feedback has been shown to be correlated with child language acquisition of specific morphemes and syntax (Baker, & Nelson, 1984; Farrar, 1990)

Figure 7. Child preference for linguistic data in recent speech (Doughty, 1994)

that negative evidence in the form of corrective recasts is reliably as-sociated with ungrammatical utterances and, most importantly, that children notice and use the information during L1 development. Thus, it may be the case that child–adult discourse, like adult–adult discourse is psycholinguistically organized by a cognitive preference for using repeating resources from recent speech.

Evidence from naturally occurring speech errors   In a study which analyzed naturally occurring speech errors (L1 adult speakers), Harley (1984) has also demonstrated that material early in conversations (e.g., speech or concepts) influences subsequent utterances. Concurring with Schenkein, Harley claims that speech errors reveal that 'speakers must hold fairly concrete representations of prior discourse throughout con-versation which either can be incorporated into or used to influence the form of new productions' (p. 199). In psycholinguistic terms, this is known as the cognitive process of *perseveration*. While Schenkein's conversational data primarily shows perseveration of speech act forms and syntactic and prosodic features, Harley's data further reveal per-severation at the lexical level, typically as an associate to an earlier concept. These speech errors are categorized as topic-based, as exem-plified in Figure 8.

Interestingly, topic-based errors show that propositional content from the prior discourse can influence the production of subsequent

C: *Helping to load books into small boxes.*

T: At least they'll be good for books.

U: At least they'll be good for boxes.

C: *After a spectacular miscue during a game of pool.*

T: I haven't a clue what went wrong there.

U: I haven't a cue what went wrong there.

C: *Had just been discussing literature, but the word read had not been used.*

T: I'm going to eat a yoghurt.

U: I'm going to read a yoghurt.

Figure 8. Topic-based errors: intrusion of material from earlier in the conversation (but not in the utterance being planned) into the intended utterance (Harley, 1984)
C = context; T = target utterance; U = actual utterance

(1) Environmental contaminants: intrusion of a lexical representation of something in the speaker's environment into the intended utterance (e.g., word substitution):

(a) from another channel
C: *Glancing up at "Clark's" shop while getting out of car.*
T: Get out of the car.
U: Get out of the clark.

(b) from another speech event
C: *Talking about dress making while interlocutor is switching off TV. Announcer is saying: "The next program is 'Bee in my Bonnet'"*
T: Why not a plain white dress?
U: Why not a bee?

(2) Content errors (i.e., intruding thoughts): whole-word substitution when the target and the substitution are in strict or loose semantic association.

C: *Talking about moving to a place where the incidence of skin cancer due to sunshine was very high.*
T: Head for the west coast and die of skin cancer.
U: Head for the west coast and die of sun cancer.

C: *Speaking to a friend who was soon due to have a cartilage removed from his knee, which meant that his knee was not in good shape. Said while offering to help carry heavy object. No mention of the surgery in earlier discourse. No mention of thinking of the word "carting."*
T: You'll need some portage help.
U: You'll need some cartilage help.

(3) Errors made because of competing speech plans

(a) Word blends
fire/flames --> flire
shut/locked --> shlocked

(b) Syntactic blends
T1: It depends where they place their limits.
T2: It does depend where they place their limits.
U: It depends where it does place their limits.

(4) Errors due to alternative plans

T1: The sky is blue.
T2: The sun is shining.
U: The sky is shining.

Figure 9. Cognitive intrusions
(Harley, 1984)
C = context; T = target utterance; U = actual utterance

utterances, even if the speakers are not explicitly attending to those items in focal attention. This suggests that message propositions, in addition to actually uttered prior speech, are available for reactivation and use in speech planning. Further examples appearing in the category of content errors (see Figure 9) show whole-word substitution when the target and the substitution are in strict or loose semantic association. Clearly, both already-encoded language and unformulated concepts that are current in thought are activated such that they affect encoding processes. This heightened level of activation may be correlated to the level of noticing that is necessary for processing for language learning.

Evidence from psycholinguistic experiments   The third source of evidence for speakers' preference for previous utterances is found in a series of psycholinguistic experiments conducted by Levelt and his colleagues, which constitute a detailed, controlled examination of this preference for words or sentence frames used earlier by a speaker and/or the interlocutor (once again, L1 adult speakers). Levelt has termed this the *correspondence* effect, and describes it as follows: 'It is as if previous talk sets up a more or less abstract frame in the mind of an interlocutor, which is then used in the formulation of the next turn' (Levelt & Kelter, 1982, p. 79).

A psycholinguistically plausible use for the correspondence effect that Levelt and Kelter propose is that of keeping track of co-reference for the correct production and interpretation of anaphora. Moreover, if speech formats somehow remain activated in memory, they reason that this generally is more cognitively economical than perpetually generating speech anew. However, acknowledging that other explanations for the correspondence effect could include rhetorical style, politeness, and theme maintenance, Levelt and Kelter have, through a carefully designed series of experiments, ruled out any pragmatic explanation and established the roles in sentence production of short-term and long-term memory in the correspondence effect. This convincing reasoning is demonstrated in their analyses of results of several experiments on the consistent matching of answer formats to question types, shown in summary form in Figure 10.

In the first experiment, the correspondence effect was simply established under minimal conditions, as in the case of asking questions in two formats (QFs) incorporating verbs that can be used with or without prepositions. Results showed that, for all four preposition types, there was a 73 per cent chance of a prepositional response over a non-prepositional response when the question was in the prepositional format. This effect is significant because such a correspondence is not obligatory. To determine whether subjects were using a strategy of matching the degree-of-elaboration of the question (rather than the correspondence effect), Levelt and Kelter checked to see whether longer questions (i.e., those in the prepositional format) were more likely to elicit answers with main verbs rather than their elliptical counterparts, which are also conversationally appropriate. According to this measure, there was no general tendency on the part of subjects to match the degree of elaboration of the question. Rather, it seemed that subjects preferred to match question and answer formats exactly.

Subsequent experiments increased the STM load in various ways (showing that matching occurs even under distraction), provided

All Experiments: Semantically & pragmatically equivalent questions:

Question Format 1 (+preposition) To whom shows Paul his violin? (Ans1 – To Mary)

Question Format 2 (-preposition) Whom shows Paul his violin? (Ans2 – Mary)

Experiment 1: Answer question about picture

Hear Question (QF1 or QF2)	View a picture	Answer the question

Experiment 2: Interference in STM

Irrelevant Question	Relevant Question	Picture	Answer the question
Relevant Question	Irrelevant Question	Picture	Answer the question

Experiment 3: in vivo – telephone questions + STM interference

Question		Answer the question
Question	Interfering Clause	Answer the question

Experiment 4: Greater STM interference

Question	Picture	Rehearse 6 digits	Answer the question

Experiment 5: LTM recall of question format

Question 1			
Question 2	Picture 1	Answer 1	"What was question 1?"
Question 3	Picture 2	Answer 2	"What was question 1?"
Question 4	Picture 3	Answer 3	"What was question 1?"

Figure 10. Controlled experimentation

similar results from a natural context, telephone questions, (showing that the effects are not due to experimental conditions), and demonstrated that subjects undergoing an extreme STM load condition could report the format of the question to which they had provided an answer matching in format (showing that long-term traces of the question format had been established). Thus, it appears from these findings that whereas the non-interference subjects could simply rely upon the STM trace to answer the question with a corresponding format, the interference groups established an LTM representation that enabled a corresponding answer to the question because the STM was dealing with the extensive interference material. This suggests the existence of a heightened, reactivatable trace in LTM. What is interesting to note is that, from a FonF perspective, the presence of extensive interfering material clearly influenced the *type* of memory that was utilized in language processing, but did not interrupt the processing itself. Future work on determining optimal pedagogical intervention points should aim to tap into the cognitive resource of heightened, recently activated portions of LTM.

The interruption issue

Is a pedagogical intervention that does not interrupt the learner's own processing for language learning even possible? Doughty and Williams' (1998a, p. 4) operational definition of focus on states that 'it should be kept in mind that the fundamental assumption of FonF instruction is that meaning and use must already be evident to the learner at the time that attention is drawn to the linguistic apparatus needed to get the meaning across.' As a strong integration position, this could be interpreted to mean that simultaneous processing of meaning, function, and forms is a necessary condition for focus on form and, hence, that the attention to form should not interrupt the ongoing and parallel meaning and function processing. However, since it is known that attentional capacity is somewhat limited, this necessitates asking whether simultaneous processing of forms, meaning and function is cognitively plausible. In SLA research, VanPatten (1989) has claimed that learners cannot attend to forms and meaning simultaneously. However, the operationalization of attention in that study – making a hash mark with pencil – may have itself competed for attentional capacity. For greater insight into the plausibility of simultaneous processing, it is useful to turn to psycholinguistic speech error analysis and experimentation.

The first source of insight into the interruption issue is the analysis of naturally occurring speech errors. Speech errors reflect an alteration to an intended speech plan that results from some external or internal interference on processing. From the point of view of focus on form as a pedagogical intervention, it is intriguing to consider the possibility that such alterations could be beneficial if they are made in the direction of the TL. In this case, of course, the changed element would be different from the element in the learner's speech plan but obviously would not be considered a speech 'error'. Furthermore, if the impetus for the speech plan alteration can be identified in the native speaker's naturally occurring speech errors, and an understanding of its cognitive nature ascertained, this could form the basis for developing particular FonF intervention techniques to be examined experimentally in SLA.

In analyzing the systematicity of naturally occurring speech errors, such as the topic-based errors already discussed (i.e., in terms of how the speech of previous discourse shapes subsequent speech plans),

Harley (1984) developed the notion of 'cognitive intrusions'. Cognitive intrusions surface as speech errors which arise from various discourse, environmental and processing sources. The method of analysis is as follows: naturally occurring speech errors are recorded as soon as they are heard. Notes about the context are made, and the natives peaker is then consulted concerning (a) intended meaning, (b) whether or not the slip was noticed during production, and (c) any awareness of thought processes that could have been responsible for the cognitive intrusion on the intended speech plan. An example of an environmental cognitive intrusion, taken from Harley (1984, p. 196), is the following:

Context: Moving boxes. A is moving a box labeled 'SLO-cooker'.
A -> B: Is that box heavy or slow?
Target: Is that box heavy or light?

Cognitive intrusions become elements now incorporated into the utterance that were not originally in the specification of the intended speech. In the case of the SLO-cooker example, information read while formulating the spoken utterance intruded into the speech plan, resulting in the substitution of the planned adjective 'light' by the read adjective 'slow'. The range and variety of such cognitive intrusions are shown above in Figure 9. In addition to the speech-plan organizing influence of previous discourse in which the interlocutor participated (shown in Figure 9), there appear to be at least four additional sources for cognitive intrusions: (1) what Harley calls 'environmental contaminants', which reflect the intrusion of input from another channel, such as the intrusion of the read word in the example above or from another speech event as seen in the example in Figure 9, in which the words of a television announcer are incorporated into the utterance; (2) intruding thoughts or images at the conceptual stage, such as the (Figure 9) example in which the speaker said 'sun cancer' instead of 'skin cancer'; (3) competing speech plans, for instance saying 'shlocked' as a consequence of retrieving both lexical items, 'shut' and 'locked'; and (4) alternative speech plans, for instance when a speaker says 'The sky is shining'.

These analyses suggest that humans can, and sometimes do, attend to, internalize, and use speech, environmental input, or conceptual information that was not originally formulated in their own speech plan in their utterance. Naturally occurring speech errors also seem to provide evidence that attention can be attracted to something in the environment without interruption of the speech plan. These kinds of intruding elements may or may not be relevant to the conversation at hand and, often, are not something the speaker was fully aware of. A mechanism proposed to explain cognitive intrusion into speech planning is *roving attention* (Garrett, 1980, cited in Harley, 1984). Roving attention is susceptible to influence from stimuli and cognition that are outside of focal attention. Noting that such a mechanism is unsatisfactory on its own because cognitive intrusions, as revealed in naturally occurring speech errors, are relatively rare Harley proposes that environmental contaminants are only able to attract roving attention and thus to intrude into speech when there is some sort of conjunction between roving attention and sufficient facilitators, 'such that the intrusion can occur in an utterance where there will be a minimum of [processing] disturbance.' Furthermore, the ability of roving attention to intrude must decay over time unless there are suitable facilitators available (otherwise there would be a far greater number of speech errors).

Most importantly, the relationship of facilitation of attraction between roving attention and intruding elements is crucial to the ability to process information outside of immediate focal attention. In examining the data, Harley discusses two cases of facilitation: that where the intruding stimulus is already in phonological form, such as in previous speech, and that when the stimulus is a visual concept or a written word. The latter is difficult to explain – the only proposal thus far is that there are other cognitive systems responsible for processing environmental input, and they must have access to the lexicon and be able to prime selection from it: 'Environmental contamination appears to involve competition between elements, and bears some resemblance to attentional dyslexia and the Stroop effect in that competing representations somehow combine in the speech stream.' (Harley, 1984)

In the data shown in Figure 9, the facilitation needed to attract roving attention to the stimulus was either phonological, semantic, or a combination of the two. To demonstrate that phonological facilitation occurs, Harley shows that the probability of a speech error occurring is greater if the target word and the intrusion or substitution are phonologically similar, as measured by sharing the first consonant in the stressed syllable, by having an equal number of syllables with identical stress pattern, or by some combination of the two. However, for all three measures in the data, the probability of phonological facilitation, as defined in this way, occurring by chance is still very low. Subsequently, the additive contribution of semantic facilitation was demonstrated by analyzing the distribution of speech errors due to both strict and loose semantic associations between targets and substitutions. Strict semantic similarity involves any one of three relationships: antonymy (e.g., dry–wet), coordinates (e.g., east–west) and hypernym-hyponym pairs (e.g., dog–poodle). Loose semantic similarity is revealed in synonyms or close associates (e.g., determination-dedication). Overall, the evidence shows that there are more whole-word substitutions in which the target and substitutions are related than could be expected by chance alone. However, it is still not entirely clear what the precise source of facilitation is, since many errors involving both semantically and phonologically related elements also occur. In summary, cognitive intrusions on the current utterance appear to be the result of a combination of one or more among the following environmental and thought 'contaminants', aided by the attraction of roving attention to phonological and/or semantic facilitation: 1. Irrelevant material from the environment; 2. Especially prominent words in the preceding conversation; 3. Competing goals that blend; 4. Internally verbalized thought; 5. Competing message plans that blend; 6. Loose semantic relations, association, encyclopedic knowledge.

In focus-on-form terms, the critical point here is that what appear to be intrusions alternatively could be considered to be momentary expansions of the limitations on attentional capacity. Such cognitive intrusions would be welcome if the 'intruding' element were cleverly introduced by the teacher to attract any available learner roving attention. Of course, future investigation of this would have to take into account the integral role of phonological and semantic facilitation in attracting attention and the capacity for the L2 learner to retain the original erroneous utterance in WM.

A second source of insight into the interruption issue concerns the nature of speech plan formulation and the planning units therein. The architecture of the overall production system is generally agreed upon in the field of psycholinguistics. For example, in the case of formulating an utterance, as shown in Figure 11, accessing words in speech to produce words or utterances is generally agreed to involve two stages (this figure represents the formulator portion of Levelt's overall speech processing model shown in its entirety in Figure 2).[8] Stage 1 is lemma access: selection of the appropriate lemma from the mental lexicon (Levelt, 1989). Stage 2 is phonological access: phonological encoding of that item, that is the computation of the phonetic plan for the item to be used in the context of the utterance, i.e., the lexeme (Kempen & Huijbers, 1983).

At present, it is undisputed that mapping must take place between a conceptual representation and a word's phonological form and that pragmatic, semantic, syntactic, and phonological information all contribute to this mapping. Nevertheless, difficult questions concerning the time-course of this mapping process remain: (1) When are the various types of linguistic information used? (2) Is their use in each

---

[8] This two-stage access model is common to all modern views of lexical access.

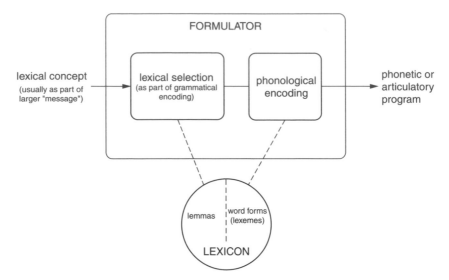

*Figure 11. Lexical access in speech production
(from Levelt, 1991: 4)*

stage organized into temporally distinct phases? (3) Or, do the various types of information exert their influence throughout the process of mapping from meaning to sound (i.e., formulation and articulation)? (4) What are the planning units? (5) How are representations planned and constructed? At present, there is a debate concerning the extent to which the two stages of cognitive processing are encapsulated (i.e., automatic and modular or discrete). A controversial question is whether phonological encoding can affect lexical selection and vice versa. From a focus-on-form point of view, automatic and encapsulated processes would be impossible to intrude upon, and any attempts to do so perhaps would have the undesirable consequence of interrupting ongoing learner processing or shifting it over to focus on forms.

The encapsulation debate centers on whether semantic information is segregated from phonological information, with semantic information being accessed and used at an earlier stage of lexical access than phonological information. There are two major hypotheses in this debate: the modular two-step hypothesis and the interactive two-step hypothesis (Dell & O'Seaghdha, 1991). In the modular, two-step hypothesis (H1) Stages 1 and 2 are non-overlapping and operate on different inputs. Semantic (but not phonological) information is active up to point of lemma access, and the reverse is true during phonological access (Butterworth, 1989; Schriefers, Meyer & Levelt, 1990). In the interactive, two-step hypothesis (H2) activation is predominantly semantic during lemma access, and activation is predominantly phonological during phonological access, however there is some activation of phonological information during lemma access and some activation of semantic information during phonological access. This interactive view is implemented in a connectionist spreading activation network (Dell, 1986; Dell & O'Seaghdha 1991, 1993).

According to Levelt (1991, p. 5) and the modular hypothesis, lexical selection proceeds in the following steps: (1) Input to the formulator is a message cast in propositional language of thought representing a speech act; (2) Grammatical encoding retrieves matching lexical items from the mental lexicon and delivers a surface structure as output, which is a hierarchical organization of syntactic phrases made up of lemmas. Lemmas are semantically and syntactically specified, but as yet unspecified for phonetic form. The syntactic specification involves category and subcategorization information, as well as the way in which grammatical subcategory functions of the lemma are mapped onto the conceptual arguments in the lemma's semantic description (e.g., thematic role assignments). The following is an example of a lemma, e.g., for the French word 'tuer,' to kill (de Bot, 1996: 539):

Conceptual specification: CAUSE (X ("DIE" Y))
Conceptual arguments: (X,Y)
Syntactic category: V
Grammatical functions: (SUBJ, DO)
Lexical pointer: 245
Diacritic parameters: tense, aspect, mood, person, number, pitch, accent

---

The semantic (i.e., conceptual) specification is the set of conceptual conditions whose fulfillment in the message is a necessary requirement for lemma retrieval. According to Levelt (1989), lexical selection then drives grammatical encoding and is more or less automatic. The units of planning are the lemmas themselves, which are activated when semantic conditions are met in the message. In their turn, lemmas call syntactic procedures that correspond to their syntactic specifications, for instance, verbs call the VP procedure (e.g., the lemma for 'tuer' above) and nouns call the NP procedure. In Levelt's words, 'Grammatical encoding is somewhat like solving a set of simultaneous equations, simultaneously realizing the appropriate thematic role assignments for all lemmas retrieved' (Levelt, 1991, p. 5). Similarly, in the third step (3) phonological encoding a word's ultimate shape is generated each time it is uttered. In other words, the phonological information is not stored in the lemma.

Although it seems inefficient to pull apart speech in this way, the process is apparently necessary in the production of connected speech (Levelt, 1989). The unit of planning at the phonological level is the phonological word, a unit that is metrical, not lexical, and is based on syllabification and stress (Levelt, 1991). To use Levelt's (1991, pp. 10–11) example, the utterance 'Black Bear gave it to him' contains two phonological words: *BlackBear gavitim*. The phonological encoding results in a compound noun plus a head verb with two cliticized nouns.

The lexical access process is not quite as simple as it might seem, however, since lemmas can become available at different times depending upon the speaker's unfolding of the message. Furthermore, some closed-class items are not conceptually driven but rather grammatical encoding drives lexical selection in these cases (e.g., the relative pronoun 'that' is called by the relative clause procedure). And some do have semantic content (gender, definiteness), however, and must also match the concept (except in cases syntactically driven by agreement).

While in agreement that lexical access is a two-stage process that is predominantly semantic in the first stage and mainly phonological in the second stage, the interaction model in hypothesis 2 allows for influence between and within the two levels. The interactive model is represented in the spreading activation network shown in Figure 12. The model utilizes the same processing units found in Levelt's production model, but these are organized into a network which allows for a bi-directional spread of activation between units at adjacent

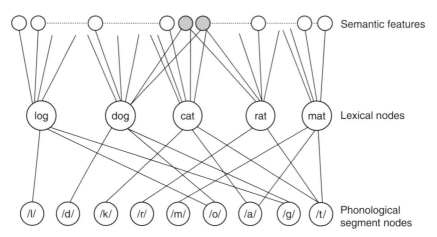

Figure 12. Spreading activation during lexical access in speech production (from Dell & O'Seaghdha, 1991: 294)

levels. The steps in lexical access in spreading activation accounts are as follows (Dell & O'Seaghdha, 1991, p. 295):

1. The semantic units of the concept-to-be-lexicalized receive external inputs.
2. Activation spreads in an unconstrained fashion throughout the network.
3. The most highly activated word unit is selected. In the case of sentence production, selection entails the linkage of this unit to the developing syntactic frame for the sentence ... and is followed by post-selection inhibition of other units (activation $= 0$).
4. When the word is ready for phonological encoding, it is given a triggering jolt of activation. For multi-word utterances, which require advance planning, the timing of this external signal is controlled by the syntactic frame slot (the lemma) that the unit is linked to.
5. Activation continues to spread, but because of the extra activation of the selected word unit the appropriate phonological units at the adjacent level become significantly activated.
6. The most active phonological units are selected and linked to slots in a constructed phonological wordshape frame, a data structure analogous to a syntactic frame.

In comparison, the lexical access and modular models are similar, differing primarily in positions taken regarding the interaction or lack thereof between lexical selection and phonological encoding: Levelt envisions the various stages of lexical retrieval and phonological encoding as largely encapsulated or modular, whereas Dell and Reich (1981) claim that speech error work, such as that of Harley (1984) (see Figures 8 & 9) shows that errors of lexical selection and of phonological encoding are not independent. For instance, there is an observed lexical bias effect – that is, errors in phonological encoding more often result in real words than in non-words. According to Dell and Reich, only forward and backward spreading activation can account for this.

Priming and interference techniques are used to study the encapsulation debate (also referred to as the discreteness question or the question of modularity in lexical access). In the standard interference paradigm researchers superimpose an interfering word on a picture to be named. However, a common variation of this procedure involves naming pictures in the presence of an auditorily presented interfering word. Several conditions of interfering words are included in the design to examine all possible (non)interactions of phonological and semantic encoding processes, as shown here:

semantic	cat-dog (picture-interfering word)
phonological	fog-dog
unrelated	roof-dog
silence	no interference

Priming studies have employed one of a number of variations of the basic paradigm to investigate the time-course of semantic and phonological encoding during lexical access. In work by Schriefers et al. (1990), subjects named pictures in the presence of semantically or phonologically related spoken words, or in a variety of control conditions. To examine the time-course of semantic and phonological access, the relative onsets of pictures and words were varied such that the word onset preceded the picture by 150 ms, coincided with it, or lagged it by 150 ms. The findings revealed evidence of semantic interference (relative to unrelated controls) when the words preceded the pictures, but not in the two later word presentation conditions. In contrast, there was evidence of facilitation for phonologically related words relative to the control for the two later word onset conditions, but no effect when the word onset precedes the picture. These findings are taken to support convincingly a distinction between phases.[9]

In their discussion of this and other work Dell and O'Seaghdha (1991) point out that findings to date converge on three phenomena to be explained: 1. Early semantic activation without phonological activation; 2. Absence of mediated semantic-phonological priming; 3. Presence of phonological priming in the absence of late semantic priming. Schriefers et al. (1990) argue for the discrete, modular, two-step account of lexical access. However, looking at the same data, Dell and O'Seaghdha argue that it is compatible with the interactive spreading activation view which, for them, is the account to be preferred because it can also handle speech errors, while the modular account cannot do so. To determine the status of semantic-phonological priming, Dell and O'Seaghdha modeled spreading activation under the following conditions: 'cat'—intended word; 'dog'—semantically related; 'mat'—phonologically related; 'rat'—semantically and phonologically related (mixed word); 'log'—related only through mediation of the semantic relative (mediated word).

After ten cycles, 'cat' received the highest activation, followed by 'rat'. 'Dog' and 'mat' received intermediary activation, whereas 'log',

---

[9] To explain the finding of facilitation in phonological encoding, it was suggested that related words in this study shared initial segments with the names resulting in little time for the conflicting later segments to interfere.

with the smallest number of shared features, was least activated. These results can be shown to be related to distribution of the naturally occurring speech error types representing the same conditions. The critical result is that there is approximately a tenfold difference in activation levels between the mixed condition (rat) and the mediated condition (log). Dell and O'Seaghdha claim that this is because, in the spreading activation model, the mixed condition achieves convergent, additive activation from semantic and phonological sources, whereas the mediated condition receives divergent activation in which the contributions of semantic and phonological relations are diluted. In the mixed case, 'rat' receives activation from semantic and phonological nodes shared with 'cat'. But in the mediated case, 'log' results in only phonological activation from the mediating word 'dog', and this activation is scaled down by the relatively weak activation of the mediator.

Thus, the general answer to the question of the time-course of semantic and phonological encoding seems to be that the production system appears to be globally modular (e.g., in the terms shown in Figure 2, encoding during acoustic processing/articulation is distinct from that during parsing/formulation), but locally interactive (e.g., grammatical and phonological encoding processes during parsing/formulation may influence each other) (Dell & O'Seaghdha, 1991). While, as has been argued by Levelt (1989), linguistic rule systems supply external activation to discrete levels of the lexical network, this does not mean that interaction within the lexical network can be entirely discounted. Speech errors suggest that interaction in the lexical system allows for exchange of activation at adjacent levels. Mingling is most evident when activation sources converge. This account gives the spreading activation model the ability to account for interactive error effects such as mixed errors.

This interpretation is encouraging for focus on form, given that encapsulation of encoding would represent an insurmountable cognitive obstacle to effective pedagogical intervention seeking to supply information to the forms-function-meaning mapping process. Another important question concerning the time-course of encoding – one that is also vital for focus on form intervention – is that of how far ahead utterances are planned. The time-course matters become more complex when addressed within the advance planning context of sentence production. Time-course of utterance planning experiments reveal that speakers plan further ahead semantically than phonologically, but it is not yet known how far ahead of articulation on either plane the speech plan goes. It has been found, however, that the size and nature of the sentence fragment that speakers encode phonologically before utterance onset do not correspond to syllables or words but rather to sentence structure (Ferreira, 1991). What is not clear is whether this sentence structure encompasses a syntactic unit (e.g., a lemma) or a prosodic unit (e.g., a phonological word). Accordingly, the focus of interest in studies of utterance planning is the time-course of the construction of 'syntactic' and sublexical representations. This concerns the order of accessing lemmas (L) and phonological forms (P). There are three hypotheses concerning this ordering (Dell & O'Seaghdha, 1991):

H1 The lemma buffering hypothesis: several lemmas are selected before the corresponding phonological forms are filled in.
   (Kempen & Huijbers, 1983)
//L(1) L(2) L(3) / P(1) P(2) P(3)//
H2 The structurally determined lemma-buffering hypothesis: as above, but takes into account major structural boundaries:
// L(1) L(2) / P(1) P(2) // L(3) / P(3)//
H3 The word-by word hypothesis: as above, proceeds but word by word:
// L(1) P1) // L(2) P(2) // L(3) P(3)//

Speech error data provide the evidence for lemma buffering and shows that, in general, the extent of advance planning at the syntactic level exceeds the extent of planning at the phonological level. Furthermore, lemmas within a clause may be simultaneously processed, but those in separate clauses typically are not. Most psycholinguists make a distinction between initial activation of lemmas due to conceptual activation and eventual insertion of lemmas into syntactic tree. Whereas the clause is likely the domain of advance planning at the syntactic level, the extent of the domain of phonological planning is not yet known. There are also three hypotheses concerning phonological planning; however, there is not enough evidence to distinguish among these. (Dell & O'Seaghdha, 1991, pp. 305–6):

H1 The word-by-word hypothesis: only the word about to be uttered and the following word are prepared, regardless of the structure of the sentence. This view has the advantage of simplicity and it may be all that is needed in order to accommodate phonological and phonetic rules. Only forms of adjacent words need be known to get the proper phonological form of a word (Levelt, 1989).
H2 The syntactic-structure hypotheses: words are phonologically planned in accordance with syntactic units. Given that phonological advance planning should be less extensive than syntactic, the most common proposal has been that phonological forms are retrieved in subclausal chunks corresponding to major syntactic phrases.

H3 The prosodic-structure hypothesis: phonological words are
concatenated to form phonological phrases which are,
prototypically, a content word and any preceding function
words. One or more phonological phrases may then constitute
an intonational phrase, a level of analysis over which
intonational contours are computed. For the most part,
however, prosodic units such as phonological phrases
correspond to syntactic phrases.

Production priming experiments are currently employed in an effort
to understand the time-course of multi-word utterance planning. First,
a subject views a display whose purpose is to induce the preparation
of an utterance. The display can be one of four types: (1) Reiteration,
in which subjects are instructed to repeat a single displayed utterance;
(2) Choice procedure, in which subjects are given two utterances to
view, but are only asked to prepare one for production; (3) Construction, in which subjects are given ingredients and are directed to
combine them into an utterance; and (4) Pictorial displays, in which
carefully selected and normed pictures are presented for descriptions.
This latter display type elicits more natural speech production. On
viewing the display, of whatever type, the subject prepares the utterance. Subsequently, on most trials, the subject simply produces the
prepared utterance, but on critical trials, a target word is displayed.
The subject responds to the target and may or may not be required
to produce the prepared utterance before the trial ends. Latency and
accuracy of response are the dependent measures. The design is shown
here (* refers to the first of the four display types outlined above):

View	Prepare 2/3 trials:	See * and say utterance
Display	Utterance 1/3 trials:	See and respond to target, then see * and say utterance

The logic is that production plans serve as primes, and the extent to
which the primes influence responses to related targets assesses the
extent and nature of the utterance plans. Target sentences that reflect
differing plans are embodied in active and passive sentences. Example
primes are REMOVE (BOXER, COAT) or REMOVE (BY BOXER,
COAT). Dell and O'Seaghdha carried out these production experiments using the construction and reiteration types of planning shown
above to investigate both phonological and semantic priming. The
findings pertaining to phonological priming effects show that when
the critical word was early in the sentence (as in passives: *The coat
was removed by the boxer*), responses to phonologically related targets
were significantly inhibited. In contrast, when the critical word was
late in the sentence (as in actives: *The boxer removed the coat*), there

was a significant facilitatory effect for phonologically related primes. Dell and O'Seaghdha take this to mean that there are differences in the phonological plan for early and late words in an utterance. The inhibitory effects found are indicative of a state in which access to the phonological form of the prime is complete or nearly complete. As Dell and O'Seaghdha explain, similarity-based competition occurs only when both the initial and the contrasting segment of the prime are present. More specifically, in the passive condition, phonological planning of the second word is quite advanced. In contrast, the facilitatory effect in the active condition, in which the critical word is last, reflects a lesser degree of planning of the word. The contrasting segments are not present in sufficient strength, and so there is no inhibition. Rather, there is an opportunity for facilitation by those (similar) segments that are preliminarily activated. In sum, inhibition indicates a great deal of progress toward a word's phonological form, whereas facilitation indicates a much lesser degree of preparation.

In an experiment using the reiteration display format described above, results were essentially the same as in the construction experiment, but there was a semantic effect this time. The semantic effect differed in nature, however, from the phonological effect in that position had much less influence on the amount and direction of semantic priming than it did with phonological priming. Dell and O'Seaghdha (1991, pp. 310–11) claim that 'this is exactly what one would expect if planning at the lemma level exceeds that at the phonological level.' In other words, the significant semantic and phonological facilitation in the active condition, where the critical word was late, can be taken as evidence of lemma retrieval. Phonological access associated with inhibition lags behind lemma retrieval, giving evidence for some kind of lemma buffering. Dell and O'Seaghdha (pp. 311–12) interpret their findings as follows:

Our conclusions are, for the most part, in agreement with the standard view of production (e.g., Garrett, 1975; Levelt, 1989) in which the production system distinguishes between form-related and meaning-related processes. The reach of advance planning appears to be different for meaning and form, and meaning and form also appear to be separable over the time-course of the retrieval of individual words. Though this evidence tends to favor the idea of discrete stages in production, we believe that a degree of local interaction in the course of lemma and phonological access is necessary to account for mixed semantic-phonological speech errors. These effects can be accounted for entirely by assuming that the phonological and semantic-syntactic representations of words are connected in a lexical network. That is, the interaction is a product of lexical retrieval processes, not of the way that syntactic and phonological rules are represented and used.

In summary, a convincing case has been made that the overall encoding stages of speech plan processing (see Figure 2) are largely modular, but there do appear to be small cognitive windows of opportunity for 'intrusions' and interactions among meaning (for instance semantic) and forms (for instance phonological) components within lexical access and during advance planning for utterance production. An intriguing question is the extent to which such opportunities, heretofore discussed in terms of fully mature, native-speaker speech processing, exist and could be exploited in the case of a learner's developing speech-processing system. At present, there exists no SLA research in this domain.

The timing issue

Precisely 'when', in cognitive terms, should the focus on form pedagogical intervention occur? The timing issue follows on directly from the noticing and interruption issues. Whereas Doughty and Williams (1998a) imply in their operational definition of focus on form that optimal timing results in simultaneous attention to forms, meaning, and function (see first option below), there are three other logical (weaker integration position) possibilities, provided they occur within an appropriate cognitive window: (1) Simultaneous, implicit attention to forms, meaning, and function (Doughty & Williams, 1998a) at precisely the time when the learner need arises; (2) Implicit or explicit attention to forms shortly in advance of learner need arising (DeKeyser, 1998; Lightbown, 1998); (3) A brief, implicit or explicit *shift* of attention from meaning and function to forms at precisely the time when the learner need arises (Long & Robinson, 1998); (4) Implicit attention to forms immediately contingent upon the evident learner need (Doughty & Varela, 1998; Ortega & Long, 1997).

The pedagogical components of the timing issue involve such dilemmas as the feasibility of lesson planning if attention to form must occur only at moments when a previously unidentified need has arisen, or how the teacher is to assess pervasiveness and remediability of errors online in daily classroom interaction (Doughty & Williams, 1998b). The matters at hand for present purposes are whether the recommended 'simultaneous processing', or 'occasional shifts of learners' attention' needed to draw attention to linguistic form briefly during overall processing for meaning are feasible in cognitive processing terms, as well as whether the more logistically feasible advance and contingent focus on form might respectively block or fail to engage important cognitive microprocesses, such as cognitive comparison leading to mapping.

Simultaneous processing of forms, meaning, and function   The issues of relevance in this timing proposal are essentially analogous to the interruption issue discussed in the previous section; thus, only one point will be reiterated here. Although an entirely new area of consideration and, hence, somewhat speculative, it appears that, while in the main, language processing is highly automatic, there may be some small opportunity for the attraction of attention to forms during message formulation given that speakers have been shown to do so inadvertently. If the cognitive mechanism for this is roving attention, then a key issue for FonF pedagogical intervention is that of providing facilitation factors for the attraction of roving attention to linguistic forms while the remainder of selective attention remains engaged in processing meaning.

Focus on form in advance   This view holds that if attention to form *during* meaning processing is to be brief and unobtrusive, then learners may need some advance organizers to assist them in recognizing what to pay attention to. Two cognitive constructs lend support to this proposal: expectation and orientation. It is well established that expectation affects how selective attention is allocated. This interacts with the observation that, as measured by electrodermal indices of reacting to changes in stimuli, orienting to physical traits (e.g., phonological) is automatic, but orienting to semantic traits requires directed attention (Hulstijn, 1979). Thus, it appears entirely plausible that some kind of cognitive preparation for focus on form would facilitate learner noticing of relevant input.

The critical question, however, is what should the learner be prepared to expect? Thus far, the proposals have involved utilizing what amounts to focus on forms as the advance preparation for noticing during focus on form. Lightbown (1998), for instance, recommends brief, explicit grammar lessons that would later be recalled during meaningful processing by extralinguistic means, such as hand signals or facial expressions (Schachter, 1981). In other words, the forms needed in the communicative endeavor could be brought into STM as needed if the learner had been alerted in advance to the possibility that these forms might become useful during a communicative task. While it is clear that the advantage of this approach would be the minimization of processing interruption, what is not yet demonstrated is whether learners *ever* can utilize metalinguistic information during forms-meaning-function mapping. A similar proposal is for the solid establishment of declarative knowledge in advance of its use, a major tenet in the well-known skill-acquisition model, ACT-*, already outlined (see DeKeyser, this volume). In focus on form terms, the cognitive window in which forms, meaning, and function can be compared is envisioned to be far greater than is assumed in most models of focus on form (Doughty & Williams, 1998b). DeKeyser (1998) suggests that earlier criticisms of skill-building models were unwarranted because they were based on empirical studies which did not allow for the development of sufficiently elaborated LTM representation of declarative knowledge before the learner was expected to be able to begin to deploy that knowledge procedurally. Whereas in the small-window models of focus on form (e.g., Figures 2 and 3 above) noticing is claimed to occur on-line and primarily in STM, the effect of established declarative knowledge would have to involve interaction between the LTM store and current processing in STM.

In contrast to these views, it remains entirely possible that the optimal advance preparation for focus on form involves not expectation for, and orientation to, forms, but rather expectation for, and explicit orientation to, the event structure of an upcoming task, as is the case in child expectation for and interpretation of event scene highlights. L2 learners could be instructed to pay close attention when they are trying to interpret or express particular meanings. This kind of task-orienting has been shown to affect depth of processing (Cowan, 1995). Furthermore, this kind of orientation to event representation would be in accordance with Slobin's/Andersen's OPs. To date, however, both the forms-based and the event-structure-based proposals for advance focus on form remain completely untested in SLA.

Shifts of attention during processing   At least one type of study has demonstrated that subjects can temporarily shift a portion of their attention away from a primary processing task to attend to (and notice) other stimuli without compromising ongoing meaningful macro-processing. Cross-modal processing studies reveal the complexity of WM and are indicative of the potential for the kind of simultaneous attention to forms, function and meaning that would embody non-interruptive processing for language learning. One such study – a study of syllable processing during whispered reading – shows that there is considerable memory for input that is not uniquely attended (Cowan, 1993). During these experiments, subjects whisper-read[10] a novel and occasionally hear syllables through headphones. Periodically, the subjects are interrupted and asked to identify from a list of ten the most recently heard syllable which will have occurred either 1, 5, or 10 seconds prior to the interruption. They then write the sentence most recently read, and carry on with reading the novel. Subsequently,

---

[10] Subjects are asked to whisper to ensure that they are, in fact, engaged in reading.

they are given a comprehension test, which they expect throughout the study. Subjects are reasonably good at identifying the interrupting syllables, although the ability for identification decays somewhat from 1 to 10 seconds.

The essential finding is that subjects can remember input that was not at the center of selective attention. In other words, the not uniquely attended input retained some sort of activated status in STM which lasted up to 10 seconds. Even more fascinating for present purposes, however, was the discovery of small shifts of subjects' attention and the effect that this had on recall. These shifts of attention were revealed through analyzing the whispered reading in conjunction with the syllable presentation. Frequently, subjects would pause in their whispering within about one second of hearing the target syllable. On such trials, they showed a 20% improvement on recall. This benefit, like the overall recall ability, decayed over the 1 to 10 second interval. None the less, the shifts of attention appeared to enhance performance on syllable identification without detriment to comprehension. Cowan conducted a second follow-up experiment in which the subjects were directed to press a button every time they heard a syllable while doing the same whispered reading tasks. The task was somewhat more demanding, but even so, there was still a 60 per cent detection rate. Strikingly, of those syllables detected, there was very little forgetting, even after the full 10 seconds. These findings can be interpreted to suggest that the shifts of attention advocated in focus on form pedagogy may, indeed, have a cognitive basis in the demonstrated ability of attentional shifting to enhance recall performance.

In her comprehensible output hypothesis, Swain (1995, 1998) claims that learners need to shift globally (not just briefly) from what she calls a more semantically oriented kind of processing that is typical of comprehension to a beneficial mode of syntactic processing that is required for production. Her claim essentially is that learners' own pushed output can serve as an attention-getting device which brings to their awareness something that they need to know. In other words, the requirements of utterance formulation forces learners to analyze the form of their utterances in ways that would not be necessary during comprehension alone. This kind of noticing the gap, Swain claims, may be prerequisite to learning processes, such as extending L1 meanings to L2 contexts, extending L2 meanings to new contexts, and IL system hypothesis formation and testing (Swain & Lapkin, 1995).

Immediately contingent focus on form   Perhaps the most compelling proposal for a solution to the timing issue involves tapping the powerful cognitive resources that enable learners to make use of recently occurring utterances. The evidence and arguments for these resources were presented in detail in the discussion of the noticing issues. If the verbatim format of recent speech remains activated in memory and available for use in subsequent utterance formulation, this can be taken to be an important cognitive underpinning for facilitating the opportunity to make cognitive comparisons. With regard to the timing of the information to be compared, the most efficient means to promoting cognitive comparison would seem to be provision of immediately contingent recasts.

The fundamental psycholinguistic underpinning of recasting is the hypothesized value of drawing learners' attention to differences in recently produced (especially contingent) speech. From the learner's perspective, this implies simply that mismatches (a) between his or her own intentions and the linguistic resources available to express them (holes) or (b) between his/her own IL utterance and a contingent TL utterance in the discourse (gaps) be made noticeable, since the learner presumably can already hold in memory a representation of both the output utterance (his or her own or the interlocutor's) and of the contingent input. Therefore, a key issue to consider is precisely what would make a component of a contingent utterance salient enough to be noticed and subsequently used in a cognitive comparison.

In L1 controversies concerning the contribution of recasts to acquisition, there have been a number of criticisms, mainly from the point of view of noticeability (cited in Saxton, 1997, p. 144): a) there is an unwarranted emphasis on adult response CATEGORY rather than response CONTENT (Saxton, 1993); b) adult response categories are probably too difficult for the child to identify (Marcus, 1993); c) adult categories provide only an indeterminate source of information, since they are contingent on both correct and incorrect child utterances (Bowerman, 1988); d) the child would have to repeat an utterance a great many times in order to utilize the corrective information available in differential response rates (Marcus, 1993); e) computation of a differential response rate is probably beyond the child's processing capacity; f) adult response categories such as recasts can never reveal the precise locus of ungrammaticality within a particular child's sentence (Pinker, 1989b).

Some of these criticisms have also been leveled against recasts in the L2 classroom. Lyster (1998), in discussing the distribution of recasts versus repetitions in immersion classes, claims that the two discourse types occupy the same discourse context and, therefore, are confusing to learners (as evidenced by immediate uptake failure). Doughty (1998) has argued that, whereas this may be the case in immersion classes, it does not follow logically that there is not a way to deliver recasts that would, in fact, be noticeable and useable by learners. Doughty and Varela (1998) have documented the effective use of what they term corrective recasting and have argued that certain features of the recasts enabled ESL learners to notice that material was being presented to them which they were to utilize in their own production. Subjects in the recasting condition, in comparison with no-recast controls, improved both in attempts at the recast target (expression of past) and in advancement toward targetlike use.

Moreover, as Saxton points out, even if differential response categories and response rates are not the explanation for why children seem to notice parental reformulations (or learners the teachers'), two fundamental factors remain which could be explanatory: (1) the specific linguistic content of the individual adult responses; and (2) the proximity of the corrective responses to the child's errors. Saxton has incorporated these factors into the direct contrast hypothesis[11], which states that when the child produces an utterance containing an erroneous form, which is responded to immediately with an utterance containing the correct adult alternative to the erroneous form (i.e., when negative evidence is supplied), then the child may perceive the adult form as being in CONTRAST with the equivalent child form. Cognizance of a relevant contrast can then form the basis for perceiving the adult form as a correct alternative to the child form. An example from Saxton's data illustrates the immediately contingent recast (tone = mock argumentation):

Child: Well, I feeled it.
Adult: I felt it.
Child: I felt it.
(Saxton, 1997: 155)

Saxton (1997) demonstrated in an experiment which manipulated the input to children acquiring irregular past tense forms that the children were able to recover from overgeneralized hypotheses when given recasts of errors better than when provided positive input models in advance of their errors. This advantage for recasts over models has also been found for L1 English learners of L2 Spanish adverb placement (Doughty, Izumi, Maciukaite & Zapata, 1999; Ortega & Long, 1997). In other words, these studies suggest that child and adult learners do have the cognitive resources necessary to notice the difference between an old utterance and a new utterance, particularly where the forms of the two utterances are similar and the recast technique of focus on form places them in a contingent relationship, thereby fitting into what may be a tight window of opportunity for making a cognitive comparison.

---

[11] Saxton bases the direct contrast hypothesis on the work of Nelson (1987) on the rare event theory of cognitive comparison.

Doughty (2000) also suggests that the information provided to L2 learners in recasts should be targeted in a combination of ways. In particular, the learner needs some guidance as to what the something is when recognizing that the teacher is seeking something. In Lyster's classrooms, the learners seemed, at least, to be wondering whether the teacher was commenting on the length, the meaning or the form of the utterance. This was particularly difficult since the teachers used so many discourse moves, each signaling all of these things. To remedy this, the reformulation needs to be consistent. In my view, what Lyster calls the isolated interrogative recast and what Doughty and Varela call corrective recasting are good candidates for the provision of negative evidence because these contingent recasts often contain the clear signaling factor of rising intonation, follow immediately upon the learner error and, by not expanding the utterance too much, provide a direct contrast of forms.

In immersion classes, anything and everything seemed to attract teacher reformulation. Faced with this kind of diffuse feedback, it is hardly a wonder if learners become confused. Recasting is most likely to be effective when it is targeted at only one or a few features. Furthermore, on the basis of work by Pienemann and others, the targeted features need to be aspects of language for which the learners are developmentally ready for pedagogical intervention, as evidenced by findings of numerous effect-of-instruction studies which have shown that any kind of pedagogical intervention that is too far in advance of IL development is ineffective. To target recasts properly, Doughty and Varela (1998) carried out an IL analysis in the classroom to see what kinds of learning problems the students were having. Added to this was a separate concern to be able to test the effect of recasting in classroom tasks in which the need for the targeted form would be very natural and thus likely to occur frequently. Through this preliminary analysis, they settled upon expressing past events – real and hypothesized – in the reporting of science experiments, already a frequent activity in this science class. Finally, and this departs quite a bit from the kinds of recasts that Lyster examined, Doughty and Varela's recasting technique involved an initial attention-getting phase that, in effect, pointed more clearly to the learner error. As can be seen in this example, the teacher sometimes repeated the learner's error with a clear signal of rising intonation to indicate that there was a problem with the learner utterance – a kind of intonational focus considered to draw the learner's attention directly to the problem area:

Context:	*Jose is reporting on his experiment.*
Jose:	I think that the worm will go under the soil.
T:	I *think* that the worm *will* go under the soil?

Jose: (no response)
T: I *thought* that the worm *would* go under the soil.
Jose: I thought that the worm would go under the soil.

The teacher always gave the student an opportunity to try again, but if he did not repair, then she would consistently provide the targeted reformulation. In this way, if the student is successful after being invited to try again after an error has been put into focus, then the kind of cognitive comparison that he would make would be between his own two attempts at the utterance. If the student was unable to repair, then the material for the comparison would be the learner utterance and the teacher reformulation.

In addition to the targeting of the recasts to a small number of learning problems, in classrooms it seems to be the case that intensive recasting is necessary. The responses to learners in Doughty and Varela's study were consistently provided to learners in one of two ways throughout the treatment phase (e.g., straight recast or repetition plus recast), and the teacher rarely let a learner error of past or past conditional go by without eliciting a successful repair or providing the recast herself. Finally it should be noted that this kind of consistent, targeted, intensive, and focused recasting was carried out over six weeks in the ESL science class that met daily for about one hour. To conclude, this examination of studies in and out of L2 classrooms leads to the observation that recasts are only ambiguous when they are just one type among many reformulations moves used by teachers in immersion classes to respond to a wide range of learner error types. This by no means provides any justification for the abandonment of recasts as an effective means to draw learner attention to form (i.e., a relatively implicit, non-interruptive provision of negative evidence) and certainly does not justify a focus on forms approach, such as negotiation of form. Rather, given the promising findings from the wide range of studies showing preference for recent speech in subsequent language processing – which all support the notion that L2 learners have the cognitive resources to notice the gap – it is far better to adjust the recasting technique that teachers employ. In this way, learners will be clear about what the material is that they need to be utilizing in these cognitive comparisons (see Long, 1999, for extensive review of these issues).

Conclusion

After noting that much of the discussion of focus on form issues is often couched primarily in pedagogical rather than psycholinguistic

terms and then raising the need for establishing the psychological reality of putative focus on form processes, this chapter has presented
a working taxonomy of cognitive correlates to familiar pedagogical
notions, each supported by psycholinguistic studies. The cognitive
correlates – concentrating mainly on memory, attention, cognitive
comparison, mapping, and restructuring – were utilized in considering the three processing concerns of (a) cognitive resources involved in
noticing the gap, (b) the feasibility of non-interruptive pedagogical interventions, and (c) the timing of focus on form, each of which arises
from pedagogical recommendations. By examining psycholinguistic
models and empirical research on memory and speech processing, we
have seen that the cognitive resources of L2 learners are potentially
great. Working memory is longer in duration and more complex in
both its connection to LTM resources and its capacity to be attracted
to language input that is outside of immediate focal attention. We have
also seen that speech processing, while normally relatively automatic
in operation, is not entirely encapsulated, hence that speech plans are
amenable to modification, if the conditions for cognitive intrusions on
utterance planning are facilitative and non-interruptive.

Finally, it has been suggested that, although there are some claims
that the size of the cognitive window of opportunity for pedagogical
intervention is even greater than psycholinguistic studies pointing to
a window of something well under one minute, it is more prudent
to assume that one of the most promising kinds of intervention is an
immediate contingent recast, which can easily fit into WM along with
the original utterance to which it is to be compared. Results of recast
studies suggest that such cognitive comparison does lead to forms-
function-meaning mapping and, hence, can be considered a successful
means to promoting processing for language learning. An important
caveat must be raised, however. With the exception of the recast studies, the experimental work discussed in this chapter has been carried
out with subjects possessing a mature, fully developed, fully functioning speech processing system. It remains for cognitive SLA research to
carry out similar studies to discover whether speech processing of a developing L2 system is as robust as are fully developed systems in terms
of memory capacity and preferences and of the possibility for unin-
terrupted processing of forms, meaning, and function leading toward
targetlike mapping. If it is the case that IL speech processing is much
the same as native-language speech processing, then the potential benefits of psycholinguistically motivated pedagogical interventions are,
indeed, promising.

9 Intentional and incidental second language vocabulary learning: a reappraisal of elaboration, rehearsal and automaticity

Jan H. Hulstijn[1]

Introduction

Most learners of a second language (L2) feel concerned with the burden of vocabulary learning and worry about the question of how to cope with the formidable task of learning thousands of words. This has been documented by a number of questionnaire, interview and case studies (Gu & Johnson, 1996; Jones, 1995; Lawson & Hogden, 1996; Porte, 1988; Sanaoui, 1995). Because of the sheer magnitude of the vocabulary learning task it is only quite natural that many L2 teachers feel uncertain about how to guide their students. Should they require their students to learn words intentionally, perhaps even by rote, or should they believe the rumours that intentional learning is not conducive to language learning? How much credence should they give to ideas like 'new vocabulary must be presented in context' and 'the best way to acquire vocabulary is by "picking up" words incidentally, as a by-product of being exposed to large amounts of L2 input in reading and listening tasks'?

This chapter will look at what various theories have to say about incidental and intentional vocabulary learning. It will focus especially on three issues of key importance for L2 pedagogy: (1) the quality of information processing when an unfamiliar word is first encountered; (2) the quantity and quality of rehearsal activities needed for a word to be permanently available; and (3) the training of automatic access to word knowledge necessary for fluent language use. This last issue will

[1] I am deeply indebted to the following scholars for their highly valuable comments on an earlier version of this text: Rene Appel (Amsterdam), Theo Bongaerts (Nijmegen), Ineke van de Craats (Tilburg), Kees de Bot (Nijmegen), Marijke Huizinga (Amsterdam), Anne-Mieke Janssen-van Dieten (Nijmegen), John de Jong (Arnhem), Batia Laufer (Haifa), Paul Meara (Swansea), Paul Nation (Wellington), Lydius Nienhuis (Utrecht), Peter Robinson (Tokyo), Peter Scherfer (Wuppertal), Henny van Egmond (The Hague), Hans van de Velde (Brussels), and Mari Wesche (Ottawa). Obviously, I am the sole person responsible for authorship of this text.

receive special attention in this chapter as it appears to be neglected in current L2 pedagogy.

The chapter comprises three main sections. Section 1 provides some background information on vocabulary knowledge and learning, leading the way to sections 2 and 3, which form the heart of the chapter. Section 2 is concerned with theoretical, methodological and pedagogical uses of the notions of incidental and intentional vocabulary learning. Section 3 discusses the pedagogical implications of the considerations entertained in the two previous sections, with respect to (1) elaboration at initial exposure, (2) rehearsal, and (3) automaticity.

Vocabulary knowledge, learning and use

This section aims at providing some background information necessary for an understanding of the notions of incidental and intentional learning discussed in the following section, and instructional practices with respect to elaboration, rehearsal and automaticity training discussed in the final section. It does so by briefly addressing issues of vocabulary knowledge, vocabulary learning difficulty, vocabulary size, and automatic use of vocabulary.

What does it mean to know a word?

The dominant view on vocabulary knowledge, in a first (L1) and second language (L2), avails itself of the pervasive metaphor of a dictionary-like mental lexicon consisting of lexical entries. A lexical entry in the lexicon of the average adult, literate, native speaker contains semantic, pragmatic, stylistic, collocational, syntactic, categorial, morphological, phonological, articulatory and orthographic features. According to Levelt, Roelofs and Meyer (1998), the process of uttering a word proceeds along four stages: (1) conceptual preparation, (2) lemma selection (i.e. selection of syntactic information), (3) morphonological encoding, and (4) computation of a phonetic-articulary gesture. The major rift in the system lies between the conceptual/syntactic domain (stages 1 and 2) and the morphonological/articulary domain (stages 3 and 4). Crossing the rift is not a trivial matter, illustrated by the well-known tip-of-the-tongue phenomenon, i.e. the momentary inability to retrieve the word form, given an already selected lemma.

The features of a lexical entry are intrinsically or associatively related to each other and to features of other entries while the strength of these relationships may vary (Aitchison, 1994, Ch. 17; Levelt, 1989, Ch. 6; Scherfer, 1994a). In the case of bilingual speakers, lexical features may also be connected between languages (Kroll & De Groot, 1997), but there is only one conceptual system common to both languages (Paradis, 1997).

Theories vary in their assumptions on how items in the mental lexicon are accessed for language use (see also Doughty, this volume, for discussion). According to Seidenberg (1995), there are two types of models – functional architecture-style models and connectionist models – which differ in basic assumptions about how lexical knowledge is represented and processed. In functional architecture-style models, based on the dictionary metaphor, recognizing a word involves successfully 'accessing' its entry in the mental lexicon, i.e. all its features are becoming available (total access), albeit in two stages (Levelt, 1993). In connectionist models, however, there can be partial activation of word knowledge because lexical knowledge is represented in a distributed way, allowing meanings, spellings, pronunciations, etc. to be accessed as patterns of activation over sublexical featuress (Seidenberg, 1995). Thus, connectionists have dropped the metaphor of dictionary-like mental entries.

Entries are accessed through a process of activation spreading along their interconnections. An entry is accessed if the sum of positive impulses exceeds that of negative impulses to an extent sufficient to allow it to reach its activation threshold and all competitors have been sufficiently inhibited. Processes of activation and inhibition are, therefore, a matter of degree. Different entries will require varying amounts of activation, so it will be easier to recall some words than others (Paradis, 1997).

The acquisition of an entry's features in L1 is generally believed to take place in an incremental way (Nagy & Herman, 1987), consisting of the filling of various 'slots' of entries in the mental lexicon (de Bot, Paribakht & Wesche, 1997), but to date no specific claims have been made concerning the order in which L2 lexical features must or may be acquired.[2] Beginning L2 learners, learning the first few hundred L2 vocabulary items, often appear to link the L2 word form directly to a corresponding L1 word form. In a later stage, the L2 word form is directly linked to its meaning.[3] Thus, initially, L2 lexical entries are often

---

[2] Meara (1993: 295) noted that 'the study of the bilingual lexicon is just not well enough developed for it to be able to tell practitioners what to do in classrooms'. Unfortunately, this statement still appears to be true.

[3] The dependency of L2 lexical items on L1 lexical items has traditionally been referred to with the term *subordinate* bilingualism (Weinreich, 1953). The direct linking of L2 forms to their meanings was either called *compound* or *coordinate* bilingualism: compound when an L2 word form and a corresponding L1 word form shared an identical meaning, coordinate when they shared similar but not identical and therefore essentially

coded as phonological or orthographic extensions of L1 lexical entries. This may explain why beginners have been found to confuse phonologically similar words more often and semantically similar words less often than do advanced learners (Henning, 1973). For any lexical entry, an individual's mental lexicon will often comprise both less and more than the information included in the corresponding lemma of a normal, monolingual, college dictionary. On the one hand, it may be less because the individual, even if he or she is a highly educated native speaker, may not know all the word's meanings and usages. On the other hand, it will be more because the average mental entry will exhibit various types of connections to other entries whereas the average dictionary's lemma will contain few, if any, cross-references.

How difficult is it to learn a new word?

There are many factors affecting the learning difficulty of words. Overviews are given by Nation (1990, Ch. 3), Laufer (1997), and Rodgers (1969). Two of these factors are worth mentioning in a chapter on elaboration, rehearsal and automatization. The first of these two factors is *codability* of the morphonological form of words. Word forms may differ in difficulty for coding and storing depending on the learner's prior phonotactic knowledge. When a L2 learner embarks on the learning of an entirely new language, morphonologically and phonetically unrelated to any language already known to him or her, he or she may experience great difficulties in storing isolated as well as clustered sounds or letters. Learning the first 15 content words of a new L2 language may take the beginning learner several hours. However, three months of daily study later, he or she may easily add another hundred new words to his or her medium-sized vocabulary in one hour simply because, by that time, letters and sounds are no longer encoded as single units but in now familiar chunks of phonemes, morphemes, syllables and prosodic patterns. The learner now implicitly knows which sequences and combination of elements are legal and which ones are not (see the chunking example of 'headache' in Ellis's chapter in this volume; see also Ellis & Beaton, 1993a).

Several studies have shown that repetition of L2 word forms in the form of overt or silent articulation, briefly held in working

separate meanings. More recent theories, however, especially those adopting a connectionist approach, would not make a principled distinction between these three forms of bilingualism. Instead, they in principle allow for the existence of any connections between features of L1 and L2 lexical items at all levels of representation (concept, meaning, and form). However, the relative strength of these connections may increase and decrease over the course of the L2 learning process.

memory (the so-called 'phonological loop' in Baddeley's Working Memory Model, see Baddeley, 1997, and Ellis, this volume) promotes their long-term retention. Papagno, Valentine, and Baddeley (1991) showed that preventing rehearsal practice by means of articulatory suppression (subjects tried to learn L2 words from a list of L1–L2 word pairs while repeatedly uttering the sound 'bla') interfered with the learning of L2 vocabulary. Similarly, Ellis and Sinclair (1996) demonstrated that English students' acquisition of Welsh vocabulary and morphology was facilitated by encouraging learners to repeat utterances and was hindered by articulatory suppression.[4] Thus, the evidence of all these studies suggests that the codability and hence the memorability of the forms of new words is contingent upon the learner's prior familiarity with various aspects of the linguistic system.

The second subjective, knowledge-dependent factor affecting a word's memorability is the *arbitrariness of the form-meaning link*, i.e., arbitrariness in terms of existing lexical knowledge. If a new word appears to the learner as having a form unrelated to its meaning it will need more attention and mental elaboration than if it has a transparent appearance. For example, suppose someone was trying to coin a new word in the English language referring to a door made of opaque glass. Suppose, furthermore, this person considered three alternatives: 'fogdoor', 'rog' and 'dorricor', then clearly for people already familiar with the words 'fog', 'door' and 'corridor', 'fogdoor', being a non-arbitrary and transparent word form, would be easy to learn, while 'rog' and 'dorricor' would be more difficult to learn, 'rog' being a fully arbitrary word form, and 'dorricor' being what Laufer (1991) has called a 'synform', likely to be confused with 'corridor'.

How many words do L2 learners need to know?

Although, as has been argued by Hazenberg and Hulstijn (1996), it is unlikely that a principled answer to the question of how many words L2 learners need to know will ever be attained, there is sufficient empirical evidence that the receptive vocabulary of English-speaking university undergraduates is in the range of 14,000–17,000 words (Zechmeister, D'Anna, Hall, Paus & Smith, 1993). In the literature on L2 learning a receptive knowledge of 5,000 base words is generally considered to be a minimal learning target with respect to the comprehension of the main points of non subject-specific texts (Nation, 1990,

---

[4] It has been suggested that phonological-loop capacity, although increasing with practice, differs between individuals, thereby constituting an important, but often neglected component of language learning aptitude (Atkins & Baddeley, 1998; Carroll, 1985; Ellis & Beaton, 1993a; Meara, 1993; MacWhinney, 1995).

1993; Laufer, 1992).[5] This may not be enough, however. Hirsh and Nation (1992) have convincingly argued that for such comprehension to be attained readers generally need to be familiar with 95 per cent of the words in a text. Hazenberg and Hulstijn (1996), in their study of text coverage and vocabulary knowledge, however, have given empirical evidence for the claim that if adults with secondary education want to be familiar with 95 per cent of the words contained in the large variety of non-specialist texts encountered in their daily lives, they must know at least 10,000 base words.[6]

Even more difficult than estimating required levels of receptive vocabulary knowledge is the estimation of the number of words that L2 learners need to know productively (Laufer & Nation, 1995). However, one could safely argue that the bottom line for speaking proficiency at what in the European context is commonly referred to as the Waystage Level (Van Ek & Trim, 1991) contains some 1,000 base words.[7] In conclusion, L2 learning objectives will almost always include receptive and productive knowledge of large numbers of lexical items; that is, learners must learn to activate components of lexical information in various directions: from orthographical or acoustic form to meaning, or from meaning to orthographic or phonetic form.

Skill in automatic word access

Knowing the meaning of a word form or knowing the word form belonging to a certain meaning is not enough. Learners learn words in order to be able to listen, read, speak and write. The basic facts of vocabulary use are:

(a) Normal, fluent speech proceeds at a speed of two to three words per second (Levelt, 1989 p. 22).

(b) Humans have a capacity for consciously focusing their attention on only a very limited amount of information (Baddeley, 1997, Ch. 6).

[5] This figure pertains to Germanic and Romance languages and might not be valid for other languages. A base word is any word whose meaning cannot be predicted on the basis of its components. For instance, 'bright' is a base word but 'brighter', 'brightest', 'brightly', 'brightish', 'brightness' and 'brighten' are not. See Bauer and Nation (1993) for a full treatment of this issue.

[6] The evidence produced by Hazenberg and Hulstijn (1996) pertained to the acquisition of the Dutch language. It is likely that a similar figure (roughly ten thousand base words) is required for learners of most other Indo-European languages, such as English and Spanish.

[7] The 'Common European Framework of Reference for Language Learning and Teaching' distinguishes the following six levels: Breakthrough, Waystage, Threshold, Vantage, Effective Operational Proficiency, and Mastery.

(c) If speaking is to proceed at two to three words per second and only little information can be held under conscious attention, then the speech production process must largely take place automatically. Thus, in normal speech production, the speaker only pays attention to the message (the concepts) conveyed while leaving the processes of formulation and articulation to automatically operating modules.

(d) A similar state of affairs applies to the listener. For speech comprehension to be successful, word recognition processes have to take place automatically (at a speed of two to three words per second) so that the listener's attention can be focused exclusively on the interpretation of the information conveyed by the message.

(e) A similar argument also applies to reading (and to writing – although perhaps to a lesser extent). Normal fluent reading proceeds at a speed of 200 to 350 words per minute, i.e. three to six words per second (Rayner & Pollatsek, 1989: 440). Carver (1990: 14) distinguishes five basic types of reading processes: scanning, skimming, rauding, learning and memorizing, with respective reading rates for college students of 600, 450, 300, 200 and 138 words per minute. Rauding, with an average rate of 300 words per minute, is the predominant reading mode, involving the recognition of all words and the integration of all words to comprehend the complete thought contained in each sentence.

(f) Many words do not consist of an uninflected lexical root but are composed of a root plus affixes (derivation) or of more than one lexical root (composition). Languages differ considerably in this respect. Thus, depending on the degree of agglutination of the language, speakers have to develop procedural skills to be capable of encoding and decoding multimorphemic words (Levelt, 1989: 186).

The conclusion to be drawn from these observations is that the processes involved in accessing lexical entries in the mental lexicon must take place automatically for communication to proceed efficiently.

'Automatic processes are executed without intention or conscious awareness. They also run on their own resources, i.e. they do not share processing capacity with other processes. Also, automatic processing is usually quick, even reflex-like; the structure of the process is wired in, either genetically or by learning (or both). This makes it both efficient and, to a large extent, inflexible; it is hard to alter automatic processes. Since automatic processes do not share resources, they can run in parallel without mutual interference' (Levelt, 1989: 20–21).

Word recognition in reading is a process using orthographic information as its primary basis. Phonological representations emerge during the process of lexical access, and are either utilized (the so-called indirect route to lexical access) or not (Taft, 1993: 91). Word recognition takes place in an interactive way via the activation of sublexical units ranging from (components of) letters to morphemes. Activation passes both up and down the different levels of representation, as well as between orthographic and phonological units at the same level (Taft, 1993: 119).

What is important to note in the present context of L2 learning is that fluent word recognition during normal reading and listening, although it is an interactive process including top–down spreading of activation, takes place exclusively at *sublexical* levels, i.e., it is unaffected by the meaning of the word itself or of words in the immediate context. Only less skilled readers use contextual information in word recognition (Stanovich, 1980). When readers become more skilled their reliance on context decreases (Rayner & Pollatsek, 1989: 385–386). Only when a text is visually degraded (e.g., in the case of a poor-quality copy of a faxed or photocopied text) do skilled readers use contextual information in the same way as unskilled readers (Schwantes, 1981). Thus, in normal listening and reading, lexical access is *not* subject to top–down influence from syntactic and semantic processing; the processing of a word is largely driven by the input code itself rather than by contextual information (Cutler, 1995: 114; Seidenberg, 1995: 165).

Empirical evidence for the crucial importance of automaticity in L2 reading has been provided by Segalowitz (reviewed in Segalowitz, 1997 and in Segalowitz, 2000) and Koda (reviewed in Koda, 1996). Segalowitz and his associates showed that inefficient word recognition reduces L2 reading performance in otherwise fluent bilinguals (Favreau & Segalowitz, 1983; Segalowitz, Poulsen, & Komoda, 1991). Koda (1996) argues that there is ample evidence for a causal relationship between word recognition efficiency and reading comprehension both in L1 and in L2. Her own research has demonstrated that the acquisition of L2 word recognition skills is facilitated by the degree to which L1 and L2 orthographic systems share structural similarities.

Many L2 course materials, following the view of Goodman (1971), play down the importance of automatic word recognition. Instead, they aim to train the transfer of higher-order, top–down comprehension strategies from L1 reading in order to compensate for any lack of L2 knowledge. Alderson (1984), however, advanced the so-called threshold hypothesis according to which knowledge of reading goals, text characteristics and reading strategies (such as inferring the meaning of unknown words from context), cannot compensate for a lack of language knowledge if the latter remains below a certain threshold level. The empirical evidence for the threshold hypothesis has been provided by Schoonen, Hulstijn and Bossers (1998).[8] Thus, learning to apply reading strategies should not take precedence over establishing a core of automatically accessible lexical items (Coady, 1997b; Huckin & Coady, 1999).

Fluency develops over time, primarily through extensive experience.[9] What is gained by such extensive practice is the automatization of many of the components underlying the skill. This automatization reduces the burden on short-term memory (STM) and facilitates the chunking of information into higher-level units (Segalowitz, 1997: 103). Ellis and Sinclair (1996) showed that as L2 learners hear and produce L2 words, they implicitly acquire knowledge of the statistical frequencies and sequential probabilities of the phonotactics of the L2. The more they repeat words, the more these are consolidated in long-term memory (LTM). Acquisition of fluency is influenced by frequency, recency, and regularity. The frequency effect is simply that of 'practice makes perfect' (Ellis & Laporte, 1997).

Incidental and intentional learning

In the literature on L1 and L2 vocabulary acquisition it has become customary to say (a) that most vocabulary items are acquired 'incidentally', that is, as a by-product of the learner being engaged in a listening, reading, speaking or writing activity, and (b) that few words are acquired by an act of 'intentional' learning, as in the learning of a bilingual vocabulary list (Coady, 1997a; R. Ellis, 1994b; Hatch & Brown, 1995 p. 368; Nagy & Herman, 1987; Nation, 1990 p. 178; Schmidt, 1994a; Shu, Anderson & Zhang, 1995; Sternberg, 1987). Some educationalists have therefore advocated the use of activities conducive to incidental vocabulary learning (i.e. massive reading and

---

[8] Meara (personal communication, December 1997) suggests that the breakdown of text comprehension due to a deficiency in word recognition could be investigated adapting traffic flow models. The basic idea is that the crash doesn't necessarily occur at the point where the problem manifests itself. Comprehension breakdown can occur at a site that is remote from the position of the most difficult words.

[9] What fluency actually is also depends on one's theoretical standpoint (see Schmidt's chapter in this volume). Current psychological theories appear to agree that there is rigid, reflex-like automaticity at lower levels of information processing and more flexible, adaptive fluency at higher levels of processing (Segalowitz, 2000).

listening activities) while discouraging procedures of intentional vocabulary learning (Krashen, 1989). As will be demonstrated below,
this practice is based on an ill-informed understanding of the terms
'incidental' and 'intentional' learning. In a review of a wide variety of
empirical studies which all claimed to have investigated 'incidental'
learning of L2 vocabulary, Singleton (1999: 161) observes, 'Clearly,
in order for the debate about incidental vocabulary learning to proceed with any degree of coherence in the future, a consensus will have
to be reached about what is to be included and what is to be excluded under the term "incidental".' This section intends to clarify
the issue. Its main line of argument will be that: (1) theoretically, the
distinction between incidental and intentional learning has become difficult to maintain; (2) methodologically, the distinction is essential for
any researcher intending to design a vocabulary learning experiment;
(3) pedagogically, the distinction may have something to offer provided that teacher and learner are aware of points (1) and (2).

Incidental and intentional learning
in the psychological literature

Let us begin with a partly hypothetical example from L2 learning.
We ask a group of L2 learners to read a L2 text (containing some
presumably unfamiliar words) and then answer some comprehension
questions. There are two reading conditions: Group 1 has the unfamiliar words glossed in the margin by means of L1 translations; Group 2
is given four alternative L1 translations in the margin (one correct
and three incorrect translations) for each unfamiliar word, and has to
choose which one is the correct translation. The differences in information processing being manipulated are Meaning Given (Group 1)
and Meaning to be Inferred (Group 2). Unexpectedly, students in both
groups are tested afterwards with a recall test of the meaning of the
unfamiliar words.

  This is an example of incidental learning. If Group 2 was found to
perform better than Group 1, one could conclude that inferral leads
to better retention than simply being given a word's meaning.[10] However, if we told Groups 1 and 2 in advance that they would be tested
on their knowledge of these words (whose meaning was given or had
to be inferred), we would have invoked processes of intentional learning, whose effect may well have overridden the effect of incidental
learning.[11] Thus, telling or not telling students that they will be tested

---

[10] See Hulstijn (1992) for details. That study shows that things are not as simple as suggested
   in this example.
[11] This was demonstrated in Experiment IV of the same study (Hulstijn, 1992).

afterwards on their knowledge is the critical operational feature distinguishing incidental from intentional learning.

The use of the terms incidental and intentional learning in the psychological literature (not to be confused with the notions of implicit and explicit learning or with implicit and explicit memory, see Ellis, 1994a, Schmidt, this volume) goes back to the beginning of the 20th century and has served experimental psychology a long time. Hundreds of experiments on incidental and intentional learning have been conducted. Classical readings are Ebbinghaus (1964), Postman (1964), McLaughlin (1965) and Eysenck (1982).

In operational terms, incidental and intentional learning can simply be distinguished in terms of the use of prelearning instructions that either do, or do not, forewarn subjects about the existence of a subsequent retention test (Eysenck, 1982: 198). Two basic experimental methods have evolved in the study of incidental and intentional learning. The Type I design is characteristic of the earlier studies. Subjects in the incidental condition perform an orienting task on the stimulus materials but they are given no instructions to learn and they are unexpectedly given a retention test afterwards. Subjects in the intentional conditions are told in advance that they will later be tested. Early research, in the first few decades of the century, aimed at demonstrating (1) that incidental learning did indeed exist and (2) that intentional learning was superior to incidental learning. In the Type II design, which was adopted in most later studies, all subjects are instructed to learn some of the stimuli that are presented to them; but additional stimuli, which subjects are not told to learn, are presented at the same time. Retention of these additional stimuli is unexpectedly tested afterwards. Thus, in the Type II design, subjects are their own controls, serving both under intentional and incidental conditions of learning, being exposed to two categories of stimuli, while expecting to be tested on only one of these. Also, in the example at the beginning of this section, learners serve under an intentional condition as far as they read the text in order to prepare for answering the upcoming comprehension question, but they simultaneously serve under an incidental condition in that they are being exposed to unfamiliar words (with or without glosses) without expecting to be tested on their retention of these words.

Until about 1965, hundreds of experiments were conducted in order to investigate the effect on learning of (1) the manipulation of stimulus materials, and (2) intrasubject differences (e.g., age). While the distinction between incidental and intentional learning is fairly straightforward in operational terms, psychologists have had longstanding problems in coming to grips with conceptual definitions and have debated the underlying conceptual issues for many decades. As McGeoch (1942: 304) already noted, one cannot prove that subjects in incidental conditions did *not* have a motive, self-instruction, or 'set' to learn. McGeoch's point was that it was hazardous to assert that there is incidental learning in an absolute sense.[12] Postman (1964), whose work marked the end of the 'Dark Ages' of memory research (Eysenck, 1982: 198), accepted McGeoch's point. He abandoned the dichotomous distinction between incidental and intentional learning while focusing on the 'functional relations between the instruction stimulus on the one hand and measures of learning and retention on the other' (p. 185), acknowledging the important role of the orienting task (p. 188) and the meaningfulness of the stimulus materials (p. 191) in this functional relationship. Thus, to return to our example, for Postman it would be important to study the interaction between various instructions (e.g., 'After reading, hand in the text to the teacher and summarize the text in very broad terms' vs 'After reading, hand in the text to the teacher and summarize the text in as much detail as you can') and the meaningfulness of the unfamiliar words (presence vs absence of marginal glosses).

A major turn in this debate came when psychology witnessed, in the 1960s and early 1970s, a shift from the behaviourist paradigm towards the cognitive paradigm. Cognitive psychologists were more interested in the nature of the way in which subjects process stimulus information than by the difference in learning outcomes caused by the presence or absence of an advance warning that a retention test will be administered afterwards. A seminal paper by Craik and Lockhart (1972) has been of considerable influence. It generated a renewed interest in incidental learning with the introduction of the concept of 'depth of processing'. Craik and Lockhart argued that the chance that some piece of new information will be stored into LTM is not determined by the length of time that it is held in STM but rather by the shallowness or depth with which it is initially processed. They further postulated several levels of processing depth. For instance, processing the meaning of a new lexical item takes places at a rather deep level whereas processing the phonological form takes place at a rather shallow level. Craik and Lockhart were initially successful in providing evidence that semantic processing of lexical items resulted in higher retention than phonological or orthographical processing. The levels of processing

---

[12] Similar debates have emerged more recently concerning the questions of whether there exists such a thing as completely unattentional learning or virtually implicit learning. Different performance on different tasks, such as *implicit* and *explicit memory* tasks, need not necessarily be attributed to different underlying systems (see Schmidt's chapter in this volume).

theory, however, was challenged, refined and modified, and eventually even abolished, in the succeeding years. Two of the problems were: (1) What exactly constitutes a 'level' of processing, and (2) How do we know that one level is 'deeper' than another? For instance, can 'non-semantic' processing tasks still be meaningful activities? In other words, to be meaningful, an orienting task need not involve thinking about the meaning of a word; it could just as well involve thinking about its pronunciation or spelling.

Craik and Tulving (1975) suggested that what is critical to retention is not simply the presence or absence of semantic encoding, but the richness with which the material is encoded. A major obstacle facing all proposals resides in the difficulty of providing an unambiguous, operationable definition of any notion proposed as a replacement for depth of processing, be it 'encoding specificity', 'distinctiveness of encoding', 'degree of elaboration', 'cognitive effort', 'degree of richness', etc.[13]. Yet, cognitive psychologists remained unified in their view that 'memory performance is determined far more by the nature of the processing activities engaged in by the learner than it is by the intention to learn per se' (Eysenck, 1982: 203). Thus, although researchers of knowledge representation, information encoding and retrieval, attention, and memory have not yet succeeded in providing adequate theoretical explanations of phenomena of human learning and memory in terms of quality (type) and quantity (duration and frequency) of information processing (see the chapters by Schmidt, Ellis, Harrington, and DeKeyser in this volume), they all agree that processing new lexical information more elaborately (e.g., by paying careful attention to the word's pronunciation, orthography, grammatical category, meaning and semantic relations to other words) will lead to higher retention than by processing new lexical information less elaborately (e.g., by paying attention to only one or two of these dimensions). This is true not only for intentional but also for incidental learning. Thus, incidental learning will be more successful with more than with less elaborate processing.[14]

---

[13] Overviews of the course of this debate over the years are given in many psychology textbooks. A lucid description is given by Zechmeister and Nyberg, 1982, Ch. 12. Baddeley, 1997, provides a more recent and up-to-date review.

[14] Note that it is therefore perfectly possible for learning to be both incidental and involving explicit memory. When a L2 reader encounters a new word in a L2 text and looks up the meaning of this word in a dictionary solely for the purpose of comprehending the current text (and not for the purpose of vocabulary learning) this mental event can be categorized both as incidental learning, as defined in the present chapter, and as involving explicit memory and conscious attention, as defined in Schmidt's chapter. However, *explicit learning*, as defined by Schmidt, will normally take place under conditions of intentional learning.

Incidental and intentional learning in L2 pedagogy

As the terms incidental and intentional learning have been in use for almost a century, witnessing a behaviourist-cognitive paradigm shift and, subsequently, a fundamental evolution within the cognitive paradigm, it is not surprising that the meanings of these terms have changed accordingly. Currently, in the applied domains of L1 and L2 pedagogy, incidental vocabulary learning refers to the learning of vocabulary as the by-product of any activity not explicitly geared to vocabulary learning, with intentional vocabulary learning referring to any activity aiming at committing lexical information to memory.[15]

Influential in this respect have been publications by Nagy and Anderson (1984), Nagy, Herman and Anderson (1985), and Nagy and Herman (1987). These researchers showed that American high school students know between 25,000 and 50,000 words, or even more (Nagy & Anderson, 1984 p. 324).[16] They argued that such a large number of words cannot have been learned solely by means of explicit vocabulary instruction; rather, most words are learned in an incremental way through repeated encounters during extensive reading.[17] Nagy, Herman and Anderson (1985: 234) acknowledge that it is still an open question how all this incidental learning takes place.[18] As possible causes they mention the contribution of conversation with adults or peers, watching television, classroom discussion, school reading and

---

[15] This subsection will be limited to the use of incidental and intentional learning in the *vocabulary* learning literature. In Hulstijn (forthcoming), the two terms are also discussed in the context of *grammar* learning.

[16] These figures are substantially higher than the estimations of Zechmeister et al. (1993), referred to earlier. The discrepancy is mainly due to differences among investigators in conservativeness concerning the operationalization of the notion of 'word'. Nagy and his associates count different word meanings as different words more readily and count semitransparent derivations and compositions (such as 'casualty' vs 'casual', and 'sidewalk' vs 'side' and 'walk') more readily as separate words than do Zechmeister et al. (see Nagy, 1997 for a discussion of this issue).

[17] Meara (1997) suggests that the rate of incidental vocabulary expansion through extensive reading may vary with proficiency: a low, high, and low rate respectively at beginning, intermediate and highly advanced proficiency levels. Meara also considers the role of learner and language variables as potential intervening factors in the rate of expansion. Nagy (1997: 76) points to some differences in this respect between L1 and L2 incidental vocabulary expansion: (1) L2 learners usually have to learn at a faster rate than the 'natural' rate of L1 acquisition, (2) early stages of L2 acquisition involve a relatively small number of high frequency words, for which there is a greater pay-off instructionally, and (3) L2 learners encounter unfamiliar words (and word meanings) at a greater rate than L1 learners and may therefore have a greater need to use context (and learn words incidentally).

[18] Landauer and Dumais (1997) have proposed a formal theory, the Latent Semantic Analysis (LSA) theory, to simulate incidental vocabulary learning from reading: see Ellis, this volume, for discussion of LSA.

free reading. Yet the pedagogical thrust of their argument has been that vocabulary growth is largely determined by reading and that students must be encouraged to spend much time on reading: 'Incidental learning of words during reading may be the easiest and single most powerful means of promoting large-scale vocabulary growth' (Nagy & Herman, 1987: 27). It is this message that most other educationalists have concentrated upon, neglecting the acknowledgement of Nagy et al. (1985) and Nagy (1997) that it is an open question how incidental learning takes place.

The vocabulary-acquisition-through-reading argument is a default argument: because relatively few words are explicitly taught, most words are acquired from reading. As Nagy (1997: 70) points out, 'This argument is far from airtight.' It may well be that the explosive growth of vocabulary between the ages of 6 to 16 (in countries where young people go to school during these years) is not solely the result of reading for pleasure but rather stems from a variety of oral and written tasks which not only expose students to new words and concepts, but also force them to process this lexical information repeatedly. In other words, instructional programmes of most subject matter, knowledge and skill avail themselves of language, and hence vocabulary, as their primary vehicle. Although this vocabulary is learned 'incidentally', i.e., through the performance of subject-related tasks, these tasks often require learners to process words elaborately and repeatedly.[19] Hence, since it is the quality and the frequency of the way in which new words are processed that determine their acquisition, it may be too simple to conclude that the only thing students need is extensive reading.

Another influential paper, with a catching title that lends itself readily as a slogan for L1 and L2 pedagogy ('Most vocabulary is learned from context'), written by an influential psychologist (Sternberg, 1987), has also contributed to the recommendation of extensive reading. However, Sternberg deals in quite some detail with the cognitive processes, contextual cues, and moderating variables which determine incidental vocabulary acquisition. Sternberg warns that presentation of words in context and hence extensive reading is not enough. Students need theory-based instruction concerning the role of the processes, cues and moderating variables involved (p. 96). In other words, vocabulary acquisition will benefit from reading only when readers consciously engage in inferring the meaning of unfamiliar words, and when the text does contain cues allowing the meaning of unfamiliar words to be inferred. Or, as Prince (1996: 489) has put it, 'Effective

---

[19] Corson (1997) emphasizes the role of group work and other dialogue activities in class ('talking about text'), providing the necessary elaboration on and reconceptualization of word meanings, for adolescents to increase their vocabularies.

learning of words requires a stage in which the word is in fact isolated from its context and submitted to elaborative processing.'

Nagy's and Sternberg's claims have been widely referred to in the L2 pedagogic literature on vocabulary learning. They have led, however, to various pedagogical interpretations (Coady, 1997b; Huckin & Coady, 1999). Some educationalists claim that students will learn all the vocabulary they need from context by reading extensively (Krashen, 1989). Others, however, while acknowledging the usefulness, even necessity, of extensive reading, have emphasized the importance of making L2 learners aware of their vocabulary learning task and of teaching explicit strategies for vocabulary learning (Ellis & Sinclair, 1989; Hulstijn, 1997; Oxford & Crookall, 1989; Sökmen, 1997) as well as of the importance of teaching the linguistic principles of the target language's lexical system (e.g., Carter & McCarthy, 1988; Lewis, 1994). In most published teaching materials for learners at beginning and intermediate levels (textbooks, multimedia software), a selected core vocabulary is explicitly taught and rehearsed through a wide variety of techniques and activities (as illustrated in publications such as Allen, 1983; Gairns & Redman, 1986; Morgan & Rinvolucri, 1986; Nation, 1990, 1993; Nation & Newton, 1997; Scherfer, 1994b). Coady (1993) advocates explicit teaching of a base vocabulary at an early stage of acquisition, which should be learned to the point of automaticity, with contextual learning during the later stages.

Concerning the use of the labels incidental and intentional learning, when L2 educationalists advocate incidental vocabulary learning while devaluating the role of intentional learning, what they probably mean is that the former procedure leads to information processing of a higher quality, and hence to better retention, than the latter procedure. However, as this section has tried to demonstrate, this is not necessarily the case. One could think of an incidental task (i.e., a task without forewarning that a retention test will follow) allowing learners to process new vocabulary only superficially or even skip new words altogether (e.g., 'Read the following text and summarize its contents in about five sentences') and one could think of an intentional task (i.e., a task with forewarning of an upcoming retention task) forcing learners to process new vocabulary elaborately (e.g., 'Read the following text, look up the meaning of any words you don't know in your dictionary, summarize the text's contents in about five sentences, and learn the new words looked up. You will later be tested on your knowledge of the words in this text'). The last ten years have witnessed the publication of a number of studies giving empirical evidence for the claim that L2 vocabulary acquisition during reading will be substantially enhanced when learners' attention is oriented towards unfamiliar words, e.g., when the meaning of unfamiliar words is given by means of marginal glosses or has to be looked up in a dictionary, or when reading is combined or supplemented with a simple fill-in exercise (Chun & Plass, 1996; Hulstijn, 1992, 1993; Hulstijn, Hollander & Greidanus, 1996; Hulstijn & Laufer, 1998; Hulstijn & Trompetter, 1999; Jacobs, Dufon & Fong, 1994; Knight, 1994; Krantz, 1991; Laufer & Osimo, 1991; Laufer & Shmueli, 1997; Mondria & Wit-de Boer, 1991; Paribakht & Wesche, 1999; Watanabe, 1997).[20] Huckin and Coady (1999: 183–184) refer to a number of empirical studies suggesting that attention for new words is governed in large part by task demands.

As will be further illustrated in the next section, in L2 pedagogy it is important to design tasks that focus learners' attention on vocabulary learning and to make them aware of the importance of efficient vocabulary learning strategies. From an educational point of view, simply encouraging learners to spend much time on reading and listening, although leading to some incidental vocabulary learning, will not be enough in itself.[21]

---

[20] Most of the experiments conducted by Hulstijn and his associates on incidental vocabulary learning were designed with only an immediate post-test to measure retention of word knowledge; they did not include one or more delayed post-tests. Vocabulary learning experiments containing no delayed post-test(s) have been criticized on methodological grounds by Wang, Thomas and Ouellette (1992). However, the present author is of the opinion that a distinction should be made between measuring the effect of information processing during initial exposure to new (lexical) information (e.g., incidental vocabulary learning during the performance of a L2 reading comprehension task) and measuring the effect of presence or absence of information processing after initial exposure (e.g., whether or not, and if, how and how often, words encountered during reading are encountered again, e.g., through rehearsal). If the aim of the investigation is to assess incidental learning taking place during initial exposure, an immediate post-test is all one needs. Obviously, people tend to forget information without additional exposure or rehearsal and therefore, under such circumstances, performance on a delayed post-test will generally be lower than performance on an immediate post-test. This fall in performance, however, is irrelevant from a theoretical perspective (when the research question focuses on the differential effect of various types of information processing during initial exposure) and trivial from an educational perspective (because all teachers and learners know that rehearsal is highly recommendable for successful long-term retention of information). Delayed post-tests, therefore, are appropriate only if the research question focuses on what happens with information *after* initial exposure under various conditions of rehearsal or re-exposure.

[21] As Schmidt (this volume) observes, N.C. Ellis (1994c) claims that attention (but not awareness) is necessary and sufficient for learning the perceptual aspects of word forms, whereas learning word meanings requires both attention and explicit awareness. This difference, however, may be of little practical value because, as has already been argued in the first section, for words to be useful tools for language learners and users, they must be represented in their users' mental lexicons as *combinations* of formal and semantic information. Thus, successful acquisition of words in this combinatory sense will almost always require attention *and* awareness.

To sum up, the labels incidental and intentional learning no longer reflect a major theoretical distinction. It is the quality and frequency of the information processing activities (i.e. elaboration on aspects of a word's form and meaning, plus rehearsal) which determine retention of new information, far more than the question of whether learners are forewarned of an upcoming retention test or the question of whether they process lexical information without or with the intention to commit it to memory. Thus, both the experimental researcher and the language teacher can still make use of the labels in their methodological and educational senses, but they must be aware of the fact that neither the presence or absence of a post-test nor the presence or absence of a learning intention determine the retention of information.

Pedagogic consequences

This section is concerned with the pedagogic consequences of the psycholinguistic insights mentioned in the two previous sections. It will examine the role of elaboration, rehearsal and automatization in the attainment of vocabulary knowledge and use. The recommendations in this section are based on the view, exposed in the previous section, that, from an educational (as opposed to a theoretical) point of view, incidental and intentional vocabulary learning should be treated as *complementary* activities which *both* deserve to be practised.

Vocabulary learning activities

As was mentioned in the first section, most teaching materials for L2 learners at beginning and intermediate levels explicitly teach and rehearse a target core vocabulary of up to around 2,000 high-frequency words, to be selected on the basis of frequency and range and perhaps also on some secondary criteria such as coverage, availability, centre of interest, and difficulty/learnability (Nation & Waring, 1997; O'Dell, 1997). Many current multimedia language learning programs have built-in components dealing with vocabulary learning, offering opportunities:

1. to look up various kinds of lexical information in an electronic vocabulary list;
2. to paste this information into a personal vocabulary data base;
3. to organize such a personal list into several categories (such as 'well known and not in need of further practice', 'known but still

in need of occasional practice', 'not yet known well enough & in need of frequent practice');
4. to offer a variety of vocabulary exercises (using an algorithm that repeats incorrectly answered items at shorter intervals than items correctly answered);
5. to offer vocabulary tests with immediate feedback on performance;
6. to offer learners the opportunity to request additional rehearsal of words they felt they did not know well.

However, most L2 learners have to learn large numbers of words beyond a core vocabulary, words to which they are not frequently exposed during normal reading or listening activities. For the retention of these words it is necessary that learners are made aware of the nature and extent of their formidable word learning task and are taught effective strategies for coding and memorizing new words (e.g., Bogaards, 1994; G. Ellis & B. Sinclair, 1989; Esser & Nowak, 1990; Harley, 1995; Hatch & Brown, 1995, Ch. 15; Hulstijn, 1997; Lewis, 1994; Oxford & Crookall, 1989; Scherfer, 1994a, 1994b; Schmitt, 1997).

A well-known technique, to be applied when learners encounter an unfamiliar word while reading a L2 text, is to figure out the meaning of an unfamiliar word while using various inferencing strategies, such as analyzing the word's form and using contextual information (Nation & Coady, 1988; Nation, 1990, Ch. 10). This is a useful activity because it requires learners to process the relevant information elaborately, and elaborative processing is potentially conducive to retention. It is now common practice to make the teaching of such elaboration techniques an integral part of the L2 learning curriculum (e.g., Brown, 1994). However, as has been pointed out by some researchers (e.g., Coady, 1997b; Hulstijn, 1997; Lawson & Hogden, 1996; and the sources referred to in these papers) elaborating on a new word's meaning in itself may not suffice to have it available for later access. High quality information processing when a word is first encountered as such is not predictive of retention outcomes. Rather, as some word forms are less codable and more arbitrary than others (see the first section of this chapter) they need deliberate rehearsal.

A classic and approved rehearsal technique is to write down a word's form (its orthographic form) on one side of an index card, while writing all other information on the reverse side, and to review the cards (in varying order) at regular intervals (Mondria & Mondria-de Vries, 1993; Wallace, 1982: 61). The information on the reverse side may include:

- morphology (gender, flection, derivation, composition);
- pronunciation and prosody;
- meaning(s), including the word's translation in L1;
- typical examples of usage;
- any associations, common as well as bizarre, general as well as personal, verbal as well as non-verbal, that may strengthen the word's codability and memorability.

Many L2 learners will find it cumbersome to carry around index cards for rehearsal. Good alternatives are a loose-leaf, alphabetically ordered vocabulary notebook or a personal, electronic database on a (preferably portable) PC. The advantage of an electronic database over a hard copy notebook is that it allows (depending on the software) multiple orderings of its entries and the establishment of inter-entry linkages, whereas the hard copy notebook allows only one ordering (usually the alphabetical order). The ideal software program would combine the function of a personal lexical database (to be stored with lexical information by the learner himself/herself) with the function of a drill master, providing opportunities for rehearsal while keeping a record of the learner's performance and putting each lexical entry in categories such as 'well known', 'known but still in need of regular rehearsal', 'not known and in need of frequent rehearsal'.

Rehearsal regimes

Landauer and Bjork (1978) distinguish between the repetition of new information (e.g., when a L2 learner is being exposed to a target word repeatedly, beyond his or her own volition), and the testing of new information (e.g., when a L2 learner, after having encountered a target word, has deliberately decided to test him or herself repeatedly). In a name-learning experiment using college students, these researchers found that uniform spacing was better in the former case and a pattern of increasing intervals in the latter case. The educational implication of this finding would be that incidental vocabulary learning benefits from regular and frequent exposure whereas intentional vocabulary learning benefits from self tests with increasing intervals.

Studies by Bloom and Shuell (1981) and Dempster (1987) on L2 vocabulary learning have shown, not surprisingly, that if some 40 vocabulary items (consisting of a L2 word form and a L1 translation) had to be learned in a single learning session, massed presentation or practice (e.g., the presentation of each target item three times immediately after each other) had much less effect than did spaced presentation.[22] Furthermore, 'maintenance rehearsal' in STM (as when one repeats a name or telephone number, thereby continuing to prime an existing representation) does not lead to long-term learning, in contrast to 'elaborative rehearsal', involving the formation of connections between the new information and information already known (Baddeley, 1997: 123). Quite remarkable in this respect are the investigations of Bahrick and his associates and relatives (Bahrick, 1984; Bahrick & Phelps, 1987; H. P. Bahrick, L. E. Bahrick, A. S. Bahrick & P. E. Bahrick, 1993). Bahrick (1984) first conducted a cross-sectional study among 800 Americans who had learned Spanish in high school or college. The results show that Spanish vocabulary will be recallable for more than 25 years if the vocabulary is not lost during the first 5 years following training. Bahrick and Phelps (1987) then conducted a longitudinal study involving 35 individuals who learned and relearned 50 English–Spanish word pairs under ten different retraining regimes. For instance, in condition 1, subjects were administered six retraining sessions on the same day in which they had first learned the words, whereas in condition 10, subjects were administered seven retraining sessions with 30-day intervals. Approximately 8 years after the termination of training, subjects' retention was tested. Recall was 15%, 8% and 6% for subjects who had trained with intervals of 30, 1 and 0 days respectively. The results of this study clearly demonstrate that retention probability is greatly enhanced for words that are well encoded in one or two presentations and are subsequently accessed several times at intervals of 30 days. In the study published in 1993, the four members of the Bahrick family report the results of a 9-year longitudinal investigation conducted on themselves. Each of the four subjects learned six sets of 50 English–French or English–German word pairs (300 words in total). Relearning sessions were administered at intervals of 14, 28 or 56 days and continued for 13 or 26 sessions, yielding a 3 × 2 factorial design. Retention was tested for 1, 2, 3 or 5 years after training had terminated. The results show that retention benefited from both independent variables. Best retention – 5 years after termination of relearning – was attained when words had been retrained with 56-day intervals (60%), and worst retention was attained when words had been retrained with 14-day intervals. This result was offset, however, by a slower acquisition under the 56-day regime than under the 28 and 14-day regimes.

---

[22] For details concerning optimal block sizes per training session for the learning of bilingual word lists see the monumental study of Crothers and Suppes (1967). Vocabulary block size refers to the number of word pairs per training session. Crothers and Suppes found that, generally, either the largest or the smallest block size are optimal.

Although the validity of the Bahrick studies is limited because subjects in the two longitudinal studies did not use the L2 during the long duration of the investigation, and the number of words to be learned was relatively small, the studies provide support for the suggestions that optimal retention will be attained if new vocabulary is initially rehearsed with frequent intervals (e.g. one day apart) and with intervals gradually becoming longer until they are approximately one month apart.

Mathematical models simulating word knowledge gains under various assumptions suggest that there are at least two independent factors determining learning/forgetting curves: the time interval between trials for a particular word, and the number of interfering words (personal communication, Dr. T. Chessa, Psychology Department of the University of Amsterdam). Learning/forgetting curves are further determined by word characteristics (e.g., concrete words are better retained than abstract words; see the first section) and by a retrieval practice effect: words correctly remembered on one test are more likely to be remembered than words not remembered but followed by feedback (Meara, 1989). In an incidental vocabulary learning study, in which EFL learners read an English novel and were subsequently surprised with a vocabulary test, Horst, Cobb and Meara (1998) obtained some evidence suggesting that learners with larger vocabulary knowledge profited more from reading the novel than learners with smaller vocabularies, suggesting that the 'rich get richer'.

Pimsleur (1967) proposed a L2 vocabulary memory schedule according to which the learner should be reminded of the new word with intervals increasing in length by a factor of two, i.e. after approximately 5 sec., 25 sec., 2, 10 and 50 minutes, 5 hours, 1 day, 5 days, 20 days. Bjork (1988) proposed the following retrieval practice for the maintenance of knowledge: 'A nearly immediate first rehearsal could be followed by additional rehearsal at successively longer delays (. . .). In principle, if one were able to do so, one should schedule each successive retrieval just prior to the point where one would otherwise lose access to the item in memory' (p. 399).[23]

Obviously, for any particular word there is no way of knowing when the point of losing access would be reached, because words differ in learning difficulty. But the gist of the recommendation is clear:

---

[23] Bjork quotes the following verse, written by the famous psychologist Ulric Neisser during a conference:
   1. 'You can get a good deal from rehearsal
   2. If it just has the proper dispersal.
   3. You would just be an ass
   4. To do it *en masse*: your remembering would turn out much worsal.'

distributed practice with increasing intervals after correct retrievals and short intervals after incorrect retrievals generates much higher retention than does massed practice (Baddeley, 1997: 112–113) and 'items that are difficult to learn should be overlearned to ensure long-term retention' (Atkins & Baddeley, 1998: 549).

The computer, obviously, must be considered as a welcome aid in the implementation of a well-designed rehearsal regime, since, as Van Bussel (1994) demonstrated, it can be easily programmed to keep track of the learner's performance on every individual word, retesting less well known words more often than well known words. Nation and Waring (1997) stress the importance of achieving a balance between meaning-focused, form-focused and fluency-focused rehearsal activities (see also Gatbonton & Segalowitz, 1998; Segalowitz & Gatbonton, 1995).

Rote learning and learning by heart

At this point, it is appropriate to address the much-debated issue of 'rote learning' (as in the learning of lists of isolated L2/L1 word pairs) and 'learning by heart' (as in memorizing a poem or dialogue). If by rote learning is meant repetition of information without understanding the meaning of the information being repeated, then rote learning will hardly have a useful place in the L2 curriculum. However, to the extent that rote learning implies that information is repeated with an understanding of its meaning, it may certainly have a place, among many other information processing techniques geared towards repetition with understanding. Affected by the behaviourist-cognitivist paradigm shift of the 1960s, most authors of publications on L2 pedagogy in the last 25 years hold rote learning in abhorrence.[24] This

---

[24] Behaviourists investigating verbal learning, however, did not equate language learning with reflex-type habit formation. They considered habit formation by classical conditioning of limited applicability to language learning (Anisfeld, 1966). Even the famous Benton Underwood, who conducted innumerable verbal learning experiments, considered the picture of a subject in a rote learning experiment as being a *tabula rasa* as archaic. Rather, the subject 'actively calls upon all the repertoire of habits and skills to outwit the investigator' (Underwood, 1964: 52). And John B. Carroll, psychologist and long-time investigator of L2 learning, who personally witnessed and actively co-executed the behaviourist-cognitive paradigm shift, sees 'automatization' and 'habit formation' as being essentially the same thing. Initial coding, according to Carroll (1986: 107), involves the putative cognitive event of 'noticing'. Over time, as the number of occasions on which a given regularity is noticed increases, the speed and accuracy of any responses that depend on this regularity also increase. 'Such increases are referred to by the term "habit formation"; they may also be described in terms of automatization' (Schneider & Shiffrin, 1977: 107). Carroll then quotes from Schneider and Shiffrin (1977), calling their description of an 'automatic process', 'particularly apt as a description of the formation of linguistic habits' (ibid.).

is illustrated by a memorable statement of Stevick, quoted with approval by Lewis (1994: 118): 'If you want to forget something, put it in a list'. This unqualified rejection of rote learning of information kept in a list format, however, may be unwarranted. For instance, suppose a learner has encountered some new vocabulary items in a meaningful reading or listening task and has done all of the following: tried to infer their meaning, checked these inferences by consulting a dictionary, and listed the word forms (along with other relevant lexical information) in a personal notebook. It would then only be profitable for him or her to regularly consult that list and rehearse its contents. That is, although it would not make sense to learn the entire list (so that the learner could spontaneously recall all items in the listed order), it would make sense to learn each individual item on the list.

If one were to conduct a study comparing the effect of learning isolated word pairs versus the effect of learning words in contexts deemed to be 'functional' (e.g., in a real-life communicative situation) one would fall victim to the same error as was made some fifty years ago in studies comparing incidental and intentional conditions of learning (as discussed above). The technique or task as such will not be decisive; its effect will rather be determined by the nature of the information processing, and that may vary within techniques and tasks.[25] Thus, to take two examples from past and current L2 classroom practice, to have L2 learners learn a dialogue by heart (even if in a mimicry fashion, cf. Rivers, 1967: 183–184) or to have L2 learners learn a L1–L2 list of isolated vocabulary items, may be effective or ineffective to the extent that learners realize what they are doing. If a dialogue were learned by heart and followed by later role play (enacting the situation), or if the words of a list were rehearsed and followed up by a communicative task in which they were to be used meaningfully, then there is no reason why these activities should be condemned.

Skill in automatic word access

As was explained in the first section of this chapter, it is not enough to 'know' a word; one must also be able to use word knowledge quickly in order to be able to listen or speak at a speed of two to three words per second and to read at a speed of three to six words per second. The training of automaticity appears to be a neglected component in

---

[25] It is important to keep this in mind in interpreting the ongoing debate concerning the task-based approach (see Skehan & Foster, and Robinson, this volume). It is not the task itself but rather the information processing activities with which it is being executed that must be taken into account in order to assess its usefulness.

many current L2 curricula. This may be caused by the following two trends in current L2 pedagogy:

1. The claim that language learning is primarily driven by the processing of large quantities of new, but level-appropriate input which will therefore hopefully be 'comprehensible' at the so-called 'i plus one' level (Krashen, 1982). This means that new input should ideally contain many familiar elements as well as some new elements whose meaning and function may become clear with the help of the familiar ones. On this basis L2 specialists and material writers encourage L2 learners to proceed with considerable speed through the chapters and lessons of their course materials and not to reprocess old materials too extensively. Learners are urged not to worry too much if not all the contents of one lesson have been mastered or not all the exercises and tasks of one lesson have been completed before the next lesson is embarked upon. Learners are assured that acquisition proceeds not in an instantaneous but in an incremental fashion and that many words and other linguistic elements not yet acquired will recur in later lessons.

2. The claim that for the comprehension of a text read or heard it is not necessary to know all the words, that it is in fact very likely that L2 learners will be exposed to authentic reading or listening texts containing many unfamiliar words for a considerable time, and that it is therefore important to develop intelligent, task-appropriate comprehension strategies to compensate for their lack of vocabulary knowledge. Examples of such compensatory strategies are: concentrating on familiar words deemed to be relevant, activating background knowledge, inferring the meaning of unknown words from the verbal and nonverbal context, as well as consulting authoritative sources such as dictionaries, teachers, native speakers and other experts.

Pedagogic practices based on both these claims are important and welcome ingredients of any up-to-date L2 curriculum and their theoretical foundations are sound in principle. But, as so often in educational practice, they run the risk of being overemphasized and applied to the detriment of other sound principles. As for the first trend of pushing for a certain speed in the presentation of new input, this should not mean that rehearsal of 'old input' for the benefit of training automaticity should be abandoned. And the second trend, of making top–down inferring strategies at the word, text and non-verbal context levels an integral part of the L2 curriculum, should not mean that the training of automatic word recognition at sublexical levels should be abandoned. It is in this *complementary* spirit that the practical suggestions in the following subsection are recommended.

Training tasks for automatic word recognition in listening and reading, or processing at the 'i minus one' level

Units of most L2 course materials for students at beginning and intermediate levels are normally constructed around a listening or a reading text. Such a text usually contains a number of new elements (words, expressions for certain speech acts, discourse features, grammatical structures, intonational patterns), most of which are exploited in various ways (explanations, exercises) after their presentation. Normally these texts, together with a number of comprehension questions, are presented as a listening or reading comprehension task. Thus it is a comprehension task that normally provides the setting in which students encounter and explore the new elements. After this exploration, students proceed to other tasks and seldom return to the text from where they started. Yet, for the sake of training automatic word recognition, it would be desirable that students be repeatedly exposed to the original text thereafter, not only while working on the current unit (which began with the original text) but also when they have moved on to later units. In the case of a listening text, the instruction could be formulated as:

'Now that you are familiar with all the elements of this text, train yourself to recognize *all* the words in it. Pay attention to how the words sound in concatenated speech. (In normal speech, words are pronounced without pauses in between. A word may sound a little different each time, depending on the preceding and following words [assimilation] and on speaker factors such as accent and emotional state.) Play the text, utterance by utterance, and check whether you recognized every word in it by consulting the printed text. A simple way of doing this is by whispering every word to yourself or by counting the number of words. If an utterance is too long to do this, cut it up into sections short enough for you to remember. Do this as long as is necessary. In the end you should be able to understand *every* word without looking at the printed text.'

Rereading or relistening to an old text will seldom be motivating to students because it does not contain any new information and therefore does not arouse their curiosity. Ideally, each unit of the course materials should therefore contain at least one 'new' listening and one 'new' reading text which contains only 'old' words and constructions but which has the advantage over 'old' texts in that it has the appeal of new information.[26] Some publishers have published reading materials graded at levels of increasing vocabulary difficulty. These readers lend themselves excellently for the purpose of increasing reading speed (for writing and selection guidelines, see Hatch & Brown, 1995: 408–412). Much less common, unfortunately, are such graded texts in aural form. For some foreign languages, however, there is a monthly magazine with articles on a wide variety of topics, including topics of the day, produced in both a written and an aural format. Texts should contain as little vocabulary beyond the 2,000 most frequent words as is possible to just remain interesting and appealing.

Reading or listening to 'new' texts containing 'old' elements, a type of input processing at the 'i minus one' level (a phrase suggested by, among others, Day & Bamford, 1998, in contrast to Krashen's famous 'i plus one' input), might boost students' motivation by giving them the experience of being able to understand (almost) everything (almost) effortlessly upon a first encounter, just like hearing or reading a text in L1. Thus, instead of being boring, automaticity training in the form of hearing or reading 'new' texts containing 'old' elements should give students experiences of pleasure and satisfaction, thereby combining business with pleasure. Some of the following tasks, designed to foster reading speed, might be manipulated to do just that:

*Tell the difference
Learners listen to a text and have the printed text simultaneously available. However, the printed text deviates now and then from the oral input: some words have been (a) deleted, (b) added, or (b) substituted by another word. Both the oral and the written input are grammatical, however. The text should not contain unfamiliar words. Learners have to spot the deviations. This forces them to read quickly (i.e. in the speed of the speech delivery).[27]

*Silent reading
Learners silently read *short* texts (e.g., interesting newspaper clippings of approximately 200 words) during the first five minutes of a class period. Then follows a brief discussion of maximally five minutes, *not* focusing on vocabulary but on learners' opinion. At the end of

---

[26] However, it must be acknowledged that as soon as such a 'new' practice-for-automaticity text containing 'old' elements is repeated, its semantic content is not 'new' to the students either.

[27] Examples:
1. Learners hear 'You must do this very fast' but hear 'You must do this fast'.
2. Learners hear 'You must do this fast' but hear 'You must do this very fast'.
3. Learners hear 'You must do this very fast' but hear 'You must do this quickly'.

the class period the text will be read once again, silently, in only two minutes.

*Fun reading
Learners are given assignments for extended reading *at their linguistic level* (e.g., using so-called 'graded readers'). They must be given a wide variety of topics to choose from. The texts should not be too long. Learners are given rewards that they themselves perceive as a real reward.

*Bimodal input
Learners watch television programs both spoken and subtitled in L2 (so-called 'bimodal input'). Repetition is highly recommendable. Learners are forced to read with the speed of subtitle presentation.

*Reversed subtitling
Learners watch television programmes spoken in their L1 but under-titled in L2. This is called 'TV with reversed subtitles'. Repetition is highly recommendable. Learners are forced to read with the speed of subtitle presentation.

Conclusion

There is some confusion in current L2 pedagogy concerning the question of what to adopt and what to reject of behaviourist and cognitive psychology and to what extent the principles of these two paradigms can or cannot coexist. The present chapter aimed to give a balanced answer to this question as far as vocabulary learning is concerned. What L2 pedagogy can and should adopt from cognitive psychology is the basic proposition that it is the nature of information processing which primarily determines retention (*elaboration*). The more a learner pays attention to a word's morphonological, orthographic, prosodic, semantic and pragmatic features and to intraword and interword relations, the more likely it is that the new lexical information will be retained. It is not important whether the learner does so with the explicit intention to commit the information to memory and not to forget it (*intentional learning*) or with the intention to use the information for the successful completion of a listening, reading, speaking or writing activity (potentially resulting in *incidental learning*). Thus, encountering new words in context and extensive reading, as advocated in current L1 and L2 pedagogy, are neither necessary nor sufficient for efficient vocabulary expansion. Readers should apply a variety of decontextualization skills and write down the lexical information encountered during reading.

Rich, elaborate processing, however, is not enough either. New information will seldom leave a lasting trace in memory if not frequently reactivated. Reactivation of high-frequency words will occur naturally when learners frequently engage in listening, reading, speaking and writing activities. The reactivation of targeted low-frequency words encountered during extensive reading, and subsequently written down on index cards, in a hard-copy notebook or in a computer program, must take place by means of deliberate *rehearsal* activities, because the likelihood of these words reoccurring soon during normal extensive reading activities is too small. Deliberate vocabulary rehearsal should begin with short intervals and level off at approximately monthly intervals.

In order to attain *automaticity* in accessing high-frequency words, it is important that learners are exposed to reading and listening texts which contain only familiar words (the 'i minus one' level). Rereading a text until a speed of 300 words per minute is reached while the contents of the text is comprehended should be a major learning target. Similarly, learners should relisten to oral texts until they recognize all words.

'Intentional learning', 'rehearsal', 'practice', 'drill', and 'automaticity' are terms which often elicit negative connotations among L2 specialists, being associated with the superficial parroting of meaningless stimuli, as in practices based on behaviourist psychology. However, several decades of psycholinguistic research have made it clear that lexical information simply must be reactivated regularly for it to remain quickly accessible. Therefore, these terms deserve to be updated in the jargon of the L2 specialist, albeit with the note that the nature of the processing during a rehearsal event will determine the likelihood of the information being rescued from the fate of oblivion. With this proviso in mind, it is legitimate to conclude that 'intentional vocabulary learning' as well as 'drill and practice' must have a place in the L2 curriculum, complementary to (not instead of) the well-established principles of incidental and contextual learning. Fortunately, as the final section has tried to show, there are plenty of ways of making intentional learning and drill & practice activities interesting and appealing, with the help of the (multimedia) computer serving in a role for which it is well suited, namely that of the ideal slave, stuffed with the most precious of all resources: human imagination.

10 Task complexity, cognitive resources, and syllabus design: a triadic framework for examining task influences on SLA

Peter Robinson

Introduction

In this chapter I describe a theoretical rationale for and, where possible, empirical research into criteria to be adopted when progressively increasing the cognitive demands of second language (L2) tasks. These criteria, I argue, provide a basis for decisions about sequencing tasks in a task-based syllabus as well as a framework for studying the effects of increasing L2 task complexity on production, comprehension and learning. I distinguish task *complexity* (the task dependent and proactively manipulable cognitive demands of tasks) from task *difficulty* (dependent on learner factors such as aptitude, confidence, motivation, etc.) and task *conditions* (the interactive demands of tasks), arguing that these influences on task performance and learning are different in kind, and have not been sufficiently distinguished in previous approaches to conceptualizing the options in, and consequences of, sequencing tasks from the syllabus designer's perspective. My focus in this chapter is on the issue of task complexity, which I argue should be the sole basis of prospective sequencing decisions since most learner factors implicated in decisions about task difficulty can only be diagnosed *in situ* and in process, so cannot be anticipated in advance of implementation of a syllabus and therefore can be of no use to the prospective materials and syllabus designer. Those learner factors which can be diagnosed in advance of syllabus implementation (e.g., aptitude and cognitive style) have not to date been shown to have stable effects on task performance at the different levels of complexity proposed here. However, if assessed *in situ*, learner factors contributing to task difficulty could potentially influence on-line methodological choice of options, such as how to pair and group learners under differing task conditions, though here again there is little research evidence to date suggesting how this could be done most effectively.

With these issues and distinctions in mind, in the first section I review the issue of task complexity from a pedagogical and from a

287

theoretical perspective. From a pedagogical perspective I relate task complexity, cognitively defined, to options in syllabus design and to other issues in the implementation and assessment of task-based instruction. I then summarize previous approaches to conceptualizing and theorizing task complexity, particularly work by G. Brown, Anderson, Shillcock and Yule (1984), Brindley (1987), Candlin (1987), Nunan (1989), and Prabhu (1987) (see also Skehan & Foster, this volume). While there is some overlap between the proposals reviewed there is also considerable disparity between them in scope, theoretical motivation and research support. In the second section, therefore, I propose a narrower but, I believe, more operationalizable framework for studying task complexity and for the design of language learning materials and task-based syllabuses that draws on some previous SLA research as well as on some current work in applied cognitive psychology. I also relate this framework to issues in the study of memory, attention, automaticity, and the processes implicated in focus on form during task performance which are discussed in greater detail by N. Ellis, Schmidt, DeKeyser and Doughty (this volume). After summarizing findings from the few studies to date based on this theoretical framework, I briefly consider further implications of the framework and findings described for sequencing tasks in task-based approaches to syllabus design.

Task-based language teaching: the grading and sequencing issue

Pedagogical perspectives

Syllabus design is based essentially on a decision about the *units* of classroom activity, and the *sequence* in which they are to be performed, and these two decisions have consequences for the *role* of the learner in assimilating the language encountered in classrooms. A brief summary of options in choice of unit, sequence and learner role is given here in order to contrast two contemporary task-based approaches, those of Long (1985, 1998; Long & Crookes, 1992) and Skehan (1996, 1998a, 1998b; Skehan & Foster, this volume), with other approaches to pedagogy and syllabus design.

There are options in the units to be adopted in syllabus design. Units can be based on an analysis of the *language* to be learned, in terms of grammatical structures, as in R. Ellis (1993, 1997); lexical items and collocations, as in Willis (1990); propositional relations, as in Crombie (1985); or notions and functions, as in Wilkins (1976) and Finocchiaro and Brumfit (1983). Units may also be based on an analysis of the components of *skilled behavior* in the L2, such as the reading microskills described by Richards (1990) and J. D. Brown (1995), or the communicative skills forming part of Munby's (1978) communicative needs profiler, and Johnson's (1996) recent work. In contrast, in task-based approaches to instruction, particularly as described by Long and Skehan, units of analysis are *pedagogic tasks* or gradual approximations to real world target tasks, such as serving meals on an airplane (Long, 1985, 1998); finding a journal article in a library using library technology (Robinson & Ross, 1996); or taking part in an academic discussion (Robinson, Strong, Whittle & Nobe, 2001). Long argues a needs analysis is necessary to identify real world target tasks for specific groups of learners and based on these the syllabus designer plans a series of pedagogic tasks; '... these are a series of initially simple, progressively more complex approximations to the target task' (Long, 1998: 10).

While Long places great importance on the needs analysis stage of task-based instruction, and on the opportunities to focus on form in the context of meaningful interaction that task work provides, in line with his 'interactionist' theory of L2 development (Long, 1996), Skehan takes a more cognitive, information processing, approach to task-based instruction and the criteria for selecting and sequencing tasks, acknowledging a needs analysis is desirable, but not always possible (Skehan, 1998a: 96). Like Long, Skehan rejects linguistic grading as a criterion for task and syllabus design, defining a task as an activity in which, 'Meaning is primary; there is some communication problem to solve; there is some sort of relationship to comparable real-world activities; task completion has some priority; the assessment of the task is in terms of outcome' (Skehan, 1998a: 95). Skehan concludes that this definition rules out 'an activity that focuses on language itself' such as a transformation drill, or the consciousness raising tasks described by R. Ellis (1997), and many of the tasks in Nunan (1989) which fall within the category of tasks Skehan describes as 'structure-trapping', i.e., designed as a context for the display and practice of linguistic items and which therefore form part of the implementation of a linguistic, structural syllabus.

Along with choices in the units to be adopted, there are choices in the sequence in which they can be presented. A syllabus can consist of a *prospective* decision about what to teach, and in what order. In this case the syllabus will be a definition of the contents of classroom activity. A sequencing decision can also be made *on-line*, during classroom activity, as in Breen's 'process' syllabus (Breen, 1984; Clarke, 1991). In this case the initial syllabus will only guide, but not constrain, the classroom activities. Finally, Candlin has proposed that a syllabus can be *retrospective,* in which case no syllabus will emerge until after the course of instruction. In this case the syllabus functions only as a record of what was done, imposing no controlling constraint on the classroom negotiation of content (Candlin, 1984; Clarke, 1991). In the task-based proposals of Long and Skehan sequencing is based in large part on a prospective decision about the increasing complexity of pedagogic tasks for the learner, although I will suggest that implementational factors may result in on-line adjustments to these decisions for reasons described later in this chapter.

Another distinction in conceptualizing options in syllabus design was made initially by Wilkins (1976; see also R. White, 1988) and refers to the learner's role in assimilating the content provided during group instruction and applying it individually to real world language performance and interlanguage (IL) development. *Synthetic* syllabuses involve a focus on specific elements of the language system, often serially and in a linear sequence, such as grammatical structures or language functions. The easiest, most learnable, most frequent, or most communicatively important (sequencing decisions can be based on each of these ultimately non-complementary criteria, and on others) are presented before their harder, later learned, less frequent, and more communicatively redundant counterparts. These syllabuses assume the learner will be able to put together, or synthesize in real world performance, the parts of the language system they have been exposed to separately.

In contrast, *analytic* syllabuses, of which task-based syllabuses are one variety, do not divide up the language to be presented in classrooms but involve holistic use of language to perform communicative activities. The learner's role in these syllabuses is to analyze or attend to aspects of language use and structure as the communicative activities require them to, in line with: a) their developing *interlanguage systems*; b) preferred *learning style* and *aptitude profile*; and c) to the extent that they are *motivated* to develop to an accuracy level which may not be required by the communicative demands of the task. For these reasons Long (1998) and Skehan (1998a, 1998b) have argued that analytic approaches to syllabus design are more sensitive to SLA processes and learner variables than their synthetic counterparts.

While there are some differences of scope and implementational detail in their rationales for task-based instruction, Long and Skehan are in broad agreement about the SLA motivation for analytic syllabuses, and task-based syllabuses in particular, citing research showing three problems for sequencing decisions in synthetic approaches to syllabus design that adopt language items as units of analysis. Firstly, SLA research has revealed evidence of restructuring and the non-linearity, and punctuated equilibrium (cf. Eldredge & Gould, 1972) of acquisition processes. Learners appear to restructure IL in line with developmental constraints, producing progressively more complex grammatical forms (Cazden, Cancino, Rosansky & Schumann, 1975; Kanagy, 1994; Mackey, 1999; Pienemann, 1989), lexis (Laufer, 1997), and pragmatic behavior (Kasper & Schmidt, 1996), while at each stage in the restructuring process producing many forms which are non-targetlike. However, developmental restructuring is not an additive linear process, as synthetic structural syllabuses seem to imply, since there is evidence of backsliding and U-shaped learning, demonstrating an apparent unlearning of earlier acquired forms and functions (Kellerman, 1985; Larsen-Freeman & Long, 1991), as well as sudden shifts in development. Secondly, SLA research has shown that learners differ with respect to rate of development through certain syntactic and morphological domains, making it problematic to treat learners homogeneously over time (R. Ellis, 1994a; Skehan, 1989). Thirdly, there is insufficient evidence about the learnability of the majority of functions and structures in English, so acquisition-sensitive sequencing decisions – even were they feasible given individual differences (IDs) in rate of progress – could only be made for a small portion of English (Paulston, 1981; White & Robinson, 1995; Widdowson, 1990). Additionally, as Long (1998) and Widdowson (1978) have pointed out, linguistic grading as required by many synthetic structural approaches, at least in the early stages, results in simplified classroom language and texts which are functionally and linguistically impoverished, prohibiting exposure to forms and functions learners may be ready to learn, or need to use.

Task-based approaches differ from language-based approaches to syllabus design in the following respects. They have a performance emphasis and are not predicated on the assumption that levels of target-like accuracy (bench marks of synthetic structural syllabuses) will be achieved in an accumulative manner following lock-step instruction targeted at specific units of language (an unrealistic assumption given the non-linearity of restructuring processes and IDs in rate of progress through developmental sequences referred to above). Achievement during task-based instruction is therefore performance, not system-referenced, and based on a decision about whether and to what degree learners can successfully perform the pedagogic and target tasks that are the focus of instruction (Baker, 1990; Carroll, 1980; Hauptman, LeBlanc & Wesche, 1985; McNamara, 1996; Norris, Brown, Hudson & Yoshioka, 1998; Robinson et al., 2001; Robinson & Ross, 1996). Consequently, in task-based approaches such as those of Long, exposure to target language form predominantly takes place in the context of communicative pair or group work activities, making functional co-ordinates of grammatical structure (as well as speech acts and lexis) available to learners, along with their purely formal aspects, thus potentially providing rich 'cues' to learners (MacWhinney, this volume), and opportunities for elaborative processing (Hulstijn, this volume) of form-function 'mappings' (Doughty, this volume). While synthetic syllabuses adopting linguistic units of analysis may also be implemented by a methodology which provides considerable opportunities for communicative practice, this is usually less common than in task-based approaches, and in many cases practice is focused on functionally and linguistically simplified texts and dialogues encouraging recognition, and repetition of forms targeted for explanation in an earlier presentation phase (see Willis, 1996; Skehan & Foster, this volume). Finally, and particularly in the approach of Long, adopting tasks as the unit of analysis helps to ensure a high degree of real-world relevance, since they are based on a needs analysis of target performance objectives, thereby most likely increasing student interest and motivation in classroom pedagogic activities, and the possibility of direct transfer of the abilities developed in classrooms to similar situational contexts.

Decisions about sequencing based on the relative complexity of pedagogic task content are one element in the delivery of task-based instruction. Task complexity is related to other elements, such as methodology and assessment in Figure 1. Both materials and syllabus design are decisions about *task content* which begin with collection of language input data relevant to target task performance. An option in decisions about language input is whether to simplify, linguistically or elaboratively, the authentic data to facilitate processing by less proficient learners (see Chaudron, 1988; Lynch, 1996; Yano, Long & Ross, 1994). Task conditions refers to the interactive demands of pedagogic tasks, i.e., the distribution of information and the extent of collaboration required to reach a solution (see Duff, 1986; Long, 1989; Pica, Kanagy & Falodun, 1993). Choice of pedagogic task conditions is constrained by the nature of the target task being approximated. For example, listening to an after-hours taped telephone description of bank opening and closing times and other services would best be approximated via a series of one-way closed tasks. Making actual transactions and enquiries over the counter during banking hours would require two-way tasks. Task complexity is represented as a series of options which can be manipulated to progressively increase the cognitive demands of pedagogic tasks, so they approach the full complexity of the target task. Research into those identified here is described in more

Task content	Methodological sequence	Focus on form /assessment
1.Data simple/authentic reading/listening	1. Language input------------------------>	Proactive e.g., flooding
2.Task condition e.g., one/two-way open/closed convergent/divergent	2. Pedagogic task------------------------> performance	Reactive e.g., recasts/rules
3.Task complexity e.g.,+/- single task +/- prior knowledge +/- planning time +/- few elements/steps +/- no reasoning demands +/- here-and-now	3. Assessment of target task---------> (performance-referenced)	Assessment of language (system-referenced)

Figure 1. Elements in the delivery of pedagogic tasks

detail in the following sections of this chapter. The *methodological sequence* of task components requires language input to be followed by pedagogic task performance, and ultimately by assessment of target task abilities using performance-referenced tests. Linked to the language input stage are *proactive* options in focus on form, and linked to the task performance stage are *reactive* options in focus on form (Doughty, this volume; Doughty & Williams, 1998b). Target language ability, in terms of stage of development, accuracy and fluency, can also be assessed via system-referenced tests periodically throughout the course of instruction as a way of examining the extent to which success in achieving performance objectives is calibrated with gains in knowledge of the language system (see Bachman & Palmer, 1996; Baker, 1990; Robinson & Ross, 1996).

A triadic framework for investigating task influences on SLA

If tasks are to be sequenced on the basis of their relative complexity, and not on the basis of linguistic criteria, how is this to be done? Figure 2 distinguishes three groups of factors, which interact to influence task performance, and learning. The first group of factors concern task complexity. These are represented as dimensions, plus or minus a

Task complexity (cognitive factors)	Task conditions (interactive factors)	Task difficulty (learner factors)
a) resource-directing	a) participation variables	a) affective variables
e.g., +/- few elements	e.g., one-way/two-way	e.g., motivation
+/- here-and-now	convergent/divergent	anxiety
-/+ no reasoning demands	open/closed	confidence
b) resource-depleting	b) participant variables	b) ability variables
e.g., +/- planning	e.g., gender	e.g., aptitude
+/- single task	familiarity	proficiency
+/- prior knowledge	power/solidarity	intelligence

Sequencing criteria_____Methodological criteria
Prospective decisions   On-line decisions
about task units   about pairs and groups

Figure 2. A triad of task complexity, condition and difficulty factors

feature, but can also be thought of in some cases as continuums, along which relatively more of a feature is present or absent. Each of these is discussed in more detail later in this paper. These dimensions of complexity, I argue, are design features of tasks and their implementation which can be manipulated to increase or lessen the cognitive demands tasks make on the learner during task performance. For example, tasks requiring simple description of events happening now, in a shared context (+ here and now), where few elements (+ few elements) have to be described and distinguished are less consuming of attentional, memory and reasoning resources than tasks requiring reference to events that happened elsewhere (− here and now), in the past, where many elements have to be distinguished (− few elements), and where reasons have to be given to support statements made (+ reasoning). Similarly, tasks where planning time and prior knowledge are available, requiring a single activity (for example, describing a route from A to B drawn on a map of a familiar area) are less cognitively demanding than tasks without planning time, or prior knowledge support, requiring learners to simultaneously perform two steps in the task (for example, quickly thinking up and describing the direction from A to B on a map of an unfamiliar area). Research into the effects of these dimensions of complexity on language production is reported later in this paper.

It is important to note, however, a further distinction made between these dimensions in Figure 2. Some *resource-directing* dimensions of complexity increase the demands made on learners' cognitive resources, while at the same time potentially directing their resources to aspects of language code that can be utilised in completing the task (for example, using present or past tense forms to describe things happening now versus in the past, or using attributive adjectives and/or relative clauses to distinguish between many similar elements). On the other hand, tasks can increase in complexity along *resource-depleting* dimensions, and make extra resource demands (relative to tasks simpler along these dimensions) which cannot be met through the use of any particular features of the language code. Such is the case when making a task more complex by removing prior knowledge support, or making it a dual, not single task.

The factors contributing to task *complexity*, then, are design features of tasks, which are proactively manipulable by the task designer, and can be used as the basis of sequencing decisions. Following Spilsbury, Stankov and Roberts (1990) I argue that these factors need to be distinguished from the learner factors contributing to task *difficulty*. Task difficulty concerns learners' *perceptions* of the demands of the task, and these are determined by both *affective* variables (such as motivation to complete the task) and by *ability* factors such as aptitude. Two learners, that is, differing in motivation, or aptitude, may find the same task easier or more difficult than each other as a result of these differences between them – more motivated learners, or learners higher in aptitude finding the task easier than less motivated learners, or those with lower aptitude. Task difficulty should therefore help explain variation in task performance *between any two learners* performing the same task (simple or complex), whereas task complexity should help explain *within learner* variation in performance on any two tasks (simple and complex). Since affective variables contributing to task difficulty are hard, or impossible, to diagnose in advance of engagement with the task in context, and can sometimes be unpredictably influenced by participant variables, they can therefore play little role in *a priori* decisions about task sequencing, although they are extremely important to assess on-line during classroom activity.

Finally, as briefly described above, task *condition* factors concern the nature of the *participation* required on task (e.g., whether information goes one way, or two ways, whether the task solution is closed or open), and also *participant* variables, such as whether the groups or pairs are same/different gender, or previously familiar/unfamiliar with each other. As argued above, choice of pedagogic task conditions is largely constrained by the nature of the target task being approximated. Therefore, once again, I would suggest, participation and participant factors are unlikely to be a useful basis for *a priori* sequencing decisions, since they will largely have been specified on the basis of the needs analysis, and fidelity to the target task performance the pedagogic tasks are aiming to facilitate.

Historical perspectives

The distinction made above between task complexity and task difficulty has not been adopted in previous proposals for grading and sequencing tasks. While I acknowledge that task complexity and task difficulty, as well as task condition factors, interact to determine performance outcomes, they must in principle be distinguished in order to establish a clear basis for *a priori* task sequencing decisions. However, previous discussion of this area has tended to conflate all three factors. An important early contribution to research into task-based teaching, and the issue of grading and sequencing tasks, is that of Prabhu (1987) who describes the theoretical rationale for, and procedures used to deliver, the Bangalore project between 1979 and 1984. This project implemented a task-based 'procedural' syllabus in a number of high schools in South East India which rejected linguistic grading of materials and the provision of grammar rules and explanations or explicit corrective feedback as methodological procedures for focusing learners' attention on form. The project used tasks (such as understanding and using railway or school curriculum timetables) to promote development of the 'means' of communication, identified as the procedures deployed in successfully conveying information, giving reasons and expressing opinions. Prabhu's claim is that the effort expended by learners in using these procedures 'to work out meaning content is . . . a condition which is favorable to the subconscious abstraction – or cognitive formation – of language structure' (1987: 70), a claim which potentially conflicts with Schmidt's arguments (this volume) for the importance of noticing in SLA, and for the rationale offered by Doughty (this volume) for the importance of focus on form. Prabhu's criteria for grading and sequencing tasks are based on a distinction between three task-types; information gap (simple transfer of information); reasoning gap (information transformation requiring inferencing, deduction and other reasoning skills); and opinion gap (expression of preferences, attitudes, feelings and beliefs). Prabhu describes sequencing criteria, established as a result of his observation of this long term project, in the following way.

There may be a case for moving generally from information gap to
reasoning gap to opinion gap activity as learners progress in their language
acquisition, though genuine opinion gap activity is likely to be feasible only
at very advanced stages . . . tasks within a given sequence (i.e., tasks of the

same type forming the basis of several lessons) were ordered by a
commonsense judgement of increasing complexity, the later tasks being
either inclusive of the earlier ones or involving larger amounts of
information, or an extension of the kind of reasoning done earlier.

(Prabhu, 1987, pp. 64 & 39).

These are admittedly intuitive and limited, but also *limiting* conclusions about sequencing criteria. To base sequencing decisions on a
shift from information gap to reasoning gap and then opinion gap
tasks constrains the options available to the task designer in developing pedagogic tasks to approximate the performance objectives of
target tasks since, as mentioned previously, certain real world target
task objectives may require practice under one variety of task conditions, open versus closed or one-way versus two-way, but not others.
Similarly, the distinction between amounts of information, and the
reasoning demands of tasks limits the task designer in the complexity
differentials they can manipulate in designing tasks to meet a variety of
performance objectives. I have also argued above that the distinction
between information and reasoning gap versus opinion gap, is essentially one between task conditions (closed versus open tasks), with the
former necessarily requiring more interaction and interlocutor participation than the latter. The commonsense criteria Prabhu refers to,
such as differences in the amount of information on task, or the reasoning demands of tasks, are *different in kind* from the information
and reasoning gap versus opinion gap distinction, since these do refer to the cognitive demands of tasks, defined independently of task
conditions, and clearly make differential demands on the attentional
and memory resources of the learner. An important empirical issue,
then, not addressed by Prabhu at this early stage, is whether changing
the nature of the solution to the task (from closed to open) does interact with and compound the effects of increasing cognitive complexity.
Recent research (described in the following section) has begun to examine the interaction of task complexity and condition on measures
of learner performance. Other research into the interaction of task
condition and task difficulty (also described in the following section)
suggests, contrary to Prabhu's speculation, that closed tasks may lead
to greater 'difficulty' for learners than open tasks when affective variables such as anxiety and motivation are assessed, since closed tasks
may lead to greater anxiety (Holthouse, 1995) and one study has found
them to be significantly less motivating than open tasks (Jacob, 1996).
Research has also shown that differentials in ability variables such as
the proficiency levels of partners can significantly affect the probability of success on closed tasks (Yule & MacDonald, 1990). In other

words, while being a restricted and constraining basis for sequencing tasks, the claim that open, opinion gap tasks are more demanding than closed information gap tasks is also a simplification, ignoring the potential interaction of learner factors with these task conditions.

Similar criteria for sequencing tasks to those described by Prabhu were identified by controlled experimental research into task performance by G. Brown et al. (1984) taking place concurrently with the Bangalore project. Aimed at producing grading and assessment criteria for tasks to promote the development of speaking skills by native English speaking Scottish school children, G. Brown et al. conclude that:

We have found that different *types* of tasks elicit different types of language and pose different communicative problems for the speaker. From our studies of pupils' performances we have found that there is an ascending scale of difficulty among different task types. Tasks which involve the speaker in describing static relationships among objects are fairly easy to communicate to a hearer, if there are relatively few objects and the relationships among them are fairly simple. Tasks which involve dynamic relationships among people or objects, where a speaker has to describe events which change over time and space, are more difficult. Tasks which require the speaker to communicate abstract notions, for instance in argument or justifications, are more difficult again.

(G. Brown et al., 1984:51).

Additionally, G. Brown et al. claim that tasks of each type can be made more complex by increasing the amount of information on tasks, i.e., that tasks with many elements, relationships and characters are harder than those with fewer elements, relationships and characters. G. Brown et al.'s research was not intended to address the issue of sequencing L2 tasks and like the conclusions of Prabhu regarding sequencing criteria these distinctions alone are undoubtedly too limiting for materials and syllabus designers concerned with sequencing pedagogic tasks to meet a wide variety of real world objectives. It is also true that a large part of G. Brown et al.'s work is concerned with the effect of manipulating a third group of learner factors not included in Figure 2, which are power/solidarity variables such as age, status, interlocutor familiarity and gender, and their effects on interactive task performance. I will not be concerned with these variables here, for reasons of space and since the focus of this chapter is on cognitive factors (though for some work in this area see G. Brown, 1995; Gass & Varonis, 1986; Plough & Gass, 1993).

Following the suggestive early empirical work of Prabhu and G. Brown et al. a number of speculations about task sequencing and complexity were made by researchers working together at MacQuarie University in the mid and late 1980s. In contrast to the limited scope of earlier proposals, Candlin (1987), Brindley (1987) and Nunan (1989) raise a much wider range of issues. Candlin briefly describes six criteria 'to promote discussion and experiment' (1987: 15) but with no guidance about how these are to be operationalized. The first, *cognitive load*, 'a gradual increase in cognitive complexity' is essentially the criterion for sequencing tasks proposed in this chapter, as illustrated in Figures 1 and 2, and described in the following section. However, Candlin's example of such an increase – tasks following a clear chronological sequence and involving individual actions of individual characters, versus more complex and cognitively demanding tasks without a clear chronological development, with multiple actions and actors – compounds a number of separable processing dimensions (referring to events over time, and number of elements/characters and actions). Other suggested sequencing criteria include *communicative stress*, as described by G. Brown et al. (1984), i.e., the communicative difficulties posed by differences in interlocutor power/solidarity; *code complexity and interpretive density*, i.e., the linguistic and argumentative complexity of texts used on tasks; process *continuity*, i.e., learners' own decisions about sequencing learning tasks; *content continuity*, i.e., the extent to which the pedagogic task is modeled on, and approximates, the real world target task; and *particularity and generalizability*, the novelty and situation specificity, versus non specificity of tasks. Clearly this is a disparate collection of criteria which, as Skehan (1998a) notes, offer no transparent guidelines to materials and syllabus designers and which are non-complementary in many ways. For example, a task which closely approximates real world performance (and is therefore easier, Candlin argues, having more content continuity), may well involve greater communicative stress (and so be more difficult) than a simplified, less content continuous version of the task where real world differentials in power relationships between interlocutors have been equalized or nullified.

Brindley (1987) and Nunan (1989) propose more parsimonious, and essentially identical, classifications of factors in their proposals for sequencing decisions. Brindley distinguishes Learner, Task and Text factors, whereas Nunan distinguishes Learner, Activity and Input factors. Brindley's learner factors include confidence and motivation, along with prior learning experience, ability to learn at the pace required, and possession of necessary language skills and relevant cultural knowledge. Having all of these, Brindley claims, makes tasks easier, and I would agree, since they affect 'difficulty', but are of limited use to prospective decisions about sequencing tasks, being hard or impossible to diagnose in advance of instruction. Task factors include degree of cognitive complexity, number of steps, amount of context support, and amount of time provided. These I would argue are of use to prospective syllabus designers and contribute to task complexity along some of the dimensions illustrated in Figure 1 and described in the following section. Brindley's proposed text factors include the length, clarity and familiarity of texts used on tasks. However, the textual language input to tasks, I have argued, while an element in the decisions made about task content (see Figure 1) is independent of the cognitive demands of tasks, and can be adjusted to learner factors such as proficiency level without affecting the design and sequencing of tasks themselves. Johnson (1996) too stresses the independence of task complexity and linguistic input factors:

In the past, grading has generally been in terms of language content. An exercise was considered more or less difficult than another one largely in terms of what language items it included. So exercises expecting the present perfect passive would, for example, be regarded as more complex than those expecting the present simple. It is central to a processing approach to language teaching, however, that what learners are expected to do with language is as important as the actual content of that language. From this standpoint it is perfectly feasible to have a challenging, difficult exercise that uses relatively simple structures – and an easier exercise which uses more complex language.

(Johnson, 1996: 150–151).

There is a danger, also, that using linguistic text factors to grade and sequence tasks may result in those structure-trapping tasks described by Skehan, which use tasks to implement a linguistic syllabus. Nunan (1989) clearly advocates this position. He argues the written input to a task may be more or less complex; the activity required (e.g., ticking an answer or writing it out in sentence or paragraph form) may be more or less complex; and that degree of learner motivation and confidence makes tasks more complex, then concludes that the job of the task designer is to 'create an interesting/relevant text or task at the appropriate level of difficulty', and then see what items on the linguistic syllabus can be taught through it. In Widdowson's terms Nunan advocates the use of tasks to 'realize' or implement a linguistic syllabus.

Recognizing this and other problems with the proposals to date regarding the issue of task complexity and sequencing Widdowson

(1990) wrote:

> But the use of problem solving tasks as units of syllabus content, as distinct from activities for syllabus realization, encounters a number of difficulties. By what criteria, for example, are such tasks to be sequentially arranged? If the sequence is to be in accord with natural learning, as it would only be consistent to require, then reliable information is needed about cognitive development at different stages of maturation, about the conditions, psychological and social, which attend the emergence in the mind of general problem solving capabilities. Armed with such information, we could perhaps relate these capabilities to certain task types, analyzed into their constituent features, and then given token realizations and arranged in an order of increasing complexity. Such information is not, to my mind, currently available.
>
> (Widdowson, 1990: 147–148).

In line with the above observations of Widdowson and Johnson, and complementary to Long's (1985, 1998) proposals for task-based language teaching, in the following section I describe research into a framework for analyzing pedagogic tasks into their cognitive 'constituent features' so they can be arranged in 'an order of increasing complexity' for the learner.

Cognitive dimensions of task complexity

The cognition hypothesis of task-based L2 development

Gradually increasing the cognitive demands of tasks so they approach the full complexity of authentic, real world performance can be justified by the rationale that it enables learners to achieve the 'ends' of learning identified by a needs analysis, i.e., ability to complete a range of performance objectives. This rationale for adopting the approach to syllabus design proposed here is no different from that underlying educational decision making in other domains such as pilot training or mathematics education which approach the development of complex skills and problem-solving abilities (landing an aircraft in a blizzard, doing calculus) through practice on initially simple, then progressively more complex tasks. But this says nothing about language development and the process of L2 learning. A corollary of this approach, then, is the claim that scheduling tasks for language learners in terms of their increasing cognitive complexity will facilitate the 'means' of language learning, and therefore lead to a transition in the learner's knowledge states. This is because tasks making increasing conceptual/communicative demands increasingly engage cognitive resources,

Task demands	Cognitive resources	Learning mechanisms	Performance effects
more cognitively —> demanding tasks	more attention—> to input /output and noticing/ rehearsal in memory	more rule and —> instance learning/ stage shifts/ proceduralization/ cue strengthening	more incorporation of input more modification of output

Figure 3. Tasks, resources, learning and performance

which progressively exploit learning mechanisms leading to greater analysis, modification and restructuring of IL with consequent performance effects (fully articulated, this amounts to what Gregg, this volume, following Cummins, 1983, refers to as a transition theory). Figure 3 summarizes these relationships and in what follows I speculate about the effects of increasing task complexity on learning and performance.

Task demands are the attentional, memory and reasoning demands of tasks that increase the mental workload the learner engages in performing the task. These demands are operationalized as dimensions of complexity (illustrated in Figure 1 and described in more detail below) and can be increased, for example, when the learner performs tasks with little planning time, without sufficient readily accessible background knowledge, or is forced to divide attention when performing one or two secondary tasks simultaneously with the main task. As illustrated in Figure 3, increases in task complexity are proposed to have performance effects; *modification of output*, and *incorporation of input*. While these are related, they are separable phenomena, since the latter logically entails the former, though the reverse is not true. I will deal first with output modification.

Task complexity and output modification

Increasing the cognitive and conceptual demands of the task, I suggest, may lead the learner to push output (Swain, 1985, 1995) to meet those demands causing reanalysis and restructuring of current linguistic resources. There are two motivations for this claim; the *communicative consequences*, and the *functional requirements* of increasing task complexity. Firstly, Swain and Lapkin (1995) note that pushed output can be externally induced by an interlocutor giving external feedback about difficulties in comprehension, and it is likely that increasing the cognitive demands of tasks would often have these communicative consequences, resulting in increasing comprehension difficulty and greater numbers of clarification requests and comprehension checks (Robinson, 2001). Pushed output can also be induced by internal feedback or self monitoring and correction, involving cognitive comparison of learner utterance and input models or recasts as described by Doughty (this volume). Swain and Lapkin speculate that such internal or external feedback caused by communication difficulty:

> ... 'pushes' the learner to modify his/her output. In doing so, the learner may sometimes be forced into a more syntactic processing mode than might occur in comprehension. Thus, output may set 'noticing' in train, triggering the mental processes that lead to modified output ... producing language forces learners to recognize what they do not know or know only partially. This may trigger an analysis of incoming data, that is, a syntactic analysis of the input, or it may trigger an analysis of existing internal linguistic resources, in order to fill the knowledge gap.
>
> (Swain & Lapkin, 1995: 372 & 375).

A second motivation for the claim that more cognitively complex tasks may lead to more pushed and modified output concerns the functional requirements of tasks. Givon (1985, 1989; see also Sato, 1988, 1990) has argued that structural complexity tends to accompany functional complexity in discourse and it is therefore reasonable to assume that in many cases increasingly cognitively demanding tasks will make increasing functional demands on the learner, with their attendant linguistic consequences. Increasing the complexity of tasks on *some* of the dimensions of Figure 2 has been shown to have just these functional and linguistic consequences, i.e., removing contextual support, increasing the number of elements in a task that need to be distinguished and referred to, and increasing the reasoning demands of tasks. These are what I have referred to above as resource-directing, as opposed to resource-depleting dimensions. So, for example, performing a narrative describing events that happened in the past, somewhere else (and therefore with no context support), is facilitated by control over a wider range of morphology (past tense) and syntax (embedded adverbials of time and location, sentence connectors), compared to describing events that are happening now, in context, before our eyes (Sachs, 1983; Meisel, 1987). This latter, functionally less demanding Here-and-Now narrative is also less cognitively complex, making fewer demands on memory resources than the former There-and-Then narrative. Similarly, performance on a task that requires the learner to distinguish one person from a group of four or five similar people is facilitated by control over the use of a wide range of deictic expressions, relative clauses and therefore production of more complex syntax when compared to a task requiring the description of a single person, while also being more attentionally demanding (G. Brown, 1995; G. Brown et al., 1984).

Task complexity and incorporation of input

The differential communicative consequences and functional requirements of simple versus complex tasks can also be expected to affect learner perceptions of input salience and subsequent incorporation of input into production following the arguments above. A number of studies have examined the effects of increasing input salience via interventionist techniques such as underlining or highlighting of forms in written input to tasks (Alanen, 1995; Doughty, 1991; Shook, 1994, J.White, 1998) or via targeted recasts of ungrammatical learner written (Doughty & Varela, 1998) and oral production (Doughty & Varela, 1998; Lyster & Ranta, 1997; Oliver, 1995). While some of these studies have shown positive effects for learner uptake and incorporation of targeted forms made salient in these ways, others have not (e.g., Shook, 1994; J. White, 1998). I would suggest that task complexity is likely to be a factor here, not examined to date in such studies, and that uptake and incorporation of forms is more likely to be evident on more complex tasks, since these more effectively direct learner attention to the targeted input due to their greater communicative consequences (manifested, as described above, in communication breakdowns, comprehension checks and clarification requests), and functional (and therefore structural) requirements. That is, increasingly complex tasks may prompt learners to look for more and more help in the input, attending to facilitative forms made salient by teacher intervention using one or more of the focus on form techniques described by Doughty (this volume).[1]

---

[1] These claims can be seen as a variant of Cromer's (1991, Ch. 1) cognition hypothesis of L1 development, with the difference that for adult L2 development, it is not (as in childhood) cognitive maturation and development that creates the conceptual impetus for language change (see e.g., Gopnik & Meltzoff, 1984; Mandler, 1992; Weist, Lyytinen, Wysocka & Atanassova, 1997) but the demands of the task, which by increasing in complexity may in some cases recapitulate the course of conceptual change over time in childhood (e.g., by requiring reference first to the Here-and-Now, and then to the There-and-Then). Whether such ontogenetically motivated incremental changes in task complexity also provide optimum contexts for the development of needed (task relevant) form function mappings in the L2 is an interesting question. Note, Cromer (1991, Ch. 2) came to reject the strong form of his cognition hypothesis, accepting that innate, informationally encapsulated knowledge also guided L1 development, independently of general cognitive maturation. However the availablity of such knowledge to adult L2 learners is disputed (see Gregg, this volume, and also Ellis, and MacWhinney, for different perspectives).

In summary, the relationships illustrated in Figure 3 suggest that the greater the *cognitive demands* of a task, the more they engage *cognitive resources* (attention and memory), and so are likely to focus attention on input and output, which will have *performance effects*. More complex tasks should lead to more pushing of output, and analysis of IL than simpler counterparts. This should lead to more 'noticing' (as defined by Schmidt, this volume) of relevant forms in the input, and problematic forms in the output, leading to more incorporation (of forms in the input) and modification (of problematic forms in output). While I have described potential relationships between task demands, cognitive resources and performance effects, I have omitted mention of the third component of Figure 3, *learning mechanisms*. I will not specify these in detail here, though there are a number of candidates, many of which are described elsewhere in more detail in this volume. One is strengthening of instance representation in memory, important to instance theories of knowledge representation and access (DeKeyser, this volume; Logan, 1988) – a mechanism likely to be affected by techniques to facilitate incorporation of input, such as flooding, or textual highlighting of forms. Another is proceduralization and production compilation, important to rule-based theories of skill development and automaticity (Anderson, 1993; DeKeyser, 1997, this volume) – a mechanism likely to be implicated in attempts to push output. A third is cue-strengthening, important to the competition model of MacWhinney (this volume) and to other connectionist approaches to knowledge representation (N. Ellis, and Harrington, this volume). All of these putative mechanisms require attention to input and rehearsal in memory (Hulstijn, and Schmidt, this volume), as does (though to a lesser extent) a fourth candidate, Universal Grammar, which holds that attention to aspects of input can trigger parameter resetting of aspects of core grammar (Gibson & Wexler, 1994; and Gregg, this volume).

Admittedly, these relationships between task complexity, resources, learning mechanisms and performance effects are speculative, with few findings yet in many of the areas described. However, findings regarding the effect of task complexity on the accuracy, fluency and complexity of language production have been obtained from a number of studies adopting the framework proposed in this chapter. Before summarizing these, it is necessary to motivate directional hypotheses for the effects of task complexity on measures of accuracy, complexity and fluency, and also to describe the units of analysis adopted in this research. These are the subjects of the following section.

Effects of task complexity on language production

Validating proposed dimensions of complexity for L2 tasks involves predicting differential effects of simple and complex tasks (along a dimension) on performance, both *generally* in terms of whether and to what extent the *task outcome* was achieved, and *specifically* in terms of their effects on *learner language*. There are a number of general indices used by applied cognitive psychologists to assess the effects of task difficulty and mental workload on task performance (see Gopher, 1992; Sanders, 1998; Wickens, 1992) that can be applied, with some modifications, to validating complexity dimensions of L2 tasks. Such measures include whether or not the task was completed, and if so the time taken to task completion, the learners' ratings of task difficulty, and the extent of interference and intrusion on the main task by secondary tasks. Complex tasks are less likely to be successfully completed; take longer than simple counterparts; are rated by learners as more difficult; have physiological consequences (e.g., pupillary dilation, increased heart rate); and are more susceptible to interference from competing tasks. Surprisingly, no studies of L2 task complexity to date have adopted these general indices, despite their obvious relevance, and despite the fact that the workload models themselves which incorporate and weight these separate indices (e.g., *Time Line Analysis and Prediction*, Parks & Boueck, 1989; and *Workload Index*, North & Riley, 1989) are often supported by sophisticated theoretical models of attention and attention switching.

With regard to task effects on language production, the outcome measures are often classified in terms of accuracy, fluency and complexity of learner language. Skehan has suggested, using supporting evidence from performance on planned and unplanned tasks, that accuracy and complexity may be in competition for attentional resources (see Skehan & Foster, this volume) but makes no firm predictions about the effects of task complexity on these measures. Skehan does argue, following VanPatten (1990) – and adopting, like Van Patten, a limited-capacity, single-resource model of attention – that more complex tasks require more attention to content and that this likely involves withdrawal of attention to form. However, the assumptions of limited-capacity, single-resource models are questioned by recent research into the role of attention in perception and task performance (e.g., Navon, 1989; Neumann, 1987, 1996) and, as Sanders (1998) notes, 'present-day theorizing on dual-task performance and divided attention is rapidly moving away from the limited-capacity processor' (1998: 357). Consequently, I would argue that form and content need not always be in competition for scarce attentional

monologic tasks

simple	complex
+ fluency, - complexity, - accuracy	- fluency, + accuracy, + complexity

interactive tasks

simple	complex
+ fluency, - accuracy,	- fluency, + accuracy,
- comprehension checks/	+ comprehension checks/
clarification requests	+ clarification requests

Figure 4. Proposed effects of task complexity on accuracy, fluency and complexity along resource-directing dimensions

resources (Robinson, 1995b, to appear), and that alternative models of attention and time-sharing based on multiple resource theory (Navon & Gopher, 1980; Wickens, 1989), which do not entail this assumption, may be suitable for L2 task research, in the same way they have been applied to studies of effects of divided attention and dual task performance in other domains (Allport, Antonis & Reynolds, 1972; Gopher, Brickner & Navon, 1982; Sarno & Wickens, 1995). This view proposes there are no general capacity constraints on attention (Neumann, 1987), and therefore no competition for attention, unless this involves attention switching (an executive/action control problem, not a capacity problem) between resource pools (Wickens, 1989). Consequently, where tasks are made increasingly complex simultaneously along dimensions which draw on different resource pools, there should be no competition for attentional resources.

It is, of course, an empirical question whether stable effects on learner output (and incorporation of input) can be achieved by manipulating dimensions of a task's complexity, and which model of attentional resources can best accommodate these findings. Acknowledging this, and in the interests of promoting SLA-motivated research into task effects on output and comparisons of findings across studies, predictions for L2 speech production on simple and complex versions of *monologic* tasks are illustrated in Figure 4, based on the following assumptions: a) structural complexity tends to accompany functional complexity in discourse (Givon, 1985, 1989; Sato, 1988, 1990) and therefore complexity of oral production will develop in response to the increasingly complex functional demands the learner has as a developing communicator; b) greater attention to SL speech, induced by the communicative demands of specific tasks, often results in higher levels of accuracy on task-relevant, non-communicatively redundant language (Hulstijn, 1989; Loschky & Bley-Vroman, 1993; Tarone, 1985; Tarone & Parrish, 1988); and c) high communicative and cognitive task demands can lead learners to 'push production' (Swain, 1985, 1995), 'stretch interlanguage' (Long, 1989) and expend the additional 'mental effort' on production that leads to destabilization of stabilized forms (Schmidt, 1983).

The predictions for *interactive* tasks must take account of the fact that greater complexity is likely to lead to greater amounts of negotiation for meaning, and hence greater numbers of clarification requests and comprehension checks (Long, 1983a). This should have the effect of reducing the overall length and complexity of utterances on complex versus simple tasks (since there will be many phrasal or one word responses to clarification requests and comprehension checks). That is, greater amounts of interaction, triggered by the complex task, will often lead participants to interrupt, and so mitigate their attempts at syntactic complexity. However, the predictions for accuracy and fluency on monologic tasks should still hold.

These effects should be found when increasing complexity along those cognitive dimensions identified in Figure 2 which make increasing functional demands on the language user, i.e., +/− here-and-now, +/− few elements, +/− no reasoning demands since increasing complexity along these dimensions, as mentioned previously, is a means of *directing* resources to a wider range of functional and linguistic requirements. In contrast, tasks manipulating +/− planning time, +/− prior knowledge, or +/− single task demands leads to a *depletion* of attentional and memory resources on more complex versions. Synergistic effects of simultaneously increasing complexity along these *resource-directing* and *resource-depleting* dimensions can be expected and research is needed to investigate these issues. In general the research findings summarized below show the predictions for fluency to hold fairly consistently, across all dimensions, on monologic tasks, with less clear results for accuracy and complexity. However, there have been very few studies of the effects of these dimensions of complexity on interactive, non-monologic task production (though see Robinson, 2001).

One obvious caveat to the claim about accuracy is that it should ideally be assessed with reference to the learner's current level of ability and stage of development, and not necessarily with reference to the target language (Bley-Vroman, 1983) since SLA research has shown consistently that in many domains learners progress through a series of developmental stages before acquiring native-like control over forms, each stage being evidence of learning but characterized by ungrammaticality and error when compared to native speaker norms (cf. Doughty & Varela's, 1998, interlanguage analysis of past tense use). It must also be stressed that choice of the unit of analysis is determined in large part by its validity as a measure of the differences in complexity hypothesized for the task, given its interactive, input and output modality demands. The issue of which units of analysis to adopt in research into the effects of task production is currently a problematic one as Skehan and Foster (this volume) also acknowledge, though full discussion of this issue is beyond the scope of this chapter.

Task demands and task production: previous research

Research findings concerning the effects of increasing task complexity along the dimensions illustrated in Figure 2 have accumulated in recent years, but have tended to focus on the issue of effects on monologic task production. The dimension of $+/-$ *here-and-now* has been studied by Robinson (1995a) and partially replicated by Rahimpour (1997, 1999), who operationalized it as a distinction between narratives performed in the Here-and-Now, when learners describe a series of events in the present tense while looking at pictures illustrating them, versus narratives performed in the There-and-Then, when learners first view the illustration, then are required to perform the narrative from memory without looking at the pictures, and deliver it in the past tense. Motivated by studies of L1 development which show displaced, past time reference to emerge later than present tense, context-supported reference (e.g., Cromer, 1991; Eisenberg, 1985; Sachs, 1983), and by similar findings from SLA research (Meisel, 1987), and also in part by the work of Tarone (1985) on effects of attention to speech on accuracy, Robinson (1995a) found the complex There-and-Then condition elicited more accurate speech, with a trend to greater dysfluency, but with no significant findings for syntactic complexity. However, there was significantly greater lexical complexity in the There-and-Then condition. Accuracy was measured via Targetlike-use (TLU) analysis of articles (Pica, 1984); fluency by numbers of pauses and numbers of words per utterance (Lennon, 1990); and complexity by multipropositional utterances (Sato, 1990), S-nodes per T-unit (Bardovi-Harlig, 1992; Crookes, 1990) and by a measure of lexical complexity, the ratio of lexical to grammatical words.

Similar findings emerged from Rahimpour's (1997, 1999) partial replication of the study. Adopting the same measures as Robinson, with the addition of a general measure of accuracy, percentage of error-free T-units (Larsen-Freeman, 1978), Rahimpour found complex There-and-Then narratives to be significantly more accurate (in terms of error-free T-units, but not TLU of articles), and more dysfluent.

Going beyond Robinson's earlier study Rahimpour also crossed the task complexity factor with a task condition factor – open versus closed tasks. Half of the simple and complex tasks were performed under the open conditions adopted in Robinson's study (where the narrator simply described the sequence of events illustrated in the pictures) and half were performed in a closed condition (where the speaker was instructed to deliver the narration so that the listener could place the sequence of pictures in the correct order). Rahimpour found that open conditions, for both Here-and-Now and There-and-Then narratives, elicited more fluent production, with no effects for accuracy or complexity. These findings partially confirm the predictions for the effects of increasing cognitive complexity on task production made above. Unfortunately, no general measures of the effects of task complexity were obtained in these studies, such as learner ratings of difficulty, time taken to completion, error rate, etc. However, findings for the production data suggest that this is a valid operationalization of an important dimension of the cognitive demands of tasks – the amount of context support speakers and hearers receive (cf. also G. Brown et al.'s (1984) similar conclusions based on their studies of narrative performance).

Only one, unpublished, study has examined another candidate dimension of L2 task complexity, $+/-$ *single task demand*. However, a considerable amount of research in other domains of applied psychological enquiry offers theoretical support for the validity of this dimension (see e.g., Heuer, 1996; Sanders, 1998; Stankov, 1987; Wickens, 1992). In such research, performance on a primary task is examined to see to what extent decrements in performance occur when a secondary task is added. The aim of this research is to examine the relative difficulty, and attentional demands of primary tasks (more attention-demanding tasks are more susceptible to interference from the secondary task), and to examine the extent to which primary and secondary tasks draw on separate attentional resource pools, and so can be successfully time-shared. Robinson and Lim (1993) operationalized single versus dual task performance for L2 learners in the following way. Using a repeated measures design, with order of single and dual-task conditions counterbalanced, speakers were asked to give directions from point A to point B on a map to a partner who had only point A marked on the map. In the single-task condition the route was marked on the map for the speaker, while in the dual-task condition the route was not marked, following the thinking that in this latter condition the speaker would have to both think up the best route and describe it (two tasks) compared to simply describing an identified route (one task). Robinson and Lim found performance on the route-not-marked map task was less fluent than on the route-marked task, with no differences for accuracy and complexity, using the same measures adopted in Robinson (1995a). This is clearly a dimension of complexity in need of further research, and one which is relatively easy to manipulate in L2 materials design, falling within, perhaps, the area Skehan (1996, 1998a) has called the 'degree of structure' task materials impose on learner performance. This dimension is also related to work in mainstream educational psychology (of potential relevance to materials writers and task designers) into the effects of increasing 'cognitive load' on academic task performance, for example, the work of Sweller (1988) who has examined ways of optimizing the integration of illustrations and explanations in physics, maths and other texts, finding that certain arrangements minimize division of attention between explanatory text and diagram, reducing cognitive load (and the dual-task demands of reading separated text and illustration) and thus improving learning and performance.

In contrast to the above described dimensions of task complexity, a growing body of L2 research has examined the effects of manipulating +/− *planning time*. Since findings from this research are described in great detail by Skehan and Foster, this volume, only a brief summary is given here. While there have been differences across studies in critical features of the operationalization of this dimension, such as length of planning time allowed, and whether a task familiarization phase was allowed in both conditions, or not (see Ortega, 1999, for an overview), in general, findings from the studies regarding accuracy and complexity have been in the reverse direction to those predicted in Figure 4. When learners are given time to think, and plan what they will say or write (the simple condition), there is some evidence of gains in accuracy and complexity. R. Ellis (1987) found more accurate production of past tense morphemes on planned versus unplanned narratives, and Crookes (1989) found a trend for more complex syntax on planned versus unplanned information gap tasks. Foster and Skehan (1996) found planning time led to increases in fluency, accuracy and complexity. Ortega (1999) and Wendel (1997) also found increased accuracy as a result of allowing planning time. However, Ting (1996; Robinson, Ting & Urwin, 1995) found equivalent accuracy and complexity on planned and unplanned speaking and writing tasks, but with greater fluency on planned speaking tasks. Undoubtedly, giving planning time, and furthermore focusing attention during planning time on relevant aspects of task structure (Skehan, 1998a), makes a task easier. The effects for greater accuracy on simpler planned tasks along this dimension are possibly due in part to learner avoidance of problematic forms (Schachter, 1974) and to a narrowing of their productive repertoire to the tried and trusted.

A fourth dimension of complexity +/− *prior knowledge* receives considerable support from previous research both within and outside (see for example, Anderson, 1981; Britten & Tresser, 1982; Joseph & Dwyer, 1984) the field of SLA. There is evidence that prior knowledge of formal and content schemata both facilitate L2 reading (e.g., Carrell, 1987), and that prior knowledge of the role of the listener makes speaking tasks easier (G. Brown, 1995; G. Brown et al., 1984; Yule & MacDonald, 1990), as does prior knowledge of, and familiarity with, the content domain of the speaking task (Selinker & Douglas, 1985). Robinson (2001) showed that prior knowledge of an area described by a map led to more fluent (more words per communication unit) production on a direction giving task, compared to no prior knowledge, but this had no effect on accuracy or syntactic complexity. Results also showed significantly greater amounts of negotiation (measured in confirmation checks and clarification requests) on the no prior knowledge task. However, type of prior knowledge (e.g., of form or content) may have differential effects on L2 comprehension. In a study of the effect of prior knowledge on academic listening task performance, Urwin (1999) found that prior knowledge of the content of an academic lecture (given during a pre-task which involved listening to a lecture in a schematically similar domain) led to greater *inferencing* ability than did prior knowledge of form (given during a pre-task to familiarize subjects with its organizational structure). Both prior knowledge groups were equivalent in recall of facts, and both outperformed a no prior knowledge control group on both measures of listening comprehension.

Research by G. Brown et al. (1984; G. Brown & Yule, 1983) and the observations of Prabhu (1987) regarding task difficulty in the Bangalore project are inferential support for the remaining dimensions of complexity proposed in Figure 1, +/− *reasoning demands* and +/− *many elements*. Both G. Brown et al. and Prabhu claim that tasks requiring selective information transmission plus reasoning to establish causality, and justification of beliefs based on abstract concepts, such as morality, goodness, appropriacy, are more complex than tasks requiring non-selective information transmission, without these demands, and that tasks which require few clearly different elements to be described and distinguished from each other (e.g., apples, trees and clouds), are simpler than tasks which require many similar elements to be distinguished from each other (e.g., cars in a traffic jam, buildings and streets on a map, or suspects in a police line-up). Complex tasks on both of these dimensions would seem likely to require the learner to use a wider range of linguistic resources than simpler counterparts (e.g., greater using of logical connectors and subordinate clauses, more complex noun phrases and a wider variety of attributive adjectives, and relative clauses, see G. Brown, 1995, pp. 138–139; G. Brown & Yule, 1983: 135).

In a study of the effects of increasing reasoning demands on narrative task production, Niwa (2000; Robinson & Niwa, to appear) found that the most complex narrative of four produced (in a repeated measure design, using four picture strip sequences from the picture arrangement subtest of the Wechsler Adult Intelligence Scale as prompts for the narratives) resulted in more complex production than the least complex narrative, measured in S nodes per T unit. However, contrary to the predictions made, there were no differences in speech rate, and even greater fluency on the most complex versus least complex narrative, measured as longer mean length of period of phonation. Interestingly, Niwa (2000) additionally found that IDs in ability factors; aptitude, WM capacity, and intelligence, correlated significantly with five measures of production on the most complex narrative, compared to only one on the simplest narrative, suggesting that as tasks increase in their cognitive demands, so IDs in relevant cognitive abilities increasingly differentiate performance. This was so especially for fluency. Those with higher aptitude and WM capacity were significantly less fluent on the most complex version.

Further studies of the cognitive dimensions of complexity described above are much needed, as are theoretically motivated studies of other dimensions of complexity that can be applied to task design. The cognitive dimensions I have described are non-overlapping, and consequently pedagogic tasks can be made more complex on an increasing number of them, as illustrated in Figure 5. In this task learners are initially presented with a map of a small area they are familiar with, with the route marked on, and are given planning time to decide how to describe the route to a partner. Task complexity can be increased by first removing planning time, then asking learners to give directions from a map without a route marked on, then doing the same with a map of an unfamiliar area, and finally increasing the size of the map so that many elements (houses, roads, and other landmarks) have to be distinguished. By increasing pedagogic task complexity in this way, learners gradually approximate the performance demands of real world target tasks.

Sequencing, workload, automaticity and affect

The proposals for task sequencing described above raise a number of complex and important issues which can only be touched on briefly here. Staged, cumulative increases in the cognitive demands of tasks,

	simple				complex
dimensions of complexity	1	2	3	4	5
planning time (before speaking)	+	-	-	-	-
single task (route marked)	+	+	-	-	-
prior knowledge (of a familiar area)	+	+	+	-	-
few elements (a small area)	+	+	+	+	-
	(simplified data/map)				(authentic data/map)

Figure 5. Increasingly complex versions of a map task

in the manner illustrated in Figure 5, are likely to have at least two positive consequences for L2 learners not so far considered; *efficient* scheduling of task elements for the learner leading to gains in automatization (DeKeyser, this volume), functional mapping and restructuring (Doughty, this volume), and *equilibration of perceived workload* across performance on simple and final complex versions leading to positive effects on affective variables such as anxiety and motivation.

Efficient scheduling of component steps in tasks is necessary to increase the efficiency of, and the probability of, success during task performance. For example, in the task described by Figure 5, the learner has to both look at the map to think up the best route, and then describe it. By removing the need to perform the first step (thinking up the route) on the first two versions of the task the learner is able to focus more attention on, practise and so automatize the description step before performing under the dual task conditions of thinking up at the same time as describing. As Sanders (1998) notes, '... scheduling and coordinating task elements is a skill that develops over time and adds to proficient dual-task performance as well as to the impressive effects of practice' (1998: 347). The task sequence described by Figure 5 supports the learner in the development of this scheduling ability. In Bialystok's terms (1994a), efficient scheduling of component steps during pedagogic task practice may be seen as important to developing 'control' of language used, thus facilitating the restructuring and greater 'analysis' of language use (as indexed by syntactic complexity and accuracy effects, as predicted earlier in this chapter) on more complex and subsequent target task versions. That is, staged increases in the complexity of tasks would be more likely to facilitate those cognitive macroprocesses of mapping and restructuring, discussed by Doughty, this volume, with more of this taking place on complex versions.

Gradually approximating real world target task demands rather than moving directly from simple to complex versions would also be likely to reduce stress, or subjective perceptions of difficulty, so having positive effects on affective variables such as levels of anxiety, confidence and motivation. Ergonomics research by Hancock, Williams and Manning (1995) has shown that perceptions of task difficulty are influenced by the demands of prior tasks. This suggests, for example, that a learner performing versions 1 then 5 in Figure 5 above would rate 5 to be much more difficult than they would when performing versions 3 then 5, or 4 then 5. In their research Hancock et al. used the Subjective Workload Index (Reid & Nygren, 1988), a weighted index of learner ratings of the mental, temporal, performance and affective demands of tasks. The development of such an index for SL task research is an important agenda item since complexity and sequencing effects on task 'difficulty' affective variables needs to be put on an empirical footing: two recent studies (Robinson, 2001; Robinson & Niwa, to appear) have attempted to do this.

In a repeated measures design with 44 Japanese learners of English, with task sequence (Simple to Complex, and Complex to Simple) counterbalanced, Robinson (2001) assessed perceptions of task difficulty, anxiety, interest level, motivation, and perceptions of ability on version 3 and version 5 of the map task in Figure 5. He did this by asking participants to complete Likert rating scale questionnaire items assessing participants' perceptions of each of these factors immediately following version 3 and version 5 map task performance. Results showed that, regardless of sequence, participants rated the complex version 5 map task to be more difficult overall, and more stressful, but ratings of interest in and motivation to complete the tasks did not differ significantly on the two versions. Robinson and Niwa (to appear) found the same results for responses to the questionnaire following performance on narratives that increased in their reasoning demands. Narratives requiring complex reasoning were rated more difficult and stressful, and confidence in ability was lower on them than on simpler narratives. However, the complexity of the reasoning demands required by the narratives did not negatively affect interest or motivation to complete them. These results suggest that, at least on the dimensions of cognitive complexity operationalized in these studies, learner perceptions of difficulty do appear to correspond with increases in cognitively defined complexity. However, Robinson (2001) did not confirm the findings of Hancock et al. (1995) for L2 learning task performance since learners performing the version 3 map tasks then version 5 map tasks (see Figure 5) in the sequence Simple-Complex, did not rate version 5 less difficult than they did when they performed version 5 and then version 3 in the sequence Complex-Simple.

Other SLA research has examined the affects of anxiety and motivation on the task *conditions* illustrated in Figure 1. Holthouse (1995) in a study of SL task anxiety under closed and open, one-way and two-way conditions and using a repeated measures design, counterbalanced for sequencing and carrier content, found only a non-significant trend to greater anxiety (measured by a modified version of the Foreign Language Classroom Anxiety Scale, Horwitz, Horwitz & Cope, 1986) under closed, two-way conditions versus others. Similar findings emerged from Jacob's (1996) study of L2 task performance in Singaporean schools. Again, using a repeated measures design counterbalanced for task sequence and content, and using holistic (see MacIntyre & Gardner, 1991) as well as analytic (questionnaire) measures of anxiety and motivation along with interview data, Jacob found no significant difference in anxiety levels on open and closed task conditions, but significantly higher levels of motivation (using only the holistic measure) for performance on open tasks.

In summary, the only findings in this area (Robinson, 2001; Robinson & Niwa, to appear) show that learner perceptions of difficulty are not affected by sequencing decisions that result in a gradual approximation of the cognitive complexity of target tasks. Regardless of the sequence in which they are performed, cognitively more complex versions of tasks are judged by learners to be more difficult than simpler versions, using some measures (such as ratings of overall difficulty, and stressfulness) but not others (interest in and motivation to complete the task). In addition, two studies to date (Holthouse, 1995; Jacob, 1996) have shown that task condition factors, such as open or closed solutions, or one or two-way interaction, have unpredictable effects on perceptions of difficulty. These findings support the position advocated in this chapter that task complexity alone (cognitively defined) be the basis of prospective syllabus design and sequencing decisions.

Conclusion

Research into the effects of task complexity on L2 learning has barely begun but it is an area of great consequence for the development of theories of instructed SLA, and for pedagogic decisions about grading and sequencing tasks for learners. I have proposed a framework to guide this research which distinguishes between task complexity, task difficulty and task conditions. The first, I have argued, should be the basis of decisions about grading and sequencing in prospective task-based syllabus design. Research into all three areas and their effects on language learning is needed, as well as research into potential interactions between them. A brief summary is given here of four issues this research could address.

1. Dimensions of task complexity   I have distinguished between two categories of the cognitive demands of tasks which contribute to their complexity: resource-depleting dimensions such as allowing or withdrawing planning time, and resource-directing dimensions, such as referring to events happening now, in a shared context versus referring to events displaced in time and space. Transitions from simple to complex on the former dimensions increases the authenticity of pedagogic tasks by gradually approximating the processing constraints on real time target task performance. Transitions on the latter dimensions increases the functional demands of tasks with possible linguistic consequences. More studies of the effects of each of these dimensions on measures of learner production are needed. These could address performance on simple and complex tasks on one of the proposed dimensions, or examine the synergy between them by studying the effects of increasing task complexity on a number of dimensions simultaneously, as illustrated in Figure 5. The six dimensions I have proposed in this paper should lend themselves easily to manipulations in task demands made by classroom teachers and materials designers. However, further dimensions will probably need to be proposed, motivated and studied to complement them.

2. Task complexity, noticing, restructuring and uptake   It will be important to assess the effects of task complexity, not only on comprehension and production, but also on noticing, restructuring, and uptake of new linguistic information. The Cognition Hypothesis I have described in this chapter broadly predicts that the greater cognitive demands of complex tasks along resource-directing dimensions will lead to greater attentional allocation to, and rehearsal of, input in memory; greater functional differentiation of language use; and also more extensive noticing of mismatches between learner output and target input (see Doughty, this volume).

3. Interactions of complexity and ability variables   How is performance on simple and complex tasks on these dimensions affected by differences between learners in ability variables such as aptitude and WM capacity? The only study to date (Niwa, 2000) shows that IDs in WM, aptitude, and intelligence, increasingly differentiate performance – especially fluency of production – as narrative tasks increase in the complexity of their reasoning demands. Will this trend be found for complex tasks on other proposed dimensions? Pursuing this issue will take SLA research beneath the surface of studies of the global effects of aptitude on learning, or of the interactions of components of aptitude with different learning conditions (de Graaff, 1997; Robinson, 1997a; Skehan, 1998a), enabling interactions of task factors and ability variables to be charted (Robinson, in press; Robinson & Niwa, to appear; Snow, 1994). This will contribute much to our understanding of task complexity and ability variables alike.

4. Effects of complexity and sequencing on automaticity and affect
The issues raised briefly in the final section of this paper are important and in need of research. What are the effects of staged increases in the cognitive complexity of tasks on automaticity and skill development? What are the effects of such sequencing decisions on motivation and anxiety, and learner perceptions of difficulty? I have speculated, with some support from studies outside the area of SLA, and from one study assessing L2 task performance (Robinson, 2001), that such sequencing decisions provide optimum conditions for skill development and efficient scheduling of the components of task performance, but do not affect learner perceptions of difficulty. Further SLA studies of these issues are much needed.

Many other issues remain, and must go untreated here. Enough issues have been raised in this paper, however, to guide future research into task complexity – research which would contribute much to establishing an empirical basis for decisions about grading and sequencing tasks, as well as to our understanding of the effects of task-based instruction on L2 development.

11 Aptitude, individual differences, and instructional design

Mark Sawyer and Leila Ranta

Introduction: a paradox in SLA research

Individuals who attempt to learn a foreign language differ dramatically in their rates of acquisition and in their ultimate attainment. This is perhaps the clearest fact about SLA that we currently have, and of course it is particularly striking in relation to the relative uniformity of learning rate and ultimate success in L1 acquisition. Bley-Vroman (1989), among other scholars, has argued that these differences demonstrate that the underlying L1 and L2 acquisition processes must be fundamentally different. Whether or not L1 and L2 acquisition develop in completely different ways, it is important for both theoretical and practical reasons to attempt to specify and understand the sources that contribute to differences among second language (L2) learners.

The paradox is that despite this importance, L2 research into the sources of individual differences (IDs) has lagged far behind research seeking universal principles. With the exception of the social psychologically oriented work on motivation and other affective variables pursued by Robert Gardner (see Gardner & MacIntyre, 1992, 1993, for an overview), no major research program focusing on IDs and integrating them within a model of SLA has yet been developed. This is partly due to limitations inherent in the correlational research designs favored by earlier studies, and the difficulty of finding reliable and valid measures of both the learner traits and the L2 learning outcomes (Larsen-Freeman & Long, 1991; Lightbown & Spada, 1993). Another difficulty with doing research into IDs is the complexity of the interaction between learner traits and characteristics of the context of learning. It is also the case that overly influential early work and measurement instruments have tended to blind later researchers to potentially more fruitful approaches. With little theoretical foundation to stand on, new researchers are less likely to be attracted to IDs than they are to areas where relatively intensive study has led to some initial progress. If the field of SLA is to attain explanatory

319

adequacy, however, the exploration of how different learner traits lead to different learning outcomes needs to be a focus of future research activity.

Though the L2 IDs literature has remained relatively uninfluential, it is by no means scarce. Over the past 30 years, various researchers have identified and argued for the importance of a wide range of IDs, including intelligence, aptitude, strategies, attitudes, motivation, anxiety, risk taking, introversion/extroversion, cognitive style, and ego permeability. In the brief review below, it will be seen that, among the variables studied to date, language aptitude is the one that contributes most to accounting for differential success of individual learners.

Language aptitude

Foreign language learning aptitude has been defined by John Carroll, the most prominent scholar in this area, as 'some characteristic of an individual which controls, at a given point of time, the rate of progress that he will make subsequently in learning a foreign language' (1974). Studies investigating L2 success in relation to language aptitude have generally yielded correlation coefficients in the .4 to .6 range (Carroll, 1981: 93). These are considered moderate to strong correlations, and although they imply that considerable learner variation remains to be explained by additional factors, they also demonstrate that language aptitude has consistently been the single best predictor of subsequent language learning achievement.

Motivation

Motivation is also clearly important in a difficult, often never-ending, task like L2 learning. However, measuring it directly is more difficult than measuring an ability factor like language aptitude, so motivation research has relied heavily on self-report questionnaires. Robert Gardner and colleagues developed the Attitudes and Motivation Test Battery (AMTB), which has since been the basis for numerous studies (for reviews see Gardner, 1986; Gardner & MacIntyre, 1993). As one example, a median correlation coefficient of $r = .37$ between motivation as measured by AMTB and language achievement (French grades) was reported by Gardner (1986) in a large-scale survey in Canada. Correlations of that magnitude are not unusual, but numerous other studies have also produced lower and sometimes even negative correlations between self-reported motivation and achievement. Besides the inherent limitations of self-report data, the AMTB strongly reflects Gardner's emphasis on attitudes toward target language speakers and his distinction between integrative and instrumental orientations, and these may not generalize well to a wide range of contexts. For a critique of Gardner's line of research, see Au (1988); Crookes and Schmidt (1991) provide suggestions for new, more productive lines of motivation research, and Oxford (1996) contains some studies pursuing these lines. Dornyei (1998) provides a comprehensive survey and integration of several diverse lines of motivation research.

Cognitive style

The term cognitive style has been used to label a variety of phenomena of interest to different scholars, but the bulk of L2 research using the concept has been based on the opposing styles of field independence (FI) and field dependence (FD). FI individuals are those adept at distinguishing figure from ground on visual tasks, while FD individuals are those who tend to perceive in a more holistic fashion. In L2 learning, it is thought that FI learners have an advantage in analyzing language material, while FD learners are better at developing interpersonal skills. Important to the concept of style is that it refers to differences in tendency rather than categorical differences in processing abilities; furthermore, it is assumed that neither end of the style continuum is inherently better than the other. Unfortunately, the test that has been used in nearly all the L2 research on FI/D, the Group Embedded Figures Test (GEFT) (Oltman, Raskin & Witkin,1971), is clearly an ability rather than a style measure. Individuals who are able to quickly and accurately recognize simple familiar figures embedded in complex configurations of lines are labeled FI, and those who have less of this ability are labeled FD. There is no corresponding interpersonal task to confirm any advantages for FD; instead, FD is simply the absence of FI. Largely due to ease of administration, many studies have been conducted using the GEFT, often producing correlation coefficients between field independence and language achievement measures in the $r = .30$ range, and sometimes as high as .43 (Stansfield and Hansen, 1983). On the other hand, different studies have found little or no relationship between GEFT scores and learning, and Hansen (1984) found that high correlations in the .40 range essentially disappeared when the effects of academic ability were factored out (see Chapelle & Green, 1992, for an overview of these studies).

Skehan (1989), R. Ellis (1994a), and Griffiths and Sheen (1992) have all suggested abandoning further efforts to investigate FI/D in relation to L2 learning, but Chapelle (1992; Chapelle & Green, 1992) has argued that FI/D is worthy of further study, though not so much in terms of style but rather in terms of a better understanding of the 'cognitive restructuring ability' that seems to underlie performance on embedded figures tests. Extending these arguments, Skehan (1998a) has proposed a framework that attempts to illuminate the relationships between aptitude, cognitive style, and task demands.

Personality traits

The effect of personality traits on L2 achievement is the area that has perhaps been the most disappointing in ID research, producing few clear findings. Ellis (1985: 120) suggests that identification and measurement of relevant variables is particularly difficult in personality research, whereas Skehan (1989: 105) views the problem more in terms of over-reliance on the feeder discipline of psychology. Both of these views are opposed by Griffiths (1991b), who sees the adoption of a clear theoretical framework, specifically that of H. J. Eysenck (Eysenck & Eysenck, 1985), as a first step to progress in the area. Other researchers have made use, at least implicitly, of a Jungian view of personality structure, which underlies the Myers-Briggs Type Indicator (MBTI) (Myers & McCaulley, 1985). Ehrman (1990) is an example of research that has used the MBTI to attempt to relate personality-based learning styles to L2 achievement, but without quantitatively clear patterns emerging.

Below are brief summaries of results in three sub-areas of personality research: risk-taking; social style, sociability, and introversion/extroversion; and anxiety.

Risk-taking as an individual difference has been discussed by Beebe (1983) and put to empirical test by Ely (1986). In Ely's study, risk-taking (measured by a 6-item self-assessment) correlated at .39 with observed classroom participation, but then classroom participation had a significant relationship with achievement on only one of the achievement measures that Ely used.

Social style, sociability, and introversion/extroversion are overlapping personality traits that have over the years been used in numerous studies. A wide variety of results have been reported, only about half of them indicating positive relationships. As observed by Skehan (1989: 104), the results have tended to follow from the methodology – observation studies have yielded positive results, and questionnaire studies have produced null findings. A good example of the former is Strong (1984), who found that child learners' observed talkativeness and responsiveness produced strong correlations with their communicative language measures. An example of no such relationship is Ely's (1984) study, where sociability was an even poorer predictor of achievement than risk-taking.

Anxiety is potentially a very important individual difference, but perhaps the most difficult to generalize about, starting from the question of whether it can even be called a personality trait. Some people habitually tend to be more anxious than others, so there is something that can be called a trait, but everyone undergoes anxiety in some situations, though these situations vary according to the individual. The effects of the anxiety also vary, sometimes being facilitative, sometimes debilitative, and the relationship between anxiety and performance need not be linear (Scovel, 1978). A little bit may help, but too much will hurt. Gardner and colleagues (e.g., MacIntyre & Gardner, 1991) have conducted numerous studies assessing the effect of anxiety, and in general the questionnaire-based studies by them and others have produced low-strength negative correlations in the $r = -.20$ to $-.30$ range with language achievement measures.

The nature of language aptitude

Carroll's (1962) four factor model

Language aptitude first became the object of widespread interest and serious research in the 1950s, with the development of Carroll and Sapon's (1959) Modern Language Aptitude Test (MLAT), concurrent efforts by the US Army to develop a cost-effective aptitude test (e.g., Berkhouse, Mendelson & Kehr, 1959), and the beginning of work that led to the Pimsleur Language Aptitude Battery (PLAB) (Pimsleur, 1966). The PLAB was designed specifically for junior high school learners, and though it sometimes surpassed the MLAT in predictive validity for this population, these validities might be inflated by the inclusion of past Grade Point Average and self-assessed interest in foreign languages (Carroll, 1981: 94). The US government has also continued to develop aptitude tests, namely the Defense Language Aptitude Battery (DLAB) (Petersen & Al-Haik, 1976), and VORD (Parry & Child, 1990), but neither has demonstrated superiority over MLAT.

Given the hybrid nature and limited target group of the PLAB, and the restricted availability of the DLAB, the MLAT has become something of a standard for research in aptitude for foreign language learning. Based on factor and regression analyses of a large number of candidate tests for the prediction of language learning success, Carroll developed the following four component model of aptitude:

1. Phonetic coding ability[1] – an ability to identify distinct sounds, to form associations between those sounds and the symbols representing them, and to retain these associations.
2. Grammatical sensitivity – the ability to recognize the grammatical functions of words (or other linguistic entities) within sentences.
3. Rote learning ability for foreign language materials – the ability to learn the associations between sounds and meanings rapidly and efficiently, and to retain these associations.
4. Inductive language learning ability – the ability to infer or induce the rules governing a set of language materials, given samples of language materials that permit such inferences. (Carroll, 1981: 105)

Given these empirically derived factors, the next step was to choose sub-tests that could sample each of them effectively and efficiently, while overlapping as little as possible with other subtests. The subtests selected in this way are described below.

Sections of the MLAT

Part 1: Number Learning.   In the learning phase, the words for the numbers in a novel language are taught by way of a tape recording: first 1, 2, 3, and 4 are learned and rehearsed, then 10, 20, 30, and 40; and finally 100, 200, 300, and 400. In the testing phase, test-takers need to recognize and write down one-, two-, and three-digit numbers presented orally. According to Carroll (1981: 108–109), this part contributes to the measurement of rote learning ability, and possibly of inductive language learning ability. The latter is arguably invoked through sensitivity to the morphological regularities in the number system that can help to remember the words for the numbers, and by recognition of exceptions to those regularities.

Part 2: Phonetic Script.   In the learning phase, sound-symbol correspondences for a novel orthography are taught in sets of four nonsense syllables, each set containing one vowel and one consonant contrast. In the testing phase, test-takers hear a subset of the syllables they have learned, and attempt to recognize which among four written representations each oral stimulus corresponds to. This part clearly is intended to measure phonetic coding ability. Carroll (1990: 18) mentions that

---

[1] Skehan (e.g., 1989, 1998) consistently refers to this factor as *phonemic* coding ability rather than *phonetic* coding ability. No explanation is given for the change in terminology. We will use the term *phonemic* unless referring to Carroll directly.

it seems to tap general intellectual ability and memory as well. He also speculates that low phonetic coding ability may be closely related to dyslexia in the L1. Two further noteworthy features of the Phonetic Script subtest are that all of the sounds used are sounds that exist in English, and the novel orthography is actually the Smith-Trager transcription system.

Part 3: Spelling Clues. Test-takers must rapidly recognize English words that have been spelled creatively, and match each word with the correct synonym among four choices. Unlike other parts of the MLAT, Spelling Clues is highly speeded, such that most test-takers fall short of completing all the items. Performance on this section is doubtless the main factor in distinguishing among high-aptitude learners, as few test-takers even manage to finish the section. (Perfect scores on any of the other sections are quite common, except Words in Sentences, where perfect scores are rare, but near-perfect scores are not unusual.)

Carroll (1981: 106) suggests that Spelling Clues measures both phonetic coding ability and L1 vocabulary knowledge, justifying the inclusion of the latter in the test by claiming that it is indicative of the ability to learn the more advanced lexical aspects of a foreign language. Spelling Clues also appears to measure some sort of cognitive flexibility, in that the creatively spelled English words violate spelling regularities of English, and perhaps also measures a sort of strategic competence (Bachman, 1990; Chapelle & Green, 1992) in that completing the section within the available time is unlikely without a conscious analysis of the required pace of performance.

Part 4: Words in Sentences. Each item consists of a stimulus sentence that has one word underlined, and a second sentence that has four words underlined. Test-takers must choose the one word among the four that serves the same grammatical function as the underlined word in the stimulus sentence. This part is clearly intended to measure grammatical sensitivity, without requiring the use of any grammatical terminology. However, it is still open to criticism that it favors test-takers who have experienced formal grammar instruction. Carroll (1981, 1990) has acknowledged that performance on Words in Sentences has been found to correlate with knowledge of grammatical categories, but not with amount of formal grammar instruction.

Part 5: Paired Associates. In the learning phase, test-takers attempt to memorize 24 Kurdish words paired with their English counterparts. A two-minute practice phase follows, and then a 24-item multiple choice test, in which the Kurdish stimulus word needs to be matched with the appropriate English equivalent from among four candidates. This part is clearly intended to measure rote learning for foreign language materials. Carroll (1990: 20–21) admits that validities of this section fluctuate considerably for different samples, and emphasizes that there are many other types of memory that might be predictive of language achievement.

Variations of the MLAT

Several tests based on the MLAT for different populations are currently available. For researchers working with younger populations (ages 8–11), the Modern Language Aptitude Test – Elementary (EMLAT) (Carroll, 1981) is appropriate. Translations exist in Italian (Ferencich, 1964), French (Wells, Wesche & Sarrazin, 1982), and Hungarian (Otto, 1996). A Japanese translation (Murakami, 1974) no longer exists, but more recently a new language aptitude test has been developed for native speakers of Japanese. Sasaki's (1996) Language Aptitude Battery for Japanese (LABJ) contains a translation of Paired Associates from MLAT, a variation of the Inductive Language Learning subtest from the Pimsleur Language Aptitude Battery, and an original test of Sound-Symbol Association.

Carroll's conception of aptitude as speed of learning

Carroll operationalizes aptitude in terms of rate (i.e., speed) of learning a foreign language in the context of some sort of formal instruction, either a language course or program of self-study. According to this view, learners with aptitude are those who learn the fastest. It is important to understand that Carroll's conception of a specialized talent for learning a L2 reflects the specific period and place in which the MLAT was developed. There was a need at that time in the United States to train a large number of people in foreign languages, a process which was very costly to the public purse, so it was necessary to find a way of ensuring that those individuals streamed into language training would succeed. These courses tended to be intensive in nature, consisting of full-time study for a period of eight to twelve months (Carroll, 1962). In such a setting, it is fairly clear why speed of learning would be the operationalization of talent. This contrasts with the choice made by some other researchers, generally working in second language rather than foreign language contexts, who operationalize talent as native-like attainment (e.g., Ioup, Boustagui, El Tigi, & Moselle, 1994; Novoa, Fein, & Obler, 1988; Schneiderman & Desmarais, 1988).

Carroll's model of school learning

In addition to his componential model of aptitude, Carroll (1963) sought to account for the interaction between learner and instructional variables in his Model of School Learning. He offers a formalization of possible interactions between the factors of time, quality of instruction and IDs in order to predict learning outcomes in a classroom setting. The instructional variables include adequacy of presentation of learning tasks, and opportunities allowed for learning tasks. The individual difference variables include general intelligence, aptitude (reflecting the time required by the individual to learn a task), and motivation (representing the maximum amount of time that the individual is willing to devote to learning). In situations where ample time is available, a motivated person with low aptitude is able to attain success despite requiring more time to learn because she is willing to devote the maximum amount of time to studying. In contrast, a learner with high aptitude will require less time to learn, and thus can succeed even with low levels of motivation. Carroll also proposes that high quality instruction may make aptitude less significant. Although more than 30 years old, the Model of School Learning still has unfulfilled potential in relation to SLA research.

The concept of aptitude: problems and solutions

As mentioned earlier, the concept of aptitude has not been the object of as widespread research attention as might be expected given its demonstrated capability to predict L2 achievement. The discussion below presents five problems surrounding aptitude research that have reduced its attractiveness to researchers. Following these are accounts of progress that has been made toward solving these problems.

Problem 1: unclear relationship between testing instrument and factors

One readily apparent problem with Carroll's conception of language aptitude in relation to how it is measured is the mismatch between his four putative factors and the five subtests of the MLAT. The mismatch is especially clear given his admission that one of the factors – inductive language learning ability – is not really measured on the MLAT, and one of the sections – Spelling Clues – has at best a tenuous conceptual connection to any of the factors as Carroll himself conceptualized them.

Toward a solution: *clarifying the components of language aptitude*

One step toward solving this problem is to reconceptualize inductive language learning ability and grammatical sensitivity not as two separate factors, but rather merely as two facets of the same underlying language analytical ability. Skehan (1989, 1998a) has argued for this approach, suggesting that the two abilities differ only in emphasis. Indeed, the cognitive operations required by Words in Sentences are similar to those required by inductive learning tests. The first requires the examinee to analyze the grammatical patterns of sentences in a well-known language (the L1), while the second involves extracting grammatical patterns from a small set of sentences in an unknown language.

On the other hand, in a recent study of British university students by Alderson, Clapham, and Steel (1997), the MLAT's Words in Sentences task did not correlate with their measure of inductive language learning ability, a task requiring the translation of a short Swahili text, following the pattern of the first few sentences for which the translation was already provided (Davies, 1971). Since different measures of inductive language learning were used in the studies by Alderson et al., and by Skehan, it is not possible to draw firm conclusions, but the widely divergent results indicate that much more research is needed into the nature of language analytic abilities.

Concerning the issue of what aptitude component is measured by Spelling Clues, it is clear that Phonetic Coding Ability is involved, but that L1 vocabulary knowledge plays at least as important a role. Although this situation appears anomalous in the context of the particular four factors that Carroll (1962) proposed, Skehan's (1986b) follow-up of the Bristol study provides some evidence that perhaps L1 vocabulary knowledge deserves further study in its relationship to language aptitude. Skehan found that vocabulary knowledge measured at age 39 months turned out to be a good predictor of a full range of language aptitude measures (EMLAT 1, EMLAT 2, York Language Aptitude Test, PLAB 5, PLAB 6) administered at age 13–14. The larger question brought up by this study is the extent to which L2 learning aptitude is a residue of variation in first language ability. Though an accurate characterization of the components of language aptitude remains a problem, recent attempts to rethink the nature of aptitude have provided a good starting point for future research. Skehan (1998a) makes a particularly interesting attempt to specify the roles of three aptitude factors within an overall framework of L2 learning.

Problem 2: aptitude tests really measure intelligence

If language aptitude is really general intelligence as applied to the task of learning a language, there is not much point in examining it as a unique learner trait. This basic equivalence of intelligence and language aptitude has been argued by numerous scholars, most notably Oller (1983).

Solution: distinguishing aptitude from intelligence

There is abundant empirical evidence showing differences between aptitude and intelligence. This evidence is of two types. Firstly, there are studies such as those reported in Carroll (1981) which showed that measures of L2 aptitude and measures of intelligence do not exhibit the same pattern of correlations with L2 achievement. Secondly, there are studies examining the correlation of IQ and aptitude measures themselves. Gardner and Lambert (1972) and Skehan (1982) reported low to moderate strength correlations (around $r = .4$), with the aptitude tests also showing higher correlations with L2 proficiency measures than with IQ. On the other hand, Wesche, Edwards and Wells (1982) and Sasaki (1996) found moderate to strong relationships between aptitude and IQ. However, in both cases, a second-order factor analysis was needed to bring out this relationship; the first order factors suggested some degree of separation. Skehan (1998a) suggests that the difference between the earlier and later studies may be due to the fact that the Lambert and Gardner and the Skehan studies were conducted with fairly unselected groups while the Wesche et al. and Sasaki studies made use of subjects who had been streamed in some way. Skehan concludes provisionally that aptitude is not completely distinct from general cognitive abilities, as represented by intelligence tests, but it is not the same thing either. Furthermore, he argues that the relationship between aptitude and cognitive abilities appears to be strongest when dealing with language analytic rather than with memory or with phonetic coding ability. Here we see that treating L2 aptitude in a monolithic way obscures the nature of the relationship between general cognitive abilities and specific linguistic ones.

Problem 3: aptitude is not a trait, but a matter of skill development

In his earlier writings, Carroll (1973) argued for the innateness of L2 aptitude, linking it to the Critical Period in which the learner has a 'heightened capacity to learn ANY language' (p. 6), which implies that IDs in aptitude arise because of different rates of decline in this capacity. Later, he took a more neutral position:

An aptitude might be at least in part innate, or it could have developed over a long period as a result of the individual's experience and activities. In any case, aptitudes are regarded as being relatively enduring. Although it may be possible to improve an individual's aptitudes by special instruction or training, this is not easily done, and there seem to be limits to how far aptitudes can be changed. (Carroll, 1985: 84–85)

In recent years support for the innateness or at least stability of aptitude has come from two sources: (1) a study examining the relationship between rate of L1 development and L2 aptitude later in life, and (2) studies investigating the effect of language learning experiences on L2 aptitude. We begin with the first strand of evidence provided by Skehan (1986b, 1989, 1990) who reports on the findings from the follow-up study to the Bristol Language Project (Wells, 1985).

Solution 1: the relationship between L1 abilities and L2 abilities

The aim of Skehan's (1986b, 1989, 1990) study was to investigate the three-way relationship between L1 development in early childhood, performance on L2 aptitude tests, and success in L2 learning in secondary school. Skehan was able to administer aptitude and L2 proficiency tests to 103 of the individuals who had participated in the Bristol Language Project (Wells, 1985) as young children. In the original longitudinal study, Wells and his colleagues collected data from two samples of children (N = 128), one group from the age of 15 months until the age of 42 months and the other from age 39 to 60 months. A stratified sample was obtained by selecting children from a range of family backgrounds. Each child was audio-recorded once every three months by a recording set-up that was preprogrammed to sample at frequent but irregular intervals over the course of a day without there being an outside observer present. In addition to the spontaneous production data, tests of different kinds were administered in conjunction with each observation. Parental interviews also provided other types of information such as the quality of literacy-based activities the children were exposed to.

The follow-up phase to the Bristol Project involved administering (1) measures of different components of L2 aptitude (verbal intelligence, grammatical sensitivity, inductive language learning ability and phonetic coding ability); and (2) standardized tests of speaking, listening, writing, and reading in French or German. Skehan found that aptitude and L2 achievement were strongly related to each other. On the other hand, L1 development and L2 success were not found to be directly related to each other. What is interesting is that strong correlations were found between some measures of L1 development and many of the L2 aptitude measures, particularly the more 'language analytic' tasks. For example, significant, moderate-strength correlation coefficients in the range of .4–.5 were found between grammatical sensitivity and 'MLU at 42 months', between grammatical sensitivity and 'range of adjectives and determiners', and between inductive language learning ability and 'vocabulary at 39 months' (Skehan, 1990; note that only the results for the first cohort (n = 53) of the original sample have been reported). In other words, speed of L1 learning was correlated with tests that purportedly measured speed of L2 learning. However, a simple innatist explanation is not the only interpretation of the results, since 'nurture' variables such as family background indices also correlated moderately with grammatical sensitivity. Based on regression analyses using the wide variety of L1 developmental indices from Wells' data, Skehan concluded that aptitude is a product of two separate groups of influences: one which reflects an innate capacity for learning that is a 'residue' of L1 development, and the other which reflects the development of the ability to handle language in a decontextualized way, which is influenced by family background factors such as parental literacy.

Solution 2: studies of L2 aptitude and L2 learning experience

Many people believe that the more languages a person knows, the more successful that person will be in further L2 learning. As we shall see, research investigating this issue has not unequivocally confirmed this belief. The discussion will begin with the correlational studies and then move on to experimental studies.

Eisenstein (1980) studied the relationship between the language aptitude of 93 college students and their past language learning experiences. She found that both bilingualism and previous (generally high school) language training led to greater language aptitude as measured by MLAT. Polylinguals (defined as bilinguals who had learned more than one additional language before age 10) showed a trend toward advantage over simple bilinguals, though the difference fell short of statistical significance. She also claimed that among bilinguals there was a trend toward an advantage for those with formal education in a second language.

In contrast to Eisenstein's study, two other studies did not find an effect for experience. Sawyer (1992) administered the MLAT and a language experience questionnaire to a group of 129 students beginning short intensive courses in various Southeast Asian languages. Both correlational and principal components analyses were performed to examine the relationships among language learning experience, aptitude, and L2 proficiency. Aptitude correlated moderately with final course grades and with some of the L2 proficiency measures. It did not, however, correlate with biographical variables such as the amount of exposure to other languages. Language learning experience, aptitude and proficiency all emerged as independent factors in the principal components analysis.

Harley and Hart (1997) compared the aptitude and L2 proficiency of learners who had had either an early or a late start to L2 learning. Four grade 11 French immersion classes (N = 65) were involved in the study; the students in two of the classes were continuing in a partial immersion program that had begun in grade 1 (the early group), while the students in the other two classes were continuing in a partial immersion program that had begun in grade 7 (the late group). A variety of tests were administered, including two memory measures, the Language Analysis subtest from the PLAB, and various L2 tests (more will be said about this study in later sections). Results showed that the early immersion students did not have higher levels of aptitude overall, despite having 12 years of exposure to French compared to the 4 years of the late immersion students.

A recent teaching experiment that has shown a positive effect for language learning experience on aptitude was conducted by Sparks, Ganschow, Fluharty, and Little (1995). In earlier research, Sparks, Ganschow and colleagues (e.g., Sparks & Ganschow, 1993) documented that students who have strong L1 skills generally have strong L2 aptitude and achieve higher grades in foreign languages at school, and that those who experience difficulties in L2 courses at school exhibit overt or subtle L1 problems that are similar to those found in learning-disabled students. Sparks et al. (1995) compared changes in aptitude scores of learning-disabled and of non-learning-disabled high school students after they had studied Latin. Additionally, they examined whether using a 'multisensory, structured language approach' to L2 teaching would improve the aptitude scores of the learning-disabled students. This method is characterized by direct and explicit teaching of the phonology/orthography of the L2 in a step-by-step approach, providing students with opportunities to hear, see and write the sound-symbols simultaneously. The MLAT was administered at the beginning and at the end of the school year; there were significant improvements on the aptitude test for the non-learning-disabled students following the regular Latin program, and for the learning-disabled students who had the multisensory structured treatment in Latin, but not for the learning-disabled students who had the regular Latin program. The learning-disabled students who improved still scored well below the mean for the non-learning disabled. This improvement in aptitude test scores may be due to the positive effect that studying Latin grammar would have on performing the type of sentence analysis involved in the Words in Sentences task. Unfortunately, Sparks et al. (1995) do not report the subtest scores for the MLAT to confirm this.

Two lab experiments made use of the Reber experimental paradigm (Reber, 1989) to investigate the issue of whether the experience of being bilingual leads to language learning 'expertise' (see McLaughlin, 1995 for general discussion of this approach).

Nation and McLaughlin (1986) compared monolinguals, bilinguals, and multilinguals on learning an artificial language, under two different conditions: implicit and explicit. They found no significant differences when learning under explicit conditions but superior multilingual performance when learning under implicit conditions. They interpreted this finding to mean that the multilinguals are better able to abstract structural information from linguistic stimuli that they are exposed to when there is no instruction or obvious reason to do so. In information processing terms, this means that multilinguals may 'habitually exert more processing effort in making sense of verbal stimuli.' (p. 52) This finding is consistent with Skehan's (1986a, b) idea of the good language learner being able to abstract from experience in order to handle decontextualized material. However, since the multilinguals did no better than the monolinguals when the learning task included instructions, and since the multilingual advantage in the implicit condition did not extend to the bilingual group, this study provides minimal evidence that language experience contributes significantly to language learning aptitude.

Nayak, Hansen, Krueger, & McLaughlin (1990) further explored differences between monolinguals and multilinguals in a study which involved learning a different type of artificial language, this time a phrase-structure grammar. Monolingual and multilingual subjects were randomly assigned to either the Memory condition or to the Rule-discovery condition. The Memory group was instructed to memorize each sentence presented while subjects in the Rule-discovery condition were told, as in the earlier study by Nation and McLaughlin, that the order of the words in the sentences was based on a complex set of rules, and that they should try and discover the rules. Although multilinguals were observed to exhibit a wider variety of strategies and use them more flexibly, there were no significant differences between the monolinguals and multilinguals in either vocabulary or rule learning in either of the two learning conditions.

Summary of findings on the aptitude-experience relationship

As this review has shown, a wide range of studies have probed the relationship between language aptitude and language experience. Although Eisenstein's (1980) correlational study and Sparks et al.'s (1995) experimental study showed effects for previous experience on aptitude scores, numerous other correlational and experimental studies have found no such effect despite clear differences in language experience among participants. Especially compelling are Skehan's (1986b, 1989, 1990) results showing the degree to which language aptitude could be predicted from L1 development measures taken as many as 10 years earlier. Until further research sorts out which aspects of aptitude are susceptible to what sorts of experience, the interim conclusion should be that aptitude is much more than a matter of skill development.

Problem 4: aptitude is only related to formal instruction

Based on his Monitor Model, Krashen (1981) claimed that aptitude can only predict language learning achievement in formal (classroom) situations, and as measured by tests permitting Monitor use. Attitude, conversely, will be more predictive in informal settings when the focus is on communication, and when Monitor-free measures of proficiency are used. Gardner (1986) has made similar statements. Cook (1996) dismisses the relevance of aptitude tests for present-day L2 teaching contexts:

Such tests are not neutral about what happens in the classroom nor about the goals of language teaching. They assume that learning words by heart is an important part of L2 learning ability, that the spoken language is crucial, and that grammar consists of structural patterns. In short MLAT mostly predicts how well a student will do in a course that is predominantly audiolingual in methodology rather than in a course taught by other methods. (Cook, 1996: 101)

As we shall see, such a dismissal of aptitude and the MLAT is unwarranted – many studies conducted in different L2 learning/ teaching contexts point to the relevance of this cognitive learner trait.

Solution: the relevance of aptitude in a range of learning environments

The relationship between L2 aptitude and L2 learning in grammar-based instructional settings was established in the validation testing of the MLAT and the PLAB in the 1960s (Carroll, 1963; Pimsleur, 1966) and confirmed by such studies as Gardner and Lambert (1972), Gardner, Smythe, Clément, and Gliksman (1976) and Bialystok and Fröhlich (1978). But even when instruction is mainly form-oriented, aptitude measures have proven to be associated with more than performance on discrete-point items or metalinguistic rules. Consider the Bristol Language Project follow-up study reported in Skehan (1986b, 1989, 1990). The subjects had been studying French or German for 1–2 years at the secondary school level in the UK. Testing included measures of different aspects of aptitude and achievement in French or German as measured by standardized tests of reading, writing, listening and speaking. Aptitude and all L2 achievement measures were found to be strongly related to each other. For example, the tests of speaking ability correlated strongly with both the measure of grammatical sensitivity (r = .66) and with the test of inductive language learning ability (r = .68).

There is also evidence that aptitude is a good predictor when grammatical structure is not the focus, as in informal learning, immersion, and communication-oriented classrooms, as well as in implicit learning under controlled laboratory conditions.

Informal learning

A study that has been cited (e.g. Skehan, 1998a) as the only existing research into the relationship between aptitude and L2 learning in an informal setting is Reves (1983). The interesting design feature here is that she was able to compare formal and informal learning in the same learners. The subjects were Arabic L1 speakers in Israel who were learning Hebrew informally, and studying English in the classroom. While Reves found that correlations between all of the predictors and the criterion measures were lower in the informal setting than in the formal setting, it was none the less the case that aptitude proved to be a better predictor of learning success in Hebrew than other learner factors such as motivation, cognitive style and use of learning strategies. The problem with interpreting this study as corroborating the relationship between aptitude and informal learning is that in fact the learners were not acquiring Hebrew purely through naturalistic exposure. In addition to that exposure, the learners had received instruction in written Hebrew for 6–7 years.

French immersion

Harley and Hart (1997) demonstrated the relevance of aptitude when the L2 is learned through content-based teaching. They examined the relationship between components of aptitude and L2 learning for two types of learners in French immersion: grade 11 students who had begun French immersion in grade 1 vs. those who began in grade 7. The researchers administered the 'Language Analysis' subtest of the PLAB (Pimsleur, 1966) and two measures of memory: the Paired Associates subtest from the MLAT and a measure of learners' memory for prose. The L2 proficiency measures included a range of both formal and communicative tasks. Harley and Hart found that aptitude was related to performance on the L2 measures, although the two groups of learners differed in the pattern of relationships between the components of aptitude and different L2 tasks. This might reflect the influences of age of onset of acquisition, programmatic differences, or population differences. However, for the purposes of the present discussion, Harley and Hart's study shows that aptitude is relevant even in an immersion setting where there is greater quantity of input than in traditional foreign language classrooms, and where the focus is on the learning of subject matter content.

Communicative L2 instruction

Horwitz (1987) sought to distinguish the abilities that facilitate the development of grammatical competence from those that facilitate the development of communicative competence. She hypothesized that the social cognitive abilities associated with a learner factor called 'conceptual level' (Hunt, Butler, Noy, & Rosser, 1978) would be associated with communicative competence, while aptitude would be associated with grammatical competence. Conceptual level provides 'an index of a person's cognitive complexity and interpersonal maturity', in terms of stages from 'self-centeredness,' through 'concern with social acceptability' and 'tolerance of ambiguity and difference of opinion', to a mature sense of empathy and interdependence (Horwitz, 1987: 148).

American high school students in their second year of French (n = 61) completed the MLAT, a measure of conceptual level, a French grammar test, and three oral production tasks; these last were recorded and later rated for communicative effectiveness. Classroom observation ensured that all the learners had comparable experiences of communicative activities in the L2 classroom. Horwitz found that the MLAT correlated significantly and moderately with the grammar test (r = .41), and conceptual level correlated with communicative competence (r = .54) as measured by the oral tasks. Unexpectedly, there was also a similar strength relationship between aptitude and communicative competence on the one hand, and between conceptual level and grammatical competence on the other. Significant for this discussion is that there was a clear relationship between a component of aptitude as measured by the MLAT and the ratings of oral language performance achieved through communicative instruction. However, the shared variance that Horwitz found between grammatical sensitivity and interpersonal sensitivity is also something worthy of future investigation.

Ehrman and Oxford (1995) found a positive relationship between aptitude measures and L2 success in a more recent large-scale study. They examined relationships between a variety of learner variables (i.e., aptitude, learning strategies, learning styles, personality traits, motivation and anxiety) and proficiency ratings in speaking and reading a foreign language. The subjects were 855 US government employees who had participated in intensive language instruction that was largely communicative but also included some features of audiolingual teaching such as drills and dialogues. However, data were not collected from everyone on all measures; for example, only 282 people completed the MLAT. Ehrman and Oxford found that the MLAT and an 'observed aptitude' rating by the instructor were the predictor variables that were most strongly correlated with the Foreign Service Institute ratings of speaking and reading. These proficiency measures correlated with the grammatical sensitivity subtest at around r = .4, and with the MLAT as a whole at r = .5, which is in keeping with the ranges found by Carroll during the audiolingual era. The authors conclude that aptitude is still a good predictor of L2 learning success even when teaching is communicative in orientation.

Research in the laboratory

The studies reviewed so far in this section have each represented one particular type of instruction or learning environment. In contrast, the lab studies reviewed here manipulated learning conditions so that the interaction of language aptitude and type of instruction could be examined in one controlled experiment. De Graaff (1997) studied the learning by Dutch university students of a modified version of Esperanto called 'eXperanto'. The participants (N = 54) were randomly assigned to either an implicit or an explicit learning condition.

Aptitude was measured as a pre-test variable using Dutch versions of the MLAT Words in Sentences and Paired Associates subtests, and a lexical inferencing test. All three aptitude measures were collapsed into one variable for the correlations with the proficiency measures. The learning materials which were presented on a computer consisted of 10 lessons of approximately 1.5 hours each. The rules were embedded in dialogues which were contextualized in a setting. Learning activities included translation and production exercises. In addition, the explicit group received grammatical explanations of the target structures. Proficiency measures were administered three times: once during the instructional phase, and twice after the treatment. These measures included sentence judgements, a gap-filling task, a translation task, and a sentence correction task.

De Graaff found that participants in the explicit instruction condition outperformed those in the implicit learning condition, and that aptitude correlated with performance on the proficiency measures. There was no interaction between the influence of aptitude and treatment condition: aptitude affected test performance in both conditions to the same extent. In other words, his findings support the idea that aptitude is relevant in both implicit and explicit instructional settings.

In contrast to de Graaff's use of an artificial language, Robinson (1997a) used English in his learning experiment. Two syntactic rules were chosen for the study: one was judged by 15 ESL teachers to be an 'easy' rule based on its structural complexity and the complexity of the pedagogical explanation it would require; the other rule was judged to be 'hard' by the same criteria. The participants in the study were 104 learners of English as a L2, most of whom had Japanese as their L1. Only those who showed by their performance on a pre-test that they were unfamiliar with the target structures were selected for the study. Aptitude was measured using the English version of Words in Sentences and Paired Associates subtests of the MLAT.

Subjects were randomly assigned to one of four training groups: implicit, incidental, rule-search, and instructed conditions. All subjects were presented with sentences on a computer for the same length of time. What they did after viewing the sentences varied according to the condition. In the implicit condition, participants were told that they were to perform a memory task, and were asked questions concerning the location of words in sentences. The incidental group answered yes/no comprehension questions and received feedback concerning the content of their responses. Subjects in the rule-search condition were told to try and find the rules in the sentences, and then were asked after each sentence whether they had found the rules or were still looking;

no feedback was provided. Finally, in the instructed group, participants began by viewing explanations of the easy and hard rules and were asked to apply the rule to each sentence as they saw it. Following each sentence, there was a metalinguistic question to which they responded with a 'yes' or 'no' and were given feedback. Learning was evaluated by a grammaticality judgement task administered after the training.

On the post-test, the instructed group outperformed all the other groups with respect to the easy rule, but its advantage on the hard rule reached significance only in relation to the rule-search group. With respect to the role of aptitude, the results on the grammaticality judgement task revealed that grammatical sensitivity was significantly correlated with learning in the implicit, rule-search, and instructed conditions, but not in the incidental condition. Indeed the strongest correlations were with accuracy on the easy and hard rules in the implicit condition ($r = .69$ and $.75$, respectively). In this condition, those who responded that they had looked for rules, and those who were able to verbalize rules were more accurate on the judgement task. Furthermore, those who were able to look for rules or could verbalize the rules were significantly better on Words in Sentences. In other words, those with higher aptitude claimed higher levels of awareness and demonstrated higher levels of learning.

On the surface, it looks as if learners who had grammatical sensitivity were able to derive explicit knowledge out of a stimulus which was not structured to promote learning. In fact, the task demands in the implicit condition, which involved responding to questions such as, 'Were the words X and Y next to each other?' required careful processing of the form of the stimulus sentences. Robinson concludes that task demands determine the role IDs in grammatical sensitivity and memory played in each learning condition. When an individual's abilities matched the demands of the task 'aptitude often led to awareness, which often was associated with superior levels of learning' (Robinson, 1997a: 81).

Summary of findings on the relationship between aptitude and learning setting

From this brief review we can see that the predictive value of the aptitude measures has been maintained even when L2 learning takes place in a variety of settings which do not involve a metalinguistic analysis of language rules. Moreover, in controlled laboratory studies, aptitude was relevant to L2 learning in both implicit and explicit conditions.

Problem 5: the concept of aptitude has no clear relationship to acquisition processes

As many scholars have pointed out over the years (e.g., R. Ellis, 1994a; Larsen-Freeman & Long, 1991; Skehan, 1986b), theoretical accounts of IDs can never be adequate unless they are linked to a theoretical model of the acquisition process (and vice versa). In the past aptitude was associated with the behavioristic learning theory current at the time of the development of the MLAT; when that learning theory was discredited, interest in language aptitude commensurately withered. However, the componential model of aptitude developed by Carroll need not be limited to a stimulus-response account of language learning. In 1981, Carroll himself linked the components of aptitude to the then current information processing model including short- and long-term memory. Skehan (1998a) has gone further with this linkage of aptitude to psycholinguistic processes in his information-processing model which incorporates more recent theorizing in cognitive psychology. His model of acquisition consists of three stages: input processing, central processing, and output. The operations at each stage are then linked to the three components of aptitude (as discussed earlier, Skehan has collapsed grammatical sensitivity and inductive language learning ability into 'language analytic ability'). This recent conceptualization of aptitude has not been put to the empirical test, but research in the area of working memory (WM) capacity has begun to lend plausibility to some aspects of the model.

Solution 1: aptitude and working memory capacity

Working memory capacity may be the key to elaborating the concept of language aptitude itself and to clarifying its relationship to the second language acquisition (SLA) process (see Ellis, this volume). Working memory, first proposed in cognitive psychology by Baddeley and Hitch (1974), differs from the traditional concept of short-term memory (STM) in two fundamental ways: (1) whereas STM is often seen as a way station to long-term memory, WM is an independent temporary cognitive workspace used for sequential cognitive processes, such as the comprehension and production of language; (2) whereas STM is generally seen to have a passive storage function, WM includes both temporary storage and ongoing processing functions. Thus, in comprehending a spoken utterance, for example, a listener must store relevant units of information from earlier in the utterance while processing subsequent units of information in order to derive an accurate and complete representation of the utterance's meaning. Once this representation has been formed, the stored earlier partial products can be forgotten. In fact, the earlier bits of low level information must be purged to some extent, so that full WM capacity will remain available for processing subsequent speech.

Whereas a limited behavioristic understanding of memory underlay Carroll's work on the MLAT, WM depended on later developments in cognitive psychology, most importantly the capacity theory of attention (Kahneman, 1973; Schneider & Shiffrin, 1977). Baddeley and Hitch's contribution was a proposal for how attentional capacity limitations worked: once those limits were reached, there would be a trade-off between the total amount of information that could be stored and the efficiency with which later information would be processed. Consequently, some of the stored information would be forgotten, and/or processing would be slowed down or rendered inaccurate. Although the relationship between the two components is conceptualized as a trade-off whereby one is sacrificed to allow the other to continue to function, it is not difficult to imagine how decrements in either part of performance would actually contribute to decrements in the other in a snowballing fashion, since both are essential, especially in ongoing rapid aural comprehension of language. It is also probable that L2 learners frequently find themselves in situations where their WM limitations are being exceeded.

To find out if WM capacity was a viable individual difference that might explain why individuals differed in their level of comprehension of reading passages (in their L1), Daneman and Carpenter (1980) developed the Reading Span task. The Reading Span task was designed to simultaneously draw on the storage and processing resources of WM. On this task, subjects would have to read increasing long series of sentences, and then after each series they would be asked to recall the final word from each sentence in the series. The reasoning behind the task is that individuals with more WM capacity should have more capacity left to hold the relevant words in storage after comprehending the sentences than individuals with less WM capacity. In numerous experiments, Daneman and Carpenter obtained high correlations in the range of .5 and .6 between WM and aspects of comprehension (such as verbal SAT scores). Importantly, they were also able to obtain similar results with a listening version of the Reading Span task, showing that the differences were generalizable to language processes rather than restricted to reading processes.

The potential of WM capacity for explaining differences in language comprehension having thus been established, Harrington and Sawyer (1992) undertook a study to examine individual WM capacity differences among L2 learners in relationship to their reading comprehension. To high intermediate-advanced Japanese learners of English, they gave a battery of tests that included L1 and L2 Digit Span, Word Span, and Reading Span tasks, two parts of the Test of English as a Foreign Language (TOEFL), and a cloze task. The purpose of the Digit and Word Span tasks was to establish that any effects attributed to WM were not merely caused by simple short term storage capacity. The main findings were correlations of .57 between Reading Span and TOEFL Part 2 (Grammar), and .54 between Reading Span and TOEFL Part 3 (Reading). These results demonstrated a fairly strong relationship between WM capacity and L2 proficiency. This relationship was further validated by the lack of significant correlation between L2 proficiency and simple STM spans (Digit and Word).

Subsequent studies by Osaka and Osaka (1992), Osaka, Osaka, and Groner (1993), Berquist (1998), and Miyake and Friedman (1998), have confirmed the relationship between WM capacity and L2 achievement, and also between L1 and L2 WM capacity. To overcome the inability of correlational research to establish a clear direction of influence between two related variables, Harrington (1992a), using stepwise regression, and Miyake and Friedman (1998), using path analysis, have obtained evidence for a causal role for WM capacity in relation to aspects of L2 proficiency. Additionally, Sagarra's (1998) longitudinal study of achievement differences among learners of Spanish in relation to WM, found differences only between 'truly low' WM and 'probably low' memory groups after 1.5 years of instruction. Sagarra's result, if replicable, may have important implications for instruction. Working memory capacity, and perhaps other aspects of aptitude as well, may not be crucial when they are not challenged. It thus becomes important to attempt to identify the threshold at which learners' capacities are exceeded.

If further research confirms WM capacity to be a stable individual difference among learners, its potential importance in SLA will be clear. Assuming that noticing is crucial to learning, and attention is required for noticing, and attention at any moment is limited by WM capacity, then there must logically be a close relationship between amount of learning and size of WM. It is also likely that WM serves as an arena in which the effects of other components of aptitude are integrated. To the extent that phonemic coding, grammatical sensitivity, and memorial access to lexicon are respectively inefficient, processing will be slower and more laborious. Meanwhile, the temporary storage of information for comprehension or production as an utterance proceeds is likely to be incomplete or incorrect, and will therefore be less helpful to subsequent processing, further decreasing efficiency. Under conditions of WM overload, or even simply full capacity, there will be few if any attentional resources available for learning.

Solution 2: aptitude and noticing

The view of aptitude embodied in the earlier cited quote by Cook (1996) reflects the zeitgeist of the 1970s when the new field of SLA turned away from behaviourist models of learning and embraced the research methods and goals of L1 acquisition (Corder, 1967). Research focused on the universal characteristics of language learning across languages and learners; similarities in the acquisition process were found between L1 and L2 learners, between child and adult L2 learners, and between learners from different L1 backgrounds (Dulay, Burt, & Krashen, 1982). It was proposed that the process is the same in all cases: the learner must process the input in such a way as to 'break the code' of the target language through input processing and hypothesis-testing and thus arrive at a grammar (i.e., internalized system) of the target language (Cook, 1996). Since the child acquiring an L1 does this intuitively, without conscious analysis, then the same must be true for the older L2 learners. The fact that the 'little linguist in the head' didn't use the methods of 'the big linguist', as Sharwood Smith (1994b) puts it, meant that the role of metalinguistic knowledge in L2 learning was minimized. However, the present climate in L2 teaching and research circles has favoured the renewal of interest in the role of formal instruction and the conscious involvement of the learner in the acquisition process.

There is a now general consensus in SLA theory that access to comprehensible input, and processing for meaning alone are not sufficient conditions for attaining native-like knowledge of a L2, and that some attention to language form is necessary (see Long & Robinson, 1998; Spada, 1997; and Doughty, this volume). The basis for this rests on many types of evidence such as the logical arguments concerning the limitations of input (White, 1987), the learning outcomes of immersion programs (Harley & Swain, 1984; Swain, 1985), of communicative intensive ESL programs (Lightbown & Spada, 1993) and of comprehension-based instruction (Lightbown, 1992a). These and other researchers conclude that learners need to have their attention focused on formal aspects of the L2 during, immediately following, or preceding communicative activity (see Doughty's discussion of the 'timing' issue in focus on form, this volume), and that noticing the 'gap' between what they themselves can, or have said, and the production of native, or more competent non-native speakers is necessary for subsequent learning (see Schmidt, this volume). Evidence in support of the important role of selectively attending to, and noticing formal details of the L2 during SLA comes from Schmidt's diaries documenting his experiences learning Portuguese in Brazil (Schmidt & Frota, 1986). A careful analysis of his own retrospective accounts in comparison to analyses of the input he received and samples of his oral production indicated a relationship between what Schmidt noticed in the input and what was found in his output (Schmidt, 1990). Further evidence for the role of noticing, and higher levels awareness such as rule understanding, is found in laboratory studies that have contrasted explicit learning conditions to implicit learning conditions (DeKeyser, 1995; N. Ellis, 1993; Robinson, 1996b). These studies have tended to show that the explicit conditions, in which subjects attend to and are aware of formal rules, lead to superior results in short-term learning, although these effects have been more obvious on easy rules than on hard rules.

Thus, various strands of theory and research in SLA are consistent with the notion that L2 learners need to focus attention on the form of the target language in some way. It then seems likely that this process will be facilitated by the learner's ability to focus on form, and this brings us back to the concept of L2 aptitude, specifically to the component of language analytic ability (i.e., grammatical sensitivity and inductive language learning ability). This notion was explored by Ranta (1998) who studied grade 6 learners participating in an intensive ESL program in which instruction focused almost exclusively on the development of interpersonal communication skills. She hypothesized that learners with higher levels of grammatical sensitivity would be at an advantage in some aspects of L2 learning. Indeed, she found that the performance of learners who scored higher on a test of grammatical sensitivity in the L1 (French) was associated with higher stages of grammatical development in L2 oral production (i.e., question forms and the possessive determiners *his/her*).

Further evidence is provided by the results of the implicit learning experiment conducted by Robinson (1996b, 1997a), described previously, in which it appears that those implicit learners (instructed to simply memorize a display in order to subsequently identify whether two words had co-occurred together) who had greater levels of grammatical sensitivity were also those who searched for, found and successfully derived accurate explicit knowledge from language stimuli which were not structured to promote learning.

Such findings support the link between aptitude and the concept of noticing. It follows from the reconceptualization of aptitude in terms of information-processing that an important function of form-focused instruction is to compensate for learners' deficiencies in phonemic coding, and/or grammatical sensitivity. Drawing learners' attention in the appropriate directions may not only facilitate learning of the particular features of language, but may ease the overall burden on WM so that more attention is available for additional learning. Needless to say, more work is needed to explore the relationship between aptitude and the processing involved in L2 acquisition.

Section 4: aptitude and instructional treatments

The review of the aptitude literature makes it clear that abilities that have been labeled as L2 aptitude have a direct impact on L2 learning outcomes. It is thus important for course designers to take aptitudinal differences into account in order to maximize learners' potential for success. One way of taking aptitude into account is to include as an instructional objective the enhancement of learners' aptitude. Another option is to modify language instruction so that it accommodates learners' aptitude profiles in some way.

Option 1: enhancing the abilities of L2 learners

There are two ways in which L2 learning capabilities could potentially be enhanced. The first is through training that might directly increase one or more of the abilities that comprise language aptitude. However, if the characterization of language aptitude earlier in this chapter is accurate, such training should not be effective, and indeed it has not shown itself to be. Although there have been no recent training programs that we know of, there were several attempts to train language aptitude soon after the development of the MLAT. Pike (1959) and Yeni-Komshian (1965) were not successful in improving phonetic coding ability. In the case of Pike's students, large differences remained after 45 hours of training. Politzer and Weiss (1969) attempted to train both phonetic coding ability and grammatical sensitivity. Not only were they unable to show clear advantages for their experimental groups over their control groups, but the training also generated dissatisfaction among the learners, who did not perceive it as relevant or worthwhile.

In the last 10–15 years, another interesting possibility for improving language learning ability has emerged. Language learning (or learner) strategies have generated a steadily increasing amount of interest among teachers. The rationale is that, whether or not ability can be increased, poor learners may be able to achieve more by consciously learning about and practising the strategies used by successful language learners. One view of learning strategies sees them as possibly synonymous with aptitude. In their review of learning strategies instruction, O'Malley and Chamot (1990: 162) state that 'individuals with a special aptitude for learning foreign languages may simply be learners who have found on their own the strategies that are particularly effective for efficient language learning.' Prescriptions (e.g., Oxford, 1990) and materials (e.g. Ellis & Sinclair, 1989) for teaching learner strategies have become abundant, though research on the effectiveness of such programs has lagged behind.

The few studies of learner strategy training that have been published to date have not yielded impressive results, but none of the researchers have concluded that the area is any less promising. One of the earliest attempts to measure the effects of strategy training was that of O'Malley, Chamot, Stewner-Manzares, Kupper and Russo (1985), who gave eight days of training (50 minutes per day) to beginning/intermediate junior high school age ESL students. One group worked on cognitive and socio-affective strategies, another group on those two types plus metacognitive strategies, and a control group received special reading instruction, irrelevant to the vocabulary list learning, speaking, and listening tasks that the strategies were to be applied to. The results showed that neither the metacognitive *self-evaluation* nor the cognitive *imagery* and *grouping* tasks made any difference on vocabulary list learning. Likewise, none of the listening strategies – metacognitive *selective* attention, cognitive *note taking*, and socio-affective *cooperation* – led to improvement on the lecture listening post-test. On the speaking task, however, the metacognitive *functional planning* along with *cooperation* produced better presentations than *cooperation* alone, and *cooperation* only produced better results than the control group achieved. Unfortunately, even these positive results do not provide unambiguous support for the role of learned strategies, since *cooperation* involved a rehearsal of the presentation in front of the same audience that it was soon to be delivered to, and the metacognitive instruction was rather closely related to the organizational criteria upon which the presentations were evaluated. Positive results on the listening or vocabulary tasks, for which much more generally applicable strategies had been taught, would have established more transferability of the learned strategies.

A very interesting finding emerged from O'Malley et al.'s study when the vocabulary learning results were broken down by ethnicity. Among the Asian students, the control group, who reportedly relied on rote memory techniques according to their teachers, scored better than the two treatment groups, who were reluctantly trained in imagery and grouping techniques. The opposite pattern occurred among the Hispanic students, who were more receptive to the new strategies.

These results underscore the difficulty of determining categorically that one strategy or combination of strategies is better than another, and suggest caution in deciding that learners should be induced to modify their existing strategic behavior.

Learner resistance played an even larger role in Wenden's (1987) learner training program for two classes of advanced ESL students. Two out of 20 hours per week in a seven-week intensive program were devoted to strategies instruction, through mini-lectures and readings on learner strategies, with follow-up comprehension exercises and discussions in class, and practice tasks and focused diary writing outside of class. Resistance to the strategy training was severe enough that it was abandoned in one of the classes after three weeks, and was received with only dutiful cooperation in the second. At the end, less than half of the students agreed that the learner training tasks had been useful. Wenden's interpretation of the disappointing results was that the materials suffered from not being sufficiently integrated or focused on particular language tasks. This suggestion is consistent with the pattern of O'Malley et al.'s (1985) results, but if learner training needs to be closely tied to specific tasks, it diminishes in transferability and becomes less likely to play an important role as a surrogate for language aptitude.

The most ambitious program of strategy training to date is probably that conducted by Cohen, Weaver, and Li (1998) with foreign language learners at an American university. Four classes of intermediate French learners and two classes of intermediate Norwegian learners (total N = 55) were designated as either experimental or comparison classes (intact groups). The experimental classes featured strategies-based instruction (SBI), which 'includes not only the typical presentation, discussion, promotion, and practice of strategies, but also the added element of explicit (as well as implicit) integration of training into the very fabric of the instructional program' (Cohen, 1998: 82). The teachers of the experimental classes had all undergone 30 hours of training in SBI. To test the effectiveness of SBI and the use of particular strategies in relation to speaking performance, learners performed three speaking tasks in a language laboratory before and after instruction. Soon after completing each task, learners completed corresponding strategies checklists, tailored to the specific task (Self-Description, Story Retelling, City Description). Oxford's (1990) Strategy Inventory for Language Learning (SILL) was also administered pre/post for additional information. To test the effects of the SDI, judges' overall ratings of the taped post-test performances were analyzed by ANCOVA. The experimental classes performed significantly better on the aggregate ratings for one of the three tasks (City Description). Broken down by subscale, the experimental group's mean rating was significantly higher on one of the eight subscales ('Grammar' on the City Description), and when broken down further by language, the French experimental classes outperformed the comparison classes on 'Vocabulary' on the Self-description. Although these results are far from overwhelming, they represent a small measure of success in the most rigorous test of learner training effectiveness attempted so far.

Another innovative feature of Cohen et al.'s (1998) study is their examination of the relationship between gains in task performance and increase in the use of various strategies, as tabulated from the strategy checklists completed by the learners after every task. The checklists each assessed three stages of strategy use: (1) preparation before using the language skill; (2) self-monitoring during the use of the skill; and (3) self-reflection afterwards. Some of correlations between performance and strategy use are intriguing, but are very hard to interpret, since (1) out of hundreds of correlations (2 groups × 3 tasks × 2–3 scales × 3 stages of strategy use × 10–15 checklist items), some are sure to be significant by chance; (2) nearly one-third of the significant correlations are negative; and (3) two-thirds of the significant correlations involve the comparison rather than the experimental group. To take one example from the results of the City Description, the preparation strategy of having practised pronunciation of specific words before recording began correlated at $r = .43$ with Self-Confidence ratings and $r = .50$ with Grammar ratings for the Experimental group, but $r = -.42$ with Vocabulary for the Comparison group. Perhaps the safest interpretations are that learners' use of strategies are not easily predicted on the basis of training or lack thereof, and that the effectiveness of particular strategies varies greatly according to task and learner.

If Cohen et al.'s (1998) work represents the state-of-the-art in learner strategy training, it is clear that the value of such training is far from clearly established. Although there is an intuitive appeal to O'Malley and Chamot's (1990: 162–163) account of the four components of language aptitude in terms of cognitive and metacognitive strategies that should logically promote learning in the same way, an empirical demonstration of such an equivalence remains elusive, as does an indication that strategies can be meaningfully taught. Rather than trying to reduce aptitude to strategy use, it may be more productive to consider the extent to which effective strategy use depends on the language aptitude of the user. In any case, another possibility for facilitating efficient language learning is to adapt instruction to maximize learner aptitudinal strengths and to compensate for weaknesses.

Option 2: modifying L2 instruction to accommodate learner differences

The most straightforward way of accommodating learner aptitude profiles is to teach to learners' strengths, that is, to match learner characteristics with instructional characteristics. The componential character of aptitude makes it possible to identify patterns of learner strengths and weaknesses (Skehan, 1989). Some individuals may be strong or weak in all of the components while others may be stronger in one particular component. An example of how learner profiles can be used to individualize L2 instruction is reported in Wesche (1981). The language training program for Canadian civil servants assigned students to a compatible teaching approach based on their aptitude profile. Students entering language training in English or French were given several placement tests including the MLAT, parts of the PLAB, and an interview. This placement procedure made it possible to classify learners as being analytic or memory-oriented or as having a 'flat profile'. On the basis of this assessment, students were then placed in an appropriate course: those who had a high score on the grammatical sensitivity subtest of the MLAT, but a low score on the memory subtest were placed in a grammar-based Analytic class, those with the reverse profile were placed in the Functional class which was organized around communicative functions, and those who had no clear strengths or weaknesses were placed in the Audiolingual class which was the default program at the time. Wesche reports that such streaming led to greater student and teacher satisfaction. Indeed, when comparisons were made between 'analytic' students placed in the Audiolingual class (i.e., mismatched learners) and those in an Analytic class (i.e., matched learners), significant differences in favor of the matched learners were found in both L2 achievement and in attitudes.

Wesche's study remains one of the few to demonstrate the benefits of matching learners to instruction. However, given the predominance of the communicative approach to L2 teaching, it is relatively unlikely that learners would have the option of taking a grammar-based or audiolingual course. Matching is most likely to take place daily as teachers choose the most appropriate learning activities for their students.

Another approach to accommodating learners' aptitudinal differences is to adopt a compensatory approach and teach to remediate learners' weaknesses. For example, Sparks and Ganschow (1991) have written extensively on the L2 learning problems faced by individuals who have weak phonemic coding ability (i.e., the Linguistic

Decoding Deficit Hypothesis). They argue that such learners flounder in a naturalistic learning environment and require some kind of structured approach, and recommend more direct forms of L2 instruction such as the multisensory structured language approach (Sparks, Ganschow, Kenneweg, & Miller, 1991), and this type of instruction was found to be effective for learning-disabled students studying Latin (Sparks et al., 1995).

While Sparks et al. (1991) were concerned with populations who display clear deficits with respect to the norm, a similar proposal has been made by Skehan (1998a) with respect to learner style differences in normal populations. He argues that in communication-oriented instructional settings, learners who are analysis-driven will be able to impose structure on meaningful input on their own, whereas memory-driven learners will not be able to perform such structural analyses without assistance – they need to have a focus on form provided for them. While little empirical research has directly addressed this question, a study by Ranta (1998) is suggestive. She studied 150 grade 6 students in an intensive ESL school in Quebec where students received L2 instruction that focused exclusively on the development of interpersonal communication skills. Observations and questionnaires confirmed that form-focused instruction was not a regular part of the program. Students were given a measure of grammatical sensitivity in the L1 and a variety of proficiency measures administered at three time intervals. Ranta found through a cluster analysis that the best learners were characterized by above average performance on all the L2 measures administered including the ones that required a focus on form; the other learners performed relatively poorly on tasks that required higher levels of analyzed knowledge of English. She suggests that the non-analytic learners might benefit from the provision of more form-focused instruction.

Conclusion

The relationships among language aptitude, additional IDs, and instructional treatments provide an abundance of overlapping areas where future work is likely to be productive. It is only in the last few years that widespread interest in the study of IDs has developed, and the above review shows that though intriguing suggestions have been forthcoming, conclusive findings are still rare. Some of the most immediately promising areas of future endeavor are sketched out below.

1. The measurement of language learning abilities

The most fundamental research need in this area is a fresh look at the nature and measurement of language aptitude, both in an absolute sense and in relation to progress in language pedagogy. Carroll (1990) himself admits the data for the factor analysis that led to the 4-factor model was not optimal, and that the resulting test (MLAT) did not match those factors closely. Furthermore, the test was designed to predict speed of learning in audiolingual methodology, a goal that is arguably irrelevant today. (This is not to say, however, that the test does not have predictive value in non-audiolingual settings, since we have provided abundant evidence to the contrary.) Carroll has suggested particularly that new measures of different types/aspects of memory might be useful, and we have discussed WM as one direction to move in. Additional possibilities are suggested by Skehan (1982, 1998a), and still other possibly relevant forms of memory have not yet been researched at all in relation to L2 learning.

Of the many new research technologies that have become available subsequent to the time when the early language aptitude studies were done, reaction time measurements could be especially revealing in bringing out IDs in language processing efficiency. This methodology seems an even more obvious choice to the extent that one accepts Carroll's (1962) view of language aptitude as a speed function. Although the Number Learning and Phonetic Script sections of the MLAT measure learners' ability to learn language material delivered at a certain pace, and the Spelling Clues section needs to be performed extremely rapidly to be completed, none of the currently available aptitude tests attempt a direct measure of variation in processing speed among learners. The studies by Robinson (1996b, 1997a) and de Graaf (1997), reviewed earlier, include reaction time measures. de Graaf does not discuss reaction times specifically in relation to aptitude, and Robinson (1996b: 151) found few significant correlations between reaction time and aptitude measures. However, Robinson's task provided no incentive for learners to favour speed over accuracy.

2. Learner profiles

Another area where more research is needed urgently in order to use aptitude information for course design purposes is the corroboration and refinement of learner profiles. The work by Wesche (1981) and Skehan (1986a) provides techniques for how learners can be grouped according to similar patterns of learning strengths and weaknesses, and the former demonstrated that such grouping led to pedagogical benefits, but it would be dangerous to generalize too far on the strength of these two pieces of research. One reason for caution is that in both Wesche's and Skehan's studies, extraneous variables, most notably age, played an important role in defining the profiles. Another reason is that phonetic coding ability did not play a major role in defining the contrasting profiles in either study. In other words, although there are nine possible combinations of strengths and weaknesses in the three main components of aptitude, both studies focused on only two of them: strong analysis/weak memory, and strong memory/weak analysis, plus a flat profile with no contrast. It is likely that in the earlier stages of L2 learning, phonemic coding ability will be even more relevant than the other two components.

3. The relationships between abilities and performances on particular tasks

Based on more sophisticated knowledge of learner profiles, we need many more studies of how aptitude differences affect the outcome of instruction in general and specific language learning tasks in particular. In fact, not only aptitude differences, but a full range of potentially important learner variables, need to be investigated in relation to instructional outcomes and the learning processes that lead to those outcomes. The study of aptitude-treatment interactions, as well as the interactions of other learner variables with instructional treatments, represents a huge and surprisingly uncharted area of important L2 research. As we suggested earlier, especially helpful will be more studies along the lines of Ranta (1998), where the effect of IDs was examined in relation to a model of language processing.

4. Individualized instructional treatments

In terms of designing instruction to cope effectively with IDs, one clearly promising direction is computerized instruction. Computer programs can be written to provide virtually limitless possibilities for variety in the choice, modification, and sequencing of language learning tasks. A study by Doughty (1991) provides some suggestions of the relative effects of differentially focused computerized instruction on learner comprehension and grammatical knowledge. Since her study did not include any measures of IDs, however, it is impossible to tell how different treatments may have interacted with learner variables. Another pioneering study is that by R. Sawyer (1994), who studied learner differences in navigational patterns through a computerized learning environment in relation to differences of field dependence/independence, and how those variables interacted with learning outcomes (recognition of Japanese syllabary characters). Although the short instructional period and small sample size precluded clear-cut findings, Sawyer's design points the way for larger scale research and instructional efforts in the future.

5. Task-based language learning

Though computerized instruction makes possible a degree of individual customization that generally cannot be matched in the teacher-fronted classroom, there are numerous reasons why computers cannot and should not completely replace the traditional classroom learning environment, and it thus makes sense to consider the full range of possibilities for adapting classroom instruction to the IDs of the students. One fertile area where research is already active is that of task-based language learning, where the learning effects of different task specifications are being increasingly investigated. The next step is to look carefully at how different sorts of tasks affect different types of learners, and how the different roles in cooperative task performance could be manipulated so as to maximize the benefits to each. One other fundamental issue that needs much further study is that of whether learner-sensitive instruction should best aim to remediate learner weaknesses, or rather to circumvent those weaknesses by catering to the learner's strengths. Among the studies discussed earlier, Ranta's (1998) research would indicate the former course, while Wesche (1981) demonstrated the viability of the latter. Again, further experimental research is needed.

The reawakening of interest in language aptitude, and of IDs in general, comes at an opportune time. Future work can now benefit from, as well as inform, new developments in the study of the cognitive processes universally involved in SLA, such as those outlined in other chapters of this book. Likewise, ID research can be guided by progress in language pedagogy, such as the identification of effects of task feature variation, and can be expected to reciprocate with exciting new instructional possibilities.

12 Cognition, instruction and protocol analysis

Renée Jourdenais

Introduction

If we desire to better understand the processes involved in second language (L2) learning and to make claims regarding learners' attention to and processing of different types of linguistic input, it is important to examine the cognitive processes of interest to us as directly as possible. One method of data collection which allows researchers to do this is protocol analysis, in which verbal reports are collected from the language learner.

While this method has been used for over a century in the field of psychology in order to investigate problem-solving and memory skills, it is only within the past few decades that SLA researchers have begun to use protocols to observe the cognitive processes utilized in language behaviours and tasks. As Schmidt has pointed out, 'The problem in applied linguistics has not been over reliance on first-person reports and data, but an almost total neglect of them' (1994c: 22).

The goal of this paper is to address this situation by examining the strengths of protocol analysis as a method for looking at a variety of cognitive processes of interest to second language acquisition (SLA) researchers. The methods involved in the collection and analysis of protocols will be addressed, followed by a discussion of various linguistic studies which have utilized protocols and how the information gained from such research can inform SLA theory. Finally, both the limitations and benefits of this method of data collection for language acquisition research will be considered.

Types of protocol analysis

There are primarily three different types of protocol reports which can be collected from learners: introspective, retrospective, and think-aloud. Each of these elicits a different type of information from the learner. Introspective reports, for example, require that learners

Table 1. *Types of protocol reports*

	Concurrent with task	Subsequent to task	Asks learners to report processes
Retrospective		*	*
Introspective	*		*
Think-aloud	*		

explain their processing strategies simultaneously with their performance of a task. Retrospective reports, on the other hand, are collected upon completion of a task as learners are prompted to think back upon and report the processes they used and thoughts they had as the task was being completed. Think-alouds, like introspective reports, are also collected during the execution of a task, but unlike introspective and retrospective protocols, do not ask learners to interpret their cognitive behaviours. Rather, learners are asked to simply 'think aloud' as they perform a task, verbalizing whatever comes to mind as they complete the activity. Table 1 summarizes the features of these different types of protocols.

The basic assumption underlying the use of protocols is that information most recently attended by the learner is available for verbal report. According to models of memory and information processing (see Ellis, this volume), this accessible information is comprised of the contents of working, or short-term, memory, in which information is initially processed and stored before (possibly) being further incorporated into long-term memory (e.g., Craik & Lockhart, 1972; McLaughlin, Rossman, & McLeod, 1983; Robinson, 1995b). Introspective and think-aloud reports are designed to tap directly into working memory, as they are collected simultaneously with the performance of a task. Retrospective reports, if given immediately upon completion of a task, may attempt to collect information from the learners' short-term memory as well, but as information remains available for only a very limited time, the retrospective protocol may also require that learners retrieve information from long-term memory for this type of verbalization.

Designing prompts and training learners

When designing data collection procedures which utilize the protocol technique, the type of information desired from the learner must be considered. Requests, for example, that a learner report his or her thought processes during the performance of a task will require that the learner attend to the types of strategies and processes he or she utilizes, and provide verbal accounts of these behaviours. Concerns exist, however, as to the ability of learners to accurately interpret and report such behaviours (these concerns will later be discussed in more detail), and the desire that learners may have to 'please the researcher' and report behaviours that they believe would be of interest to the researcher, or behaviours that they believe they *should* be using as 'good' learners, rather than the actual strategies and processes employed (e.g., Birdsong, 1989; Stratman & Hamp-Lyons, 1994; van Lier, personal communication). To avoid such problems associated with self-interpretation and report, learners can be instructed to simply 'think aloud', saying everything that comes to mind during the task, rather than to introspect about the processes involved, for example: '... say aloud *everything* that you say to yourself silently. Just act as if you're alone in the room speaking to yourself' [original emphasis] (Ericsson & Simon, 1993: 376). Such instructions may discourage learners from attempting to interpret or explain their behaviours, and researchers can avoid issues of whether or not learners have, or are able to accurately report, metalinguistic and/or metacognitive awareness of their linguistic processing.

As the prompt for protocoling may affect the information reported by the learner, the timing and phrasing prompts become of particular importance for the collection of retrospective protocols (e.g., Cohen, 1996; Ericsson & Simon, 1993; Greene & Higgins, 1994). If, for example, retrospective protocols are not collected immediately upon completion of a task, the learner may no longer recall the behaviours utilized during task performance, and may have to rely upon inferences of what 'must have happened' or utilize past experiences and knowledge to guide the report, rather than provide information about what actually *did* happen. Nisbett and Wilson (1977) found, in fact, that when asked to report cognitive processes, learners tended to hypothesize about the processes rather than report actual behaviours:

When reporting on the effects of stimuli, people may not interrogate a memory of the cognitive processes that operated on the stimuli; instead, they may base their reports on implicit, a priori theories about the causal connection between stimulus and response. (p. 233)

By requiring immediate reporting and providing careful retrieval cues, however, this problem can be minimized (e.g., Cohen, 1996; Ericsson & Simon, 1993; Greene & Higgins, 1994; Harri-Augstein & Thomas, 1984; P. White, 1980).

Asking focused, yet open-ended questions and providing contextual cues 'to help [the learner] reconstruct the situation and the specific strategies used, without cueing particular responses' (Greene & Higgins, 1994: 124) may provide the learner with sufficient guidance to provide accurate accounts of what actually occurred during task performance. The phrasing of these prompts must be carefully considered, however. For example, prompts such as 'Did you use strategy X?' may bias the learners' response and elicit untruthful reports (Ericsson & Simon, 1993: 23). Even a prompt such as 'What types of strategies did you use?' may encourage the learner to recall, or perhaps even to invent, 'strategies' that he/she feels are appropriate to report, rather than what he/she actually did. Likewise, asking learners to hypothesize as to *why* they performed in certain ways requires them to search for possible explanations, rather than to report actual behaviours.

Utilizing the actual task performance of the learner to prompt reporting may be a means of providing sufficient information to the learner to help him/her recall task performance without prompting for specific behaviours. For example, Greene and Higgins (1994) suggest beginning with focused open-ended questions and then following learner responses with specific questions on 'threads' provided by the learners themselves:

Researcher:
1. What goals, if any, did you have when you began to write this argument paper?

Writer:
2. It was important to use my own ideas.

Researcher:
3. So how did you use your own ideas? Show me . . .
   (Greene & Higgins, 1994: 26)

Similarly, Harri-Augstein and Thomas (1984) employed the data collected from a Brunel Reading Recorder to prompt L2 readers to recall the reasons behind their pauses and regressions while reading. By making use of the learners' actual performances to provide context, information is made more accessible to the protocol provider and more meaningful to the researcher.

Recent research looking at communication strategies of L2 learners has utilized the contextual information provided by audio- and video-tapes of learner interactions to prompt the learners to recall their decisions and behaviours during the performance of tasks (e.g., Cohen & Olshtain, 1993; Mackey (personal communication);

Tyler & Davies, 1990). The use of such prompts provides learners with the information they may need to extract particular behaviours from memory. In one example, taken from Cohen and Olshtain (1993), we see that a video-taped replay of an interaction can lead to reports of interesting details by the learner:

Galit wanted to make a polite request and was uncertain as to whether she could ask, *Do you have any room in the car?* As she put it:

It has a lot of meanings and I wasn't sure that it was correct, so I changed my tactic, and decided she would understand better if I said, *I want to drive with you.* I thought of *lift*, but didn't know how to use it in a sentences so I left it out. (p. 40)

Particular behaviours such as these may easily be omitted as a learner recalls a speech event, but with careful elicitation techniques, such as those provided by presenting learners with samples of their actual linguistic behaviours in the form of written, audio-, and/or video-taped documentation, learners may be able to offer researchers various types of detailed and reliable information regarding their linguistic decisions.

Training learners to provide protocols may also assist them in providing more complete and accurate portrayals of their behaviours (e.g., Ericsson & Simon, 1993; Pressley & Afflerbach, 1995). This, however, is a practice little reported upon in protocol research, if, in fact, performed at all. One type of training described in protocol research is that provided by the sample scripts in Ericsson and Simon (1993). These scripts introduce learners to thinking aloud and retrospective protocoling by asking them to perform sample problem-solving tasks. For simultaneous think-aloud protocols, for example, asking learners to solve a mathematical problem and an anagram may mimic certain problem-solving behaviours required of learners during their own task performance:

... before we turn to the real experiment, we will start with a couple of practice problems. I want you to talk aloud while you do these problems. First, I will ask you to multiply two numbers in your head.
So *talk aloud* while you multiply 24 times 34!
Good!
Now I would like you to solve an anagram. I will show you a card with scrambled letters. It is your task to find an English word that consists of all the presented letters. For example, if the scrambled letters are KORO, you may see that these letters spell the word ROOK. Any questions? Please 'talk aloud' while you solve the following anagram!
<NPEPHA = HAPPEN>
(Ericsson & Simon, 1993: 376, original emphasis)

Similarly, for retrospective protocols, learners can be asked to solve a multiplication problem, count rooms in a house, and/or name 20 animals. Upon providing the answers to these questions, the learner is then prompted to 'tell me all that you can remember about your thinking' (Ericsson & Simon, 1993: 377). These types of activities provide learners with some guidance as to what is expected of them during a protocol, modelling basic problem-solving and retrospective techniques, without biasing learners to perform or report any behaviours particular to the task at hand. However, whether or not this type of practice is facilitative for subsequent reporting of language behaviour is unclear.

More detailed training can also be provided by modelling behaviours that are similar to those that the learners will be performing. This was, in fact, done by Rosa and O'Neill (1999) who modelled protocol behaviour with a distractor puzzle task similar to that which the learners would be completing in their research study. Unfortunately, they do not report upon the details of this task, and it is, therefore, not clear exactly what types of behaviours were modelled.

In order to encourage her learners to reflect on their behaviours throughout their reading tasks, Cavalcanti (1987) trained her learners with a series of tasks which encouraged them to think-aloud whenever they faced a pause in their reading, rather than only report retrospectively at the end of the reading task, as they tended to do. Nyhus (1994) went a step further than this and provided her protocol subjects with quite detailed training for their reading protocols. They watched a video in which the researcher performed the same type of reading task as the learners. In the video-tape, various types of reading behaviours, such as questioning, inferencing, pausing, making regressions, and offering opinions about the text were modelled. Similar protocoling practice with reading tasks was also reported in several other research studies surveyed by Pressley and Afflerbach (1995). Whether or not these practice tasks may lead learners to report behaviours that they would not otherwise comment on, or even perhaps utilize, certainly merits further investigation. Thus, while some type of training for learners may prove beneficial in that it provides the opportunity to practise the somewhat unusual task of talking aloud and reporting task activities, researchers must also consider the potential effects of such training on the contents of the protocol reports themselves.

Analyzing protocol reports

As analyzing protocol reports is largely an interpretative undertaking on the part of the researcher, it is vital that reliability of the protocol analysis be established by a variety of means. Comparison of verbalizations with actual learner production is one such way of doing so. For example, drafts of written production can be compared with the verbal reports of the learner as the drafts were written in order to determine when and where changes were made in the composing processes. Likewise, Harri-Augstein and Thomas (1984) utilize data collected on a Brunel Reading Recorder, along with flow diagrams, and retrospective reports (or 'talk-backs', as the authors refer to them) to examine reading behavior. By incorporating multiple sources of information regarding learners' behavior, researchers can be more confident in their analyses.

Cognitive processes identified by the researcher should also reflect a theoretical approach to the processes under investigation. For example, in order to study the task-related thoughts of writers over a variety of treatment conditions, Smagorinsky (1994) determined that he 'needed to identify statements related to the protocols' *content* and to the *processes* engaged in by the writers' [original emphasis] (p. 9). For 'content', Smagorinsky (1994) looked for examples of students discussing the substance of their essays. For 'processes', the researcher identified segments of the protocols when the students did such things as re-read their assignment, 'experienced a block in their thinking, made a decision to rewrite or re-read, [and] initiated a memory search' (p. 9). As these behaviours are reflective of hypothesized models of writing (e.g., Swarts, Flowers, & Hayes, 1984), they may therefore be expected to be seen in the verbalizations provided by writers.

Analyses of protocol data may also be data-driven. For example, Hayes and Flowers (1980) formulated a theory of composition processes on the basis of protocols collected from a variety of learners. Similarly, Hosenfeld (1977) collected reading protocols from both successful and less successful readers in order to identify strategies which lead to effective reading in a foreign language. Likewise, Leow (1997) identified different levels of attention to linguistic output by learners when examining protocol data in his research. Such information gleaned from protocol analyses can then be utilized to guide further investigations of learners' processing behaviours.

Once cognitive behaviours have been identified – whether through theory-driven or data-driven analyses – it is also important that the reliability of these categories be assessed through the use of additional reviewers of the data. With carefully defined categories of behaviours, the protocol data can be reliably analyzed by multiple researchers, thereby making any claims based upon analyses of the protocols less subjectively interpretative (e.g., Ericsson & Simon, 1993; Greene & Higgins, 1994; Smagorinsky, 1994).

Protocol analysis in language learning research

During the past several decades, researchers in the cognitive sciences have conducted studies in which protocol data have been collected for the investigation of cognitive processes and constructs such as problem-solving procedures (e.g., Flaherty, 1974; Newell & Simon, 1972), memory (e.g., Loftus, 1972), and attention and awareness (e.g., Dulany, Carlson, & Dewey, 1984, 1985; Hsiao & Reber, 1998; Reber, 1989). Results of these studies have demonstrated the value of protocol use in cognition research.

As many such cognitive processes are presumed similar to those used in language processing, it makes sense that protocol analysis also be used to examine the behaviours involved in the use and acquisition of language. In such a spirit, researchers have collected protocol data to explore the cognitive processes involved in writing and reading in both a first and second language (e.g., Cohen & Calvalcanti, 1987; Cumming, 1989, 1994; Davis & Bistodeau, 1993; Greene & Higgins, 1994; Hayes & Flower, 1980; Haastrup, 1987; Hosenfeld, 1977; Raimes, 1994; Swarts et al., 1984), strategies for language use and interpretation[1] (e.g., Cohen, 1996; Cohen & Olshtain, 1993; Einstein & Bodman, 1987; Mangubhai, 1991; Sasaki, 1996; Tyler & Davies, 1980), and attention to and awareness of both linguistic input and output (e.g., Alanen, 1995; Jourdenais, 1995, 1998; Jourdenais et al., 1995; Leow, 1997; Rosa & O'Neill, 1999; Swain & Lapkin, 1995).

We will now discuss the findings yielded in the protocol data collected from some of the above-mentioned studies in light of support for existing and developing theories of language processing and acquisition, as well as for information which may be useful to guide the development of classroom instructional practices and materials.

Writing research

One of the areas in which protocol data has been employed extensively is that of writing research. Researchers have made use of both concurrent and retrospective protocols to inform general models of composition (e.g., Hayes & Flower, 1980; Swarts et al., 1984), and to investigate the cognitive processes of L1 and L2 writers (e.g., Cumming, 1989, 1994; Raimes, 1985, 1994; Swain & Lapkin, 1995).

A particular goal of writing research has been to identify the composing processes of 'good' writers. A composition model put forth by

---

[1] See also Faerch and Kasper (1987) for a collection of research studies on translation which employ various types of protocol data.

Hayes and Flower (1980) identified three main composing processes on the basis of protocol data analysis: planning the text, translating ideas into words, and reviewing the text for editing purposes, as well as sets of subprocesses (generating, organizing, and goal-setting; evaluating and revising) also used in the creation of written texts (Hayes & Flower, 1980: 10–11). In order to assess the accuracy of this model in more detail, Hayes and Flowers (1980) analyzed the think-aloud protocol provided by one writer in depth. They found that the writer first generated ideas, noting comments such as, 'And what I'll do now is to simply jot down random thoughts . . . ' and 'Topics as they occur randomly are . . . ' (p. 21). She then worked to organize her thoughts, making remarks such as, 'Now this isn't the overall organization. This is just the organization of a subpart' and 'I can imagine the possibility of an alternate plan' (p. 22). And she finally translated her ideas into words, constructing the body of the text itself: 'But let's build on this plan and see what happens with it' (p. 22). Each of the composing processes proposed in their model of composition were, in fact, identified in the protocol report collected from this one writer, and coding of the protocol data by independent raters also provided further support for the reliable classification of the observed writing behaviours, indicating that the model proposed by Hayes and Flowers (1980) was supported in the data collected from this successful writer. Although the protocol of one writer can hardly be used to definitively determine the success of any particular model, it can be used to provide evidence in support of a model or to refine such a model. Analyses of protocols in other writing research have, in fact, demonstrated similar categories of writing strategies in both L1 and L2 composition (e.g., Cumming, 1989, 1994; Raimes, 1985, 1994). Raimes (1994), for example, collected protocol data from L2 writers at two different levels of English proficiency to determine how their composition processes compared to one another as well as to those of first language writers. Identifying six composing strategies in the think-aloud protocols of the learners, Raimes concluded that L1 and L2 writers share common strategies, such as minimal planning, prewriting, and considerable rescanning of the text, but differ in that L2 writers appear more willing to edit their writing, and that they rehearse extensively in order to generate content, syntax, and vocabulary:

'I can talk about girls-boys relationship . . . or I can talk about the relation between parents and how a man has a problem back home and a man has a problem here, the differences. Yeah, that's good. I can say what's the difference between my father, the feelings, the relationship – no, that's too specific. I can talk about how here people are more close . . . .' (example of rehearsing, Raimes, 1994: 156)

She also found, however, that the more remedial ESL students were actually less likely to revise and edit their texts than were the more fluent students. Raimes suggests that awareness of such writing strategies employed by students can be used to guide classroom instruction and to provide students with information on improved composing strategies.

In the think-aloud protocols collected by Raimes (1994), as well as those collected by Cumming (1989, 1994), information was also provided about the relationship between general language proficiency and writing proficiency. The researchers determined, as based on correlating the evidence from L2 proficiency measures with the strategies demonstrated in the writing protocols, that while second language proficiency may facilitate writing in the L2, second-language writing success is more likely to be attributed to L1 writing experiences than to general L2 proficiency measures. These results indicate that there are cognitive behaviours associated with writing that are developed separately from those associated with the development of language. In fact, Cumming (1994) suggests that 'writing expertise and second-language proficiency are psychologically different' (p. 201). Such findings from protocol research have implications, not only for a definition of 'language proficiency', but also for decisions regarding the focus of writing instruction and assessment in the classroom.

The above examples demonstrate that the use of protocol data in composition research enables researchers to systematically gather and access information otherwise unavailable through analyses of the written products alone. This information regarding the writing processes of learners in both first and second languages and at varying levels of writing proficiency can be used to guide classroom instruction, as well as to inform and construct models of composition and theories of written language acquisition.

Reading research

Language research has also relied upon protocol data collection to further contribute to theories of reading development. Studies have assessed models of text processing (e.g., Pressley & Afflerbach, 1995), bottom–up and top–down reading processes (Davis & Bistodeau, 1993), vocabulary recognition (Haastrup, 1987), and reading strategies (e.g., Cohen and Calvalcanti, 1987; Cohen, Glasman, Sosenbaum-Cohen, Ferrara, & Fine, 1979; Harri-Augstein & Thomas, 1984; Hosenfeld, 1977).

Surveying 38 primary research studies of reading which utilized protocol analysis data, Pressley and Afflerbach (1995) concluded that current models of text processing, including reader response theory (e.g., Rosenblatt, 1978), metacognitive theory (Baker & Brown, 1984), schema theory (Anderson & Pearson, 1984), discourse comprehension (van Dijk & Kintsch, 1983), text inferential processes (e.g., Graesser & Bower, 1990), and sociocultural theories of reading (e.g., Beach & Hynds, 1991; Fish, 1980), are insufficient to account for the complexity and richness of strategies employed by readers. Reviewing the protocol data from various studies, Pressley and Afflerbach (1995) conclude that 'all of the processes favored in these various theories…in fact, are part of skilled reading' (1995: 115), but that a more comprehensive theory would better account for the varied behaviours revealed in the protocol verbalizations. Such a claim emphasizes that while an individual protocol study may yield certain insights as to readers' processing of texts, a compilation and examination of various protocol data may permit researchers to gain a yet more comprehensive view of reader behaviour. Pressley and Afflerbach (1995) utilize the information from their survey to establish a new 'constructively responsive' theory of text comprehension, which incorporates the findings of numerous protocol reading studies.

To examine whether text processing differs at varying levels of reading proficiency and for first and second-language readers, Davis and Bistodeau (1993) also utilized think-aloud protocols. The researchers identified thirteen processing strategies employed by readers, which they divided into two larger groups: bottom–up strategies, which focused on intrasentential features, and top–down strategies, which included inferencing, prediction, and evaluation (among others). Davis and Bistodeau (1993) found that processing strategies did, in fact, differ depending upon proficiency. The more proficient L2 readers employed both top-down and bottom-up processing equally when reading in both their L1 and L2, while the less proficient L2 readers utilized bottom-up processing more in their L2 reading than they did in their L1 reading. These findings provide empirical evidence for models of language processing and comprehension in which low-proficiency learners are hypothesized to rely on bottom–up strategies, gradually expanding to top–down processing as language proficiency increases (e.g., Bialystok, 1994a; Clarke, 1980; McLaughlin et al., 1983; Stanovich, 1984). The importance of individual performance, however, is also highlighted in this research as a factor in reading development as some of the lower-proficiency readers made more equal use of both top–down and bottom–up processing as evidenced in their protocol verbalizations than might otherwise have been expected. The protocol data in this study thus provides evidence in favour of certain text processing strategies, while simultaneously emphasizing the need to consider individual differences in learner behaviours.

Hosenfeld (1977) made similar observations as she researched whether there were specific processes utilized by more successful readers which were lacking in the repertoires of less successful readers. She collected both introspective and retrospective reading protocols in order to identify 'successful' and 'nonsuccessful' L2 reading strategies (Hosenfeld, 1977). Analyzing the protocol data, she found the behaviours of the two levels of readers to be quite different. The 'successful' reader maintained the central meaning of the passage throughout the activity, enabling him to skip words he deemed less important for the understanding of the story:

Steven: (Pause)
It's the day of departure. Lucien is at the international airport...at Orly that is situated south-east of Paris. He waits for the departure...of something... something... number 250 for Martinique. Uh...he's at the airport so it must be flight number 250 for Martinique. Why choose Martinique? Uh...I don't know what a-t-il means but he's going to Martinique...
...and then they say *Why choose Martinique? At the lycée Lucien is a serious* something ... something ... *history of France and geography.* Uh...wait a minute...I can get this. Uh...it must be *a serious student of the history of France and geography...it's geography.* I don't know what surtout means. (Continuing) He...

Interviewer: (Interrupting) Would you look up surtout?
Steven: No. You don't really need it.
(Hosenfeld, 1977, p. 116)

The 'nonsuccessful' reader, on the other hand, concentrated on word-level meaning, rather than sentence or paragraph-level comprehension, and devoted equal time and energy to each and every word. Strategies for solving unknown lexical items also differed considerably. While the successful learner used the context of the reading to decode unfamiliar words, the less successful reader stopped at each unknown word to use a dictionary, and only after establishing word meaning, continued on with the remainder of the text:

Student: Uh...well...I understand *Pourquoi*...why...and I'm looking up *choisi.* (He looks up choisi in the back of the book.) To choose. *Why did you* ... no. (Pause)
Interviewer: What are you stuck on?
Student: (He points to *a-t-il.*) *Why are you choose.* I don't understand the sentence. (Pointing to choisi) This means to choose...right?
Interviewer: You looked it up?

Student:	Right. (Pointing to *Pourquoi*) And that's why. And *a-t-il* . . . oh yeah . . . *why did you* . . . no. What is confusing me is the *il.* (Pause)
Interviewer:	So what would you do?
Student:	Well . . . *il a* is avoir which means *to have.* (Pause) Maybe if I read the first paragraph again I'd understand this part better.
Interviewer:	The first paragraph?
Student:	Yeah. The first paragraph might give me a clue to the sentence I'm having so much trouble with.
	(Hosenfeld, 1977: 115)

By examining these two protocol transcripts, the differences in reading strategies employed by the two learners were evident. Collecting protocols such as these, and analyzing the text processing strategies utilized by both successful and less successful L1 and L2 readers, researchers and instructors are thus better informed about reading behaviours which may either hamper or lead to increased reading proficiency. This information can then utilized to inform theories of text processing, as well as lead to improved reading instruction which will be better able to meet the needs of both L1 and L2 readers at varying levels of proficiency.

Research on language use and interpretation

Protocol analysis has also provided language acquisition researchers with information as to the types of processes employed by language learners when interpreting and using their L2. Of particular interest has been an investigation of learners' attention to the meaning, in contrast to the grammatical form, of utterances (cf., VanPatten, 1990, 1994), as well as an investigation of the relationship between information processing and L2 proficiency (e.g., Cohen, 1984; Hosenfeld, 1977; Mangubhai, 1991; Sasaki, 1996). Hosenfeld (1977), for example, investigated learner performance on grammatical tasks through the use of think-aloud and retrospective protocols and found that learners do not necessarily attend to the meaning of utterances on traditional grammar tasks. Rather, the learners' protocols indicate that they were able to complete more traditional tasks without utilizing sentential information, but rather by simply looking at the provided targeted items and then filling in the blanks. Meaning and other information provided at sentence-level was not utilized by the learner if it was not essential for task completion. Likewise, Cohen's (1984) investigation of test-taking techniques of language learners found that the immediate environment of the targeted word had the largest impact on learners' response, not the more extensive information which may be provided by the extended context of the testing item.

Based on the findings from such protocol studies, it appears that when meaning is needed in order to complete the task successfully, learners may choose to translate from their L2 into their first language in order to interpret sentences, rather than rely on L2 knowledge. This translation then provides the explanation for many grammatical errors on tasks as the learners supply responses on the basis of their L1, disregarding the potential inappropriateness of the particular form in the L2 (Hosenfeld, 1977). Such reliance on local strategies and on L1 structure during test performance, rather than on information provided by the L2 and more global strategies for text interpretation, may not always be evident from learner performance (although it may be, in some cases, suggested by particular inaccuracies), but becomes more clearly apparent when think-aloud protocols collected during task performance are examined.

Similar findings were also noted in the concurrent think-aloud and immediate retrospective reports collected by Mangubhai (1991), who investigated strategy use in the learning of Hindi as a second language. He found that less proficient learners spent more time on word-level interpretations than did the more successful learners who devoted considerable time to understanding the meaning of the utterances in Hindi, rather than translating word-by-word back to English.

Sasaki (1996) also investigated the relationship between proficiency level and cognitive processing (cf., Bachman & Palmer, 1982) by comparing the test-taking processes of learners at three levels of L2 proficiency. The researcher collected protocols from learners after the completion of each test item on tests of L2 proficiency (short and long multiple-choice, cloze, and free composition), foreign language aptitude (an adapted Language Aptitude Battery for Japanese), and intelligence (Kyoto University New NX-15 Intelligence Test). These protocols yielded information on the amount of textual information used by the learners to successfully complete each test item (Sasaki, 1996), as well as information on the relationship between the learner's level of proficiency and the cognitive processing requirements of tasks on each test (cf. Carroll, 1985). The researcher found that the tests appeared to be assessing the skills that they claimed to test, but that the amount of processing employed by the learner did not necessarily correlate with levels of L2 proficiency. Learners at high and low proficiency levels did, however, differ in the types of textual information they utilized to solve tasks and with the test-taking strategies they employed. High-level learners relied on the wider context of items and used multiple strategies when problem-solving, while low level learners were more limited in their range of processing approaches.

Findings from these protocol studies highlight the importance of determining whether a task truly elicits the type of language behaviour we seek to examine from learners at varying proficiency levels. This information is not only of interest to L2 researchers, but also to testing specialists and pedagogues alike. Protocol data can provide us with information on task behaviour that may not be apparent from learners' responses alone. This information can then be used to guide task design, to inform theories about learners' processing mechanisms, as well as to serve as an empirical foundation for further research.

Discourse research

Protocol research has also been used to inform various types of discourse research. Cohen (1996), for example, states, 'Along with the study of the development of speech act ability, there is a need to investigate the processes underlying the planning and execution of speech act utterances' (p. 256). Recent research has sought to go beyond a description of speech act development and to examine the sociocultural and sociolinguistic strategies of L2 learners through the collection of retrospective protocols. By analyzing the protocol data collected from learners, researchers and instructors are better able to:

interpret sociocultural and sociolinguistic successes and failures . . . we need to know the sociocultural context in which the given realization of the speech act appeared, why it was performed in that way, what processes contributed to generating the specific sociolinguistic forms that were produced, and how the utterance was comprehended by the listeners(s). (Cohen, 1996: 263)

Einstein and Bodman (1987), for example, did just this as they collected retrospective data to investigate learners' linguistic decisions as they expressed gratitude in their second language. Cohen and Olshtain (1993) also collected retrospective protocol reports from language learners performing various speech acts (apologies, requests, and complaints). They found that learners spent very little time planning the vocabulary and grammar of their utterances, and utilized knowledge of speech act behaviour from other languages when choosing how to express themselves (Cohen & Olshtain, 1993: 46).

While the above studies focused on speech act behavior, Tyler and Davies (1990) examined actual video-taped classroom discourse in order to establish the reasons behind areas of communication difficulty for international teaching assistants (ITAs). Analyzing the tapes and transcripts for various discourse strategies and collecting retrospective data from both the concerned teaching assistant and from a group of native-English speaking student consultants, the researchers were able to identify areas of cross-cultural differences in discourse structure and participant schemas which contributed to communication misunderstandings in the classroom. With the collection of protocol data, such as that discussed in the studies above, researchers are better able to determine the source of particular speech behaviours, and may thus be able to utilize this information to inform classroom instruction and guide learners to improved communicative competence.

Research on attention and awareness

While the above discussion has centred on the use of protocols for the identification of learner's processing strategies, protocol data has also been collected in order to offer support for more theoretical constructs such as attention and awareness (c.f., Ellis, N., 1993, 1994c; Schmidt, 1990, 1993a, 1994c, this volume; Rutherford & Sharwood Smith, 1985; Sharwood Smith, 1981, 1993; van Lier, 1994). In recent research, protocols have been collected and analyzed in order to examine language learners' attentional focus on linguistic input, and to determine the effects of particular types of input enhancement and instruction (Alanen, 1995; Jourdenais, 1996, 1998; Jourdenais et al., 1995; Leow, 1997; Rosa & O'Neill, 1999).

Arguing that 'noticing' is a conscious behaviour necessary for language learning to take place, Schmidt (1990, 1993a, 1994c) has operationalized noticing as being 'available for self report' at or immediately after the point of noticing (1990: 32). Following this definition, protocol analysis becomes a perfect candidate for investigation of the hypothesis, as it is based on the assumption that the information in focal attention is available for verbal report (Ericsson & Simon, 1993). Protocol reports collected concurrently with the performance of a task may thus provide researchers with a means for observing what input the learners 'notice' or attend to, and whether this appears related to their subsequent language performance.

Swain and Lapkin (1995), for example, utilized think-aloud writing protocols in an attempt to investigate whether learners, as Schmidt and Frota (1986) suggest, must 'notice a gap' in their interlanguage (IL) prior to making a change in any hypotheses they may hold. Analyzing think-aloud protocols collected from L2 learners of French as they wrote in their second language, Swain and Lapkin documented numerous language-related episodes in the writing processes of L2 learners in which the learners noticed a gap in their IL abilities and then made an attempt to address it in order to express themselves more clearly. This protocol evidence not only provides support for Schmidt and

Frota's (1986) 'notice-the-gap' hypothesis, but also raises the question as to whether or not learners' attention can then be directed towards particular input forms where 'gaps' occur.

Research aimed at drawing learners' attention to problematic linguistic forms via a variety of input enhancement techniques (Sharwood Smith, 1981, 1993) has made claims regarding the success of various methods in directing learners' attention to such gaps (e.g., Carroll & Swain, 1993; Doughty, 1991, this volume; Doughty & Varela, 1998; Fotos, 1993, 1994; Izumi, Bigelow, Fujiwara, & Fearnow, 1998; Shook, 1994; White, Spada, Lightbown, & Ranta, 1991; J. White, 1998). In these studies, however, learners' actual processing of and attention to the input has not been observed. Rather, learners' attention has been assumed on the basis of their subsequent task performance. Protocol analysis, however, affords us a means of examining learners' on-line processing of input more directly.

In a small study conducted with several of my colleagues (Jourdenais et al., 1995), we attempted to provide information about the effectiveness of one type of input enhancement technique, textual enhancement (e.g., bolding, underlining, typeface changes), on learners' cognitive processing of targeted linguistic forms: the Spanish preterit and imperfect aspect. Analysis of both protocol and written data indicated that learners in the study who had been provided with the textually enhanced input performed differently than did learners who received no enhancement in their texts. While neither group utilized the input forms in their written production in a more target-like manner than did the other, the think-aloud protocols of the learners in the enhancement group indicated that they made more explicit references to the preterit and imperfect forms as they composed their essays. They were also more likely to use the targeted forms in their written compositions than were the learners who did not receive the enhanced input. While accuracy of suppliance thus yielded no differences between the two groups, the protocol verbalizations and the frequency of suppliance of the targeted forms suggest that the method of textual enhancement may have had an effect on the processing of input by the learners.

The small number of learners (ten) participating in the Jourdenais et al. (1995) study led to an expanded study – Jourdenais (1998) – in which protocol data was collected from 61 of the 116 learners of Spanish participating in the study. As with the earlier study, evidence from the protocols indicated that the learners were attending to the targeted verb forms both explicitly (i.e., metalinguistically) and implicitly as they composed their essays:

Explicit:	'Let's see Aladin started to um imperfect *Aladin empezaba...*'
	'I'm not sure if that's preterit *estuvo o estaba...*'
	'um Aladin pone no poner in the past it's *puso...*'
Implicit:	'In the next picture *hab í an* ooh *hubieran muchas joyas en el piso.*'
	'*sabiendo que va a morir, no va, que iba a morir en la cueva.*'
	' "*Es tan bonita*" *dice el,* no not *dice dec í a* oh *diciste -ijo.*'

However, differences in group performance due to the presence of textual enhancement were not readily apparent. These protocol findings differed from those of Jourdenais et al. (1995), suggesting that textual enhancement may not be a sufficient means of drawing learners' attention to the subtleties of aspectual use, as had been indicated in the smaller study.[2]

While research in these two studies focused on the effects of only one particular type of input enhancement, the comparative effectiveness of different *focus on form* techniques is also of great interest to SLA researchers. Alanen (1995), for example, utilized think-aloud protocols to compare effectiveness of different types of input enhancement on learners' attention to and processing of prepositional morphology: explicit information regarding the forms and implicit textual enhancement. She found that the protocol data provided evidence in favour of the explicit information regarding the forms, as learners receiving this type of input were able to discuss rules guiding their use of the morphology, but the protocol data also indicated that implicit enhancement may be effective as well, as it also lead the learners to formulate some type of rules regarding the use of the forms.

Recent research by Leow (1997) and Rosa and O'Neill (1999) using protocols has demonstrated that different types of information provided by learners in think-aloud reports may correlate with different accuracies in their performance on subsequent receptive and productive language tasks. Upon analyzing the think-aloud protocols provided by learners during a crossword puzzle task, Leow (1997) found that different levels of awareness of stem-changing verb forms in Spanish lead to different levels of performance. Learners who made metacomments about the targeted forms and stated some type of rule guiding the stem change (e.g., '... *ellos repitieron?* I think it has a stem change, down, *ir*, yes!...') performed more accurately on subsequent tasks than did those who mentioned the forms, but stated no rules (e.g., 'the form of the verb of *repetir* is *repetieron, re-pe-ti-eron...*').

---

[2] The Jourdenais (1998) study, although similar, was not a direct replication of the Jourdenais et al. (1995) study, and thus many other variables must also be considered when examining the findings.

This latter group, however, despite a lack of rules found in the protocols, still performed better than learners who made no mentions of the forms whatsoever in their protocols. According to Leow (1997), 'the findings provide empirical support for the facilitative effects of awareness on foreign language behavior'(p. 495).

A similar investigation conducted by Rosa and O'Neill (1999) also reported that think-aloud protocols collected during a problem-solving linguistic task provides evidence of different levels of awareness on the part of the learners. In this study, learners who reported rules for the formation of the past subjunctive in Spanish in their protocols provided the forms in a more target-like manner than did learners who simply acknowledged that the past subjunctive was needed for completion of their puzzle tasks.

Results such as those discussed in the studies above suggest that protocols may be able to provide language researchers with not only evidence for better defining theoretical constructs such as 'awareness' and 'noticing', but also with information regarding different levels of attention that learners devote to different types of linguistic input and the effects that these varying levels of attention may have on subsequent task performance. This information might then be utilized to determine which types of treatment and which types of attention correlate most strongly with more successful language use and acquisition.

Concerns about protocol use

Despite all of the benefits offered by the collection of protocol data from language learners, there is no denying that concerns have been raised as to whether or not protocols can truly provide a reliable and complete means of assessing learners' cognitive processing. Criticisms of this method of data collection include concerns regarding learners' memory constraints, that is, whether or not learners are able to accurately recall the thoughts they have during task completion (required for retrospective and introspective reports, in particular); the reliability of the protocols, in that learners may report what they feel the researcher wants to hear, rather than what is actually experienced; the completeness of the reports provided by the learners; elicitation techniques, which may lead learners to report certain behaviours but not others; and finally, whether or not the learner actually has access to the metalinguistic information and/or the metalinguistic ability to describe his or her own behaviours (for a more detailed discussion of these criticisms see also Ericsson & Simon, 1993; Seliger, 1983; Stratman & Hamp-Lyons, 1994).

As mentioned earlier, some of these concerns are diminished by the use of careful elicitation procedures which will prompt the learner to remember and report relevant (and real) behaviours. Some problems may also be eased, or eliminated entirely, by gathering different types of protocol data. Collecting concurrent think-alouds, for example, in which the learners provide verbalizations simultaneously with the performance of a task, rather than retrospectively, will alleviate concerns about memory constraints. Also, concurrent think-alouds do not require the learner to interpret or explain behaviours, as do retrospective and introspective reports. By eliminating such concerns, these think-aloud protocols may provide researchers with a more accurate picture of learners' on-line processing.

Think-aloud protocols may not, however, be appropriate for some types of data collection, for example during communicative tasks, when they would interfere with the task at hand. As discussed earlier, carefully designed prompts and video- and audio-tapes of learners' language behaviour may also lead learners to provide accurate recollections of their linguistic decisions.

Concerns have also been raised about the possible effects of the simultaneous reporting of thoughts and task performance required by think-aloud protocols. Questions have been asked as to whether or not reporting thoughts aloud while performing a task may actually change the task itself, thereby influencing learners' cognitive processing (Jourdenais, 1995; Seliger 1983, 1984; Stratman & Hamp-Lyons, 1994). In fact, in Jourdenais (1998), the learners who provided protocols during their written task performance were significantly less likely to employ the targeted linguistic forms than were the learners who did not have the additional task of protocoling during the composition of their essays. Thus, it appears that the think-aloud data collection method itself acts as an additional task which must be considered carefully when examining learner performance. If the data collection method affects task performance, we must be very careful about any claims we make regarding what it is that we are measuring.

There is also a possibility that concurrent verbalization may affect the task in a different manner, perhaps by providing additional input for the learner. Swain's (1985) Output Hypothesis, for example, suggests that the learners' opportunity to produce comprehensible output may create a means for the learner to notice gaps in his/her IL and make adjustments in order to approximate the target language. As many such learning opportunities (or 'language episodes', as defined by Swain & Lapkin, 1995) have been noted in concurrent protocols provided by learners (Jourdenais, 1998; Jourdenais et al., 1995; Swain & Lapkin, 1995), it may be that the verbalizations act as an additional form of linguistic input for the learner, thereby adding another variable to the data collection situation.

Questions have also been raised as to the overall completeness of protocol data and whether or not learners are actually able to verbalize everything that they are thinking. Certainly, as more automatic processes take over, learners may not be aware of some of the processing they undergo when performing a task (Anderson, 1982; McLaughlin et al., 1983; Shiffrin & Schneider, 1977), and therefore may not report some behaviours. Additionally, learners' individual abilities and attentional preferences may also contribute to inconsistencies in protocol reporting (see Sawyer & Ranta, and Skehan & Foster, this volume). Learners who are less willing to take risks, for example, may be less inclined to produce language which leads them to address IL gaps. Likewise, those who are more field independent may attend more to details of their language production, such as grammatical form. Cohen and Olshtain (1993), for example, identified three production styles in their speech act research and were able to classify learners as *metacognizers*, *avoiders*, and *pragmatists*, each of whom approached the speech act task from a different perspective. The *metacognizers* attended to possible production errors and monitored grammar and pronunciation in their output. The *avoiders*, on the other hand, circumlocuted in order to avoid producing problematic forms. The *pragmatists* were more interested in providing comprehensible output than they were in monitoring exact forms, and thus were willing to approximate targeted output if they felt it could be understood by their interlocutors. The comfort level of learners with this type of task (as with any other) and their ability to provide protocols must also be considered. Despite training learners to think-aloud or provide introspective or retrospective reports, some learners may not be able to provide detailed information regarding their performances, and others may simply be very uncomfortable with this type of task. In Jourdenais (1998), for example, some learners had to be prompted to 'keep talking', while others had no hesitations in their protocols and verbalized constantly throughout their tasks. Several learners also indicated that they felt very awkward providing the protocol report. This, too, may have an impact on protocol content and should be addressed when analyzing verbalizations.

While there are admittedly a number of concerns regarding the use of protocol data collection and analyses, many of these can be overcome through careful design of studies, elicitation of verbalizations, and coding of data. As I have argued throughout this chapter, verbal reports are a potentially valuable source of information about L2 learning processes, and can be used to research such issues as:

the effect of L1 knowledge on L2 processes; the various strategies employed by learners as they produce and attend to linguistic information; and the manner in which different instructional tasks and treatment materials may impact on language acquisition. All of these are issues of central importance to SLA theory and pedagogy alike.

References

Abney, S. (1989). A computational model of human parsing. *Journal of Psycholinguistic Research, 18,* 129–144.

ACTFL. (1986). *The ACTFL proficiency guidelines.* New York: American Council on the Teaching of Foreign Languages.

Aitchison, J. (1994). *Words in the mind.* Oxford: Blackwell.

Alanen, R. (1995). Input enhancement and rule presentation in second language acquisition. In R. Schmidt (Ed.), *Attention and awareness in foreign language learning and teaching* (pp. 259–302). Honolulu, HI: University of Hawaii Press.

Alderson, J. C. (1984). Reading in a foreign language: A reading or a language problem? In J. C. Alderson & A. H. Urquhart (Eds.), *Reading in a foreign language* (pp. 1–24). London: Longman.

Alderson, J. C., Clapham, C., & Steel, D. (1997). Metalinguistic knowledge, language aptitude and language proficiency. *Language Teaching Research, 1,* 93–121.

Allen, V. F. (1983). *Techniques in teaching vocabulary.* Oxford: Oxford University Press.

Allport, D. A., Antonis, B., & Reynolds, P. (1972). On the division of attention: A disproof of the single-channel hypothesis. *Quarterly Journal of Experimental Psychology, 24,* 225–235.

Altmann, G., & Steedman, M. (1988). Interaction with context during human sentence processing. *Cognition, 30,* 191–238.

Andersen, R. (1984). The One-to-One Principle of language construction. *Language Learning, 34,* 77–95.

Andersen, R. (1989). The theoretical status of variation in interlanguage development. In S. Gass, C. Madden, D. Preston, & L. Selinker (Eds.), *Variation in second language acquisition, Vol. 1: Psycholinguistic issues,* (pp. 46–64). Clevedon, Avon: Multilingual Matters.

Anderson A., & Lynch, T. (1988). *Listening.* Oxford: Oxford University Press.

Anderson, J. R. (1976). *Language, memory and thought.* Hillsdale, NJ: Erlbaum.

Anderson, J. R. (1981). Effects of prior knowledge on memory for new information. *Memory and Cognition, 9,* 237–246.

Anderson, J. R. (1982). Acquisition of cognitive skill. *Psychological Review,* *89,* 369–406.

Anderson, J. R. (1983). *The architecture of cognition.* Cambridge, MA: Harvard University Press.

Anderson, J. R. (1987). Skill acquisition: Compilation of weak-method problem solutions. *Psychological Review, 94,* 192–210.

Anderson, J. R. (1992). Automaticity and the ACT theory. *American Journal of Psychology, 105,* 165–180.

Anderson, J. R. (1993). *Rules of the mind.* Hillsdale, NJ: Erlbaum.

Anderson, J. R. (1995). *Learning and memory: An integrated approach.* New York: John Wiley.

Anderson, J. R., & Fincham, J. M. (1994). Acquisition of procedural skills from examples. *Journal of Experimental Psychology: Learning, Memory and Cognition, 20,* 1322–1340.

Anderson, J. R., Fincham, J. M., & Douglass, S. (1997). The role of examples and rules in the acquisition of a cognitive skill. *Journal of Experimental Psychology: Learning, Memory and Cognition, 23,* 932–945.

Anderson, J. R., & Lebiere, C. (1998). *The atomic components of thought.* Mahwah, NJ: Erlbaum.

Anderson, N. (1982). *Methods of information integration theory.* New York: Academic Press.

Anderson, R., & Pearson, P. (1984). A schema-theoretic view of basic processes in reading. In P. Pearson, R. Barr, M. Kamil & P. Mosenthal (Eds.), *Handbook of reading research* (pp. 225–291). New York: Longman.

Anderson, R., Wilson, P., & Fielding, L. (1988). Growth in reading and how children spend their time outside of school. *Reading Research Quarterly, 23,* 285–303.

Andonova, E. (1998). Sentence interpretation in Bulgarian: The contribution of animacy. *Proceedings of the 20th Annual Meeting of the Cognitive Science Society,* (pp. 54–58). Mahwah, NJ: Erlbaum.

Anisfeld, M. (1966). Psycholinguistic perspectives on language learning. In A. Valdman (Ed.), *Trends in language teaching* (pp. 107–119). New York: McGraw-Hill.

Arevart, S., & Nation, P. (1991). Fluency improvement in a second language. *RELC Journal, 22,* 84–94.

Aston, G. (1986). Troubleshooting interaction with learners: the more the merrier? *Applied Linguistics, 7,* 128–143.

Atkins, P. W. B., & Baddeley, A. D. (1998). Working memory and distributed vocabulary learning. *Applied Psycholinguistics, 19,* 537–552.

Atkinson, M. (1982). *Explanations in the study of child language development.* Cambridge: Cambridge University Press.

Atkinson, M. (1992). *Children's syntax: an introduction to principles and parameters theory.* Cambridge: Cambridge University Press.

Au, S. Y. (1988). A critical appraisal of Gardner's social-psychological theory of second-language (L2) learning. *Language Learning, 38,* 75–100.

Baars, B. J. (1988). *A cognitive theory of consciousness*. Cambridge: Cambridge University Press.

Baars, B. J. (1996). *In the theater of consciousness*. New York: Oxford University Press.

Bachman, L., & A. Palmer (1982). The construct validation of some components of communicative proficiency. *TESOL Quarterly, 16*, 449–465.

Bachman, L. (1990). *Fundamentals of language testing*. Oxford: Oxford University Press.

Bachman, L., & Palmer, A. (1996). *Language testing in practice: developing and designing useful language tests*. Oxford: Oxford University Press.

Baddeley, A. (1986). *Working memory*. Oxford: Clarendon Press.

Baddeley, A. (1997). *Human memory: Theory and practice (revised edition)*. Hove: Psychology Press.

Baddeley, A. D., & Hitch, G. J. (1974). Working memory. In G. Bower (Ed.), *The psychology of learning and motivation: Vol. 8*, (pp. 47–90). New York: Academic Press.

Baddeley, A., Papagno, C., & Vallar, G. (1988). When long-term learning depends on short-term storage. *Journal of Memory and Language, 27*, 586–595.

Baddeley, A., Thomson, N., Buchanan, M. (1975). Word length and the structure of short-term memory. *Journal of Verbal Learning and Verbal Behavior, 14*, 575–589.

Bahrick, H. P. (1984). Semantic memory content in permastore: Fifty years of memory for Spanish learned in school. *Journal of Experimental Psychology: General, 113*, 1–29.

Bahrick, H. P., Bahrick, L. E., Bahrick, A. S., & Bahrick, P. E. (1993). Maintenance of foreign language vocabulary and the spacing effect. *Psychological Science, 4*, 316–321.

Bahrick, H. P., & Phelps, E. (1987). Retention of Spanish vocabulary over 8 years. *Journal of Experimental Psychology, 13*, 344–349.

Bailey, D., Feldman, J., Narayanan, S., & Lakoff, G. (1997). Modelling Embodied Lexical Development. *Proceedings of the cognitive science conference 1997*. Cognitive Science Society, Pittsburgh, PA.

Baker, D. (1990). *A guide to language testing*. London: Arnold.

Baker, L., & Brown, A. (1984). Metacognitive skills and reading. In P. D. Pearson, R. Barr, M. Kamil, & P. Mosenthal (Eds.), *Handbook of reading research* (pp. 353–394). New York: Longman.

Baker, N., & Nelson, K. (1984). Recasting and related conversational techniques for triggering syntactic advances by young children. *First Language, 5*, 3–22.

Bardovi-Harlig, K. (1992). A second look at t-unit analysis: Reconsidering the sentence. *TESOL Quarterly, 26*, 390–395.

Bargh, J. A. (1992). The ecology of automaticity: Toward establishing the conditions needed to produce automatic processing effects. *American Journal of Psychology, 105*, 181–199.

Barsalou, L. W. (1992). *Cognitive psychology: An overview for cognitive scientists.* Hillsdale, NJ: Erlbaum.

Barton, M., & Tomasello, M. (1991). Joint attention and conversation in mother-infant-sibling triads. *Child Development, 62,* 517–29.

Bates, E. (1984). Bioprograms and the innateness hypothesis. *Behavioral and Brain Sciences, 7,* 188–190.

Bates, E., Chen, S., Tzeng, O., Li, P., & Opie, M. (1991). The noun-verb problem in Chinese aphasia. *Brain and Language, 41,* 203–233.

Bates, E., & MacWhinney, B. (1981). Second language acquisition from a functionalist perspective. In H. Winitz (Ed.), *Native language and foreign language acquisition, Annals of the New York Academy of Sciences, 379,* 190–214.

Bates, E., McNew, S., MacWhinney, B., Devescovi, A., & Smith, S. (1982). Functional constraints on sentence processing: A cross-linguistic study. *Cognition, 11,* 245–299.

Bates, E., Thal, D., & Marchman, V. (1991). Symbols and syntax: A Darwinian approach to language development. In N. A. Krasnegor, D. M. Rumbaugh, R. L. Schiefelbusch, & M. Studdert-Kennedy (Eds.), *Biological and behavioral determinants of language development* (pp. 29–66). Hillsdale, NJ: Erlbaum.

Bauer, L., & P. Nation. (1993). Word families. *International Journal of Lexicography, 6,* 253–279.

Bavin, E., & Shopen, T. (1989). Warlpiri children's processing of transitive sentences. In B. MacWhinney & E. Bates (Eds.), *The crosslinguistic study of sentence processing,* (pp. 185–208). New York: Cambridge University Press.

Bazell, C. E., Catford, J. C., Halliday, M. A. K., & Robins, R. H. (Eds.) (1966). *In memory of J. R. Firth.* London: Longman.

Beach, R., & S. Hynds (1991). Research on response to literature. In R. Barr, M. Kamil, P. Mosenthal & P. Pearson (Eds.), *Handbook of reading research* (pp. 453–489). New York: Longman.

Becker, A. L. (1983). Toward a post-structuralist view of language learning: A short essay. *Language Learning, 33,* 217–220.

Beebe, L. (1983). Risk-taking and the language learner. In H. W. Seliger & M. H. Long (Eds.), *Classroom oriented research in second language acquisition.* Rowley, MA: Newbury House.

Bellugi, U., A. Bihrle, T. Jernigan, D. Trauner, & S. Doherty. (1991). Neuropsychological, neurological, and neuroanatomical profile of Williams Syndrome. *American Journal of Medical Genetics Supplement, 6,* 115–125.

Berkhouse, R. G., Mendelson, M. A., & Kehr, C. (1959). *Comparison of the Army Language Aptitude Test with a commercial language aptitude test.* Washington, DC: Personnel Research and Procedures Division, Adjutant General's Office, Research Memorandum 59–63.

Berquist, B. (1998). Working memory models applied to second language acquisition. *Paper presented at the Annual conference of the American Association of Applied Linguistics,* Seattle, March.

Berry, D. C. (1994). Implicit and explicit learning of complex tasks. In N. C. Ellis (Ed.), *Implicit and explicit learning of languages* (pp. 147–164). London: Academic Press.

Berwick, R. (1985). *The acquisition of syntactic knowledge.* Cambridge, MA: MIT Press.

Berwick, R. C., Abney, S. C., & Tenny, C. (Eds.), (1991). *Principle-based parsing: Computational and psycholinguistics.* Dordecht: Kluwer.

Bever, T. G. (1970). The cognitive basis of linguistic structure. In J. R. Hayes (Ed.), *Cognition and the development of language.* New York: Wiley.

Bever, T. G. (1988). Empty categories access their antecedents during comprehension. *Linguistic Inquiry, 19,* 35–43.

Bever, T. G. (1992). The demons and the beast – Modular and nodular kinds of knowledge. In R. G. Reilly & N. E. Sharkey (Eds.), *Connectionist approaches to natural language processing* (pp. 213–252). Hove: Erlbaum.

Bialystok, E. (1990). The competence of processing: classifying theories of second language acquisition. *TESOL Quarterly, 24,* 635–648.

Bialystok, E. (1993). Symbolic representation and attentional control in pragmatic competence. In G. Kasper & S. Blum-Kulka (Eds.), *Interlanguage pragmatics* (pp. 43–57). Oxford: Oxford University Press.

Bialystok, E. (1994a). Analysis and control in the development of second language proficiency. *Studies in Second Language Acquisition, 16,* 157–168.

Bialystok, E. (1994b). Representation and ways of knowing. In N. Ellis (Ed.), *Implicit and explicit learning of languages,* (pp. 549–69). London: Academic Press.

Bialystok, E., & Fröhlich, M. (1978). Variables of classroom achievement in second language learning. *Modern Language Journal, 62,* 327–336.

Bialystok, E., & Mitterer, J. (1987). Metalinguistic differences among three kinds of readers. *Journal of Educational Psychology, 79,* 147–153.

Birdsong, D. (1989). *Metalinguistic performance and interlinguistic competence.* Berlin: Springer-Verlag.

Birdsong, D. (Ed.) (1999). *Second language acquisition and the Critical Period Hypothesis.* Mahwah, NJ: Erlbaum.

Bjork, R. A. (1988). Retrieval practice and the maintenance of knowledge. In M. M. Gruneberg, P. E. Morris, & R. S. Sykes (Eds.), *Practical aspects of memory: Current research and issues* (pp. 396–401). Chichester: Wiley.

Bjorklund, D. F., & Harnishfeger, K. K. (1995). The evolution of inhibition mechanisms and their role in human cognition and behavior. In F. N. Dempster & C. J. Brainerd (Eds.), *Interference and inhibition in cognition* (pp. 141–173). San Diego, CA: Academic Press.

Blackwell, A., & Bates, E. (1995). Inducing agrammatic profiles in normals: Evidence for the selective vulnerability of morphology under cognitive resource limitation. *Journal of Cognitive Neuroscience, 7,* 228–257.

Bley-Vroman, R. (1983). The comparative fallacy in interlanguage studies: The case of systematicity. *Language Learning, 33,* 1–17.

Bley-Vroman, R. (1986). Hypothesis testing in second language acquisition. *Language Learning, 36*, 353–376.

Bley-Vroman, R. (1990). The logical problem of foreign language learning. *Linguistic Analysis, 20*, 3–49.

Bley-Vroman, R. (1991). Processing, constraints on acquisition, and the parsing of ungrammatical sentences. In L. Eubank (Ed.), *Point counterpoint: Universal Grammar in the second language*, (pp. 191–198). Amsterdam: Benjamins.

Bley-Vroman, R. (1997). Features and patterns in foreign language learning. *Paper presented at the Second Language Research Forum*, Michigan, October.

Bley-Vroman, R., & Chaudron, C. (1994). Elicited imitation as a measure of second-language competence. In E. Tarone, S. Gass, & A. Cohen (Eds.), *Research methodology in second-language acquisition*, (pp. 245–262). Hillsdale, NJ: Erlbaum.

Block, D. (1996). Not so fast: Some thoughts on theory culling, relativism, accepted findings, and the heart and soul of SLA. *Applied Linguistics, 17*, 63–83.

Bloom, K. C., & Shuell, T. J. (1981). Effects of massed and distributed practice on the learning and retention of second-language vocabulary. *Journal of Educational Research, 74*, 245–248.

Bloom, L. (1974). Talking, understanding, and thinking. In R. Schiefelbusch & L. Lloyd (Eds.), *Language perspectives: Acquisition, retardation, and intervention*. Baltimore: University Park Press.

Bogaards, P. (1994). *Le vocabulaire dans l'apprentissage des langues étrangères*. Paris: Didier.

Bohannon, J., & Stanowitz, L. (1988). The issue of negative evidence: Adult responses to children's language errors. *Developmental Psychology, 34*, 684–9.

Boland, J. E. (1997). The relationship between syntactic and semantic processes in comprehension. *Language and Cognitive Processes, 12*, 423–484.

Boland, J. E., Tanenhaus, M. K., & Garnsey, S. M., (1990). Evidence for the immediate use of verb control information in sentence processing. *Journal of Memory and Language, 29*, 413–432.

Boland, J. E., Tanenhaus, M. K., Garnsey, S. M., & Carlson, G. N. (1995). Verb argument structure in parsing and interpretation: Evidence from wh-questions. *Journal of Memory and Language, 34*, 774–806.

Booth, J. R., MacWhinney, B., Feldman, H. M., Thulborn, K. R., Sacco, K., & Voyvodic, J. (1999). Functional activation patterns in adults, children, and pediatric patients with brain lesions: Whole brain MRI imaging during three different cognitive tasks. *Progress in Neuro-Psychopharmacology and Biological Psychiatry, 23*, 669–682.

Borer, H., & K. Wexler. (1987). The maturation of syntax. In. T. Roeper & E. Williams (Eds.), *Parameter setting*, (pp. 123–172). Dordrecht: Reidel.

Bowerman, M. (1987). Commentary: Mechanisms of language acquisition. In B. MacWhinney (Ed.), *Mechanisms of language acquisition*. Hillsdale, NJ: Erlbaum.

Bowerman, M. (1988). The 'No Negative Evidence' problem: How do children avoid constructing an overly general grammar. In J. Hawkins (Ed.), *Explaining language universals* (pp. 73–101). Oxford: Blackwell.

Bowerman, M. (1996). Learning how to structure space for language: A cross-linguistic perspective. In P. Bloom, M. Peterson, L. Nadel, & M. Garrett (Eds.), *Language and space* (pp. 385–436). Cambridge, MA: MIT Press.

Breen, M. (1984). Process syllabuses for the language classroom. In C. Brumfit (Ed.), *General English syllabus design* (pp. 47–60). Oxford: Pergamon.

Bresnan, J. W. (1978). A realistic transformational grammar. In M. Halle, J. Bresnan, & G. Miller (Eds.), *Linguistic theory and psychological reality*. Cambridge, MA: MIT Press.

Brindley, G. (1987). Factors affecting task difficulty. In D. Nunan (Ed.), *Guidelines for the development of curriculum resources* (pp. 45–56). Adelaide National Curriculum Resource Centre.

Britten, B., & Tresser, A. (1982). Effects of prior knowledge on the use of cognitive capacity in three complex tasks. *Journal of Verbal Learning and Verbal Behaviour, 21*, 421–436.

Broadbent, D. E. (1958). *Perception and communication*. London: Pergamon.

Broadbent, D. E. (1984). The Maltese Cross: A new simplistic model for memory. *The Behavioral And Brain Sciences, 7*, 55–94.

Brown, G. (1995). *Speakers, listeners and communication*. Cambridge: Cambridge University Press.

Brown, G., & Yule, G. (1983). *Teaching the spoken language*. Cambridge: Cambridge University Press.

Brown, G., Anderson, A., Shillcock, R., & Yule, G. (1984). *Teaching talk: Strategies for production and assessment*. Cambridge: Cambridge University Press.

Brown, G. D. A., & Hulme, C. (1992). Cognitive psychology and second-language processing: the role of short-term memory. In R. Harris (Ed.), *Cognitive processing in bilinguals* (pp. 105–122). North Holland: Elsevier.

Brown, H. D. (1994). *Teaching by principles: An interactive approach to language pedagogy*. Englewood Cliffs, NJ: Prentice Hall.

Brown, J. D. (1995). *Elements of language curriculum*. Boston, MA: Heinle & Heinle.

Brown, R. (1991). Group work, task difference and second language acquisition. *Applied Linguistics, 11*, 1–12.

Brumfit, C. (1984). *Communicative methodology in language teaching*. Cambridge: Cambridge University Press.

Bruner, J. (1992). Another look at New Look 1. *American Psychologist, 47*, 780–783.

Butler, C. (1995). Between lexis and grammar: Repeated word sequences and collocational frameworks in Spanish. *Paper presented to the 5th Dyffryn Conference on Vocabulary and Lexis*, Cardiff, March.

Butterworth, B. (1989). Lexical access in speech production. In W. Marslen-Wilson (Ed.), *Lexical representation and process*. Cambridge, MA: MIT Press.

Bybee, J. (1985). *Morphology*. Amsterdam: Benjamins.

Bybee, J. (1995). Regular morphology and the lexicon. *Language and Cognitive Processes, 10*, 425–455.

Bygate, M. (1988). *Speaking*. Oxford: Oxford University Press.

Bygate, M. (1996). Effects of task repetition: Appraising the developing language of learners. In J. Willis and M. Willis (Eds.), *Challenge and change in language teaching* (pp. 136–146). Oxford: Heinemann.

Candlin, C. (1984). Syllabus design as a critical process. In C. Brumfit (Ed.), *General English syllabus design* (pp. 29–46). Oxford: Pergamon.

Candlin, C. (1987). Towards task-based language learning. In C. Candlin, & D. Murphy (Eds.), *Language learning tasks* (pp. 5–22). London: Prentice Hall.

Carlson, R. A. (1997). *Experienced cognition*. Mahwah, NJ: Erlbaum.

Carlson, R. A., & Dulany, D. E. (1985). Conscious attention and abstraction in concept learning. *Journal of Experimental Psychology: Learning, Memory, and Cognition, 11*, 45–58.

Carlson, R. A., Sullivan, M. A., & Schneider, W. (1989). Practice and working memory effects in building procedural skill. *Journal of Experimental Psychology: Learning, Memory and Cognition, 15*, 517–526.

Caron, J. (1992). *An introduction to psycholinguistics*. Toronto: University of Toronto Press.

Carpenter, P. A., Miyake, A., & Just, M. A. (1995). Language comprehension: Sentence and discourse processing. *Annual Review of Psychology, 46*, 91–120.

Carr, T. H., & Curran, T. (1994). Cognitive factors in learning about structured sequences: Applications to syntax. *Studies in Second Language Acquisition, 16*, 205–230.

Carrell, P. (1987). Content and formal schemata in ESL pedagogy. *TESOL Quarterly, 21*, 461–481.

Carroll, B. (1980). *Testing communicative performance*. Oxford: Pergamon.

Carroll, J. B. (1962). The prediction of success in intensive foreign language training. In R. Glaser (Ed.), *Training research and education* (pp. 87–136). Pittsburgh, PA: University of Pittsburgh Press.

Carroll, J. B. (1963). A model of school learning. *Teachers College Record, 64*, 723–733.

Carroll, J. B. (1973). Implications of aptitude test research and psycholinguistic theory for foreign language teaching. *International Journal of Psycholinguistics, 2*, 5–14.

Carroll, J. B. (1974). The aptitude-achievement distinction: the case of foreign language aptitude and proficiency. In D. Green (Ed.), *The aptitude-achievement distinction* (pp. 289–303). Monterey, CA: McGraw-Hill.

Carroll, J. B. (1981). Twenty-five years of research on foreign language aptitude. In K. C. Diller (Ed.), *Individual differences and universals in language learning aptitude*, (pp. 83–118). Rowley, MA: Newbury House.

Carroll, J. B. (1985). Second-language abilities. In R. Sternberg (Ed.), *Human abilities* (pp. 83–101). New York: W.H. Freeman.

Carroll, J. B. (1990). Cognitive abilities in foreign language aptitude: Then and now. In T. Parry & C. Stansfield (Eds.), *Language aptitude reconsidered* (pp. 11–29). Englewood Cliffs, NJ: Prentice Hall.

Carroll, J. B., & Sapon, S. M. (1959). *Modern Language Aptitude Test*. New York: The Psychological Corporation/Harcourt Brace Jovanovich.

Carroll, S. (2000). *Input and evidence*. Amsterdam: Benjamins.

Carroll, S. (1995). The hidden dangers of computer modelling: remarks on Sokolik and Smith's connectionist learning model of French gender. *Second Language Research, 11*, 193–205.

Carroll, S., & J. Meisel. (1990). Universals and second language acquisition: some comments on the state of current theory. *Studies in second language Acquisition, 12*, 201–208.

Carroll, S., & Swain, M. (1993). Explicit and implicit negative feedback: an empirical study of the learning of linguistic generalizations. *Studies in Second Language Acquisition, 15*, 357–86.

Carter, R., & McCarthy, M. (1988). Lexis and structure. In R. Carter, & M. McCarthy (Eds.), *Vocabulary and language teaching* (pp. 18–38). Harlow: Longman.

Carver, C. P. (1990). *Reading rate*. San Diego, CA: Academic Press.

Casey, B. J., Gordon, C. T., Mannheim, G. B., & Rumsey, J. M. (1993). Dysfunctional attention in autistic savants. *Journal of Clinical and Experimental Neuropsychology, 15*, 933–946.

Cavalcanti, M. (1987). Investigating FL reading performance through pause protocols. In C. Faerch, & G. Kasper (Eds.), *Introspection in second language Research* (pp. 230–250). Philadelphia, PA: Multilingual Matters.

Cazden, C., Cancino, H., Rosansky, E., & Schumann, J. (1975). *Second language acquisition sequences in children, adolescents and adults*. Final report, Project No. 730744, National Institute of Education.

Chapelle, C. (1992). Disembedding 'Disembedded figures in the landscape …': An appraisal of Griffiths and Sheen's 'Reappraisal of L2 research on field dependence / independence'. *Applied Linguistics, 13*, 375–384.

Chapelle, C. (1998). Multimedia CALL: Lessons to be learned from research on instructed SLA. *Paper presented at the Invitational Symposium on Advancing Technology Options in Language Learning*, Honolulu, February.

Chapelle, C., & Green, P. (1992). Field independence/dependence in second-language acquisition research. *Language Learning, 42*, 47–83.

Charniak, E. (1993). *Statistical language learning*. Cambridge, MA: MIT Press.

Chaudron, C. (1988). *Second language classrooms*. New York: Cambridge University Press.

Cheng, P. (1985). Restructuring vs. automaticity: Alternative accounts of skill-acquisition. *Psychological Review, 92*, 414–23.

Chomsky, N. (1965). *Aspects of the theory of syntax.* Cambridge, MA: MIT Press.

Chomsky, N. (1976). *Reflections on language.* London: Temple Smith.

Chomsky, N. (1981). *Lectures on Government and Binding.* Dordrecht: Foris.

Chomsky, N. (1986). *Knowledge of language.* New York: Praeger.

Chomsky, N. (1989). Some notes on economy of derivation and representation. *MIT working papers in Linguistics, 10*, 43–74.

Chomsky, N. (1995). *The Minimalist Program.* Cambridge, MA: MIT Press.

Chun, D. M., & Plass, J. L. (1996). Effects of multimedia annotations on vocabulary acquisition. *The Modern Language Journal, 80*, 183–198.

Clark, A. (1989). *Microcognition: philosophy, cognitive science, and parallel distributed processing.* Cambridge, MA: MIT Press.

Clark, E. (1987). The principle of contrast: a constraint on language acquisition. In B. MacWhinney (Ed.), *Mechanisms of language acquisition.* Hillsdale, NJ: Erlbaum.

Clark, H. H. (1992). *The arena of language.* Chicago, IL: University of Chicago Press.

Clarke, D. (1991). The negotiated syllabus: What is it and is it likely to work? *Applied Linguistics, 12*, 13–28.

Clarke, M. (1980). The 'short circuit' hypothesis of ESL reading or when language competence interferes with reading performance. *Modern Language Journal, 64*, 203–09.

Clifton, C. Jr., Frazier, L., & Rayner, K. (Eds.), (1994). *Perspectives on sentence processing.* Hillsdale, NJ: Erlbaum.

Clifton, C. Jr., Speer, S., & Abney, S. P. (1991). Parsing arguments: Phrase structure and argument structure as determinants of initial parsing structures. *Journal of Memory and Language, 30*, 251–271.

Coady, J. (1993). Research on ESL/EFL vocabulary acquisition: Putting it in context. In T. Huckin, M. Haynes, & J. Coady (Eds.), *Second language reading and vocabulary learning* (pp. 3–23). Norwood, NJ: Ablex.

Coady, J. (1997a). L2 vocabulary acquisition through extensive reading. In J. Coady & T. Huckin (Eds.), *Second language vocabulary acquisition* (pp. 225–237). Cambridge: Cambridge University Press.

Coady, J. (1997b). L2 vocabulary acquisition: A synthesis of the research. In J. Coady & T. Huckin (Eds.), *Second language vocabulary acquisition* (pp. 273–290). Cambridge: Cambridge University Press.

Cohen, A. (1984). On taking language tests: What the students report. *Language Testing, 1*, 70–81.

Cohen, A. (1996). Developing the ability to perform speech acts. *Studies in Second Language Acquisition, 18*, 253–267.

Cohen, A. (1998). *Strategies in learning and using a second language.* New York: Longman.

Cohen, A., & Cavalcanti, M. (1987). Feedback on compositions: teacher and student verbal reports. In B. Kroll (Ed.), *Second language writing.* (pp. 155–177). New York: Cambridge University Press.

Cohen, A., Glasman, H., Sosenbaum-Cohen, P., Ferrara, J., Fine, J. (1979). Reading English for specialized purposes: Discourse analysis and the use of student informants. *TESOL Quarterly, 13,* 551–564.

Cohen, A., & Olshtain, E. (1993). The production of speech acts by ESL learners. *TESOL Quarterly, 27,* 33–56.

Cohen, A., Weaver, S. J., & Li, T.-Y. (1998). The impact of strategies-based instruction on speaking a foreign language. In A. Cohen (Ed.), *Strategies in learning and using a second language* (pp. 107–156). New York: Longman.

Cohen, D. D., Perlstein, W. M., Braver, T. S., Nystrom, L. E., Noll, D. C., Jonides, J., & Smith, E. (1997). Temporal dynamics of brain activation during a working memory task. *Nature, 386,* 604–608.

Cohen, J. D., Dunbar, K., & McClelland, J. L. (1990). On the control of automatic processes: A parallel distributed processing account of the Stroop effect. *Psychological Review, 97,* 332–361.

Cohen, J. D., Servan-Schreiber, D., & McClelland, J. (1992). A parallel distributed processing approach to automaticity. *American Journal of Psychology, 105,* 239–269.

Collins Cobuild. (1996). *Grammar patterns 1: Verbs.* London: Collins.

Cook, V. (1979). Aspects of memory in secondary school language learners. *Interlanguage studies bulletin – Utrecht, 4,* 161–172.

Cook, V. (1996). *Second language learning and language teaching* (2nd ed.). London: Arnold.

Corder, S. P. (1967). The significance of learners' errors. *IRAL, 5,* 161–170.

Corder, S. P. (1973). *Introducing applied linguistics.* Harmondsworth: Penguin.

Corson, D. (1997). The learning and use of academic English words. *Language Learning, 47,* 671–718.

Cottrell, G., & Plunkett, K. (1994). Acquiring the mapping from meaning to sounds. *Connection Science, 6,* 379–412.

Coughlan, P., & Duff, P. (1994). Same task, different activities: analysis of an SLA task from an activity theory perspective. In J. Lantolf, & G. Appel (Eds.), *Vygotskyan approaches to second language research,* (pp. 173–194). Norwood, NJ: Ablex.

Cowan, N. (1988). Evolving conceptions of memory, storage, selective attention, and their mutual constraints within the human information processing system. *Psychological Bulletin, 104,* 163–191.

Cowan, N. (1992). Verbal memory span and the timing of spoken recall. *Journal of Memory and Language, 31,* 668–684.

Cowan, N. (1993). Activation, attention, and short-term memory. *Memory and Cognition, 21,* 162–167.

Cowan, N. (1995). *Attention and memory: An integrated framework.* New York: Oxford University Press.

Cowan, N. (1996). Short-term memory, working memory, and their importance in language processing. *Topics in Language Disorders, 17,* 1–18.

Craik, F. I. M., & Lockhart, R. S. (1972). Levels of processing: A framework for memory research. *Journal of Verbal Learning and Verbal Behavior, 11,* 671–684.

Craik, F. I. M., & Tulving, E. (1975). Depth of processing and the retention of words in episodic memory. *Journal of Experimental Psychology: General, 104,* 268–294.

Crain, S., & R. Thornton. (1998). *Investigations in Universal Grammar.* Cambridge, MA: MIT Press.

Crain, S., Ni, W., & Conway, S. (1994). Learning, parsing, and modularity. In C. Clifton, L. Frazier, & K. Rayner, (Eds.), *Perspectives on sentence Processing* (pp. 443–467). Hillsdale, NJ: Erlbaum.

Crain, S., & Steedman, M. (1985). On not being led up the garden path: The use of context by the psychological parser. In D. R. Dowty, L. Kartunnen, & A. Zwicky (Eds.), *Natural language parsing: Psychological, computational and theoretical perspectives* (pp. 320–357). Cambridge: Cambridge University Press.

Crocker, M. W. (1994). On the nature of the principle-based parser. In C. J. Clifton, L. Frazier, & K. Rayner (Eds.), *Perspectives on sentence processing* (pp. 245–266). Hillsdale, NJ: Erlbaum.

Crombie, W. (1985). *Discourse and language learning: A relational approach to syllabus design.* Oxford: Oxford University Press.

Cromer, R. (1991). *Language and thought in normal and handicapped children.* Oxford: Blackwell.

Crookes, G. (1989). Planning and interlanguage variation. *Studies in Second Language Acquisition, 11,* 367–383.

Crookes, G. (1990). The utterance and other basic units for second language discourse analysis. *Applied Linguistics, 11,* 183–199.

Crookes, G. (1991). Second language speech production research: A methodologically oriented review. *Studies in Second Language Acquisition, 13,* 113–132.

Crookes, G., & Schmidt, R. (1991). Motivation: Reopening the research agenda. *Language Learning, 41,* 469–512.

Crosby, M. (1998). The influence of modality in multimedia software for foreign language learning. *Paper presented at the Invitational Symposium on Advancing Technology Options in Language Learning,* Honolulu, February.

Crothers, E. J., & Suppes, P. (1967). *Experiments in second-language learning.* New York: Academic Press.

Crystal, D. (1987). *The Cambridge encyclopaedia of language.* Cambridge: Cambridge University Press.

Cumming, A. (1989). Writing expertise and second language proficiency. *Language Learning, 39,* 81–141.

Cumming, A. (1994). Writing expertise and second-language proficiency. In A. Cumming (Ed.), *Bilingual performance in reading and writing* (pp. 173–221). Ann Arbor, MI: Benjamins.

Cummins, R. (1983). *The nature of psychological explanation.* Cambridge, MA: MIT Press.

Curran, T., & Keele, S. W. (1993). Attentional and nonattentional forms of sequence learning. *Journal of Experimental Psychology: Learning, Memory, and Cognition, 19,* 189–202.

Curtiss, S. (1977). *Genie: A psycholinguistic study of a modern-day wild child.* New York: Academic Press.

Cutler, A. (1995). Spoken word recognition and production. In J. Miller, & P. Eimas (Eds.), *Speech, language, and communication* (pp. 97–136). San Diego, CA: Academic Press.

Dalrymple-Alford, E. C., & Budayr, B. (1966). Examination of some aspects of the Stroop color-word test. *Perceptual & Motor Skills, 23,* 1211–1214.

Daneman, M., & Carpenter, P. (1980). Individual differences in working memory and reading. *Journal of Verbal Learning and Verbal Behavior, 19,* 450–466.

Daugherty, K. G., & Seidenberg, M. S. (1994). Beyond rules and exceptions: A connectionist approach to inflectional morphology. In S. Lima, R. Corrigan, & G. Iverson (Eds.), *The reality of linguistic rules* (pp. 353–388). Amsterdam: Benjamins.

Davies, A. (1971). Language aptitude in the first year of the U.K. secondary school. *RELC Journal, 2,* 4–19.

Davis, J., & Bistodeau, L. (1993). How do L1 and L2 reading differ? Evidence from think aloud protocols. *The Modern Language Journal, 77,* 459–72.

Dawkins, R. (1976). Hierarchical organisation: A candidate principle for ethology. In P. P. G. Bateson & R. A. Hinde (Eds.), *Growing points in ethology* (pp. 7–54). Cambridge: Cambridge University Press.

Dawkins, R. (1986). *The blind watchmaker.* Harlow: Longman.

Day, R. R. (Ed.). (1986). *Talking to learn; conversation in second language acquisition.* Rowley, MA: Newbury House.

Day, R. R., & Bamford, J. (1998). *Extensive reading in the second language classroom.* New York: Cambridge University Press.

de Bot, K. (1996). Review article: The psycholinguistics of the output hypothesis. *Language Learning, 46,* 3, 529–555.

de Bot, K., & van Montfort, R. (1988). 'Cue validity' in het Hederlands als eerste en tweede taal. *Interdisciplinair Tijdschrift vor Taal en Tekstwetenschaap, 8,* 111–120.

de Bot, K., Paribakht, T. S., & Wesche, M. B. (1997). Toward a lexical processing model for the study of second language vocabulary acquisition: Evidence from ESL reading. *Studies in Second Language Acquisition, 19,* 309–329.

de Graaff, R. (1997a). The eXperanto experiment: Effects of explicit instruction on second language acquisition. *Studies in Second Language Acquisition, 19,* 249–275.

de Graaff, R. (1997b). *Differential effects of explicit instruction on second language acquisition.* The Hague: Holland Institute of Generative Linguistics.

de Houwer, A. (1995). Bilingual language acquisition. In P. Fletcher, & B. MacWhinney (Eds.), *The handbook of child language,* (pp. 219–250). London: Blackwell.

Deacon, T. (1991). Brain-language co-evolution. In J. H. M. Gel-Man (Ed.), *The evolution of languages,* (pp. 48–83). New York: Addison-Wesley.

DeKeyser, R. M. (1995). Learning second language grammar rules: An experiment with a miniature linguistic system. *Studies in Second Language Acquisition, 17,* 379–410.

DeKeyser, R. M. (1996). Critical period effects as a function of verbal aptitude. *Paper presented at the Second Language Research Forum,* University of Arizona, Tucson.

DeKeyser, R. M. (1997). Beyond explicit rule learning: Automatizing second language morphosyntax. *Studies in Second Language Acquisition, 19,* 195–222.

DeKeyser, R. M. (1998). Beyond focus on form: Cognitive perspectives on learning and practicing second language grammar. In C. Doughty, & J. Williams (Eds.), *Focus on form in classroom second language acquisition* (pp. 42–63). New York: Cambridge University Press.

DeKeyser, R. M., & Sokalski, K. (1996). The differential role of comprehension and production practice. *Language Learning 46,* 613–642.

Delaney, P. F., Reder, L. M., Staszewski, J. J., & Ritter, F. E. (1998). The strategy-specific nature of improvement: The power law applies by strategy within task. *Psychological Science, 9,* 1–7.

Dell, G. (1986). A spreading activation theory of retrieval in language production. *Psychological Review, 93,* 283–321.

Dell, G., & O'Seaghdha, P. (1991). Stages of lexical acquisition in language production. In W. Levelt (Ed.), *Lexical access in speech production,* (pp. 287–314). Cambridge, MA: Blackwell.

Dell, G., & O'Seaghdha, P. (1993). Inhibition in interactive activation models of linguistic selection and sequencing. In Dagenbach, D., & Carr, T. (Eds.), *Inhibitory processes in attention, memory, and language* (pp. 409–453). New York: Academic Press.

Dell, G., & Reich, P. (1981). Stages in sentence production: An analysis of speech error data. *Journal of Verbal Learning and Verbal Behavior, 20,* 611–629.

Demetras, M., Post, K., & Snow, C. (1986). Feedback to first language learners: the role of repetitions and clarification requests. *Journal of Child Language, 13,* 275–92.

Dempster, F. N. (1987). Effects of variable encoding and spaced presentations on vocabulary learning. *Journal of Educational Psychology, 79,* 162–170.

Dempster, F. N. (1995). Interference and inhibition in cognition: An historical perspective. In F. N. Dempster, & C. J. Brainerd (Eds.), *Interference and inhibition in cognition* (pp. 3–26). San Diego, CA: Academic Press.

DeSchepper, B., & Treisman, A. (1996). Visual memory for novel shapes: Implicit coding without attention. *Journal of Experimental Psychology: Learning, Memory, and Cognition, 22*, 27–47.

Deutsch, J. A., & Deutsch, D. (1963). Attention: Some theoretical considerations. *Psychological Review, 70*, 80–90.

Dijkstra, T., & di Smedt, K. (Eds.), (1996). *Computational psycholinguistics: AI and connectionist models of human language processing*. Bristol, PA: Taylor & Francis.

Dornyei, Z. (1998). Motivation in foreign and second language learning. *Language Teaching, 31*, 117–135.

Doughty, C. (1991). Second language instruction does make a difference: Evidence from an empirical study of SL relativization. *Studies in Second Language Acquisition, 13*, 431–469.

Doughty, C. (1994). Fine tuning of feedback by competent speakers to language learners. In J. Alatis (Ed.), *Strategic interaction and language acquisition: Theory, practice, and research* (pp. 96–108). Washington, DC: Georgetown University Press.

Doughty, C. (1997). Meeting the criteria of focus on form. *Paper presented at the Second Language Research Forum*, Michigan State University, October.

Doughty, C. (1998). Corrective recasts in and out of classrooms. *Paper presented at the Edith Cowan Language Round Table*, Edith Cowan University, June.

Doughty, C. (2000). Negotiating the linguistic environment. *University of Hawaii Working Papers in ESL, 18*, 47–85.

Doughty, C., Izumi, S., Maciukaite, S., & Zapata, G. (1999). Recasts, focused recasts, and models: Effects on L2 Spanish word order. *Paper presented at the Second Language Research Forum*, Minnesota, September.

Doughty, C., & Varela, E. (1998). Communicative focus on form. In C. Doughty, & J. Williams (Eds.), *Focus on form in classroom SLA.* (pp. 114–138). New York: Cambridge University Press.

Doughty, C., & Williams, J. (1998a). Issues and terminology. In C. Doughty & J. Williams (Eds.), *Focus on form in classroom second language acquisition* (pp. 1–11). New York: Cambridge University Press.

Doughty, C., & Williams, J. (1998b). Pedagogical choices in focus on form. In C. Doughty & J. Williams (Eds.), *Focus on form in classroom second language acquisition* (pp. 197– 262). New York: Cambridge University Press.

Driver, J., & Baylis, G. C. (1993). Cross-modal negative priming and interference in selective attention. *Bulletin of the Psychonomic Society, 31*, 45–48.

Duff, P. (1986). Another look at interlanguage talk: Taking task to task. In R. Day (Ed.), *Talking to learn: Conversation in second language development* (pp. 147–181). Rowley, MA: Newbury House.

Dulany, D., Carlson R., & Dewey, G. (1984). A case of syntactical learning and judgment: How conscious and how abstract? *Journal of Experimental Psychology, 113*, 541–55.

Dulany, D., Carlson R., & Dewey, G. (1985). On consciousness in syntactic learning and judgment: A reply to Reber, Allen and Regan. *Journal of Experimental Psychology, 114*, 25–32.

Dulay, H., Burt, M., & Krashen, S. (1982). *Language 2*. New York: Oxford University Press.

Ebbinghaus, H. (1964). *Memory: A contribution to experimental psychology.* New York: Dover.

Eckman, F., Bell, L., & Nelson, D. (1988). On the generalization of relative clause instruction in the acquisition of English as a second language. *Applied Linguistics, 9*, 10–20.

Ehrman, M. (1990). Owls and doves: Cognition, personality, and learning success. In J. E. Alatis (Ed.), *Linguistics, language teaching, and language acquisition: The interdependence of theory, practice, and research* (pp. 423–437). Washington, DC: Georgetown University Press.

Ehrman, M., & Oxford, R. (1995). Cognition plus: Correlates of language learning success. *Modern Language Journal, 79*, 67–89.

Eich, E. (1984). Memory for unattended events: Remembering with and without awareness. *Memory and Cognition, 12*, 105–111.

Einstein, M., & Bodman, J. (1987). 'I very appreciate': Expressions of gratitude by native and non-native speakers of American English. *Applied Linguistics, 7*, 167–85.

Eisenberg, A.R. (1985). Learning to describe past experiences in conversation. *Discourse Processes, 8*, 177–204.

Eisenstein, M. (1980). Childhood bilingualism and adult language learning aptitude. *International Review of Applied Psychology, 29*, 159–174.

Elredge, N., & Gould, S. (1972). Punctuated equilibrium: An alternative to phyletic gradualism, in T. Schopf (Ed.), *Models in paleobiology*, (pp. 211–282). San Francisco, CA: Freeman.

Ellis, G., & Sinclair, B. (1989). *Learning to learn English: A course in learner training*. Cambridge: Cambridge University Press.

Ellis, N. C. (1990). Reading, phonological processing and STM: Interactive tributaries of development. *Journal of Research in Reading, 13*, 107–122.

Ellis, N. C. (1993). Rules and instances in foreign language learning: Interactions of implicit and explicit knowledge. *European Journal of Cognitive Psychology, 5*, 289–319.

Ellis, N. C (1994a). Implicit and explicit language learning: an overview. In N. Ellis (Ed.), *Implicit and explicit learning of languages* (pp. 1–31). London: Academic Press.

Ellis, N. C. (1994b). Vocabulary acquisition: The implicit ins and outs of explicit cognitive mediation. In N. Ellis (Ed.), *Implicit and explicit learning of languages* (pp. 211–282). London: Academic Press.

Ellis, N. C. (1994c). Consciousness in second language learning: Psychological perspectives on the role of conscious processes in vocabulary acquisition. *AILA Review, 11*, 37–56.

Ellis, N. C. (1994d) (Ed.). *Implicit and explicit learning of languages*. New York: Academic Press.

Ellis, N. C. (1996a). Sequencing in SLA: Phonological memory, chunking, and points of order. *Studies in Second Language Acquisition, 18*, 91–126.

Ellis, N. C. (1996b). Analyzing language sequence in the sequence of language acquisition: Some comments on Major and Ioup. *Studies in Second Language Acquisition, 18*, 361–368.

Ellis, N. C. (1998). Emergentism, connectionism and language learning. *Language Learning, 48*, 631–664.

Ellis, N. C., & Beaton, A. (1993a). Factors affecting the learning of foreign language vocabulary: Imagery keyword mediators and phonological short–term memory. *Quarterly Journal of Experimental Psychology, 46A*, 533–558.

Ellis, N. C., & Beaton, A. (1993b). Psycholinguistic determinants of foreign language vocabulary learning. *Language Learning, 43*, 559–617.

Ellis, N. C., & Laporte, N. (1997). Contexts of acquisition: Effects of formal instruction and naturalistic exposure on second language acquisition. In A. M. B. de Groot and J. F. Kroll (Eds.), *Tutorials in bilingualism: Psycholinguistic perspectives* (pp. 53–83). Hillsdale, NJ: Erlbaum.

Ellis, N. C., & Large, B. (1987). The development of reading: as you seek so shall you find. *British Journal of Psychology, 78*, 1–28.

Ellis, N. C., & Schmidt, R. (1997). Morphology and longer-distance dependencies: Laboratory research illuminating the A in SLA. *Studies in Second Language Acquisition, 19*, 145–171.

Ellis, N. C., & Schmidt, R. (1998). Rules or associations in the acquisition of morphology? The frequency by regularity interaction in human and PDP learning of morphosyntax. *Language and Cognitive Processes, 13*, 307–336.

Ellis, N. C., & Sinclair, S. (1996). Working memory in the acquisition of vocabulary and syntax: Putting language in good order. *Quarterly Journal of Experimental Psychology, 49A*, 234–250.

Ellis, R. (1985). *Understanding second language acquisition.* Oxford: Oxford University Press.

Ellis, R. (1987). Interlanguage variability in narrative discourse: Style shifting in the use of the past tense. *Studies in Second Language Acquisition, 9*, 1–20.

Ellis, R. (1989). Are classroom and naturalistic acquisition the same? A study of the classroom acquisition of German word order rules. *Studies in Second Language Acquisition, 11*, 305–328.

Ellis, R. (1993). The structural syllabus and second language acquisition. *TESOL Quarterly, 27*, 91–113.

Ellis, R. (1994a). *The study of second language acquisition.* Oxford: Oxford University Press.

Ellis, R. (1994b). Factors in the incidental acquisition of second language vocabulary from oral input: A review essay. *Applied Language Learning, 5*, 1–32.

Ellis, R. (1997). *SLA research and language teaching.* Oxford: Oxford University Press.

Ellison, T. M. (1997). Acquisition, learnability and distributional information. *Paper presented at the 5th International Cognitive Linguistics Conference,* Amsterdam, July.

Elman, J. L. (1990). Finding structure in time. *Cognitive Science, 14,* 179–212.

Elman, J. L., Bates, E. A., Johnson, M. H., Karmiloff-Smith, A., Parisi, D., & Plunkett, K. (1996). *Rethinking innateness: A connectionist perspective on development.* Cambridge, MA: MIT Press.

Elman, J. L., & McClelland, J. (1984). Speech perception as a cognitive process: The interactive activation model. In N. Lass (Ed.), *Speech and language* (pp. 337–374). Mahwah, NJ: Erlbaum.

Elman, J. L., & Zipser, D. (1988). Learning the hidden structure of speech. *Journal of the Acoustic Society of America, 83,* 1615–1626.

Ely, C. (1986). An analysis of discomfort, risktaking, sociability, and motivation in the L2 classroom. *Language Learning, 36,* 1, 1–35.

Epstein, S. D., S. Flynn, & G. Martohardjono. (1996). Second language acquisition: theoretical and experimental issues in contemporary research. *Behavioral and Brain Sciences, 19,* 677–758.

Epstein, W. (1967). The influence of syntactical structure on learning. In N. J. Slamecka (Ed.), *Human learning and memory: Selected readings* (pp. 391–395). New York: Oxford University Press.

Ericsson K., & Simon H. A. (1987). Verbal reports in thinking. In Faerch C., & Kasper G. (Eds.), *Introspection in second language research* (pp. 24–53). Clevedon, Avon: Multilingual Matters.

Ericsson, K. A., & Simon, H. A. (1993). *Protocol Analysis: Verbal reports as data.* Boston, MA: MIT Press.

Eriksen, C. W., & St. James, J. D. (1986). Visual attention within and around the field of focal attention: A zoom lens model. *Perception and Psychophysics, 40,* 225–240.

Esser, U., & Nowak, U. (1990). Cognitive training of second-language learning strategies: The formation of a new research approach in foreign-language learning psychology. *Glottodidactica, 20,* 15–20.

Eubank, L. (Ed.). (1991). *Point counterpoint: Universal Grammar in the second language.* Amsterdam: Benjamins.

Eubank, L., & K. R. Gregg. (1995). "Et in amygdala ego"? UG, (S)LA, and neurobiology. *Studies in Second Language Acquisition, 17,* 35–57.

Eubank, L., & K. R. Gregg. (1999). Critical periods and (second) language acquisition: *Divide et impera.* In D. Birdsong (Ed.), *Second language acquisition and the Critical Period Hypothesis.* Mahwah, NJ: Erlbaum.

Eysenck, H. J., & Eysenck, M. W. (1985). *Personality and individual differences: A natural science approach.* New York: Plenum.

Eysenck, M. W. (1982). Incidental learning and orienting tasks. In C. R. Puff (Ed.), *Handbook of research methods in human memory and cognition* (pp. 197–228). New York: Academic Press.

Faerch C., & Kasper G. (Eds.) (1983). *Strategies in interlanguage communication,* London: Longman.

Faerch, C., & G. Kasper, (Eds.) (1987). *Introspection in second language research*. Philadelphia, PA: Multilingual Matters.

Fantuzzi, C. (1993). Connectionism: explanation or implementation. *Issues in Applied Linguistics, 3*, 319–340.

Farrar, M. (1990). Discourse and the acquisition of grammatical morphemes. *Journal of Child Language, 17*, 3, 607–24.

Farrar, M. (1992). Negative evidence and grammatical morpheme acquisition. *Developmental Psychology, 25*, 1, 62–75.

Farrar, M., Friend, J., & Forbes, J. (1993). Event knowledge and early language acquisition. *Journal of Child Language, 20*, 591–606.

Farrar, W., & Kawamoto, A. (1993). The return of visiting relatives: Pragmatic effects in sentence processing. *Quarterly Journal of Experimental Psychology, 46A*, 463–487.

Fausett, L. (1994). *Fundamentals of neural networks*. Englewood Cliffs, NJ: Prentice Hall.

Favreau, M., & Segalowitz, N. (1983). Automatic and controlled processes in the first and second language reading of fluent bilinguals. *Memory and Cognition, 11*, 565–574.

Feldman, J., Lakoff, G., Bailey, D., Narayanan, S., Regier T., & Stolcke. A. (1996). L0: The first five years of an automated language acquisition project. *Artificial Intelligence Review, 10*, 103–129.

Ferencich, M. (Ed.). (1964). *Reattivo di attitudine linguistica*. Florence: Organizzazioni Speciali.

Ferguson, C. (1975). Towards a characterization of English foreigner talk. *Anthropological Linguistics, 17*, 1–14.

Ferreira, R. (1991). Effects of length and syntactic complexity on initiation times for prepared utterances. *Journal of Memory and Language, 30*, 210–233.

Ferreira, F., & Clifton, C. (1986). The independence of syntactic processing. *Journal of Memory and Language, 25*, 348–368.

Fillmore, C. C. (1977). Topics in lexical semantics. In R. W. Cole (Ed.), *Current issues in linguistic theory* (pp. 76–138). Bloomington, IN: Indiana University Press.

Finch, S., & Chater, N. (1994). Learning syntactic categories: A statistical approach. In M. Oaksford & G. D. A. Brown (Eds.), *Neurodynamics and psychology* (pp. 295–321). London: Academic.

Finer, D. L. (1991). Binding parameters in second language acquisition. In L. Eubank (Ed.), *Point counterpoint: Universal Grammar in the second language*. Amsterdam: Benjamins.

Finocchiaro, M., & Brumfit, C. (1983). *The Functional-notional approach: From theory to practice*. Oxford: Oxford University Press.

Firth, A., & J. Wagner. (1997). On discourse, communication, and (some) fundamental concepts in SLA research. *Modern Language Journal, 81*, 285–300.

Firth, J. R. (1957). *Papers in linguistics 1934–1951*. London: Oxford University Press.

Fish, S. (1980). *Is there a text in this class? The authority of interpretive communities.* Cambridge, MA: Harvard University Press.

Fisk, A. D., & Schneider, W. (1984). Memory as a function of attention, level of processing, and automatization. *Journal of Experimental Psychology: Learning, Memory, and Cognition, 10,* 181–197.

Fitts, P., & Posner, M. (1967). *Human performance.* Belmont: Brooks/Cole.

Flaherty, E. (1974). The thinking aloud technique and problem solving ability. *Journal of Educational Research, 68,* 223–225.

Flege, J. (1991). Perception and production: The relevance of phonetic input to L2 phonological learning. In T. Heubner & C. A. Ferguson (Eds.), *Crosscurrents in second language acquisition and linguistic theories* (pp. 249–289). Amsterdam: Benjamins.

Flege, J., & Davidian, R. (1984). Transfer and developmental processes in adult foreign language speech production. *Applied Psycholinguistics, 5,* 323–347.

Flege, J., Takagi, J., & Mann, V. (1995). Japanese adults can learn to produce English "r" and "l" accurately. *Language Learning, 39,* 23–32.

Flynn, S., G. Martohardjono, & W. O'Neil, (Eds.) (1998). *The generative study of second language acquisition.* Mahwah, NJ: Erlbaum.

Fodor, J. A. (1981). Special sciences. In J. A. Fodor (Ed.), *Representations.* Cambridge, MA: MIT Press.

Fodor, J. A. (1983). *The modularity of mind: An essay on faculty psychology.* Cambridge, MA.: MIT Press.

Fodor, J. A., & Pylyshyn, Z. (1988). Connectionism and cognitive architecture: A critical analysis. *Cognition, 28,* 3–71.

Fodor, J. D. (1989). Empty categories in sentence processing. *Language and Cognitive Processes, 4,* 155–209.

Fodor, J. D. (1998). Unambiguous triggers. *Linguistic Inquiry, 29,* 1–36.

Fodor, J. D., & S. Crain. (1987). Simplicity and generality of rules in language acquisition. In B. MacWhinney (Ed.), *Mechanisms of language acquisition.* Hillsdale, NJ: Erlbaum.

Ford, M., Bresnan, J., & Kaplan, R. M. (1982). A competence-based theory of syntactic closure. In J. Bresnan (Ed.), *The mental representation of grammatical relations.* Cambridge, MA: MIT Press.

Foster, P. (1998). A classroom perspective on the negotiation of meaning. *Applied Linguistics, 19,* 1–23.

Foster, P., & Skehan, P. (1996). The influence of planning and task type on second language performance. *Studies in Second Language Acquisition, 18,* 299–324.

Foster, P., & Skehan, P. (1999a). The influence of source of planning and focus of planning on task-based performance. *Language Teaching Research, 3,* 215–247.

Foster, P., & Skehan, P. (1999b). Inducing selective effects on accuracy: the role of post-task dictation activities. *Paper presented at the British Association for Applied Linguistics Conference,* Edinburgh, August.

Foster, P., Tonkyn, A., & Wigglesworth, G. (1997). A unit for all reasons: assessing complexity in spoken language performance. *Paper presented at the joint CALS/CALR Conference*, Reading, October.

Fotos, S. (1993). Consciousness-raising and noticing through focus on form: grammar task performance vs. formal instruction. *Applied Linguistics, 14*, 385–407.

Fotos, S. (1994). Integrating grammar instruction and communicative language use through grammar consciousness-raising tasks. *TESOL Quarterly, 28*, 323–351.

Fotos, S., & Ellis, R. (1991). Communicating about grammar: A task-based approach. *TESOL Quarterly, 25*, 608–628.

Frazier, L. (1987). Sentence processing: A tutorial review. In M. Coltheart (Ed.), *Attention and performance XII: The psychology of reading* (pp. 601–681). Hillsdale, NJ: Erlbaum.

Frazier, L. (1989). Against lexical generation of syntax. In W. Marslen-Wilson (Ed.), *Lexical representation and process* (pp. 505–528). Cambridge, MA: MIT Press.

Frazier, L. (1995). Constraint satisfaction as a theory of sentence processing. *Journal of Psycholinguistic Research, 24*(2), 437–468.

Frazier, L., & Clifton, C. (1996). *Construal*. Cambridge, MA: MIT Press.

Frazier, L., & De Villiers, J. (1990). Introduction. In L. Frazier & J. De Villiers (Eds.), *Language processing and language acquisition* (pp. 1–11). Dordecht: Kluwer.

Frazier, L., & Fodor, J. D. (1978). The sausage machine: A new two-stage parsing model. *Cognition, 6*, 1–34.

Frazier, L., & Rayner, K. (1987). Resolution of syntactic category ambiguities: Eye movements in parsing lexically ambiguous sentences. *Journal of Memory and Language, 26*, 505–526.

Frazier, L., & Rayner, K. (1990). Taking on semantic commitments: Processing multiple meanings vs. multiple senses. *Journal of Memory and Language, 29*, 181–200.

Gairns, R., & Redman, S. (1986). *Working with words: A guide to teaching and learning vocabulary*. Cambridge: Cambridge University Press.

Gardner, R. (1986). *Social psychology and second language learning*. London: Arnold.

Gardner, R., & Lambert, W. (1972). *Attitudes and motivation in second-language learning*. Rowley, MA: Newbury House.

Gardner, R., & MacIntyre, P. (1992). A student's contribution to second language learning. Part I: Cognitive variables. *Language Teaching, 25*, 211–220.

Gardner, R., & MacIntyre, P. (1993). A student's contribution to second language learning. Part II: Affective variables. *Language Teaching, 26*, 1–11.

Gardner, R., Smythe, P., Clément, R., & Gliksman, L. (1976). Second-language learning: A social psychological perspective. *Canadian Modern Language Review, 32*, 198–213.

Garrett, M. (1975). The analysis of sentence production. In G. Bower (Ed.), *The psychology of learning and motivation, Vol. 9* (pp. 133–175). New York: Academic Press.

Garrett, M. (1980). Levels of processing in sentence production. In B. Butterworth (Ed.), *Language production* (pp. 177–210). London: Academic Press.

Garrett, M. (1990). Sentence processing. In D. N. Osherson & H. Lasnik (Eds.), *An invitation to cognitive science*. Cambridge, MA: MIT Press.

Gass, S. (1982). From theory to practice. In M. Hines & W. Rutherford (Eds.), *On TESOL 81* (pp. 129–139). Washington, DC: TESOL.

Gass, S. (1987). The resolution of conflicts among competing systems: A bidirectional perspective. *Applied Psycholinguistics, 8*, 329–350.

Gass, S. (1988). Integrating research areas: A framework for second language studies. *Applied Linguistics, 9*, 198–217.

Gass, S. (1997). *Input, interaction, and the second language learner*. Mahwah, NJ: Erlbaum.

Gass, S., & Madden, C. (Eds.) (1985). *Input in second language acquisition*. Rowley, MA: Newbury House.

Gass, S., & Selinker, L. (1994). *Second language acquisition: An introductory course*. Mahwah, NJ: Erlbaum.

Gass, S., & Varonis, E. (1986). Variation in native speaker speech modification to non native speakers. *Studies in Second Language Acquisition, 7*, 37–58.

Gass, S., & Varonis, E. (1994). Input, interaction, and second language production. *Studies in Second Language Acquisition, 16*, 283–302.

Gasser, M. (1990). Connectionism and universals of second language acquisition. *Studies in Second Language Acquisition, 12*, 179–199.

Gatbonton, E., & Segalowitz, N. (1988). Creative automatization: Principles for promoting fluency within a communicative framework. *TESOL Quarterly, 22*, 473–492.

Gathercole, V., & Baddeley, A. (1993). *Working memory and language*. Hillsdale, NJ: Erlbaum.

Gazzaniga, M. (Ed.) (1997). *The cognitive neurosciences*. Cambridge, MA: MIT Press.

Gerver, D. (1974). The effects of noise on the performance of simultaneous interpreters: Accuracy of performance. *Acta Psychologica, 38*, 159–167.

Geschwind, N. (1970). The organization of language and the brain. *Science, 170*, 940–944.

Gibson, E., Hickok, G., & Schütze, C. (1994). Processing empty categories: A parallel approach. *Journal of Psycholinguistic Research, 23*, 381–405.

Gibson, E., & Wexler, K. (1994). Triggers. *Linguistic Inquiry, 25*, 407–454.

Givon, T. (1985). Function, structure, and language acquisition. In D. Slobin (Ed.), *The crosslinguistic study of language acquisition: Vol 1* (pp. 1008–1025). Hillsdale, NJ: Erlbaum.

Givon, T. (1989). *Mind, code and context: Essays in pragmatics.* Hillsdale, NJ: Erlbaum.

Gold, E. (1967). Language Identification in the Limit. *Information and Control, 16,* 447–474.

Goodman, K. S. (1971). Psycholinguistic universals in the reading process. In P. Pimsleur & T. Quinn (Eds.), *The psychology of second language learning* (pp. 135–142). Cambridge: Cambridge University Press.

Gopher, D. (1992). Analysis and measurement of mental workload. In G. d'Ydewalle, P. Eelen & P. Bertelson (Eds.), *International perspectives on psychological science: Vol. 2, State of the art* (pp. 265–291). Hillsdale, NJ: Erlbaum.

Gopher, D., Brickner, M., & Navon, D. (1982). Different difficulty manipulations interact differently with task emphasis: Evidence for multiple resources. *Journal of Experimental Psychology: Human Perception and Performance, 8,* 146–157.

Gopnick, A., & Meltzhoff, A. (1984). Semantic and cognitive development in 15–21-month-old children. *Journal of Child Language, 11,* 495–513.

Graesser, A., & G. Bower (1990). *Inferences and text comprehension.* San Diego, CA: Academic Press.

Grainger, J., & Dijkstra, T. (1992). On the representation and use of language information in bilinguals. In R. Harris (Ed.), *Cognitive processing in bilinguals.* Amsterdam: North-Holland.

Greene, S., & Higgins, L. (1994). "Once Upon a Time": The use of retrospective accounts in building theory in composition. In P. Smagorinsky (Ed.), *Speaking about writing: Reflections on research methodology* (pp. 115–140). Thousand Oaks, CA: Sage.

Greenwald, A. G. (1992). New look 3: Unconscious cognition reclaimed. *American Psychologist, 47,* 766–779.

Gregg, K. R. (1984). Krashen's monitor and Occam's razor. *Applied Linguistics, 5,* 79–100.

Gregg, K. R. (1993). Taking explanation seriously; or, Let a couple of flowers bloom. *Applied Linguistics, 14,* 276–294.

Gregg, K. R. (1996). The logical and developmental problems of second language acquisition. In W. C. Ritchie & T. Bhatia (Eds.), *Handbook of second language acquisition* (pp. 49–81). San Diego, CA: Academic Press.

Grice, P. (1975). Logic and conversation. In P. Cole & J. Morgan (Eds.), *Syntax and semantics, Volume 3, Speech acts.* New York: Academic Press.

Griffiths, R. (1991a). Pausological research in an L2 context: A rationale, and review of selected studies. *Applied Linguistics, 12,* 345–364.

Griffiths, R. (1991b). Language learning and the Japanese personality: Hypotheses from the psychological literature. *Paper presented at the IUJ Conference on Second Language Research in Japan,* Tokyo, January.

Griffiths, R., & Sheen, R. (1992). Disembedded figures in the landscape: A reappraisal of L2 research on field dependence/independence. *Applied Linguistics, 13,* 133–148.

Grosjean, F. (1982). *Life with two languages: An introduction to bilingualism.* Cambridge, MA: Harvard University Press.

Gu, Y., & Johnson, R. K. (1996). Vocabulary learning strategies and language learning outcomes. *Language Learning, 46,* 643–679.

Haastrup, K. (1987). Using thinking aloud and retrospection to uncover learners' lexical inferencing procedures. In C. Faerch & G. Kasper (Eds.), *Introspection in second language research* (pp. 197–211). Philadelphia, PA: Multilingual Matters.

Haider, H., & Frensch, P. (1996). The role of information reduction in skill acquisition. *Cognitive Psychology, 30,* 304–337.

Hakuta, K. (1974). Prefabricated patterns and the emergence of structure in second language acquisition. *Language Learning, 24,* 287–298.

Hakuta, K. (1982). Interaction between particles and word order in the comprehension of simple sentences in Japanese children. *Developmental Psychology, 18,* 62–76.

Hancin-Bhatt, B. (1994). Segment transfer: a consequence of a dynamic system. *Second Language Research, 10,* 241–269.

Hancock, P., Williams, G., & Manning, C. (1995). Influence of task demand characteristics on workload and performance. *The International Journal of Aviation Psychology. Special Issue on Pilot Workload: Contemporary Issues, 5, 1,* 63–86.

Hansen, L. (1984). Field dependence-independence and language testing. *TESOL Quarterly, 18,* 65–78.

Harel, D. (1992). *Algorithmics: the spirit of computing.* New York: Addison-Wesley.

Harley, B. (1995). The lexicon in language research. In B. Harley (Ed.), *Lexical issues in language learning* (pp. 1–28). Amsterdam: Benjamins.

Harley, B., Allen, J. P. B., Cummins, J., & Swain, M. (Eds.) (1990). *The Development of second language proficiency.* Cambridge: Cambridge University Press.

Harley, B., & Hart, D. (1997). Language aptitude and second language proficiency in classroom learners of different starting ages. *Studies in Second Language Acquisition, 19,* 379–400.

Harley, B., Howard, J., & Hart, D. (1995). Second language processing at different ages: Do younger learners pay more attention to prosodic cues to sentence structure? *Language Learning, 45,* 43–71.

Harley, B., & Swain, M. (1984). The interlanguage of immersion and its implications for second language teaching. In A. Davies, C. Criper, & A. Howatt (Eds.), *Interlanguage* (pp. 291–311). Edinburgh: Edinburgh University Press.

Harley, T. (1984). A critique of top-down independent levels models of speech production: Evidence from non-plan internal speech errors. *Cognitive Science, 8,* 191–219.

Harmer, J. (1983). *The practice of English language teaching.* London: Longman.

Harnishfeger, K. K. (1995). The development of cognitive inhibition: Theories, definitions, and research evidence. In F. N. Dempster &

C. J. Brainerd (Eds.), *Interference and inhibition in cognition* (pp. 175–204). San Diego, CA: Academic Press.

Harri-Augstein, S., & Thomas, L. (1984). Conversational investigations of reading: the self-organized learner and the text. In J. C. Alderson & A. Urquhart (Eds.), *Reading in a foreign language* (pp. 250–80). New York: Longman.

Harrington, M. (1987). Processing transfer: language-specific strategies as a source of interlanguage variation. *Applied Psycholinguistics, 8*, 351–378.

Harrington, M. (1992a). Working memory capacity as a constraint on L2 development. In R. J. Harris (Ed.), *Cognitive processing in bilinguals* (pp. 123–135). Amsterdam: Elsevier.

Harrington, M. (1992b). Review of MacWhinney, B., & Bates, E. (Eds.) *The crosslinguistic study of sentence processing. American Journal of Psychology, 105*, 484–492.

Harrington, M. (forthcoming). *Input-matching models of second language learning*. Mahwah, NJ: Erlbaum.

Harrington, M., & Sawyer, M. (1992). L2 working memory capacity and L2 reading skill. *Studies in Second Language Acquisition, 14*, 25–38.

Harris, R. (1987). The grammar in your head. In C. Blakemore & S. Greenfield (Eds.), *Mindwaves* (pp. 507–516). Oxford: Blackwell.

Hasher, L., Stolzfus, E. R., Zacks, L. T., & Rypma, B. (1991). Age and inhibition. *Journal of Experimental Psychology, 17*, 163–169.

Hasher, L., & Zacks, R. T. (1979). Automatic and effortful processes in memory. *Journal of Experimental Psychology: General, 108*(3), 356–388.

Hatch, E. (1978). Discourse analysis and second language acquisition. In E. Hatch (Ed.), *Second language acquisition; a book of readings*. Rowley, MA: Newbury House.

Hatch, E. (1983a). Simplified input and second language acquisition. In R. Andersen (Ed.), *Pidginization and creolization as language acquisition*. Rowley, MA: Newbury House.

Hatch, E. (1983b). *Psycholinguistics: A second language perspective*. Cambridge, MA: Newbury House.

Hatch, E., & Brown, C. (1995). *Vocabulary, semantics, and language education*. New York: Cambridge University Press.

Hauptman, P., LeBlanc, R., & Wesche, M. (1985). *Second language performance testing*. Ottawa: University of Ottawa Press.

Hayes, J., & Flower, S. (1980). Identifying the organization of writing processes. In L. Gregg & E. Steinberg (Eds.), *Cognitive processes in writing* (pp. 3–30). Hillsdale, NJ: Erlbaum.

Hazenberg, S., & Hulstijn, J. H. (1996). Defining a minimal receptive second-language vocabulary for non-native university students: An empirical investigation. *Applied Linguistics, 7*, 145–163.

Healey, A., & Bourne, L. (1998) (Eds.) *Foreign language learning: Psycholinguistic studies on training and retention*. Mahwah, NJ: Erlbaum.

Heath, S. B. (1983). *Ways with words*. Cambridge: Cambridge University Press.

Hempel, C. G. (1966). *Philosophy of natural science.* Englewood Cliffs, NJ: Prentice Hall.

Henning, G. H. (1973). Remembering foreign language vocabulary: Acoustic and semantic parameters. *Language Learning, 23,* 185–196.

Heuer, H. (1996). Dual-task performance. In O. Neumann & A. Sanders (Eds.), *Handbook of perception and action, Vol. 3: Attention* (pp. 113–148). New York: Academic.

Higgs, T. V. (1984). (Ed.) *Teaching for proficiency, the organizing principle.* Lincolnwood, IL: National Textbook Company.

Hirsh, D., & Nation, P. (1992). What vocabulary size is needed to read unsimplified texts for pleasure? *Reading in a Foreign Language, 8,* 689–696.

Holthouse, J. (1995). *Anxiety and second language learning task type.* Unpublished M.A. dissertation, University of Queensland, Australia.

Horst, M., Cobb, T., & Meara, P. (1998). Beyond a Clockwork Orange: Acquiring second language vocabulary through reading. *Reading in a Foreign Language, 11,* 207–223.

Horwitz, E. (1987). Linguistic and communicative competence: Reassessing foreign language aptitude. In B. VanPatten, T. Dvorak, & J. Lee (Eds.), *Foreign language learning* (pp. 146–157). Cambridge, MA: Newbury House.

Horwitz, E. K., Horwitz, M. B., & Cope, J. (1986). Foreign language classroom anxiety. *Modern Language Journal, 70,* 125–132.

Hosenfeld, C. (1977). A preliminary investigation of the reading strategies of successful and nonsuccessful second language learners. *System, 5,* 110–123.

Hsaio, A. T., & Reber, A. S. (1998). The role of attention in implicit sequence learning: Exploring the limits of the cognitive unconscious. In M. A. Stadler & P. A. Frensch (Eds.), *Handbook of implicit learning,* (pp. 471–494). London: Sage.

Huang, J. (1971). *A Chinese child's acquisition of syntax.* Unpublished Ph.D. dissertation. UCLA.

Huckin, T., & Coady, J. (1999). Incidental vocabulary acquisition in a second language: A review. *Studies in Second Language Acquisition, 21,* 181–193.

Hulstijn, J. (1990). A comparison between the information processing and analysis/control approaches to language learning. *Applied Linguistics, 11,* 30–45.

Hulstijn, J. H. (1989). A cognitive view on interlanguage variability. In M. Eisenstein (Ed.), *The dynamic interlanguage* (pp. 17–32). New York: Plenum Press.

Hulstijn, J. H. (1992). Retention of inferred and given word meanings: Experiments in incidental vocabulary learning. In P. J. Arnaud & H. B joint (Eds.), *Vocabulary and applied linguistics* (pp. 113–125). London: Macmillan.

Hulstijn, J. H. (1993). When do foreign-language readers look up the meaning of unfamiliar words? The influence of task and learner variables. *Modern Language Journal, 77,* 139–147.

Hulstijn, J. H. (1997). Mnemonic methods in foreign-language vocabulary learning: Theoretical considerations and pedagogical implications. In J. Coady & T. Huckin (Eds.), *Second language vocabulary acquisition: A rationale for pedagogy* (pp. 203–224). Cambridge: Cambridge University Press.

Hulstijn, J. H. (forthcoming). Incidental and intentional learning. In C. Doughty & M. H. Long (Eds.), *Handbook of second language acquisition.* Oxford: Blackwell.

Hulstijn, J. H., & de Graaff, R. (1994). Under what conditions does explicit knowledge of a second language facilitate the acquisition of implicit knowledge? A research proposal. *AILA Review, 11*, 97–113.

Hulstijn, J. H., Hollander, M., & Greidanus, T. (1996). Incidental vocabulary learning by advanced foreign language students: The influence of marginal glosses, dictionary use, and reoccurrence of unknown words. *Modern Language Journal, 80*, 327–339.

Hulstijn, J. H., & Hulstijn, W. (1984). Grammatical errors as a function of processing constraints and explicit knowledge. *Language Learning, 34*, 23–43.

Hulstijn, J. H., & Laufer, B. (1998). What leads to better incidental vocabulary learning: Comprehensible input or comprehensible output? *Paper presented at the 3rd Pacific Second Language Research Forum, Tokyo,* March.

Hulstijn, J. H., & Trompetter, P. (1999). Incidental learning of second-language vocabulary in computer-assisted reading and writing tasks. In D. Albrechtsen, B. Henrikse, I. M. Mees, & E. Poulsen (Eds.), *Perspectives on foreign and second language pedagogy* (pp. 191–200). Odense: Odense University Press.

Hulstijn, W. (1979). Selective attention and the orienting response. In H. Kimmel, E. Van Olst, & J. Orlebeke (Eds.), *The orienting reflex in humans,* (pp. 557–566). Hillsdale, NJ: Erlbaum.

Hunt, D., Butler, L., Noy, J., & Rosser, M. (1978). *Assessing conceptual level by the paragraph completion method.* Toronto: OISE.

Hyams, N. (1987). The theory of parameters and syntactic development. In T. Roeper & E. Williams (Eds.), *Parameter setting* (pp. 1–22). Dordrecht: Reidel.

Ijaz, I. (1986). Linguistic and cognitive determinants of lexical acquisition in a second language. *Language Learning, 36*, 401–451.

Ioup, G., Boustagui, E., El Tigi, M., & Moselle, M. (1994). Reexamining the Critical Period Hypothesis: A case study of successful adult SLA in a naturalistic environment. *Studies in Second Language Acquisition, 16*, 73–98.

Izumi, S., Bigelow, M., Fujiwara, M., & Fearnow, S. (1999). Testing the output hypothesis: Effects of output on noticing and second language acquisition. *Studies in Second Language Acquisition, 21*, 421–452.

Jacob, A. (1996). *Anxiety and motivation during second language task performance in Singaporean schools.* Unpublished M.A. dissertation, National University of Singapore/RELC, Singapore.

Jacobs, B. (1988). Neurobiological differentiation of primary and secondary language acquisition. *Studies in Second Language Acquisition, 10*, 303–337.

Jacobs, B., & Schumann, J. H. (1992). Language acquisition and the neurosciences: towards a more integrative perspective. *Applied Linguistics, 13*, 282–301.

Jacobs, G. M., Dufon, P., & Fong, C. H. (1994). L1 and L2 vocabulary glosses in L2 reading passages: Their effectiveness for increasing comprehension and vocabulary knowledge. *Journal of Research in Reading, 17*, 19–28.

Jacoby, L. L., Lindsay, D. S., & Toth, J. P. (1992). Unconscious influences revealed: Attention, awareness, and control. *American Psychologist, 47*, 802–809.

James, W. (1890). *Principles of psychology*. New York: Holt.

Johnson, J., & Newport, E. (1989). Critical period effects in second language learning: The influence of maturational state on the acquisition of English as a second language. *Cognitive Psychology, 21*, 60–99.

Johnson, J., & Newport, E. (1991). Critical period effects on universal properties of language: the status of subjacency in the acquisition of a second language. *Cognition, 39*, 215–258.

Johnson, K. (1996). *Language teaching and skill learning*. Oxford: Blackwell.

Jones, F. R. (1995). Learning an alien lexicon: A teach-yourself case study. *Second Language Research, 11*, 95–111.

Joseph, J. H., & Dwyer, F. M. (1984). The effects of prior knowledge, presentation mode, and visual realism on student achievement. *Journal of Experimental Education, 52*, 110–121.

Jourdenais, R. (1995). Input processing and textual enhancement. *Paper presented at the Annual Conference of the American Association of Applied Linguistics*, Chicago, March.

Jourdenais, R. (1998). *The effects of textual enhancement on the acquisition of the Spanish preterit and imperfect*. Unpublished Ph.D. dissertation, Georgetown University, Washington, DC.

Jourdenais, R., M. Ota, S. Stauffer, B. Boyson, & C. Doughty (1995). Does textual enhancement promote noticing? A think-aloud protocol analysis. In R. Schmidt (Ed.), *Attention and awareness in foreign language learning* (pp. 183–216). Honolulu, HI: University of Hawaii Press.

Juffs, A. (1996). *Learnability and the lexicon: Theories and second language acquisition research*. Amsterdam: Benjamins.

Juffs, A. (1998). Main verb versus reduced relative clause ambiguity resolution in L2 sentence processing. *Language Learning 48*, 1, 107–147.

Juffs, A., & Harrington, M. (1995). Parsing effects in L2 sentence processing: Subject and Object asymmetries in WH-extraction. *Studies in Second Language Acquisition, 17*, 483–512.

Juffs, A., & Harrington, M. (1996). Garden path sentences and error data in second language sentence processing research. *Language Learning, 46*, 286–324.

Juliano, C., & Tanenhaus, M. (1994). A constraint-based lexicalist account of the subject/object attachment preference. *Journal of Psycholinguistic Research, 23,* 459–471.

Just, M., & Carpenter, P. (1992). A capacity theory of working memory: Individual differences in comprehension. *Psychological Review, 99,* 122–149.

Kahneman, D. (1973). *Attention and effort.* Englewood Cliffs, NJ: Prentice Hall.

Kahneman, D., & Treisman, A. (1984). Changing views of attention and automaticity. In R. Parasuraman & D. R. Davies (Eds.), *Varieties of attention* (pp. 29–61). New York: Academic Press.

Kail, M. (1989). Cue validity, cue cost, and processing types in French sentence comprehension. In B. MacWhinney & E. Bates (Eds.), *The crosslinguistic study of language processing,* (pp. 77–117). New York: Cambridge University Press.

Kanagy, R. (1994). Developmental sequences in acquiring Japanese: negation in L1 and L2. In T. Fujimura, Y. Kato, M. Leong & R. Uehara (Eds), *Proceedings of the 5th conference on second language research in Japan* (pp. 109–126). Tokyo: ICU.

Kane, M., Hasher, L., Stolzfus, E. R., Zacks, R. T., & Connelly, S. L. (1994). Inhibitory attentional mechanisms and aging. *Psychology & Aging, 9,* 103–112.

Kaplan, R. (1983). An introduction to the study of written text: The "Discourse Compact". *Annual Review of Applied Linguistics, 3,* 138–151.

Karmiloff-Smith, A. (1992). *Beyond modularity: A developmental perspective on cognitive science.* Cambridge, MA: MIT Press.

Kasper, G., & Kellerman, E. (Eds.) (1997). *Communication Strategies: Psycholinguistic and sociolinguistic perspectives.* London: Longman.

Kasper, G., & Schmidt, R. (1996). Developmental issues in interlanguage pragmatics. *Studies in Second Language Acquisition, 18,* 145–163.

Kawamoto, A. H. (1993). Nonlinear dynamics in the resolution of lexical ambiguity: a parallel distributed processing account. *Journal of Memory and Language, 32.*

Keane, M. T. (1990). Production systems. In M. W. Eysenck (Ed.), *The Blackwell dictionary of cognitive psychology* (pp. 288–293). Oxford: Blackwell.

Kellerman, E. (1985). Input and second language acquisition theory. In S. Gass & C. Madden (Eds.), *Input in second language acquisition* (pp. 345–353). Rowley, MA: Newbury House.

Kellogg, R. T., & Dare, R. S. (1989). Explicit memory for unattended information. *Bulletin of the Psychonomic Society, 27,* 409–412.

Kempe, V., & MacWhinney, B. (1998). The acquisition of case-marking by adult learners of Russian and German. *Studies in Second Language Acquisition, 20,* 543–587.

Kempen, G., & Huijbers, P. (1983). The lexicalization process in sentence production and naming: Indirect selection of words. *Cognition, 14*, 185–209.

Kihlstrom, J. (1984). Conscious, subconscious, unconscious: A cognitive perspective. In K. Bowers & D. Meichenbaum (Eds.), *The unconscious reconsidered* (pp. 149–211). New York: Wiley.

Kilborn, K. (1989). Sentence processing in a second language: The timing of transfer. *Language and Speech, 32*, 1–23.

Kilborn, K., & Ito, T. (1989). Sentence processing in Japanese-English and Dutch-English bilinguals. In B. MacWhinney & E. Bates (Eds.), *The crosslinguistic study of sentence processing* (pp. 257–291). New York: Cambridge University Press.

King, J., & Just, M. (1991). Individual differences in syntactic processing: the role of working memory. *Journal of Memory and Language, 30*, 580–602.

Kirsner, K. (1994). Implicit processes in second language learning. In N. Ellis (Ed.), *Implicit and explicit learning of languages* (pp. 283–312). London: Academic Press.

Kirsner, K., Lalor, E., & Hird, K. (1993). The bilingual lexicon: Exercise, meaning & morphology. In R. Schreuder & B. Weltens (Eds.), *The bilingual lexicon*. Amsterdam: Benjamins.

Kiss, G. R. (1973). Grammatical word classes: A learning process and its simulation. In G. H. Bower (Ed.), *The psychology of learning and motivation: Advances in research and theory*: Vol. 7. New York: Academic Press.

Klapp, S. T., Boches, C. A., Trabert, M. L., & Logan, G. D. (1991). Automatizing alphabet arithmetic: II. Are there practice effects after automaticity is achieved? *Journal of Experimental Psychology: Learning, Memory and Cognition, 17*, 196–209.

Knight, S. (1994). Dictionary: The tool of last resort in foreign language reading? A new perspective. *Modern Language Journal, 78*, 285–299.

Koda, K. (1994). Second language reading research: Problems and possibilities. *Applied Psycholinguistics, 15*, 1–28.

Koda, K. (1996). L2 word recognition research: A critical review. *The Modern Language Journal, 80*, 450–460.

Kosslyn, S. (1983). *Ghosts in the mind's machine: Creating and using images in the brain*. New York: Norton.

Krantz, G. (1991). *Learning vocabulary in a foreign language: A study of reading strategies*. Göteborg, Sweden: Acta Universitatis Gothburgensis.

Krashen, S. (1981). Aptitude and attitude in relation to second language acquisition and learning. In K. C. Diller (Ed.), *Individual differences and universals in language learning aptitude* (pp. 155–175). Rowley, MA: Newbury House.

Krashen, S. (1982). *Principles and practice in second language acquisition*. Oxford: Pergamon.

Krashen, S. (1989). We acquire vocabulary and spelling by reading: Additional evidence for the input hypothesis. *The Modern Language Journal, 73,* 440–464.

Kroll, J., & de Groot, A. M. B. (1997). Lexical and conceptual memory in the bilingual: Mapping form to meaning in two languages. In A. M. B. de Groot & J. F. Kroll (Eds.), *Tutorials in bilingualism: Psycholinguistic perspectives* (pp. 169–199). Mahwah, NJ: Erlbaum.

Kroll, J., & Sholl, A. (1992). Lexical and conceptual memory in fluent and nonfluent bilinguals. In R. Harris (Ed.), *Cognitive processing in bilinguals* (pp. 191–206). Amsterdam: North-Holland.

LaBerge, D. (1995). *Attentional processing: The brain's art of mindfulness.* Cambridge, MA: Harvard University Press.

LaBerge, D., & Samuels, S. J. (1974). Toward a theory of automatic information processing in reading. *Cognitive Psychology, 6,* 293–323.

Lachter, J., & Bever, T. (1988). The relation between linguistic structure and associative theories of language learning: A constructive critique of some connectionist learning models. *Cognition, 28,* 195–247.

Lado, R. (1965). Memory span as a factor in second language learning. *IRAL, III,* 123–129.

Lakoff, G. (1987). *Women, fire, and dangerous things.* Chicago, IL: University of Chicago Press.

Lakoff, G., & Johnson, M. (1980). *Metaphors we live by.* Chicago, IL: University of Chicago Press.

Landauer, T. K., & Bjork, R. A. (1978). Optimum rehearsal patterns and name learning. In M. M. Gruneberg, P. E. Morris, & R. N. Sykes (Eds.), *Practical aspects of memory* (pp. 625–632). London: Academic Press.

Landauer, T. K., & Dumais, S. T. (1997). A solution to Plato's problem: The latent semantic analysis theory of acquisition, induction, and representation of knowledge. *Psychological Review, 104,* 211–240.

Langacker, R. W. (1987). *Foundations of cognitive grammar, Vol. 1: Theoretical prerequisites.* Stanford, CA: Stanford University Press.

Langacker, R. W. (1991). *Foundations of cognitive grammar, Vol. 2: Descriptive application.* Stanford, CA: Stanford University Press.

Larsen-Freeman, D. (1976). An explanation for the morpheme acquisition order of second language learners. *Language Learning, 26,* 125–134.

Larsen-Freeman, D. (1978). An ESL index of development. *TESOL Quarterly, 12,* 439–448.

Larsen-Freeman, D. (1980). *Discourse analysis in second language research.* Rowley, MA: Newbury House.

Larsen-Freeman, D. (1995). On the teaching and learning of grammar: Challenging the myths. In F. Eckman, D. Highland, P. W. Lee, J. Mileham, & R. R. Weber (Eds.), *Second language acquisition theory and pedagogy* (pp. 131–50). Mahwah, NJ: Erlbaum.

Larsen-Freeman, D., & Long, M. (1991). *An introduction to second language acquisition research.* New York: Longman.

Laufer, B. (1991). *Similar lexical forms in interlanguage*. Tübingen: Gunter Narr.

Laufer, B. (1992). How much lexis is necessary for reading comprehension? In P. Arnaud & H. Béjoint (Eds.), *Vocabulary and Applied Linguistics* (pp. 126–132). London: Macmillan.

Laufer, B. (1997). What's in a word that makes it hard or easy: some intralexical factors that affect the learning of words. In N. Schmitt & M. McCarthy (Eds.), *Vocabulary: Description, acquisition and pedagogy* (pp. 140–155).Cambridge: Cambridge University Press.

Laufer, B., & Nation, P. (1995). Vocabulary size and use: Lexical richness in L2 written production. *Applied Linguistics, 16*, 307–322.

Laufer, B., & Osimo, H. (1991). Facilitating long-term retention of vocabulary: The second-hand cloze. *System, 19*, 217–224.

Laufer, B., & Shmueli, K. (1997). Memorizing new words: Does teaching have anything to do with it? *RELC Journal, 28*, 89–108.

Lawson, M. J., & Hogden, D. (1996). The vocabulary-learning strategies of foreign-language students. *Language Learning, 46*, 101–135.

Lee, J. F., Cadierno, T., Glass, W. R., & VanPatten, B. (1997). The effects of lexical and grammatical cues on processing past temporal reference in second language input. *Applied Language Learning, 8*, 1–23.

Lehman, J. F., Laird, J. E., & Rosenbloom, P. (1998). A gentle introduction to SOAR: An architecture for human cognition. In D. Scarborough & S. Sternberg (Eds.), *An invitation to cognitive science. Vol. 4: Methods, models and conceptual issues* (pp. 211–253). Cambridge, MA: MIT Press.

Lenneberg, E. H. (1967). *Biological foundations of language*. New York: Wiley.

Lennon, P. (1990). Investigating fluency in EFL: A quantitative approach. *Language Learning, 40*, 387–417.

Leow, R. (1993). To simplify or not to simplify: a look at intake. *Studies in Second Language Acquisition, 15*, 333–55.

Leow, R. (1997). Attention, awareness, and foreign language behavior. *Language Learning, 47*, 467–505.

Levelt, W. (1989). *Speaking: From intention to articulation*. Cambridge, MA: MIT Press.

Levelt, W. (1991). Accessing words in speech production: Stages, processes, and representations. In W. Levelt (Ed.), *Lexical access in speech production* (pp. 1–22). Cambridge, MA: Blackwell.

Levelt, W. (1993). Language use in normal speakers and its disorders. In G. Blanken, J. Dittman, H. Grimm, J. Marshall, & C. Wallesch (Eds.), *Linguistic disorders and pathologies: An international handbook* (pp. 1–15). Berlin: de Gruyter.

Levelt, W., & Kelter, S. (1982). Surface form and memory in question answering. *Cognitive Psychology, 14*, 78–106.

Levelt, W. J. M., Roelofs, A., & Meyer, A. S. (1998). *A theory of lexical access in speech production*. Nijmegen: Max Planck Institute.

Levy, J. P., Bairaktaris, D., Bullinaria, J. A., & Cairns, P. (Eds.) (1995). *Connectionist models of memory and language*. London: UCL Press.

Lewis, M. (1994). *The lexical approach*. Hove: Language Teaching Publications.

Lieven, E. V. M., Pine, J. M., & Baldwin, G. (1997). Lexically-based learning and early grammatical development. *Journal of Child Language, 24*, 187–219.

Lieven, E. V. M., Pine, J. M., & Dresner Barnes, H. (1992). Individual differences in early vocabulary development: Redefining the referential-expressive dimension. *Journal of Child Language, 19*, 287–310.

Lightbown, P. (1992a). Can they do it themselves? A comprehension-based ESL course for young children. In R. Courchène, J. St. John, C. Therrien, & J. Glidden (Eds.), *Comprehension-based language teaching: Current trends*. Ottawa: University of Ottawa Press.

Lightbown, P. (1992b). Getting quality input in the second and foreign language classroom. In C. Kramsch & S. McConnell-Ginet (Eds.), *Text and context: Cross-disciplinary and cross-cultural perspectives on language study*. Lexington, MA: DC Heath.

Lightbown, P. (1998). The importance of timing in focus on form. In C. Doughty & J. Williams (Eds.), *Focus on form in classroom second language acquisition* (pp. 177–196). New York: Cambridge University Press.

Lightbown, P., & Spada, N. (1993). *How languages are learned*. Oxford: Oxford University Press.

Lightbown, P., & Spada, N. (1994). An innovative program for primary ESL in Quebec. *TESOL Quarterly, 28*, 563–579.

Lightfoot, D. (1989). The child's trigger experience: Degree-0 learnability. *Behavioral and Brain Sciences, 12*, 321–375.

Linacre, J. M. (1992). *A User's Guide to FACETS*, Chicago, Ill.: Mesa Press.

Liu, H., Bates, E., & Li, P. (1992). Sentence interpretation in bilingual speakers of English and Chinese. *Applied Psycholinguistics, 13*, 451–484.

Locke, J. L. (1995). Development of the capacity for spoken language. In P. Fletcher & B. MacWhinney (Eds.), *The handbook of child language*. Oxford: Blackwell.

Loftus, E. F., & Klinger, M. R. (1992). Is the unconscious smart or dumb? *American Psychologist, 47*, 761–765.

Loftus, G. (1972). Eye fixations and recognition memory for pictures. *Cognitive Psychology, 7*, 1–19.

Logan, G. D. (1988). Toward an instance theory of automatization. *Psychological Review, 95*, 492–527.

Logan, G. D. (1990). Repetition priming and automaticity: Common underlying mechanisms? *Cognitive Psychology, 22*, 1–35.

Logan, G. D. (1992). Shapes of reaction-time distributions and shapes of learning curves: A test of the instance theory of automaticity. *Journal of Experimental Psychology: Learning, Memory and Cognition, 18*, 883–914.

Logan, G. D., & Etherton, J. L. (1994). What is learned during automatization? The role of attention in constructing an instance. *Journal of Experimental Psychology: Learning, Memory and Cognition, 20,* 1022–1050.

Logan, G. D., & Klapp, S. T. (1991). Automatizing alphabet arithmetic: I. Is extended practice necessary to produce automaticity? *Journal of Experimental Psychology: Learning, Memory and Cognition, 18,* 883–914.

Logan, G. D., Taylor, S. E., & Etherton, J. L. (1996). Attention in the acquisition and expression of automaticity. *Journal of Experimental Psychology: Learning, Memory and Cognition, 22,* 620–638.

Lombardi, L., & Potter, M. (1992). The regeneration of syntax in short term memory. *Journal of Memory and Language, 31,* 713–733.

Long, M. H. (1983a). Linguistic and conversational adjustments to non-native speakers. *Studies in Second Language Acquisition, 5,* 177–193.

Long, M. H. (1983b). Does second language instruction make a difference? A review of the research. *TESOL Quarterly, 17,* 359–382.

Long, M. H. (1985). A role for instruction in second language acquisition: Task-based language teaching. In K. Hyltenstam & M. Pienemann (Eds.), *Modelling and assessing second language acquisition* (pp. 77–99). Clevedon, Avon: Multilingual Matters.

Long, M. H. (1988). Instructed interlanguage development. In L. Beebe (Ed.), *Issues in second language acquisition: Multiple perspectives* (pp. 115–141). New York: Newbury House.

Long, M. H. (1989). Task, group, and task-group interactions. *University of Hawaii Working Papers in ESL, 8,* 1–25.

Long, M. H. (1990). Maturational constraints on language development. *Studies in Second Language Acquisition, 12,* 251–285.

Long, M. H. (1991). Focus on form: A design feature in language teaching methodology. In K. de Bot, D. Coste, R. Ginsberg, & C. Kramsch (Eds.), *Foreign language research in cross-cultural perspectives* (pp. 39–52). Amsterdam: Benjamins.

Long, M. H. (1992). Input, focus on form, and second language acquisition. *Paper presented at the American Association of Applied Linguistics,* Seattle, March.

Long, M. H. (1993). Assessment strategies for second language acquisition theories. *Applied Linguistics,14,* 225–249.

Long, M. H. (1996). The role of the linguistic environment in second language acquisition. In W. C. Ritchie & T. K. Bhatia (Eds.), *Handbook of second language acquisition* (pp. 413–468). San Diego, CA: Academic Press.

Long, M. H. (1998). Focus on form in task-based language teaching. *University of Hawaii Working Papers in ESL, 16,* 49–61.

Long, M. H. (1999). Recasts: The story so far. To appear in *Problems in SLA.* Mahwah, NJ: Erlbaum.

Long, M. H., & Crookes, G. (1992). Three approaches to task-based syllabus design. *TESOL Quarterly, 26,* 27–56.

Long, M. H., & Robinson, P. (1998). Focus on form: Theory, research, and practice. In C. Doughty & J. Williams (Eds.), *Focus on form in classroom second language acquisition* (pp. 15–41). New York: Cambridge University Press.

Loschky, L., & Bley-Vroman, R. (1993). Grammar and task-based methodology. In G. Crookes & S. Gass (Eds.), *Tasks in Language Learning: Integrating Theory and Practice* (pp. 123–167). Clevedon, Avon: Multilingual Matters.

Luria, A. R. (1961). *The role of speech in the regulation of normal and abnormal behavior.* New York: Liveright.

Lynch, T. (1996). *Communication in the classroom.* Oxford: Oxford University Press.

Lyons, J. (1975). Deixis as a source of reference. In E. Keenan (Ed.), *Formal semantics of natural language.* Cambridge: Cambridge University Press.

Lyster, R. (1998). Recasts, repetition, and ambiguity in L2 classroom discourse. *Studies in Second Language Acquisition, 20,* 51–81.

Lyster, R., & Ranta, L. (1997). Corrective feedback and learner uptake: Negotiation of form in communicative classrooms. *Studies in Second Language Acquisition, 19,* 37–66.

MacDonald, M. C. (1993). The interaction of lexical and syntactic ambiguity. *Journal of Memory and Language, 32,* 692–715.

MacDonald, M. C. (1994). Probabilistic constraints and syntactic ambiguity. *Language and Cognitive Processes, 9,* 157–201.

MacDonald, M. C. (Ed.). (1997). *Lexical representations and sentence processing.* Hove: Psychology Press.

MacDonald, M. C., Just, M., & Carpenter, P. (1992). Working memory constraints on the processing of syntactic ambiguity. *Cognitive Psychology, 24,* 56–98.

MacDonald, M. C., & MacWhinney, B. (1990). Measuring inhibition and facilitation from pronouns. *Journal of Memory and Language, 29,* 469–492.

MacDonald, M. C., Pearlmutter, N. J., & Seidenberg, M. S. (1994). Syntactic ambiguity resolution as lexical ambiguity resolution. In C. Clifton, L. Frazier, & K. Rayner (Eds.), *Perspectives on sentence processing.* Hillsdale, NJ: Erlbaum.

MacIntyre, P. D., & Gardner, R. (1991). Language anxiety: Its relationship to other anxieties and to process in native and second languages. *Language Learning, 41,* 513–534.

MacIntyre, P. D., & Noels, K. A. (1996). Using social-psychological variables to predict the use of language learning strategies. *Foreign Language Annals, 29,* 373–386.

MacKay, D. G. (1982). The problems of flexibility, fluency, and speed-accuracy trade-off in skilled behavior. *Psychological Review, 89,* 483–506.

MacKay, D. G. (1990). Perception, action, and awareness: A three-body problem. In O. Neumann & W. Prinz (Eds.), *Relationships between perception and action: Current approaches* (pp. 269–303). Berlin: Springer.

Mackey, A. (1999). Input, interaction and second language development. *Studies in Second Language Acquisition, 21,* 557–587.

Mackworth, A. K. (1977). Consistency in networks of relations. *Artificial Intelligence, 8,* 99–118.

MacWhinney, B. (1974). *How Hungarian children learn to speak.* Berkeley, CA: University of California Press.

MacWhinney, B. (1987). The Competition Model. In B. MacWhinney (Ed.), *Mechanisms of language acquisition* (pp. 249–308). Hillsdale, NJ: Erlbaum.

MacWhinney, B. (1992). Transfer and competition in second language learning. In R. J. Harris (Ed.), *Cognitive processing in bilinguals* (pp. 371–390). Amsterdam: North Holland.

MacWhinney, B. (1995). Language-specific prediction in foreign language learning. *Language Testing, 12,* 292–320.

MacWhinney, B. (1998). Models of the emergence of language. *Annual Review of Psychology, 49,* 199–227.

MacWhinney, B., & Bates, E. (1978). Sentential devices for conveying givenness and newness: A cross–cultural developmental study. *Journal of Verbal Learning and Verbal Behavior, 17,* 539–558.

MacWhinney, B., & Bates, E. (Eds.) (1989). *The crosslinguistic study of sentence processing.* New York: Cambridge University Press.

MacWhinney, B., Bates, E., & Kliegl, R. (1984). Cue validity and sentence interpretation in English, German, and Italian. *Journal of Verbal Learning and Verbal Behavior, 23,* 127–150.

MacWhinney, B., & Leinbach, J. (1991). Implementations are not conceptualizations: Revising the verb learning model. *Cognition, 40,* 121–157.

MacWhinney, B. J., Leinbach, J., Taraban, R., & McDonald, J. L. (1989). Language learning: Cues or rules? *Journal of Memory and Language, 28,* 255–277.

MacWhinney, B., & Pléh, C. (1988). The processing of restrictive relative clauses in Hungarian. *Cognition, 29,* 95–141.

MacWhinney, B., & Pléh, C. (1997). Double agreement: Role identification in Hungarian. *Language and Cognitive Processes, 12,* 67–102.

Mandler, J. (1992). How to build a baby: II. Conceptual primitives. *Psychological Review, 99,* 589–604.

Mangubhai, F. (1991). The processing behaviours of adult second language learners and their relationship to second language proficiency. *Applied Linguistics, 12,* 268–97.

Marantz, A. (1995). The minimalist program. In G. Webelhuth (Ed.), *Government and binding theory and the minimalist program* (pp. 349–382). Oxford: Blackwell.

Maratsos, M., & Chalkley, M. (1980). The internal language of children's syntax: The ontogenesis and representation of syntactic categories. In K. Nelson (Ed.), *Children's language: Volume 2* (pp. 127–214). New York: Gardner.

Marcel, A. J. (1983). Conscious and unconscious perception: An approach to the relations between phenomenal experience and perceptual processes. *Cognitive Psychology, 15,* 238–302.

Marchman, V. A. (1993). Constraints on plasticity in a connectionist model of the English past tense. *Journal of Cognitive Neuroscience, 5*, 215–234.

Marchman, V. A., & Bates, E. (1994). Continuity in lexical and morphological development: a test of the critical mass hypothesis. *Journal of Child Language, 21*, 339–366.

Marcus, G. (1993). Negative evidence in language acquisition. *Cognition, 46*, 53–69.

Marcus, G., Brinkmann, U., Clahsen, H., Wiese, R., & Pinker, S. (1995). German inflection: The exception that proves the rule. *Cognitive Psychology, 29*, 198–256.

Marslen-Wilson, W. C. (1993). Issues of process and representation. In G. Altmann & R. Shillcock (Eds.), *Cognitive models of speech processing*. Hillsdale, NJ: Erlbaum.

Marlsen-Wilson, W., & Tyler, L. K. (1980). On the temporal structure of spoken language understanding. *Cognition, 8*, 1–71.

Marlsen-Wilson, W., & Tyler, L. K. (1987). Against modularity. In J. L. Garfield (Ed.), *Modularity in knowledge representation and natural language understanding*. Cambridge, MA: MIT Press.

Marlsen-Wilson, W., & Tyler, L. K., Warren, P., Grenier, P., & Lee, C. S. (1992). Prosodic effects in minimal attachment. *Quarterly Journal of Experimental Psychology, 45*, 73–87.

Massaro, D. (1987). *Speech perception by ear and eye*. Hillsdale, NJ: Erlbaum.

Maurice, K. (1983). The fluency workshop. *TESOL Newsletter, 17*(4), 29.

McCawley, J. D. (1983). Execute criminals, not rules of grammar. *Behavioral and Brain Sciences, 6*, 410–411.

McClelland, J. L., Rumelhart, D. E., & Hinton, G. (1986). The appeal of parallel distributed processing. In D. E. Rumelhart & J. L. McClelland, (Eds.), *Parallel distributed processing* (pp. 3–44). Cambridge, MA: MIT Press.

McDonald, J. L. (1986). The development of sentence comprehension strategies in English and Dutch. *Journal of Experimental Child Psychology, 41*, 317–335.

McDonald, J. L. (1987a). Assigning linguistic roles: The influence of conflicting cues. *Journal of Memory and Language, 26*, 100–117.

McDonald, J. L. (1987b). Sentence interpretation in bilingual speakers of English and Dutch. *Applied Psycholinguistics, 8*, 379–414.

McDonald, J. L. (1989). Acquisition of cue-category mappings. In B. MacWhinney & E. Bates (Eds.), *The crosslinguistic study of language processing* (pp. 375–396). New York: Cambridge University Press.

McDonald, J. L., & Heilenman, K. (1991). Determinants of cue strength in adult first and second language speakers of French. *Applied Psycholinguistics, 12*, 313–348.

McDonald, J. L., & MacWhinney, B. (1989). Maximum likelihood models for sentence processing research. In B. MacWhinney & E. Bates (Eds.), *The crosslinguistic study of sentence processing*, (pp. 397–421). New York: Cambridge University Press.

McDonald, J. L., & MacWhinney, B. J. (1995). The time course of anaphor resolution: Effects of implicit verb causality and gender. *Journal of Memory and Language, 34,* 543–566.

McGeoch, J. A. (1942). *The psychology of human learning.* New York: Longman.

McLaughlin, B. (1965). "Intentional" and "incidental" learning in human subjects: The role of instructions to learn and motivation. *Psychological Bulletin, 63,* 359–376.

McLaughlin, B. (1982). Second-language learning and bilingualism in children and adults. In S. Rosenberg (Ed.), *Handbook of applied psycholinguistics: Major thrusts of research and theory,* Hillsdale, NJ: Erlbaum.

McLaughlin, B. (1987). *Theories of second language learning.* London: Arnold.

McLaughlin, B. (1990). Restructuring. *Applied Linguistics, 11,* 113–128.

McLaughlin, B. (1995). Aptitude from an information-processing perspective. *Language Testing, 12,* 370–387.

McLaughlin, B., & Heredia, R. (1996). Information-processing approaches to research on second language acquisition and use. In W. C. Ritchie & T. K. Bhatia (Eds.), *Handbook of second language acquisition* (pp. 213–228). San Diego, CA: Academic Press.

McLaughlin, B., Rossman, T., & McLeod, B. (1983). Second language learning: an information-processing perspective. *Language Learning, 33,* 135–158.

McLeod, B., & McLaughlin, B. (1986). Restructuring or automaticity? Reading in a second language. *Language Learning, 36,* 109–123.

McNamara, T. (1996). *Second language performance testing.* London, New York: Longman.

Meara, P. (1989). Matrix models of vocabulary acquisition. *AILA Review, 6,* 66–74.

Meara, P. (1993). The bilingual lexicon and the teaching of vocabulary. In R. Schreuder & B. Weltens (Eds.), *The bilingual lexicon* (pp. 279–297). Amsterdam: Benjamins.

Meara, P. (1997). Towards a new approach to modelling vocabulary acquisition. In N. Schmitt & M. McCarthy (Eds.), *Vocabulary: Description, acquisition and pedagogy* (pp. 109–121). Cambridge: Cambridge University Press.

Mehnert, U. (1998) The effects of different lengths of time for planning on second language performance. *Studies in Second Language Acquisition, 20,* 83–108.

Meisel, J. (1987). Reference to past events and actions in the development of natural second language acquisition. In C. Pfaff (Ed.), *First and second language acquisition processes* (pp. 206–225). Rowley, MA: Newbury House.

Mellow, D. (1996). A cognitive account of L2 development: The automatization of form-function mappings. *Paper presented at the Second Language Research Forum,* Tucson, September.

Melton, A. W. (1963). Implications of short-term memory for a general theory of memory. *Journal of Verbal Learning and Verbal Behavior, 2,* 1–21.

Merikle, P. M., & Cheesman, J. (1987). Current status of research on subliminal perception. In M. Wallendorf & P. F. Anderson (Eds.), *Advances in consumer research, Vol. XIV* (pp. 298–302). Provo, UT: Association for Consumer Research.

Merikle, P. M., & Daneman, M. (1998). Psychological investigations of unconscious perception. *Journal of Consciousness Studies, 5,* 5–18.

Miller, G. A. (1956). The magical number seven, plus or minus two: Some limits on our capacity for processing information. *Psychological Review, 63,* 81–97.

Mitchell, D. C. (1994). Sentence parsing. In M. Gernsbacher (Ed.), *Handbook of psycholinguistics,* (pp. 375–410). San Diego, CA: Academic Press.

Mitchell, D. C., Corley, M. M. B., & Garnham, A. (1992). Effects of context in human sentence processing: evidence against a discourse-based proposal mechanism. *Journal of Experimental Psychology: Learning, Memory, and Cognition, 18,* 69–88.

Miyake, A., Carpenter, P., & Just, M. (1994). A capacity approach to syntactic comprehension disorders: Making normal adults perform like aphasic patients. *Cognitive Neuropsychology, 11,* 671–717.

Miyake, A., & Friedman, N. F. (1998). Individual differences in second language proficiency: Working memory as "language aptitude". In A. F. Healy & L. E. Bourne (Eds.), *Foreign language learning: Psycholinguistic studies on training and retention.* (pp. 339–364). Mahwah, NJ: Erlbaum.

Möhle, D. (1984). A comparison of the second language speech of different native speakers. In H. Dechert, D. Möhle, & M. Raupach (Eds.), *Second language productions* (pp. 28–49). Tübingen: Gunter Narr.

Mondria, J-A., & Mondria-de Vries, S. (1993). Efficiently memorizing words with the help of word cards and "hand computer": Theory and applications. *System, 22,* 47–57.

Mondria, J-A., & Wit-de Boer, M. (1991). The effects of contextual richness on the guessability and the retention of words in a foreign language. *Applied Linguistics, 12,* 249–267.

Morgan, J., & Rinvolucri, M. (1986). *Vocabulary.* Oxford: Oxford University Press.

Morton, J. (1967). A singular lack of incidental learning. *Nature, 215,* 203–204.

Munby, J. (1978). *Communicative syllabus design.* Cambridge: Cambridge University Press.

Murakami, K. (1974). A language aptitude test for Japanese. *System, 2*(3), 31–47.

Muranoi, H. (1996). *Effects of interaction enhancement on restructuring of interlanguage grammar: A cognitive approach to foreign language instruction.* Unpublished Ph.D dissertation, Georgetown University, U.S.A.

Myers, I. B., & McCaulley, M. H. (1985). *A guide to the development and use of the Myers-Briggs Type Indicator.* Palo Alto: Consulting Psychologists Press.

Myles, F. (1995). Interaction between linguistic theory and language processing in SLA. *Second Language Research, 11,* 235–265.

Myles, F., Hooper, J., & Mitchell, R. (1998). Rote or rule? Exploring the role of formulaic language in classroom foreign language learning. *Language Learning, 48,* 323–364.

Myles, F., Mitchell, R., & Hooper, J. (1999). Interrogative chunks in French L2: A basis for creative construction. *Studies in Second Language Acquisition, 20,* 49–80.

Nagy, W. (1997). On the role of context in first- and second-language vocabulary learning. In N. Schmitt & M. McCarthy (Eds.), *Vocabulary: Description, acquisition and pedagogy* (pp. 64–83). Cambridge: Cambridge University Press.

Nagy, W. E., & Anderson, R. C. (1984). How many words are there in printed school English? *Reading Research Quarterly, 19,* 304–330.

Nagy, W. E., & Herman, P. A. (1987). Breadth and depth of vocabulary knowledge: Implications for acquisition and instruction. In M. G. McKeown & M. Curtis (Eds.), *The nature of vocabulary acquisition* (pp. 19–35). Hillsdale, NJ: Erlbaum.

Nagy, W. E., Herman, P. A., & Anderson, R. A. (1985). Learning words from context. *Reading Research Quarterly, 20,* 233–253.

Narayanan, S. (1997).Talking the talk is like walking the walk: A computational model of verb aspect. *Proceedings of the Cognitive Science Conference 1997.* Pittsburgh, PA.: Cognitive Science Society.

Nation, P. (1990). *Teaching and learning vocabulary.* New York: Newbury House.

Nation, P. (1993). Vocabulary size, growth, and use. In R. Schreuder & B. Weltens (Eds.), *The bilingual lexicon* (pp. 115–134). Amsterdam: Benjamins.

Nation, P., & Coady, J. (1988). Vocabulary and reading. In R. Carter & M. McCarthy (Eds.), *Vocabulary and language teaching* (pp. 97–110). Harlow: Longman.

Nation, P., & Newton, J. (1997). Teaching vocabulary. In J. Coady & T. Huckin (Eds.), *Second language vocabulary acquisition: A rationale for pedagogy* (pp. 238–254). Cambridge: Cambridge University Press.

Nation, P., & Waring, R. (1997). Vocabulary size, text coverage and word lists. In N. Schmitt & M. McCarthy (Eds.), *Vocabulary: Description, acquisition and pedagogy* (pp. 6–19). Cambridge: Cambridge University Press.

Nation, R., & McLaughlin, B. (1986). Experts and novices: An information processing approach to the good language learner problem. *Applied Psycholinguistics, 7,* 41–56.

Nattinger, J. R., & DeCarrico, J. S. (1992). *Lexical phrases and language teaching.* Oxford: Oxford University Press.

Navon, D. (1989). The importance of being visible: On the role of attention in a mind viewed as an anarchic intelligence system. *European Journal of Cognitive Psychology, 1*, 191–238.

Navon, D., & Gopher, D. (1980). Task difficulty, resources and dual-task performance. In R.S. Nickerson (Ed.), *Attention and performance VIII* (pp. 297–315). Hillsdale, NJ: Erlbaum.

Nayak, N., Hansen, N., Krueger, N., & McLaughlin, B. (1990). Language-learning strategies in monolingual and multilingual adults. *Language Learning, 40*, 221–244.

Neill, W. T., & Valdes, L. A. (1992). The persistence of negative priming: Steady-state or decay? *Journal of Experimental Psychology: Learning, Memory, and Cognition, 18*, 565–576.

Neill, W. T., Lissner, L. S., & Beck, J. L. (1990). Negative priming in same-different matching: Further evidence for a central locus of inhibition. *Perception & Psychophysics, 48*, 398–400.

Neill, W. T., Valdes, L. A., & Terry, K. M. (1995). Selective attention and the inhibitory control of cognition. In F. N. Dempster & C. J. Brainerd (Eds.), *Interference and inhibition in cognition* (pp. 207–261). San Diego, CA: Academic Press.

Neisser, U. (1967). *Cognitive psychology*. New York: Appleton-Century-Crofts.

Neisser, U. (1976). *Cognition and reality: Principles and implications of cognitive psychology*. San Francisco, CA: Freeman.

Nelson, K. (1987). Some observations from the perspective of the rare event cognitive comparison theory of language acquisition. In K. Nelson & A. vanKleeck (Eds.), *Children's language*. Norwood, NJ: Erlbaum.

Nelson, K., Denninger, M., Bonvillian, J., Kaplan, J., & Baker, N. (1984). Maternal adjustments and non-adjustments as related to children's linguistic advances and to language acquisition theories. In A. Pellegrini & T. Yawkey (Eds.), *The development of oral and written language: Readings in developmental and applied linguistics* (pp. 31–56). New York: Ablex.

Neumann, O. (1987). Beyond capacity: A functional view of attention. In H. Heuer & A. Sanders (Eds.), *Perspectives on perception and action*. Berlin: Springer.

Neumann, O. (1990). Visual attention and action. In O. Neumann & W. Prinz (Eds.), *Relationships between perception and action: Current approaches* (pp. 227–267). Berlin: Springer.

Neumann, O. (1996). Theories of attention. In O. Neumann & A. Sanders (Eds.), *Handbook of perception and action Vol. 3: Attention* (pp. 389–446). San Diego, CA: Academic Press.

Newell, A. (1990). *Unified theories of cognition*. Cambridge, MA: Harvard University Press.

Newell, A., & Rosenbloom, P. S. (1981). Mechanisms of skill acquisition and the law of practice. In J. R. Anderson (Ed.), *Cognitive skills and their acquisition* (pp. 1–55). Hillsdale, NJ: Erlbaum.

Newell, A., Rosenbloom, P. S., & Laird, J. E. (1989). Symbolic architecture for cognition. In M. I. Posner (Ed.), *Foundations of cognitive science*. Cambridge, MA: MIT Press.

Newell, A., & Simon, H. A. (1972). *Human problem solving*. Englewood Cliffs, NJ: Prentice Hall.

Newmeyer, F. J. (1983). *Grammatical theory; its limits and possibilities*. Chicago, IL: University of Chicago Press.

Newport E. (1990). Maturational constraints on language learning. *Cognitive Science, 14,* 11–28.

Ni, W., Crain, S., & Shankweiler, D. (1996). Sidestepping garden paths: Assessing the contributions of syntax, semantics, and plausibility in resolving ambiguities. *Language and Cognitive Processes, 11,* 283–334.

Nicol, J., & Swinney, D. A. (1989). The role of structure in coreference assignment during sentence comprehension. *Journal of Psycholinguistic Research, 18,* 5–19.

Nisbett, R. E., & W. T. D. Wilson (1977). Telling more than we can know: Verbal reports on mental processes. *Psychological Review, 84,* 231–59.

Nissen, M., & Bullemer, P. (1987). Attentional requirements of learning: Evidence from performance measures. *Cognitive Psychology, 19,* 1–32.

Niwa, Y. (2000). *Reasoning demands of L2 tasks and L2 narrative production: Effects of individual differences in working memory, aptitude and intelligence*. Unpublished M.A. dissertation, Aoyama Gakuin University, Tokyo, Japan.

Norman, D. A. (1980). Cognitive engineering and education. In D. T. Tuma & F. Reif (Eds.), *Problem solving and education: Issues in teaching and learning*. Hillsdale, NJ: Erlbaum.

Norris, J., Brown, J. D., Hudson, T., & Yoshioka, J. (1998). *Developing second language performance tests*. Honolulu: University of Hawaii Press.

North, R. A., & Riley, V. A. (1989). W/INDEX: A predictive model of operator workload. In G. R. McMillan, D. Beevis, E. Sala, M. H. Strub, R. Sutton, & L. Van Breda (Eds.), *Applications of human performance models to system design* (pp. 81–89). New York: Plenum.

Nosofsky, R. M. (1986). Attention, similarity, and the identification-categorization relationship. *Journal of Experimental Psychology: General, 115,* 39–57.

Nosofsky, R. M., & Palmeri, T. J. (1997). An exemplar-based random walk model of speeded classification. *Psychological Review, 104,* 266–300.

Novoa, L., Fein, D., & Obler, L. (1988). Talent in foreign languages: A case study. In L. Obler & D. Fein (Eds.), *The exceptional brain* (pp. 294–302). New York: Guildford Press.

Nunan, D. (1989). *Designing tasks for the communicative classroom*. Cambridge: Cambridge University Press.

Nyhus, S. (1994). *Attitudes of non-native speakers of English toward the use of verbal report to elicit their reading comprehension strategies*. Unpublished Master's Thesis, University of Minnesota.

O'Dell, F. (1997). Incorporating vocabulary into the syllabus. In N. Schmitt & M. McCarthy (Eds.), *Vocabulary: Description, acquisition and pedagogy* (pp. 258–278). Cambridge: Cambridge University Press.

Oden, G., & Massaro, D. (1978). Integration of featural information in speech perception. *Psychological Review, 85*, 172–191.

O'Grady, W. (1987). *Principles of grammar and learning.* Chicago, IL: University of Chicago Press.

O'Grady, W. (1996). Language acquisition without Universal Grammar: a general nativist proposal for L2 learning. *Second Language Research, 12*, 374–397.

O'Grady, W. (1997). *Syntactic development.* Chicago, IL: University of Chicago Press.

Oliver, R. (1995). Negative feedback in child NS/NNS conversation. *Studies in Second Language Acquisition, 17*, 459–483.

Oller, J. (1983). *Issues in language testing research.* Rowley, MA: Newbury House.

Oltman, P., Raskin, E., & Witkin, H. (1971). *Group Embedded Figures Test.* Palo Alto, CA: Consulting Psychologists Press.

O'Malley, J., & Chamot, A. (1990). *Learning strategies in second language acquisition.* Cambridge: Cambridge University Press.

O'Malley, J. M., Chamot, A. U., Stewner-Manzares, G., Kupper, L., & Russo, R. P. (1985). Learning strategies used by beginning and intermediate ESL students. *Language Learning, 35*, 21–46.

O'Malley, J. M., Chamot, A. U., & Walker, C. (1987). Some applications of cognitive theory to second language acquisition. *Studies in Second Language Acquisition, 9*, 287–306.

Ortega, L. (1999). Planning and focus on form in L2 oral discourse. *Studies in Second Language Acquisition, 20*, 103–135.

Ortega, L., & Long, M. (1997). The effects of models and recasts on the acquisition of object topicalization and adverb placement in L2 Spanish. *Spanish Applied Linguistics, 1*(1), 65–86.

Osaka, M., & Osaka, N. (1992). Language-independent working memory as measured by Japanese and English reading span tests. *Bulletin of the Psychonomic Society, 30*, 287–289.

Osaka, M., Osaka, N., & Groner, R. (1993). Language-independent working memory: Evidence from German and French span tests. *Bulletin of the Psychonomic Society, 31*, 117–118.

Otto, I. (1996). *Hungarian language aptitude test: Words in sentences.* Budapest: Department of English Applied Linguistics, Eotvos University.

Oxford, R. (1990). *Language learning strategies: what every teacher should know.* New York: Newbury House.

Oxford, R. (Ed.) (1996). *Language learning strategies around the world: crosscultural perspectives.* Honolulu, HI: University of Hawaii Press.

Oxford, R., & Nyikos, M. (1989). Variables affecting choice of language learning strategies by university students. *The Modern Language Journal, 73*, 291–300.

Oxford, R., & Crookall, D. (1989). Research on language learning strategies: Methods, findings, and instructional issues. *The Modern Language Journal, 73*, 404–419.

Palmer, S. E., & Kimchi, R. (1986). The information processing approach to cognition. In T. J. Knapp & L. C. Robertson (Eds.), *Approaches to cognition: Contrasts and controversies* (pp. 37–77). Hillsdale, NJ: Erlbaum.

Palmeri, T. J. (1997). Exemplar similarity and the development of automaticity. *Journal of Experimental Psychology: Learning, Memory and Cognition, 23*, 324–354.

Papagno, C., Valentine, T., & Baddeley, A. (1991). Phonological short-term memory and foreign-language vocabulary learning. *Journal of Memory and Language, 30*, 331–347.

Paradis, M. (1994). Neurolinguistic aspects of implicit and explicit memory: Implications for bilingualism and SLA. In N. Ellis (Ed.), *Implicit and explicit learning of languages* (pp. 393–419). London: Academic Press.

Paradis, M. (1997). The cognitive neuropsychology of bilingualism. In A. M. B. de Groot & J. F. Kroll (Eds.), *Tutorials in Bilingualism: Psycholinguistic perspectives* (pp. 331–354). Mahwah, NJ: Erlbaum.

Paribakht, T. S., & Wesche, M. (1999). Reading and "incidental" L2 vocabulary acquisition: An introspective study of lexical inferencing. *Studies in Second Language Acquisition, 21*, 195–224.

Parks, D., & Boueck, G. (1989). Workload prediction, diagnosis and continuing challenges. In G. R. McMillan, D. Beevis, E. Sala, M. H. Strub, R. Sutton, & L. Van Breda (Eds.), *Applications of human performance models to system design* (pp. 47–64). New York: Plenum.

Parry, T., & Child, J. (1990). Preliminary investigation of the relation between VORD, MLAT and proficiency. In T. Parry & C. Stansfield (Eds.), *Language aptitude reconsidered* (pp. 126–178). New Jersey: Englewood Cliffs.

Paulston, C. B. (1981). Notional syllabuses revisited: Some comments. *Applied Linguistics, 2*, 93–95.

Paulston, C. B., & Bruder, M. N. (1976). *Teaching English as a second language: Techniques and procedures*. Cambridge, MA: Winthrop.

Pavlov, I. P. (1927). *Conditioned reflexes*. London: Clarendon Press.

Pawley, A., & Syder, F. H. (1983). Two puzzles for linguistic theory: Nativelike selection and nativelike fluency. In J. C. Richards & R. W. Schmidt (Eds.), *Language and communication*. London: Longman.

Peters, A. M. (1983). *The units of language acquisition*. Cambridge: Cambridge University Press.

Peters, S. (1998). Evaluating language learning technology from a linguist's perspective. *Paper presented at the Invitational Symposium on Advancing Technology Options in Language Learning*, Honolulu, February.

Petersen, C., & Al-Haik, A. (1976). The development of the Defense Language Aptitude Battery (DLAB). *Educational and Psychological Measurement, 36*, 369–380.

Phillips, J. G., & Hughes, B. G. (1988). Internal consistency of the concept of automaticity. In A. M. Colley & J. R. Beech (Eds.), *Cognition and action in skilled behavior* (pp. 317–331). Amsterdam: North-Holland.

Pica, T. (1984). Methods of morpheme quantification: Their effect on the interpretation of second language data. *Studies in Second Language Acquisition, 6*, 69–78.

Pica, T. (1994). Research on negotiation: What does it reveal about second-language learning conditions, processes, and outcomes? *Language Learning, 44*, 493–527.

Pica, T. (1997). Second language teaching and research relationships: a North American view. *Language Teaching Research, 1*, 48–72.

Pica, T., Kanagy, R., & Falodun, J. (1993). Choosing and using communication tasks for second language teaching and research. In G. Crookes & S. Gass (Eds.), *Tasks in language learning: Integrating theory and practice* (pp. 9–34). Clevedon, Avon: Multilingual Matters.

Pienemann, M. (1985). Learnability and syllabus construction. In K. Hyltenstam & M. Pienemann (Eds.), *Modelling and assessing second language acquisition* (pp. 23–75). Clevedon, Avon: Multilingual Matters.

Pienemann, M. (1989). Is language teachable? *Applied Linguistics, 10*, 52–79.

Pienemann, M., & Johnston, M. (1987). Factors influencing the development of language proficiency. In D. Nunan (Ed.), *Applying second language acquisition research* (pp. 45–141). Adelaide: National Curriculum Resource Centre.

Pienemann, M., Johnston, M., & Brindley, G. (1988). Constructing an acquisition based procedure for second language assessment. *Studies in Second Language Acquisition, 10*, 217–244.

Pike, E. V. (1959). A test for predicting phonetic ability. *Language Learning, 9*, 35–41.

Pimsleur, P. (1966). *The Pimsleur Language Aptitude Battery.* New York: Harcourt Brace Jovanovitch.

Pimsleur, P. (1967). A memory schedule. *The Modern Language Journal, 51*, 73–75.

Pimsleur, P. (1968). Language aptitude testing. In A. Davies (Ed.), *Language testing symposium: a psycholinguistic perspective.* Oxford: Oxford University Press.

Pine, J. M., & Lieven, E. V. M. (1997). Slot and frame patterns in the development of the determiner category. *Applied Psycholinguistics, 18*, 123–138.

Pinker, S. (1979). Formal models of language learning. *Cognition, 7*, 217–283.

Pinker, S. (1984). *Language learnability and language development.* Cambridge, MA: Harvard University Press.

Pinker, S. (1989a). [Review of D. I. Slobin (Ed.), *The crosslinguistic study of language acquisition.*] *Journal of Child Language, 16*, 456–466.

Pinker, S. (1989b). *Learnability and cognition: the acquisition of argument structure.* Cambridge, MA: MIT Press.

Pinker, S. (1991). Language acquisition. In L. Gleitman & M. Liberman (Eds.), *An invitation to cognitive science: volume 1, Language* (pp. 107–134). Cambridge, MA: MIT Press.

Pinker, S. (1994). *The language instinct.* New York: William Morrow.

Pinker, S. (1995). Language acquisition. In L. Gleitman & M. Liberman (Eds.), *An invitation to cognitive science, vol. 1* (pp. 135–187). Cambridge, MA: MIT Press.

Pinker, S., & Prince, A. (1988). On language and connectionism: Analysis of a parallel distributed processing model of language acquisition. *Cognition, 29,* 195–247.

Pinker, S., & Prince, A. (1994). Regular and irregular morphology and the psychological status of rules. In S. Lima, R. Corrigan, & G. Iverson (Eds.), *The reality of linguistic rules* (pp. 321–351). Philadelphia, PA: Benjamins.

Plough, I., & Gass, S. (1993). Interlocutor and task familiarity: Effects on Interactional structure. In G. Crookes & S. Gass (Eds.), *Tasks in language learning: Integrating theory and practice* (pp. 95–122). Clevedon, Avon: Multilingual Matters.

Plunkett, K. (1998). Language acquisition and connectionism. *Language and Cognitive Processes, 13,* 97–104.

Plunkett, K., & Marchman, V. (1993). From rote learning to system building: acquiring verb morphology in children and connectionist nets. *Cognition, 48,* 21–69.

Politzer, R. L., and Weiss, L. (1969). *An experiment in improving achievement in foreign language learning through learning of selected skills associated with language aptitude.* Stanford, CA: Stanford University.

Porte, G. (1988). Poor language learners and their strategies for dealing with new vocabulary. *English Language Teaching Journal, 42,* 167–172.

Posner, M. I. (1992). Attention as a cognitive and neural system. *Current Directions in Psychological Science, 1,* 11–14.

Posner, M. I. (1994). Attention in cognitive neuroscience: An overview. In M. Gazzaniga (Ed.), *The cognitive neurosciences* (pp. 615–624). Cambridge, MA: MIT Press.

Posner, M. I., & Peterson, S. E. (1990). The attentional systems of the human brain. *Annual Review of Neuroscience, 13,* 25–42.

Posner, M. I., & Snyder, C. R. (1975). Facilitation and inhibition in the processing of signals. In P. Rabbitt & S. Dornic (Eds.), *Attention and performance, Volume 5.* (pp. 669–682). Hillsdale, NJ: Erlbaum.

Posner, M. I., Walker, J. A., Friedrich, F. J., & Rafal, R. D. (1987). How do the parietal lobes distribute attention? *Neuropsychologia, 25,* 135–145.

Postman, L. (1964). Short-term memory and incidental learning. In A.W. Melton (Ed.), *Categories of human learning* (pp. 145–201). New York: Academic Press.

Prabhu, N. (1987). *Second language pedagogy.* Oxford: Oxford University Press.

Prasada, S., Pinker, S., & Snyder, W. (1990). Some evidence that irregular forms are retrieved from memory but regular forms are rule–governed. *Paper presented at the 31st Meeting of the Psychonomic Society*, New Orleans, November.

Pressley, M., & Afflerbach, P. (1995). *Verbal protocols of reading: The nature of constructively responsive reading.* Hillsdale, NJ: Erlbaum.

Prince, P. (1996). Second language vocabulary learning: The role of context versus translations as a function of proficiency. *The Modern Language Journal, 80*, 478–493.

Pritchett, B. (1992). *Grammatical competence and parsing performance.* Chicago, IL: University of Chicago Press.

Pulvermuller, F., & J. H. Schumann. (1994). Review article: Neurobiological mechanisms of language acquisition. *Language Learning, 44*, 681–734.

Pylyshyn, Z. W. (1984). *Computation and cognition.* Cambridge, MA: MIT Press.

Quartz, S. R., & Sejnowski, T. J. (1997). The neural basis of cognitive development: A constructivist manifesto. *Behavioral and Brain Sciences, 30*, 537–556.

Rabinowitz, M., & Goldberg, N. (1995). Evaluating the structure-process hypothesis. In F. Weinert & W. Scheider (Eds.), *Memory performance and competencies* (pp. 225–242). Mahwah, NJ: Erlbaum.

Radford, A. (1990). *Syntactic theory and the acquisition of English syntax.* Oxford: Blackwell.

Radford, A. (1997). *Syntax. A minimalist introduction.* Cambridge: Cambridge University Press.

Rahimpour, M. (1997). *Task condition, task complexity and variation in oral L2 discourse.* Unpublished Ph.D. dissertation, University of Queensland, Australia.

Rahimpour, M. (1999). Task complexity and variation in interlanguage. In N. Jungheim & P. Robinson (Eds.), *Pragmatics and pedagogy: Proceedings of the 3rd Pacific Second Language Research Forum, Vol. 2* (pp. 115–134). Tokyo: PacSLRF.

Raimes, A. (1985). What unskilled ESL students do as they write: A classroom study of composing. *TESOL Quarterly, 19*, 229–258.

Raimes, A. (1994). Language proficiency, writing ability, and composing strategies: A study of ESL college student writers. In A. Cumming (Ed.), *Bilingual performance in reading and writing* (pp. 139–172). Ann Arbor, MI: Benjamins.

Ranta, L. (1998). *Focus on form from the inside: The significance of grammatical sensitivity for L2 learning in communicative ESL classrooms.* Unpublished Ph.D. Dissertation, Concordia University, Montreal.

Raupach, M. (1987). *Procedural learning in advanced learners of a foreign language.* Duisburg: Universität Duisburg Gesamthochschule.

Rayner, K., Carlson, M., & Frazier, L. (1983). The interaction of syntax and semantics during sentence processing: Eye movements in the analysis of semantically ambiguous sentences. *Journal of Verbal Learning and Verbal Behavior, 22,* 358–374.

Rayner, K., & Pollatsek, A. (1989). *The psychology of reading.* Englewood Cliffs, NJ: Prentice Hall.

Reason, J. (1984). Lapses of attention in everyday life. In R. Parasuraman and D. Davies (Eds.), *Varieties of attention* (pp. 515–549). Orlando, FL: Academic Press.

Reber, A. (1989). Implicit learning and tacit knowledge. *Journal of Experimental Psychology: General, 118,* 219–235.

Regier, T. (1996). *The human semantic potential: Spatial language and constrained connectionism.* Cambridge, MA: MIT Press.

Reid, G. B., & Nygren, T. E. (1988). The subjective workload assessment technique: A scaling procedure for measuring mental workload. In P. A. Hancock & N. Meshtaki (Eds.), *Human mental workload* (pp. 185–214). Amsterdam: Elsevier.

Reves, T. (1983). *What makes a good language learner?* Unpublished Ph.D. dissertation, Hebrew University of Jerusalem, Israel.

Richards, J. (1990). *The language teaching matrix.* New York: Cambridge University Press.

Rickard, T. (1997). Bending the power law: A CMPL theory of strategy shifts and the automatization of cognitive skills. *Journal of Experimental Psychology: General, 126,* 288–311.

Rivers, W. M. (1967). *Teaching foreign-language skills.* Chicago: University of Chicago Press.

Robinson, P. (1995a). Task complexity and second language narrative discourse. *Language Learning, 45,* 99–140.

Robinson, P. (1995b). Attention, memory and the 'noticing' hypothesis. *Language Learning, 45,* 283–331.

Robinson, P. (1996a). Learning simple and complex second language rules under implicit, incidental, rule-search, and instructed conditions. *Studies in Second Language Acquisition, 18,* 27–67.

Robinson, P. (1996b). *Consciousness, rules and instructed second language acquisition.* New York: Lang.

Robinson, P. (1997a). Individual differences and the fundamental similarity of implicit and explicit adult second language learning. *Language Learning, 47,* 45–99.

Robinson, P. (1997b). Generalizability and automaticity of second language learning under implicit, incidental, enhanced and instructed conditions. *Studies in Second Language Acquisition, 19,* 223–247.

Robinson, P. (2001). Task complexity, task difficulty, and task production: Exploring interactions in a componential framework. *Applied Linguistics, 22,* 27–57.

Robinson, P. (in press). Individual differences, cognitive abilities, aptitude complexes, and learning conditions: An Aptitude Complex/Ability Differentiation framework for researching input processing during SLA. *Second Language Research, 17.*

Robinson, P. (to appear). Attention and memory during SLA. To appear in C. Doughty & M. H. Long (Eds.), *Handbook of second language acquisition*. Oxford: Blackwell.

Robinson, P., & Ha, M. (1993). Instance theory and second language rule learning under explicit conditions. *Studies in Second Language Acquisition, 13*, 413–438.

Robinson, P., & Lim, J. J. (1993). *Cognitive load and the route-marked not-marked map task*. Unpublished data, University of Hawaii at Manoa, Department of ESL, Honolulu, U.S.A.

Robinson, P., & Niwa, Y. (to appear). Task complexity, production and the reasoning demands of L2 narratives; What role do intelligence, aptitude, working memory, and perceptions of task difficulty play? In P. Robinson & P. Skehan (Eds.), *Individual differences and second language instruction*. Amsterdam: Benjamins.

Robinson, P., & Ross, S. (1996). The development of task-based testing in English for Academic Purposes programs. *Applied Linguistics, 17*, 523–549.

Robinson, P., Strong, G., Whittle, J., & Nobe, S. (2001). The development of EAP discussion ability. In J. Flowerdew & M. Peacock (Eds.), *Research perpectives on english for academic purposes* (pp. 255–271). New York: Cambridge University Press.

Robinson, P., Ting, S., & Urwin, J. (1995). Investigating second language task complexity. *RELC Journal, 25*, 62–79.

Rock, I., & Gutman, D. (1981). The effect of inattention and form perception. *Journal of Experimental Psychology: Human Perception and Performance, 7*, 275–285.

Rodgers, T. S. (1969). On measuring vocabulary difficulty: An analysis of item variables in learning Russian-English vocabulary pairs. *IRAL 7*, 327–343.

Rosa, E., & O'Neill, M. (1999). Explicitness, intake, and the issue of awareness: Another piece to the puzzle. *Studies in Second Language Acquisition, 21*, 511–566.

Rosenblatt, L. (1978). *The reader, the text, the poem: The transactional theory of literary work*. Carbondale, IL: Southern Illinois University Press.

Rosenbloom, P., & Newell, A. (1987). Learning by chunking: A production system model of practice. In D. Klahr, P. Langley, & R. Neches (Eds.), *Production system models* (pp. 221–286). Cambridge, MA: MIT Press.

Rounds, P., & Kanagy, R. (1998). Acquiring linguistic cues to identify agent: Evidence from children learning Japanese as second language. *Studies in Second Language Acquisition, 20*, 509–542.

Rumelhart, D. E. (1989). The architecture of mind: A connectionist approach. In K. Posner (Ed.), *Foundations of cognitive science* (pp. 133–159). Cambridge, MA: MIT Press.

Rumelhart, D., & McClelland, J. (1986). On learning the past tense of English verbs. In D. E. Rumelhart & J. L. McClelland (Eds.), *Parallel distributed processing: Explorations in the microstructure of cognition.* Vol. 2: *Psychological and biological models* (pp. 272–326). Cambridge, MA: MIT Press.

Rutherford, W. E., & Sharwood Smith, M. (1985). Consciousness-raising and universal grammar. *Applied Linguistics, 6,* 274–82.

Rutherford, W. E. (1989). Preemption and the learning of L2 grammars. *Studies in Second Language Acquisition, 11,* 441–457.

Sachs, J. (1983). Talking about the there-and-then: The emergence of displaced reference in parent-child discourse. In K. Nelson (Ed.), *Children's language Vol. 4* (pp. 1–28). New York: Gardner Press.

Saffran, J. R., Aslin, R. N., & Newport, E. L. (1996). Statistical learning by 8-month-old infants. *Science, 274,* 1926–1928.

Sagarra, N. (1998). The role of working memory in adult L2 development: A longitudinal study. *Paper presented at the Annual Conference of the American Association for Applied Linguistics,* Seattle, March.

Sampson, G. (1987). Probabilistic models of analysis. In R. Garside, G. Leech & G. Sampson (Eds.), *The computational analysis of English.* Harlow, Essex: Longman.

Sampson, G. R. (1980). *Making sense.* Oxford: Oxford University Press.

Samuda, V., Gass, S., & Rounds, P. (1996). Two types of task in communicative language teaching. *Paper presented at the TESOL convention,* Chicago, March.

Sanaoui, R. (1995). Adult learners' approaches to learning vocabulary in second languages. *The Modern Language Journal, 79,* 15–28.

Sanders, A. (1998). *Elements of human performance.* Mahwah, NJ: Erlbaum.

Sarno, K., & Wickens, C. (1995). Role of multiple resources in predicting time-sharing efficiency: Evaluation of three workload models in a multiple task setting. *The International Journal of Aviation Psychology. Special Issue on Pilot Workload: Contemporary Issues, 5, 1,* 107–130.

Sasaki, M. (1996). *Second language proficiency, foreign language aptitude, and intelligence.* New York: Lang.

Sasaki, Y. (1991). English and Japanese interlanguage comprehension strategies: An analysis based on the competition model. *Applied Psycholinguistics, 12,* 47–73.

Sasaki, Y. (1994). Paths of processing strategy transfers in learning Japanese and English as foreign languages. *Studies in Second Language Acquisition, 16,* 43–72.

Sasaki, Y. (1997). Individual variation in a Japanese sentence comprehension task: Form, functions, and strategies. *Applied Linguistics, 18,* 508–537.

Sato, C. (1988). Origins of complex syntax in interlanguage development. *Studies in Second Language Acquisition, 10,* 371–395.

Sato, C. (1990). *The syntax of conversation in interlanguage development.* Tubingen: Gunter Narr.

Sawyer, M. (1992). Language aptitude and language experience: Are they related? *The Language Programs of the International University of Japan Working Papers, 3,* 27–45.

Sawyer, M. (1993). *The Modern Language Aptitude Test: A Rasch analysis of its performance with Japanese learners of English.* Unpublished manuscript, University of Hawaii, Honolulu.

Sawyer, R. (1994). *Individual differences in linear/non-linear CALL environments.* Unpublished M.A. thesis, University of Hawaii, Honolulu.

Saxton, M. (1993). Does negative input work? In J. Clibbens & B. Pendleton (Eds.), *Proceedings of the 1993 Child Language Seminar.* Plymouth: University of Plymouth.

Saxton, M. (1997). The contrast theory of negative input. *Journal of Child Language, 24,* 1, 139–155.

Schachter, J. (1974). An error in error analysis. *Language Learning, 27,* 205–214.

Schachter, J. (1981). The hand-signal system. *TESOL Quarterly, 15,* 125–38.

Schachter, J. (1990). On the issue of completeness in second language acquisition. *Second Language Research, 6,* 93–124.

Schachter, J. (1996). Maturation and the issue of Universal Grammar in second language acquisition. In W.C. Ritchie & T.K. Bhatia (Eds.), *Handbook of second language acquisition.* San Diego, CA: Academic Press.

Schachter, J., Rounds, P. L., Wright, S., & Smith, T. (1996). *Comparing conditions for learning syntactic patterns: Attentional, nonattentional and aware.* Eugene, OR: University of Oregon, Institute of Cognitive & Decision Sciences (Technical Report No. 96–08).

Schachter, J., & Yip, V. (1990). Why does anyone object to subject extraction? *Studies in Second Language Acquisition, 12,* 379–392.

Schacter, D. L. (1991). Memory. In M. I. Posner (Ed.), *Foundations of cognitive science* (pp. 683–726). Cambridge MA: MIT Press.

Schank, R. C. (1982). *Dynamic memory: A theory of reminding and learning in computers and people.* Cambridge: Cambridge University Press.

Schenkein, J. (1980). A taxonomy for repeating action sequences in natural conversation. In B. Butterworth (Ed.), *Language production, Vol 1. Speech and talk* (pp. 21–47). New York: Academic Press.

Scherfer, P. (1994a). Ueberlegungen zu einer Theorie des Vokabellernens und -lehren. In W. Berner & K. Vogel (Eds.), *Kognitive linguistik und fremdsprachenerwerb* (pp. 185–215). Tübingen: Gunter Narr.

Scherfer, P. (1994b). Ein vorschlag zur systematisierung der wortschatzarbeit im fremdsprachenunterricht. In S. Merten (Ed.), *Von lernenden menschen: Erst- und zweitspracherwerbsprozesse* (pp. 132–159). Rheinbreitbach: Dörr & Kessler.

Schmidt, R. (1983). Input, acculturation and the acquisition of communicative competence. In N. Wolfson & E. Judd (Eds.), *Sociolinguistics and second language acquisition* (pp. 137–174). Rowley, MA: Newbury House.

Schmidt, R. (1988). The potential of PDP for SLA theory and research. *University of Hawaii Working Papers in ESL, 11,* 441–457.

Schmidt, R. (1990). The role of consciousness in second language learning. *Applied Linguistics, 11,* 129–158.

Schmidt, R. (1992). Psychological mechanisms underlying second language fluency. *Studies in Second Language Acquisition, 14*, 357–385.

Schmidt, R. (1993a). Awareness and second language acquisition. *Annual Review of Applied Linguistics, 13*, 206–226.

Schmidt, R. (1993b). Consciousness, learning, and interlanguage pragmatics. In G. Kasper & S. Blum-Kulka (Eds.), *Interlanguage pragmatics* (pp. 21–42). Oxford: Oxford University Press.

Schmidt, R. (1994a). Deconstructing consciousness: In search of useful definitions for Applied Linguistics. *AILA Review, 11*, 11–26.

Schmidt, R. (1994b). Implicit learning and the cognitive unconscious: Of artificial grammars and SLA. In N. Ellis (Ed.), *Implicit and explicit learning of languages* (pp. 165–209). London: Academic Press.

Schmidt, R. (1994c). Consciousness and SLA: Cognitive perspectives on intention, attention, awareness, and control. *Paper presented at the Annual Conference of the American Association of Applied Linguistics,* Baltimore, March.

Schmidt, R. (1995a). Consciousness and foreign language learning: A tutorial on the role of attention and awareness in learning. In R. Schmidt (Ed.), *Attention and awareness in foreign language learning* (pp. 1–63). Honolulu, HI: University of Hawaii Press.

Schmidt, R. (1995b). *Attention and awareness in foreign language learning.* Honolulu, HI: University of Hawaii Press.

Schmidt, R., & Frota, S. (1986). Developing basic conversational ability in a second language: A case study of an adult learner of Portuguese. In R. Day (Ed.), *Talking to learn: Conversation in second language acquisition* (pp. 237–322). Rowley, MA: Newbury House.

Schmidt, R., Jacques, S., Kassabgy, O., & Boraie, D. (1997). Motivation, reported strategy use, and preferences for activities in foreign language classes. *Paper presented at the TESOL convention,* Orlando, March.

Schmitt, N. (1997). Vocabulary learning strategies. In N. Schmitt & M. McCarthy (Eds.), *Vocabulary: Description, acquisition and pedagogy* (pp. 199–227). Cambridge: Cambridge University Press.

Schneider, W. (1985). Toward a model of attention and the development of automatic processing. In M. I. Posner & O. S. Marin (Eds.), *Attention and performance XI* (pp. 475–492). Hillsdale, NJ: Erlbaum.

Schneider, W., & Detweiler, M. (1988). The role of practice in dual-task performance: Toward workload modeling in a connectionist/control architecture. *Human Factors, 30*, 539–566.

Schneider, W., Dumais, S. T., & Shiffrin, R. M. (1984). Automatic and controlled processing and attention. In R. Parasuraman & D. R. Davies (Eds.), *Varieties of attention* (pp. 1–27). New York: Academic Press.

Schneider, W., & Shiffrin, R. M. (1977). Controlled and automatic human information processing: I. Detection, search, and attention. *Psychological Review, 84*, 1–66.

Schneider, W., & Shiffrin, R. M. (1985). Categorization (restructuring) and automatization: Two separable factors. *Psychological Review, 92,* 424–428.

Schneiderman, E., & Desmarais, C. (1988). A neuropsychological substrate for talent in second-language acquisition. In L. Obler & D. Fein (Eds.), *The exceptional brain* (pp. 103–126). London: Guildford Press.

Schoonen, R., Hulstijn, J., & Bossers, B. (1998). Language-specific and metacognitive knowledge in native and foreign language reading comprehension: An empirical study among Dutch students in grades 6, 8 and 10. *Language Learning, 48,* 71–106.

Schriefers, H., Meyer, A., & Levelt, J. (1990). Exploring the time course of lexical access in language production: Picture-word interference studies. *Journal of Memory and Language, 29,* 86–102.

Schumann, J. (1978). *The pidginization process: A model for second language acquisition.* Rowley, MA: Newbury House.

Schwantes, F. M. (1981). Effect of story context on children's ongoing word recognition. *Journal of Reading Behavior, 13,* 305–311.

Schwartz, B. (1986). The epistemological status of second language acquisition. *Second Language Research, 2,* 121–159.

Schwartz, B. (1993). On explicit and negative data effecting and affecting competence and linguistic behavior. *Studies in Second Language Acquisition, 15,* 147–163.

Schwartz, B., & M. Gubala-Ryzak (1992). Learnability and grammar reorganization in L2A: against negative evidence causing the un-learning of verb movement. *Second Language Research, 8,* 1–38.

Scovel, T. (1978). The effect of affect on foreign language learning: A review of the anxiety research. *Language Learning, 28,* 129–142.

Segalowitz, N. (1997). Individual differences in second language acquisition. In A. M. B. de Groot & J. F. Kroll (Eds.), *Tutorials in bilingualism: Psycholinguistic perspectives* (pp. 85–112). Mahwah, NJ: Erlbaum.

Segalowitz, N. (2000). Automaticity and attentional skill in fluent performance. In H. Riggenbach (Ed.), *Perspectives on fluency.* Ann Arbor, MI: University of Michigan Press.

Segalowitz, N., & Gatbonton, E. (1995). Automaticity and lexical skills in second language fluency: Implications for computer assisted language learning. *Computer Assisted Language Learning, 8,* 129–149.

Segalowitz, N., Poulsen, C., & Komoda, M. (1991). Lower level components of reading skill in higher level bilinguals: Implications for reading instruction. *AILA Review, 8,* 15–30.

Segalowitz, N., & Segalowitz, S. J. (1993). Skilled performance, practice, and the differentiation of speed-up from automatization effects: Evidence from second language word recognition. *Applied Psycholinguistics, 14,* 369–385.

Segalowitz, S. J., Segalowitz, N., & Wood, A. G. (1998). Assessing the development of automaticity in second language word recognition. *Applied Psycholinguistics, 19,* 53–67.

Seidenberg, M. S. (1995). Visual word recognition: An overview. In J. Miller & P. Eimas (Eds.), *Speech, language, and communication* (pp. 137–179). San Diego, CA: Academic Press.

Seidenberg, M. S., & McClelland, J. L. (1989). A distributed developmental model of visual word recognition and naming. *Psychological Review, 96,* 523–568.

Seidenberg, M. S., Tanenhaus, M. K., Leiman, J. M., & Bienkowski, M. A. (1982). Automatic access of ambiguous words in context: Some limitations of knowledge–based processing. *Cognitive Psychology, 14,* 489–537.

Seleskovitch, D. (1976). Interpretation: A psychological approach to translating. In R. W. Brislin (Ed.), *Translation: Application and research.* New York: Gardner.

Seliger, H. (1983). The language learner as linguist: Of metaphors and realities. *Applied Linguistics, 4,* 179–191.

Seliger, H. (1989). Semantic transfer constraints on the production of English passives by Hebrew-English bilinguals. In H. Dechert & M. Raupach (Eds.), *Transfer in language production.* Norwood, NJ: Ablex.

Selinker L. (1972). Interlanguage. *IRAL, 10,* 209–231.

Selinker, L., & Douglas, D. (1985). Wrestling with context in interlanguage theory. *Applied Linguistics, 6,* 190–204.

Servan-Schreiber, E., & Anderson, J. R. (1990). Learning artificial grammars with competitive chunking. *Journal of Experimental Psychology: Learning, Memory and Cognition, 16,* 592–608.

Service, E., & Craik, F. I. M. (1993). Differences between young and older adults in learning a foreign vocabulary. *Journal of Memory and Language, 32,* 608–623.

Shapiro, K. L., Arnell, K. M., & Raymond, J. E. (1997). The attentional blink. *Trends in Cognitive Sciences, 1,* 291–296.

Sharkey, N. E. (1996). Fundamental issues in connectionist processing. In G. Brown, K. Malmkjär, & Williams, J. (Eds.), *Performance and competence in second language acquisition* (pp. 155–183), Cambridge: Cambridge University Press.

Sharwood Smith, M. (1981). Consciousness-raising and second language acquisition theory. *Applied Linguistics, 2,* 159–68.

Sharwood Smith, M. (1985). From input to intake: on argumentation in SLA. In S. Gass & C. Madden (Eds.), *Input in second language acquisition.* Rowley, MA: Newbury House.

Sharwood Smith, M. (1993). Input enhancement in instructed SLA: Theoretical bases. *Studies in Second Language Acquisition, 15,* 165–179.

Sharwood Smith, M. (1994a). *Second language learning: Theoretical foundations.* London: Longman.

Sharwood Smith, M. (1994b). The unruly world of language. In N. Ellis (Ed.), *Implicit and explicit learning of languages* (pp. 33–44). London: Academic Press.

Sharwood Smith, M. (1995). Input enhancement and the logic of input processing. *Paper presented at the 6th EUROSLA,* Nijmegen, June.

Shaw, M. L., & Shaw, P. (1978). A capacity allocation model for reaction time. *Journal of Experimental Psychology: Human Perception and Performance, 4,* 596–598.

Shiffrin, R. M., & Schneider, W. (1977). Controlled and automatic human information processing II: Perceptual learning, automatic attending, and a general theory. *Psychological Review, 84,* 127–190.

Shiffrin, R. M., & Schneider, W. (1984). Automatic and controlled processing revisited. *Psychological Review, 91*(2), 269–276.

Shirai, Y. (1992). Conditions on transfer: a connectionist approach. *Issues in Applied Linguistics, 3,* 91–120.

Shook, D. (1994). FL/L2 Reading, Grammatical Information and the Input-to-Intake Phenomenon. *Applied Language Learning, 5,* 57–93.

Shu, H., Anderson, R. C., & Zhang, H. (1995). Incidental learning of word meanings while reading: A Chinese and American cross-cultural study. *Reading Research Quarterly, 30,* 76–95.

Simon, H. A. (1962). The architecture of complexity. *Proceedings of the American Philosophical Society, 106,* 467–482.

Simon, H. A. (1969). The sciences of the artificial. Cambridge, Mass.: MIT Press.

Simon, H. A. (1980). Problem solving and education. In D. T. Tuma & F. Reif (Eds.), *Problem solving and education: Issues in teaching and learning.* Hillsdale, NJ: Erlbaum.

Simpson, G. B., & Kang, H. (1994). Inhibitory processes in the recognition of homograph meanings. In Dagenbach, D., & Carr, T. H. (Eds.), *Inhibitory processes in attention, memory, and language* (pp. 259–381). San Diego, CA: Academic Press.

Sinclair, J. (1991). *Corpus, concordance, collocation.* Oxford: Oxford University Press.

Singleton, D. (1999). *Exploring the second language mental lexicon.* Cambridge: Cambridge University Press.

Singley, M. K., & Anderson, J. R. (1989). *The transfer of cognitive skill.* Cambridge, MA: Harvard University Press.

Skehan, P. (1982). *Memory and motivation in language aptitude testing.* Unpublished doctoral dissertation, University of London.

Skehan. P. (1986a). Cluster analysis and the identification of learner types. In V. Cook (Ed.), *Experimental approaches to second language acquisition* (pp. 81–94). Oxford: Pergamon.

Skehan, P. (1986b). The role of foreign language aptitude in a model of school learning. *Language Testing, 3,* 188–221.

Skehan, P. (1989). *Individual differences in second language learning.* London: Arnold.

Skehan, P. (1990). The relationship between native and foreign language learning ability: Educational and linguistic factors. In H. Dechert

(Ed.), *Current trends in European second language acquisition research* (pp. 83–106). Clevedon: Multilingual Matters.

Skehan, P. (1992). Strategies in second language acquisition. *Thames Valley University Working Papers in English Language Teaching*, No. 1.

Skehan, P. (1996). A framework for the implementation of task-based instruction. *Applied Linguistics, 17*, 38–62.

Skehan, P. (1998a). *A cognitive approach to language learning.* Oxford: Oxford University Press.

Skehan, P. (1998b). Task-based language instruction. In W. Grabe (Ed.), *Annual Review of Applied Linguistics.* Oxford: Oxford University Press.

Skehan, P. (to appear). Task characteristics, fluency, and oral performance testing. In C. Clapham (Ed.), *Tasks and language testing.*

Skehan, P., & Foster, P. (1997). Task type and task processing conditions as influences on foreign language performance. *Language Teaching Research, 1*, 185–211.

Skehan, P., & Foster, P. (1999). Task structure and processing conditions in narrative retellings. *Language Learning, 49*, 93–120.

Skehan, P., Foster, P., & Mehnert, U. (1997). Assessing and using tasks. In Renandya, W., & Jacobs, G. (Eds.), *Learners and language learning.* Singapore: RELC Anthology Series 39.

Slobin, D. I. (1973). Cognitive prerequisites for the development of grammar. In C. A. Ferguson and D. I. Slobin (Eds.), *Studies of child language development* (pp. 175–208). New York: Holt Rinehart Winston.

Slobin, D. I. (1985). Crosslinguistic evidence for the language-making capacity. In D. I. Slobin (Ed.), *The crosslinguistic study of language acquisition, Vol. 2, Theoretical issues* (pp. 1157–1259). Hillsdale, NJ: Erlbaum.

Smagorinsky, P. (1994). Think-aloud protocol analysis: Beyond the black box. In P. Smagorinsky (Ed.), *Speaking about writing: Reflections on research methodology* (pp. 3–19). London: Sage Publications.

Smith, N., & I.-M. Tsimpli. (1995). *The mind of a savant.* Oxford: Blackwell.

Snow, C. (1995). Issues in the study of input: Finetuning, universality, individual and developmental differences, and necessary causes. In P. Fletcher & B. MacWhinney (Eds.), *The handbook of child language* (pp. 180–193). Oxford: Blackwell.

Snow, C., & C. A. Ferguson (Eds.) (1997). *Talking to children; language input and acquisition.* Cambridge: Cambridge University Press.

Snow, R. E. (1994). Abilities in academic tasks. In R. Sternberg & R. Wagner (Eds.), *Mind in context: Interactionist perspectives on human intelligence* (pp. 3–37). New York: Cambridge University Press.

Sökmen, A. J. (1997). Current trends in teaching second language vocabulary. In N. Schmitt & M. McCarthy (Eds.), *Vocabulary: Description, acquisition and pedagogy* (pp. 237–257). Cambridge: Cambridge University Press.

Sokolik, M. E. (1990). Learning without rules: PDP and a resolution of the adult language learning paradox. *TESOL Quarterly 24*, 685–696.

Sokolik, M. E., & M. E. Smith. (1992). Assignment of gender to French nouns in primary and secondary language: a connectionist model. *Second Language Research, 8*, 39–58.

Sokolov, J. L. (1988). Cue validity in Hebrew sentence comprehension. *Journal of Child Language, 15*, 129–156.

Spada, N. (1997). Form-focussed instruction and second language acquisition: A review of classroom and laboratory research. *Language Teaching Abstracts, 30*, 73–87.

Sparks, R., & Ganschow, L. (1991). Foreign language learning differences: Affective or native language aptitude differences? *Modern Language Journal, 75*, 3–16.

Sparks, R., & Ganschow, L. (1993). Searching for the cognitive locus of foreign language learning difficulties: Linking first and second language learning. *Modern Language Journal, 77*, 289–302.

Sparks, R., Ganschow, L., Fluharty, K., & Little, S. (1995). An exploratory study on the effects of Latin on the native language skills and foreign language aptitude of students with and without disabilities. *The Classical Journal, 91*, 165–184.

Sparks, R., Ganschow, L., Kenneweg, S., & Miller, K. (1991). Use of an Orton-Gillingham approach to teaching a foreign language to dyslexic/learning disabled students: Explicit teaching of phonology in a second language. *Annals of Dyslexia, 41*, 96–118.

Spilsbury, G., Stankov, L., & Roberts, R. (1990). The effects of a task's difficulty on its correlation with intelligence. *Personality and Individual Differences, 11*, 1069–1077.

Spivey-Knowlton, M., & Sedivy, J. C. (1994). Resolving attachment ambiguities with multiple constraints. *Cognition, 55*, 227–267.

Spivey-Knowlton, M., & Tanenhaus, M. (1994). Referential context and syntactic ambiguity resolution. In C. Clifton, L. Frazier, & K. Rayner (Eds.), *Perspectives on sentence processing*. Hillsdale, NJ: Erlbaum.

Stankov, L. (1987). Competing tasks and attentional resources: Exploring the limits of the primary-secondary paradigm. *Australian Journal of Psychology, 39*, 123–137.

Stanovich, K. E. (1980). Toward an interactive-compensatory model of individual differences in the development of reading fluency. *Reading Research Quarterly, 16*, 360–406.

Stanovich, K. E. (1984). The interactive-compensatory model of reading: A confluence of developmental, experimental, and educational psychology. *Remedial and Special Education, 5*, 11–19.

Stanovich, K. E., & Cunningham, A. E. (1992). Studying the consequences of literacy within a literate society: The cognitive correlates of print exposure. *Memory and Cognition, 20*, 51–68.

Stansfield, C., & Hansen, J. (1983). Field dependence-interdependence as a variable in second language cloze test performance. *TESOL Quarterly, 17*, 29–38.

Steedman, M. J., & Altmann, G. T. M. (1989). Ambiguity in context: A reply. In G. Altmann (Ed.), *Parsing and interpretation* (pp. 105–122). Hove: Erlbaum.

Sternberg, R. J. (1987). Most vocabulary is learned from context. In M.G. McKeown & M. Curtis (Eds.), *The nature of vocabulary acquisition* (pp. 89–105). Hillsdale, NJ: Erlbaum.

Stevick, E. (1976). *Memory, meaning and method.* Rowley, MA: Newbury House.

Stillings, N. A., Weisler, S. E., Chase, C. H., Feinstein, M. H., Garfield, J. L., & Rissland, E. L. (1995). *Cognitive science: An introduction.* Cambridge, MA: MIT Press.

Stratman, J. F., & L. Hamp-Lyons (1994). Reactivity in concurrent think-aloud protocols. In P. Smagorinsky (Ed.), *Speaking about writing: Reflections on research methodology* (pp. 89–112). London: Sage.

Strayer, D. L., & Kramer, A. F. (1990). An analysis of memory-based theories of automaticity. *Journal of Experimental Psychology: Learning, Memory and Cognition, 16,* 291–304.

Strong, M. (1984). Integrative motivation: Cause or result of second language acquisition? *Language Learning, 34,* 1–13.

Studdert-Kennedy, M. (1991). Language development from an evolutionary perspective. In N. A. Krasnegor, D. M. Rumbaugh, R. L. Schiefelbusch, & M. Studdert-Kennedy (Eds.), *Biological and behavioral determinants of language development.* Hillsdale, NJ: Erlbaum.

Suedfeld, P., & Coren, S. (1992). Cognitive correlates of conceptual complexity. *Personality and Individual Differences, 13,* 1193–1199.

Swain, M. (1985). Communicative competence: some roles of comprehensible input and comprehensible output in its development. In S. Gass & C. Madden (Eds.), *Input in second language acquisition* (pp. 235–53). Rowley, MA: Newbury House.

Swain, M. (1993). The output hypothesis: Just speaking and writing aren't enough. *The Canadian Modern Language Review, 50,* 158–164.

Swain, M. (1995). Three functions of output in second language learning. In G. Cook & B. Seidlhoffer (Eds.), *Principle and practice in applied linguistics: Studies in honour of H.G. Widdowson* (pp. 125–144). Oxford: Oxford University Press.

Swain, M. (1998). Focus on form through conscious reflection. In C. Doughty & J. Williams (Eds.), *Focus on form in classroom second language acquisition* (pp. 64–82). New York: Cambridge University Press.

Swain M., & Lapkin S. (1982) *Evaluating bilingual education: A Canadian case study.* Clevedon, Avon: Multilingual Matters.

Swain, M., & Lapkin, S. (1995). Problems in output and the cognitive processes they generate: A step towards second language learning. *Applied Linguistics, 16,* 370–391.

Swarts, H., Flower, L., & Hayes, J. (1984). Designing protocol studies of the writing process: An introduction. In R. Beach & L. Bridwell

(Eds.), *New directions in composition research* (pp. 53–71). New York: Guilford.

Sweller, J. (1988). Cognitive load during problem solving: Effects on learning. *Cognitive Science, 12*, 257–285.

Taft, M. (1993). *Reading and the mental lexicon.* Hove: Erlbaum.

Talmy, G. (1983). How language structures space. In H. Pick & L. Acredolo (Eds.), *Spatial orientation: Theory, research, and application.* New York: Plenum Press.

Talmy, L. (1988). Force dynamics in language and cognition. *Cognitive Science, 12*, 49–100.

Talmy, L. (1996a). The windowing of attention in language. In M. Shibatani & S. Thompson (Eds.), *Grammatical constructions: Their form and meaning* (pp. 235–287). Oxford: Oxford University Press.

Talmy, L. (1996b). Fictive motion in language and "ception". In P. Bloom, M. Peterson, L. Nadel, & M. Garrett (Eds.), *Language and space* (pp. 211–275). Cambridge, MA: MIT Press.

Talmy, L. (1997). Relating language to other cognitive systems. *Paper presented at the 5th International Cognitive Linguistics Conference, Amsterdam, July.*

Taman, H. (1993). The utilization of syntactic, semantic, and pragmatic cues in the assignment of subject role in Arabic. *Applied Psycholinguistics, 14*, 299–317.

Tanenhaus, M. K., Carslon, G. N., & Trueswell, J. C. (1989). The role of thematic structures in interpretation and parsing. *Language and Cognitive Processes, 4*, 211–234.

Tanenhaus, M. K., & Trueswell, J. C. (1995). Sentence comprehension. In J. L. Miller & P. D. Eimas (Eds.), *Speech, language, and communication* (pp. 217–262). San Diego, CA: Academic Press.

Taraban, R., & McClelland, J. L. (1988). Constituent attachment and thematic role assignment in sentence processing: Influences of content-based expectations. *Journal of Memory and Language, 27*, 597–632.

Taraban, R., & McClelland, J. L. (1990). Parsing and comprehension: A multiple constraint view. In D. A. Balota, G. B. Flores d'Arcais, & K. Rayner (Eds.), *Comprehension processes in reading.* Hillsdale, NJ: Erlbaum.

Tarone, E. (1985). Variability in interlanguage use: A study of style-shifting in morphology and syntax. *Language Learning, 35*, 373–403.

Tarone, E. (1996). Variation and cognition: The impact of social factors on interlanguage constructions. *Paper presented at the Second Language Research Forum*, Tucson, September.

Tarone, E., & Parrish, B. (1988). Task-based variation in interlanguage: The case of articles. *Language Learning, 38*, 21–44.

Terrell, T. (1991). The role of grammar instruction in a communicative approach. *The Modern Language Journal, 75*, 52–63.

Ting, Chi-chien, S. (1996). Tasks and planning time in the acquisition of Chinese as a second language. In P. Robinson (Ed.), *Task complexity and second language syllabus design: Data-based studies and speculations* (pp. 30–63). Brisbane: University of Queensland Working Papers in Applied Linguistics.

Tipper, S. P. (1985). The negative priming effect: Inhibitory priming by ignored objects. *Quarterly Journal of Experimental Psychology, 37A*, 571–590.

Tipper, S. P., & Balyis, G. C. (1987). Individual differences in selective attention: The relation of priming and interference to cognitive failure. *Personality and Individual Differences, 8*, 667–675.

Tipper, S. P., & Cranston, M. (1985). Selective attention and priming: Inhibitory and facilitatory effects of ignored primes. *Quarterly Journal of Experimental Psychology, 37A*, 581–611.

Tomasello, M. (1992). *First verbs: A case study of early grammatical development*. Cambridge: Cambridge University Press.

Tomasello, M. (1995). Language is not an instinct. *Cognitive Development, 10*, 131–156.

Tomlin, R., & Villa, V. (1994). Attention in cognitive science and second language acquisition. *Studies in Second Language Acquisition, 16*, 183–203.

Towell, R., & Hawkins, R. (1994). *Approaches to second language acquisition*. Clevedon, Avon: Multilingual Matters.

Towell, R., Hawkins, R., & Bazergui, N. (1996). The development of fluency in advanced learners of French. *Applied Linguistics, 17*, 84–119.

Trahey, M., & L. White. (1993). Positive evidence and preemption in the second language classroom. *Studies in Second Language Acquisition, 15*, 181–204.

Treiman, R., & Danis, C. (1988). Short-term memory errors for spoken syllables are affected by the linguistic structure of the syllables. *Journal of Experimental Psychology: Learning, Memory and Cognition, 14*, 145–152.

Treisman, A. (1992). Visual attention and the perception of objects. *International Journal of Psychology, 27*, 13.

Treisman, A., Vieira, A., & Hayes, A. (1992). Automaticity and preattentive processing. *American Journal of Psychology, 105*, 341–362.

Tremblay, P. F., & Gardner, R. C. (1995). Expanding the motivation construct in language learning. *The Modern Language Journal, 79*, 505–518.

Trévise, A. (1986). Is it transferable, topicalization? In K. Kellerman & M. Sharwood Smith (Eds.), *Crosslinguistic influence in second language acquisition*, (pp. 186–206). New York: Pergamon.

Trueswell, J. C., & Tanenhaus, M. K. (1994). Toward a constraint-based lexicalist approach to syntactic ambiguity resolution. In C. Clifton, L. Frazier, & K. Rayner (Eds.), *Perspectives on sentence processing*. Hillsdale, NJ: Erlbaum.

Trueswell, J. C., Tanenhaus, M. K., & Garvey, S. M. (1994). Semantic influences on parsing: Use of thematic role information in syntactic ambiguity resolution. *Journal of Memory and Language, 33*, 285–318.

Truscott, J. (1998). Noticing in second language acquisition: A critical review. *Second Language Research, 14*, 103–135.

Tyler, A., & Davies, C. (1990). Cross-linguistic communication missteps. *Text, 10*, 385–411.

Tyler, L. K., & Marslen-Wilson, W. D. (1977). The on-line effects of semantic context on syntactic processing. *Journal of Verbal Learning and Verbal Behavior, 16*, 683–692.

Underwood, B. J. (1964). The representativeness of rote verbal learning. In A. W. Melton (Ed.), *Categories of human learning*, (pp. 48–78). New York: Academic Press.

Ungerer, F., & Schmid, H. J. (1996). *An introduction to cognitive linguistics.* Harlow Essex: Addison Wesley Longman.

Urwin, J. (1999). *Second language listening task complexity.* Unpublished Ph.D. dissertation, Monash University, Melbourne, Australia.

Vaid, J., & Pandit, R. (1991). Sentence interpretation in normal and aphasic Hindi speakers. *Brain and Language, 41*, 250–274.

Valdman, A. (1976). *Introduction to French phonology and morphology.* Rowley, MA: Newbury House.

Van Bussel, F. J. J. (1994). Design rules for computer-aided learning of vocabulary items in a second language. *Computers and Human Behavior, 10*, 63–76.

Van der Heijden, A. (1981). *Short term visual information processing.* London: Routledge.

van Dijk, T., & W. Kintsch (1983). *Strategies of discourse comprehension.* NY: Academic Press.

Van Ek, J. A., & Trim, J. L. M. (1991). *Waystage 1990.* Strasbourg: Council of Europe.

van Lier, L. (1991). Inside the classroom: Learning processes and teaching procedures. *Applied Language Learning, 2*, 29–68.

van Lier, L. (1994). Language awareness, contingency, and interaction. *AILA Review, 11*, 69–82.

VanPatten, B. (1989). Can learners attend to form and content while processing input? *Hispania, 72*, 409–17.

Van Patten, B. (1990). Attending to form and content in the input: An experiment in consciousness. *Studies in Second Language Acquisition, 12*, 287–301.

VanPatten, B. (1994). Evaluating the role of consciousness in second language acquisition: Terms, linguistic features & research methodology. *AILA Review, 11*, 27–36.

VanPatten, B. (1996). *Input processing and grammar instruction.* New York: Ablex.

Varonis, E., & Gass, S. (1985). Non-native/non-native conversations: a model for the negotiation of meaning. *Applied Lingusitics, 6*, 71–90.

Velmans, M. (1991). Is human information processing conscious? *Behavioral and Brain Sciences, 14*, 651–669.

Wallace, M. (1982). *Teaching vocabulary.* London: Heinemann.

Wang, A. Y., Thomas, M. H., & Ouellette, J. A. (1992). Keyword mnemonic and retention of second-language vocabulary words. *Journal of Educational Psychology, 84,* 520–528.

Warden, M., Lapkin, S., Swain, M., & Hart, H. (1995). Adolescent language learners on a three-month exchange: Insights from their diaries. *Foreign Language Annals, 28,* 537–549.

Watanabe, Y. (1997). Input, intake, and retention: Effects of increased processing on incidental learning of foreign language vocabulary. *Studies in Second Language Acquisition, 19,* 287–307.

Weinert, R. (1995). Formulaic language in SLA: A review. *Applied Linguisitcs, 16,* 180–205.

Weinreich, U. (1953). *Languages in contact.* New York: Linguistic Circle of New York.

Weist, R., Lyytinen, P., Wysocka, J., & Antanassova, M. (1997). The interaction of language and thought in children's language acquisition: A crosslinguistic study. *Journal of Child Language, 24,* 81–122.

Wells, C. G. (1981). *Learning through interaction.* Cambridge: Cambridge University Press.

Wells, C. G. (1985). *Language development in the pre-school years.* Cambridge: Cambridge University Press.

Wells, W., Wesche, M., & Sarrazin, G. (1982). *Test d'Aptitudes aux langues.* Montreal: Institute for Psychological Research.

Wendel, J. (1997). *Planning and second language narrative production.* Unpublished Doctoral Dissertation, Temple University, Tokyo.

Wenden, A. (1987). Incorporating learner training in the classroom. In A.Wenden & J. Rubin (Eds.), *Learner strategies in language learning.* Englewood Cliffs, NJ: PrenticeHall.

Werker, J. F., Gilbert, J. H. V., Humphrey, K., & Tees, R. C. (1981). Developmental aspects of cross-language speech perception. *Child Development, 52,* 349–355.

Wesche, M. (1981). Language aptitude measures in streaming, matching students with methods, and diagnosis of learning problems. In K. C. Diller (Ed.), *Individual differences and universals in language learning aptitude* (pp. 119–154). Rowley, MA: Newbury House.

Wesche, M., Edwards, H., & Wells, W. (1982). Foreign language aptitude and intelligence. *Applied Psycholinguistics, 3,* 127–140.

Wexler, K., & Manzini, M. R. (1987). Parameters and Learnability in Binding Theory. In T. Roeper & E. Williams (Eds.), *Parameter Setting* (pp. 41–76). Dordrecht: Reidel.

White, J. (1998). Getting the learners attention: A typographical input enhancement study. In C. Doughty & J. Williams (Eds.), *Focus on form in classroom second language acquisition* (pp. 85–113). New York: Cambridge University Press.

White, L. (1987). Against comprehensible input: The input hypothesis and the development of second language competence. *Applied Linguistics, 8,* 95–110.

White, L. (1989). *Universal Grammar and second language acquisition.* Amsterdam: Benjamins.

White, L. (1991). Adverb placement in second language acquisition: some effects of positive and negative evidence in the classroom. *Second Language Research, 7,* 133–161.

White, L. (1996). Universal grammar and second language acquisition: Recent developments and new directions. In W. Ritchie & T. K. Bhatia (Eds.), *Handbook of second language acquisition* (pp. 85–120). New York: Academic Press.

White, L., Spada, N., Lightbown, P., & Ranta, L. (1991). Input enhancement and L2 question formation. *Applied Linguistics, 12,* 416–32.

White, P. (1980). Limitations on verbal reports of internal events: A refutation of Nisbett and Wilson and of Bem. *Psychological Review, 87,* 105–112.

White, R. (1988). *The ELT curriculum: Design, management and innovation.* Oxford: Blackwell.

White, R., & Robinson, P. (1995). Current approaches to syllabus design: A discussion with Ron White. *RELC Guidelines, 17,* 93–101.

Wickens, C. (1984). Processing resources in attention. In R. Parasuraman and D. R. Davies (Eds.), *Varieties of attention* (pp. 63–102). New York: Academic Press.

Wickens, C. (1989). Attention and skilled performance. In D. Holding (Ed.), *Human skills* (pp. 71–105). New York: John Wiley.

Wickens, C. (1992). *Engineering psychology and human performance: 2nd edition.* New York: Harper Collins.

Widdowson, H. G. (1978). *Teaching language as communication.* Oxford: Oxford University Press.

Widdowson, H. G. (1990). *Aspects of language teaching.* Oxford: Oxford University Press.

Wigglesworth, J. (1997). An investigation of planning time and proficiency level on oral test discourse. *Language Testing, 14,* 1, 85–106.

Wilkins, D. (1976). *Notional syllabuses.* Oxford: Oxford University Press.

Willis, D. (1990). *The lexical syllabus.* London: Collins.

Willis, D., & Willis, J. (1988). *COBUILD Book 1.* London: Collins.

Willis, J. (1996). *A framework for task-based learning.* Oxford: Longman.

Wittgenstein, L. (1969). *Preliminary studies for the philosophical investigations generally known as the blue and brown books by Ludwig Wittgenstein.* Oxford: Blackwell.

Wolfe-Quintero, K. (1992). Learnability and the acquisition of extraction in relative clauses and wh- questions. *Studies in Second Language Acquisition, 14,* 39–71.

Wong-Fillmore, L. (1976). *The second time around.* Unpublished doctoral dissertation, Stanford University.

Wray, A. (1992). *The focussing hypothesis.* Amsterdam: Benjamins.

Yano, Y., Long, M., & Ross, S. (1994). The effects of simplified and elaborated texts on foreign language reading comprehension. *Language Learning, 44,* 189–219.

Yee, P. L. (1991). Semantic inhibition of ignored words during a figure classification task. *Quarterly Journal of Experimental Psychology, 43A*, 127–153.

Yeni-Komshian, G. (1965). *Training procedures for developing auditory perceptual skills in the sound system of a foreign language.* Unpublished doctoral dissertation, McGill University.

Ying, H. G. (1996). Multiple constraints on processing ambiguous sentences: Evidence from adult L2 learners. *Language Learning, 46,* 681–711.

Yule, G., & MacDonald, M. (1990). Resolving referential conflicts in L2 interaction: The effect of proficiency and interactive role. *Language Learning, 40,* 539–556.

Zechmeister, E. B., D'Anna, C., Hall, J. W., Paus, C. H., & Smith, J.A. (1993). Metacognitive and other knowledge about the mental lexicon: Do we know how many words we know? *Applied Linguistics, 14,* 188–206.

Zechmeister, E. B., & Nyberg, S. E. (1982). *Human memory: An introduction to research and memory.* Monterey, CA: Brook/Cole.

Zobl, H. (1982). A direction for contrastive analysis: the comparative study of developmental sequences. *TESOL Quarterly, 16,* 169–183.

Zobl, H. (1988). Configurationality and the subset principle: the acquisition of 'V' by Japanese learners of English. In J. Pankhurst, M. Sharwood Smith, & P. van Buren (Eds.), *Learnability and second languages; a book of readings.* Dordrecht: Foris.

Zobl, H., & Liceras, J. (1994). Functional categories and acquisition orders. *Language Learning, 44,* 159–180.

Index

References to *figures* and *tables* are indicated by italics, those to notes by 'n.'